PHILIP'S

STREET ATLAS

UNRIVALLED DETAIL FROM THE BEST-SELLING ATLAS RANGE*

NAVIGATOR® SUFFOLK

T0301079

www.philips-maps.co.uk

published by Philip's, a division of
Octopus Publishing Group Ltd
www.octopusbooks.co.uk
Carmelite House
50 Victoria Embankment
London EC4Y 0DZ
An Hachette UK Company
www.hachette.co.uk

First edition 2023
First impression 2023
SUFFA

ISBN 978-1-84907-635-7

© Philip's 2023

This product includes mapping data licensed from Ordnance Survey® with the permission of the Controller of His Majesty's Stationery Office. © Crown copyright 2023. All rights reserved. Licence number 100011710.

No part of this publication may be reproduced, stored in a retrieval system or transmitted in any form or by any means, electronic, mechanical, photocopying, recording or otherwise, without the permission of the Publishers and the copyright owner.

While every reasonable effort has been made to ensure that the information compiled in this atlas is accurate, complete and up-to-date at the time of publication, some of this information is subject to change and the Publisher cannot guarantee its correctness or completeness.

The information in this atlas is provided without any representation or warranty, express or implied and the Publisher cannot be held liable for any loss or damage due to any use or reliance on the information in this atlas, nor for any errors, omissions or subsequent changes in such information.

The representation in this atlas of a road, track or path is no evidence of the existence of a right of way.

Ordnance Survey and the OS Symbol are registered trademarks of Ordnance Survey, the national mapping agency of Great Britain.

Post Office is a trade mark of Post Office Ltd in the UK and other countries.

*All streets named in the source Ordnance Survey dataset at the time of going to press are included in this Philip's Street Atlas.

Printed in China

CONTENTS

II **Key to map pages**

IV **Route planning**

VIII Administrative and Postcode boundaries

1 **Key to map symbols**

2 **Street maps** at 1¾ inches to 1 mile

109 **Street maps** at 3½ inches to 1 mile

154 **Street maps** of centres of Bury St Edmunds and Ipswich at 7 inches to 1 mile

156 **Index** of towns and villages, streets, hospitals, industrial estates, railway stations, schools, shopping centres, universities and places of interest

Key to map pages

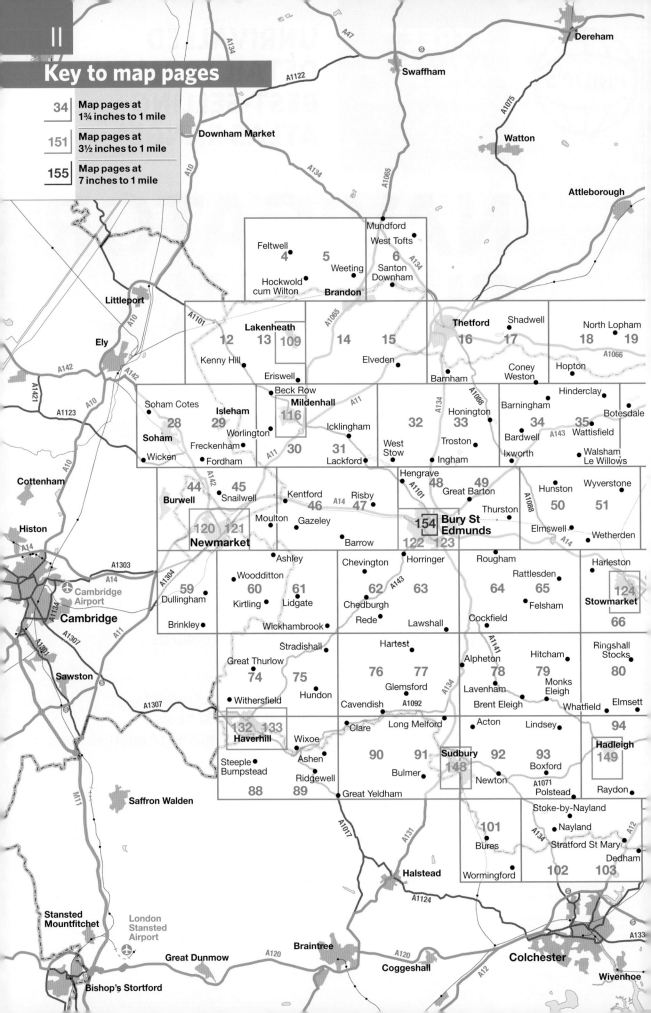

34	Map pages at 1¾ inches to 1 mile
151	Map pages at 3½ inches to 1 mile
155	Map pages at 7 inches to 1 mile

Dereham

Swaffham

Downham Market

Watton

Attleborough

Mundford
West Tofts
Feltwell
4 **5** Weeting
Hockwold Santon
cum Wilton Downham
Brandon

Littleport

Ely

12 **13** **109** **14** **15** **Thetford** Shadwell North Lopham
16 **17** **18** **19**
Lakenheath
Kenny Hill Elveden Coney Hopton
Weston
Eriswell Barnham
Beck Row Hinderclay
Mildenhall Barningham
Soham Cotes **116** Honington **34** **35** Botesdale
28 Isleham **32** **33** Bardwell Wattisfield
29 Icklingham Troston Ixworth Walsham
Soham Worlington **30** **31** West Ingham Le Willows
Freckenham Stow
Wicken Lackford
Fordham Hengrave Wyverstone
44 **45** **48** **49** Hunston
Cottenham Snailwell Kentford Risby Great Barton **50** **51**
Burwell **46** Thurston
Histon Moulton **47** Elmswell
Gazeley **154** **Bury St** Wetherden
120 **121** Barrow **Edmonds**
Newmarket **122** **123**
Cambridge Ashley Chevington Horringer Rougham Harleston
Airport Wooditton **60** **61** Rattlesden **124**
59 Kirtling Lidgate **62** **63** **64** **65** **Stowmarket**
Dullingham Chedburgh Felsham
Cambridge Brinkley Wickhambrook Rede Lawshall Cockfield **66**
Stradishall Hartest Alpheton Hitcham Ringshall
Great Thurlow **78** **79** Stocks
Sawston **74** **75** **76** **77** Lavenham Monks **80**
Withersfield Hundon Glemsford Brent Eleigh Eleigh
Cavendish Whatfield Elmsett
132 **133** Wixoe Clare Long Melford Acton Lindsey **94**
Haverhill Ashen **90** **91** **Sudbury** **92** **93** **Hadleigh**
Steeple **148** Boxford **149**
Bumpstead Ridgewell Bulmer Newton Raydon
88 **89** Great Yeldham Polstead
Saffron Walden Stoke-by-Nayland
101 Nayland
Bures Stratford St Mary
Dedham
102 **103**
Wormingford

Stansted
Mountfitchet London
Stansted
Airport
Great Dunmow **Braintree** **Colchester**
Coggeshall
Bishop's Stortford **Wivenhoe**

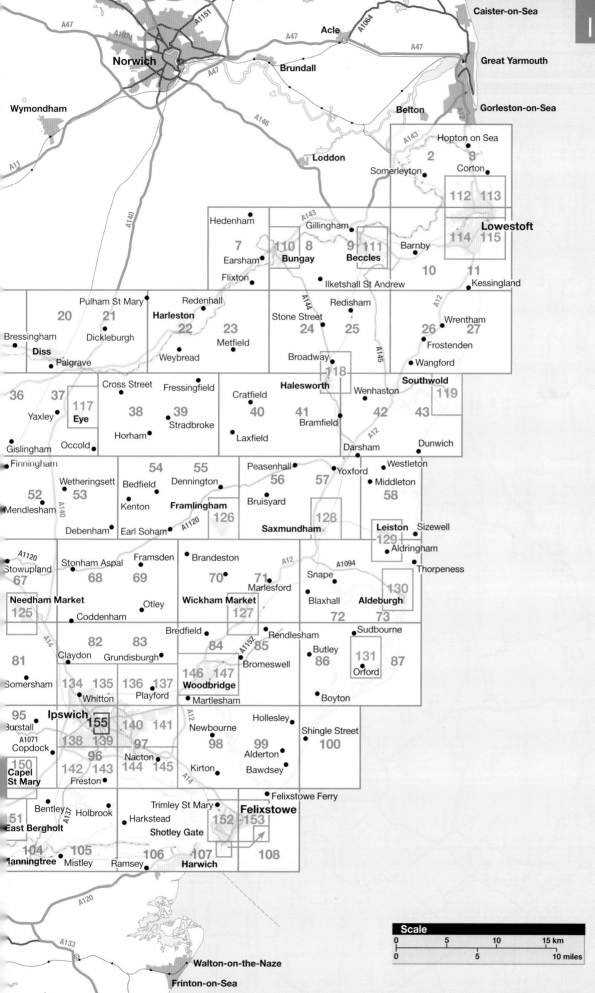

Caister-on-Sea

A47

Acle

Brundall

Great Yarmouth

Belton

Gorleston-on-Sea

Wymondham

Loddon

2

Hopton on Sea

3

Corton

Somerleyton

112 113

Lowestoft

Hedenham

Gillingham

114 115

7

110

8

9

111

Barnby

Earsham

Bungay

Beccles

10

11

Kessingland

Flixton

Ilketshall St Andrew

Pulham St Mary

Redenhall

Redisham

Wrentham

20

21

Harleston

22

23

Stone Street

24

25

26

27

Bressingham

Dickleburgh

Metfield

Frostenden

Diss

Palgrave

Weybread

Broadway

Wangford

118

36

37

Cross Street

Fressingfield

Halesworth

Wenhaston

Southwold

119

117

38

39

Cratfield

40

41

42

43

Eye

Stradbroke

Bramfield

Yaxley

Horham

Laxfield

Darsham

Dunwich

Occold

Gislingham

Finningham

Peasenhall

Yoxford

Westleton

54

55

56

57

Middleton

52

Wetheringsett

53

Bedfield

Dennington

Bruisyard

58

Mendlesham

Kenton

Framlingham

126

128

Debenham

Earl Soham

A1120

Saxmundham

Leiston

Sizewell

129

Aldringham

Stonham Aspal

Framsden

Brandeston

Snape

Thorpeness

67

68

69

70

71

Marlesford

Blaxhall

130

Aldeburgh

Needham Market

Otley

Wickham Market

72

73

125

Coddenham

127

Bredfield

Rendlesham

Sudbourne

81

82

83

84

85

Butley

86

87

Somersham

Claydon

Grundisburgh

Bromeswell

131

Orford

146 147

Woodbridge

Boyton

134 135

136 137

Martlesham

Whitton

Playford

95

Ipswich

155

140 141

Newbourne

Hollesley

Burstall

98

99

Shingle Street

100

Copdock

138 139

97

Alderton

150

96

Nacton

144 145

Kirton

Bawdsey

Capel

142 143

St Mary

Freston

Felixstowe Ferry

51

Bentley

Holbrook

Trimley St Mary

Felixstowe

East Bergholt

Harkstead

152 153

Shotley Gate

104

105

106

107

108

Manningtree

Mistley

Ramsey

Harwich

Walton-on-the-Naze

Frinton-on-Sea

Scale

0   5   10   15 km

0   5   10 miles

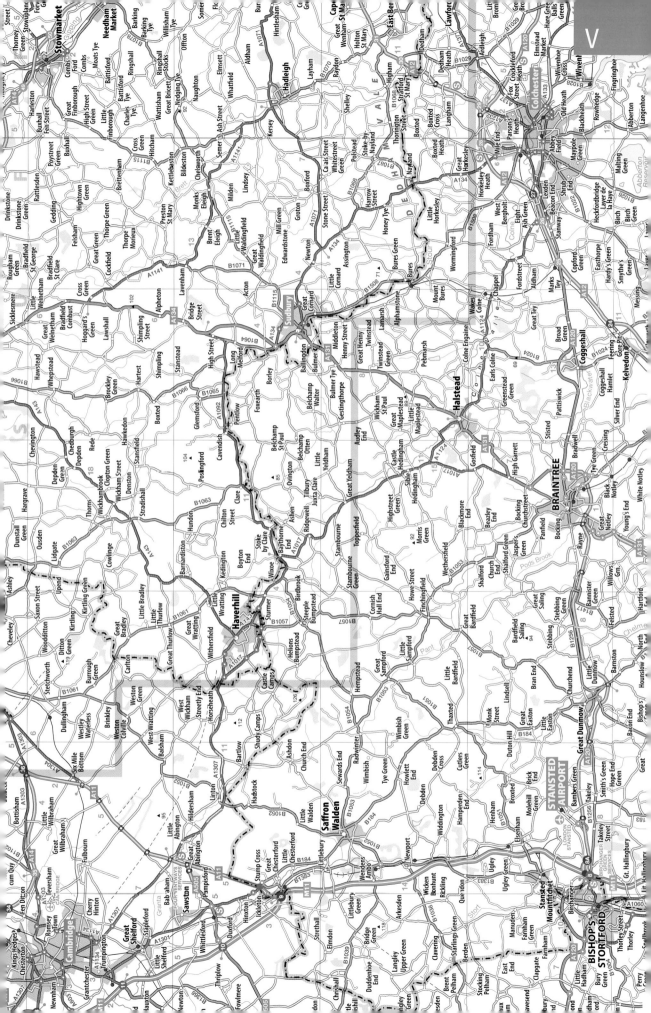

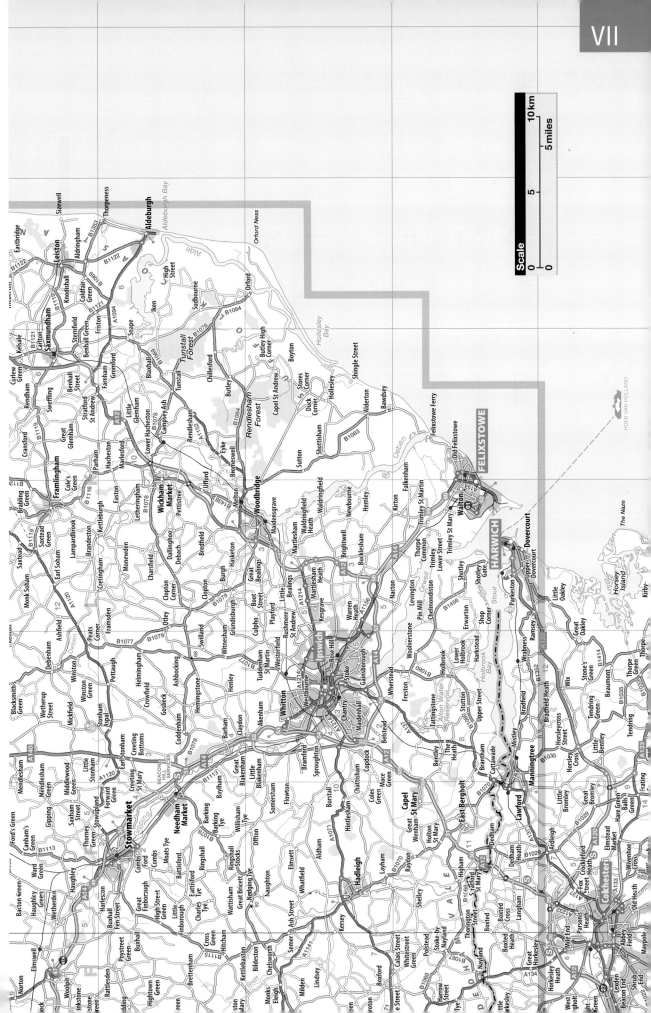

Scale

10 km

5 miles

5

0

0

Major administrative and Postcode boundaries

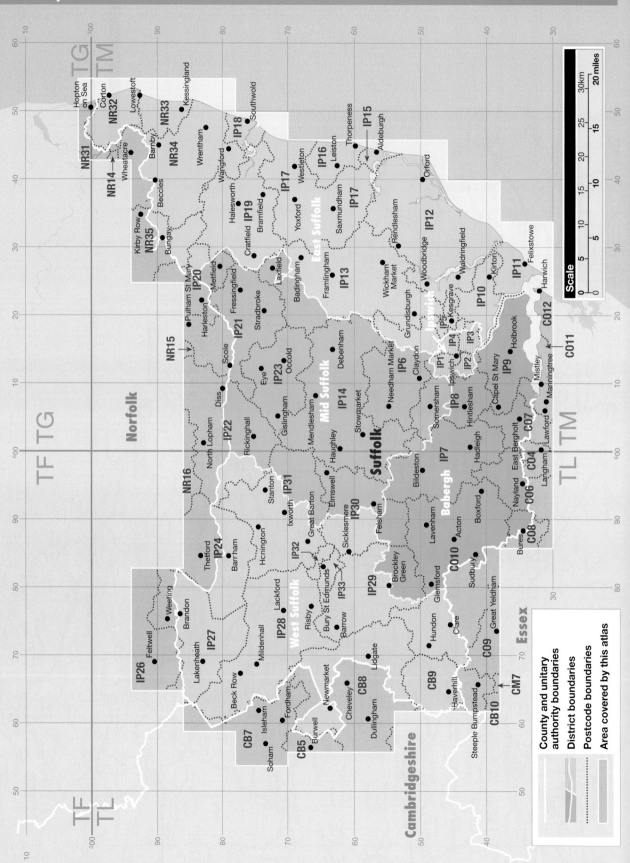

Scale

20 miles

30km

Legend:
- County and unitary authority boundaries
- District boundaries
- Postcode boundaries
- Area covered by this atlas

Key to map symbols

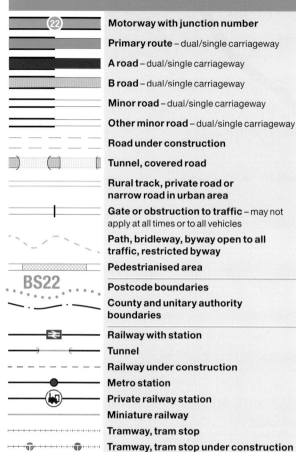

㉒	Motorway with junction number
	Primary route – dual/single carriageway
	A road – dual/single carriageway
	B road – dual/single carriageway
	Minor road – dual/single carriageway
	Other minor road – dual/single carriageway
	Road under construction
	Tunnel, covered road
	Rural track, private road or narrow road in urban area
	Gate or obstruction to traffic – may not apply at all times or to all vehicles
	Path, bridleway, byway open to all traffic, restricted byway
	Pedestrianised area
BS22	Postcode boundaries
	County and unitary authority boundaries
	Railway with station
	Tunnel
	Railway under construction
	Metro station
	Private railway station
	Miniature railway
	Tramway, tram stop
	Tramway, tram stop under construction
	Bus, coach station

◆	Ambulance station
◆	Coastguard station
◆	Fire station
◆	Police station
✚	Accident and Emergency entrance to hospital
H	Hospital
+	Place of worship
i	Information centre – open all year
P	Shopping centre, parking
P&R PO	Park and Ride, Post Office
⛺	Camping site, caravan site
⛳ ✕	Golf course, picnic site
Church ROMAN FORT	Non-Roman antiquity, Roman antiquity
Univ	Important buildings, schools, colleges, universities and hospitals
	Woods, built-up area
River Medway	Water name
	River, weir
	Stream
	Canal, lock, tunnel
	Water
	Tidal water
58 87 246	Adjoining page indicators and overlap bands – the colour of the arrow and band indicates the scale of the adjoining or overlapping page (see scales below)

The dark grey border on the inside edge of some pages indicates that the mapping does not continue onto the adjacent page

The small numbers around the edges of the maps identify the 1-kilometre National Grid lines

Enlarged maps only

	Railway or bus station building
	Place of interest
	Parkland

Abbreviations

Acad	Academy	Meml	Memorial
Allot Gdns	Allotments	Mon	Monument
Cemy	Cemetery	Mus	Museum
C Ctr	Civic centre	Obsy	Observatory
CH	Club house	Pal	Royal palace
Coll	College	PH	Public house
Crem	Crematorium	Recn Gd	Recreation ground
Ent	Enterprise		
Ex H	Exhibition hall	Resr	Reservoir
Ind Est	Industrial Estate	Ret Pk	Retail park
IRB Sta	Inshore rescue boat station	Sch	School
		Sh Ctr	Shopping centre
Inst	Institute	TH	Town hall / house
Ct	Law court	Trad Est	Trading estate
L Ctr	Leisure centre	Univ	University
LC	Level crossing	W Twr	Water tower
Liby	Library	Wks	Works
Mkt	Market	YH	Youth hostel

The map scale on the pages numbered in green is 1¾ inches to 1 mile
2.76 cm to 1 km • 1:36206

The map scale on the pages numbered in blue is 3½ inches to 1 mile
5.52 cm to 1 km • 1:18103

The map scale on the pages numbered in red is 7 inches to 1 mile
11.04 cm to 1 km • 1:9051

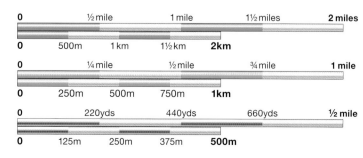

| 0 | ½ mile | 1 mile | 1½ miles | 2 miles |
| 0 | 500m | 1 km | 1½ km | 2km |

| 0 | ¼ mile | ½ mile | ¾ mile | 1 mile |
| 0 | 250m | 500m | 750m | 1km |

| 0 | 220yds | 440yds | 660yds | ½ mile |
| 0 | 125m | 250m | 375m | 500m |

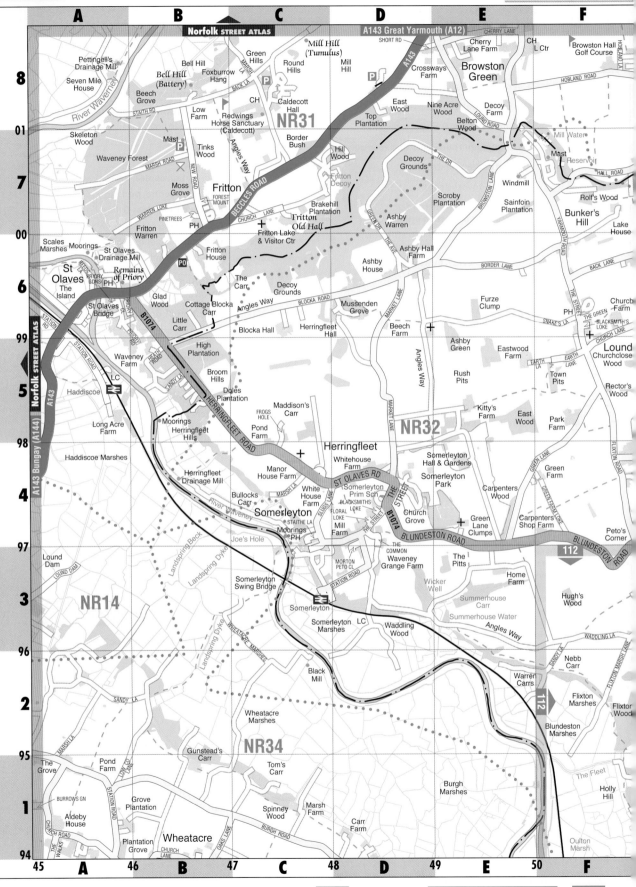

Scale: 1¾ inches to 1 mile

0 ¼ ½ mile
0 250m 500m 750m 1 km

Norfolk STREET ATLAS

A143 Great Yarmouth (A12)

SHORT RD
CHERRY LANE
Cherry Lane Farm
CH L Ctr
Browston Hall Golf Course

Pettingell's Drainage Mill
Seven Mile House
Bell Hill
Bell Hill (Battery)
Foxburrow Hang
Green Hills
Mill Hill (Tumulus)
Round Hills
Mill Hill
Crossways Farm
Browston Green
HOBLAND ROAD

Beech Grove
Low Farm
Redwings Horse Sanctuary (Caldecott)
CH
Caldecott Hall
NR31
East Wood
Top Plantation
Nine Acre Wood
Decoy Farm
Belton Wood
Mill Water
Reservoir
Mast
HALL ROAD

Skeleton Wood
Mast
Tinks Wood
Border Bush
Hill Wood
Decoy Grounds
THE DR
Windmill
Rolf's Wood
Bunker's Hill
Lake House

Waveney Forest
Moss Grove
Fritton
Fritton Decoy
Scroby Plantation
Sainfoin Plantation

Fritton Mount
Brakehill Plantation
Fritton Old Hall
Ashby Warren

PINETREES
Fritton Warren
PH
Fritton Lake & Visitor Ctr
Ashby Hall Farm
BORDER LANE
PH
THE STREET
Church Farm

Scales Marshes
Moorings
St Olaves Drainage Mill
Fritton House
Ashby House
BLACKSMITH'S LOKE
CHURCH LANE
Lound Churchclose Wood

St Olaves
The Island
Remains of Priory
PRIORY GDNS
PH
The Carr
Decoy Grounds
Mussenden Grove
Beech Farm
Rush Pits
Eastwood Farm
EARTH LA
Town Pits
Rector's Wood

St Olaves Bridge
Glad Wood
Cottage Blocka Carr
Angles Way
BLOCKA ROAD
Herringfleet Hall
Ashby Green
Kitty's Farm
East Wood
Park Farm

B1074
Little Carr
High Plantation
Blocka Hall
Angles Way
NR32
Somerleyton Hall & Gardens
Carpenters Wood
Green Farm

Waveney Farm
HEATH ROAD
SANDY LA
Broom Hills
Doles Plantation
Maddison's Carr
FROGS HOLE
Herringfleet
Somerleyton Park
Carpenters Shop Farm
Peto's Corner

Haddiscoe
LC
Long Acre Farm
Moorings
Herringfleet Hills
Pond Farm
Whitehouse Farm
St OLAVES RD
Green Lane Clumps
BLUNDESTON ROAD
112

A143 Bungay (A144)
Haddiscoe Marshes
Herringfleet Drainage Mill
Bullocks Carr
Manor House Farm
White House Farm
Somerleyton Prim Sch
BLACKSMITHS LOKE
FLORAL LOKE
Church Grove
THE STREET
Waddling Wood
Morton PETO CL
Waveney Grange Farm
The Pitts
Home Farm
Hugh's Wood

River Waveney
Joe's Hole
Moorings
PH
Mill Farm
THE COMMON
Wicker Well
Summerhouse Carr
Summerhouse Water
112
Flixton Marshes

Lound Dam
LOUND DAM
Landspring Beck
Landspring Dyke
Somerleyton Swing Bridge
Somerleyton
STATION ROAD
Somerleyton Marshes
LC
Angles Way
WADDLING LA
Nebb Carr
Flixton Wood

NR14
WHEATACRE MARSHES
Black Mill
Waddling Wood
Warren Carrs
SANDY LA

SANDY LA
Wheatacre Marshes
Burgh Marshes
Blundeston Marshes

MARSH LA
The Grove
Pond Farm
Gunstead's Carr
NR34
Tom's Carr
The Fleet
Holly Hill

BURROWS GN
Aldeby House
CHURCH ROAD
Grove Plantation
Spinney Wood
Marsh Farm
BURGH ROAD
Carr Farm
Oulton Marsh

THE WALKS
Plantation Grove
Wheatacre
CHURCH LANE

For full street detail of the highlighted area see pages 112 and 113
112

E5
1 BIRD VIEW SQ
2 OXFORD RD
3 STIRLING RD
4 WELLINGTON RD
5 LANCASTER RD
6 GREEN LA

7 VINCENT CL
8 CRABBE'S CL
9 NIGHTINGALE LA
10 CLOUGH DR
11 EDMUND MOUNDFORD RD
12 FAIRFIELD WY
13 ST JOHN'S WY

14 FAIR CL
15 FALCON RD
16 NEWCOMBE DR
17 HALL DR
18 MULBERRY CL
19 SHORT BECK
20 HILL ST

21 LAMBERTS CL
22 RAWLINGS WY
23 ST NICHOLAS DR
24 PRYERS GDNS
25 LIME KILN LA
26 ST MARY'S ST

Scale: 1¾ inches to 1 mile

0   ¼   ½ mile
0   250m 500m 750m 1 km

A   B   C   D   E   F

Norfolk STREET ATLAS

New Farm

Queen's Ground

Whiteplot Farm

WHITEPLOT LA

Airfield (dis)

Pit (dis)

TENNIS DROVE

Tennis Plantation

New Farm

HYTHE ROAD

Muriel's Farm

Jubilee Farm

Great Oulsham Drain

MOLEHILL DROVE

LITTLE OULSHAM DROVE

OLD METHWOLD ROAD

Birch Farm

LITTLE OULSHAM DRO

Little Oulsham Drain

1 CROFT HOUSE DR
2 SKYE GDNS

Feltwell Common

SOUTHERY ROAD

KETTLE LA

D5
1 CURTIS DR
2 CAMP CL
3 ARCHERS' AVE
4 WESTERN CL
5 HEREWARD WAY
6 HARVARD RD
7 PORTAL CL
8 TRENCHARD SQ
9 BLACKDYKE CL
10 CARDINGTON RD

11 SPARKES WY
12 MOAT SIDE
13 BLACKDYKE CRES
14 LIBERATOR CRES
15 OXFORD RD

MUNSON'S PL 1
MUNSON'S LA 2
ST NICHOLAS DR 3

East Hall

LODGE ROAD

FOSTER'S DROVE

PLOUGHMAN'S DV

RAF Outfall Drain

HAYHILL LA

Edmund de Moundeford VC Prim Sch

B1112

ADDISON CL

Feltwell

Sewage Works

Moat

THE BECK

OAK ST

UPCHER CL

OLD BRANDON ROAD

Works

LEONARD'S LA

Long Lane

SHORT LA

HIGH STREET

BELL ST

Mast

Southery Road Farm

White Bridge Farm

New Cut Farm

Sternshouse Farm

PH

PROVOST

PAYNE'S LA

WILTON ROAD

PO

Chy

Stake Lode

Lakenheath Mid Sch

Mast

Corkway Drove

Mid Farm

Masts

CH

FODDERFEN DRO

WHITEDIKE DROVE

IP26

White Dyke Farm

Feltwell Golf Course

Masts

WHITEDIKE DROVE

Pit (dis)

Black Dyke Farm

Field Farm

Grange Farm

Field Farm

Black Dyke Road

BOUNDARY CL 1
MAIN ST 2
COLLEGE RD 3
ST PETER'S WLK 4
PLOVERS WAY 5
PEALICK CL 6
HARRISON WAY 7
CLINGOS WAY 8

The Moat

Pumping Station

BURDOCK LANE

Cut-off Channel

SLUICE DV

BURDOCK LANE

MALT'S LANE

PO

FELTWELL ROAD

Future Farm

Blackdike Plantation

BLACKDIKE DROVE

College Farm

SOUTH STREET

PH

Sallowrow Drain

PE38

Calledge Farm

MOOR DROVE (EAST)

Hockwold Fens

CROSS DROVE

COWLES DROVE

MOOR DROVE

Heath Farm

Freedom Farm

Mast

STATION RD

Maytree Farm

HEADLAND DROVE

COWLE'S DROVE

Cowle's Drove

The Wash

Wilton Bridge

Aqueduct

IP27

Hereward Way

Little Ouse River

NEWFEN GRAVEL DRO

Lakenheath Fen Nature Reserve

Lakenheath

B1112

LC

FURTHEST DROVE

Brandon Fen

Hiss Farm

A   B   C   D   E   F

67   68   69   70   71   72

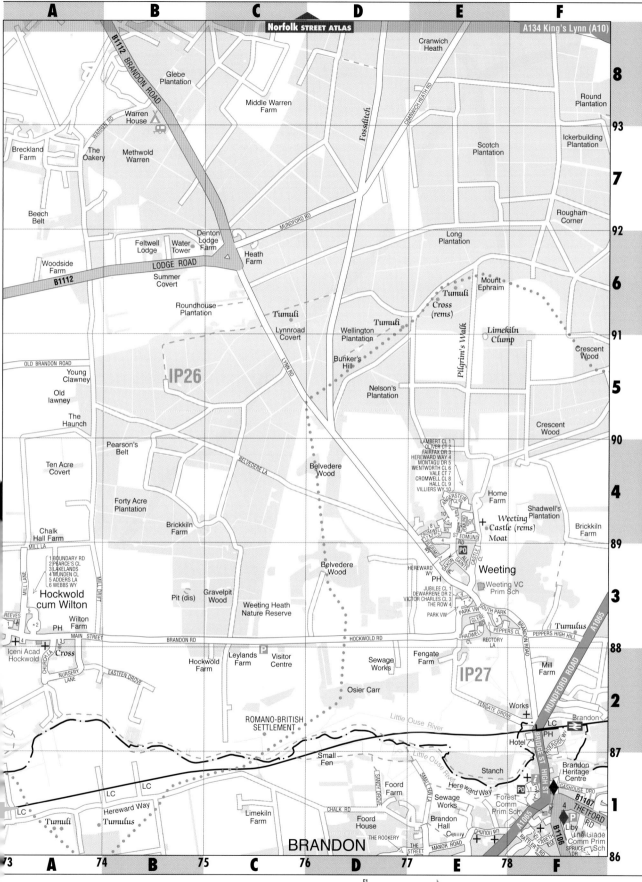

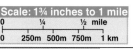

Norfolk STREET ATLAS

A134 King's Lynn (A10)

A   B   C   D   E   F

8
93
7
92
6
91
5
90
4
89
3
88
2
87
1
86

Cranwich Heath
Round Plantation
Ickerbuilding Plantation
Scotch Plantation
Rougham Corner
Long Plantation

B1112 BRANDON ROAD
Glebe Plantation
Middle Warren Farm
Fossditch
CRANWICH HEATH RD

Warren House
WARREN RD

Breckland Farm
The Oakery
Methwold Warren

Beech Belt

B1112
Woodside Farm
Feltwell Lodge
Water Tower
Denton Lodge Farm
LODGE ROAD
Heath Farm
Summer Covert
MUNDFORD RD

Mount Ephraim
Tumuli Cross (rems)
Limekiln Clump
Crescent Wood

Roundhouse Plantation
Tumuli
Lynnroad Covert
Tumuli
Wellington Plantation
Bunker's Hill
Pilgrim's Walk

OLD BRANDON ROAD
Young Clawney
Old Iawney
IP26
LYNN RD
Nelson's Plantation

The Haunch
Pearson's Belt
Crescent Wood

Ten Acre Covert
BELVEDERE LA
Belvedere Wood

LAMBERT CL 1
OLIVER CT 2
FAIRFAX DR 3
HEREWARD WAY 4
MONTAGU DR 5
WENTWORTH CL 6
VALE CT 7
CROMWELL CL 8
HALL CL 9
VILLIERS WY 10

Forty Acre Plantation
Brickkiln Farm
Home Farm
Shadwell's Plantation
Weeting Castle (rems) Moat
Brickkiln Farm
ANGERSTEIN CL
ST EDMUND RD

Chalk Hall Farm
MILL LA
1 BOUNDARY RD
2 PEARCE'S CL
3 LAKELANDS
4 MUNDEN CL
5 ADDERS LA
6 WEBBS WY
MILL DRIFT
MILL LANE

Belvedere Wood
HEREWARD WY
PH
SAXON ST
ALL SAINTS RD
CASTLE
PO
Weeting
Weeting VC Prim Sch

Hockwold cum Wilton
Pit (dis)
Gravelpit Wood
Weeting Heath Nature Reserve
JUBILEE CL 1
DEWARRENE DR 2
VICTOR CHARLES CL 3
THE ROW 4
PARK VW
SOUTH PARK
GLEBE
Tumulus
A1065

REEVES
PH
Wilton Farm
MAIN STREET
BRANDON RD
HOCKWOLD RD
PARK VW
SHADWELL CL
PEPPERS CL
BRANDON ROAD
PEPPERS HIGH HILL
RECTORY LA
Mill Farm

Iceni Acad Hockwold
Cross
CHURCH LA
NURSERY LANE
EASTFEN DROVE
Hockwold Farm
Leylands Farm
Visitor Centre
Sewage Works
Fengate Farm
IP27
MUNDFORD ROAD

Osier Carr
TENGATE DROVE
Works
LC
Brandon

ROMANO-BRITISH SETTLEMENT
Little Ouse River
Hotel
BRIDGE ST
PH
RIVERSIDE WY

LC   LC
Small Fen
Little Ouse River
Stanch
Brandon Heritage Centre
GASHOUSE DRO

LC
Hereward Way
SANDY DROVE
Foord Farm
SMALL DROVE
Sewage Works
Hereward Way
PO
HIGH ST
Forest Comm Prim Sch
A1065
B1107 THETFORD RD

LC
Tumuli
Tumulus
Limekiln Farm
CHALK RD
Foord House
THE ROOKERY
THE STREET
MANOR ROAD
Brandon Hall
Cemy
CHURCH RD
ELIZABETH CT
BATTLER'S RD
SPRUCE DR
B1106
Liby
The Glade Comm Prim Sch

BRANDON

73   74   75   76   77   78   86

For full street detail of Brandon see Philip's STREET ATLAS of Norfolk

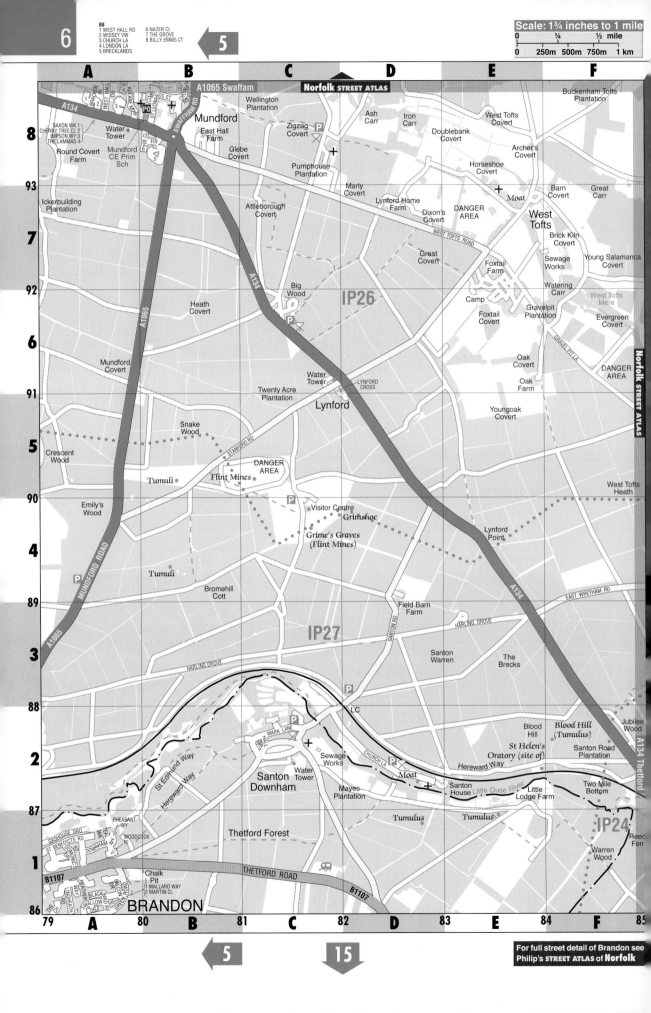

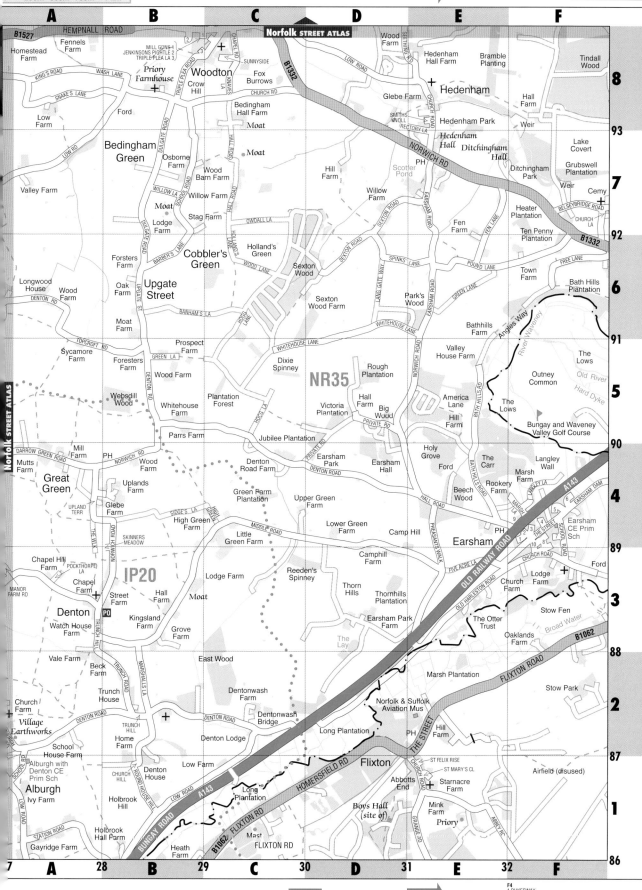

A B C D E F

Norfolk STREET ATLAS

8

Wood Farm
Moat
Tindall Hall
Belsey Bridge
Cemy
Hollybush Farm
All Hallows Farm
Home Farm
Ditchingham

The Shrub
Rayner's Lane
Kirby Cane
Hungry Hill
Old Bungay Road
Litcham La
Brick Kiln Road
Bulls Rd
Dulls Rd
Libs Rd
Bungay Road
Spion Kop Plantation
Spink's Hill
Broome Fruit Farm
New Covert
Broome Place
Rectory Road
Church Lane
Ivy House Farm
Home Farm Road
Willow Lane
Longford Bridge
Stonewall Plantation
Ellingham Hall
Old Hall Farm
Ellingham
Lodge Plantation
Wangoyl Hill

Yarmouth Rd 1
Lockhart Rd 2
Crisp Rd 3
Old Post Office La 4
Chapel La 5
Woodland Dr 6
Chapel Meadow 7

Pewter Hill
Sheepwalk Farm
The Hall
Manor Farm
School Road
Bungay Road
A143
Kirby Hill
Gravel Pit
Leet Hill
Leet Hill Farm
Kirby Row
Geldeston
West End
Yarmouth Road
School La
Newgate La
Florence Way
Henry's Plantation
Ellingham Prim Sch
Church Farm
Mill Lane
Boon's Plantation
Dockeney
Kell's Acres

Norwich Road
Belseybridge Road
Drapers Lane
Thwaite Rd
Bakers Lane
Tunneys Lane
Wildflower Wy
Hollow Rd
Station Rd
Acad
Tumuli Enclosure
Green La
Street Farm
Loddon Road
Sunley Cl
Sun Road
Yarmouth Road
Broome Common
Station Farm
Old Station La
River Waveney
Ellingham Marshes
Willow Farm

Home Farm
Broome
Broome Marshes
Valley Farm
Low Road
Low Fell
Prospect Farm
Benstead Marshes
Bensteads Farm
Alder Farm
White House Farm
Geldeston Marshes
Geldeston Lock

Old River
B1332
Sports Gd
NR35
Wainford
Dirnham Street
Muck Heap Rd
By Road Farm
Cherry Tree Farm
Shipmeadow Marshes
Manor Farm
Sewage Works
Nunnery Farm

Castle (rems)
BUNGAY
Broad St
Netherygate St
Outney Rd
Castle La
St John's Road
Hillside Rd E
Hillside Rd W
Liby
Sch
Beccles Road
Garden Cl
River Waveney
Watch Ho
HL
Beccles Rd
Beccles Rd
Mettingham
Top Farm
The Hall
Moat
Angles Way
Viewpoint
MWS
Church Farm
The Hill
B1062
Shipmeadow
Laurels Farm
NR34
High Common

Flixton Road
B1062
Upper Olland Street
Hillside Rd W
Mountain Ten Cl
Woodland Dr
Princes Rd
Kings Cl
St Margaret's Rd
Annis Hill
Trinity Farm
Grove Farm
Vicarage Lane
New Rd
Castle Farm
Moats
Round Wood
Crow's Nest Wood
Highfields Farm
Shipmeadow Common
Boundary Farm
Low Farm
Orchard Farm
Hall Rd
Clarke's Lane

St Margaret's Plantation
Manor Farm
Three Ash Farm
St Margaret's Road
Upland Hall Farm Rd
St John's Road
Halesworth Rd
Lodge Road
St Johns Lodge Farm
Castle Road
Mettingham Wood
The Firs
The Mount
Manor Farm Road
Low Road
Manor Farm
Ilketshall St Andrew
Birchams Farm
Tithe Farm
Clarke's Lane
School Rd
Chapel Road

Uplandhall Farm
Angles Way
Shadowbarn Farm
Hill Farm
Hill Farm
The Elms
Englishes La
Miles Lane
Grove Farm
Stone St
A144
Church Farm
Great Common
Great Common Lane
Green Farm
Glebe Farm
Hanna Barn Farm
Water Tower
Willow Farm
Top Road
Banters Lane
Moat Farm
St Andrew's Hall
Willow Tree Farm
Cooks Rd

33 34 35 36 37 38

A B C D E F

93 92 91 90 89 88 87 86
8 7 6 5 4 3 2 1

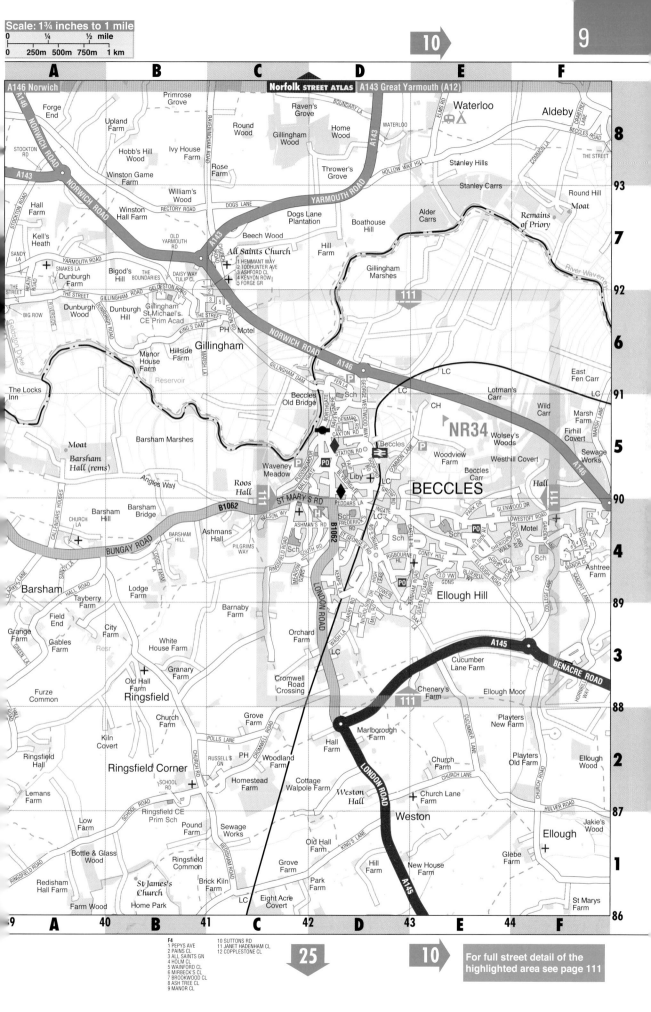

Scale: 1¾ inches to 1 mile

0 ¼ ½ mile
0 250m 500m 750m 1 km

A B C D E F

8

Three Gates Farm
CHURCH RD
Church Farm PH
CRAMP LANE
PIT LANE
Burgh St Peter
Holly Farm
Staithe
Green Farm
Windmill
WASH LANE
BURGH RD
Hall Farm
MIDDLE LANE
Waveney River Centre
Peto's Marsh
NR32
GRAVEL DAM
FISHER ROW
Moat
Oaklands Farm
Burgh End
BOONS TURN
GREEN LANE
Beech Farm
PH
CHURCH LA
112
OULTON DYKE
WAVENEY HILL
BOATHOUSE LA

93
Moneys Farm
LAburnham Farm
BECCLES RD
COMMON ROAD
DUN COW ROAD
TAYLORS RD
STAITHE ROAD
The Plantation
Share Drainage Mill
Angles Way
White Cast Marshes

7
Suttons Farm
ST MARY'S ROAD
Mast
Boon's Heath
BOONS HEATH
THE ROADWAYS
Sand & Gravel Pit
Slade Marshes
GREEN LANE
DUCKS MOUNT
Short Dam Level
Castle Drainage Mill
Share Marsh
Carlton Marshes Nature Reserve
Wildlife Centre
BUBNEL LA
P

92
College Farm
EAST END LA
Eastend Farm
Seven Mile Carr
Castle Mill
Boundary Dyke
Share Marsh
Stone End
Burnt Hill

6
Moorings
MARSH LA
East Fen Carr
Gent's Carr
Angles Way
COVE DAM
Long Dam Level
Castle Marsh
Old Broad
Ash Ground
LC
114
MARSH LA
Sallow Ground
Fairway Farm
Long Plantation
PORTHOLE CL
CABIN LA

91
Square Carr
Great Carr
East Boathouse Carr
WADEHALL OLD DAM
WADEHALL NEW DAM
NR34
Barnby Broad
Barnby Gate Crossing
LC
White House Farm
CH
Rookery Park Golf Course
Beccles Road
PH KEEL CL
ANCHOR WY
HEDLEY LA

5
Alder Carr
Three Acre Plantation
Dole's Covert
Skirts Plantation
LC
Siding Road
SIDING ROAD
A146
Eade's Farm
EADES FARM RD
WOOD BARN LA
East Anglia Transport Mus
CHAPEL ROAD

90
Hall Farm
Ash Covert
Covehall Farm
Barnby
Low Farm
Moat
Wade Hall
North Cove Comm Prim Sch
Red Oak Farm
THE GREEN
Sandy Hill
Church Farm
PH
MUTFORD WOOD
Wood Farm
NR33
Augur Grove
Priory Farm
PRIORY LA
HALL RD
CHURCH LA

4
A146
Sutton's Plantation
Musk Farm
LOWESTOFT RD
Stanley's Covert
North Cove Hall
SPINNEY CL
THE STREET
THE HILL BECCLES RD
PH
MILL LANE
SWAN LANE
NEW ROAD
Beulah Hall
Woodstock Farm
Mutford Big Wood
Wood Barn Farm
Copperfield Farm
MUTFORDWOOD LANE
FAIRHEAD LOKE
HIGHFIELD CL
114

North Cove
1 FIR CL
2 SCHOOL CL
3 WELBOURNE WAY
4 WIGGS ACRE
5 FOUNTAIN'S LA
6 WELBECK CL

Roadside Farm
Wood Barn Farm

89
Sprites Wood
Foxburrow Wood
A145
Gents Farm
Cottage Farm
BROOK ROAD
THE PIGHTLE
DAIRY LANE
Ash Farm
Manor Farm
CHURCH ROAD
Church View Farm
WELCH CL
HOLLY LA
CHAPEL ROAD
Beech Tree Farm
RUSHMERE ROAD
Gisleham Grove

3
Ellough Ind Est
Beccles Bsns Pk
COPLAND WAY
HAN LANS DR
TILIA CT
Airfield (Dis)
Highland Farm
Hill Farm
BECCLES ROAD
NEWSON AV
MILL ROAD

88
B1127
Heliport
BENACRE ROAD
Red House
HULVER ROAD
Marsh Farm
MARSH LA
Great Horns Hill Wood
HALL LA
Mutford
BLOWER'S LANE
SNAB HILL
Chestnuts Farm

2
Hill Farm
WARREN LANE
Ellough Grove
JAY'S HILL RD
PH WELL LA
SANDY LA
Mutford Hall
Hundred River
Little Horns Hill Wood
HANNERS GREEN
THE STREET
THE STREET
The Elms
Rookery Farm
BLACK LA

87
Jakie's Wood
Marsh Farm
HULVER ROAD
Valley Farm
Mill Farm
Gate Farm
CHAPEL LA
Firs Farm
HULVER RD
Lowpasture Plantation
Low Pasture Farm
TINKERS LANE
MARSH LA
Rushmere
Grange Farm
The Rookery

1
CHURCH RD
JAY'S HILL ROAD
Jay's Hill
Hulverhill Plantation
SOTTERLEY ROAD
Hulver Street
SMITHS RD
Brier Wood
B1127
Home Covert
Whitehouse Farm
Toad Row
Latymere Dam
Toadrow Farm
LATYMERE DAM LA
TOAD ROW

86
Willingham Wood
Scarls Grove
Hall Farm
The Old Sch
Henstead Arts & Crafts Ctr

45 A 46 B 47 C 48 D 49 E 50 F

For full street detail of the highlighted area see page 114

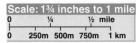

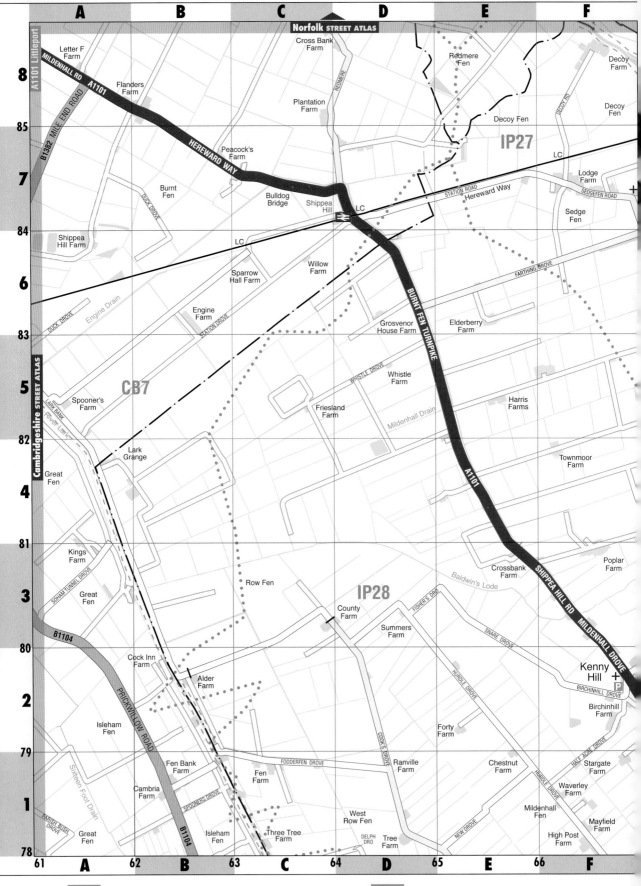

Scale: 1¾ inches to 1 mile

Norfolk STREET ATLAS

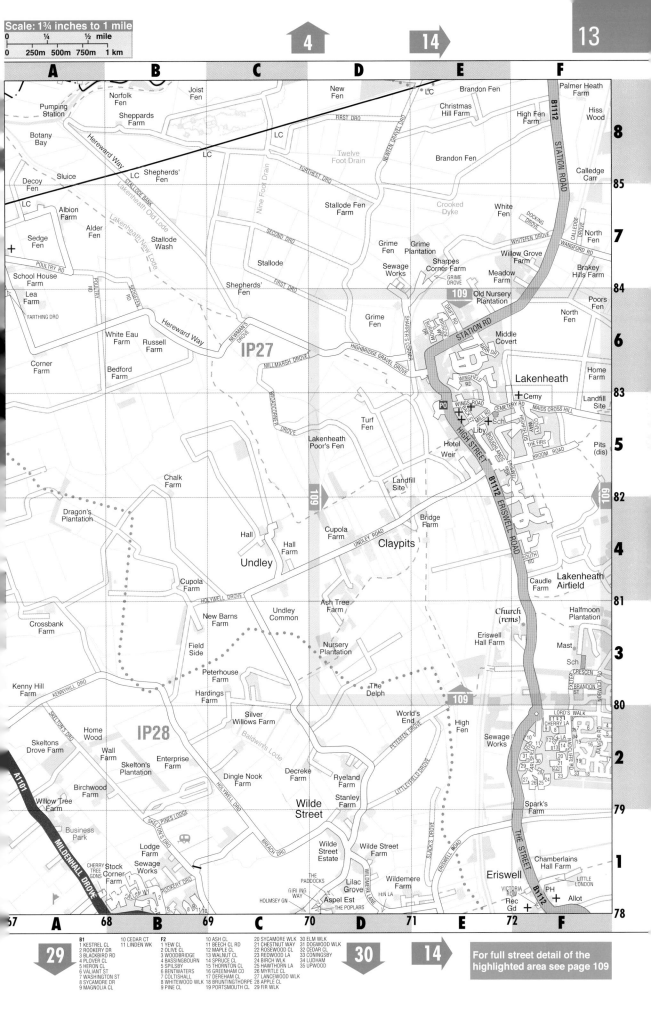

A   B   C   D   E   F

8
85
7
84
6
83
5
82
4
81
3
80
2
79
1
78

Pumping Station
Botany Bay
Sluice
Decoy Fen
LC
Sedge Fen
School House Farm
Lea Farm
FARTHING DRO
Corner Farm
POULTRY RD
Albion Farm
Alder Fen
Norfolk Fen
Sheppards Farm
Shepherds' Fen
LC
Hereward Way
STALLODE BANK
Lakenheath New Lode
Lakenheath Old Lode
Stallode Wash
POULTRY RD
SEDGE FEN
White Eau Farm
Russell Farm
Bedford Farm
Stallode
SECOND DRO
Shepherds' Fen
Stallode
FIRST DRO
Hereward Way
NEWMAN'S DROVE
MILLMARSH DROVE
IP27
Joist Fen
New Fen
FIRST DRO
LC
Twelve Foot Drain
FURTHEST DRO
Nine Foot Drain
Stallode Fen Farm
Grime Fen
Grime Fen
HIGHBRIDGE GRAVEL DROVE
Turf Fen
Lakenheath Poor's Fen
BROADCORNER DROVE
LC
Brandon Fen
Christmas Hill Farm
Brandon Fen
Crooked Dyke
Grime Plantation
Sewage Works
Sharpes Corner Farm
GRIME DROVE
109
Old Nursery Plantation
White Fen
Willow Grove Farm
Meadow Farm
STATION RD
DRIFT RD
Middle Covert
BARR DR
Lakenheath
WINGFIELD RD
Cemy
Liby
Sch
CEMETERY RD
MILL RD
MAIDS CROSS HILL
HIGHFIELDS
COXEY WAY
THE FIRS
BROOM ROAD
Pits (dis)
Hotel Weir
PO
WINGS ROAD
HIGH STREET
B1112 ERISWELL ROAD
SOUTH RD
Caudle Farm
Lakenheath Airfield
Palmer Heath Farm
Hiss Wood
High Fen Farm
Calledge Carr
North Fen
Brakey Hills Farm
Poors Fen
North Fen
Home Farm
Landfill Site
B1112 STATION ROAD
WHITEFEN DROVE
DOCKING DROVE
CALLEDGE DROVE
WANGFORD RD
Landfill Site
Cupola Farm
Undley Road
Claypits
Bridge Farm
Dragon's Plantation
Chalk Farm
Hall
Hall Farm
Undley
Cupola Farm
HOLYWELL DROVE
New Barns Farm
Undley Common
Ash Tree Farm
Field Side
Peterhouse Farm
Hardings Farm
Crossbank Farm
KENNYHILL DRO
Kenny Hill Farm
Nursery Plantation
The Delph
109
Church (rems)
Eriswell Hall Farm
Halfmoon Plantation
Mast
Sch
CRESCEN
EXETER RD
BRANDON ST
RICHMOND
109
109
Home Wood
Skeltons Drove Farm
Wall Farm
Skelton's Plantation
IP28
Enterprise Farm
SKELTON'S DRO
Baldwin's Lode
HOLYWELL DRO
Dingle Nook Farm
BREACH DRO
Silver Willows Farm
Decreke Farm
Ryeland Farm
Stanley Farm
World's End
PETEREN DROVE
LITTLEPORT DRIVE
High Fen
Sewage Works
LORD'S WALK
CHERRY LA
RADCLIFFE RD
BANGOR RD
Spark's Farm
A1101
MILDENHALL DROVE
Willow Tree Farm
Birchwood Farm
Business Park
CHERRY TREE GDNS
Stock Corner Farm
Sewage Works
Lodge Farm
PINES LODGE
ROOKERY DRO
FALCON WY
Wilde Street
Wilde Street Estate
THE PADDOCKS
GIRLING WAY
HOLMSEY GN
Aspel Est
THE POPLARS
Lilac Grove
WILDEMERE LANE
HEN LA
Wilde Street Farm
Wildemere Farm
ERISWELL ROAD
SLACKS DROVE
Chamberlains Hall Farm
LITTLE LONDON
Eriswell
VICTORIA ROW
B1112
Rec Gd
PH
Allot
THE STREET

57   A   68   B   69   C   70   D   71   E   72   F

For full street detail of the highlighted area see page 109

B1
1 KESTREL CL
2 ROOKERY DR
3 BLACKBIRD RD
4 PLOVER CL
5 HERON CL
6 VALIANT ST
7 WASHINGTON ST
8 SYCAMORE DR
9 MAGNOLIA CL
10 CEDAR CT
11 LINDEN WK

F2
1 YEW CL
2 OLIVE CL
3 WOODBRIDGE
4 BASSINGBOURN
5 SPILSBY
6 BENTWATERS
7 COLTISHALL
8 WHITEWOOD WLK
9 PINE CL
10 ASH CL
11 BEECH CL RD
12 MAPLE CL
13 WALNUT CL
14 SPRUCE CL
15 THORNTON CL
16 GREENHAM CO
17 DEREHAM CL
18 BRUNTINGTHORPE
19 PORTSMOUTH CL
20 SYCAMORE WLK
21 CHESTNUT WAY
22 ROSEWOOD CL
23 REDWOOD LA
24 BIRCH WLK
25 HAWTHORN LA
26 MYRTLE CL
27 LANCEWOOD CL
28 APPLE CL
29 FIR WLK
30 ELM WLK
31 DOGWOOD WLK
32 CEDAR CL
33 CONINGSBY
34 LUDHAM
35 UPWOOD

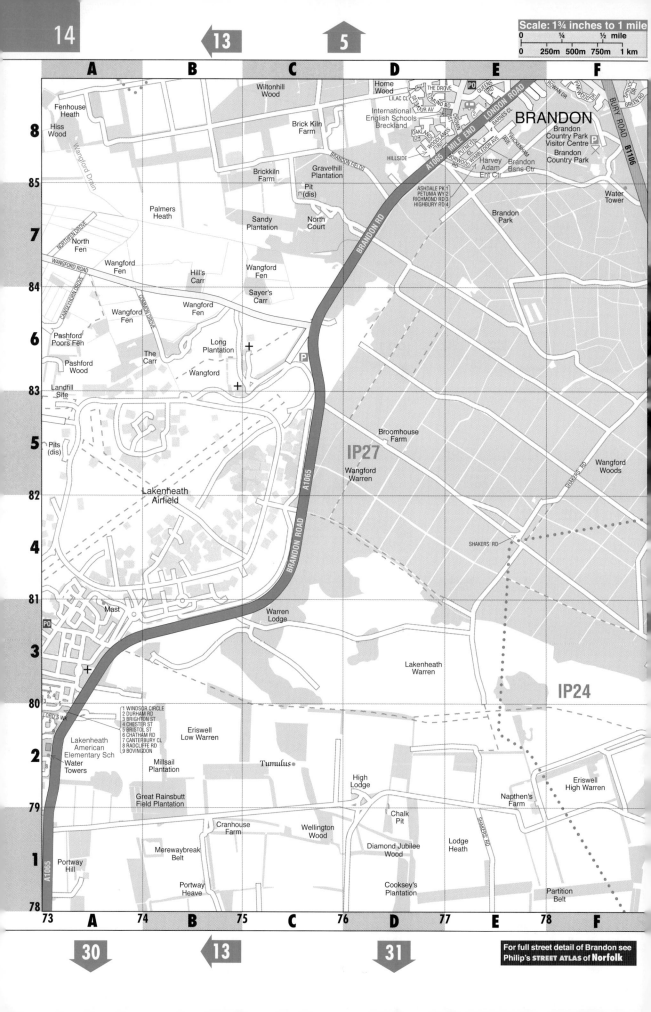

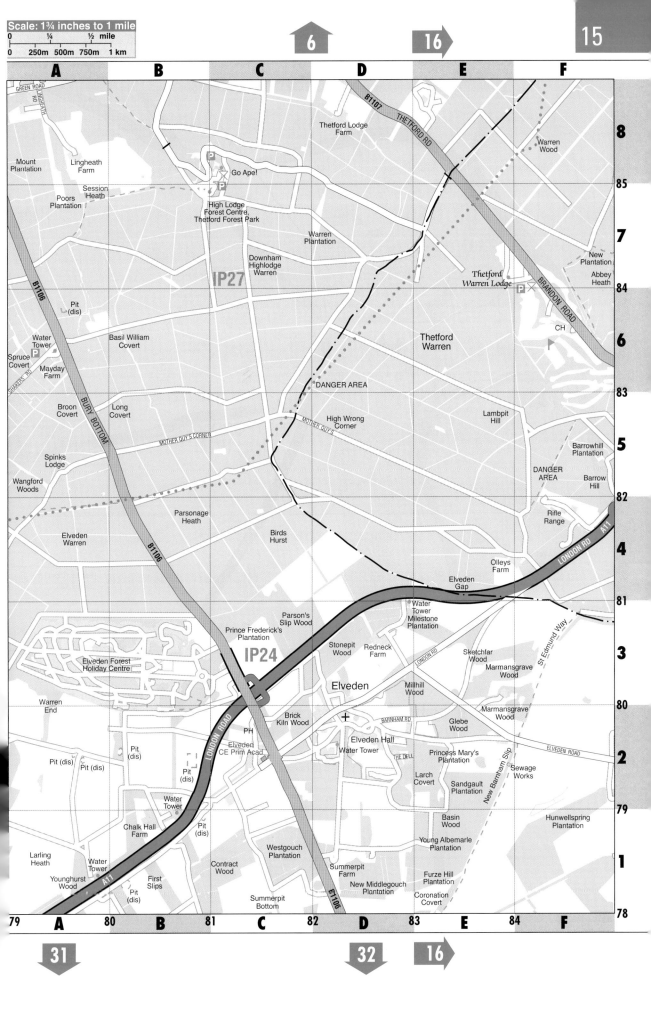

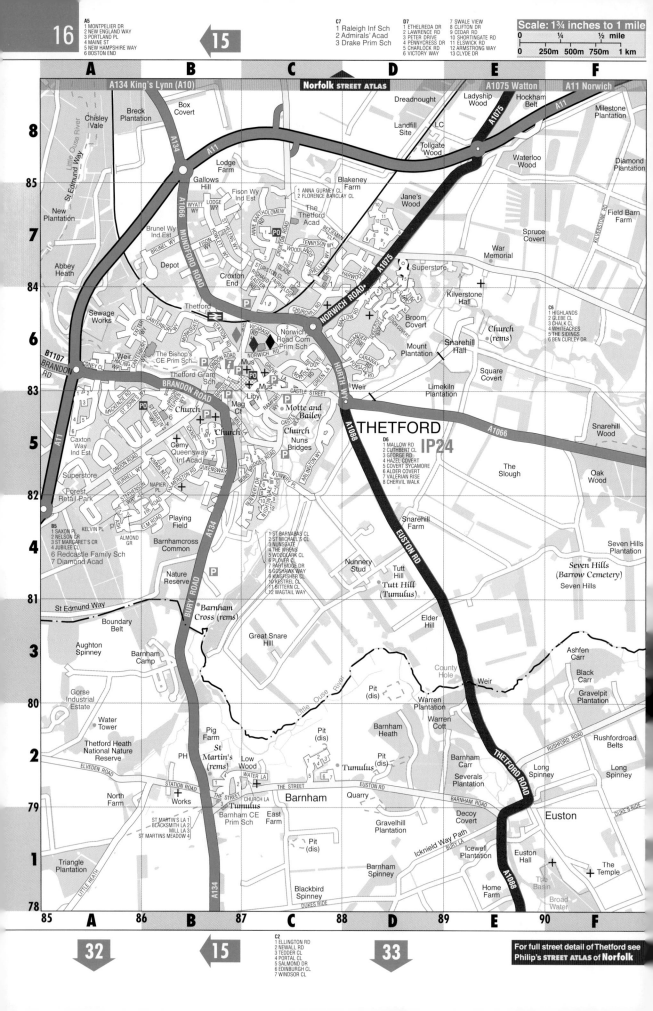

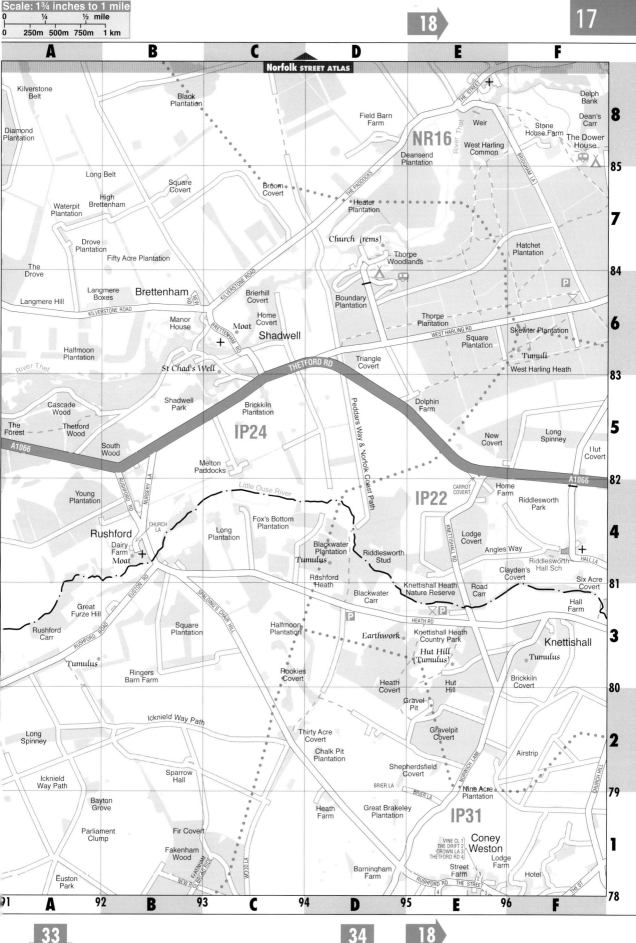

Scale: 1¾ inches to 1 mile

0   ¼   ½   mile
0 250m 500m 750m 1 km

18

A   B   C   D   E   F

Norfolk STREET ATLAS

Kilverstone Belt

Diamond Plantation

Black Plantation

Field Barn Farm

NR16

Weir

Delph Bank

Dean's Carr

The Dower House

8

Deansend Plantation

West Harling Common

Stone House Farm

85

Long Belt

Square Covert

Broom Covert

THE PADDOCKS

Heater Plantation

River Thet

BRIDGHAM LA

7

High Brettenham

Waterpit Plantation

Church (rems)

Hatchet Plantation

Drove Plantation

Thorpe Woodlands

84

Fifty Acre Plantation

The Drove

Langmere Boxes

Brettenham

KILVERSTONE ROAD

Brierhill Covert

Boundary Plantation

Thorpe Plantation

Skewter Plantation

P

6

Langmere Hill

KILVERSTONE ROAD

NEW RD

Manor House

Home Covert

Moat

Shadwell

WEST HARLING RD

Square Plantation

Tumuli

West Harling Heath

Halfmoon Plantation

BRETTENHAM RD

St Chad's Well

THETFORD RD

Triangle Covert

83

River Thet

Cascade Wood

Thetford Wood

Shadwell Park

Brickkiln Plantation

IP24

Dolphin Farm

New Covert

Long Spinney

5

The Forest

A1066

South Wood

Melton Paddocks

Peddars Way & Norfolk Coast Path

CARROT COVERT

Home Farm

Hut Covert

82

A1066

Young Plantation

RUSHFORD RD

NURSERY LA

Little Ouse River

Long Plantation

Fox's Bottom Plantation

IP22

Riddlesworth Park

KNETTISHALL RD

Lodge Covert

Angles Way

Riddlesworth Hall Sch

HALL LA

4

Rushford

CHURCH LA

Dairy Farm

Moat

Blackwater Plantation

Tumulus

Rushford Heath

Riddlesworth Stud

Clayden's Covert

Six Acre Covert

81

Great Furze Hill

EUSTON RD

Blackwater Carr

Knettishall Heath Nature Reserve

Road Carr

Hall Farm

Rushford Carr

RUSHFORD ROAD

SPALDING'S CHAIR HILL

Square Plantation

Halfmoon Plantation

P

HEATH RD

Earthwork

Knettishall Heath Country Park

P

Knettishall

Tumulus

3

Tumulus

Ringers Barn Farm

Rookies Covert

Hut Hill (Tumulus)

Brickkiln Covert

80

Icknield Way Path

Heath Covert

Hut Hill

Long Spinney

Thirty Acre Covert

Gravel Pit

Gravelpit Covert

Airstrip

CHURCH HILL

2

Icknield Way Path

Sparrow Hall

Chalk Pit Plantation

Shepherdsfield Covert

NORWICH LANE

79

Bayton Grove

Fir Covert

BRIER LA

BRIER LA

Nine Acre Plantation

IP31

1

Parliament Clump

Fakenham Wood

FAKENHAM BROAD RIDE

NEW RIDE

Heath Farm

Great Brakeley Plantation

Barningham Farm

VINE CL 1
THE DRIFT 2
CROWN LA 3
THETFORD RD 4

Street Farm

Coney Weston

Lodge Farm

Hotel

THE ST

Euston Park

RUSHFORD RD

THE STREET

78

Norfolk STREET ATLAS

Scale: 1¾ inches to 1 mile
0   ¼   ½ mile
0   250m   500m   750m   1 km

Grid columns: A B C D E F
Grid rows: 8 85 7 84 6 83 5 82 4 81 3 80 2 79 1 78

Micklemoor Hill
Settlement
Middle Harling
Mauleys Farm
Black Carr
Berdewell Hall Farm
Middle Harling Farm
Allot
Cemy
Mauleys Farm
Hill Harling Farm
Hill Harling
Grove Farm
WEST HARLING
West Harling
Town Farm
NR16
Big Wood
Flint Hall Farm
Lopham Road
Guiltcross Farm
Lodge Plantation
East Harling Road
Garboldisham Road
Privet Plantation
Tumulus
Triangle Covert
Harling Rd
Twenty Acre Plantation
Ten Acre Plantation
East Harling Heath
Tumulus
Uphall Farm
Dairy Farm
Highfield La
West Harlinghill Plantation
Roman Rd
Old Sheep Pen Plantation
Hall Farm
Cranespond Plantation
Garboldisham Manor
Stubbings's Farm
Fincham's Farm
Dickersons Farm
Fir Tree Farm
Whitebreads Farm
Hut Covert
Fir Covert
Garboldisham Heath
Sandy Betty's Plantation
Georgiana Plantation
IP22
Wilderness Plantation
Ling Farm
Orchard Farm
Gables Farm
Devil's Ditch
Tumulus
Broad Way
Long Furlong Plantation
The Hall
B1111
Garboldisham Church Prim Sch
Garboldisham
Allotments Farm
A1066
Seventeen Acre Plantation
Hill Plantation
Home Covert
Diss Road
Thetford Road
A1066
Twelve Acre Plantation
Thetford Road
Oldoak Plantation
PO
Forge Rd
Mill Pond Farm
St John's Covert
Gasthorpe
St Nicholas's Church (rems of)
Church Farm
HOPTON RD
Chapel Cl
Thomas Bole Cl
Smallworth Farm
Top Drag Way
Six Acre Covert
Lodge La
Lodge Farm
Fen Farm
Old Fen
Rec Gd
Smallworth
Three Wells Farm
Alder Carr
The Street
Angles Way
Garboldisham Common
Windmill
Boundary Farm
Broomscot Common
Clay Hall Rd
Wall Covert
Hopton Fen
Common Farm
Mill La
Hotel
Fir Covert
Willow Farm
White House Farm
Lodge Farm
All Saints Church
Common Road
Hall Farm
Church Farm
Meadowside
Manor Farm
Ash Tree Farm
Wall Covert
Dairy Farm
Manor Farm
Raydon Common
Hilldrop Farm
Middle Road
Stone La
Fen Street
Hopton
High Street
PH
Angles Way
Spring Farm
Moat
Blo' Norton
Fen Farm
Willow Farm
The Banks
Broom Covert
Robsons Farm
Thelnetham Windmill
Fen Road
IP31
Hopton Rd
Weston Fen
Hillside Farm
Hopton CE VC Prim Sch
Church Farm
Kays Farm
Thelnetham Fen (Nature Reserve)
Little Ouse River
Hinderclay Fen
Blo Norton Fen
Holiday Park
Bury Road
Church Road
Cinque Farm
Hopton End Farm
Thelnetham
Cross Green Farm
Moat
PH
St Mary's Well (Spring)
Hollow La

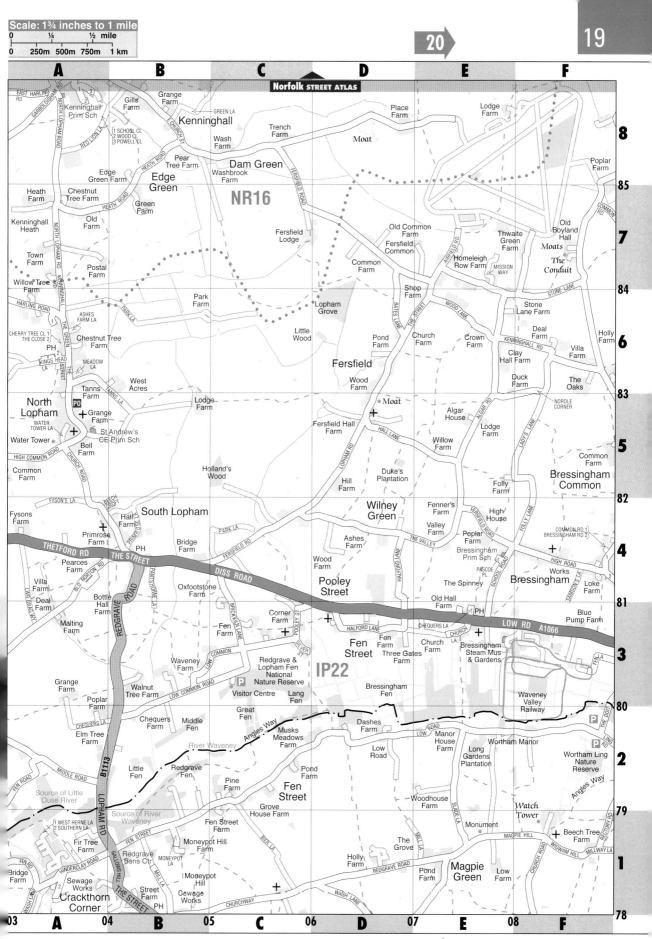

Norfolk STREET ATLAS

East Harling Rd

Kenninghall Prim Sch

Gills Farm

Grange Farm

Kenninghall

GREEN LA

Wash Farm

Trench Farm

Place Farm

Moat

Lodge Farm

Poplar Farm

1 SCHOOL CL
2 WOOD CL
3 POWELL CL

Pear Tree Farm

Dam Green

Washbrook Farm

Edge Green Farm

Edge Green

Green Farm

NR16

Fersfield Lodge

Old Common Farm

Fersfield Common

Thwaite Green Farm

Old Boyland Hall

Moats

The Conduit

Heath Farm

Chestnut Tree Farm

Old Farm

Kenninghall Heath

Town Farm

Willow Tree Farm

Postal Farm

Park Farm

Common Farm

Shop Farm

Homeleigh Row Farm

MISSION WAY

Stone Lane Farm

Deal Farm

Holly Farm

CHERRY TREE CL 1
THE CLOSE 2

Chestnut Tree Farm

Little Wood

Lopham Grove

Pond Farm

Church Farm

Crown Farm

Clay Hall Farm

Duck Farm

Villa Farm

The Oaks

PH

KINGS HEAD LA

Fersfield

Moat

Algar House

NORDLE CORNER

North Lopham

Grange Farm

Lodge Farm

Fersfield Hall Farm

Willow Farm

Lodge Farm

Common Farm

Water Tower

Bell Farm

St Andrew's CE Prim Sch

Holland's Wood

Hill Farm

Duke's Plantation

Folly Farm

Bressingham Common

Common Farm

West Acres

Wood Farm

Wilney Green

Fenner's Farm

Valley Farm

High House

COMMON RD 1
BRESSINGHAM RD 2

Fysons Farm

South Lopham

Hall Farm

Bridge Farm

Ashes Farm

Poplar Farm

Bressingham Prim Sch

THETFORD RD

THE STREET

DISS ROAD

Wood Farm

THE VALLEY

The Spinney

Bressingham

Pearces Farm

Oxfootstone Farm

Pooley Street

PASCOE PL

Works

Loke Farm

Villa Farm

Deal Farm

Bottle Hall Farm

Old Hall Farm

PH

Blue Pump Farm

LOW RD A1066

Malting Farm

Fen Farm

Corner Farm

Fen Street

Halford Lane

CHEQUERS LA

Bressingham Steam Mus & Gardens

Grange Farm

Waveney Farm

Walnut Tree Farm

Redgrave & Lopham Fen National Nature Reserve

Visitor Centre

Lang Fen

Fen Street

Three Gates Farm

Church Farm

IP22

Bressingham Fen

Waveney Valley Railway

Poplar Farm

CHEQUERS LA

Chequers Farm

Middle Fen

Great Fen

Dashes Farm

Low Road

Manor House Farm

Long Gardens Plantation

Wortham Manor

Wortham Ling Nature Reserve

Elm Tree Farm

Little Fen

Redgrave Fen

River Waveney

Angles Way

Musks Meadows Farm

Pond Farm

Angles Way

Source of Little Ouse River

Source of River Waveney

Pine Farm

Fen Street

Grove House Farm

Woodhouse Farm

SLADE LA

Watch Tower

Monument

Beech Tree Farm

1 WEST HERNE LA
2 SOUTHERN LA

Fir Tree Farm

Fen Street

Moneypot Hill Farm

The Grove

Magpie Hill

Fen Rd

Bridge Farm

Sewage Works

Redgrave Bsns Ctr

Moneypot Hill

Holly Farm

Pond Farm

Magpie Green

Low Farm

WIGWAM HILL

MILLWAY LA

Crackthorn Corner

Street Farm

Sewage Works

CHURCHWAY

WASH LANE

REDGRAVE ROAD

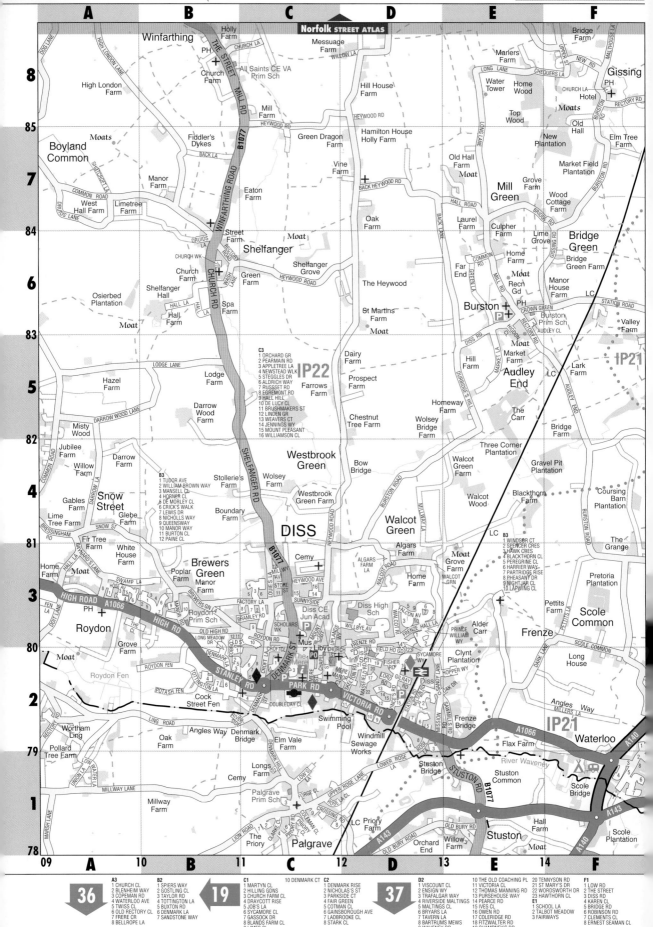

Norfolk STREET ATLAS

A **B** **C** **D** **E** **F**

Winfarthing

High London Farm

Boyland Common

Moats

West Hall Farm

Manor Farm

Limetree Farm

Holly Farm

Church Farm

PH

Church Farm

All Saints CE VA Prim Sch

Mill Farm

Fiddler's Dykes

Messuage Farm

Hill House Farm

Green Dragon Farm

Hamilton House Holly Farm

Vine Farm

Old Hall Farm Moat

Marlers Farm

Water Tower

Home Wood

Top Wood

New Plantation

Mill Green

Grove Farm

Gissing

PH

Hotel

Moats

Old Hall

Elm Tree Farm

Market Field Plantation

Wood Cottage Farm

Bridge Green

Eaton Farm

Street Farm

Shelfanger

Moat

Shelfanger Grove

Oak Farm

The Heywood

Laurel Farm

Culpher Farm

Home Farm

Far End

Lime Grove

Bridge Green Farm

Manor House Farm

LC

Osierbed Plantation

Shelfanger Hall

Church Farm

Hall Farm

Moat

Green Farm

Spa Farm

St Martins Farm

Moat

Burston

P

Burston Prim Sch

Hill Farm

Crown Green

PH

Market Farm

Moat

Audley End

Valley Farm

IP21

Hazel Farm

Lodge Farm

Farrows Farm

Prospect Farm

Dairy Farm

Lark Farm

LC

C3
1 ORCHARD GR
2 PEARMAIN CL
3 APPLETREE LA
4 NEWSTEAD WLK
5 STEGGLES DR
6 ALDRICH WAY
7 RUSSET RD
8 EGREMONT RD
9 HALL HILL
10 DE LUCY CL
11 BRUSHMAKERS ST
12 LINDEN GR
13 WEAVERS CT
14 JENNINGS WY
15 MOUNT PLEASANT
16 WILLIAMSON CL

IP22

Misty Wood

Jubilee Farm

Darrow Farm

Willow Farm

Darrow Wood Farm

Chestnut Tree Farm

Homeway Farm

Wolsey Bridge Farm

The Carr

Bridge Farm

Gables Farm

Snow Street

Glebe Farm

Lime Tree Farm

Fir Tree Farm

White House Farm

Stollerie's Farm

Wolsey Farm

Westbrook Green

Westbrook Green Farm

Bow Bridge

Boundary Farm

B3
1 TUDOR AVE
2 WILLIAM BROWN WAY
3 MANSELL CL
4 HORNER CL
5 DE MORLEY CL
6 CRICK'S WALK
7 LEWIS DR
8 NICHOLLS WAY
9 QUEENSWAY
10 MANOR WAY
11 BURTON CL
12 PAINE CL

DISS

Walcot Green

Walcot Green Farm

Walcot Wood

Three Corner Plantation

Gravel Pit Plantation

Blackthorn Farm

Coursing Barn Plantation

The Grange

B3
1 WINDSOR CT
2 SCORCER CRES
3 HAWK CRES
4 BLACKTHORN CL
5 PEREGRINE CL
6 HARRIER WAY
7 PARTRIDGE RISE
8 PHEASANT DR
9 NIGHTJAR CL
10 LAPWING CL

Home Farm

Moat

Poplar Farm

Brewers Green Manor Farm

Cemy

Algars Farm

Moat Grove Farm

Home Farm

Pretoria Plantation

Roydon

PH

Grove Farm

Moat

Roydon Prim Sch

Factory La

Sunnyside

Diss CE Jun Acad

Diss High Sch

Mus

PO

Church

Diss Inf Sch

P

Alder Carr

Clynt Plantation

Frenze

Scole Common

Long House

Pettits Farm

Scole Common

Wortham Ling

Pollard Tree Farm

Oak Farm

Angles Way

Denmark Bridge

Elm Vale Farm

Swimming Pool

Windmill Sewage Works

Frenze Bridge

A1066

Waterloo

IP21

Flax Farm

River Waveney

Angles Way

A143

Cemy

Longs Farm

Palgrave Prim Sch

The Priory

Palgrave

Stuston Bridge

Stuston Common

Stuston

Scole Bridge

Hall Farm

Moat

Scole Plantation

A140

A143

A **B** **C** **D** **E** **F**

A3
1 CHURCH CL
2 BLENHEIM WAY
3 COPEMAN RD
4 WATERLOO AVE
5 TWISS CL
6 OLD RECTORY CL
7 FRERE CR
8 BELLROPE LA

B2
1 SPIERS WAY
2 GOSTLING CL
3 TAYLOR RD
4 TOTTINGTON LA
5 BUXTON RD
6 DENMARK LA
7 SANDSTONE WAY

C1
1 MARTYN CL
2 HILLING GDNS
3 CHURCH FARM CL
4 DRAYCOTT RISE
5 JOB'S LA
6 SYCAMORE CL
7 GASSOCK DR
8 BLANDS FARM CL
9 LIMES CL

10 DENMARK CT

C2
1 DENMARK RISE
2 NICHOLAS'S ST
3 PARKSIDE CT
4 FAIR GREEN
5 COTMAN CL
6 GAINSBOROUGH AVE
7 LADBROOKE CL
8 STARK CL

D2
1 VISCOUNT CL
2 ENSIGN WY
3 TRAFALGAR WAY
4 RIVERSIDE MALTINGS
5 MALTINGS CL
6 BRYARS LA
7 TAVERN LA
8 BARTRUMS MEWS
9 WAVENEY RD

10 THE OLD COACHING PL
11 VICTORIA CL
12 THOMAS MANNING RD
13 PURSEHOUSE WAY
14 PEARCE RD
15 IVES CL
16 OWEN RD
17 COLERIDGE RD
18 FITZWALTER RD
19 CHAMPNEY'S DR

20 TENNYSON RD
21 ST MARY'S DR
22 WORDSWORTH DR
23 HAWTHORN CL

E1
1 SCHOOL LA
2 TALBOT MEADOW
3 FAIRWAYS

F1
1 LOW RD
2 THE STREET
3 DISS RD
4 KAREN CL
5 BRIDGE RD
6 ROBINSON RD
7 CLEMENTS CL
8 ERNEST SEAMAN CL

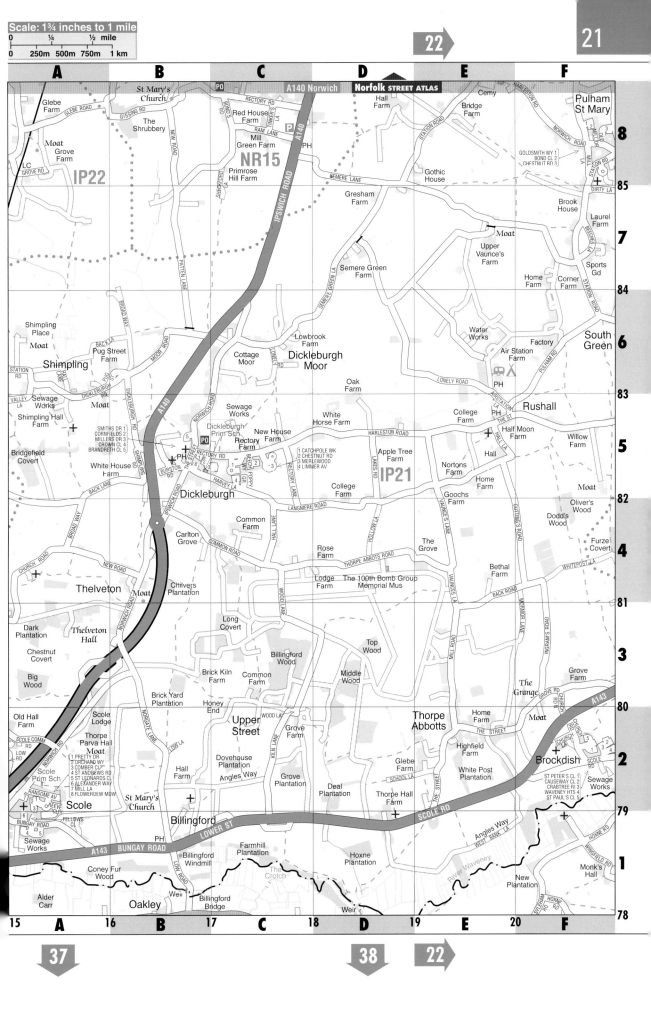

D6
1 HENRY WARD RD
2 GAWDY CL
3 BECK VW
4 POUND CL
5 HUNT CL
6 MALTINGS DR
7 PILGRIM'S WY
8 WEAVERS CROFT
9 DOUNE WY
10 CROFT CL
11 HEROLF WY
12 ALLTHORPE RD
13 PADDOCK RD
14 BULLOCK FAIR CL
15 CONSTABLE CT
16 BRIDGE CL
17 SCHOOL LA
18 CANDLER'S LA
19 STRAIGHT LA
20 BROAD ST
21 OLD MARKET PL
22 MARKET PL
23 CHURCH ST
24 MALTHOUSE CT
25 TERENCE AIREY CT
26 GLAMIS CT
27 ELIZABETH WLK
28 TITLOW RD
29 KERRIDGE WY
30 FRERE RD
31 CRANES MDW
32 EXCHANGE ST
33 MAGPIE CT
34 HOLLY CT
35 WOODLANDS
36 MENDHAM CL
37 RAINEY CT
38 MENDHAM LA
39 BRIAR RD
40 NEWLANDS CL
41 PARKLANDS WY
42 GREEN PARK
43 RUSHALL RD
44 MILLERS GN

Scale: 1¾ inches to 1 mile

0 ¼ ½ mile
0 250m 500m 750m 1 km

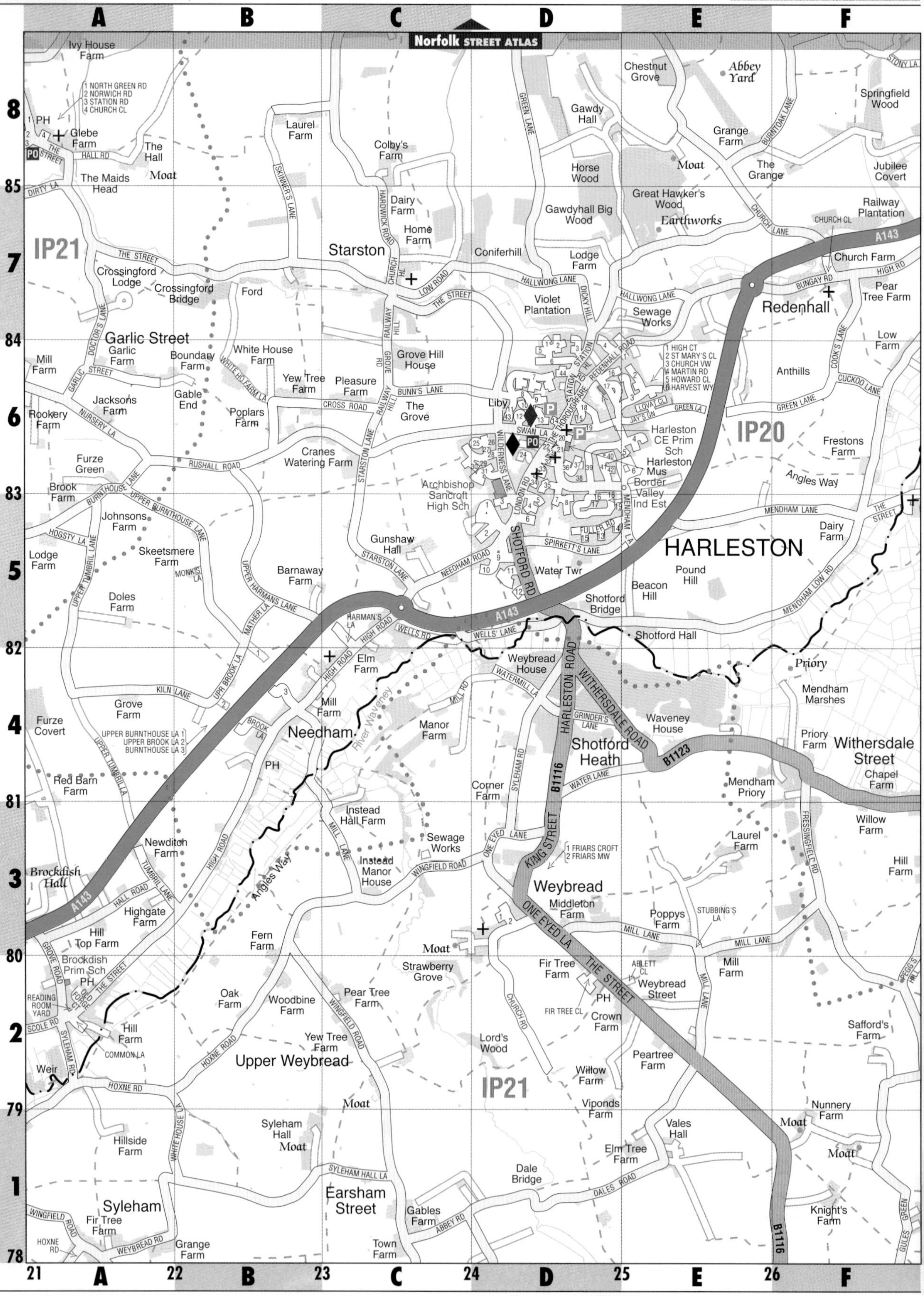

Norfolk STREET ATLAS

IP21
IP20
IP21

HARLESTON
Harleston CE Prim Sch
Harleston Mus
Border Valley Ind Est
Archbishop Sancroft High Sch

Starston
Redenhall
Needham
Weybread
Shotford Heath
Withersdale Street
Upper Weybread
Syleham
Earsham Street
Garlic Street
Brockdish

D5
1 THE COMMON
2 GOTHIC CL
3 WILDERNESS CL
4 PINE CL
5 WILLOW WLK
6 PEMBERTON RD
7 LIME CL
8 OAK TREE WY
9 DOVE CL
10 CHERRYWOOD
11 NORTHGATE
12 SOUTHGATE
13 SPEEDWELL WY
14 MAYFLOWER WY
15 CARVER WAY
16 ROBIN AVE
17 CHAFFINCH MWS
18 BLACKBIRD WAY
19 KESTREL CL

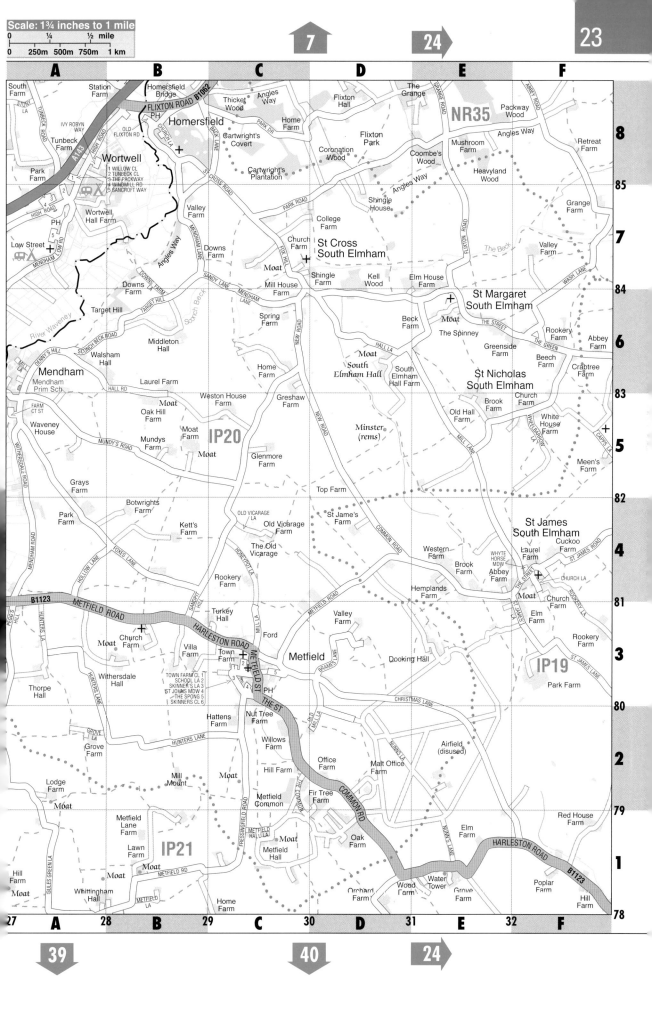

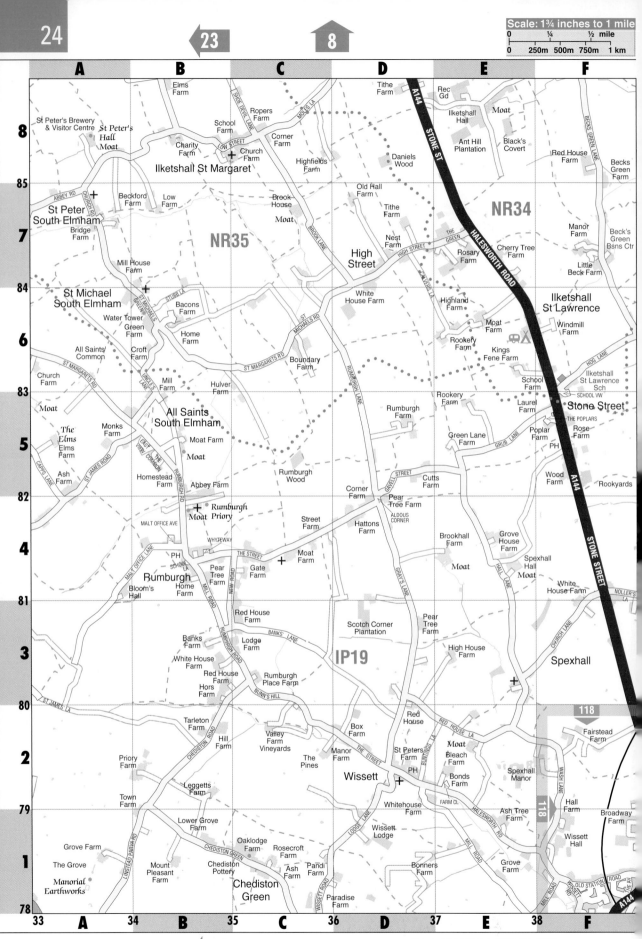

A B C D E F

8

St Peter's Brewery & Visitor Centre
St Peter's Hall Moat
St Peter South Elmham
Abbey Rd
Bridge Farm
Beckford Farm
Low Farm
Charity Farm
Elms Farm
School Farm
Ropers Farm
Corner Farm
Highfields Farm
Church Farm
Ilketshall St Margaret
Side Devil Lane
Low Street
Monks La

85

NR35

Brook House Moat
Old Hall Farm
Tithe Farm
Rec Gd
Ilketshall Hall
Moat
Ant Hill Plantation
Black's Covert
Red House Farm
Becks Green Lane
Becks Green Farm

7

St Michael South Elmham
Mill House Farm
Stubb La
Bacons Farm
Brook Lane
High Street
Nest Farm
The Green
Cherry Tree Farm
Rosary Farm
NR34
Manor Farm
Beck's Green Bsns Ctr
Little Beck Farm

84

Water Tower
Green Farm
St Michaels Green
Home Farm
St Michaels Rd
St Margarets Rd
Boundary Farm
White House Farm
Rumburgh Lane
Highland Farm
Moat Farm
Rookery Farm
Kings Fene Farm
School Farm
Ilketshall St Lawrence
Windmill Farm
Hog Lane
Ilketshall St Lawrence Sch
School VW

6

All Saints Common
Croft Farm
Lincs Lane
Mill Farm
Hulver Farm
Rumburgh Farm
Rookery Farm
Laurel Farm
Stone Street
The Poplars
Rose Farm

83

Church Farm
Moat
The Elms Elms Farm
Monks Farm
Ash Farm
East View Common
All Saints South Elmham
Moat Farm
Moat
Homestead Farm
Abbey Farm
Rumburgh Wood
Corner Farm
Gavell Street
Pear Tree Farm
Cutts Farm
Aldous Corner
Green Lane Farm
Grub Lane
Poplar Farm
PH
Wood Farm
Rookyards

5

Capps Lane
St James Road
St James Road
Rumburgh Rd
Malt Office Ave
Moat
Rumburgh Priory
Whyteway
Street Farm
Hattons Farm
Gray's Lane
Brookhall Farm
Moat
Grove House Farm
Spexhall Hall Moat
White House Farm
Noller's La

82

Malt Office Lane
PH
School La
Rumburgh
Bloom's Hall
Home Farm
The Street
Pear Tree Farm
Gate Farm
Moat Farm
Scotch Corner Plantation
Pear Tree Farm
High House Farm
Hall Lane
Spexhall
Church Lane

4

New Road
Mill Road
Red House Farm
Banks Lane

81

Banks Farm
White House Farm
Red House Farm
Hors Farm
Lodge Farm
Rumburgh Place Farm
Nunn's Hill
IP19
Red House
Fairstead Farm
118

3

St James La
Chediston Road
Tarleton Farm
Hill Farm
Valley Farm Vineyards
Box Farm
The Street
St Peters Farm
PH
Moat
Bleach Farm
Bonds Farm
Buntings La
Red House La
Halesworth Road
Spexhall Manor
Wash Lane
Hall Farm
Broadway Farm
Wissett Hall

80

Priory Farm
Town Farm
Leggetts Farm
The Pines
Manor Farm
Wissett
Whitehouse Farm
Farm Cl
Ash Tree Farm
118
Mill Road

2

Grove Farm
The Grove
Manorial Earthworks
Linstead Parva Rd
Mount Pleasant Farm
Lower Grove Farm
Chediston Green
Oaklodge Farm
Rosecroft Farm
Ash Farm
Chediston Pottery
Chediston Green
Pandi Farm
Wissett Road
Lodge Lane
Wissett Lodge
Bonners Farm
Grove Farm
Mill Road
Wissett Rd
Old Station Road
Green La
A144

79

1

78

33 A 34 B 35 C 36 D 37 E 38 F

⬇ 40

⬅ 23

⬇ 41

For full street detail of the highlighted area see page 118

118 ⬇

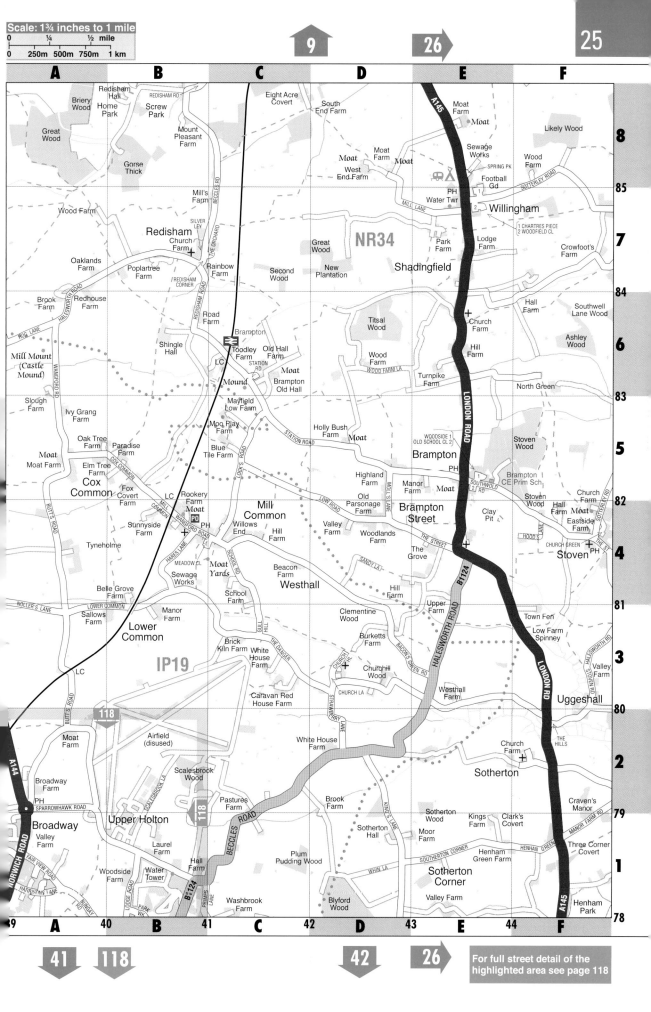

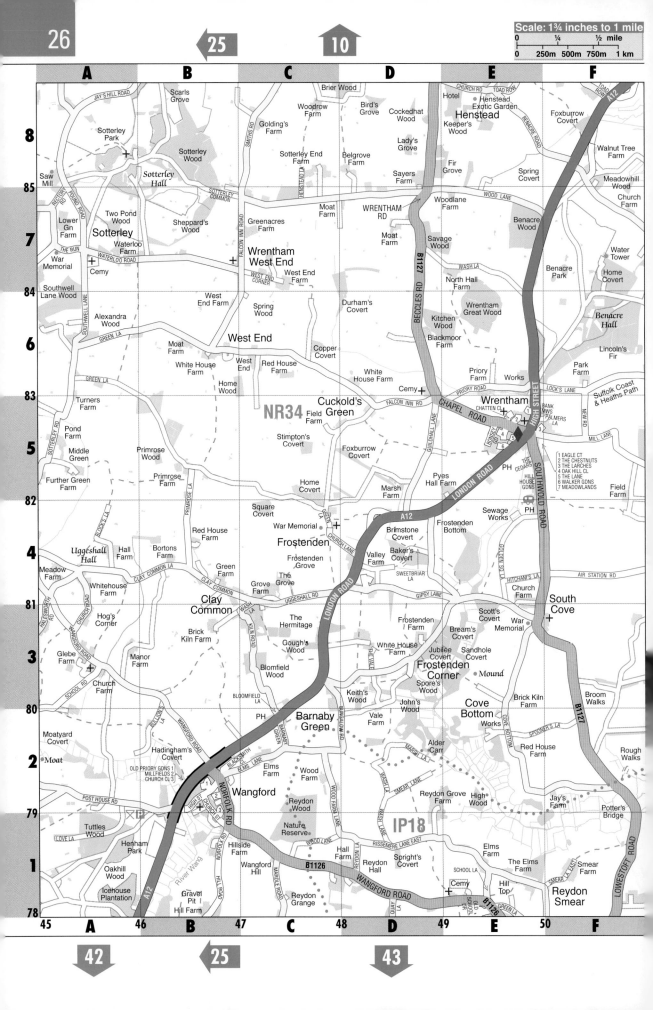

Scale: 1¾ inches to 1 mile

| 0 | ¼ | ½ | mile |
| 0 | 250m | 500m | 750m | 1 km |

A **B** **C** **D** **E** **F**

Kessingland Beach

PH
CHURCH RD

NR33

COOPERS LA.

NEW RD

MARSH LA.

BEACH RD

HOLLY GRANGE ROAD

Blackcap Wood

Churchfarm Marshes

Sewage Works

Suffolk Coast & Heaths Path

Kessingland Level

Benacre

War Memorial

THE STREET

MARSH LA.

Church Covert

Beachfarm Marshes

Northwalk Plantation

Pumping Station

The Denes

Beach Farm

Hall Farm

BACK LA.

Blackwater Covert

Alder Carr

Coney Hill

Wood Farm

Boathouse Covert

Holly Hang

Craft Plantation

Benacre National Nature Reserve

NR34

Benacre Broad

Long Covert

Holly Grove

North Common Wood

Chancel Covert

BEACH RD

St Andrew's Church

Ausgates

GREEN LA.

AIR STATION RD

Church Farm

Covehithe

Covehithe Cliffs

Porter's Farm

Green Heath

PORTERS FARM TRACK

Covehithe Broad

Warren House

Suffolk Coast & Heaths Path

The Warren

Easton Wood

Benacre National Nature Reserve

Easton Home Covert

Easton Broad

Pottersbridge Marshes

Easton Marshes

IP18

Easton Bavents

Easton Cliffs

EASTON LA.

8
85
7
84
6
83
5
82
4
81
3
80
2
79
1
78

51 A 52 B 53 C 54 D 55 E 56 F

D5
1 NORTH DR
2 ST FELIX CL
3 CALFE FEN CL
4 OLD SCHOOL CL
5 HOLMES LA
6 SNOWBERRY WY
7 FOX WOOD N
8 MARTIN CL
9 POPPY FIELDS
10 PRIMROSE LA
11 FOX WOOD S
12 CYPRIAN RUST WY
13 SHOCKSHAM TERR

Scale: 1¾ inches to 1 mile

0   ¼   ½   mile

0   250m 500m 750m 1 km

The Dunstalls
Mow Sides
Lay Clerks Farm
Harlock's Farm
Nornea Farm
Hithertree Farm
Crooked Drain
Hundred Acres
Great Fen
St John's Farm
Water Tower
Great Fen

A142 Ely
SOHAM ROAD
NORNEA LANE
Delph Bridge
Eye Hill Farm
Town Drain
Westfields Farm
Broadhill Farm
Castles Farm
Slack's Hill

Turf Fen
Blockmoor Farm
Barcham Farm
Crow Hall Farm
Broad Hill
Great Hasse Farm

TWO POLE DRO
BARWAY ROAD
A142
Blockmoor Fen
ELY ROAD
Orchard Farm
Saxon Farm
Longfield Farm
HASSE ROAD
RICK'S DROVE
Crooked Ditch

BARWAY ROAD
LC
Barway Fen
BLOCKMOOR ROAD
Orchard Farm Business Park
North Field
North Horse Fen
Hodson Farm
The Hasse

THE BIRCHES 1
CLOVERFIELD DR 2
CAMPION CL 3
BLACKTHORN CT 4
THORN CL 5
LAPWING WY 6
TEAL AVE 7
BITTERN GROVE 8
ASPEN WY 9
CADWALL WAY 10
REDSHANK CL 11

HOLTS DROVE
Soham Lode
THE COTES
THE SHADE
BARCHAM ROAD
Shade Common
Northfield Windmill
NORTHFIELD ROAD
HORSE FEN DRO
SAYER'S LANE DROVE
Granary Farm
Dolver Farm
LONG DOLVER DROVE
LITTLE HASSE DROVE
Mardon Farm
Willow Farm

Sedge Fen
NEW DROVE
SEALODES ROAD
Engine Farm
Tiled House Farm
Pantile Farm
ST SIMONS RD
BLACKBERRY LA
The Shade Prim Sch
Sewage Works
NORTHFIELD
THE SHADE PK
Bancroft Field
Soham Fen
THIRST DROVE
A142
BANCROFT DROVE
Hotel

Engine Drain
GREAT DROVE
BROAD PIECE
LC
CB7
Soham
The Weatheralls Prim Sch
EAST FEN DRO

CLARKS DRO
Middlemere Farm
SPENCER DRO
JULIUS MARTIN
East Fen Farm
Moor Farm

Mull Drain
MIDDLE DROVE
Soham Mere
Angle Common
WEST DR CR
Thomas Mews
Horse Bridge
Soham Lode
Horse Fen

Low Barn
Soham Mere
North Angle Farm
ANGLE COMMON
LC
Liby
THE CAUSEWAY
Regal La Ind Est
Wet Horse Fen

Wicken Dolves
GREAT DROVE
South Angle Farm
MILL DROVE
PO
Soham Village Coll
Ross Peers Sp Ctr
St Andrew's CE Prim Sch
ARCHERS CL
Cemy
GREENHILL'S

Twelve Foot Drain
Twelve Foot Drain
BROOKS DROVE
LC
CHERRYTREE LANE
Ash Closes
Cherry Tree Farm
FORDHAM ROAD

Horse Croft
Horse Fen
Small Path Hill
Windmill
Water Tower

The Bracks
The Bracks
NO DITCH BALK
MILITARY RD
Down Field
LARKHALL ROAD
COOPER ROAD

A1123 St. Ives
STRETHAM RD
LOWER ROAD
Football Ground
SWALLOWTAIL CL
North Corner
South Horse Fen
TORSEFEN DROVE
CALLOW BALK
Horse Fen
WICKEN ROAD
No Ditch Bridge
Block Farm
BLOCK ROAD
Down Field Windmill
Lark Hall Bridge
WINDMILL CL 1
CENTRE RD 2
CORNMILLS RD 3
MISTRAL CL 4

THE CRESCENT
NORTH ST
HIGH ST
CHAPEL LANE
DRURY LANE
Wicken
Hall
PH
Cemy
HORSEFEN DROVE
No Ditch Field
A1123
Westside Farm
A142
SOHAM ROAD

Visitor Centre
BACK LA
POND LA
Windmill
CROSS GREEN
Chancel Farm
CB5

National Trust
Moat
Little Fen

D3
1 LODE CL
2 COLLEGE RD
3 REGENT PL
4 FRANK BRIDGES CL
5 REDHOUSE GDNS
6 THE CRESCENT
7 FORDHAM RD
8 MEADOW CL
9 MILL CFT
10 BUTTS CL
11 COLLEGE CL
12 GIDNEY LA
13 ENNION CL

D4
1 ROSEBAY GDNS
2 BLUEBELL WK
3 HERBERT HUMAN CL
4 HONEYSUCKLE CL
5 NIGHTALL RD
6 CHESTNUT DR
7 GIMBERT RD
8 QUEENSWAY
9 WEATHERALLS CL
10 TEN BELL LA
11 BERRYCROFT
12 GUNTONS CL
13 BELL GDNS
14 FREDERICK TALBOT CL
15 CHURCHGATE ST
16 MARKET ST
17 ADELAIDE CL
18 EASTERN AV
19 BREWHOUSE LA
20 WHITE HART LA
21 GARDENERS LA
22 BROOK DAM CL
23 CHURCH HALL CT
24 ST ANDREWS PK
25 LINES CL
26 DIAMOND JUBILEE CL
27 MAPLE CL

44

E3
1 CELANDINE VIEW
2 VALERIAN GDNS
3 PENNYWORT
4 SYMPHONY CT
5 SUNBURST GREEN
6 MORELLO CHASE
7 GLENARE CT
8 HARDFIELDS CT
9 SKIMMER CHASE
10 PERCH CHASE
11 DACE DR
12 BLACKBERRY LA

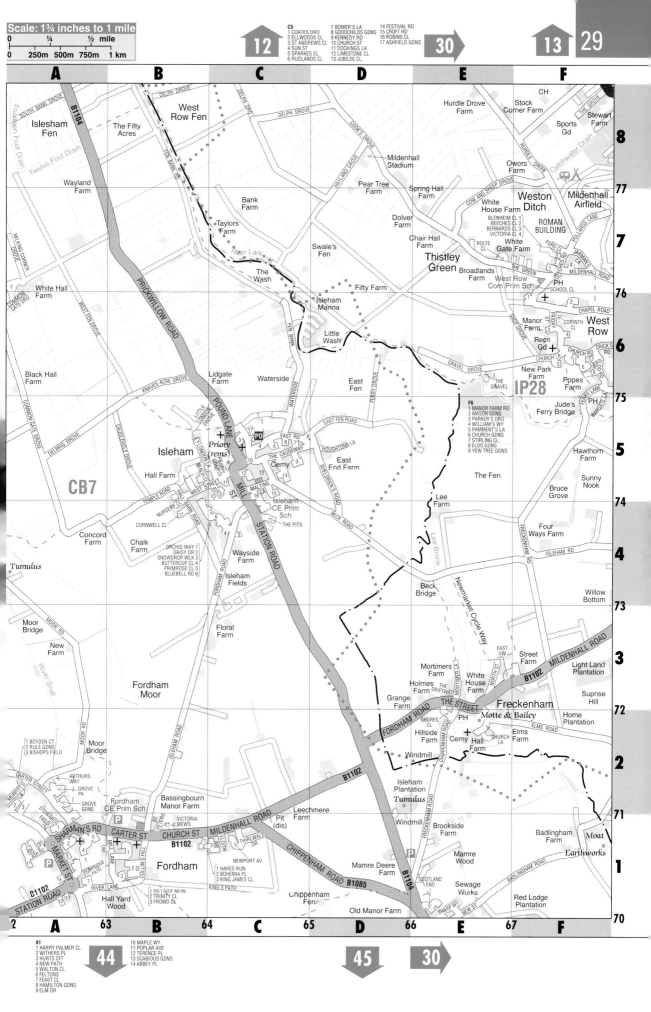

Isleham Fen

South Bank Drove

B1104

The Fifty Acres

West Row Fen

Delph Drove

Delph Dro

Delph Drove

Cook's Drove

CH

Stock Corner Farm

The Grove

Sports Gd

Stewart Farm

Fourteen Foot Drain

Twelve Foot Drain

Wayland Farm

Milking Corner Drove

Bank Farm

Taylors Farm

Fen Bank Rd

Hayland Grove

Hurdle Drove Farm

Mildenhall Stadium

Catchwater Drain

Owers Farm

Pear Tree Farm

Spring Hall Farm

Hurdle Drove

77

River Lark

The Wash

Swale's Fen

Dolver Farm

Chair Hall Farm

Cow and Sheep Drove

White House Farm

Weston Ditch

Mildenhall Airfield

Pollards Lane

7

White Hall Farm

Western Drove

Common Gate Dro

Prickwillow Road

Fifty Farm

Isleham Marina

Thistley Green

Broadlands Farm

BLENHEIM CL 1
BEECHES CL 2
BERNARDS CL 3
VICTORIA CL 4

White Gate Farm

Rolfe Cl

The Green

Ford Cl

Jarman's

Mildenhall Road

76

Black Hall Farm

Knaves Acre Drove

Delbrig Drove

Common Gate Drove

Lidgate Farm

Waterside

Little Wash

East Fen

Gravel Drove

West Row Com Prim Sch

PH

School Cl

Chapel Road

Manor Farm

Friday St

Corinth Cl

Recn Gd

Church La

New Park Farm

West Row

Crick's Rd

Eldo Rd

Poppes Fen

Ferry Lane

6

CB7

Pound Lane

Little London Drove

Fen Bank

Waterside

East Rd

East Fen Road

Houghtons La

Sheldrick's Road

The Gravel

IP28

F6
1 MANOR FARM RD
2 MASON GDNS
3 PARKER'S DRO
4 WILLIAM'S WY
5 PAMMENT'S LA
6 CHURCH GDNS
7 STIRLING CL
8 ELDO GDNS
9 YEW TREE GDNS

Jude's Ferry Bridge

Ferry Bridge

PH

Hawthorn Farm

75

Isleham

Priory rems

Hall Farm

Temple Road

Cemy

THE CAUSEWAY

East End Farm

The Fen

Bruce Grove

Sunny Nook

PO

5

Nursery Cl

West Street

MALTING LA

Isleham CE Prim Sch

THE PITS

Beck Road

Lee Farm

Four Ways Farm

Freckenham Rd

Isleham Rd

74

Concord Farm

Chalk Farm

CORNWELL CL

ORCHID WAY 1
DAISY DR 2
SNOWDROP WLK 3
BUTTERCUP CL 4
PRIMROSE CL 5
BLUEBELL RD 6

Wayside Farm

Isleham Fields

Lee Brook

Beck Bridge

4

Tumulus

Fordham Road

Floral Farm

Newmarket Cycle Way

Willow Bottom

73

Moor Bridge

New Farm

Moor Rd

River Snail

Fordham Moor

Station Road

Mortimers Farm

Holmes Farm

THE DRIFTWAY

White House Farm

Mortimell La

North St

EAST VW

Street Farm

B1102

Mildenhall Road

Light Land Plantation

Suprise Hill

3

Moor Rd

Moor Bridge

Isleham Lane

Grange Farm

Fordham Road

SHORES CL

THE STREET

Freckenham

Motte & Bailey

PH

Home Plantation

72

1 BOYDEN CT
2 RULE GDNS
3 BISHOPS FIELD

Carter Street

Arthurs Way

Grove Pk

Grove Gdns

Fordham CE Prim Sch

Bassingbourn Manor Farm

ST PETERS ST

Leechmere Farm

Hillside Farm

Cemy

Hall Farm

Church La

Elms Farm

Elms Road

2

Murfitt's La

Stewards Field

Sharman's Rd

Carter St

Church St

Mildenhall Road

Victoria Mews

NEWPORT AV

Pit (dis)

Chippenham Road

Windmill

Isleham Plantation

Tumulus

Windmill

Brookside Farm

Badlingham Farm

Moat Earthworks

71

Market St

B1102

THIRLWAL DR

ELDITH

B1104

Mamre Deere Farm

Mamre Wood

Badlingham Road

Red Lodge Plantation

1

C1102

Station Road

Ash Rd

Bridge Path

Collin's Hill

River Lane

Hall Yard Wood

1 HILLSIDE MUW
2 TRINITY CL
3 FROWD CL

1 HARES RUN
2 BOHEMIA PL
3 KING JAMES CL

KING'S PATH

Fordham

Chippenham Fen

B1085

Old Manor Farm

Scotland End

Sewage Works

Tharp Wy

New St

70

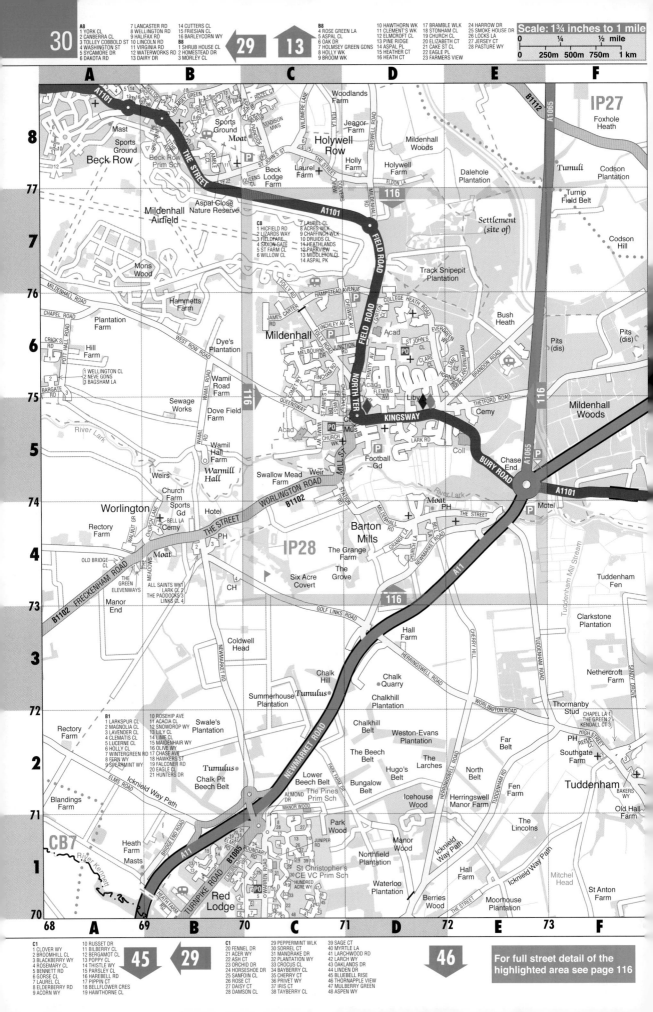

A8
1 YORK CL
2 COPPRA CL
3 TOLLEY COBBOLD ST
4 WASHINGTON ST
5 SYCAMORE DR
6 DAKOTA RD

7 LANCASTER RD
8 WELLINGTON RD
9 HALIFAX RD
10 LINCOLN RD
11 VIRGINIA RD
12 WATERWORKS RD
13 DAIRY DR

14 CUTTERS CL
15 FRIESIAN CL
B8
1 SHRUB HOUSE CL
2 HOMESTEAD DR
3 MORLEY CL

16 BARLEYCORN WY

29 **13**

B8
4 ROSE GREEN LA
5 ASPAL CL
6 OAK DR
7 HOLMSEY GREEN GDNS
8 HOLLY WK
9 BROOM WK

10 HAWTHORN WK
11 CLEMENT'S WK
12 ELMCROFT CL
13 PINE RIDGE
14 HEATHLANDS
15 HEATHER CT
16 HEATH CT

17 BRAMBLE WLK
18 STONHAM CL
19 CHURCH CL
20 ELIZABETH CT
21 CAKE ST CL
22 EAGLE PL
23 FARMERS VIEW

24 HARROW DR
25 SMOKE HOUSE DR
26 LOCKS LA
27 JERSEY CT
28 PASTURE WY

Scale: 1¾ inches to 1 mile
0   ¼   ½ mile
0   250m 500m 750m 1 km

C8
1 HICFIELD RD
2 LIZARDS WAY
3 FIELDFARE
4 SAXON GATE
5 ST FARM CL
6 WILLOW CL

7 LAUREL CL
8 ACRES WLK
9 CHAFFINCH WLK
10 DRUIDS CL
11 HEATHLANDS
12 PARKVIEW
13 MIDDLETON CL
14 ASPAL PK

B1
1 LARKSPUR CL
2 MAGNOLIA CL
3 LAVENDER CL
4 CLEMATIS CL
5 LUCERNE CL
6 HOLLY CL
7 WINTERGREEN RD
8 FERN WY
9 SPEARMINT WY

10 ROSEHIP AVE
11 ACACIA CL
12 SNOWDROP WY
13 LILY CL
14 LIME CL
15 MAIDENHAIR WY
16 OLIVE WY
17 CHASE AVE
18 HAWKERS CL
19 FALCONER RD
20 EAGLE CL
21 HUNTERS DR

C1
1 CLOVER WY
2 BROOMHILL CL
3 BLACKBERRY WY
4 ROSEMARY CL
5 BENNETT RD
6 GORSE CL
7 LAUREL RD
8 ELDERBERRY RD
9 ACORN WY

10 RUSSET DR
11 BILBERRY CL
12 BERGAMOT CL
13 THISTLE WY
14 PARSLEY CL
15 HAREBELL RD
16 PIPPIN CT
17 BELLFLOWER CRES
18 HAWTHORNE CL

45 **29**

C1
20 FENNEL DR
21 ACER WY
22 ASH CT
23 ORCHID DR
24 HORSESHOE DR
25 SANFOIN CL
26 ROSE CT
27 DAISY CT
28 DAMSON CL

29 PEPPERMINT WLK
30 SORREL CT
31 MANDRAKE DR
32 PLANTATION CL
33 CROCUS CL
34 BAYBERRY CL
35 CHERRY CT
36 PRIVET WY
37 IRIS CT
38 TAYBERRY CL

39 SAGE CT
40 MYRTLE LA
41 LARCHWOOD RD
42 LARCH WY
43 OAKLANDS DR
44 LINDEN DR
45 BLUEBELL RISE
46 THORNAPPLE VIEW
47 MULBERRY GREEN
48 ASPEN WY

46

For full street detail of the highlighted area see page 116

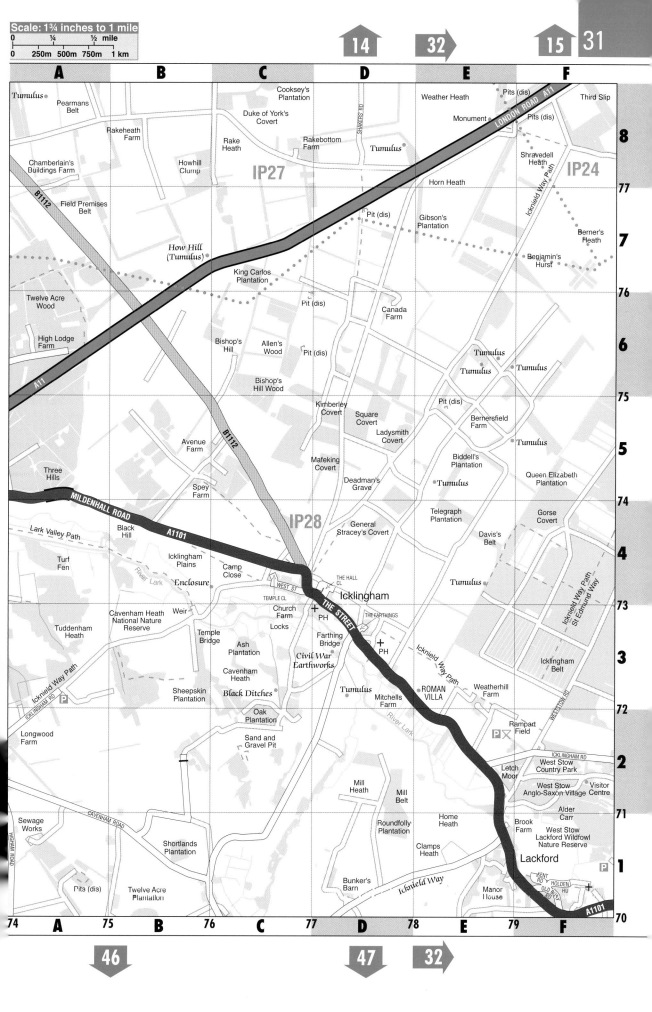

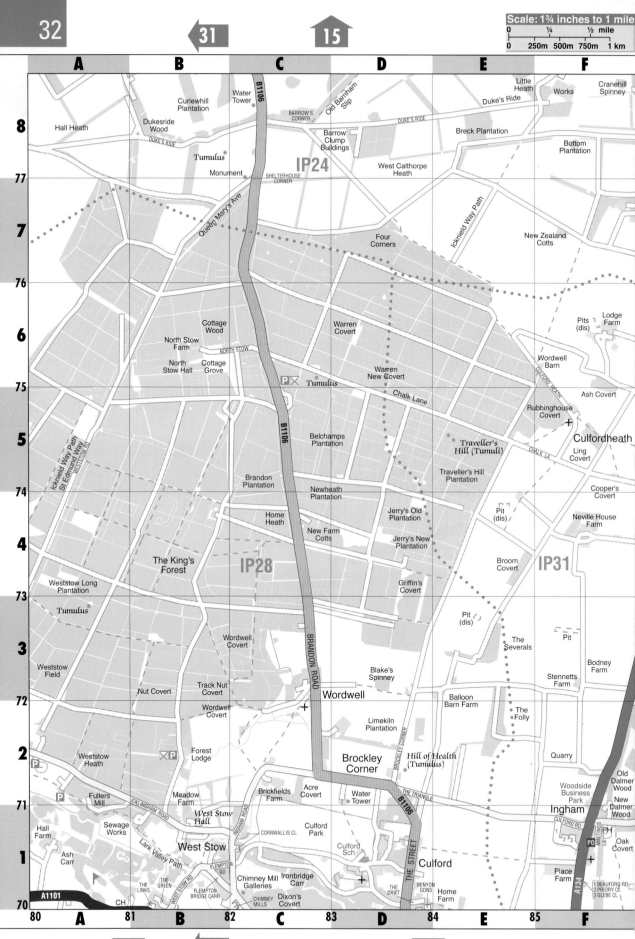

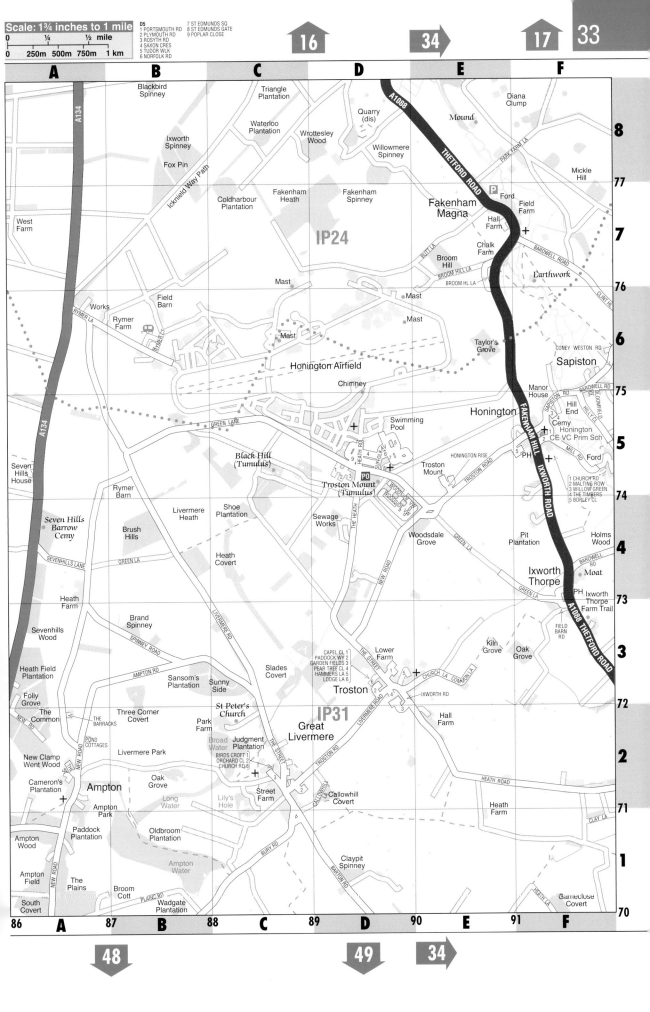

A | B | C | D | E | F

8
Fakenham Wood
Barningham Park
Coney Weston
SWAN LA 1
PADDOCK FARM 2
Willowtree Farm
Meadow Farm
THETFORD ROAD
PH
The Street
Square Plantation
Hollow Lane Farm
HOLLOW LANE
PH
B1111
Pinnocks Farm
CROW ST
Moat Plantation
SANDY LA

77
Wellmere Grove
Heath Cottages
Triangle Plantation
HEATH ROAD
NORWICH LANE
Pilgrim Shed
DAY'S LA
POUND CORNER
SANDY LANE
BISHOPS CFT
Lych Gate Cemy
CHURCH GDNS 1
ST ANDREWS CL 2
MILLERS YARD 3
Barningham CE VC Prim Sch
Barningham
HOPTON ROAD
CHURCH RD
PO
LINGWOOD CL
1 JARROLD CL
2 MILLFIELD RD
HEPWORTH ROAD

7
Park Grove
Heath Cottages
Great Grove
Lanket's Grove
White House Farm
Lodge Farm
BARDWELL ROAD
DROUT'S LA
STANTON ROAD
1
2

76
Upper Grove
Grove Farm
Water Tower
Bowbeck
Home Farm
North Common
IP22
Meadow Farm
Stanton Road Farm
Ringers Farm
NORTH COMMON

6
CLINT HILL
CONEY WESTON RD
Lanket's Grove
Dale Farm
B1111

75
BARDWELL ROAD
Little Dale Farm
Chapel Farm
DALE RD
GEORGE HILL
Hill Farm
FIELD LA

5
The Black Bourn
Pit (dis)
Mill Farm
Ford
Black Bridge
Blackwater Farm
Manor Farm
IP31
Stanton Chare
Lower Chare Farm
Little Hill Farm
HILLTOP WY
ROMAN VILLA
Little Chare Farm
Chare Farm
BARNINGHAM
Hill Farm
IP22

74
Ford
Thorpe Carr
Bardwell CE VC Prim Sch
Bardwell Windmill
SPRING LANE
SCHOOL LA
1 LAMMAS CL
2 OLD MILL CT
3 SKIMMERS LA
PO
STANTON ROAD
Dexters Farm
BARDWELL ROAD
Church
BARNINGHAM RD
A143 BURY ROAD
BOBBYS WY
GEORGE HILL
DUKE ST
CHARE FARM

4
Holms Wood
BARDWELL ROAD
IXWORTH THORPE RD
Place Farm
The Croft
CHURCH RD
QUAKER LA
UPPER ST
Bardwell
LEGION RISE
DAVEY'S LANE
PH
Stanton
OLD BURY RD
HEPWORTH ROAD
GILBERT RD
PO
VOTIERS
Stanton Post Mill
CHARITY
WILLIAM WAY
GOLDSMITH
Hall Farm
GROVE LANE
Upthorpe

73
Great Carr
Little Carr
CARR LA
LOW STREET
KNOX LANE
Rose and Crown CT
PH
Recn Gd
GLASSFIELD ROAD
Stanton Com Prim Sch
The Grundle
SHEPHERDS GROVE PK 1
DROVERS RISE 2
Mount Farm
The Grundle
Vicarage Farm
WASH LA
Pond Farm

3
THETFORD ROAD
Home Covert
The Black Bourn
BARDWELL ROAD
St John's Wood
New Grove
WYKEN ROAD
Alecock's Grave
Half Grove
Hockhouse Grove
Kiln Wood
Paddock End
NEWLANDS CL
Bromptons Farm
Sleights Wood
Park Farm
BURY LA
PARK FARM DR
Shepherd's Grove
MOUNT FARM

72
Bangrove Wood
Bardwell Manor
Dovehouse Wood
Long Grove
PADDOCK LA
Rushgreen Grove

2
Abbey Farm
Great Carr
HEATH ROAD
A1088
Ixworth
THISTLEDOWN DR
THE LANGHOLDS
STANTON ROAD
WOOLPIT ROAD
Burntfirs Plantation
Wyken Vineyard & Gardens
WYKEN LA
Wyken Hall
Wyken Wood
Ash Grove
Mulley's Grove

71
Potter's Plantation
CLAY LA
Water Twr
THE LANGHOLDS
BARDWELL RD
A143
WALSHAM ROAD
KILN LANE
STUD RD
Hillwatering Farm
Ixworth Free Sch

1
Long Carr
Rabbit Plantation
Moat
Priory (rems)
Ixworth Abbey
Hall & Liby
PO
Cemy
CROWN
Ixworth CE Prim Sch
CROWN LA
Woodstreet Farm
WOOLPIT RD
CROWN LA
Sandyways Farm
Sunny Side

70
Priory Waterfowl Farm
Bridge Farm
STOW ROAD
A1088

92 | 93 | 94 | 95 | 96 | 97
A | B | C | D | E | F

B1
1 PEDDARS CL
2 CHALK LA
3 PEASECROFT RD
4 STREET FARM LA
5 ST EDMUND CL
6 WALSHAM RD
7 COLTSFOOT CL
8 CODDINGTON WY
9 GOUGH PL
10 ABBEY CL
11 BEECHES CL
12 GARRARD PL
13 SCOTT RD
14 COMMISTER LA
15 CROWN CRES
16 THE PADDOCK
17 SADDLERS YARD
18 PEACOCK RISE
19 NEW RD

20 THOMAS CL
21 KETTLEBORROW CL
22 PLUMMER CL
23 MICKLESMERE DR
24 FORDHAM PL
25 REEVE CL
26 COPPER CT
27 LOWER FARM DR
28 PARK YD

E4
1 OLD BARNINGHAM RD
2 CAPELL WLK
3 PARKSIDE
4 CULVERS MDW
5 THE CHASE
6 GRUNDLE CL
7 DUKE ST
8 BUCKLES FIELD
9 NORTH CL
10 CATCHPOLE WY
11 LOFFT CL
12 MICHAELHOUSE WY
13 SHETLANDS
14 JACOBS CL
15 CHURCH CL
16 MEADOW CT
17 THE KNOWLE
18 FIELD WY
19 WINDMILL GN
20 SCHOOL CL
21 FORDHAMS CL
22 STURGEON WY
23 HONEYMEADE CL
24 HORSESHOE RISE
25 CONEY WLK

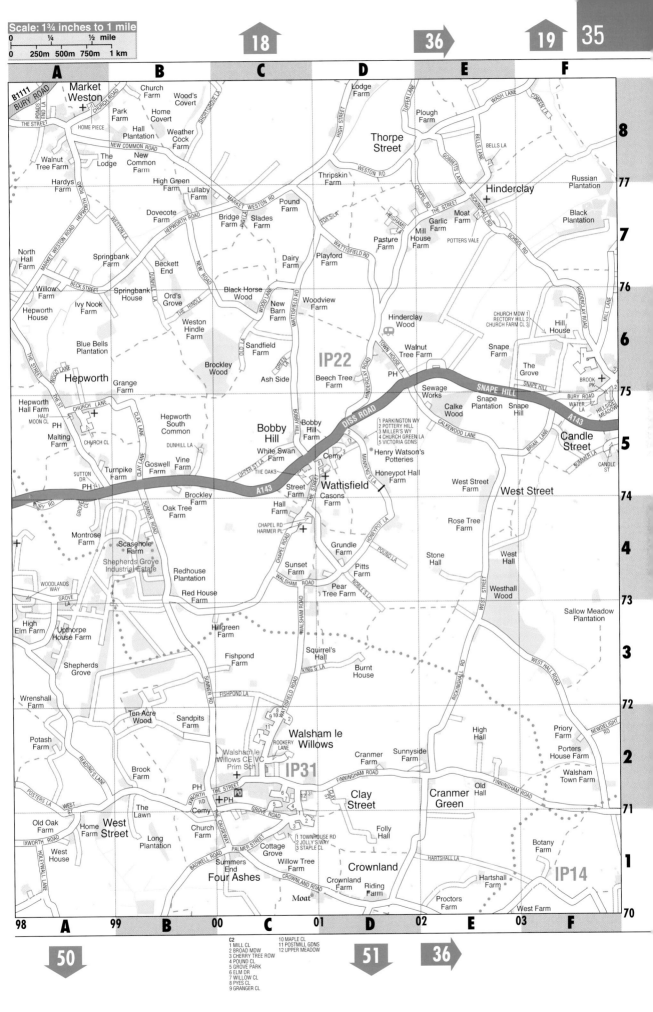

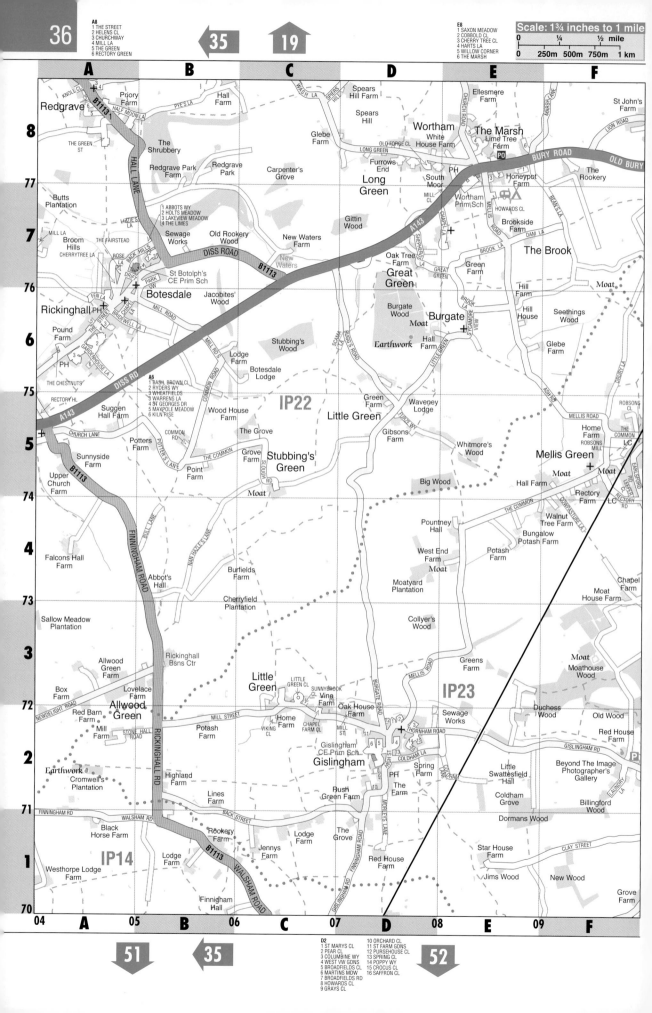

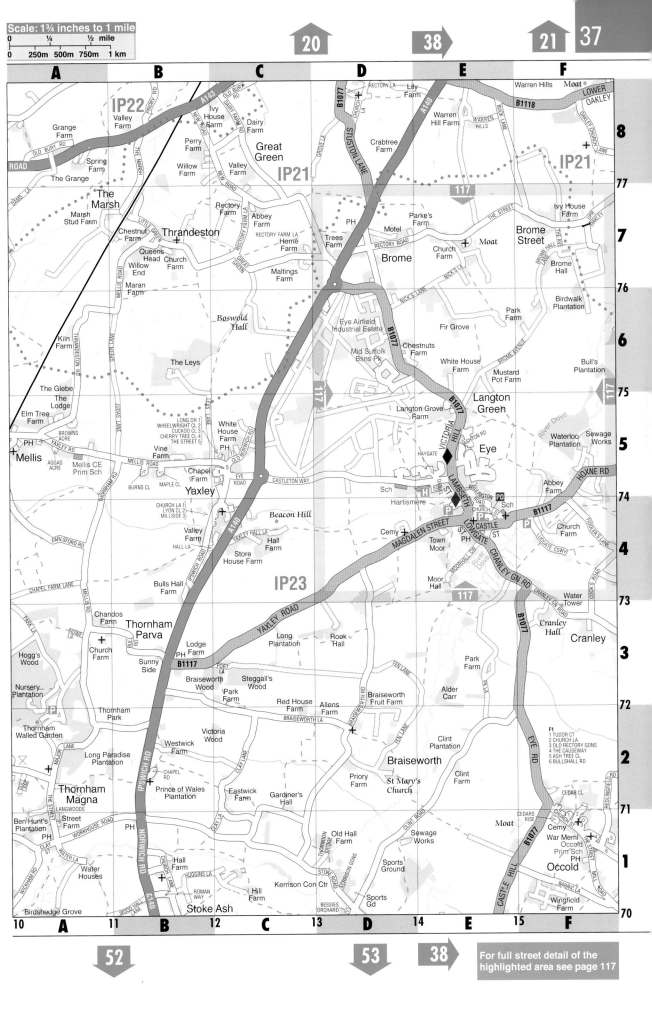

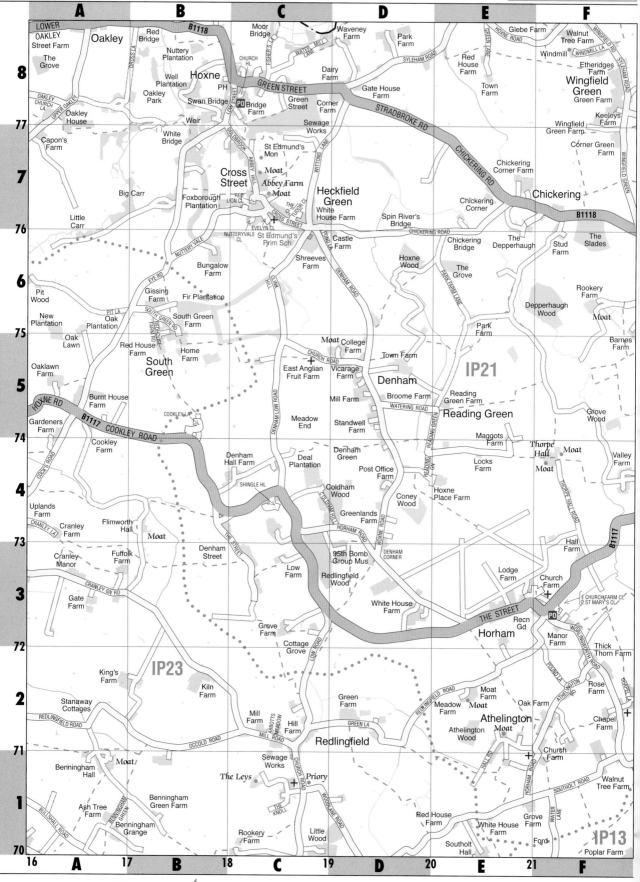

A   B   C   D   E   F

LOWER
OAKLEY
Oakley
Street Farm
The Grove

8

Oakley
Red Bridge
Nuttery Plantation
Well Plantation
Oakley Park
Swan Bridge

B1118
Moor Bridge
CHURCH HL
FISHERS LA
WATER MILL LANE
Waveney Farm
Park Farm

Hoxne
PH
PO
Bridge Farm
Green Street
Dairy Farm

Green Street
Corner Farm
Gate House Farm

SYLEHAM ROAD
Red House Farm

Glebe Farm
Walnut Tree Farm
Windmill
WINDMILL LA
Etheridges Farm

Wingfield Green
Green Farm

OAKLEY CHURCH LA
UPPER OAKLEY
Capon's Farm
Oakley House
Weir
White Bridge

77

STRADBROKE RD

Sewage Works

Town Farm

Wingfield Green Farm

Corner Green Farm

Keeleys Farm

7

Big Carr
Cross Street
Foxborough Plantation
RED LION CL
ABBEY HILL
GOLDBROOK
St Edmund's Mon
Moat
Abbey Farm
Moat
THE TUDOR CL
WITTONS LANE
Heckfield Green
White House Farm

CHICKERING RD
Chickering Corner Farm
Chickering Corner
Chickering Bridge

Chickering
B1118
The Depperhaugh
Stud Farm
The Slades

76

Little Carr
EVELYN CL
NUTTERYVALE CL
St Edmund's Prim Sch
NUTTERY VALE
Shreeves Farm
CLINK HILL
Castle Farm
Spin River's Bridge
Chickering Road

Hoxne Wood
The Grove

PARK FARM LANE
Barnes Farm
Depperhaugh Wood
Rookery Farm
Moat

6

Pit Wood
New Plantation
Oak Lawn
EYE RD
Gissing Farm
PIT LA
Oak Plantation
Bungalow Farm
Fir Plantation
South Green Farm

DENHAM ROAD
Park Farm

75

Oaklawn Farm
SOUTH GREEN RD
RECTORY RD
FARM RD
Red House Farm
South Green
Home Farm
Moat
College Farm
Town Farm

IP21

5

Burnt House Farm
COOKLEY LA
CHURCH ROAD
East Anglian Fruit Farm
Vicarage Farm
Denham
Broome Farm
Reading Green Farm
Grove Wood

HOXNE RD
Gardeners Farm
B1117 COOKLEY ROAD
Cookley Farm
Mill Farm
WATERING ROAD
Reading Green
Maggots Farm

74

COCKS ROAD
DENHAM LOW ROAD
Meadow End
Standwell Farm
Locks Farm
Thorpe Hall
Moat
Moat
Valley Farm

4

Uplands Farm
CRANLEY LA
Cranley Farm
Flimworth Hall
Moat
SHINGLE HL
Denham Hall Farm
Deal Plantation
Denham Green
Post Office Farm
READING GN
Coldham Wood
Coney Wood
Hoxne Place Farm

THORPE HALL ROAD
B1117

73

Cranley Manor
Fuffolk Farm
THE STREET
Denham Street
COLDHAM HALL
HORHAM ROAD
HOXNE ROAD
Greenlands Farm
95th Bomb Group Mus
DENHAM CORNER
Hall Farm

3

CRANLEY GN RD
Gate Farm
Low Farm
Redlingfield Wood
White House Farm
THE STREET
Lodge Farm
Church Farm
1 CHURCH FARM CL
2 ST MARYS CL
PO

Horham
Recn Gd
Manor Farm
Thick Thorn Farm

72

King's Farm
IP23
Grove Farm
Cottage Grove
LOW ROAD

WORTLINGTON ROAD
Rose Farm

2

Stanaway Cottages
REDLINGFIELD ROAD
Kiln Farm
Mill Farm
ABBOTTS MEADOW
Hill Farm
GREEN LA
Green Farm
Redlingfield Road
Meadow Farm
Moat Farm
Moat
Oak Farm
POUND LA
ATHELINGTON RD
Athelington
Moat
Chapel Farm

71

Benningham Hall
Moat
OCCOLD ROAD
MILL ROAD
Redlingfield
Athelington Wood
HORHAM RD
Church Farm

Benningham Green Farm
The Leys
CHURCH ROAD
Priory
WOODLANE ROAD
HALL RD
SOUTHOLT ROAD
Walnut Tree Farm

1

BULLSHALL ROAD
BENNINGHAM GREEN
Ash Tree Farm
Benningham Grange
The Knoll
Rookery Farm
Little Wood
Red House Farm
White House Farm
Southolt Hall
Ford
Grove Farm
WATER LANE
IP13
Poplar Farm

70

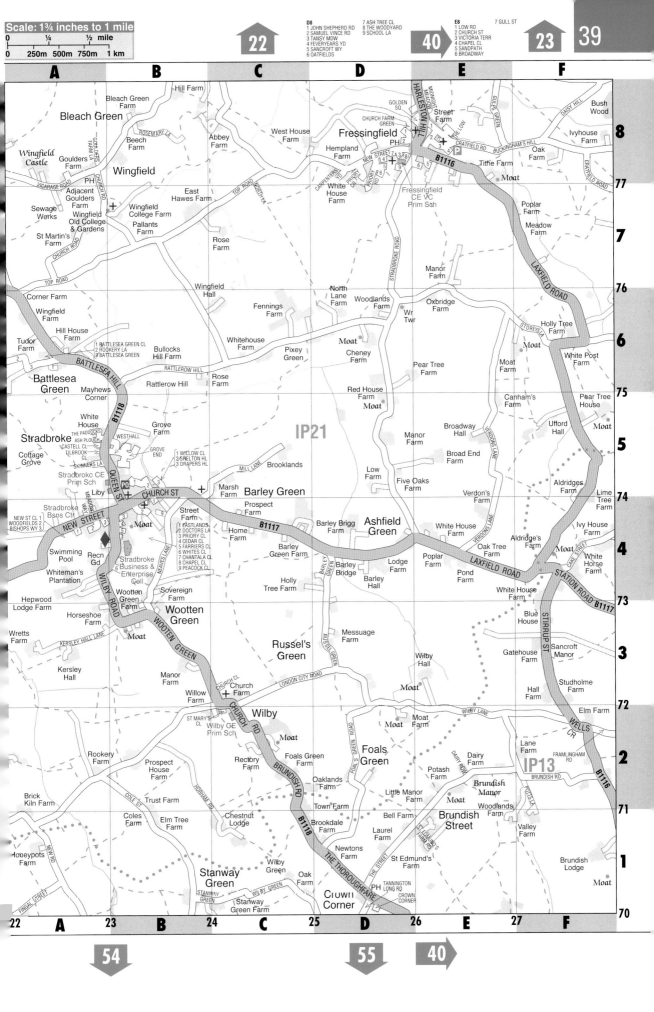

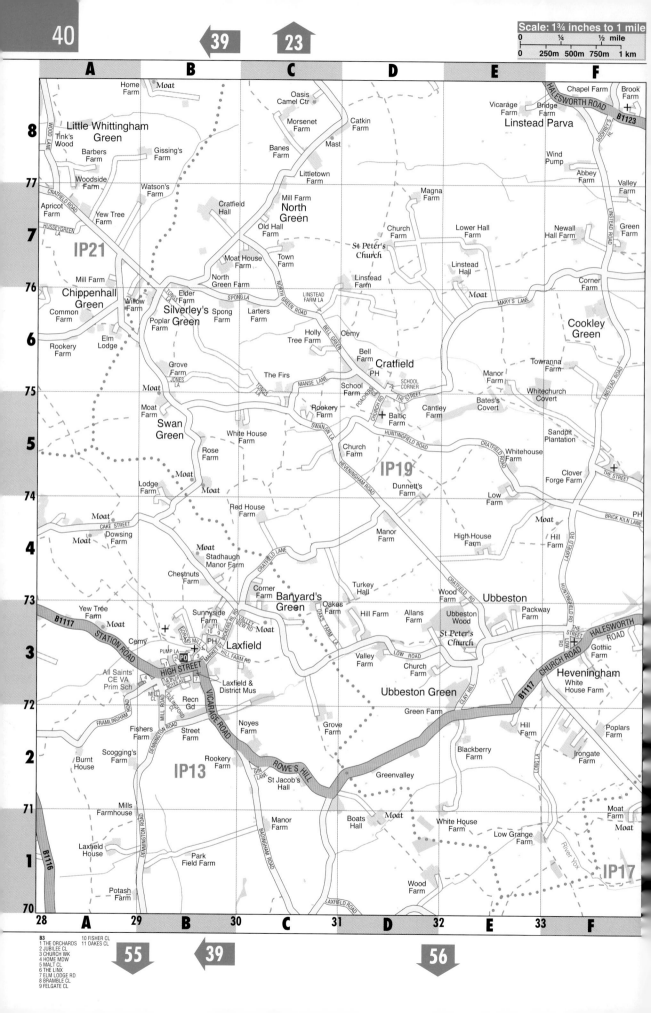

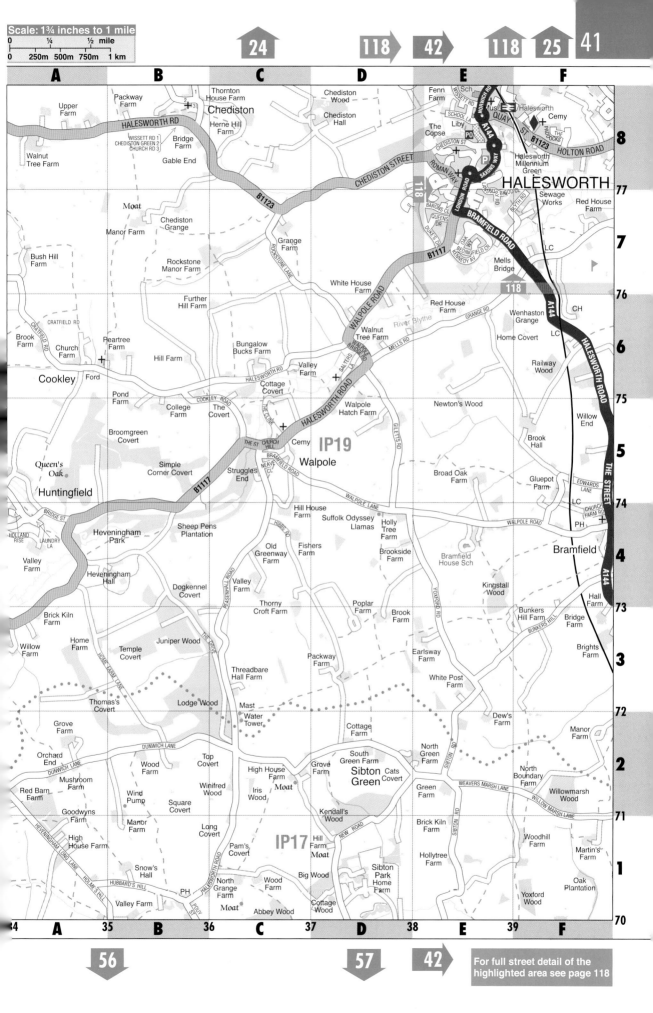

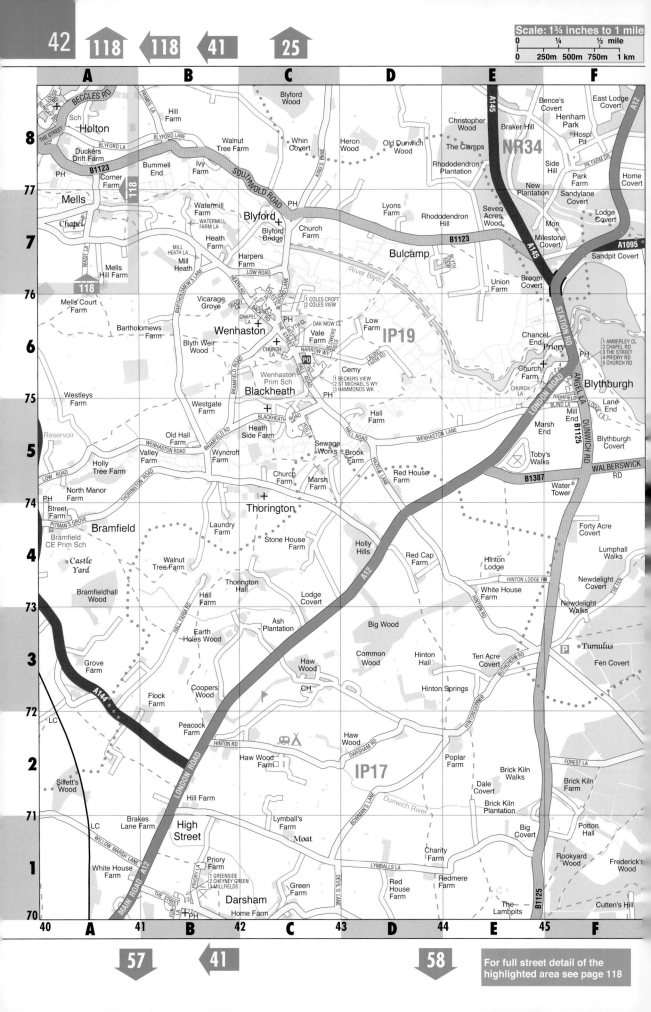

A   B   C   D   E   F

8

77

7

76

6

75

5

74

73

4

3

72

2

71

1

70

58

HILL ROAD
Alder Carr
Gravel Pit
Alder Carr Marshes
Wangford Common Covert
NR34
Scotia End
Mardle House
Lime Kiln Farm
Wolsey Bridge
Mile Walk Covert
Southwold Covert
REYDON RD
MARDLE ROAD
Hen Reed Bed Nature Reserve
Old Hall Farm
QUAY LANE
QUAY LANE
Southwold Maze
A1095
Reydon
Laurel Farm
Sch
WANGFORD RD
B1126
LOWESTOFT RD
B1127
119
SEAVIEW RD
Sole Bay
Pier
Bridge Foot Farm
NORTH RD
NORTH PAR
PIER AVE
HOTSON RD
BLYTH RD
Iby
Wr Twr
CH
Sch
HIGH ST
PO
Mus
TH
SOUTHWOLD
Gunhill Cliff
Bulcamp House
BULCAMP DRIFT
Reydon Marshes
Wind Pump
Tinker's Marshes
IP18
Buss Creek
YORK ROAD
Town Marshes
Suffolk Coast & Heaths Path
The Denes
Tinker's House
Walberswick Common
Squire's Hill
PH
FERRY RD
Hill Covert
Tinker's Covert
Eastwood Lodge Farm
Tinker's Barn
Deadman's Covert
Tumulus
Tinker's Walks
Tumulus
IP19
Suffolk Coast National Nature Reserve
Sallow Walk Covert
East Sheep Walk
LODGE RD
Walberswick
PALMER'S LA
MANOR CL
EVERETT'S LA
FERRY RD
THE STREET
B1387
Old Farm
ADAM'S LA 1
CHURCH LA 2
SEVEN ACRES LA 3
SHORT LA 4
ST ANDREWS CL 5
Hoist Covert
119
Westwood Lodge
Old Covert
Westwood Marshes
Suffolk Coast National Nature Reserve
East Hill
Dingle Great Hill
Dingle Farm
Corporation Marshes
Dunwich River
Fen Hill
Foxburrow Wood
Dingle Stone House
Sandymount Covert
Reedland Marshes
Scheiller's Grove
IP17
ST HELENA
DINGLE HILL
Dingle Marshes
St Helena Farm
Dunwich Forest
Hog's Grove
Suffolk Coast & Heaths Path
Little Dingle
Dunwich River
WESTLETON RD
Bridge Farm
Church Farm
BEACH RD
ST JAMES'S ST
SANDY LA
Sandy Lane Farm
Chapel
Mus
Dunwich
Greyfriars
The Spinney
Broom Hill
HIGH ST
Mound
MONASTERY HILL

46   47   48   49   50   51

A6
1 CHESTNUT RISE
2 APPLETREE GR
3 WESTHORPE
4 ORCHARD WY
5 NEW RD
6 KINGFISHER DR

7 HATLEY DR
8 CHANDLERS CT
9 HYTHE CL
10 MURTON CL
11 LABURNUM LA
12 PANTILE LA
13 CASBURN LA

14 NEWNHAM LA
15 BUNTINGS CR
16 MARTIN RD
17 MYRTLE DR
18 BLOSSOM CL

B6
1 TOYSE CL
2 GARDEN CT
3 THE AVENUE
4 BAKER DR
5 OLD SCHOOL CL

B5
1 HOLKHAM MEAD
2 MELFORD CL
3 KENTWELL PL
4 BAYFIELD DR
5 BURGHLEY RISE
6 MILL CL
7 MILL LA
8 BLOOMSFIELD
9 BARKWAYS
10 BEWICKS MD
11 COPPERFIELD WAY
12 CORNFIELDS
13 FIELD VW
14 SUMMERFIELD CL
15 ST MARYS MWS

A5
1 POPLARS CL
2 BOLTON CL
3 ROMAN CL
4 TUNBRIDGE CL
5 PARSONAGE CL
6 GUYATT CT
7 PRIORY CL
8 POUND CL
9 SAXON DR
10 ABBEY CL
11 MEADOWLANDS
12 THE PADDOCKS
13 WILD ACRES
14 MANDEVILLE
15 CHURCH LA
16 SCHOOL LA
17 ASH GR

A4
1 STATION GATE
2 RAILWAY CL
3 LUCUS CL
4 BURLING WY
5 ELLIS GDNS
6 LOVE LA

Cambridgeshire Street Atlas

CB5
CB7
CB8

New River
Hundred Acre Farm
Burwell Poors' Fen
Chestnut Tree Farm
The Broads
Broads Farm
Ness Farm
Tollgate Farm
West Fen
Abbey Wood
Brackland Rough
Fordham Abbey
Underdown Plantation
Fordham House
Water Tower
Limekiln Plantation
Goosehall Farm
Sewage Works
Klondyke Farm
Lark Hall Farm
Crow Hall Farm
High Ness Farm
Snailwell Fen
Little Fen
GRANTCHESTER RI 1
MASON RD 2
WATERSIDE 3
OLD STABLE CT 4
ARBOR CL 5
Broads Road Business Park
Breach Farm
Wadebridge Farm
PINE AVE
Landwade Farm
Earthworks
Moat
River Snail
Ashbridge Farm
Little Fen
LODESIDE DROVE
OLD LODE CT
Townsend Farm
HAYCROFT LA
The Hall
Landwade
Glebe Farm
The Pines Industrial Estate
Four Ponds
Lynx Business Park
ANCHOR LA
Rec Gd
Slade Farm
Bloomfield Farm
Burwell
Cemy
Burwell Village Coll Prim Sch
Sports Qtr
Liby
Parsonage Farm
Burwell Mus
Sewage Works
Plantation Stud
Burwell Castle (site of)
NEWMARKET RD
Hill Farm
Northmore Farm
MILL LA
120
37
FORDHAM RD
Crownall Farm
B1102
Eleanor Terrace
Exning
Football Gd
Dovecote
Cemy
Oaks Business Park
A142
SWAFFHAM ROAD
Lower Portland Farm
LACEY'S LANE
The Marsh
Industrial Estate
Devil's Ditch
Ditch Farm
Devils Dyke Nature Reserve
Gravel Pit Farm
St Wendred's Well
Hamilton Stud
EXNING ROAD
B1103
Warbraham Wood
Plantation Farm
Springhead Farm
120
Coll
H
Warbraham Mains Farm
HEATH ROAD
Southfields Farm
Newmarket Lawn Tennis Club
HIGH ST
B1061
Vicarage Farm
Newmarket Heath
Exercise Track
Gravelpit Farm
Sand Gallop
Rowley Mile Course
Newmarket Race Course
Millennium Grandstand
Cambridge Hill
BARBARA STRADBROKE AVENUE
A1304
Stour Valley Path
Wyck Hall Stud
Beacon
(Cesarewitch) Course
July Course
Devil's Ditch
120

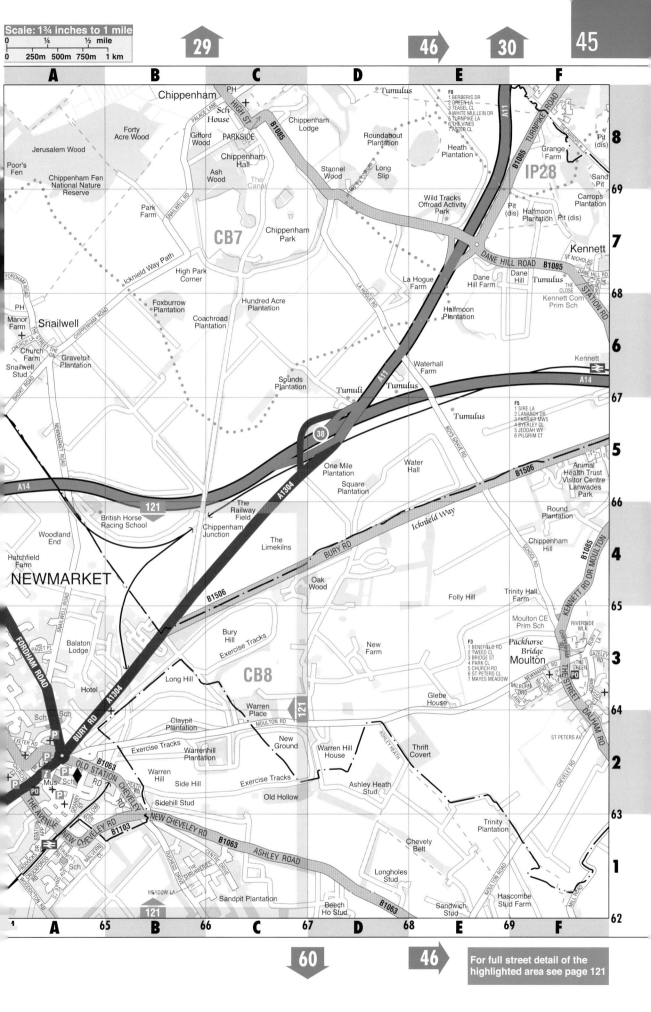

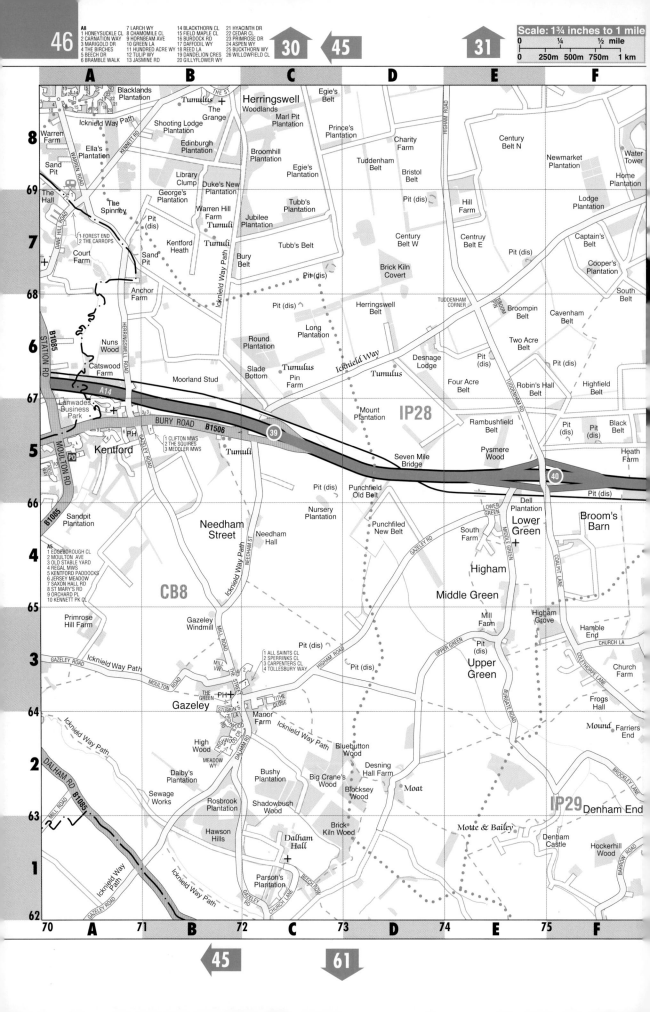

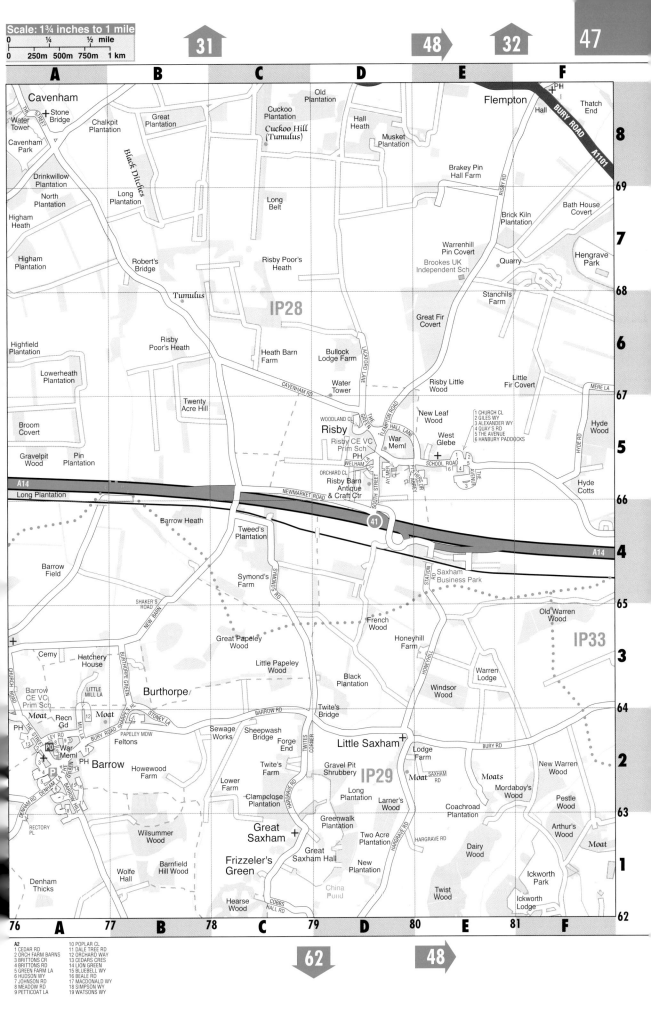

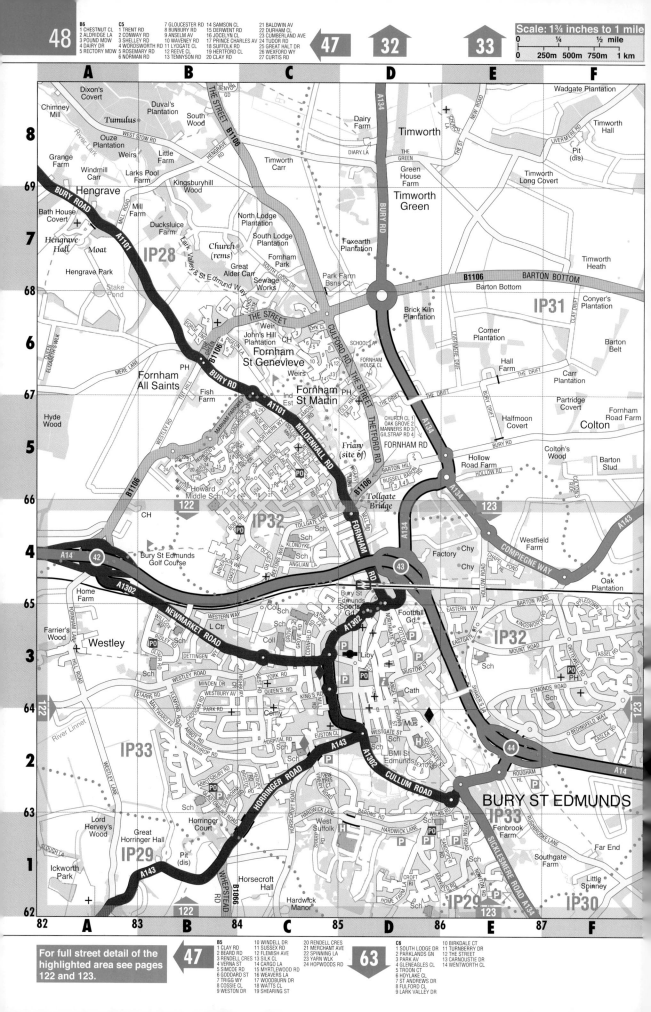

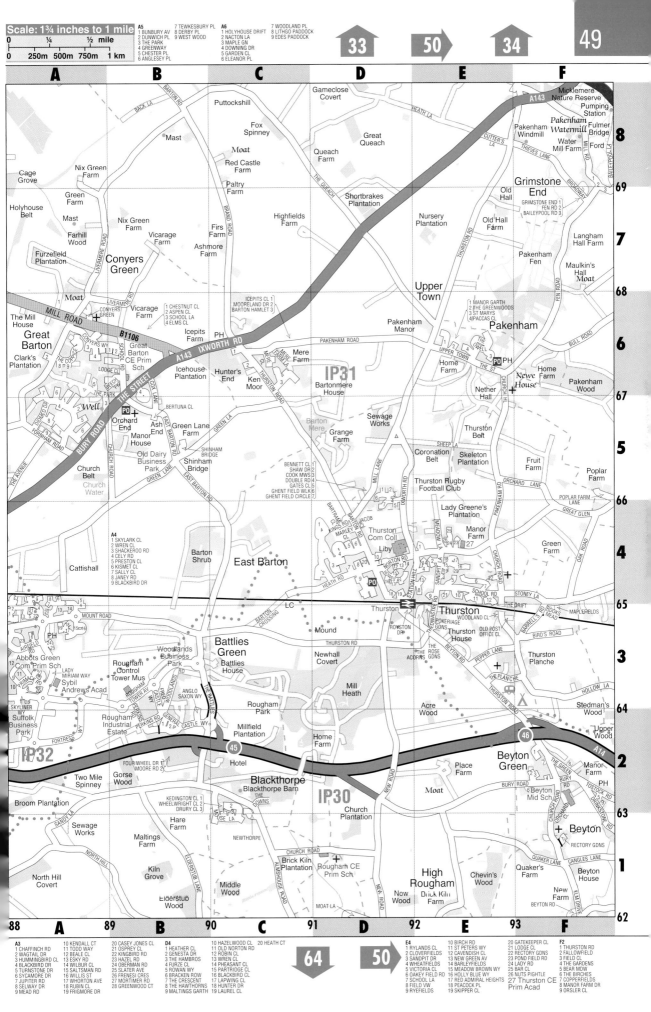

Scale: 1¾ inches to 1 mile

0   ¼   ½   mile
0   250m   500m   750m   1 km

A5
1 BUNBURY AV
2 DUNWICH PL
3 THE PARK
4 GREENWAY
5 CHESTER PL
6 ANGLESEY PL

7 TEWKESBURY PL
8 DERBY PL
9 WEST WOOD

A6
1 HOLYHOUSE DRIFT
2 NACTON LA
3 MAPLE GN
4 DOWNING DR
5 GARDEN CL
6 ELEANOR PL

7 WOODLAND PL
8 LITHGO PADDOCK
9 EDES PADDOCK

A4
1 SKYLARK CL
2 WREN CL
3 SHACKEROO RD
4 CELY RD
5 PRESTON CL
6 KISMET CL
7 SALLY CL
8 JANEY RD
9 BLACKBIRD DR

A3
1 CHAFFINCH RD
2 WAGTAIL DR
3 HUMMINGBIRD CL
4 BLACKBIRD DR
5 TURNSTONE RD
6 SYCAMORE DR
7 JUPITER RD
8 SELWAY DR
9 MEAD RD
10 KENDALL CT
11 TODD WAY
12 ESKY RD
13 ESKY RD
14 WILBUR CL
15 SALTSMAN RD
16 WILLIS ST
17 WHORTON AVE
18 RUBIN CL
19 FRIGMORE DR
20 CASEY JONES CL
21 OSPREY CL
22 KINGBIRD RD
23 HAZEL RD
24 OBERMAN RD
25 SLATER AVE
26 FRENESI CRES
27 MORTIMER RD
28 GREENWOOD CT

D4
1 HEATHER CL
2 GENESTA DR
3 THE HAMBROS
4 FURZE CL
5 ROWAN WY
6 BRACKEN ROW
7 THE CRESCENT
8 THE HAWTHORNS
9 MALTINGS GARTH
10 HAZELWOOD CL
11 OLD NORTON CL
12 WREN CL
13 ROBIN CL
14 PHEASANT CL
15 PARTRIDGE CL
16 BLACKBIRD CL
17 LAPWING CL
18 HUNTER DR
19 LAUREL CL
20 HEATH CT

E4
1 RYLANDS CL
2 CLOVERFIELDS
3 SANDPIT DR
4 WHEATFIELDS
5 VICTORIA CL
6 OAKEY FIELD RD
7 SCHOOL LA
8 FIELD VW
9 RYEFIELDS
10 BIRCH RD
11 ST PETERS WY
12 CAVENDISH CL
13 NEW GREEN AV
14 BARLEYFIELDS
15 MEADOW BROWN WY
16 HOLLY BLUE WY
17 RED ADMIRAL HEIGHTS
18 PEACOCK CL
19 SKIPPER CL
20 GATEKEEPER CL
21 LODGE CL
22 RECTORY GDNS
23 POND FIELD RD
24 LADY RD
25 BAR CL
26 NUTS PIGHTLE
27 Thurston CE Prim Acad

F2
1 THURSTON RD
2 FALLOWFIELD
3 FIELD CL
4 THE GARDENS
5 BEAR MDW
6 THE BIRCHES
7 COPPERFIELDS
8 MANOR FARM DR
9 ORSLER CL

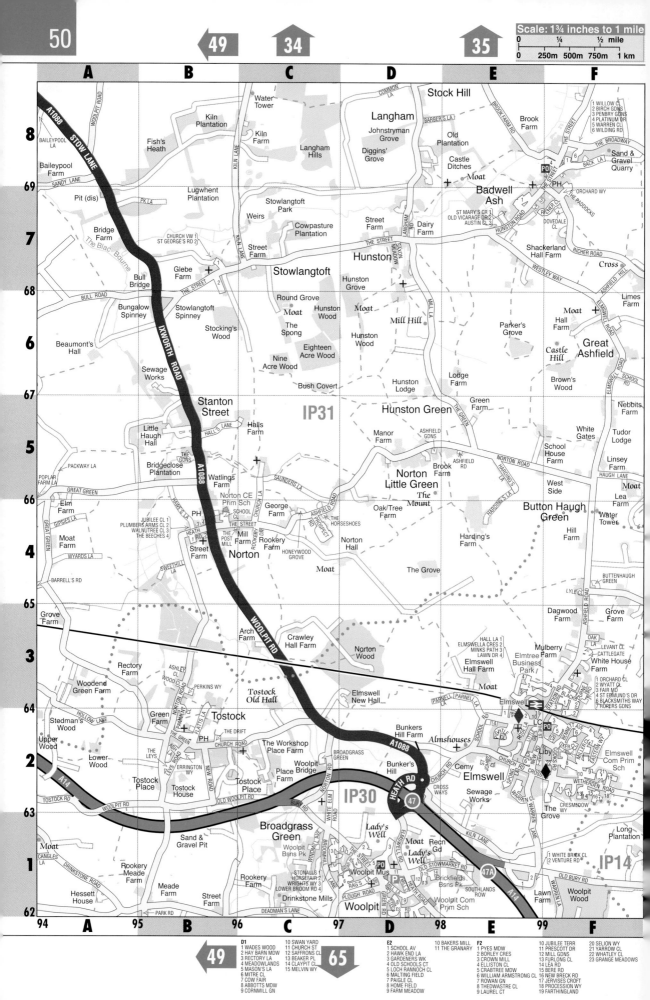

Scale: 1¾ inches to 1 mile

0   ¼   ½ mile
0   250m 500m 750m 1 km

A B C D E F

8

A1088 STOW LANE

Baileypool Farm
Baileypool La
Sandy Lane

Kiln Plantation

Water Tower

Stock Hill

Langham

Johnstryman Grove
Diggins' Grove

Old Plantation

Brook Farm

1 WILLOW CL
2 BIRCH GDNS
3 PENBRY GDNS
4 PLATINUM DR
5 WARREN CL
6 WILDING RD

THE STREET

THE BROADWAY

Fish's Heath

Kiln Hills

BARBER'S LA

Castle Ditches

Moat

PO

PH

BACK LA

Sand & Gravel Quarry

69

Pit (dis)

PK LA

Lugwhent Plantation

Stowlangtoft Park
Weirs

Cowpasture Plantation

Street Farm

Badwell Ash

ORCHARD WY

THE PADDOCKS

RICHER CL

DOVEDALE CL

7

Bridge Farm
The Black Bourne

CHURCH VW 1
ST GEORGE'S RD 2

KILN LANE

Street Farm

THE STREET

Hunston

ST MARY'S CR 1
OLD VICARAGE DR 2
AUSTIN CL 3

HUNSTON ROAD

WESTLEY WAY

Shackerland Hall Farm

Richer Road

Cross

68

Bull Bridge

Glebe Farm

THE STREET

Stowlangtoft

Hunston Grove

Round Grove

Moat

Hunston Wood

Mill Hill

Moat

Parker's Grove

Hall Farm

Moat

Limes Farm

6

Bungalow Spinney

Stowlangtoft Spinney

Stocking's Wood

The Spong

Eighteen Acre Wood

Hunston Wood

IXWORTH ROAD

Beaumont's Hall

Nine Acre Wood

Castle Hill

Great Ashfield

Brown's Wood

ELMSWELL ROAD

SCHOOL RD

Nebbits Farm

67

Sewage Works

Bush Covert

Hunston Lodge

Lodge Farm

Green Farm

White Gates

School House Farm

5

Stanton Street

Halls Farm

HALL'S LANE

IP31

Hunston Green

THE GREEN

Tudor Lodge

Linsey Farm

HAUGH LANE

Moat

Little Haugh Hall

THE GDNS

Watlings Farm

SAUNDERS LA

Manor Farm

ASHFIELD GDNS

Brook Farm

ASHFIELD RD

NORTON ROAD

HARDING'S

School House Farm

West Side

Button Haugh Green

Lea Farm

66

Packway La
POPLAR FARM LA

Elm Farm

GIPSIES LA

Great Green

Bridgeclose Plantation

Norton CE Prim Sch
SCHOOL CL

George Farm
THE STREET

Norton Little Green
The Mount

Oak/Tree Farm
The Horseshoes

Harding's Farm

Hill Farm

Water Tower

A1088

CHURCH DR

JUBILEE CL 1
PLUMBERS ARMS CL 2
WALNUTREE CL 3
THE BEECHES 4

PH

HEATH RD

4

Moat Farm

WYARDS LA

SWEETHILL LA

BARRELL'S RD

THE POST MILL

Mill Farm

Rookery Farm

HONEYWOOD GROVE

Street Farm

Norton

Moat

Norton Hall

The Grove

BUTTENHAUGH GREEN

LYLE CL

65

Grove Farm

WOOLPIT RD

Arch Farm

Crawley Hall Farm

Norton Wood

Dagwood Farm

OAK LA

LEVANT CL
CATTLEGATE

Grove Farm

ASHFIELD ROAD

3

Rectory Farm

ASHLEY CL

WOOD CL

PERKINS WY

Tostock Old Hall

Elmswell New Hall

HALL LA 1
ELMSWELLA CRES 2
MINKS PATH 3
LAWN DR 4

Elmtree Business Park

White House Farm

Woodend Green Farm

Elmswell Hall Farm

Moat

STATION RD

1 ORCHARD CL
2 WYATT CL
3 FAIR MD
4 ST EDMUND'S DR
5 BLACKSMITHS WAY
6 ROPERS GDNS

BLACKSMITHS

64

Stedman's Wood

HOLLOW LANE

Green Farm

NORTON RD

PAMMENT CL

FLATT'S LA

Tostock

THE DRIFT

Bunkers Hill Farm

Almshouses

Elmswell

LC
PO

Upper Wood

A14

Lower Wood

TOSTOCK RD

THE LEYS

THE GREEN

PH

CHURCH ROAD

ASH LA

ERRINGTON WY

NEW ROAD

The Workshop Place Farm

Woolpit Place Farm

BROADGRASS GREEN

Bunker's Hill

SCHOOL

PIGTLE

CASTLE

ROSE

CHURCH RD

Cemy

Liby

Elmswell

WETHERDEN RD

Elmswell Com Prim Sch

2

Tostock Place

Tostock House

Tostock Place

OLD WOOLPIT RD

Woolpit Bridge

Place Farm

BURY RD

WHITE ELM

IP30

HEATH RD

47

Cross Ways

Sewage Works

WARREN

CRESMEDOW WY

The Grove

63

WOOLPIT RD

Sand & Gravel Pit

Broadgrass Green

Lady's Well

Moat

Lady's Well

Recn Gd

OLD STOWMARKET RD

1 WHITE BRICK CL
2 VENTURE RD

Long Plantation

IP14

1

Moat
CANGLES LA

DRINKSTONE ROAD

Rookery Meade Farm

Meade Farm

Rookery Farm

Street Farm

Woolpit Bsns Pk

THE STREET

STONALLS 1
HORSEFAIR 2
WRIGHTS WY 3
LOWER BROOM RD 4

PO

Woolpit Mus

RAG'S LA

Brickfields Bsns Pk

SOUTHLANDS ROW

47A

OLD BURY RD

GREEN RD

Lawn Farm

Woolpit Wood

A14

62

Hessett House

PARK RD

Drinkstone Mills

DEADMAN'S LANE

Woolpit

PLOUGH ROAD

Woolpit Com Prim Sch

WARREN LA

94   95   96   97   98   99

A B C D E F

D1
1 WADES WOOD
2 HAY BARN MDW
3 RECTORY LA
4 MEADOWLANDS
5 MASON'S LA
6 MITRE CL
7 COW FAIR
8 ABBOTTS MDW
9 CORNMILL GN
10 SWAN YARD
11 CHURCH ST
12 SAFFRONS CL
13 BEAKER PL
14 CLAYPIT CL
15 MELVIN WY

E2
1 SCHOOL AV
2 HAWK END LA
3 GARDENERS WK
4 OLD SCHOOLS CT
5 LOCH RANNOCH CL
6 MALTING FIELD
7 PAIGLE CL
8 HOME FIELD
9 FARM MEADOW
10 BAKERS MILL
11 THE GRANARY

F2
1 PYES MDW
2 BORLEY CRES
3 CROWN MILL
4 ELLISTON CL
5 CRABTREE MDW
6 WILLIAM ARMSTRONG CL
7 ROWAN GN
8 THEDWASTRE CL
9 LAUREL CT
10 JUBILEE TERR
11 PRESCOTT DR
12 MILL GDNS
13 FURLONG CL
14 LEA RD
15 BERE RD
16 NEW BRECK RD
17 JERVISES CROFT
18 PROCESSION WY
19 FARTHINGLAND
20 SELION WY
21 YARROW CL
22 WHATLEY CL
23 GRANGE MEADOWS

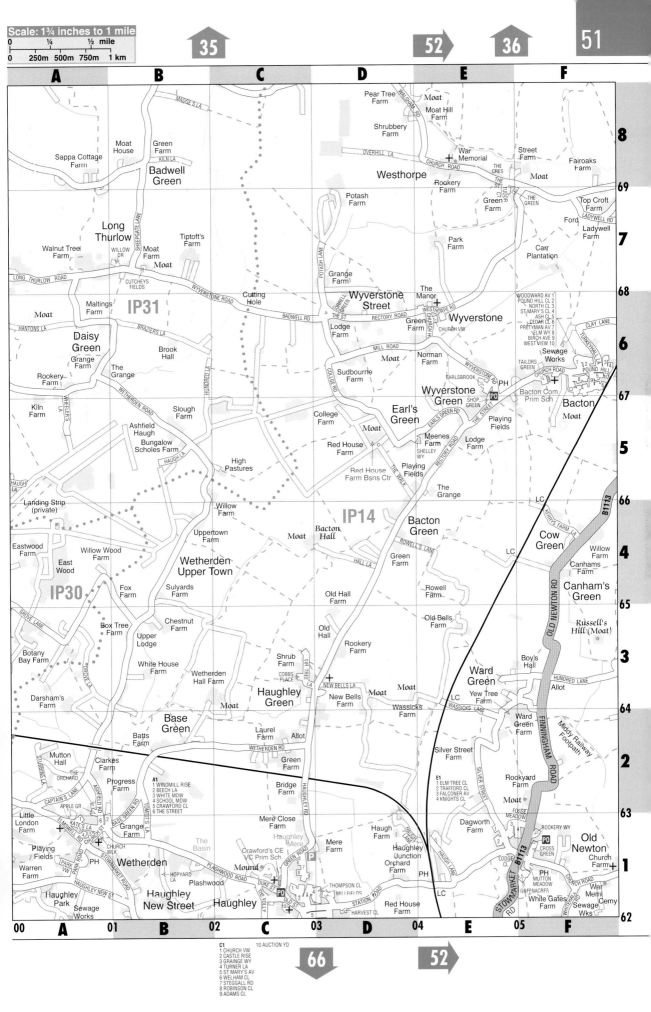

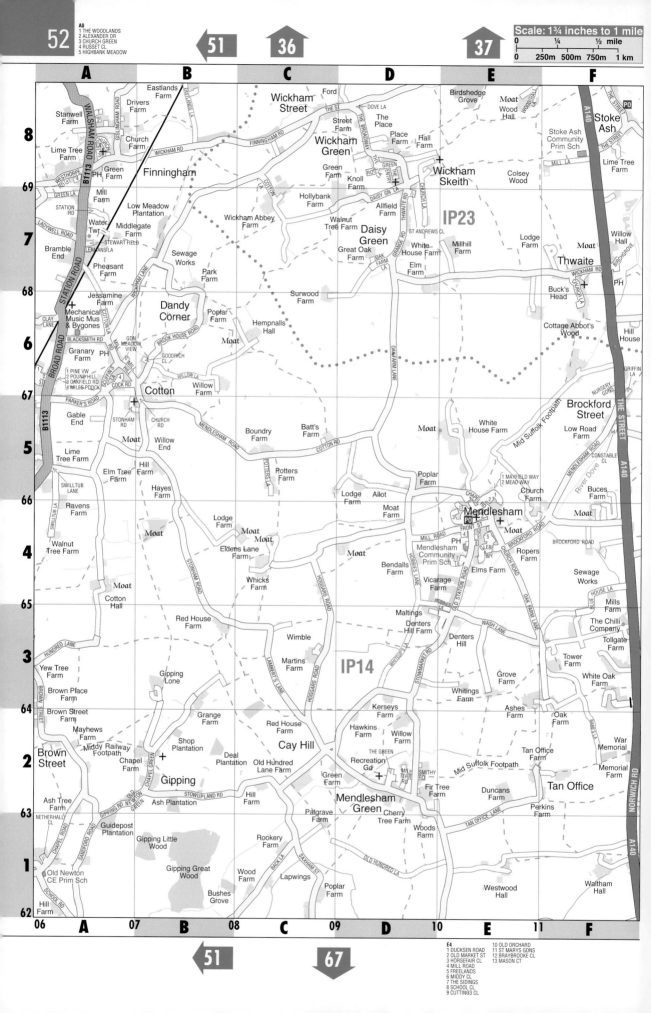

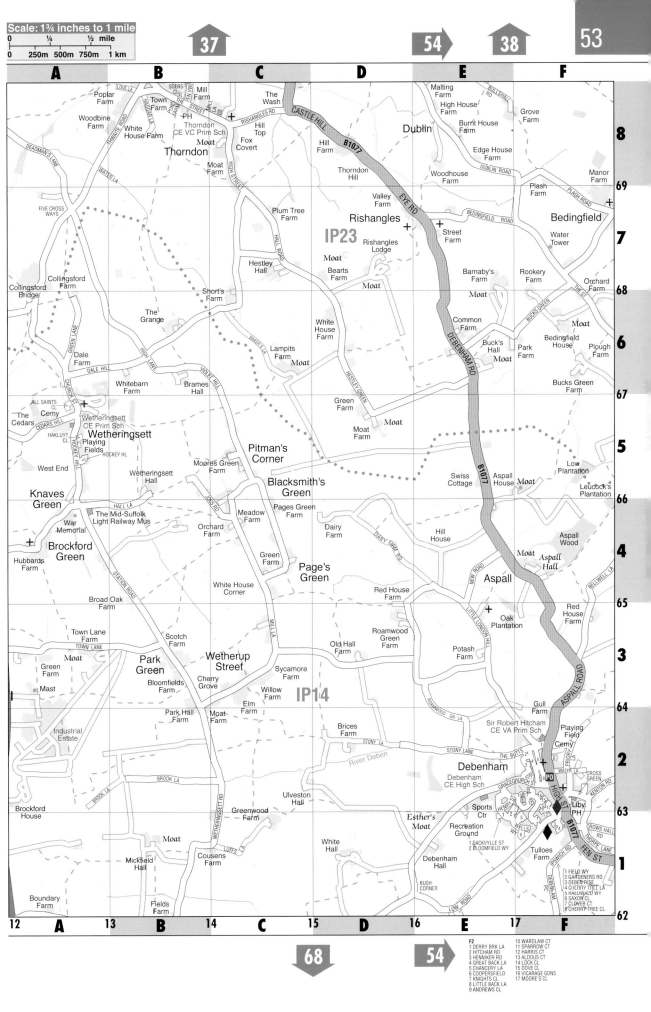

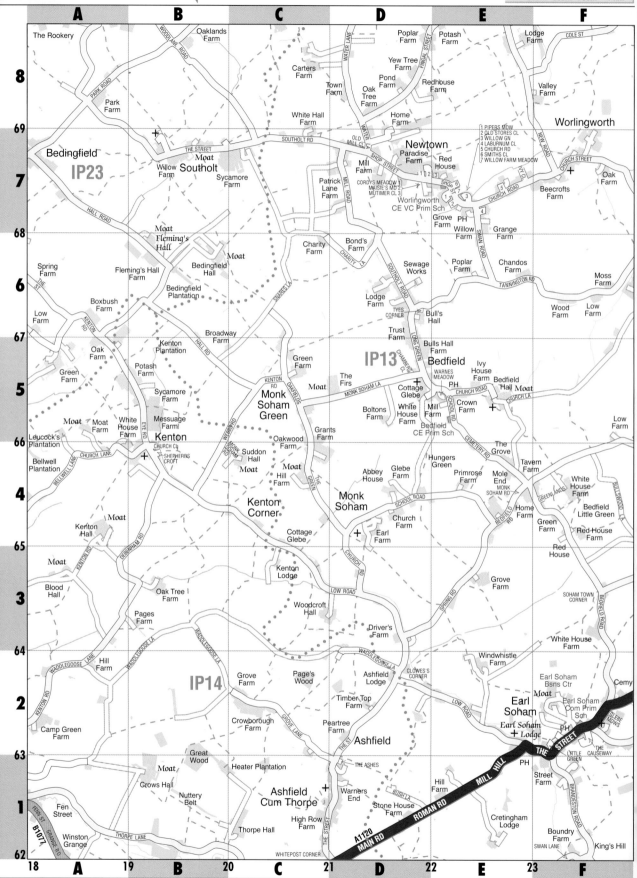

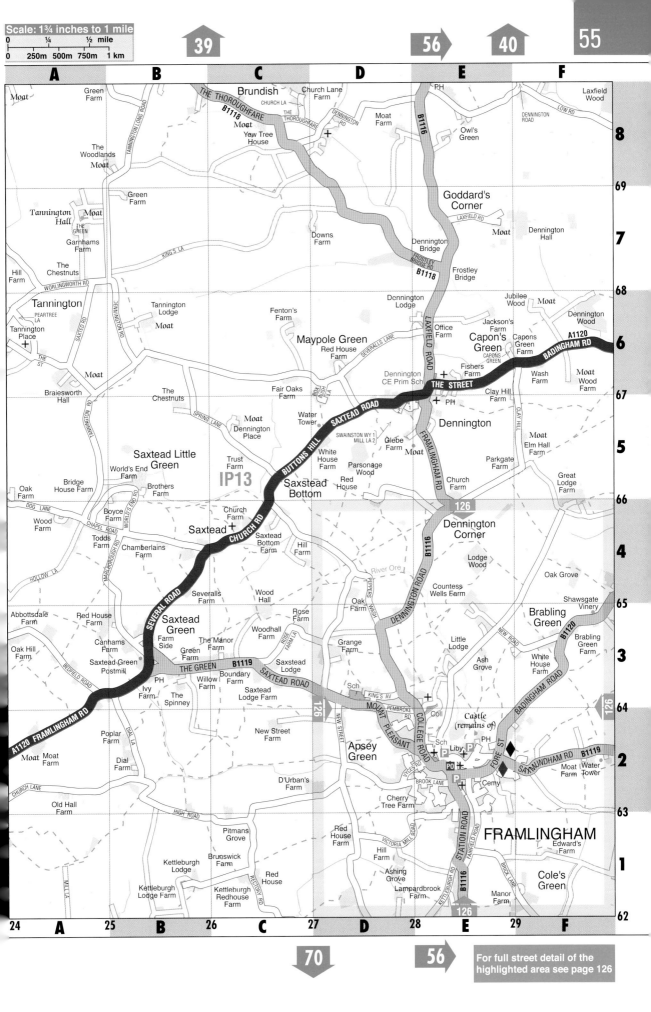

F8
1 MOUNT PLEASANT
2 MILLFIELDS
3 BROOK DR
4 WOOD VW

Scale: 1¾ inches to 1 mile
0   ¼   ½ mile
0   250m   500m   750m   1 km

A B C D E F

Laxfield Wood
Valley Farm
Sunflower Farm
Cherry Tree Farm
NEW ROAD
BADINGHAM RD
Manor House Farm
Lodge Farm
MILL ROAD
Vale Farm
Aylesbury Farm
Spring Wood
SPRINGWOOD DR
Valley Farm Spinney
Sibton Abbey
THE MOUNTS

8
LAXFIELD ROAD
Walnut Tree Farm
Wind Pump
OLD HALL ROAD
Bungalow Farm
PLUMBERS YARD
Segmore Farm
Trust Farm
RUSSELL CL
2 1
Peasenhall
SIBTON RD
PO
THE STREET
THE CAUSEWAY
4

LOW RD
White House Farm
REDHOUSE ROAD
Red House Farm
TWIN OAK DR
Bowling Green Farm
HACKNEY RD
Cemy
MILL HILL
Cottage West End

69
White House Farm
Plains Farm
Twin Oak Farm
HIGH HOUSE DR
High House Farm
Boundary Farm
Hill Farm
Hiltons Farm
BADINGHAM ROAD
BADINGHAM RD
Orchard Farm
Clare Farm
Wood Farm
Streetgrove Farm

7
Castle Farm
THE MEADOWS
ORCHARD RISE
Church Farm
RECTORY RD
Brick Kiln Farm
POUND GREEN ROAD
HIGH HOUSE DR
Chapel Farm
Pikes Farm
A1120
Lime Tree Farm
High Ash Farm
Apple Tree Farm
Shelleys Farm
Boundary Farm
The Gull

Low Farm
Bears Farm
HIGH ROAD
Broad Oak Farm
Woodlands Farm
BRUISYARD ROAD
Gales Farm

68
Badingham
The Old Rectory
HOLLOW LANE
Shrublands Farm
Hollow Lane Farm
BRUISYARD ROAD
Wood Farm
HERNSEY WOOD RD
Hernsey Wood

OLD RECTORY ROAD
Badingham House
PH
CARRS HILL
Trust Farm

6
A1120
Hill Farm
WOOD ROAD
Colston Hall
College Rd
Risings Farm
Bruisyard Wood
Hernsey Wood Farm
LINTOTTS RD
Upper Grove Farm

67
Colston Hall Wood
River Alde
OSIERBED RD
Hill Top Farm
High House Farm
MILL LANE
PEASENHALL RD
The White House Farm
PITMER RD

5
White House
Oakenhill Hall
Bruisyard Home Vineyard Farm
CHURCH ROAD
College Farm
MILL LANE
IP17
Moat
Hill Farm
Rendham Hall Farm

B1120
BADINGHAM ROAD
Oak Barn Farm
Church Farm
Bruisyard Hall
THE STREET
HILL FARM ROAD
HILL FARM RD

66
Fisk's Farm
White House Farm
Bruisyard
TINKHOUSE RD
HILL TOP

IP13
BANNOCKS LANE
Hill Farm
Sandpit Farm
LOW ROAD
RENDHAM ROAD
GRANGE FARM LA
HILL FARM ROAD
MEADHAM LA
PIPNEY HILL

4
The Moat Farm
Poplar Farm
BRUISYARD ROAD
Cransford Hall
Yew Tree Farm
BRUISYARD ROAD
Grange Farm
Manor Farm
Rookery Farm
SANDY LA
R COVERT FARM LA

65
Red House Farm
Cransford
Cottage Glebe
CRANSFORD RD
High House Farm
Sweffling Hall Farm
Pound Farm
Gables Farm
THE GREEN
BRIDGE ST
Rendham Barnes

THE ST
REDHOUSE FARM LA
BANNOCKS LA
Moat
Church Farm
Sewage Works
LODGE RD
PH
PH
Rendham
Church Farm
LOW ROAD

3
Culpho Farm
Fiddler's Hall
WEST FARM RD
Rendham Bridge

DRINKS RD
Boundary Farm
Moat
Little Lonely Farm
West Farm
FRAMLINGHAM RD
Gull Covert
Poplar Farm
MILL ROAD
Bridge Farm
RECTORY RD
Broadmeadow Covert

64
B1119
SAXMUNDHAM ROAD
B1119
The Gull
King Edward's Coronation Wood

Hatherleigh Farm
Kilderbee's Grove
LITTLE LONELY FARM RD
Broom Covert
B1119
Hill Farm
Hall Farm
HOLDANS LANE
JUBILEE CL
HOLDANS MDW
Sweffling
GLEMHAM ROAD
Burrows Hill

2
ROOKERY FARM RD
Queen Mary's Covert
Oak Farm
Gold Medal Wood
Hall Farm
CHAPEL LANE
White House Farm
Blackamoor Covert

Rookery Farm
CRANSFORD RD
Queen Mary's Plantation
Pound Farm Nature Reserve
High Grove
Valley Meadow Wood
Friar's Grove
Dodd's Wood

63
Shingle Farm
SHINGLE LA

1
Home Farm
Elm Tree Farm
Stone Farm
LOW ROAD
SIMPERS DRIFT
Low Grove
Street Farm
Haw Wood
THE GROVE
White House Farm
LOW ST
River Alde

62
North Green
Sewage Works

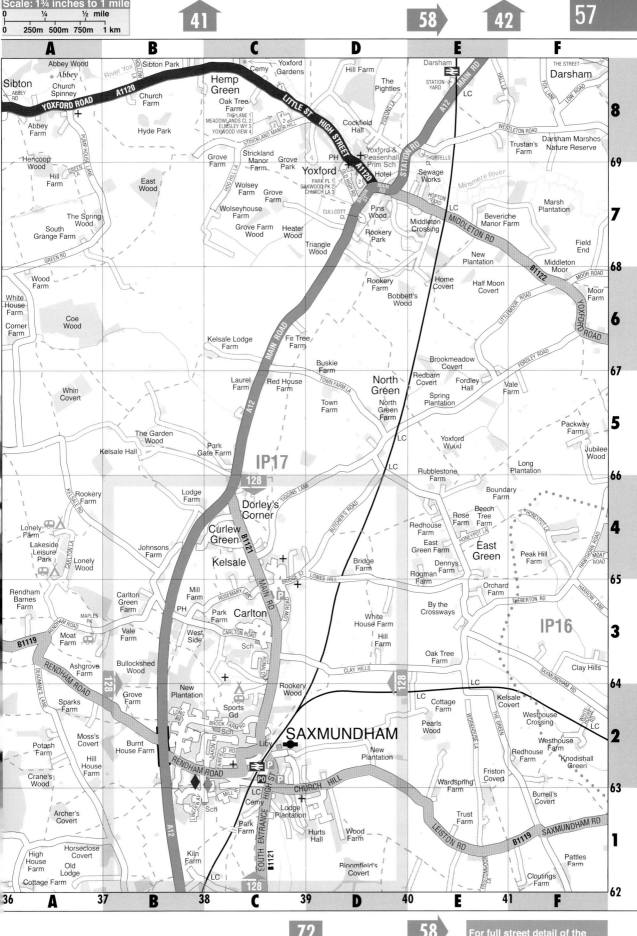

A   B   C   D   E   F

8
69
7
68
6
67
5
66
4
65
3
64
2
63
1
62

Abbey Wood
Sibton Park
Yoxford Gardens
Cemy
Hill Farm
The Pightles
Darsham
THE STREET
Darsham

Sibton
Abbey
River Yox
Church Spinney
ABBEY RD
YOXFORD ROAD
A1120
Church Farm
Hemp Green
Oak Tree Farm
THE LANE 1
MEADOWLANDS CL 2
ELMSLEY WY 3
YOXWOOD VIEW 4
LITTLE ST
HIGH STREET
Cockfield Hall
Yoxford & Peasenhall Prim Sch
Hotel
STATION YARD
LC
MAIN RD
A12
WESTLETON ROAD
Trustan's Farm
Darsham Marshes Nature Reserve
HALL LA
FOX LANE
LOW ROAD

Abbey Farm
PUMP HOUSE LANE
GREEN LA
HOLLOW LA
Hyde Park
Strickland Manor Hill
Grove Farm
Strickland Manor Farm
Grove Park
PH
Yoxford
PIGEONS LA
THURTELLS CL
STATION RD
Sewage Works
HOPTON YARD
Minsmere River
Marsh Plantation

Hencoop Wood
Hill Farm
East Wood
HOG HILL LA
Wolsey Farm
Wolseyhouse Farm
Grove Farm
Grove Farm Wood
Heater Wood
Triangle Wood
PARK PL 1
OAKWOOD PK 2
CHURCH LA 3
CULLCOTT CL
OLD HIGH RD
BYFORD RD
Pins Wood
MAIN RD
Rookery Park
Middleton Crossing
LC
MIDDLETON RD
New Plantation
Half Moon Covert
Beveriche Manor Farm
Field End
B1122
Middleton Moor
MOOR ROAD
Moor Farm
YOXFORD ROAD

The Spring Wood
South Grange Farm
GREEN RD
Wood Farm
Corner Farm
White House Farm
Coe Wood
Kelsale Lodge Farm
Fir Tree Farm
MAIN ROAD
Buskie Farm
North Green
Rookery Farm
Bobbett's Wood
Home Covert
Redbarn Covert
Spring Plantation
Brookmeadow Covert
Fordley Hall
Vale Farm
LITTLEMOOR ROAD
FORDLEY ROAD
Packway Farm

Whin Covert
Laurel Farm
Red House Farm
TOWN FARM LA
Town Farm
North Green Farm
Yoxford Wood
Rubblestone Farm
Long Plantation
Jubilee Wood

IP17
The Garden Wood
Kelsale Hall
Park Gate Farm
A12
LC
LC
Boundary Farm
HONEYPOT LA

128
Lodge Farm
Dorley's Corner
TIGGINS LANE
BUTCHER'S ROAD
Redhouse Farm
Rose Farm
Beech Tree Farm
HONEYPOT LA
East Green

Rookery Farm
KELSALE RD
Curlew Green
B1121
East Green Farm
Dennys Farm
Peak Hill Farm
HAWTHORN ROAD
MOAT ROAD

Lonely Farm
Lakeside Leisure Park
CARLTON LA
Johnsons Farm
Kelsale
Lonely Wood
BRIDGE ST
LOWES HILL
Bridge Farm
Rogman Farm
Orchard Farm
THEBERTON RD
IP16
Clay Hills

Rendham Barnes Farm
MAPLES PK
Carlton Green Farm
Mill Farm
PH
Park Farm
Carlton
MAIN RD
P
By the Crossways
Oak Tree Farm
WORKHOUSE LA
THE GREEN
HARROW LANE

B1119
RENDHAM ROAD
Moat Farm
Vale Farm
West Side
CARLTON ROAD
ROYAL LA
Sch
White House Farm
Hill Farm
CLAY HILLS
SAXMUNDHAM RD
Kelsale Covert
Westhouse Crossing
WHITE HOUSE RD
LC

DEADMAN'S LANE
Ashgrove Farm
Bullockshed Wood
Grove Farm
New Plantation
BROOK FARM RD
Sports Gd
Sch
Rookery Wood
128
LC
LC
Cottage Farm
Pearls Wood
Westhouse Farm
Redhouse Farm
Knodishall Green

Sparks Farm
Moss's Covert
LONG AV
SAXON RD
FAIRFIELD RD
SAXMUNDHAM
Liby
New Plantation
Friston Covert

Potash Farm
Hill House Farm
Burnt House Farm
RENDHAM ROAD
LINCOLN AV
MILL RD
PO
P
P
CHURCH HILL
Lodge Plantation
Wardspring Farm
Trust Farm
Burrell's Covert

Crane's Wood
Archer's Covert
A12
Cemy
Park Farm
Sch
SOUTH ENTRANCE
HIGH ST
B1121
Hurts Hall
Wood Farm
LEISTON RD
B1119
SAXMUNDHAM RD
Cloutings Farm

High House Farm
Horseclose Covert
Old Lodge
Cottage Farm
Kiln Farm
LC
128
Bloomfield's Covert
FRISTON RD
Pattles Farm

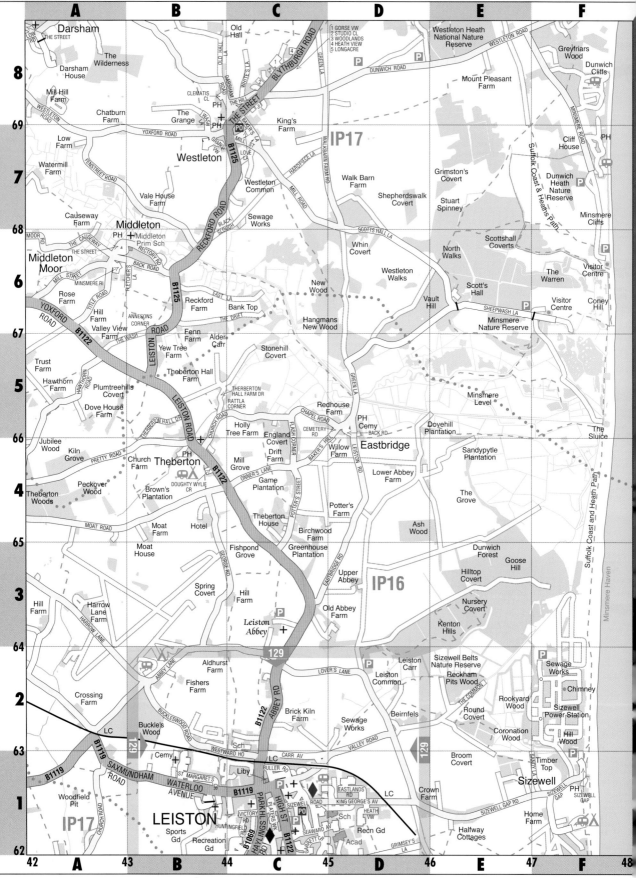

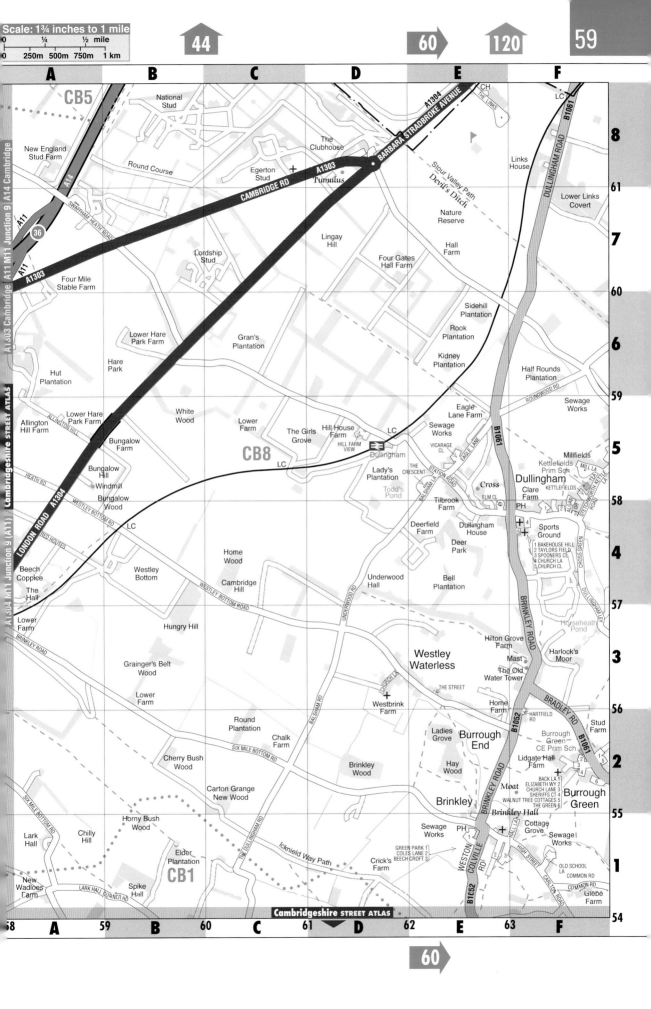

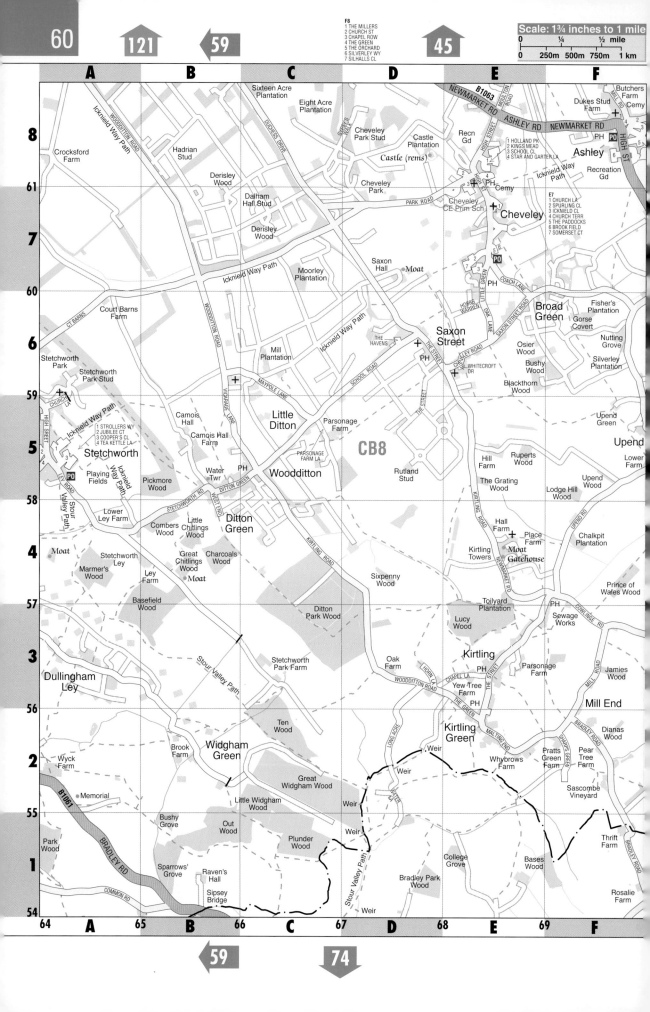

60
121
59
45

F8
1 THE MILLERS
2 CHURCH ST
3 CHAPEL ROW
4 THE GREEN
5 THE ORCHARD
6 SILVERLEY WY
7 SILHALLS CL

Scale: 1¾ inches to 1 mile
0   ¼   ½ mile
0 250m 500m 750m 1 km

A   B   C   D   E   F

Crocksford Farm
WOODDITTON ROAD
Ickfield Way Path

Sixteen Acre Plantation
Eight Acre Plantation
DUCHESS DRIVE
GRAY'S WALK
Cheveley Park Stud
Castle Plantation
Castle (rems)

B1063
NEWMARKET RD
ASHLEY RD
NEWMARKET RD
Dukes Stud Farm
Butchers Farm
Cemy
PH
HIGH ST
Ashley
Recreation Gd

8

Hadrian Stud
Derisley Wood
Dalham Hall Stud
Derisley Wood
Cheveley Park
Recn Gd
1 HOLLAND PK
2 KINGS MEAD
3 SCHOOL CL
4 STAR AND GARTER LA
PH Cemy
Cheveley CE Prim Sch
Cheveley

61

E7
1 CHURCH LA
2 SPURLING CL
3 ICKNIELD CL
4 CHURCH TERR
5 THE PADDOCKS
6 BROOK FIELD
7 SOMERSET CT

7

Ickfield Way Path
Moorley Plantation
Saxon Hall
Moat
PO
COACH LANE
PH
LITTLE GREEN
Broad Green
Fisher's Plantation
Gorse Covert

60

WOODDITTON ROAD
Court Barns Farm
CT BARNS
Mill Plantation
Ickfield Way Path
THE HAVENS
SCHOOL ROAD
Saxon Street
HOBB'S WARREN
OAK LANE
SAXON STREET ROAD
PH
THE STREET
Nutting Grove

6

Stetchworth Park
Stetchworth Park Stud
Mill Plantation
MAYPOLE LANE
VICARAGE LANE
Camois Hall
Little Ditton
Parsonage Farm
WHITECROFT DR
CHEVELEY ROAD
Osier Wood
Bushy Wood
Silverley Plantation
Blackthorn Wood

59

CHURCH LA
HIGH STREET
Ickfield Way Path
1 STROLLERS WY
2 JUBILEE CT
3 COOPER'S CL
4 TEA KETTLE LA
Stetchworth
Camois Hall Farm
PARSONAGE FARM LA
Woodditton
PH
CB8
Rutland Stud
THE STREET
Upend Green
Upend
Lower Farm

5

ELY ROAD
PO
Playing Fields
Ickfield Way Path
Pickmore Wood
Water Twr
Ditton Green
WEST END
STETCHWORTH RD
DITTON GREEN
Hill Farm
Ruperts Wood
The Grating Wood
Lodge Hill Wood
Upend Wood

Stour Valley Path
Lower Ley Farm
Combers Wood
Little Chitlings Wood
Ditton Green
KIRTLING ROAD
Hall Farm
Kirtling Towers
Place Farm
Moat
Gatehouse
Chalkpit Plantation

58

Moat
Stetchworth Ley
Ley Farm
Great Chitlings Wood
Charcoals Wood
Moat
Sixpenny Wood
KIRTLING ROAD
Toilyard Plantation
NEWMARKET ROAD
UPEND RD
Prince of Wales Wood

4

Marmer's Wood
Basefield Wood
Ditton Park Wood
Lucy Wood
Sewage Works
PH
DOWLING RD

57

Stour Valley Path
Stetchworth Park Farm
Oak Farm
HORN LA
WOODDITTON ROAD
Kirtling
THE STREET
PH
Parsonage Farm
Jamies Wood
MILL ROAD
Mill End

3

Dullingham Ley
CHAPEL LA
Yew Tree Farm
PH
Kirtling Green
THE GREEN
PH
Whybrows Farm
Pratts Green Farm
Pear Tree Farm
BRADLEY ROAD
Dianas Wood

56

Ten Wood
Brook Farm
Widgham Green
Great Widgham Wood
LONG ACRE
Weir
MALTING END
Kirtling Green
SHARPS GREEN
Sascombe Vineyard

2

Wyck Farm
B1061
Memorial
Little Widgham Wood
WATER
Weir
Weir
College Grove
Bases Wood
Thrift Farm

55

Park Wood
BRADLEY RD
Bushy Grove
Out Wood
Plunder Wood
Stour Valley Path
Weir
Bradley Park Wood
BRADLEY ROAD
Rosalie Farm

1

Sparrows' Grove
Raven's Hall
Sipsey Bridge
COMMON RD
Weir

54

64   A   65   B   66   C   67   D   68   E   69   F

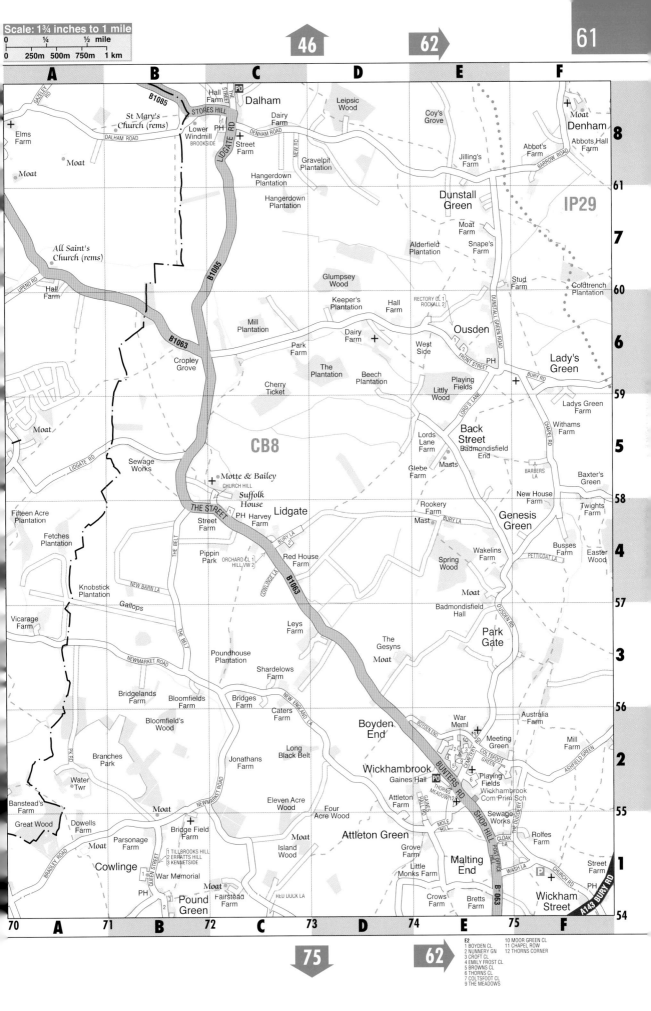

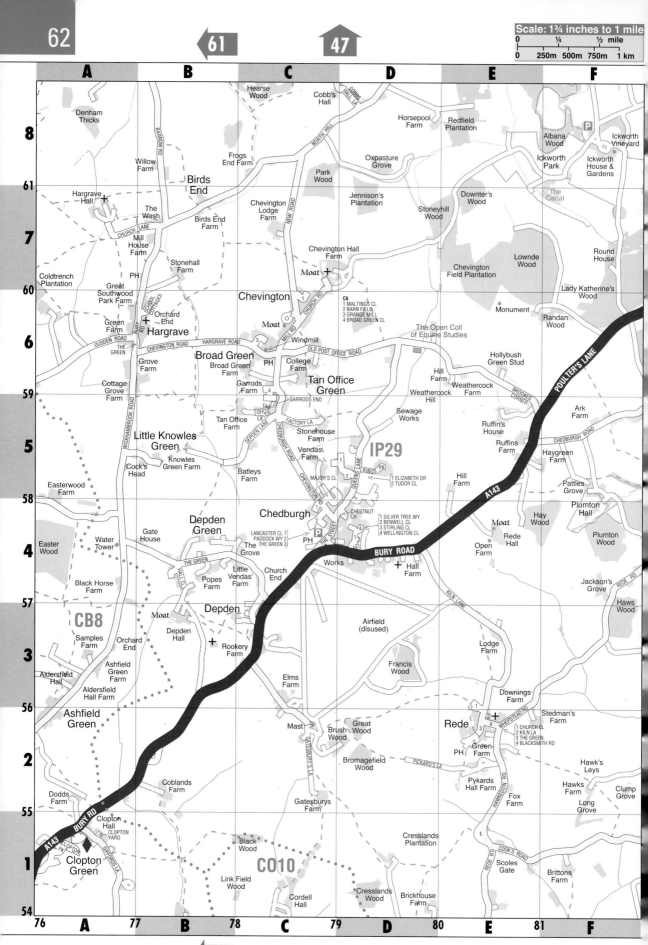

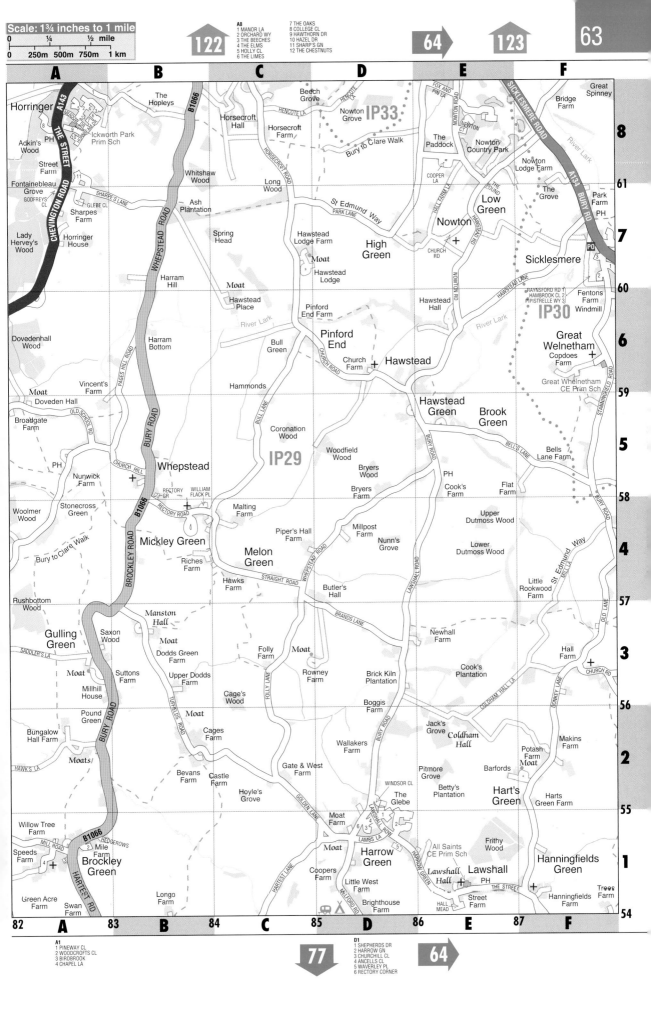

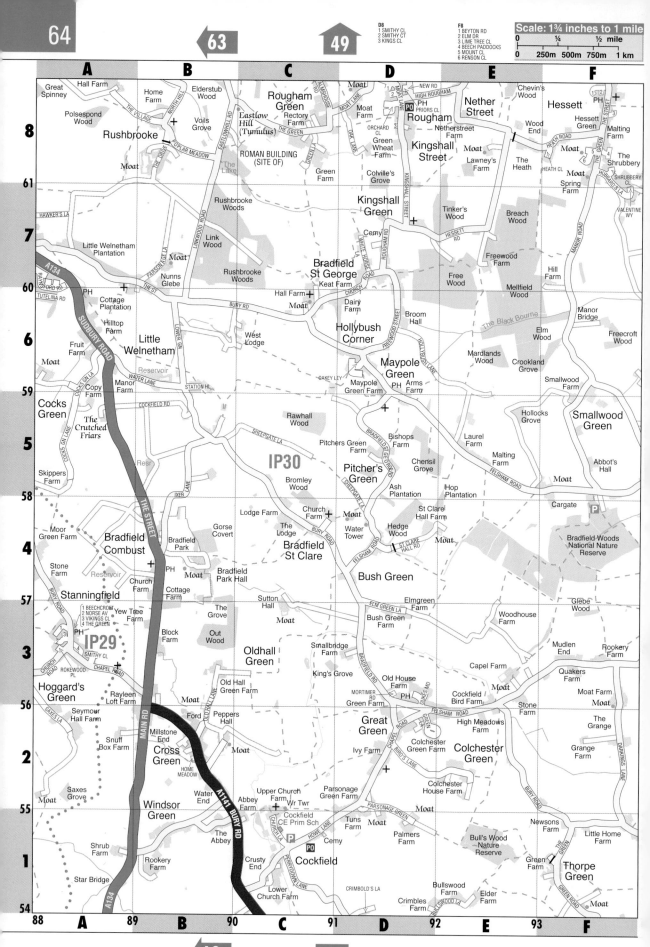

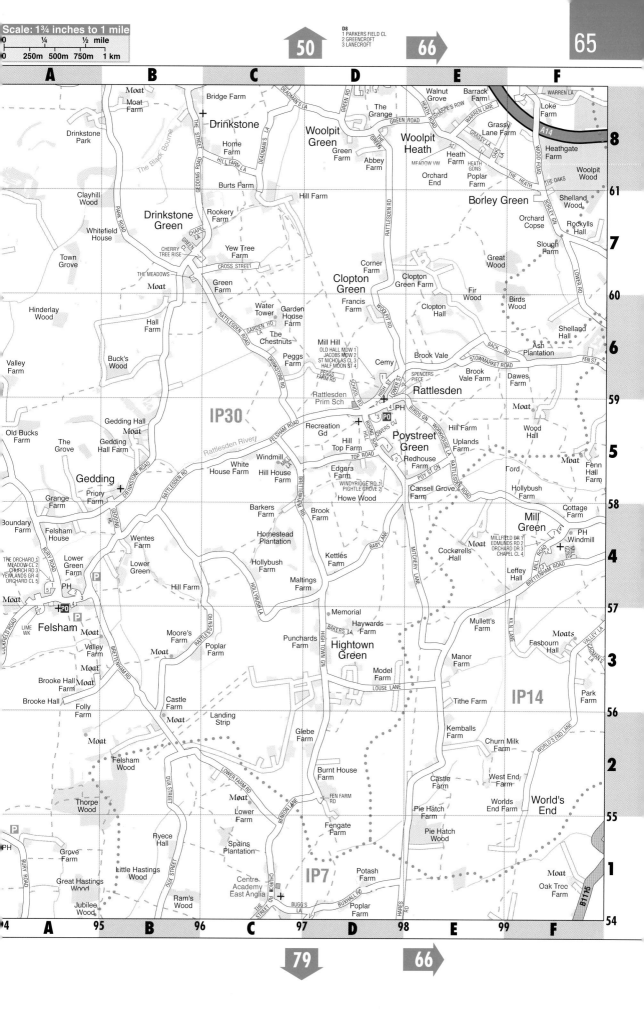

D8
1 PARKERS FIELD CL
2 GREENCROFT
3 LANECROFT

A   B   C   D   E   F

8

Moat
Moat Farm
Bridge Farm
Drinkstone
Drinkstone Park
Drinkstone
Home Farm
Burts Farm
Green Road
The Grange
Woolpit Green
Green Farm
Abbey Farm
Walnut Grove
Barrack Field
Sharpe's Row
Warren La
Warren Lane
Grassy Lane Farm
Oak La
Grassy La
Loke Farm
A14
WARREN LA
Woolpit Heath
MEADOW VW
Heath Farm
HEATH GDNS
Orchard End
Poplar Farm
THE HEATH
THE OAKS
WOOD ROAD
Heathgate Farm
Woolpit Wood

61

Clayhill Wood
The Black Bourne
Hill Farm
Rookery Farm
Hill Farm
Borley Green
Orchard Copse
Shelland Wood
Rockylls Hall
BORLEY GN

7

Whitefield House
Drinkstone Green
CHERRY TREE RISE
Yew Tree Farm
CROSS STREET
Slough Farm
LOWER RD

Town Grove
THE MEADOWS
Moat
Green Farm
Clopton Green
Corner Farm
Clopton Green Farm
Francis Farm
Clopton Hall
Fir Wood
Birds Wood
Great Wood

60

Hinderlay Wood
Hall Farm
Water Tower
Garden House Farm
GARDEN RD LA
The Chestnuts
Mill Hill
OLD HALL MDW 1
JACOBS MDW 2
ST NICHOLAS CL 3
HALF MOON ST 4
Brook Vale
STOWMARKET ROAD
BACK RD
Shelland Hall
Ash Plantation
FEN ST

6

Valley Farm
Buck's Wood
Peggs Farm
PEGGS FARM LA
Rattlesden Prim Sch
Cemy
SCHOOL RD
HIGH ST
LOWER ST
SPENCERS PIECE
Rattlesden
Brook Vale Farm
Dawes Farm
Moat

RATTLESDEN ROAD
DRINKSTONE RD
WOOLPIT RD

IP30
Gedding Hall
Moat
Gedding Hall Farm
FELSHAM ROAD
Rattlesden River
Recreation Gd
BIRDS GN
PH
POWERS CL
PO
Poystreet Green
Hill Farm
Wood Hall
WORKHOUSE LA
Uplands Farm

59

Old Bucks Farm
The Grove
Hill Top Farm
TOP ROAD
MILL LA
Redhouse Farm
POY ST CN
Ford
Moat
Fenn Hall Farm

5

Gedding
Priory Farm
White House Farm
Hill House Farm
Windmill
Edgars Farm
WINDYRIDGE RD 1
PIGTLE GROVE 2
Howe Wood
Cansell Grove Farm
RATTLESDEN RD
Hollybush Farm
Cottage Farm

Grange Farm
GEDDING HALL
BRETTENHAM RD
Barkers Farm
Brook Farm
BABY LANE
Moat
MILL RD
Mill Green
PH Windmill
BMX

58

Boundary Farm
Felsham House
Wentes Farm
Lower Green
Homestead Plantation
Hollybush Farm
Kettles Farm
Cockerells Hall
MILLFIELD DR 1
EDMUNDS RD 2
ORCHARD DR 3
CHAPEL CL 4
Leffey Hall
BRETTENHAM ROAD

THE ORCHARD 1
MEADOW-CL 2
CHURCH RD 3
YEWLANDS GR 4
ORCHARD CL 5
Lower Green Farm
BURY RD
P
Hill Farm
HOLLYBUSH LA
Maltings Farm
MITCHERY LANE

4

Moat
PH
PO
Felsham
Moat
LIME WK
Valley Farm
Moore's Farm
RATTLESDEN RD
Poplar Farm
Moat
Memorial
BAKERS LA
Haywards Farm
HIGH TOWN GN
Mullett's Farm
KILN LANE
Moats
Fasbourn Hall
VALLEY LA
JACMANS S
Park Farm

57

BRETTENHAM RD
Moat
Moat
Brooke Hall Farm
Castle Farm
Punchards Farm
Hightown Green
Model Farm
LOUSE LANE
Manor Farm
Tithe Farm
IP14

3

Brooke Hall
Folly Farm
Moat
Landing Strip
Glebe Farm
Kemballs Farm
Churn Milk Farm

56

Moat
DUX STREET
Felsham Wood
Burnt House Farm
BENTON LANE
FEN FARM RD
Castle Farm
West End Farm
WORLD'S END LANE
Worlds End Farm
World's End

2

P
Thorpe Wood
LOWER FARM RD
Moat
Lower Farm
Fengate Farm
Pie Hatch Farm
Pie Hatch Wood

55

P
PH
Grove Farm
BURY ROAD
Ryece Hall
Spains Plantation
CHURCH RD
THE STREET
IP7
Potash Farm
HARES RD
Moat
Oak Tree Farm
B1115

1

Little Hastings Wood
Great Hastings Wood
Jubilee Wood
Ram's Wood
Centre Academy East Anglia
BUGG'S LA
BUXHALL RD
Poplar Farm

54

IP7

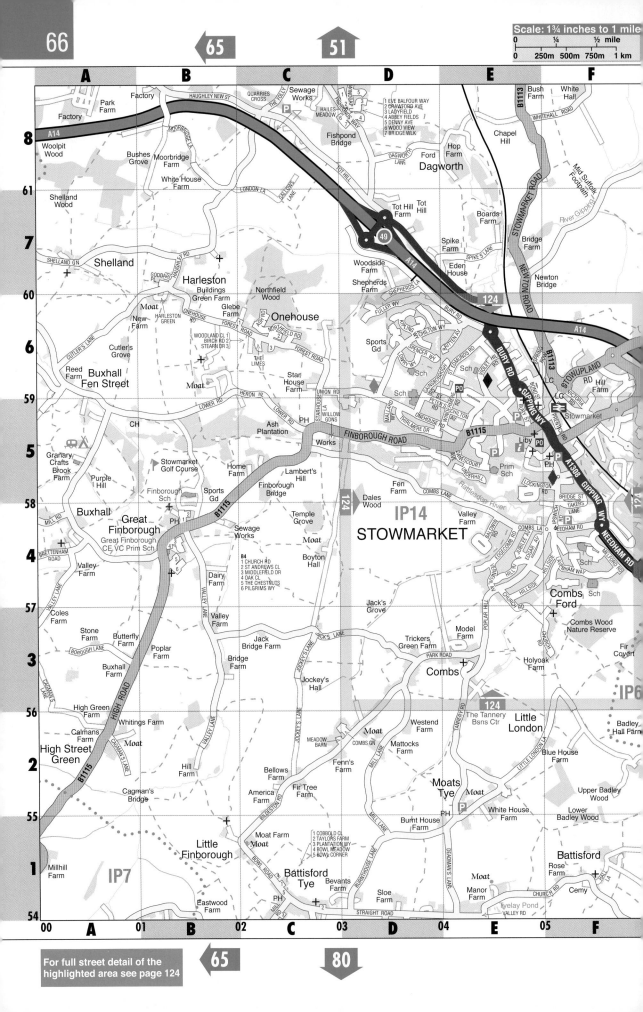

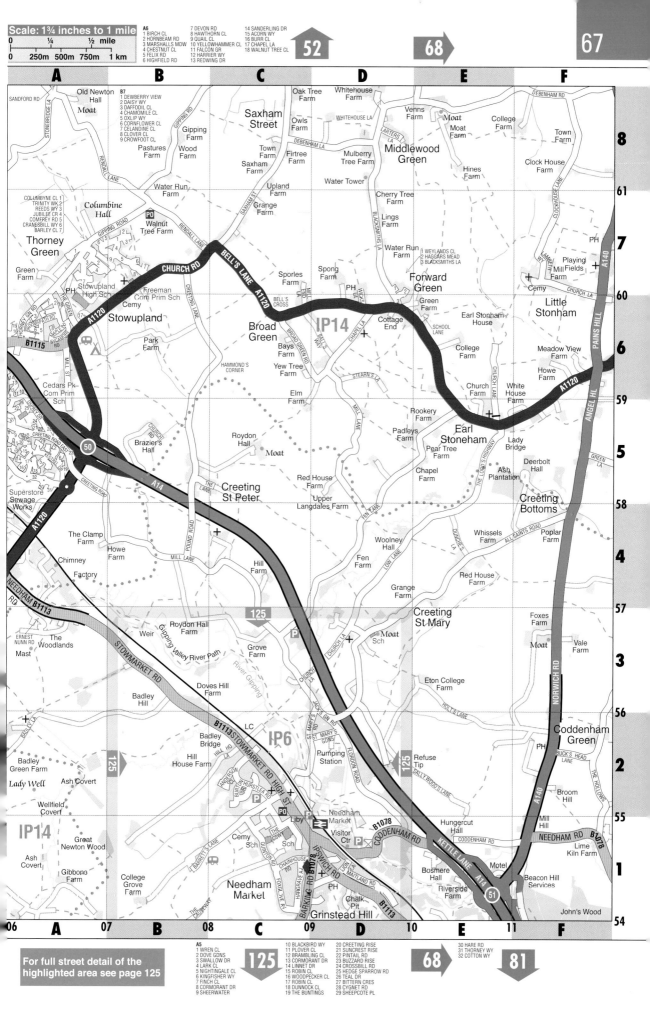

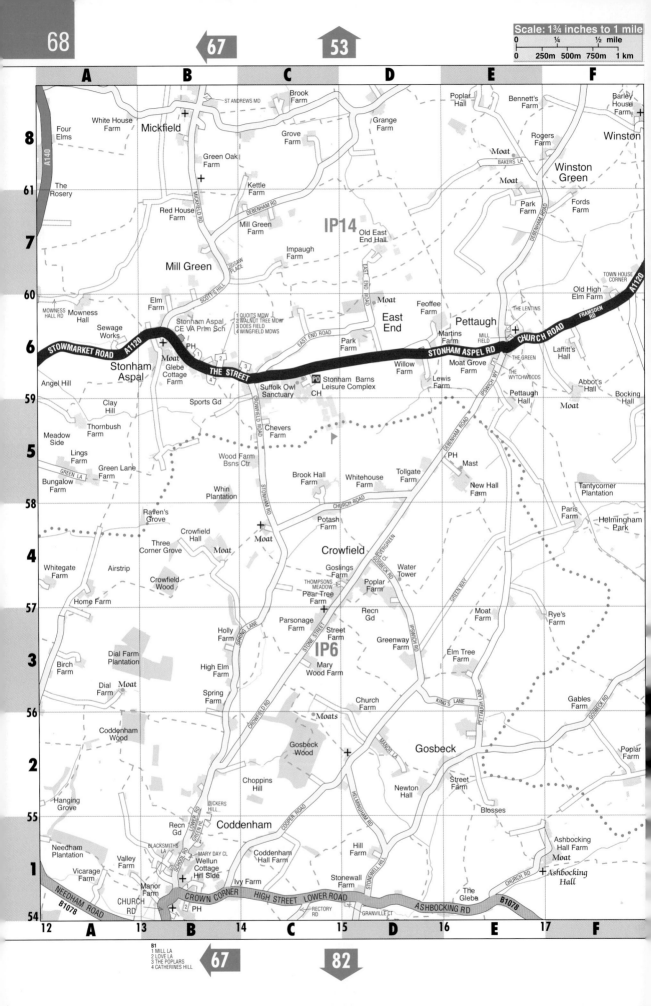

A   B   C   D   E   F

8

Four Elms

White House Farm

Mickfield

St Andrews MD

Brook Farm

Grove Farm

Grange Farm

Poplar Hall

Bennett's Farm

Barley House Farm

Winston

61

The Rosery

A140

Green Oak Farm

Kettle Farm

Mill Green Farm

DEBENHAM RD

IP14

Old East End Hall

Moat

BAKERS LA

Rogers Farm

Winston Green

Park Farm

Fords Farm

DEBENHAM ROAD

7

Mill Green

Red House Farm

MICKFIELD RD

SCOTT'S HILL

JIGSAW PLACE

Impaugh Farm

EAST END ROAD

60

Mowness Hall Rd

Mowness Hall

Elm Farm

Stonham Aspal CE VA Prim Sch

1 QUOITS MDW
2 WALNUT TREE MDW
3 DOES FIELD
4 WINGFIELD MDWS

Moat

East End

Feoffee Farm

Pettaugh

THE LENTINS

Old High Elm Farm

TOWN HOUSE CORNER

A1120

FRAMSDEN RD

Sewage Works

PH

Martins Farm

MILL FIELD

CHURCH ROAD

6

STOWMARKET ROAD   A1120

Stonham Aspal

Moat Glebe Cottage Farm

THE STREET

1

2

3

4

EAST END ROAD

Park Farm

STONHAM ASPEL RD

Willow Farm

Moat Grove Farm

IPSWICH WY

THE GREEN

THE WYTCHWOODS

Laffitt's Hall

Abbot's Hall

Bocking Hall

Angel Hill

Clay Hill

Sports Gd

CROWFIELD ROAD

Suffolk Owl Sanctuary

PO

CH

Stonham Barns Leisure Complex

Lewis Farm

Pettaugh Hall

Moat

59

Meadow Side

Thornbush Farm

Chevers Farm

DEBENHAM ROAD

5

Lings Farm

GREEN LA

Green Lane Farm

Wood Farm Bsns Ctr

Brook Hall Farm

Whitehouse Farm

Tollgate Farm

PH

Mast

New Hall Farm

Tantycorner Plantation

58

Bungalow Farm

Whin Plantation

STONHAM RD

CHURCH ROAD

Potash Farm

EVERGREEN

GOSBECK RD

Paris Farm

Helmingham Park

Raven's Grove

Crowfield Hall

Moat

Crowfield

Goslings Farm

Poplar Farm

Water Tower

GREEN WAY

4

Whitegate Farm

Airstrip

Three Corner Grove

Crowfield Wood

Moat

THOMPSONS MEADOW

Pear Tree Farm

IPSWICH RD

Moat Farm

Rye's Farm

57

Home Farm

SPRING LANE

Parsonage Farm

STONE STREET

Street Farm

Recn Gd

Greenway Farm

Elm Tree Farm

3

Birch Farm

Dial Farm Plantation

Holly Farm

IP6

Mary Wood Farm

PETTAUGH LANE

Gables Farm

GOSBECK RD

Dial Farm

Moat

High Elm Farm

CROWFIELD RD

KING'S LANE

56

Spring Farm

Moats

Church Farm

Gosbeck

Poplar Farm

2

Coddenham Wood

Gosbeck Wood

MANOR LA

Street Farm

HELMINGHAM RD

Newton Hall

Blosses

55

Hanging Grove

Choppins Hill

COOPER ROAD

Ashbocking Hall Farm

Moat

Needham Plantation

Recn Gd

BLACKSMITHS LA

LOWER RD

GREEN HL

SCHOOL RD

Coddenham

Coddenham Hall Farm

Hill Farm

STONEWELL HILL

CHURCH RD

Ashbocking Hall

1

Vicarage Farm

Valley Farm

MARY DAY CL

Wellun Cottage Hill Side

Ivy Farm

Stonewall Farm

The Glebe

B1078

Manor Farm

CHURCH RD

2

PH

CROWN CORNER

HIGH STREET

LOWER ROAD

RECTORY RD

GRANVILLE CT

ASHBOCKING RD

B1078

NEEDHAM ROAD

B1078

54

12   A   13   B   14   C   15   D   16   E   17   F

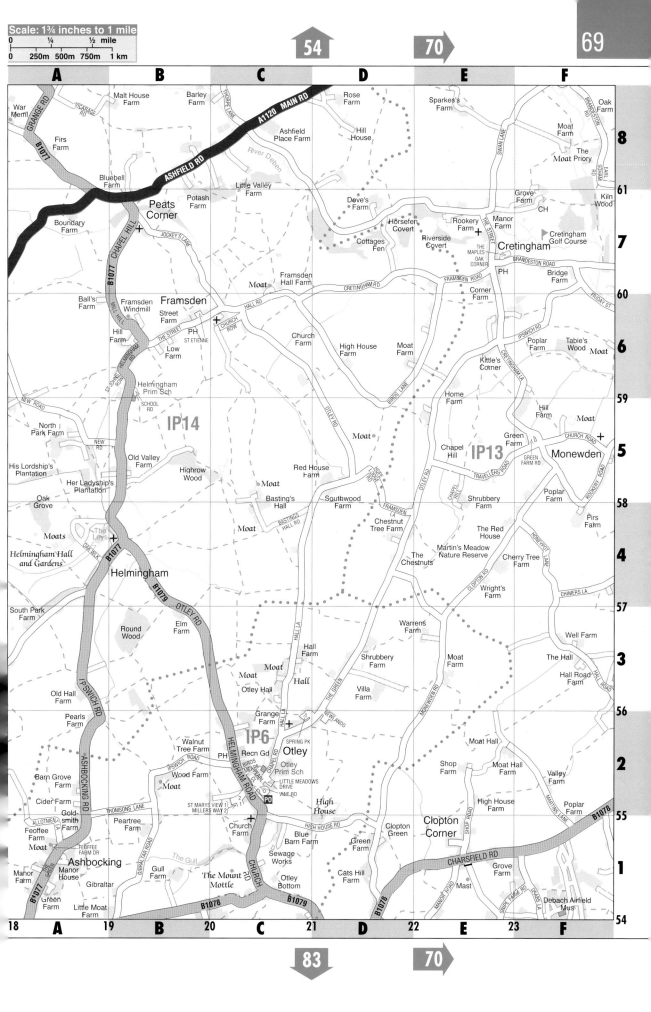

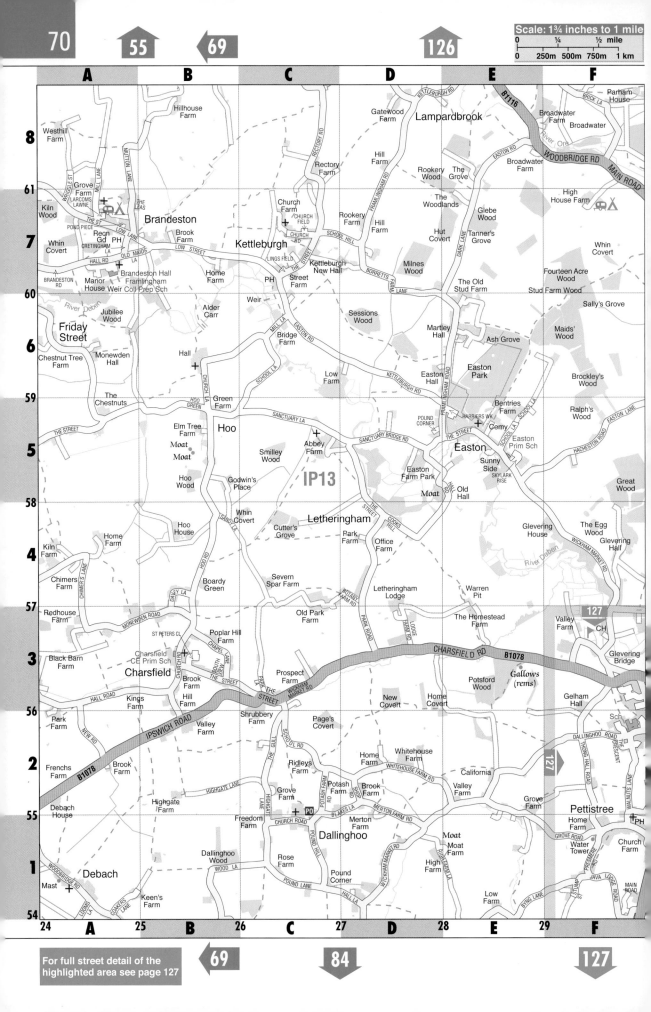

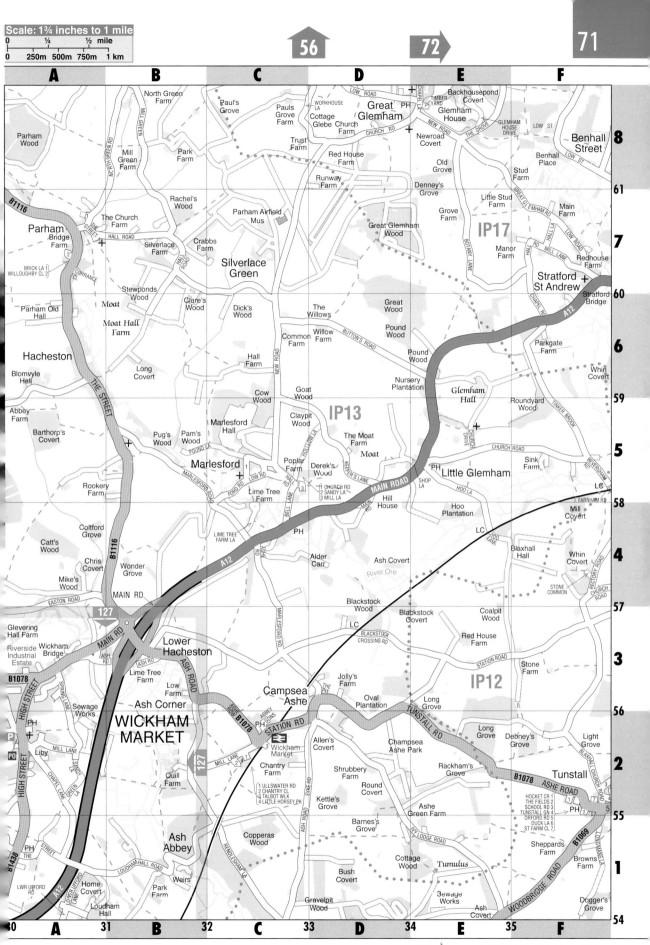

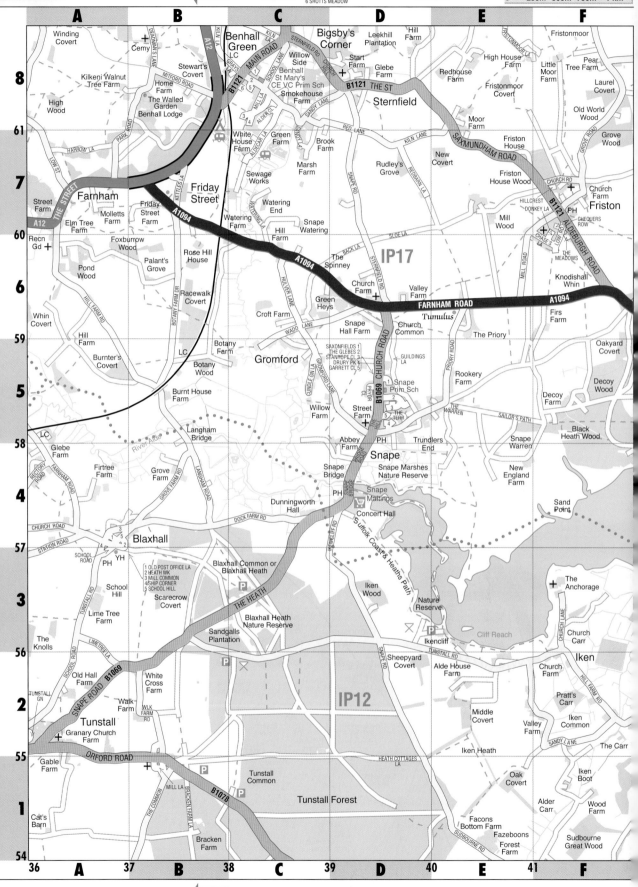

C8
1 CHALFONT DR
2 FORGE CL
3 MEADOW WK
4 FESTIVAL CL
5 THE BEECHES
6 SHOTTS MEADOW

Scale: 1¾ inches to 1 mile
0   ¼   ½ mile
0   250m 500m 750m 1 km

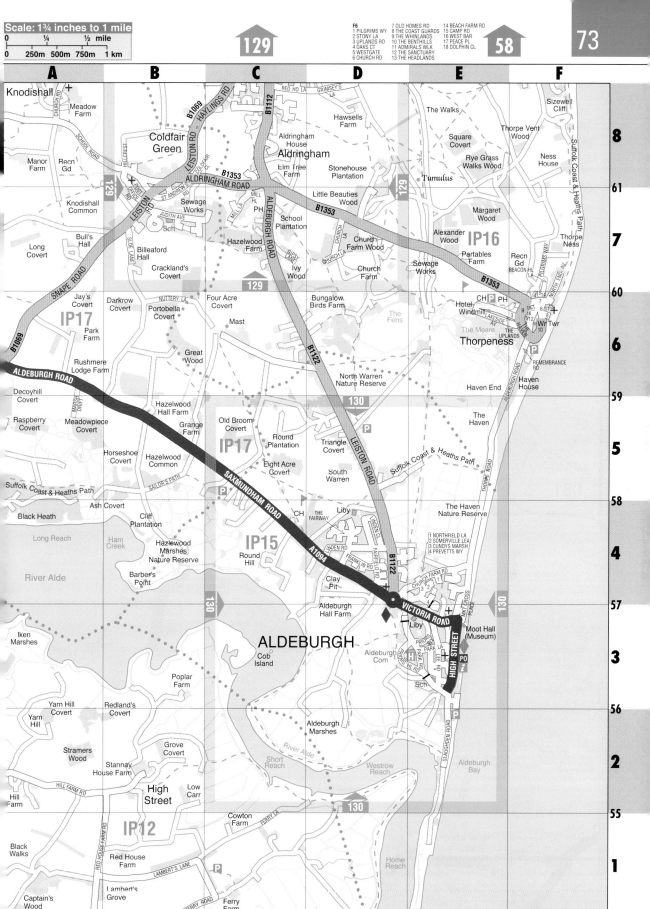

For full street detail of the highlighted areas see pages 129 and 130

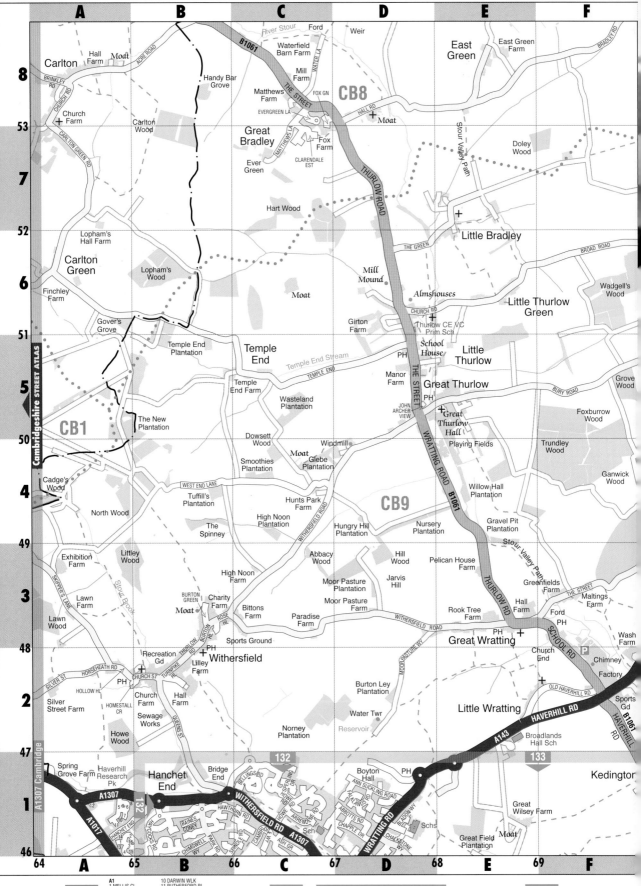

Scale: 1¾ inches to 1 mile

0   ¼   ½   mile

0   250m   500m   750m   1 km

Cambridgeshire STREET ATLAS

River Stour   Ford
Weir
B1061
Waterfield Barn Farm
Mill Farm
East Green
East Green Farm
BRADLEY RD
Carlton
Hall Farm   Moat
ACRE ROAD
Handy Bar Grove
Matthews Farm
THE STREET
FOX GN
CB8
HALL RD
Moat
Stour Valley Path
Doley Wood
BRINKLEY RD
CHURCH RD
Church Farm
CARLTON GREEN RD
Carlton Wood
EVERGREEN LA
Great Bradley
MATTHEWS LA
Fox Farm
THURLOW ROAD
Ever Green
CLARENDALE EST
Little Bradley
THE GREEN
BROAD ROAD
Lopham's Hall Farm
Hart Wood
Mill Mound
Almshouses
Little Thurlow Green
Wadgell's Wood
Carlton Green
Lopham's Wood
Moat
Girton Farm
CHURCH RD
Thurlow CE VC Prim Sch
Finchley Farm
Gover's Grove
Temple End Plantation
Temple End
Temple End Stream
TEMPLE END
School House
Little Thurlow
BURY ROAD
Grove Wood
CB1
Temple End Farm
Wasteland Plantation
PH
Manor Farm
THE STREET
Great Thurlow
Foxburrow Wood
The New Plantation
Dowsett Wood
Moat
Glebe Plantation
Windmill
JOHN ARCHER VIEW
PH
WRATTING ROAD
Great Thurlow Hall
Playing Fields
Trundley Wood
Cadge's Wood
Smoothies Plantation
West End Lane
Hunts Park Farm
CB9
Nursery Plantation
Willow Hall Plantation
Gravel Pit Plantation
Ganwick Wood
North Wood
Tuffill's Plantation
High Noon Plantation
Hungry Hill Plantation
B1061
Stour Valley Path
Exhibition Farm
Littley Wood
The Spinney
Abbacy Wood
Hill Wood
Pelican House Farm
Greenfields Farm
THE STREET
Maltings Farm
Stour Brook
High Noon Farm
Jarvis Hill
THURLOW RD
SKIPPER'S LANE
Lawn Farm
BURTON GREEN
Charity Farm
Moor Pasture Plantation
Moor Pasture Farm
Rook Tree Farm
Hall Farm
Ford
PH
Wash Farm
Lawn Wood
Moat
ROSE HL
BURTON HL
Bittons Farm
Paradise Farm
WITHERSFIELD ROAD
MOOR PASTURE WY
PH
SCHOOL RD
Great Wratting
Church End
P
Chimney Factory
SILVER ST
HORSEHEATH RD
Sports Ground
WITHERSFIELD ROAD
B1061
HAVERHILL RD
THIMBLOW RD
BURTON
Recreation Gd
PH
Withersfield
Lilley Farm
Burton Ley Plantation
OLD HAVERHILL RD
Little Wratting
HOLLOW HL
PH
CHURCH ST
TURNPIKE PL
Little Wratting
Water Twr
Reservoir
HAVERHILL RD
Sports Gd
HAVERHILL RD
Silver Street Farm
HOMESTALL CR
Church Farm
Hall Farm
Norney Plantation
A143
Broadlands Hall Sch
Kedington
QUEENS ST
Sewage Works
Howe Wood
132
Bridge End
133
Spring Grove Farm
Haverhill Research Pk
Hanchet End
BOLLINGS RD
Boyton Hall
PH
A1307 Cambridge
A1307
HANCHET END
132
WITHERSFIELD RD
HAWTHORN WY
HOWE ROAD
A1307
ANN SUCKLING ROAD
WRATTING RD
BLADON WY
CHALKSTONE WY
Schs
Great Wilsey Farm
Great Field Plantation
Moat
A1017
BAINES CONEY
CHIMSWELL RD
SPRINGFIELD RD
CAMPS RD
Sch
ABBOTT'S RD
CHAPPLE DR

64   A   65   B   66   C   67   D   68   E   69   F

A1
1 MELLIS CL
2 LANGHAM WY
3 NOTLEY DR
4 HOPTON RI
5 THREE COUNTIES WY
6 FLEMING WY
7 KELVIN DR
8 WATSON PL
9 HARVEY WLK
10 DARWIN WLK
11 RUTHERFORD PL
12 ENTERPRISE WY
13 SAXHAM CT
14 LANE END
15 BANHAM MWS
16 BENACRE

For full street detail of the highlighted area see pages 132 and 133

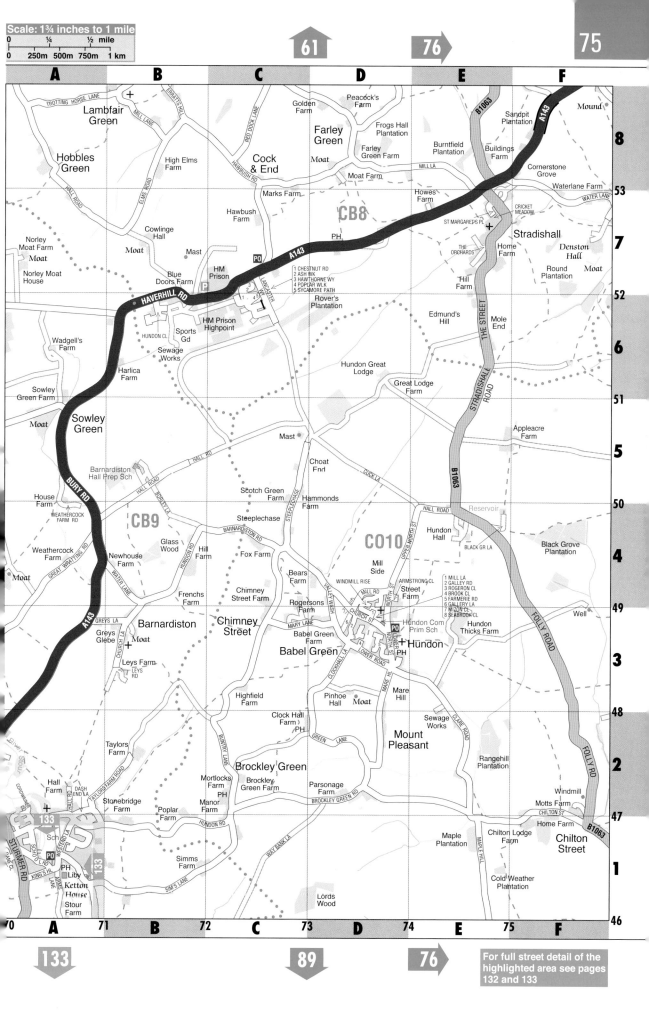

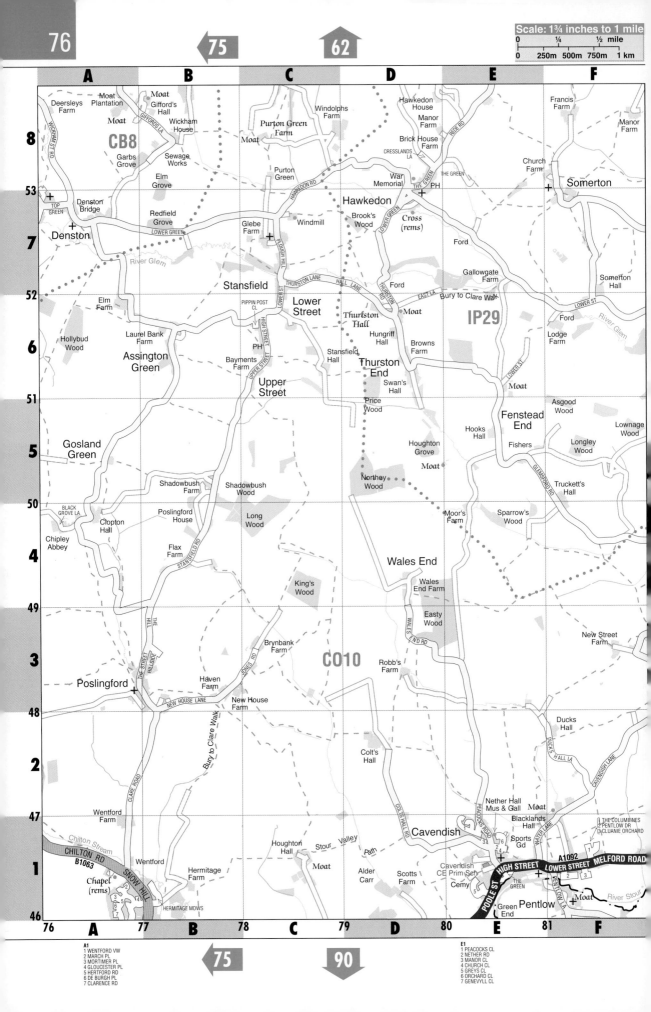

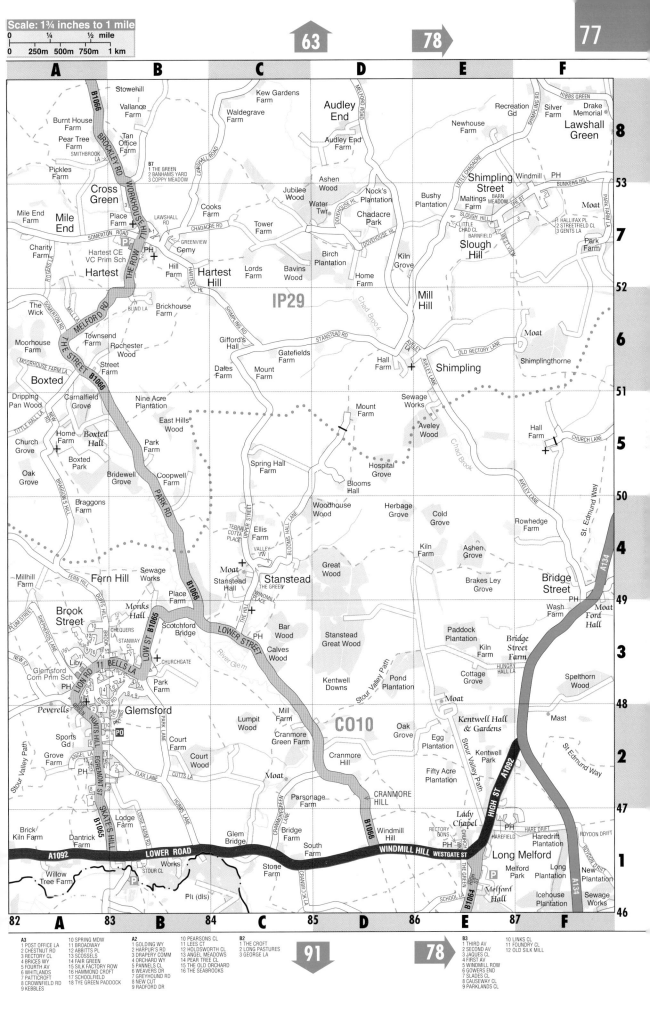

A   B   C   D   E   F

B1066
Stowehill
Vallance Farm
Kew Gardens Farm
Waldegrave Farm
Audley End
Recreation Gd
Silver Farm
Drake Memorial
Lawshall Green
HIBBS GREEN

8

Burnt House Farm
Pear Tree Farm
SMITHBROOK LA
Tan Office Farm
Newhouse Farm

BROCKLEY RD
WORKHOUSE HILL
B7
1 THE GREEN
2 BANHAMS YARD
3 COPPY MEADOW
LAWSHALL ROAD
Ashen Wood
Jubilee Wood
Nock's Plantation
Shimpling Street
Maltings Farm
Windmill
PH
BUNKERS HILL
Moat
53

Pickles Farm
Cross Green
Place Farm
LAWSHALL RD
CHADACRE RD
Cooks Farm
Greenview
Cemy
Water Twr
Chadacre Park
Bushy Plantation
SLOUGH HILL
LITTLE CHAD CL
BARNFIELD
THE ST
BARN MEADOW
LITTLE CHADACRE
WESTLEN
1 HALLIFAX PL
2 STREETFIELD CL
3 GENTS LA
7

SOMERTON ROAD
Mile End Farm
Mile End
Hartest CE VC Prim Sch
P
PH
Hill Farm
HARTEST HL
Tower Farm
Lords Farm
Bavins Wood
Birch Plantation
Home Farm
DOVEHOUSE HL
DOVEHOUSE HILL
Kiln Grove
Slough Hill
Park Farm
Charity Farm
Hartest
Hartest Hill

52

The Wick
MELFORD RD
THE STREET
BLIND LA
Brickhouse Farm
SHIMPLING RD
IP29
Chad Brook
Mill Hill
Moat
6

Moorhouse Farm
MOORHOUSE FARM LA
Townsend Farm
Rochester Wood
Gifford's Hall
STANSTEAD RD
Gatefields Farm
Hall Farm
OLD RECTORY LANE
Shimplingthorne

Boxted
B1066
Street Farm
Dales Farm
Mount Farm
Shimpling
AVELEY LANE

51

Dripping Pan Wood
Carnalfield Grove
Nine Acre Plantation
East Hills Wood
Sewage Works
Mount Farm
Aveley Wood
Chad Brook
Hall Farm
CHURCH LANE
5

Church Grove
NEW RD
TITTLE HALL LA
BRAGGON'S HILL
Home Farm
Boxted Hall
Park Farm
Spring Hall Farm
Hospital Grove
50

Oak Grove
Boxted Park
Bridewell Grove
Coopwell Farm
PARK RD
B1066
Blooms Hall
Woodhouse Wood
Herbage Grove
Cold Grove
Kiln Farm
Ashen Grove
Rowhedge Farm
ST. EDMUND WAY
A134
4

Braggons Farm
FERN HILL
DUFFS HILL
Sewage Works
UPPER STREET
TERRA COTTA PLACE
Ellis Farm
VALLEY VW
Great Wood
Brakes Ley Grove
Bridge Street
PH
49

Millhill Farm
Fern Hill
Place Farm
Moat
Stanstead Hall
THE GREEN
Stanstead
WINDMILL PLACE
THE HILL
BLOOMS HALL LANE
PH
Bar Wood
Stanstead Great Wood
Paddock Plantation
Kiln Farm
Bridge Street Farm
Wash Farm
Moat Ford Hall
3

PLUM STREET
SHEPHERDS LANE
Brook Street
Monks Hall
LOW ST
B1065
Scotchford Bridge
LOWER STREET
River Glem
Calves Wood
Stanstead Great Wood
STOUR VALLEY PATH
Pond Plantation
Cottage Grove
HUNGRY HALL LA
Spelthorn Wood
48

NEW ST
CHEQUERS LA
STANWAY CL
CHURCHGATE
Liby
BELLS LA
11
Park Farm
Kentwell Downs
CO10
Oak Grove
Moat
Kentwell Hall & Gardens
Mast
2

Glemsford Com Prim Sch
PH
LION RD
KINGS RD
PO
LANE
Court Farm
Court Wood
Lumpit Wood
Mill Farm
Cranmore Green Farm
Cranmore Hill
Egg Plantation
Kentwell Park
STOUR VALLEY PATH
A1092
HIGH ST
St Edmund Way
47

Peverells
Sports Gd
ANGEL LA
EGREMONT ST
PH
HUVTS HILL
SKATE'S HILL
FLAX LANE
CUTTS LA
Moat
Cranmore Hill
CRANMORE HILL
Fifty Acre Plantation
Lady Chapel
RECTORY GDNS
PH
HARE DRIFT
ROYDON DRIFT
46

Grove Farm
Brick Kiln Farm
Dantrick Farm
B1065
Lodge Farm
HOBBS LANE
DODRE FARM RD
Glem Bridge
Bridge Farm
South Farm
Parsonage Farm
CRANMORE GREEN LANE
Windmill Hill
B1066
Long Melford
PH
Harefield
Haredrift Plantation
A134

Willow Tree Farm
A1092
LOWER ROAD
Works
STOUR CL
P
Stone Farm
CRANBROOK LA
WINDMILL HILL WESTGATE ST
SCHOOL LA
THE GREEN
B1064
P
Melford Park
Melford Hall
Long Plantation
Icehouse Plantation
New Plantation
ROYDON DRIFT
Sewage Works
1

Plt (dis)

82   A   83   B   84   C   85   D   86   E   87   F

A3
1 POST OFFICE LA
2 CHESTNUT RD
3 RECTORY CL
4 BRICES WY
5 FOURTH AV
6 WHITLANDS
7 PATTICROFT
8 CROWNFIELD RD
9 KEBBLES
10 SPRING MDW
11 BROADWAY
12 ABBITTS PL

A2
1 GOLDING WY
2 HARPUR'S RD
3 DRAPERY COMM
4 ORCHARD WY
5 PANNELS CL
6 WEAVERS DR
7 GREYHOUND RD
8 NEW CUT
9 RADFORD DR
13 SCOSSELS
14 FAIR GREEN
15 SILK FACTORY ROW
16 HAMMOND CROFT
17 SCHOOLFIELD
18 TYE GREEN PADDOCK
10 PEARSONS CL
11 LEES CT
12 HOLDSWORTH CL
13 ANGEL MEADOWS
14 PEAR TREE CL
15 THE OLD ORCHARD
16 THE SEABROOKS

B2
1 THE CROFT
2 LONG PASTURES
3 GEORGE LA

B3
1 THIRD AV
2 SECOND AV
3 JAQUES CL
4 FIRST AV
5 WINDMILL ROW
6 GOWERS END
7 SLADES CL
8 CAUSEWAY CL
9 PARKLANDS CL
10 LINKS CL
11 FOUNDRY CL
12 OLD SILK MILL

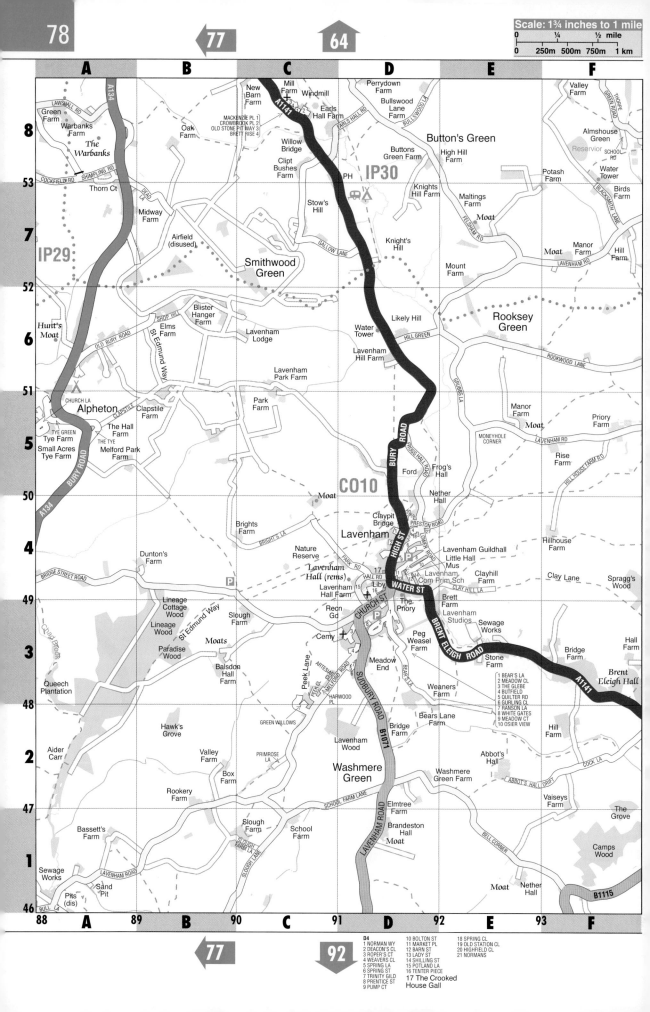

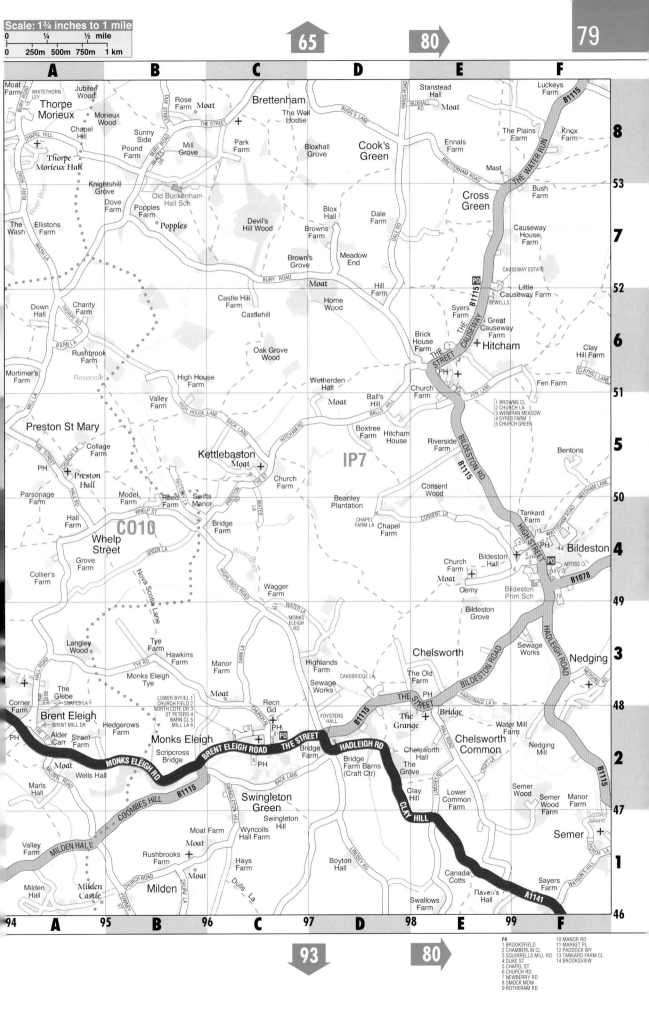

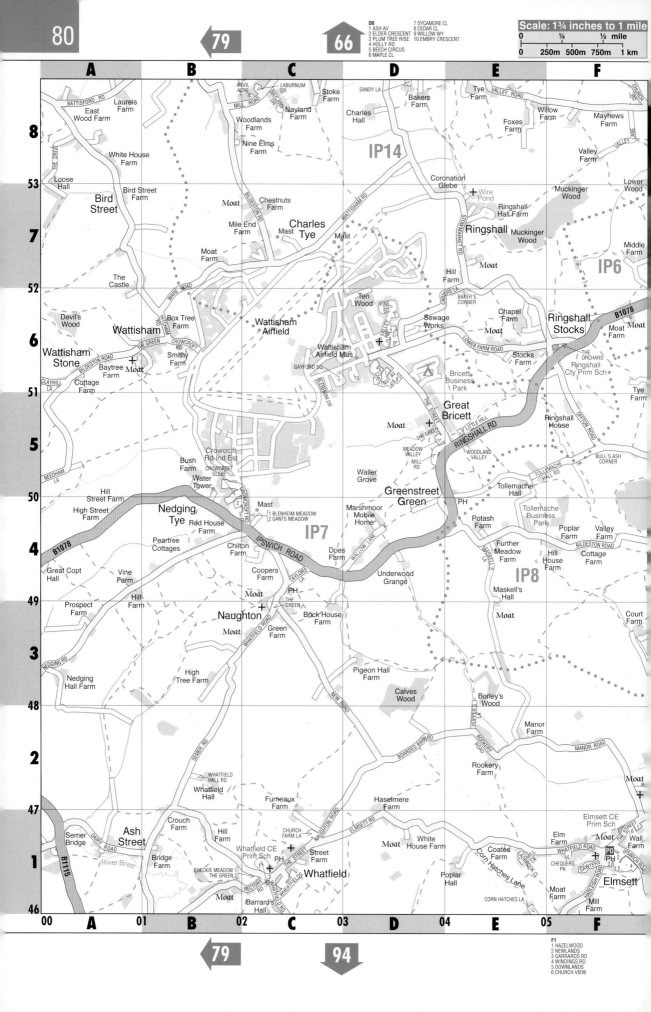

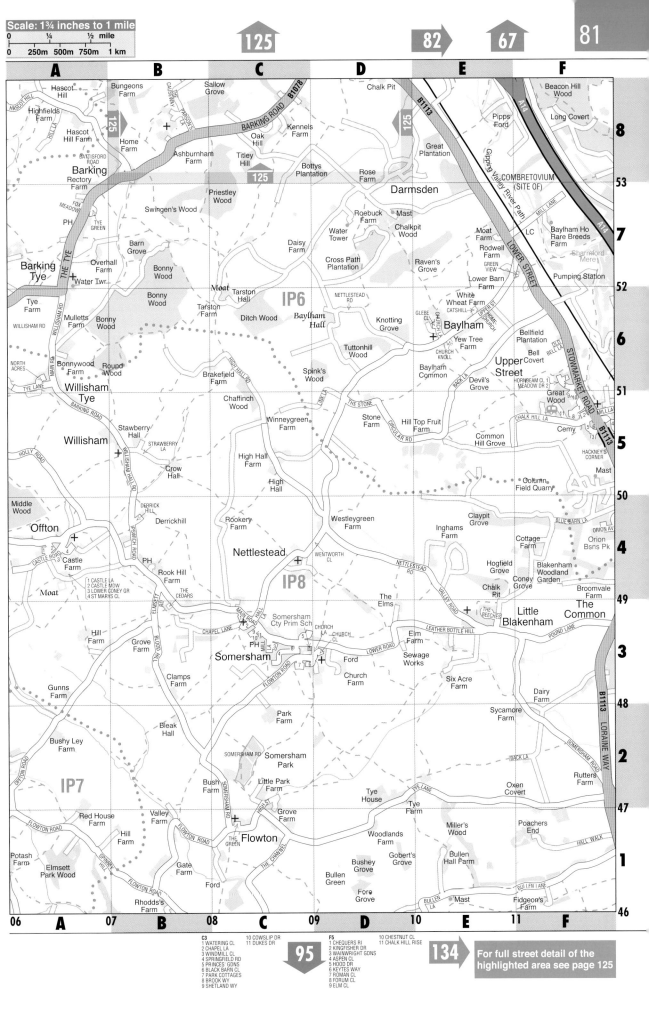

A   B   C   D   E   F

8
Hascot Hill
Highfields Farm
Hascot Hill
Bungeons Farm
Sallow Grove
Chalk Pit
Beacon Hill Wood
Pipps Ford
Long Covert
A14

53
Barking Rectory Farm
Hascot Hill Farm
Battisford Road
Ashburnham Farm
Oak Hill
Titley Hill
Kennels Farm
125
Great Plantation
Combretovium (Site of)
Mill Lane

7
PH
Fox Meadow
Tye Green
Priestley Wood
Bottys Plantation
Rose Farm
Darmsden
Moat Farm
Rodwell Farm
Green View
Bayham Ho Rare Breeds Farm
Shamford Mere
LC
Lower Street

52
Barking Tye
Overhall Farm
Water Twr.
Swingen's Wood
Daisy Farm
Roebuck Farm
Water Tower
Chalkpit Wood
Mast
Raven's Grove
Lower Barn Farm
White Wheat Farm
Catshill
Pumping Station

6
Tye Farm
Mulletts Farm
Barn Grove
Bonny Wood
Moat
Tarston Hall
Tarston Farm
Ditch Ditch Wood
Baylham Hall
Cross Path Plantation
Nettlestead Rd
Knotting Grove
Glebe Cl
Church Rd
Baylham
Yew Tree Farm
Bellfield Plantation
Bell Covert
Old Bell La

51
North Acres
Main Rd
Bonnywood Farm
Round Wood
Bonny Wood
IP6
Brakefield Farm
High Hall Rd
Spink's Wood
Tuttonhill Wood
Baylham Common
Church Knoll
Devil's Grove
Back La
Upper Street
Hornbeam Cl
Meadow Dr
Great Wood
Chalk Hill La
Stowmarket Road
B1113
Mill La

5
Willisham Tye
Tye Lane
Barking Road
Willisham
Stawberry Hall
Strawberry La
Chaffinch Wood
Winneygreen Farm
The Stone
Stone Farm
Circular Rd
Hill Top Fruit Farm
Common Hill Grove
Cemy
Hackney's Corner
Mast

50
Holly Road
Willisham Hall Rd
Crow Hall
High Hall Farm
High Hall
Column Field Quarry
Blue Barn La
Orion Av

4
Middle Wood
Offton
Castle Road
Castle Farm
Ipswich Road
Derrick Hill
Derrickhill
Rookery Farm
Nettlestead
Westleygreen Farm
Wentworth Cl
Nettlestead Rd
Inghams Farm
Claypit Grove
Hogfield Grove
Cottage Farm
Coney Grove
Orion Bsns Pk
Blakenham Woodland Garden
Broomvale Farm

49
1 Castle La
2 Castle Mdw
3 Lower Coney Gr
4 St Marys Cl
PH
Rook Hill Farm
The Cedars
IP8
The Elms
Valley Road
Chalk Pit
The Beeches
Little Blakenham
The Common

3
Moat
Elmsett
Blood Hill
Hill Farm
Grove Farm
Chapel Lane
Main Road
Somersham Cty Prim Sch
Church La
Church Cl
Elm Farm
Sewage Works
Leather Bottle Hill
Pound Lane
B1113
Loraine Way

48
Gunns Farm
Clamps Farm
Mill
PH
Somersham
Ford
Lower Road
Church Farm
Six Acre Farm
Dairy Farm

2
Bushy Ley Farm
Bleak Hall
Park Farm
Somersham Rd
Somersham Park
Little Park Farm
Somersham Rd
Back La
Sycamore Farm
Oxen Covert
Rutters Farm

47
IP7
Bush Farm
High St
Grove Farm
Tye House
Tye Lane
Miller's Wood
Poachers End
Hall Walk

1
Potash Farm
Red House Farm
Hill Farm
Valley Farm
Flowton Road
The Green
Flowton
Ford
The Channel
Woodlands Farm
Gobert's Grove
Bushey Grove
Bullen Green
Fore Grove
Bullen Hall Farm
Bullen La
Mast
Fidgeon's Farm
Bullen Lane

46
Elmsett Park Wood
Spinney Hill
Gate Farm
Ford
Flowton Road
Rhodds's Farm

06   A   07   B   08   C   09   D   10   E   11   F

C3
1 WATERING CL
2 CHAPEL LA
3 WINDMILL CL
4 SPRINGFIELD RD
5 PRINCES' GDNS
6 BLACK BARN CL
7 PARK COTTAGES
8 BROOK WY
9 SHETLAND WY

10 COWSLIP DR
11 DUKES DR

F5
1 CHEQUERS RI
2 KINGFISHER DR
3 WAINWRIGHT GDNS
4 ASPEN CL
5 HOOD DR
6 KEYTES WAY
7 ROMAN CL
8 FORUM CL
9 ELM CL

10 CHESTNUT CL
11 CHALK HILL RISE

For full street detail of the highlighted area see page 125

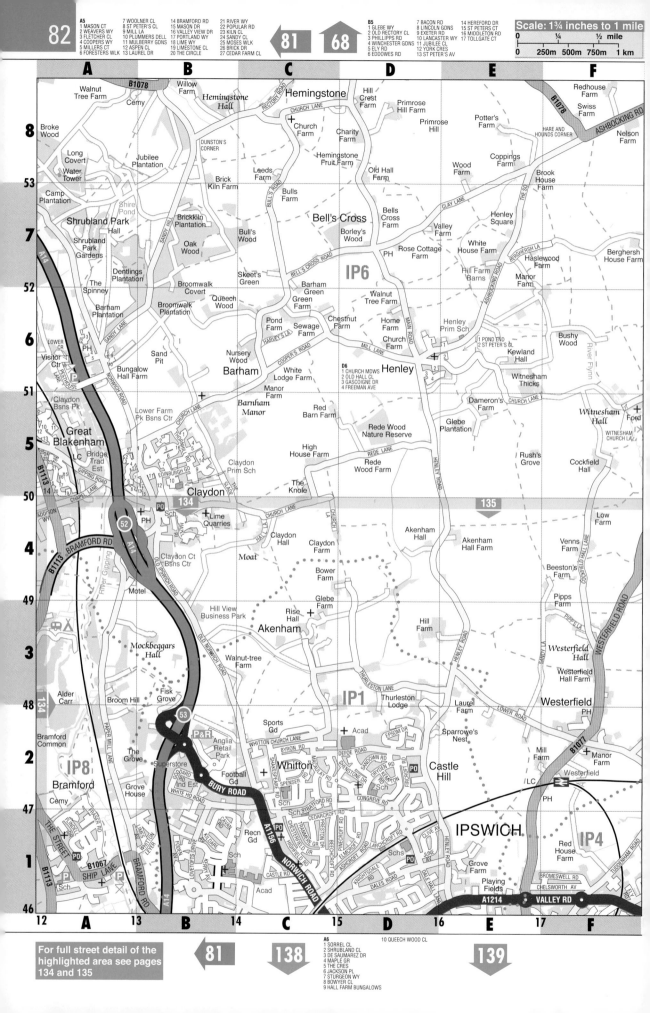

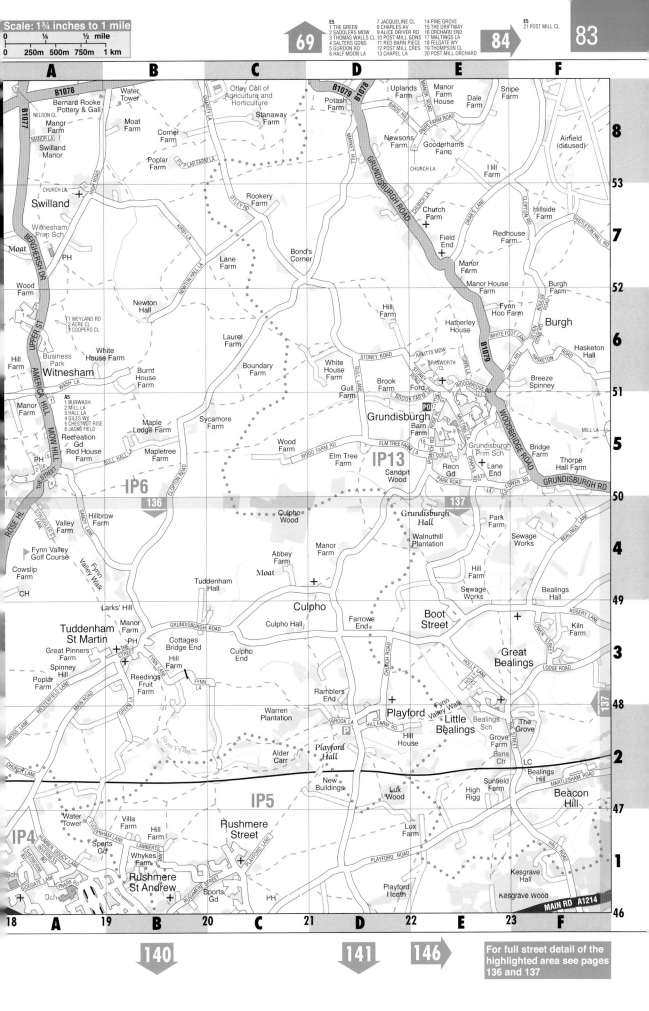

83
70

E6
1 CAGES WY
2 SCOTT LA
3 RIXON CRES
4 CLEMENTS RD
5 ST AUDRYS PARK RD
6 CALDER RD
7 BURROWS RD
8 LODGE FARM LA
9 SOUTH CL
10 UPPER MELTON TERR

F7
1 LODGE RD
2 CROWNFIELDS
3 THE WALNUTS
4 TOVELLS
5 PARKLANDS
6 LIME CL
7 NICHOLLS CL
8 UFFORD PL
9 CHURCH LA
10 REDWOOD TERR
11 NURSERY LA
12 GOLDSMITHS
13 THE WALNUTS

Scale: 1¾ inches to 1 mile

| 0 | ¼ | ½ | mile |
| 0 | 250m | 500m | 750m | 1 km |

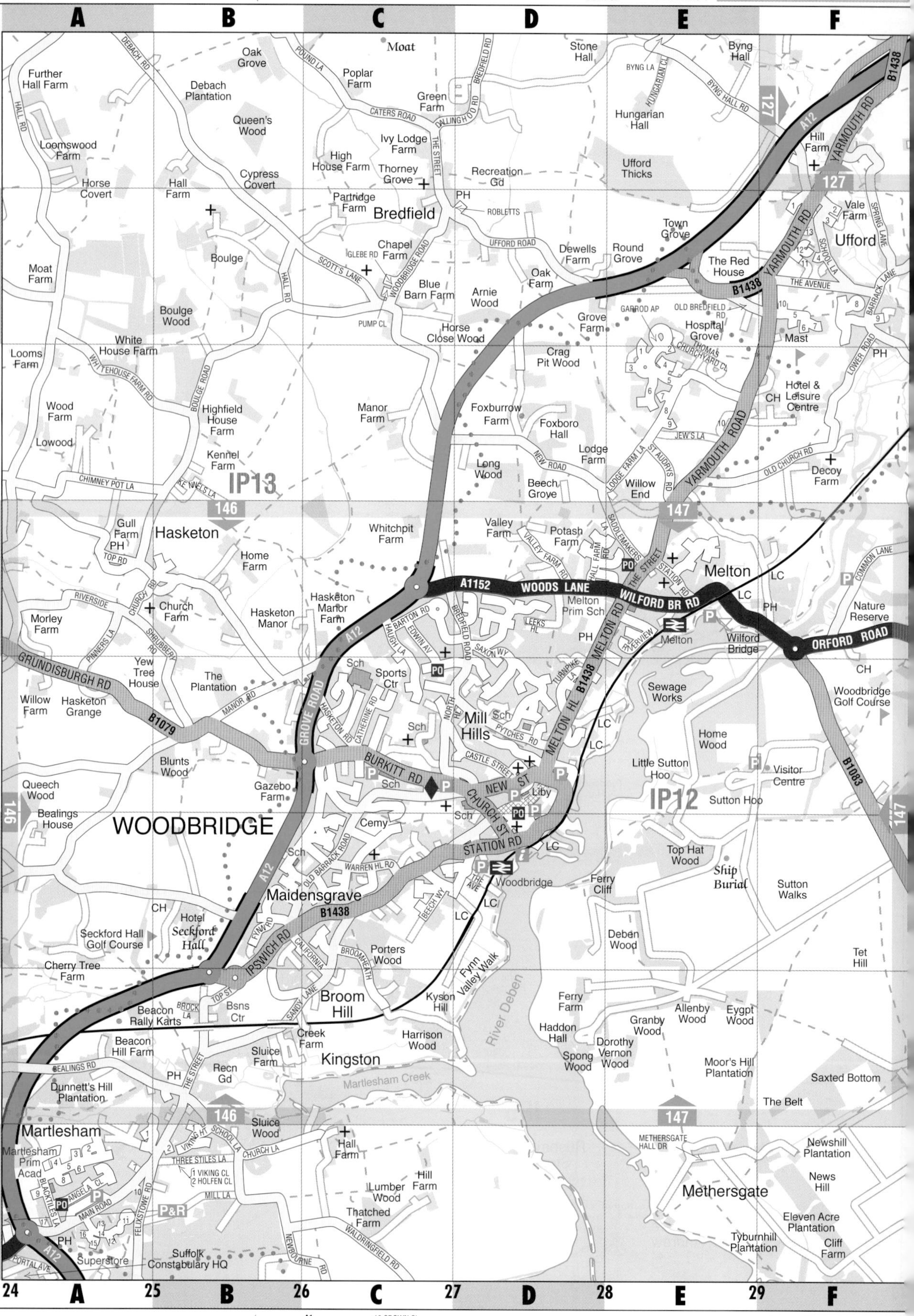

Map area labels:

8, 53, 7, 52, 6, 51, 5, 50, 4, 49, 3, 48, 2, 47, 1, 46

A B C D E F (top and bottom)

24 25 26 27 28 29 (bottom)

Further Hall Farm, Loomswood Farm, Horse Covert, Moat Farm, Looms Farm, Wood Farm, Lowood, Queech Wood, Bealings House, Willow Farm, Cherry Tree Farm, Beacon Hill Farm, Dunnett's Hill Plantation, Martlesham, Martlesham Prim Acad, Superstore, Suffolk Constabulary HQ

Debach Plantation, Oak Grove, Queen's Wood, Cypress Covert, Hall Farm, Boulge, Boulge Wood, White House Farm, Highfield House Farm, Kennel Farm, Hasketon, Home Farm, Hasketon Manor, Morley Farm, Church Farm, Yew Tree House, The Plantation, Hasketon Grange, Blunts Wood, Gazebo Farm, WOODBRIDGE, Maidensgrave, Seckford Hall Golf Course, Hotel Seckford Hall, Beacon Rally Karts, Bsns Ctr, Broom Hill, Sluice Farm, Recn Gd, Kingston, Sluice Wood, Hall Farm, Lumber Wood, Thatched Farm, Hill Farm

Moat, Poplar Farm, Green Farm, Ivy Lodge Farm, High House Farm, Thorney Grove, Partridge Farm, Bredfield, Chapel Farm, Blue Barn Farm, Pump Cl, Manor Farm, Whitchpit Farm, Home Farm, Sports Ctr, Mill Hills, Castle Stree, Cemy, Porters Wood, Harrison Wood, Creek Farm, Martlesham Creek

Horse Close Wood, Arnie Wood, Oak Farm, Foxburrow Farm, Long Wood, Beech Grove, Valley Farm, Leeks Hl, PH, Sch, New St, Liby, Station Rd, Woodbridge, Fynn Valley Walk, Kyson Hill, River Deben

Stone Hall, Recreation Gd, Ufford Thicks, Dewells Farm, Round Grove, Grove Farm, Crag Pit Wood, Foxboro Hall, Lodge Farm, Willow End, Potash Farm, Melton Prim Sch, Melton, Sewage Works, Little Sutton Hoo, Home Wood, IP12, Sutton Hoo, Top Hat Wood, Ferry Cliff, Deben Wood, Ferry Farm, Granby Wood, Haddon Hall, Dorothy Vernon Wood, Spong Wood, Moor's Hill Plantation, Methersgate, Methersgate Hall Dr

Byng Hall, Byng La, Hungarian Hall, Town Grove, The Red House, Hospital Grove, Hotel & Leisure Centre, Decoy Farm, Mast, Hill Farm, Vale Farm, Ufford, The Avenue, Nature Reserve, Woodbridge Golf Course, Visitor Centre, Ship Burial, Sutton Walks, Tet Hill, Allenby Wood, Eygpt Wood, Saxted Bottom, The Belt, Newshill Plantation, News Hill, Eleven Acre Plantation, Tyburnhill Plantation, Cliff Farm

IP13

Roads: DEBACH RD, ROUND LA, CATERS ROAD, THE STREET, HALL RD, SCOTT'S LANE, WOODBRIDGE ROAD, GLEBE RD, UFFORD ROAD, BREDFIELD RD, DALLINGHOO RD, HUNGARIAN LA, BYNG HALL RD, YARMOUTH RD, B1438, A12, B1438, THE AVENUE, SPRING LANE, BARRACK RD, LOWER RD, OLD CHURCH RD, JEW'S LA, 147, WILFORD BR RD, WOODS LANE, A1152, 146, CHIMNEY POT LA, BOULGE ROAD, WHITEHOUSE FARM RD, GRUNDISBURGH RD, B1079, PINNERS LA, SNUBBERY LA, CHURCH LA, RIVERSIDE, MANOR RD, GROVE ROAD, BURKITT RD, CHURCH ST, NEW ST, STATION RD, CASTLE STREE, PYTCHES RD, MELTON HL, THE STREET, STATION RD, ORFORD ROAD, COMMON LANE, B1083, 147, IPSWICH RD, B1438, OLD BARRACK ROAD, WARREN HL RD, BROOMHEATH, CALIFORNIA, FYNN RD, TOP ST, BROCK LA, BEALINGS RD, PORTALAVE, FELIXSTOWE RD, MAIN RD, MILL LA, SCHOOL LA, CHURCH LA, THREE STILES LA, VIKING HL, WALDRINGFIELD RD, NEWBOURNE RD

137
98

For full street detail of the highlighted area see pages 127, 146 and 147

A1
1 NUNN CL
2 ALBAN SQ
3 GREEN LA
4 BUCKINGHAM CL
5 CHANDOS DR
6 RAVENS WY
7 SHAW VALLEY RD
8 CHANDOS CT
9 CAROL AV
10 CROWN CL
11 THE COPSE
12 ELM CL
13 NIGHTINGALE WY
14 THE SANDLINGS
15 SKYLARK DR
16 NIGHTJAR GR
17 LABURNHAM GDNS

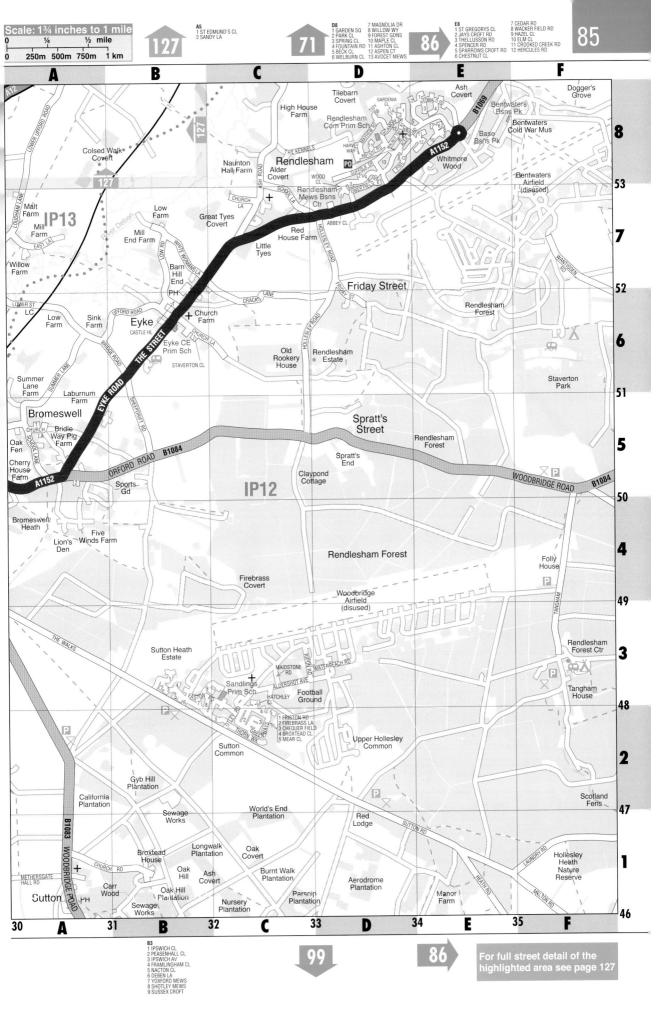

A5
1 ST EDMUND'S CL
2 SANDY LA

D8
1 GARDEN SQ
2 PARK CL
3 SPRING CL
4 FOUNTAIN RD
5 BECK CL
6 WELBURN CL

7 MAGNOLIA DR
8 WILLOW WY
9 FOREST GDNS
10 MAPLE CL
11 ASHTON CL
12 ASPEN CT
13 AVOCET MEWS

E8
1 ST GREGORYS CL
2 JAYS CROFT RD
3 THELLUSSON RD
4 SPENCER RD
5 SPARROWS CROFT RD
6 CHESTNUT CL

7 CEDAR RD
8 WACKER FIELD RD
9 HAZEL CL
10 ELM CL
11 CROOKED CREEK RD
12 HERCULES RD

A   B   C   D   E   F

8
53
7
52
6
51
5
50
4
49
3
48
2
47
1
46

30   A   31   B   32   C   33   D   34   E   35   F

B3
1 IPSWICH CL
2 PEASENHALL CL
3 IPSWICH AV
4 FRAMLINGHAM CL
5 NACTON CL
6 DEBEN LA
7 YOXFORD MEWS
8 SHOTLEY MEWS
9 SUSSEX CROFT

99

86

For full street detail of the highlighted area see page 127

IP13
Colsed Walk Covert
127
Malt Farm
Mill Farm
East La
Willow Farm
Lower St LC
Low Farm
Sink Farm
Summer Lane Farm
Laburnum Farm
Bromeswell
Oak Fen
Cherry House Farm
Church
Bridle Way Pig Farm
School La
A1152
Bromeswell Heath
Lion's Den
Five Winds Farm
California Plantation
The Walks
B1083
Woodbridge Road
Methersgate Hall Rd
Sutton
Carr Wood
Church Rd
Broxtead House
Oak Hill
Oak Hill Plantation
Sewage Works
Longwalk Plantation
Nursery Plantation
Ash Covert
Burnt Walk Plantation
World's End Plantation
Parsnip Plantation
Oak Covert
Gyb Hill Plantation
Sewage Works
Broxtead House

River Deben
Low Farm
Mill End Farm
Low Row Rd
White Woman's La
Barn Hill End
PH
Eyke
Castle Hl
The Street
Eyke Road
Bridge Road
Summer Lane
Church La
Church Farm
Eyke CE Prim Sch
Staverton Cl
Orford Road
B1084
Sheppherd Rd
Sports Gd
IP12
Sutton Heath Estate
Maidstone Rd
Waterbeach Rd
Ripon Rd
Aldershot Ave
Sandlings Prim Sch
Hatchley Cl
Football Ground
Easton Rd
Otley Rd
Thorn Wk
Green Rd
Sutton Common
1 FRISTON RD
2 FIREBRASS LA
3 CHEQUER FIELD
4 BROXTEAD CL
5 MEAR CL
Firebrass Covert
Woodbridge Airfield (disused)
Rendlesham Forest
Claypond Cottage
Spratt's End
Spratt's Street

High House Farm
Naunton Hall Farm
Alder Covert
Great Tyes Covert
Little Tyes
Red House Farm
Old Rookery House
Ash Road
School La
Church La
Tilebarn Covert
Rendlesham Com Prim Sch
The Kennels
Harvey Way
Knight Dr
Suffolk Dr
Wood Cl
Gardenia
PO
Abbey Cl
Hollesley Road
Friday St
Cracks Lane
Rendlesham
Rendlesham Mews Bsns Ctr
Rendlesham Estate
Friday Street

Ash Covert
B1069
A1152
Whitmore Wood
Bentwaters Bsns Pk
Bentwaters Cold War Mus
Base Bsns Pk
Bentwaters Airfield (disused)
Dogger's Grove
Wantisden Rd
Rendlesham Forest
Staverton Park
Rendlesham Forest
Woodbridge Road
B1084
Folly House
Tangham
Rendlesham Forest Ctr
Tangham House
Upper Hollesley Common
Sutton Rd
Red Lodge
Aerodrome Plantation
Manor Farm
Heath Rd
Laundry Rd
Hollesley Heath Nature Reserve
Scotland Fens
Milton Rd

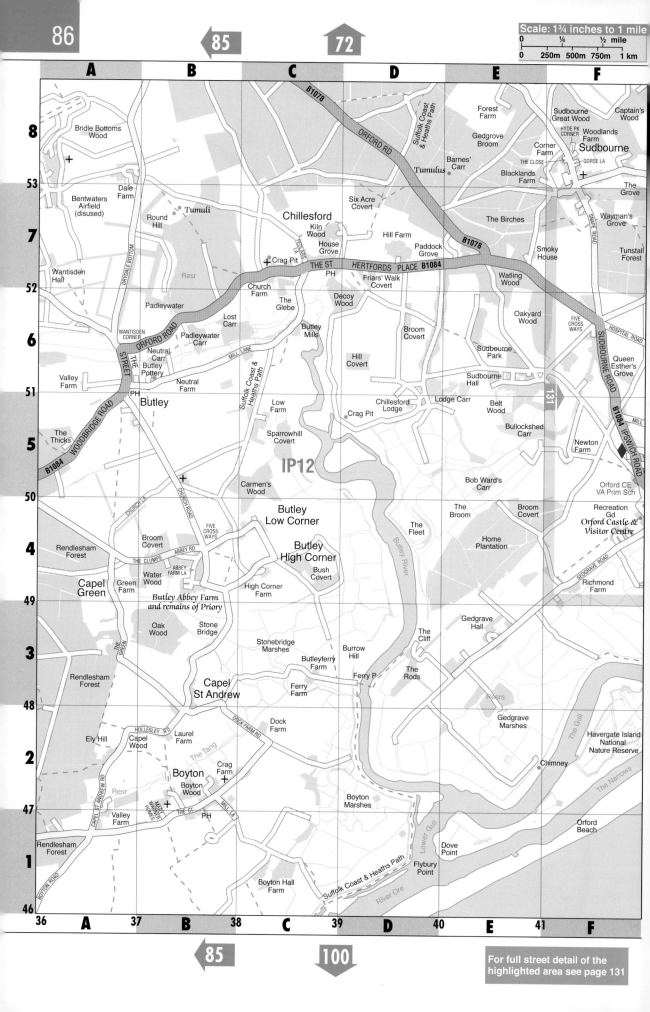

A   B   C   D   E   F

8   Bridle Bottoms Wood

B1078
ORFORD RD

Forest Farm
Sudbourne Great Wood
Captain's Wood

Gedgrove Broom
Woodlands Farm
HYDE PK CORNER

53   Bentwaters Airfield (disused)
Dale Farm
Tumuli

Corner Farm
THE CLOSE
Sudbourne
GORSE LA

Barnes' Carr
Tumulus

Blacklands Farm
The Grove

7   Round Hill
DRYSDALE BOTTOM

Chillesford
Kiln Wood
House Grove
Six Acre Covert
Hill Farm

B1078

The Birches

Wayman's Grove

Smoky House
Tunstall Forest

Wantisden Hall

Crag Pit
THE ST   HERTFORDS PLACE   B1084
PH
Friars' Walk Covert

Watling Wood

52   Church Farm
The Glebe
Decoy Wood

Padleywater

Oakyard Wood

FIVE CROSS WAYS
HOSPITAL ROAD

6   WANTISDEN CORNER
ORFORD ROAD

Lost Carr
Padleywater Carr
MILL LANE

Butley Mills

Broom Covert

Sudbourne Park

SUDBOURNE ROAD

Queen Esther's Grove

THE STREET

Neutral Carr
Butley Pottery

Hill Covert

Sudbourne Hall

131

Valley Farm

WOODBRIDGE ROAD

PH
Neutral Farm
Butley
Suffolk Coast & Heaths Path

Low Farm

Chillesford Lodge
Lodge Carr

Belt Wood

B1084 IPSWICH ROAD
MILL

5   The Thicks
B1084

CHURCH ROAD

Sparrowhill Covert

Crag Pit

Bullockshed Carr

Newton Farm

IP12

Bob Ward's Carr

Orford CE VA Prim Sch

50   FIVE CROSS WAYS

Carmen's Wood

The Broom
Broom Covert

Recreation Gd

Orford Castle & Visitor Centre

4   Rendlesham Forest
Broom Covert
THE CLUMPS
ABBEY RD
Water Wood
ABBEY FARM LA

Butley Low Corner

Butley High Corner

The Fleet

Home Plantation

GEDGRAVE ROAD

Richmond Farm

Capel Green
CHURCH LA

Green Farm

High Corner Farm
Bush Covert

Gedgrave Hall

Oak Wood
Stone Bridge

Butley Abbey Farm and remains of Priory

THE GREEN

The Cliff

3   Rendlesham Forest

Stonebridge Marshes
Butleyferry Farm

Burrow Hill

The Rods

Gedgrave Marshes

The Gull

Ferry P

Havergate Island National Nature Reserve

The Narrows

2   Ely Hill
Capel Wood
HOLLESLEY RD
Laurel Farm
DOCK FARM RD

Capel St Andrew

Ferry Farm
Dock Farm

The Tang

Chimney

CAPEL ST ANDREW RD

Boyton
Crag Farm
Boyton Wood

Boyton Marshes

Lower Gull

47   Valley Farm
MANOR HOMES
THE ST
PH
MILL LA

Orford Beach

1   Rendlesham Forest
Boyton Road

Boyton Hall Farm
Suffolk Coast & Heaths Path
River Ore

Dove Point
Flybury Point

46   36   A   37   B   38   C   39   D   40   E   41   F

For full street detail of the highlighted area see page 131

IP15

Aldeburgh Bay

River Alde

Sudbourne Beach

Firs Farm

The Firs

Longdrift Carr

Sudbourne Marshes

RED HOUSE FARM RD

The White House

SCHOOL ROAD

VALLEY FARM RD

Valley Farm

131

High House Farm

HIGH HOUSE FARM ROAD

FERRY ROAD

Elm Covert

Crag Pit

Crag Farm

CRAG FARM ROAD

Chaplin's Carr

Church Farm

Moss' Carr

Ox Carr

Blackstakes Reach

Lantern Marshes

Masts

Prettyman's Whin

IP12

131

Masts

Lodge Farm

FERRY ROAD

Cobbins Farm

Bullockshed Grove

BROADWAY

BULLOCKSHED LA

Ash Carr

Raydon Hall

RAYDON LANE

Town Marshes

Pig Pail Bridge

Wireless Station

Orford

RECTORY RD

PO

HIGH ST

DAPHNE RD

BROAD ST

King's Marshes

FRONT ST

Town Hall

P PH

P P

QUAY ST

Chantry Farm

Orfordness

River Ore

Orford Ness

Sewage Works

131

Chantry Point

Orford Ness National Nature Reserve

Stony Ditch

Orfordness Lighthouse

Stonyditch Point

Cuckold's Point

Orford Beach

For full street detail of the highlighted area see page 131

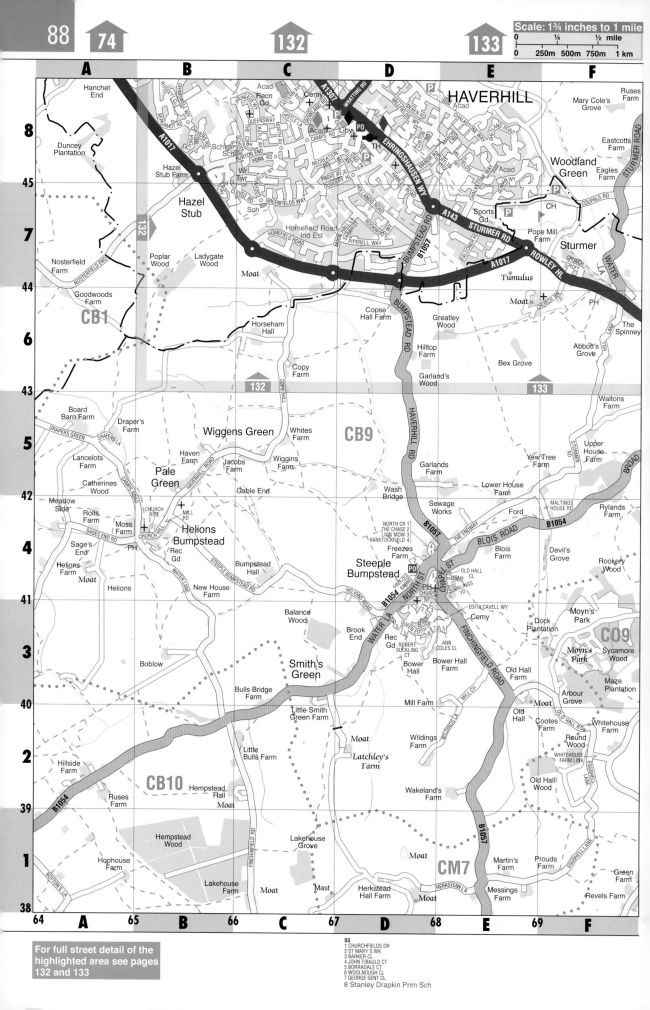

Scale: 1¾ inches to 1 mile

0   ¼   ½ mile
0   250m 500m 750m 1 km

HAVERHILL

Hanchet End

Duncey Plantation

Hazel Stub Farm

Hazel Stub

Woodland Green

Mary Cole's Grove

Ruses Farm

Eastcotts Farm

Eagles Farm

Sturmer

CB1

Nosterfield Farm

Goodwoods Farm

Poplar Wood

Ladygate Wood

Moat

Homefield Road Ind Est

Homefield Road

Piperell Way

Copse Hall Farm

Greatley Wood

Hilltop Farm

Garland's Wood

Moat

Bex Grove

Pope Mill Farm

Abbott's Grove

The Spinney

PH

Tumulus

Horseham Hall

Copy Farm

Wiggens Green

Whites Farm

CB9

Waltons Farm

Board Barn Farm

Draper's Farm

Drapers Green

Lancelots Farm

Catherines Wood

Haven Farm

Pale Green

Jacobs Farm

Wiggins Farm

Gable End

Wash Bridge

Garlands Farm

Lower House Farm

Yew Tree Farm

Upper House Farm

Rylands Farm

Meadow Side

Rolls Farm

Moss Farm

Church Rise

Helions Bumpstead

Sage's End

Helions Farm

Moat

Helions

Rec Gd

New House Farm

Bumpstead Hall

Sewage Works

Freezes Farm

Steeple Bumpstead

Ford

Blois Farm

Devil's Grove

Rookery Wood

D3
1 CHURCHFIELDS DR
2 ST MARY'S WK
3 BARKER CL
4 JOHN TIBAULD CT
5 BORRADALE CT
6 WOOLNOUGH CL
7 GEORGE GENT CL
8 Stanley Drapkin Prim Sch

Balance Wood

Brook End

Bower Hall

Smith's Green

Boblow

Bulls Bridge Farm

Little Smith Green Farm

Moat

Latchley's Farm

Wildings Farm

Bower Hall Farm

Mill Farm

Old Hall Farm

Old Hall

Moat

Cootes Farm

Arbour Grove

Moyn's Park

CO9

Sycamore Wood

Maze Plantation

Dock Plantation

Edith Cavell Wy

Cemy

Hillside Farm

Ruses Farm

CB10

Hempstead Hall

Moat

Little Bulls Farm

Wakeland's Farm

Old Hall Wood

Whitehouse Farm

Round Wood

Hophouse Farm

Hempstead Wood

Lakehouse Grove

Lakehouse Farm

Moat

Mast

Herkstead Hall Farm

CM7

Moat

Martin's Farm

Prouds Farm

Messings Farm

Revels Farm

Green Farm

For full street detail of the highlighted area see pages 132 and 133

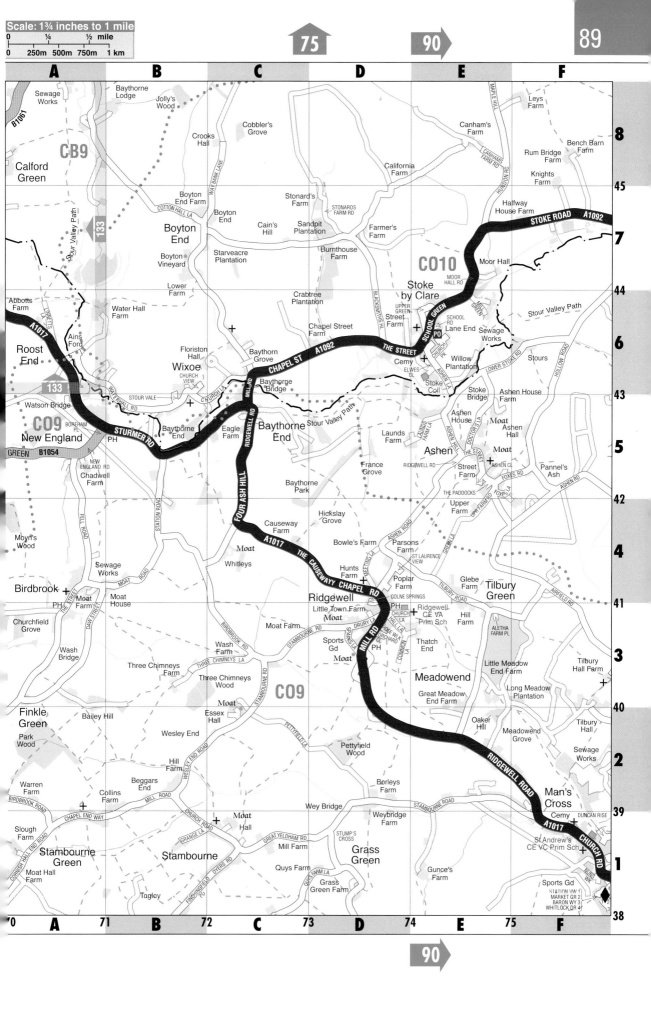

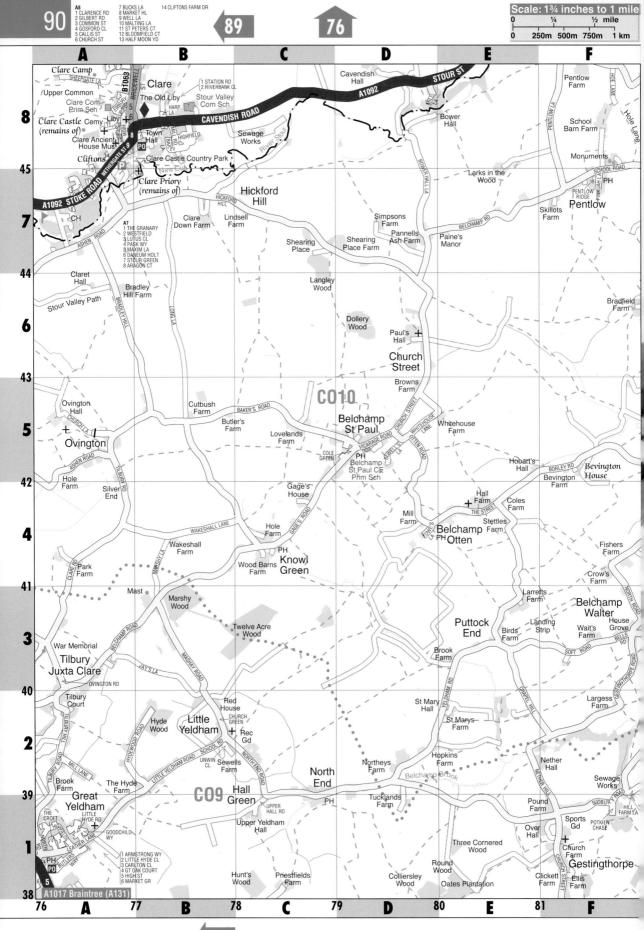

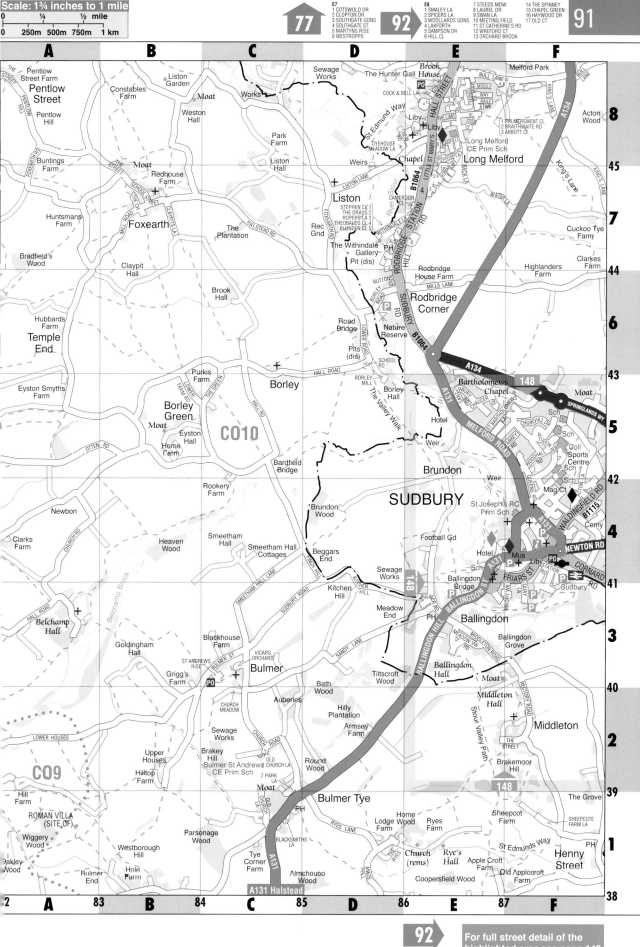

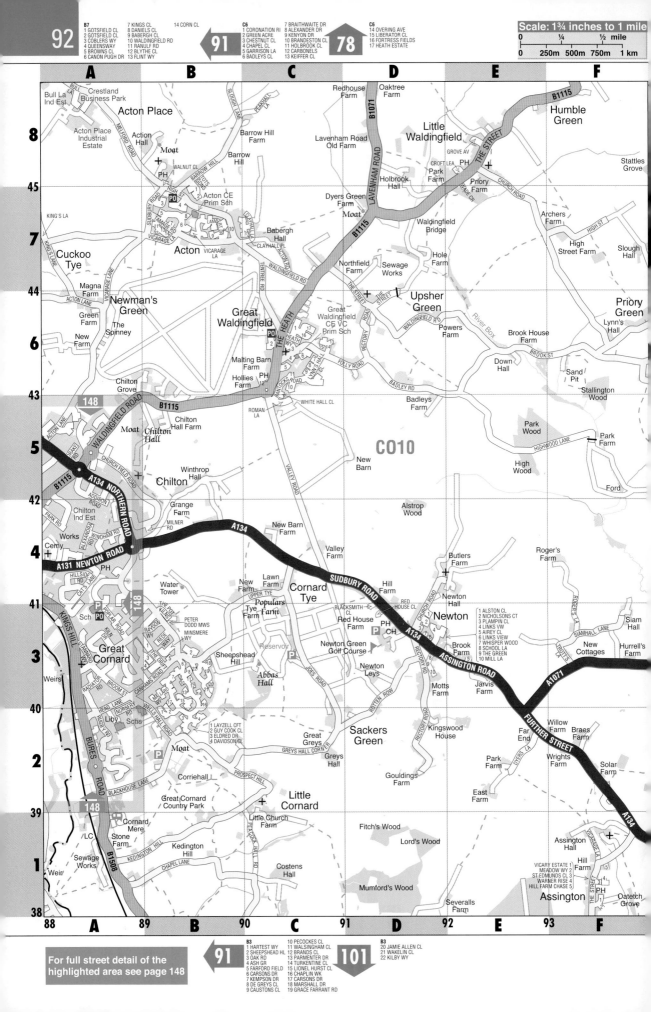

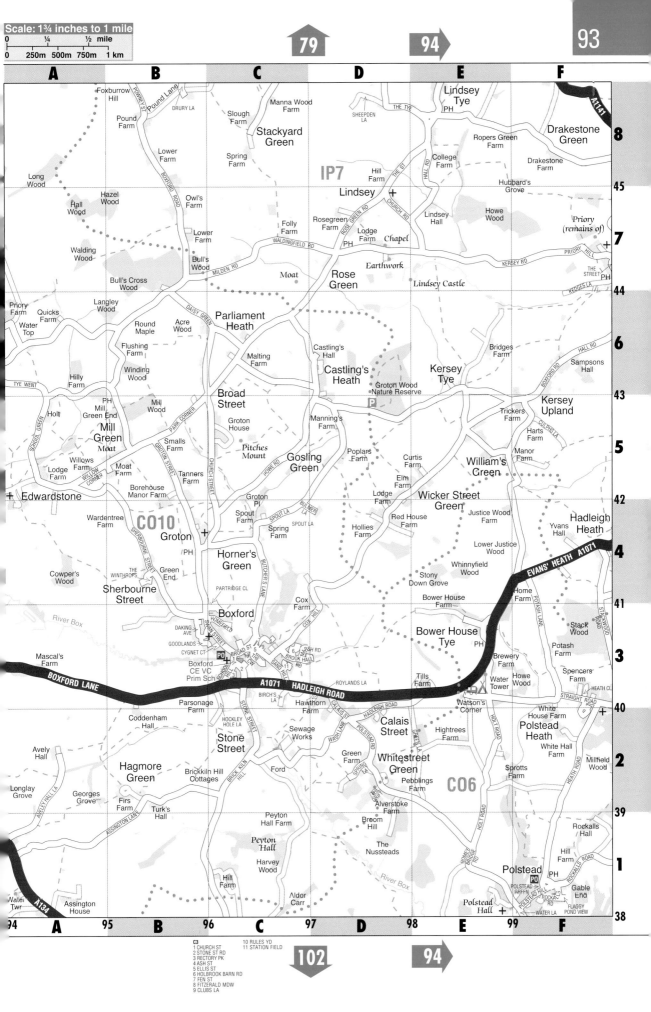

A   B   C   D   E   F

8

Foxburrow Hill
Pound Farm
Lower Farm
Long Wood
Hazel Wood
Hall Wood
Owl's Farm
Lower Farm
Walding Wood
Bull's Wood
Bull's Cross Wood

POWNEY ST
POUND LANE
DRURY LA
BOXFORD ROAD

Slough Farm
Manna Wood Farm
Stackyard Green
Spring Farm
Folly Farm

MILDEN RD
WALDINGFIELD RD

Rosegreen Farm
Lodge Farm
Moat

Sheepden La
THE TYE
THE ST
CHURCH RD
HILL RD
ROSE GREEN RD

Lindsey Tye
PH
Ropers Green Farm
College Farm
Lindsey
Lindsey Hall
Chapel
PH

Drakestone Green
Drakestone Farm
Hubbard's Grove
Howe Wood

A1141

Priory (remains of)
PRIORY HILL
KERSEY RD
THE STREET
PH
KEDGES LA

45

IP7

Lindsey

7

Earthwork
Rose Green
Lindsey Castle

44

Priory Farm
Quicks Farm
Water Top
Hilly Farm
Holt
Willows Farm
Lodge Farm
Moat Farm
Moat
Mill Green
Mill Green End
PH
Edwardstone
Wardentree Farm
Cowper's Wood
Borehouse Manor Farm
Smalls Farm
Tanners Farm

TYE WENT
SCHOOL GREEN
WILLOW CORNER
GROTON STREET
SHERBOURNE STREET
PARK CORNER
CHURCH STREET
DAISY GREEN

Langley Wood
Round Maple
Acre Wood
Flushing Farm
Winding Wood
Mill Wood

Parliament Heath
Malting Farm
Broad Street
Groton House
Pitches Mount
Gosling Green

Castling's Hall
Castling's Heath
Manning's Farm

Groton Wood Nature Reserve
P

Poplars Farm
Curtis Farm
Elm Farm
Lodge Farm

Kersey Tye
William's Green

Bridges Farm
Sampsons Hall

Kersey Upland
Trickers Farm
Harts Farm
Manor Farm

BOXFORD RD
HALL RD
CULPHO LA

6

43

5

42

CO10
Groton
PH

Horner's Green
Green End
THE WINTHROPS
Sherbourne Street
PARTRIDGE CL

Groton Pl
Spout Farm
Spring Farm
Spout La
SPOUT LA
BULMER LA

Hollies Farm
Red House Farm

Wicker Street Green
Justice Wood Farm
Lower Justice Wood
Whinnyfield Wood

Yvans Hall
Hadleigh Heath

EVANS' HEATH A1071

4

41

Cox Farm
COX HILL
BUTCHER'S LANE

Stony Down Grove
Bower House Farm
Bower House Tye
PH

Home Farm
POTASH LANE

Stack Wood
Potash Farm
Spencers Farm
HEATH CL
STRAIGHT RD

STACKWOOD ROAD

3

River Box
Mascal's Farm
BOXFORD LANE

Boxford
HOMEFIELD
SMALL STREET
DAKING AVE
GOODLANDS
CYGNET CT
PO
Boxford CE VC Prim Sch
BROAD ST
THE LOKE
SAND HILL
BROOK HALL
ASH RD

A1071 HADLEIGH ROAD
ROYLANDS LA

Tills Farm
Watson's Corner
Water Tower

Brewery Farm
Howe Wood

White House Farm
Polstead Heath

40

Parsonage Farm
Coddenham Hall
Birch's La
HOCKLEY HOLE LA
STONE STREET

Hawthorn Farm
Sewage Works
Stone Street
Ford

Green Farm
WASH LANE
POLSTEAD RD
CALAIS ST
HADLEIGH ROAD
SPRING LA
GREEN LA

Calais Street
Whitestreet Green
Hightrees Farm
Pebblings Farm

HOLT ROAD
HEATH ROAD

White Hall Farm
Sprotts Farm
Millfield Wood

2

Avely Hall
Longlay Grove
Georges Grove
Hagmore Green
Firs Farm
Turk's Hall

AVELY HILL LA
ASSINGTON LANE
BRICK KILN HILL

Brickkiln Hill Cottages
Peyton Hall Farm
Peyton Hall
Harvey Wood

Alverstoke Farm
Broom Hill
The Nussteads
River Box

CO6
POLSTEAD GREEN
HOMEY BRIDGE RD

Rockalls Hall
Hill Farm
Polstead
PO
PH
Gable End
FLAGGY POND VIEW
POLSTEAD HILL
ROCKA RD
WATER LA
ROCKALLS ROAD

39

Water Twr
A134
Assington House

Hill Farm
Peyton Hall
Aldor Carr

Polstead Hall
WATER LA

38

94   A   95   B   96   C   97   D   98   E   99   F

C3
1 CHURCH ST
2 STONE ST RD
3 RECTORY PK
4 ASH ST
5 ELLIS ST
6 HOLBROOK BARN RD
7 FEN ST
8 FITZGERALD MDW
9 CLUBS LA
10 RULES YD
11 STATION FIELD

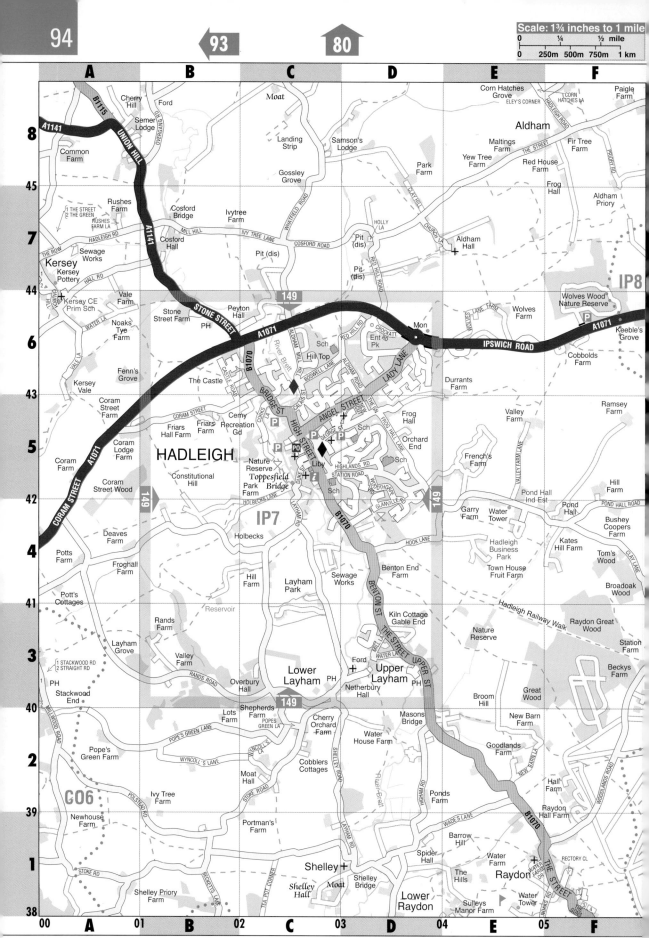

Scale: 1¾ inches to 1 mile

0   ¼   ½ mile
0 250m 500m 750m 1 km

8

45

7

44

6

5

43

42

4

41

3

40

2

1

39

38

A   B   C   D   E   F

Common Farm

Cherry Hill

Ford

Semer Lodge

A1141

B1115

UNION HILL

OVERGANG RD

Moat

Landing Strip

Samson's Lodge

Gossley Grove

Park Farm

Corn Hatches Grove

ELEY'S CORNER

Aldham

Maltings Farm

Yew Tree Farm

THE STREET

Red House Farm

HADLEIGH ROAD

CORN HATCHES LA

Paigle Farm

Fir Tree Farm

Frog Hall

PRIORY RD

1 THE STREET
2 THE GREEN
RUSHES FARM LA

Rushes Farm

Cosford Bridge

A1141

MILL HILL

Ivytree Farm

IVY TREE LANE

COSFORD ROAD

Cosford Hall

Pit (dis)

WHATFIELD ROAD

Pit (dis)

HOLLY LA

RED HILL ROAD

CLAY HILL

CHURCH LA

Aldham Hall

Aldham Priory

THE ROW

Kersey

Sewage Works

HADLEIGH RD

Kersey Pottery

HALL RD

Vale Farm

Noaks Tye Farm

Stone Street Farm

STONE STREET

Peyton Hall

PH

A1071

B1070

149

Hill Top

Sch

RED HILL RD

CROCKATT RD

Ent Pk

Mon

IPSWICH ROAD

A1071

SEVENTEEN LANE

VALLEY FARM LANE

Wolves Farm

Wolves Wood Nature Reserve

P

IP8

Keeble's Grove

Cobbolds Farm

WATER LA

CHURCH

Kersey CE Prim Sch

Kersey Vale

Fenn's Grove

VALE LA

River Brett

ALDHAM MILL HILL

BOSWELL LANE

ALDHAM ROAD

THE GREEN

FROG HALL LANE

LADY LANE

Frog Hall

Durrants Farm

Valley Farm

Ramsey Farm

Coram Street Farm

The Castle

CASTLE ROAD

COPKS LA

COQAM STREET

Cemy

Recreation Gd

CALAIS ST

ANGEL STREET

Sch

Orchard End

French's Farm

Hill Farm

Friars Hall Farm

Friars Farm

P

BRIDGE ST

HIGH STREET

P

GEORGE ST

P

Sch

Sch

HIGHLANDS RD

STATION ROAD

Pond Hall Ind Est

Pond Hall

POND HALL ROAD

Coram Lodge Farm

Coram Street Wood

HADLEIGH

PO

Liby

i

Toppesfield Bridge

Nature Reserve

Constitutional Hill

Park Farm

DUKE ST

WOODHOPE RD

GLANVILLE RD

Sch

WATER TOWER

Garry Farm

Water Tower

Hill Farm

Kates Hill Farm

Bushey Coopers Farm

Tom's Wood

Coram Farm

A1071

CORAM STREET

IP7

HOLBECKS LANE

LAYHAM RD

B1070

Holbecks

HOOK LANE

Benton End Farm

Hadleigh Business Park

Town House Fruit Farm

149

Broadoak Wood

Potts Farm

Deaves Farm

Froghall Farm

Pott's Cottages

Hill Farm

Layham Park

Reservoir

Sewage Works

BENTON ST

Hadleigh Railway Walk

Raydon Great Wood

Station Farm

Beckys Farm

Rands Farm

Valley Farm

RANDS ROAD

Layham Grove

UPPER ST

THE STREET

WATER LANE

Ford

Upper Layham

PH

Netherbury Hall

Nature Reserve

Broom Hill

Great Wood

New Barn Farm

Half Farm

1 STACKWOOD RD
2 STRAIGHT RD

PH

Stackwood End

MILLWOOD ROAD

Lower Layham

149

Masons Bridge

HIGH RD

Ponds Farm

Goodlands Farm

B1070

NEW BARN LA

Raydon Hall Farm

WOODLANDS ROAD

Pope's Green Farm

POLSTEAD RD

Ivy Tree Farm

POPE'S GREEN LANE

WYNCOLL'S LANE

Lots Farm

Shepherds Farm

POPES GREEN LA

WYNCOLL'S LA

Cherry Orchard Farm

Cobblers Cottages

SHELLEY ROAD

Water House Farm

LAYHAM RD

Water Farm

Spider Hall

Barrow Hill

The Hills

Water Farm

Raydon

RECTORY CL

WATER FARM DR

THE GDNS

THE STREET

Newhouse Farm

C06

Moat Hall

STOKE ROAD

Portman's Farm

River Brett

WADE'S LANE

Water Tower

Sulleys Manor Farm

BECKETT'S LANE

TEA. POT. CORNER

STOKE RD

Shelley

Shelley Priory Farm

Shelley Hall

Moat

Shelley Bridge

Lower Raydon

For full street detail of the highlighted area see page 149

F1
1 KING GEORGES CL
2 DUNNINGHAM DR
3 BELLS MEADOW
4 GREENGAGE CL

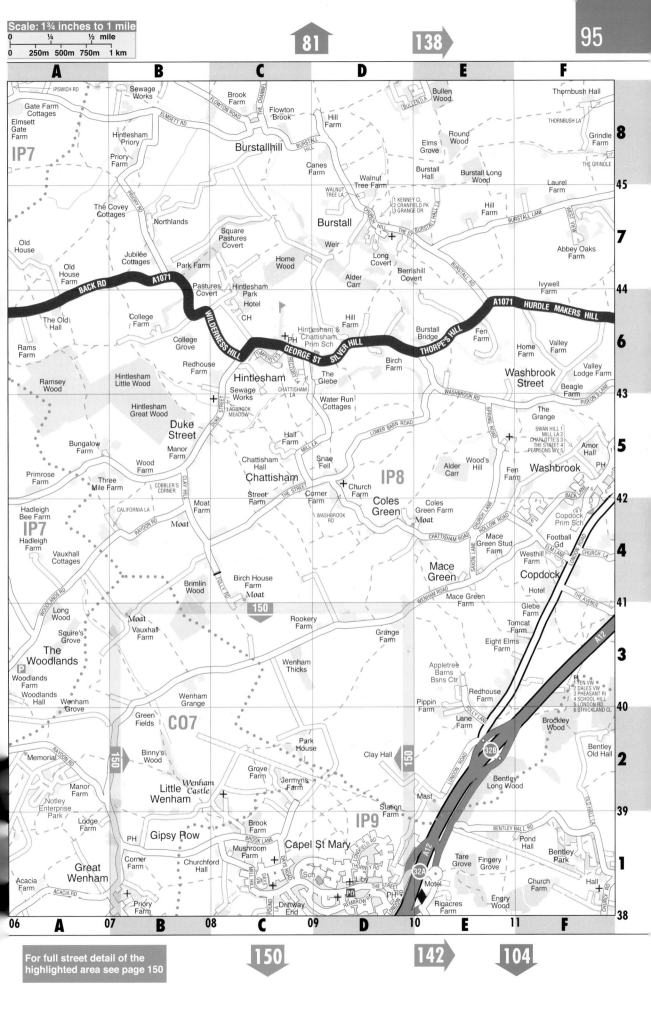

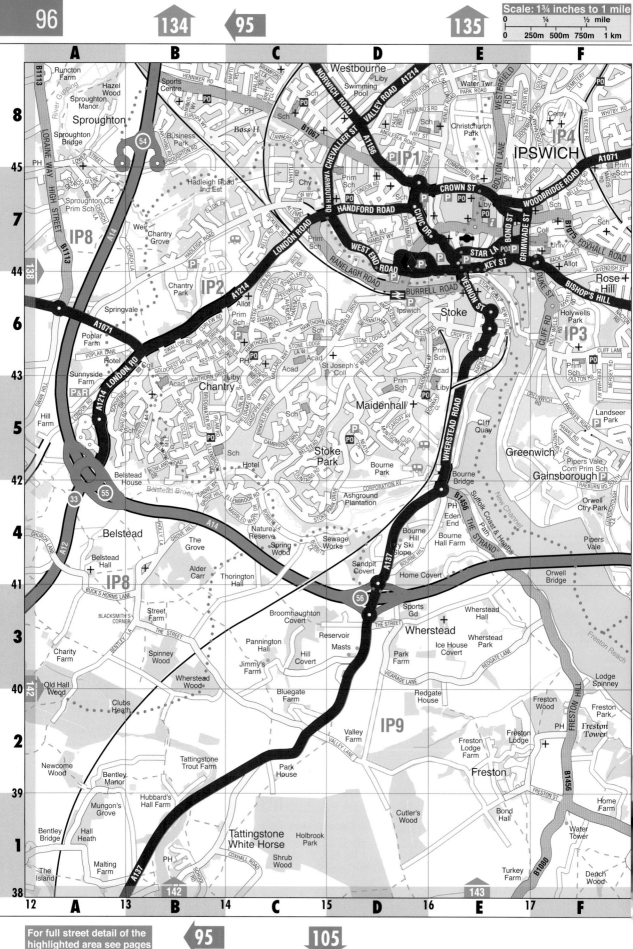

For full street detail of the highlighted area see pages 138, 139, 142 and 143

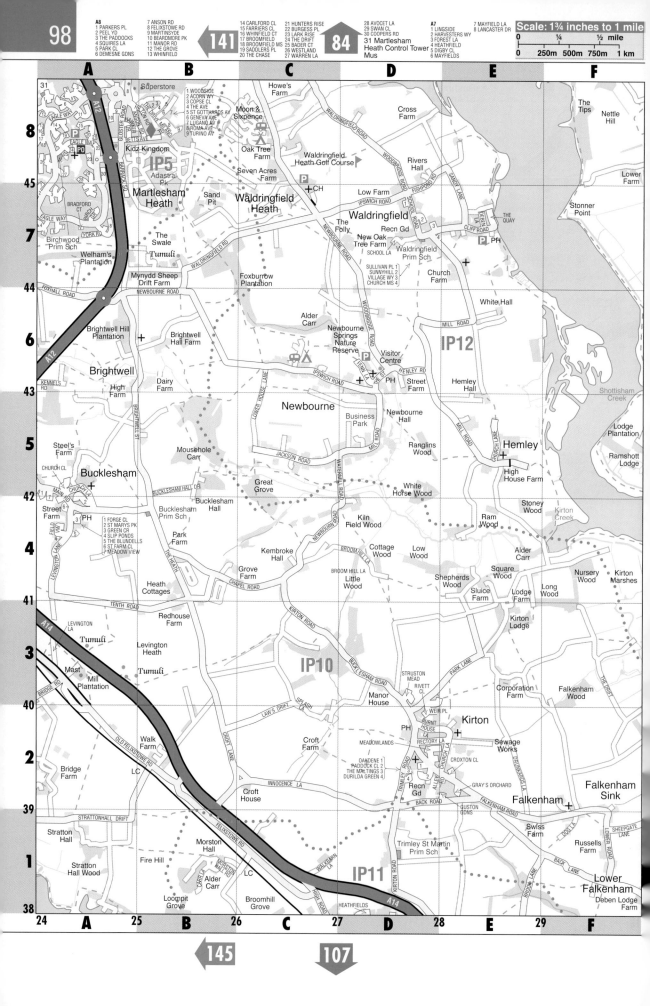

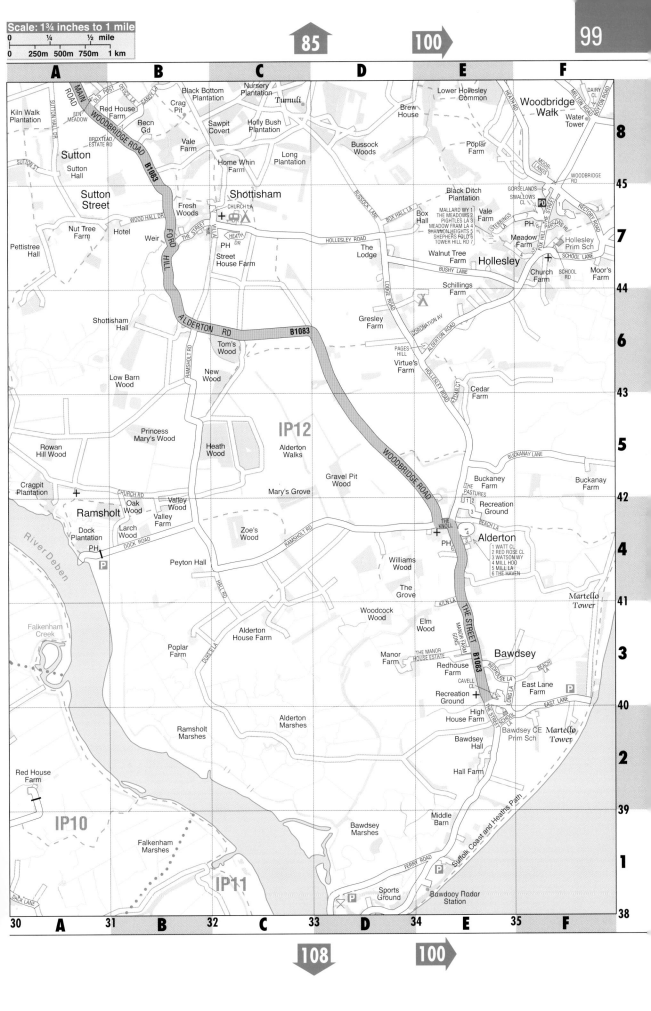

Scale: 1¾ inches to 1 mile

0   ¼   ½ mile

0   250m   500m   750m   1 km

A **B** **C** **D** **E** **F**

Oak Hill

ACORN RISE

HM Youth Custody Centre

WOODBRIDGE WALK

Sports Ground

ST DAVIDS LA

GROVER RD

Grove House

The Grove

The Suffolk Punch Trust

Hollesley Bay Colony

IP12

River Ore

COLONY RD

HM Young Offender Institution

45

Hollesley Bay

7

Orford Haven

Sewage Works

44

Oxley Dairy

SHINGLE ST

Oxley Marshes

North Weir Point

6

P

43

Shingle Street

Martello Tower

5

Suffolk Coast & Heaths Path

42

4

41

3

40

2

39

1

38

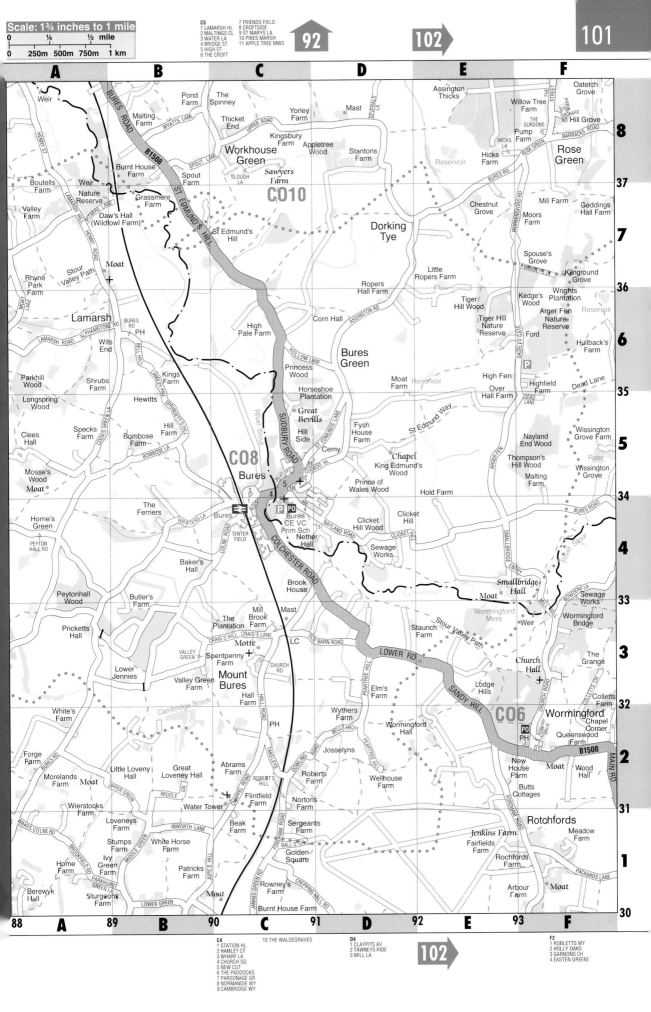

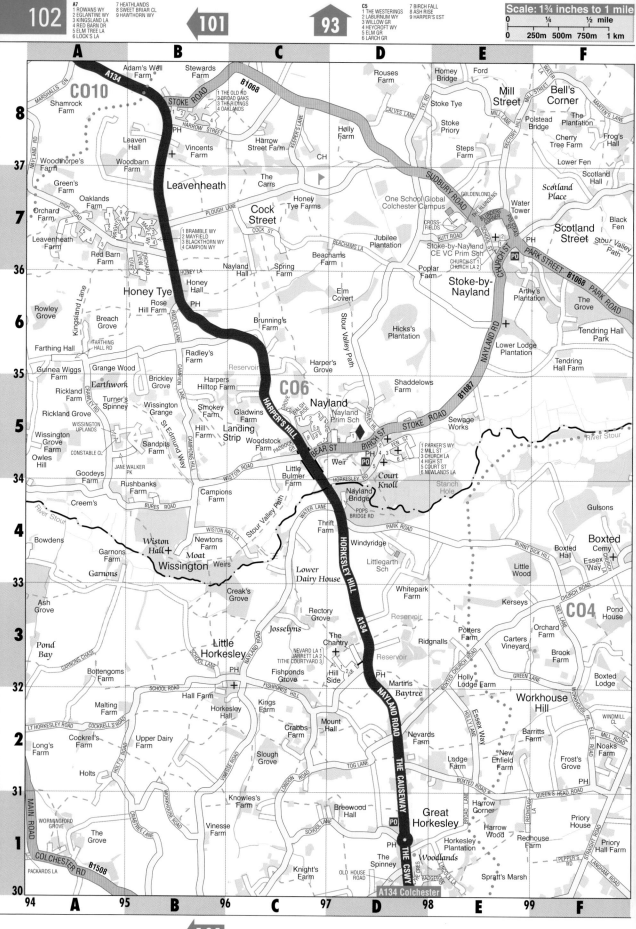

102
A7
1 ROWANS WY   7 HEATHLANDS
2 EGLANTINE WY   8 SWEET BRIAR CL
3 KINGSLAND LA   9 HAWTHORN WY
4 RED BARN DR
5 ELM TREE LA
6 LOCK'S LA

101

93

C5
1 THE WESTERINGS   7 BIRCH FALL
2 LABURNUM WY   8 ASH RISE
3 WILLOW GR   9 HARPER'S EST
4 HEYCROFT WY
5 ELM GR
6 LARCH GR

Scale: 1¾ inches to 1 mile
0   ¼   ½ mile
0   250m 500m 750m 1 km

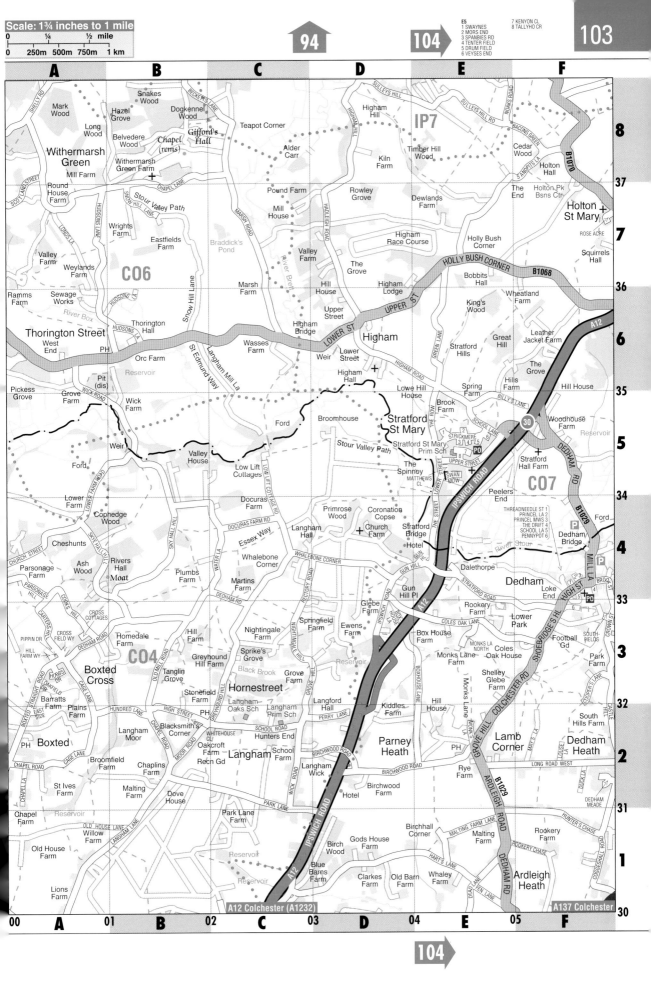

Scale: 1¾ inches to 1 mile

0   ¼   ½   mile
0   250m   500m   750m   1 km

94

104

E5
1 SWAYNES
2 MORS END
3 SPANBIES RD
4 TENTER FIELD
5 DRUM FIELD
6 VEYSES END

7 KENYON CL
8 TALLYHO CR

103

A   B   C   D   E   F

Mark Wood
Shelly Rd
Long Wood
Withermarsh Green
Mill Farm
Round House Farm
SCOT LAND STREET
Valley Farm
Weylands Farm
Ramms Farm
Sewage Works
River Box

Snakes Wood
Hazel Grove
Belvedere Wood
Chapel (rems)
Withermarsh Green Farm
CHAPEL LANE
HUDSONS LANE
SNOW HILL LANE
Wrights Farm
Eastfields Farm
C06
Thorington Hall
HUDSONS LA
HUDSONS LA

Dogkennel Wood
Gifford's Hall
BECKER'S LANE
Teapot Corner
Alder Carr
Pound Farm
Mill House
Stour Valley Path
Braddick's Pond
MARSH LANE
River Bret
Valley Farm
Marsh Farm
Hill House
Higham Bridge
LOWER ST

Higham Hill
HIGHAM HILL
Kiln Farm
Rowley Grove
Dewlands Farm
Higham Race Course
The Grove
Higham Lodge
Upper Street
UPPER ST
Higham
Lower Street
Weir

SULLEYS HILL
IP7
Timber Hill Wood
SULLEYS HILL RD
NOAKS ROAD
BACONS GREEN
SANDPITS LA
Holton Hall
Cedar Wood
The End
Holton Pk Bsns Ctr
Holton St Mary
Rose Acre
HOLLY BUSH CORNER
Holly Bush Corner
Bobbits Hall
B1068
Wheatland Farm
King's Wood
Stratford Hills
Great Hill
Leather Jacket Farm
B1070
A12
Squirrels Hall
The Grove

37

7

36

6

35

Thorington Street
West End
PH
Orc Farm
Reservoir
ST EDMUND WAY
Pit (dis)
LANGHAM MILL LA
Wasses Farm
Higham Hall
Lowe Hill House
HIGHAM ROAD
GREEN LANE
Spring Farm
THE ROW
Brook Farm
Hills Farm
Hill House
BILLY'S LANE
Woodhouse Farm
Reservoir

Pickess Grove
Grove Farm
WICK ROAD
Wick Farm
Weir
Ford
Valley House
Low Lift Cottages
LOW LIFT COTTAGE RD
Ford
Broomhouse
Stour Valley Path
Stratford St Mary
Stratford St Mary Prim Sch
STRICKMERE
SCHOOL LANE
UPPER STREET
PO
30
Stratford Hall Farm
DEDHAM RD
C07
Reservoir

Lower Farm
LOWER FARM ROAD
Cophedge Wood
Cheshunts
SKYE HALL HILL
Parsonage Farm
Ash Wood
PARSONAGE HILL
CHURCH STREET
Rivers Hall
Moat
DOCURAS FARM RD
Docuras Farm
Essex Way
WATER LA
Langham Hall
Primrose Wood
Coronation Copse
Church Farm
Stratford Bridge
Hotel
The Spinney
MATTHEWS CL
SWAN MDW
LOWER STREET
GUN ST
Dalethorpe
Peelers End
THREADNEEDLE ST 1
PRINCEL LA 2
PRINCEL MWS 3
THE DRIFT 4
SCHOOL LA 5
PENNYPOT 6
River Stour
Dedham Bridge
B1029
Ford
P
MILL LA
P
Dedham
Loke End
HIGH ST
P
PO
BROOK ST

35

5

34

4

33

COOKS HILL
CARTERS HILL
PIPPIN DR
HILL FARM WY
CROSS FIELD WY
Homedale Farm
DEDHAM ROAD
C04
Boxted Cross
CROSS COTTAGES
Hill Farm
Greyhound Hill Farm
Tanglin Grove
Plumbs Farm
Martins Farm
DEDHAM RD
Nightingale Farm
Sprike's Grove
NIGHTINGALE HILL
Black Brook
WHALEBONE CORNER
Whalebone Corner
RECTORY ROAD
Springfield Farm
Glebe Farm
Ewens Farm
Gun Hill Pl
GUN HILL
A12
STRATFORD ROAD
Rookery Farm
Box House Farm
COLES OAK LANE
Lower Park
MONKS LA NORTH
Coles Oak House
Monks Lane Farm
Shelley Glebe Farm
MONKS LANE
SHOEBRIDGE'S HL
COLCHESTER RD
Football Gd
COOPER'S LANE
Park Farm
SOUTH-FIELDS
GROVE HILL

3

32

OAKFIELD DR
HOBBS DR
BOXTED STRAIGHT ROAD
EAST SIDE
Barratts Farm
Plains Farm
PH
Boxted
CAGE LANE
Broomfield Farm
St Ives Farm
CHAPELLA
CHAPEL ROAD
Chapel Farm
Reservoir
Old House Farm
Lions Farm
OLD HOUSE LANE
Willow Farm
Old House Lane
HUNDRED LANE
Blacksmith's Corner
OLD MILL ROAD
GREYHOUND ROAD
Langham Moor
Chaplins Farm
MOOR LANE
Dove House
WHITEHOUSE CL
Oakcroft Farm
Recn Gd
Langham Oaks Sch
HIGH STREET
PH
Stonefield Farm
Grove Farm
Langham Prim Sch
SCHOOL LANE
Hunters End
Langham
School Farm
PERRY LANE
Langford Hall
Langham Wick
WICK ROAD
Malting Farm
Park Lane Farm
PARK LANE
Reservoir
BIRCHWOOD ROAD
IPSWICH ROAD
Birch Wood
Blue Barns Farm
Gods House Farm
Clarkes Farm
Parney Heath
Kiddles Farm
PH
Rye Farm
Birchwood Farm
Hotel
BIRCHWOOD ROAD
Old Barn Farm
Whaley Farm
HART'S LANE
FEN LANE
DEAD LANE
Hill House
Birchhall Corner
MALTING FARM LANE
Malting Farm
ARDLEIGH ROAD
DEDHAM RD
B1029
Rookery Farm
HUNTER'S CHASE
Rookery Chase
ROOKERY CHASE
COGGESHALL ROAD
Ardleigh Heath
Lamb Corner
LONG ROAD WEST
South Hills Farm
Dedham Heath
Dedham Meade
DUCK LA
CASTLE CL
COURSE
CROWN ST
CASTLE

2

31

1

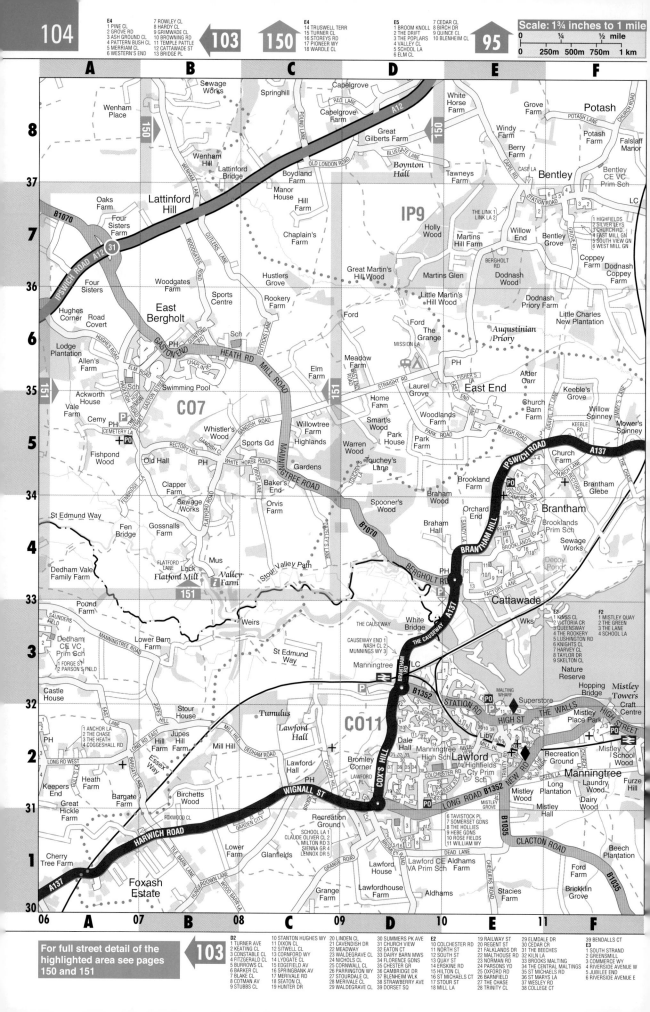

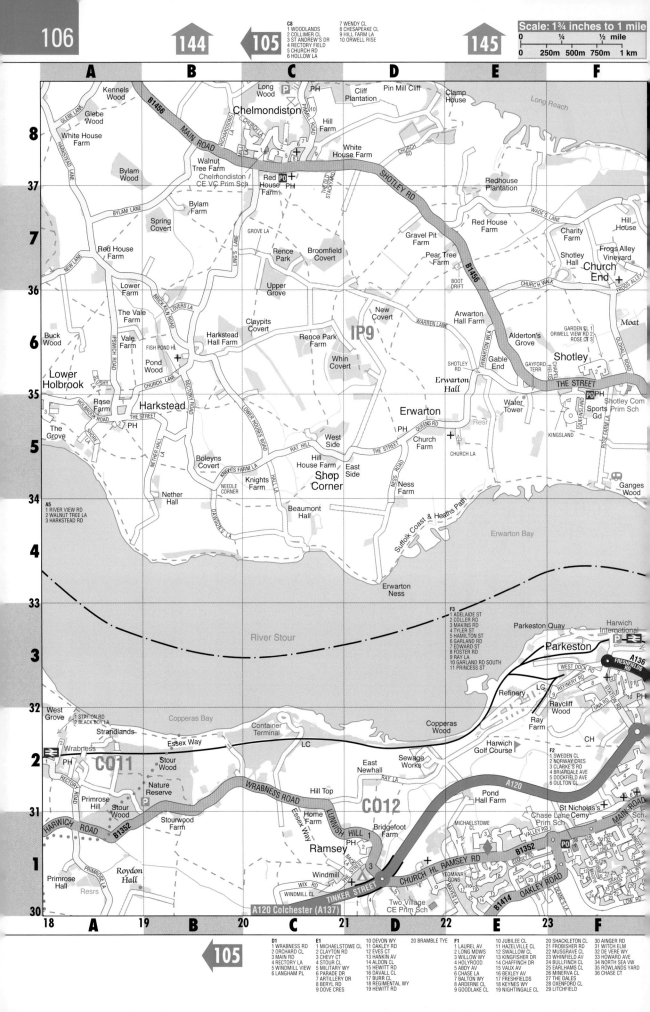

144
105
145

Scale: 1¾ inches to 1 mile
0   ¼   ½ mile
0   250m   500m   750m   1 km

C8
1 WOODLANDS
2 COLLIMER CL
3 ST ANDREW'S DR
4 RECTORY FIELD
5 CHURCH RD
6 HOLLOW LA
7 WENDY CL
8 CHESAPEAKE CL
9 HILL FARM LA
10 ORWELL RISE

A5
1 RIVER VIEW RD
2 WALNUT TREE LA
3 HARKSTEAD RD

F3
1 ADELAIDE ST
2 COLLER RD
3 MAKINS RD
4 TYLER ST
5 HAMILTON ST
6 GARLAND RD
7 EDWARD ST
8 FOSTER RD
9 RAY LA
10 GARLAND RD SOUTH
11 PRINCESS ST

F2
1 SWEDEN CL
2 NORWAY CRES
3 CLARKE'S RD
4 BRIARDALE AVE
5 DOCKFIELD AVE
6 OULTON CL

GARDEN CL 1
ORWELL VIEW RD 2
ROSE CT 3

D1
1 WRABNESS RD
2 ORCHARD CL
3 MAIN RD
4 RECTORY LA
5 WINDMILL VIEW
6 LANGHAM PL

E1
1 MICHAELSTOWE CL
2 CLAYTON RD
3 CHEVY CT
4 STOUR CL
5 MILITARY WY
6 PARADE DR
7 ARTILLERY DR
8 BERYL RD
9 DOVE CRES

10 DEVON WY
11 OAKLEY RD
12 EVES CT
13 HANKIN AV
14 ALDON CL
15 HEWITT RD
16 DAVALL CL
17 BURR CL
18 REGIMENTAL WY
19 HEWITT RD

20 BRAMBLE TYE

F1
1 LAUREL AV
2 LONG MDWS
3 WILLOW WY
4 HOLYROOD
5 ABDY AV
6 CHASE LA
7 BALTON WY
8 ARDERNE CL
9 GOODLAKE CL

10 JUBILEE CL
11 HAZELVILLE CL
12 SWALLOW CL
13 KINGFISHER DR
14 CHAFFINCH DR
15 VAUX AV
16 BEXLEY AV
17 FRESHFIELDS
18 KEYNES WY
19 NIGHTINGALE CL

20 SHACKLETON CL
21 FROBISHER RD
22 MUSGRAVE CL
23 WHINFIELD AV
24 BULLFINCH CL
25 EARLHAMS CL
26 MINERVA CL
27 THE DALES
28 OXENFORD CL
29 LITCHFIELD

30 AINGER RD
31 WITCH ELM
32 DE VERE WY
33 HOWARD AVE
34 NORTH SEA VW
35 ROWLANDS YARD
36 CHASE CT

Scale: 1¾ inches to 1 mile

0 ¼ ½ mile
0 250m 500m 750m 1 km

98 108

For full street detail of the highlighted area see page 152

107

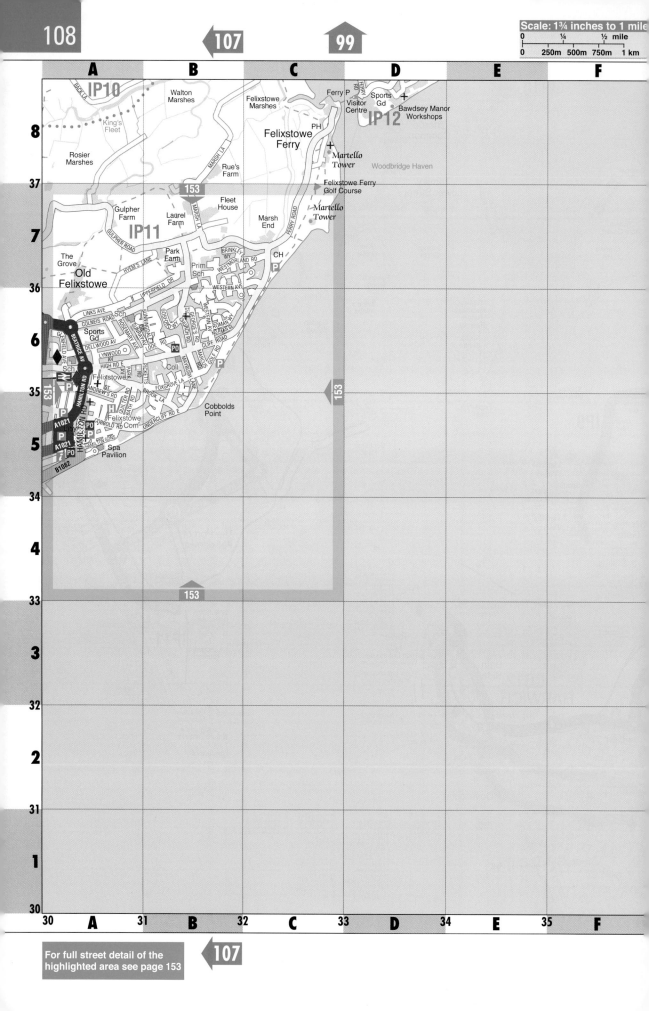

A   B   C   D   E   F

IP10

Walton
Marshes

Felixstowe
Marshes

Ferry P
Visitor
Centre

Sports
Gd

Bawdsey Manor
Workshops

IP12

King's
Fleet

8

BACK LA

Rosier
Marshes

Rue's
Farm

Felixstowe
Ferry

PH

Martello
Tower

Woodbridge Haven

37

MARSH LA

153

Fleet
House

Felixstowe Ferry
Golf Course

Gulpher
Farm

Laurel
Farm

Marsh
End

FERRY ROAD

Martello
Tower

IP11

7

GULPHER ROAD

HYEM'S LANE

The
Grove

Park
Farm

BRINKLEY WY

Prim
Sch

WESTMORLAND RD

CH

P

Old
Felixstowe

UPPERFIELD DR

WESTERN AVE

36

LINKS AVE

COLNEIS ROAD

Sch

ST GEORGE'S RD

ROMAN WY

Sports
Gd

DELLWOOD AV

ROSEMARY AVE

SUNNINGDALE AV

GOSFORD

NORMAN R

6

GENFIELD AVE

BEATRICE AV

LYNWOOD
AV

HIGH RD E

LODE RD

ST CHURCH RD

CLIFF RD

ROMAN WY

GOLF RD

PO

Sch

HAMILTON RD

Felixstowe

PARK RD

PICKETTS RD

MAYBUSH LANE

P

ST
ANDREW'S RD

QUILTER RD

Coll

35

153

153

P
A1021

QUILTER RD E

BROOK LA

FOXGROVE LA

Cobbolds
Point

COBBOLD RD

Felixstowe
Com

UNDERCLIFF RD E

P
PO
A1021

HAMILTON RD

HAMILTON GDNS

Spa
Pavilion

5

B1082

34

4

153

33

3

32

2

31

1

30

30   A   31   B   32   C   33   D   34   E   35   F

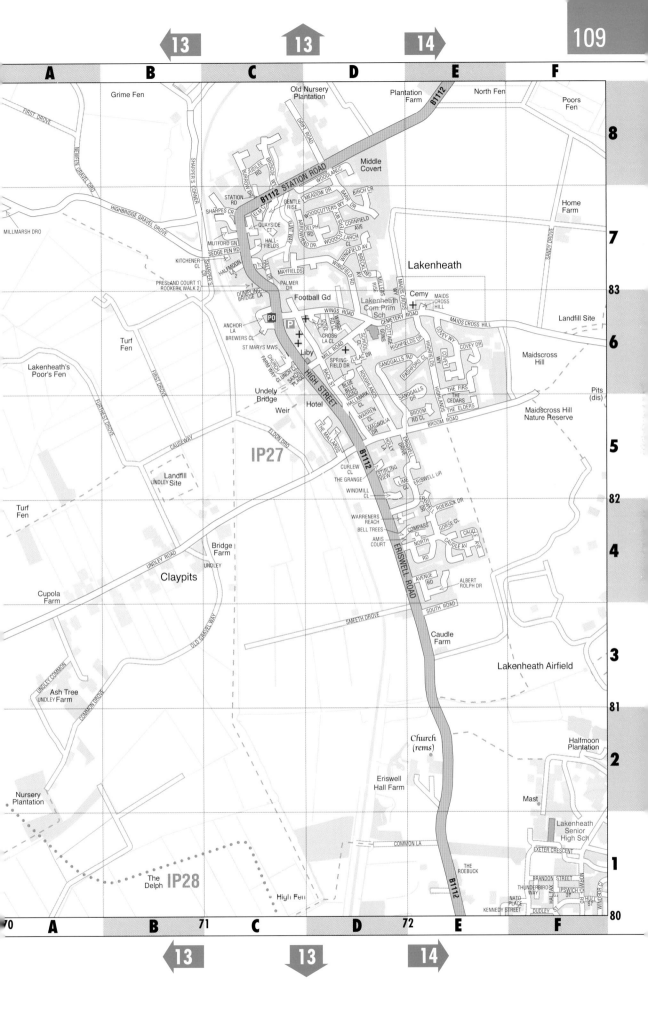

A B C D E F

Grime Fen

Old Nursery
Plantation

Plantation
Farm

North Fen

Poors
Fen

8

FIRST DROVE

NEWFEN GRAVEL DRO

HIGHBRIDGE GRAVEL DROVE

SHAPPER'S CORNER

DRIFT ROAD

B1112

Middle
Covert

B1112

Home
Farm

MILLMARSH DRO

Lakenheath

SANDY DROVE

7

STATION ROAD

B1112

STATION RD

SHARPES CR

WOODLANDS

BRISCOE WY

JUBILEE RD

ELM CL

GENTLE RISE

MEADOW DR

BARR DR

BIRCH CR

WOODCUTTERS WY

CORNFIELD AVE

QUAYSIDE CT

HALL-FIELDS

FLINT WAY

ARROWHEAD DR

DELPH

WOOD CL

AIR STATION RD

LARCH

WINGFIELD AV

MUTFORD GN

SEDGE FEN RD

BRECKLAND AV

KITCHENER CL

SHARPES CR

HALFMOON 2

MAYFIELDS

WINGFIELD RD

MILLERS RISE

83

PRESLAND COURT 1
ROOKERY WALK 2

DUMPLINGBRIDGE LA

PALMER DR

Football Gd

Cemy

MAIDS CROSS HILL

Landfill Site

Turf
Fen

ANCHOR LA

BREWERS CL

P

PO

Lakenheath
Com Prim
Sch

CEMETERY ROAD

MAIDS CROSS WY

MAIDS CROSS HILL

6

Lakenheath's
Poor's Fen

FIRST DROVE

ST MARYS MWS

Liby

CROSS LA CL

COTTAGE GDNS

SCHOOL RD

HIGHFIELDS RD

COVEY WY

COVEY

COVEY DR

Maidscross
Hill

SPRINGFIELD DR

LILAC DR

SANDGALLS RD

PASHFORD CL

HIGHFIELDS

Undely
Bridge

TURFHIST DROVE

CHURCH LA

SAXON PLACE

FARM WAY CL

LUNCH CT

BLUEBELL GDNS

ROUGHLANDS

SANDGALLS DR

THE FIRS

Pits
(dis)

Weir

Hotel

HIGH STREET

BACK ST

HALLMARK CL

WARREN CL

BROOM RD CL

THE CEDARS

THE ELDERS

Maidscross Hill
Nature Reserve

5

Undley
Site

THE BALLARDS

ELDON DRO

CAUSEWAY

IP27

MAGNOLIA DR

BROOM ROAD

HOLLY LA

ERISWELL DRIVE

B1112

CURLEW CL

THE GRANGE

STIRLING VIEW

ERISWELL DR

LIME CL

82

Turf
Fen

WINDMILL CL

ROEBUCK DR

ERISWELL

GORSE CL

CAUDLE AV

AVE

4

Bridge
Farm

UNDLEY

WARRENERS REACH

BELL TREES CL

AMIS COURT

COMPASS

NORTH RD

CAUDLE CL

ALBERT ROLPH DR

UNDLEY ROAD

Claypits

ERISWELL ROAD

AVENUE RD

SOUTH ROAD

Cupola
Farm

SMEETH DROVE

Caudle
Farm

Lakenheath Airfield

3

OLD GRAVEL WAY

Ash Tree

UNDLEY FARM

UNDLEY COMMON

COMMON DROVE

81

Halfmoon
Plantation

2

Church
(rems)

Eriswell
Hall Farm

Mast

Nursery
Plantation

Lakenheath
Senior High Sch

EXETER CRESCENT

The Delph

IP28

COMMON LA

THE ROEBUCK

B1112

BRANDON STREET

THUNDERBIRD WAY

HALFA

IPSWICH ST

NORWICH RD

WINDSOR

1

High Fen

NATO PLACE

KENNEDY STREET

DUDLEY

HULL ST

80

70 A B 71 C D 72 E F 80

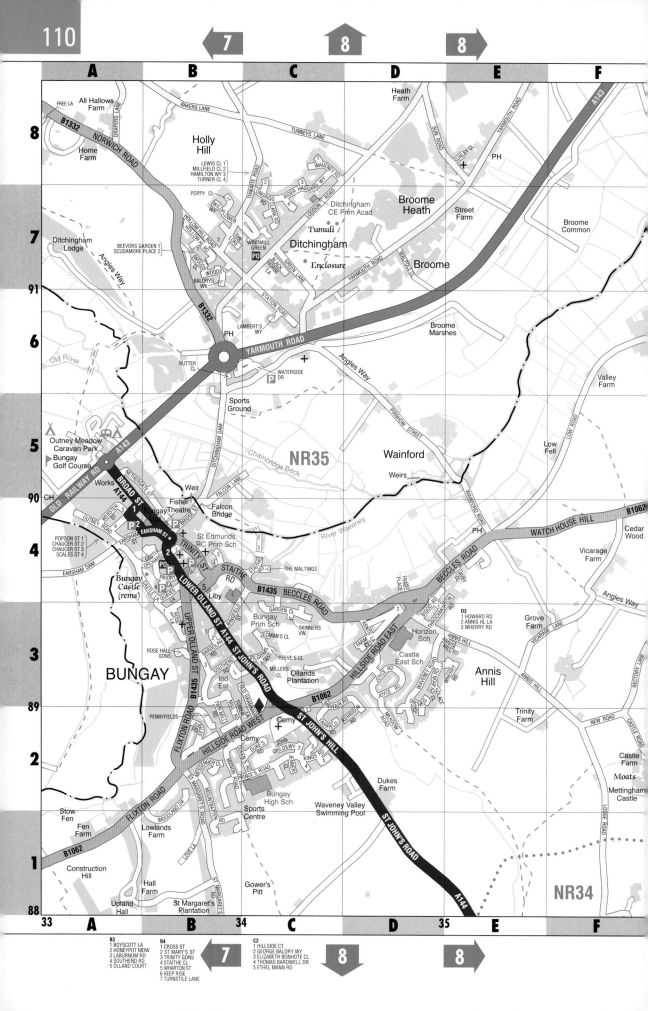

B3
1 BOYSCOTT LA
2 HONEYPOT MDW
3 LABURNUM RD
4 SOUTHEND RD
5 OLLAND COURT

B4
1 CROSS ST
2 ST MARY'S ST
3 TRINITY GDNS
4 STAITHE CL
5 WHARTON ST
6 KEEP RISE
7 TURNSTILE LANE

C2
1 HILLSIDE CT
2 GEORGE BALDRY WY
3 ELIZABETH BONHOTE CL
4 THOMAS BARDWELL DR
5 ETHEL MANN RD

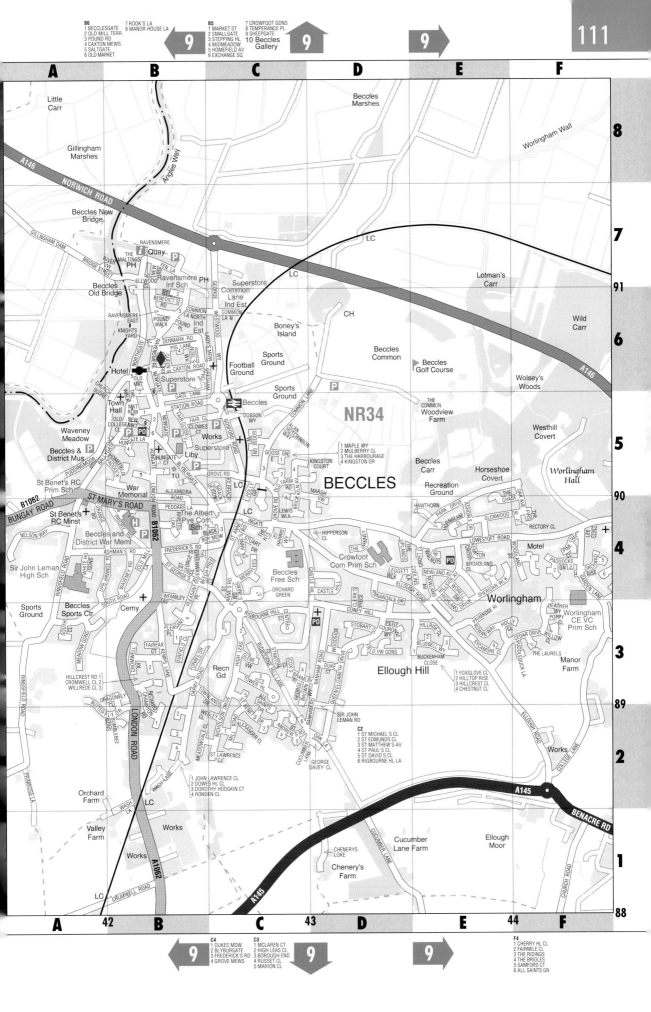

B6
1 BECCLESGATE
2 OLD MILL TERR
3 POUND RD
4 CAXTON MEWS
5 SALTGATE
6 OLD MARKET

7 ROOK'S LA
8 MANOR HOUSE LA

B5
1 MARKET ST
2 SMALLGATE
3 STEPPING HL
4 MIDMEADOW
5 HOMEFIELD AV
6 EXCHANGE SQ

7 CROWFOOT GDNS
8 TEMPERANCE PL
9 SHEEPGATE
10 Beccles
   Gallery

Little
Carr

Beccles
Marshes

Worlingham Wall

8

A146

NORWICH ROAD

Gillingham
Marshes

Beccles New
Bridge

LC

7

GILLINGHAM DAM

BRIDGE STREET

RAVENSMERE
The
MALTINGS
Quay
PH

FEN LA

Superstore
Common
Lane
Ind Est

COMMON
LA NORTH

LC

Lotman's
Carr

91

Beccles
Old Bridge

RIVER VW

ELLWOOD CL

Ravensmere
Inf Sch
PH

ST
BENEDICT'S
RD

COMMON
LA NORTH

COMMON
LA

CH

Wild
Carr

6

RAVENSMERE
EAST

POUND
WALK

GEORGE

KNIGHTS
YARD

POUND
PL

DENMARK RD

LADY'S MDW WY

WESTWOOD WY

Boney's
Island

Beccles
Common

THE
COMMON

Beccles
Golf Course

A146

PIG LANE

GRESHAM

Sports
Ground

Woodview
Farm

Wolsey's
Woods

Hotel

OLD
MKT

CHURCH
CLOSE

NORTHGATE

RAVENSMERE

NEWGATE

CAXTON RD

Superstore

Football
Ground

Sports
Ground

COMMON LANE

Westhill
Covert

5

Town
Hall

MKT
ROW

STATION ROAD

Beccles

DOBSON
WY

NR34

Worlingham
Hall

Waveney
Meadow

OLD NEW
COLLEGE MKT
CL

NEWGATE

FAIR CL

CLOWES
CT

ALAN HUTCHINSON WAY

Beccles &
District Mus

PUDDINGMOOR

HUNGATE LA

BALLYGATE

HOMEFIELD
PADDOCK

PO

GOSFORD ROAD

Works

GOOSE
GN
E

Kingston
Court

1 MAPLE WY
2 MULBERRY CL
3 THE HARBOURAGE
4 KINGSTON DR

Beccles
Carr

Horseshoe
Covert

Worlingham
Hall

St Benet's RC
Prim Sch

Superstore

Liby

B1062

BALLYGATE

GROVE RD

GOOSE GN

BECCLES

Beccles
Golf Course

Recreation
Ground

THE
CHASE

OAK AVE

THE
FIRS

90

B1062
BUNGAY ROAD

War
Memorial

LONDON ROAD

ST MARY'S ROAD

Alexandra
Road

PEDDARS LA

RIVETTS

KILBRACK

LC

BRICK KILN LA

MARSH
VW

Hawthorn

PARK DRIVE

ASHDALE DR

GLENWOOD DR

RECTORY CL

St Benet's
RC Minst

GRANGE
CL

BECCLES FREE

FREDERICK'S RD

The Albert
Pye Com
Sch

INGATE

HIPPERSON
CL

THE
SPINNEY

HORNBEAM
CL

LOWESTOFT ROAD

MOTEL

Motel

4

NELSON WAY

WHITE HO
GDNS

ASHMAN'S RD

BLACK
BOY MDW

ST ANNE'S RD

ST STUART
DR

Crowfoot
Com Prim Sch

THE
UPLANDS

NEWLAND AVE

GARSTON
CRES

PADDOCKS
GN 3

PINE TREE RISE

GARDEN CL

Sir John Leman
High Sch

RINGSFIELD GDNS

UPR GRANGE RD

WAVENEY RD

OLD MILL

BEECH DR

ST GEORGE'S RD

MERRY
LEES

ORCHARD
GREEN

CASTLE HILL

LEGGETT
WLK

COLLINS RD

BROADLAND

WOODLAND

HILLSWORELL

SHERIDAN WAY

ORCHARD CT

SAMFORD CT

Sports
Ground

Beccles
Sports Ctr

Cemy

SOUTH
CL

WEMBLEY
AV

PLEASANT
PL

ST ANNE'S RD

Beccles
Free Sch

CASTLE
HILL

CLERK'S
PIECE

Worlingham

HEATHER
WY

Worlingham
CE VC
Prim Sch

THE LAURELS

Manor
Farm

3

RINGSFIELD ROAD

MEADOW GDNS

HILLCREST RD 1
CROMWELL CL 2
WILLREDE CL 3

CROMWELL
AV

FAIRFAX
CT

KEMPS LANE

FIRFIELD CL

Recn
Gd

RIGBOURNE HILL

HIGH LEAS

RIGBOURNE HILL LANE

STANTON
CL

COX'S

CENTRE CL

WOODSIDE

Ellough Hill

STOBART
CL

PETIT
COURONE
WY

HILLRISE CL

FIELD VW GDNS

BLUEBELL WY

BUCKENHAM
CLOSE

PRIMROSE RI

ROWAN WAY

HOLLY

SYCAMORE CL

WILLOW

CEDAR DRIVE

MIDDLEDUCK LA

1 FOXGLOVE CL
2 HILLTOP RISE
3 HILLCREST CL
4 CHESTNUT CL

DRAGONFLY

BUTTERFLY DR

BUMBLEBEE

CRAMPTON RD

RICHARD
RD

TOWNLANDS RD

NICHOLSON DRIVE

MILL RD

ST PETER'S DR

ALL
SAINTS

DARBY RD

GLEBE
VW

TOWER HL

BRAMLEY RD

GEORGE
BROWN RD

DUKE
RD

QUEEN ELIZABETH DRIVE

HILLRISE CL

89

ELLOUGH ROAD

Works

2

Orchard
Farm

WESLEY RD

MEADOWVALE CL

ALEXANDER CL

ST ANDREW'S RD

ST LAWRENCE

1 JOHN LAWRENCE CL
2 DOWES HL CL
3 DOROTHY HODGKIN CT
4 RONDEN CL

WASH-LANE

WASH LA

CUCUMBER
LANE

GEORGE
DAVEY CL

C2
1 ST MICHAEL'S CL
2 ST EDMUNDS CL
3 ST MATTHEW'S AV
4 ST PAUL'S CL
5 ST DAVID'S CL
6 RIGBOURNE HL LA

Sir John
Leman RD

COLLEGE LANE

A145

BENACRE RD

A1062

CRUMWELL ROAD

LC

Valley
Farm

Works

Works

A145

CHENERYS
LOKE

Chenery's
Farm

Cucumber
Lane Farm

CUCUMBER LANE

Cucumber
Lane Farm

Ellough
Moor

CHURCH ROAD

1

88

C4
1 DUKES MDW
2 BLYBURGATE
3 FREDERICK'S RD
4 GROVE MEWS

C3
1 MCLAREN CT
2 HIGH LEAS CL
3 BOROUGH END
4 RUSSET CL
5 MARION CL

F4
1 CHERRY HL CL
2 FAIRMILE CL
3 THE RIDINGS
4 THE BRIDLES
5 SAMFORD CT
6 ALL SAINTS GN

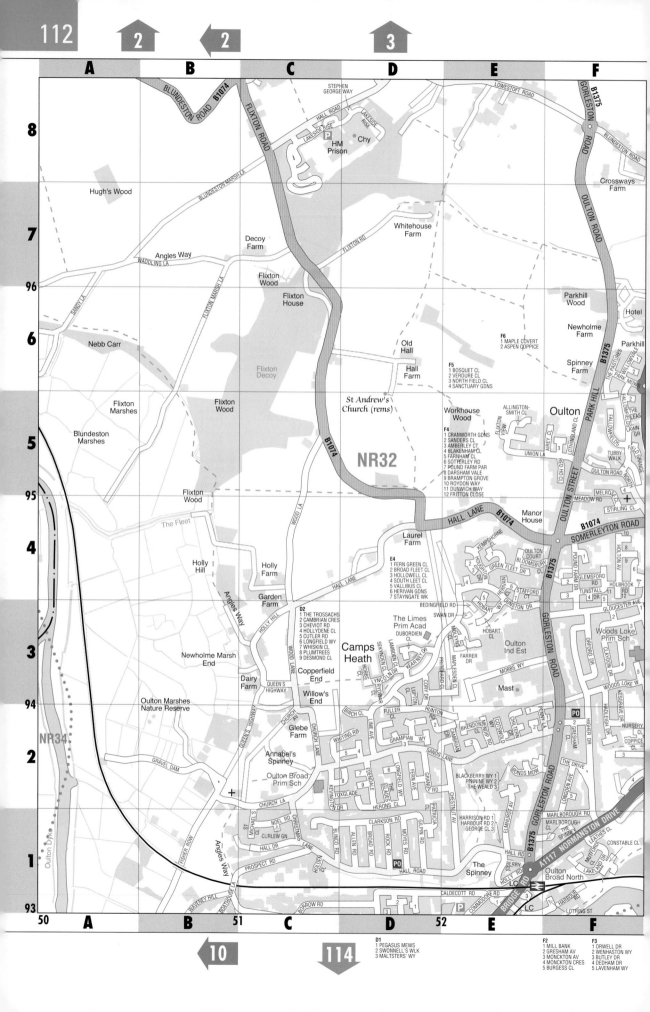

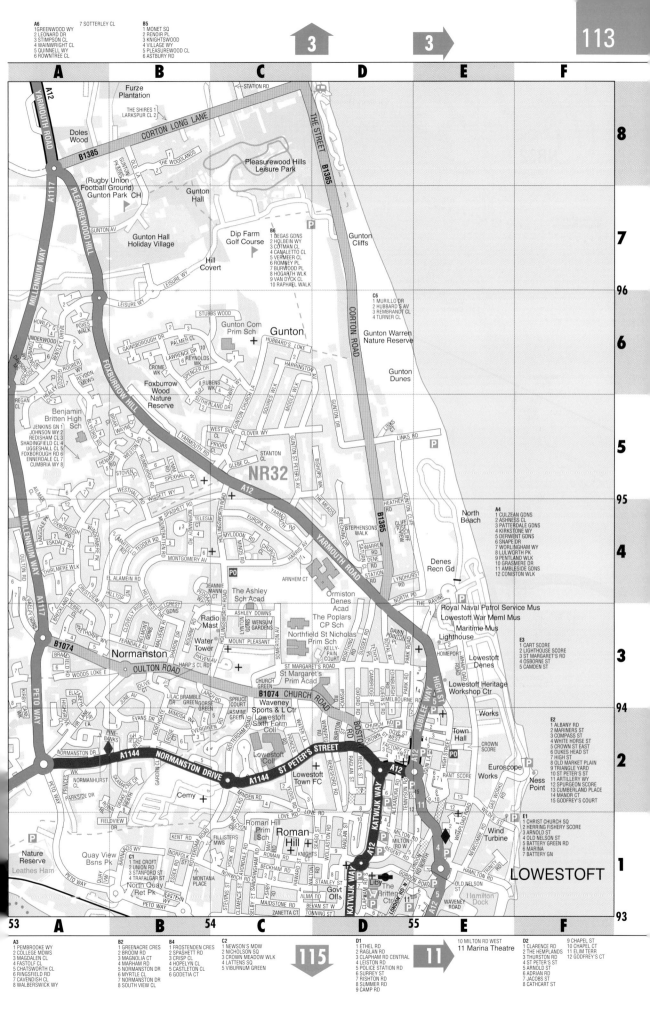

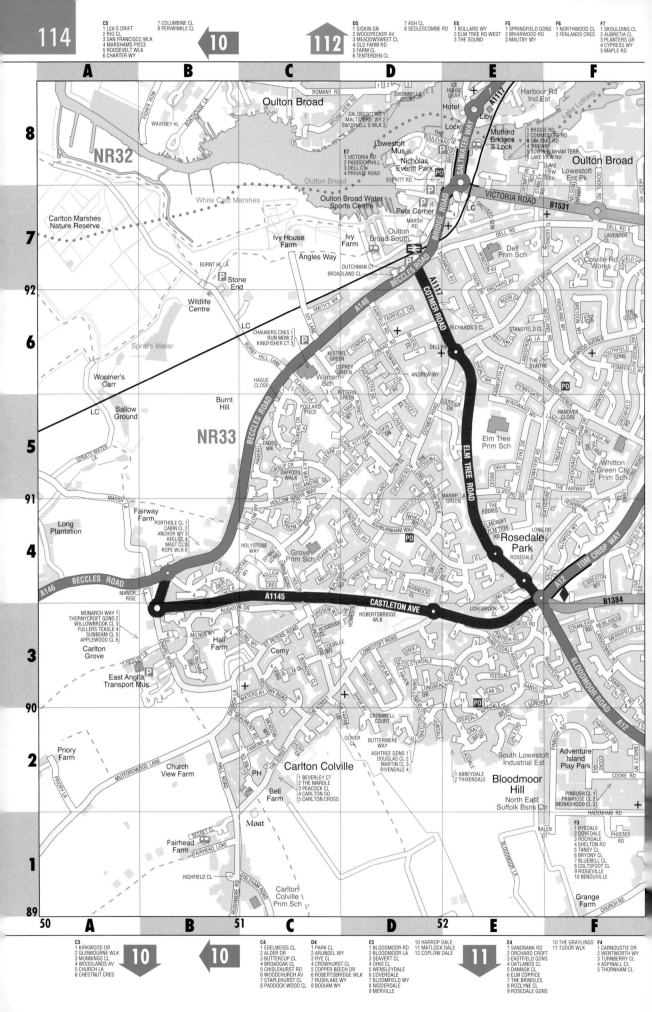

C7
1 ST LEONARD'S RD
2 LAWSON CT
3 UNION PL
4 ORCHARD TERR

D8
1 FLENSBURGH ST
2 KATWIJK WY
3 BEVAN ST E
4 SURREY ST
5 GROVE RD
6 BEACH MS

7 BON MARCHE
8 LONDON RD N
9 DENMARK RD
10 WAVENEY RD
11 STATION SQ
12 FYFFE WY
13 PARADE RD N

14 HERRING MARKET

113

11

115

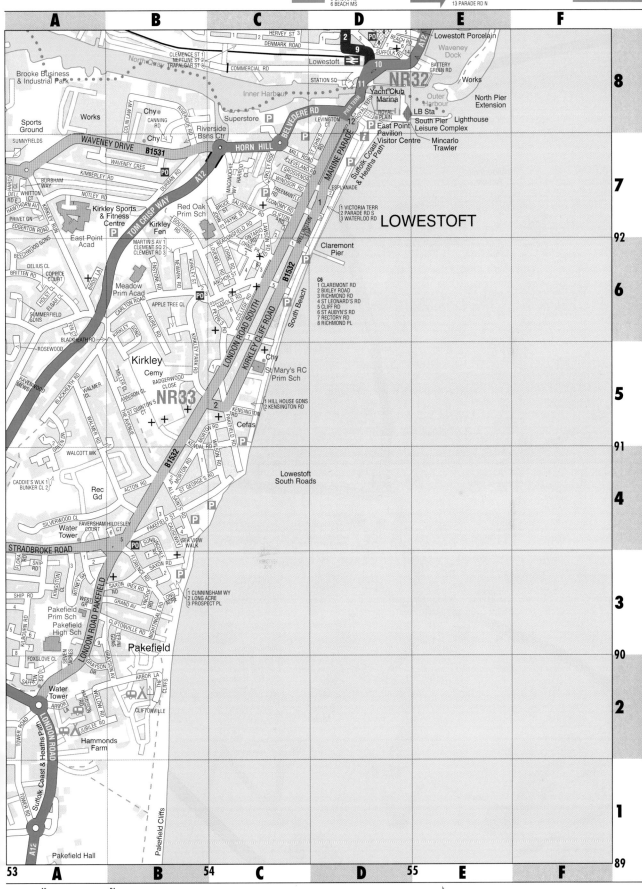

A3
1 NELSON RD
2 WELLINGTON RD
3 WITNEY RD
4 CRANFIELD CL
5 MARSDEN CL
6 KILBOURN RD
7 SPEEDWELL CL
8 HONEYSUCKLE CL

B4
1 ROCHESTER RD
2 SHORT ST
3 DOLPHIN CL
4 KIRKDALE CT
5 ASHURST PL
6 STRADBROKE RD

11

11

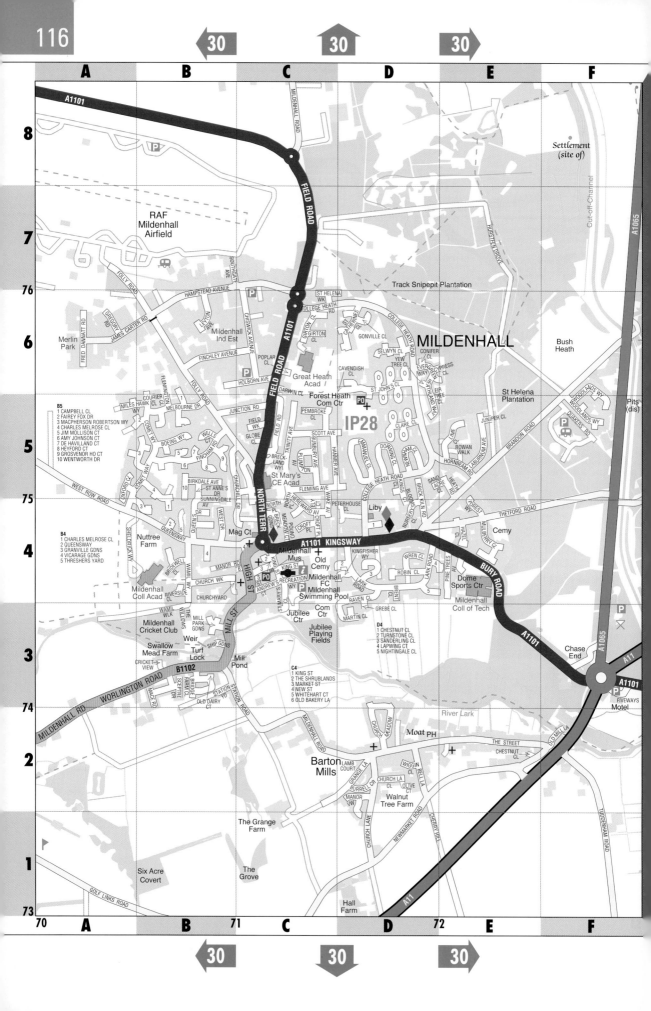

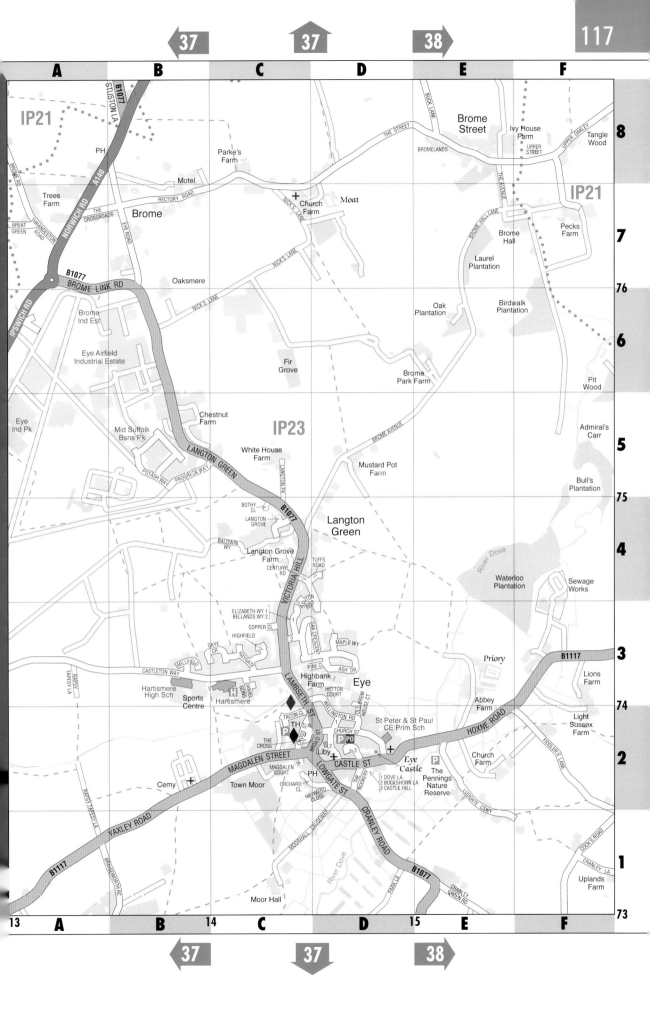

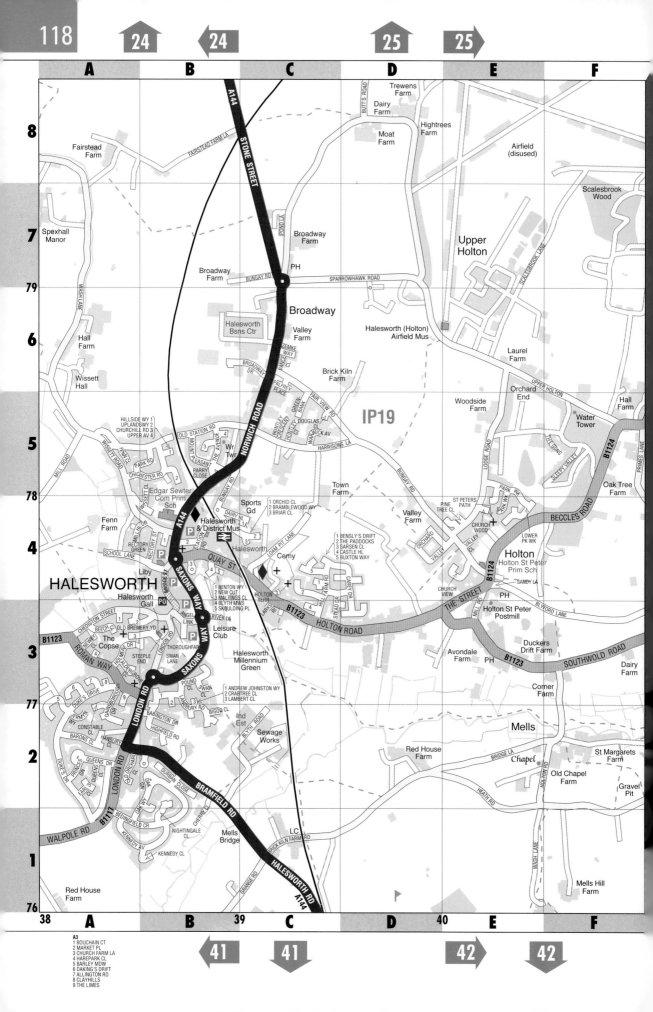

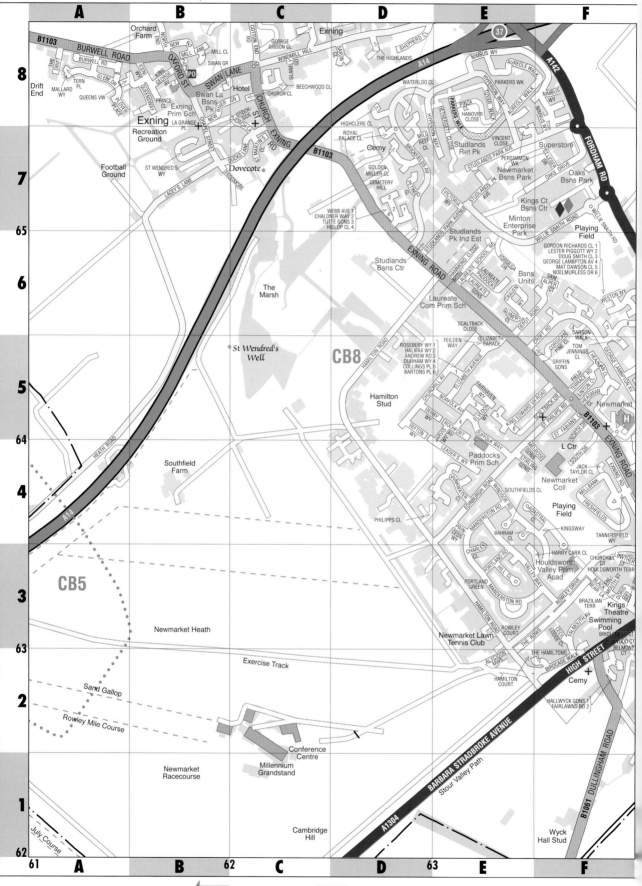

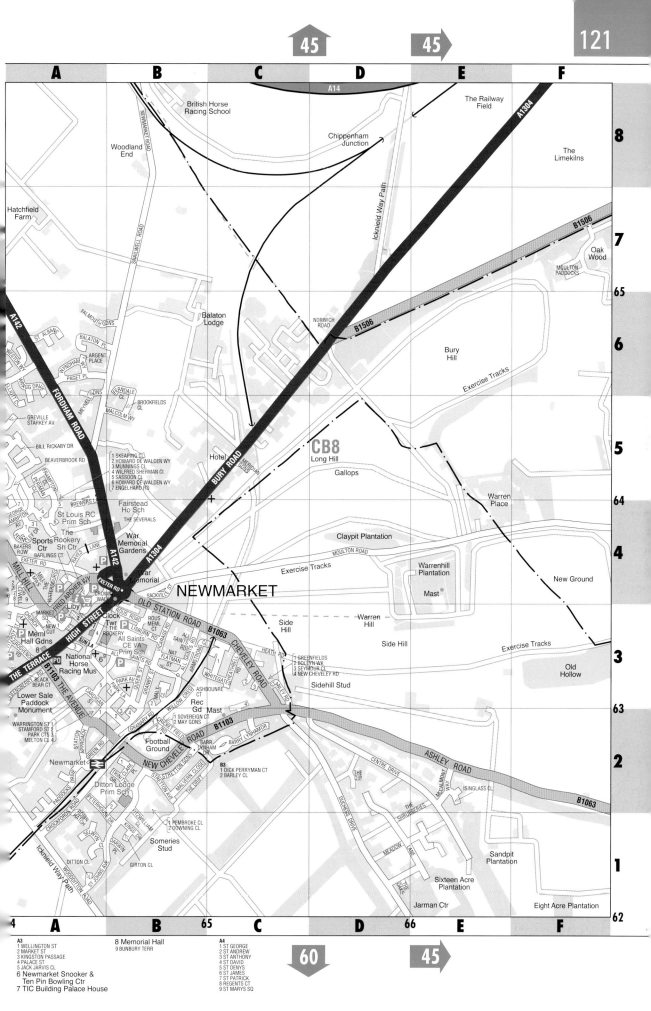

A B C D E F

8

7

65

6

5

64

4

3

63

2

1

62

A14

The Railway Field

A1304

Chippenham Junction

British Horse Racing School

Woodland End

Icknield Way Path

The Limekilns

B1506

Oak Wood

MOULTON PADDOCKS

Hatchfield Farm

NEWMARKET ROAD

SMALLWELL ROAD

Balaton Lodge

NORWICH ROAD

B1506

Bury Hill

Exercise Tracks

A1142

FALMOUTH GDNS

ST ALBANS
WESTON WY
WYAGG DRIVE
ELLIOT CL

GREVILLE
STARKEY AV

BILL RICKABY DR

BEAVERBROOK RD

FORDHAM ROAD

BALATON PL

ARGENT PLACE
PAGET PL

WYNDHAM RD

FERNDALE CL

BROOKFIELDS CL

MALCOLM WY

MELWOOD GDNS

CB8
Long Hill

Hotel

BURY ROAD

MERIDIAN GDNS

1 SKEAPING CL
2 HOWARD DE WALDEN WY
3 MUNNINGS CL
4 WILFRED SHERMAN CI
5 SASSOON CL
6 HOWARD DE WALDEN WY
7 ENGELHARD RD

Gallops

Warren Place

64

Claypit Plantation

St Louis RC Prim Sch

Fairstead Ho Sch

THE SEVERALS

The Rookery Sh Ctr

Sports Ctr

BARLINGS CT
BREWERS CT

GEORGE LAMBTON AV
KEENE CT

BAKERS ROW

EXETER RD

A1142

War Memorial Gardens

A1304

MOULTON ROAD

Exercise Tracks

Warrenhill Plantation

Mast

New Ground

MILL HILL

THE WATERHOUSE

FRED ARCHER WY

War Memorial

EXETER RD

CROWN WALK

NEWMARKET

Side Hill

Warren Hill

Side Hill

Exercise Tracks

Old Hollow

CHURCH LANE
GROSVENOR
MEML HALL GDNS

MARKET SQ

NEW CUT

Clock Twr

Liby

OLD STATION ROAD

ROUS ROAD
ROUS MEML CT

SACKVILLE ST

THE ROOKERY

LISBURN RD

B1063

VICARAGE RD

NAT FLATMAN
ALL SAINTS RDNS

ALL SAINTS RD

All Saints CE VA Prim Sch

HEATH RD

Sidehill Stud

1 GREENFIELDS
2 BOLEYN WK
3 SEYMOUR CL
4 NEW CHEVELEY RD

CHEVELEY ROAD

LANLEY RD

WHITEGATES

HEATHBEL

ASHBOURNE CT

National Horse Racing Mus

THE TERRACE

B1103 THE AVENUE

QUEENSBERRY RD
BLACK BEAR CT

Lower Sale Paddock Monument

WARRINGTON ST 1
STAMFORD ST 2
PARK CTS 3
MELTON CL 4

STATION APPROACH

GREEN RD

PARK AV
QUEEN ST
GRANBY ST
MALT
WILLOW CRES

CARDIGAN ST

PARK LA

Rec Gd

Mast

1 SOVEREIGN CT
2 MAY GDNS

B1103

ASHLEY ROAD

B1063

Newmarket

PADDOCKS DRIVE

CROCKFORDS ROAD

DITTON CL

PETERHOUSE DR

PETERHOUSE DR

TRINITY CLOSE
STRETTON GDNS
STRETTON AVE

Football Ground

NEW CHEVELEY ROAD

MALVERN CLOSE

THE DRIFT

CRICKET RD

GRANARY RD

BARR LYNHAM DR

Barry Lynham Dr

B3
1 DICK PERRYMAN CT
2 BARLEY CL

CENTRE DRIVE

McCALMONT WAY

ISINGLASS CL

THE SHRUBBERIES

DUCHESS DRIVE

THE DIP

Ditton Lodge Prim Sch

ETHERILLAM DR
KINGS DR
DARWIN AV
ST JOHNS AVE

WOODDITTON ROAD

GIRTON CL

Someries Stud

1 PEMBROKE CL
2 DOWNING CL

MEADOW LANE

Sixteen Acre Plantation

Jarman Ctr

Sandpit Plantation

Eight Acre Plantation

Icknield Way Path

A B 65 C D 66 E F

A3
1 WELLINGTON ST
2 MARKET ST
3 KINGSTON PASSAGE
4 PALACE ST
5 JACK JARVIS CL

6 Newmarket Snooker &
  Ten Pin Bowling Ctr
7 TIC Building Palace House

8 Memorial Hall
9 BUNBURY TERR

A4
1 ST GEORGE
2 ST ANDREW
3 ST ANTHONY
4 ST DAVID
5 ST DENYS
6 ST JAMES
7 ST PATRICK
8 REGENTS CT
9 ST MARYS SQ

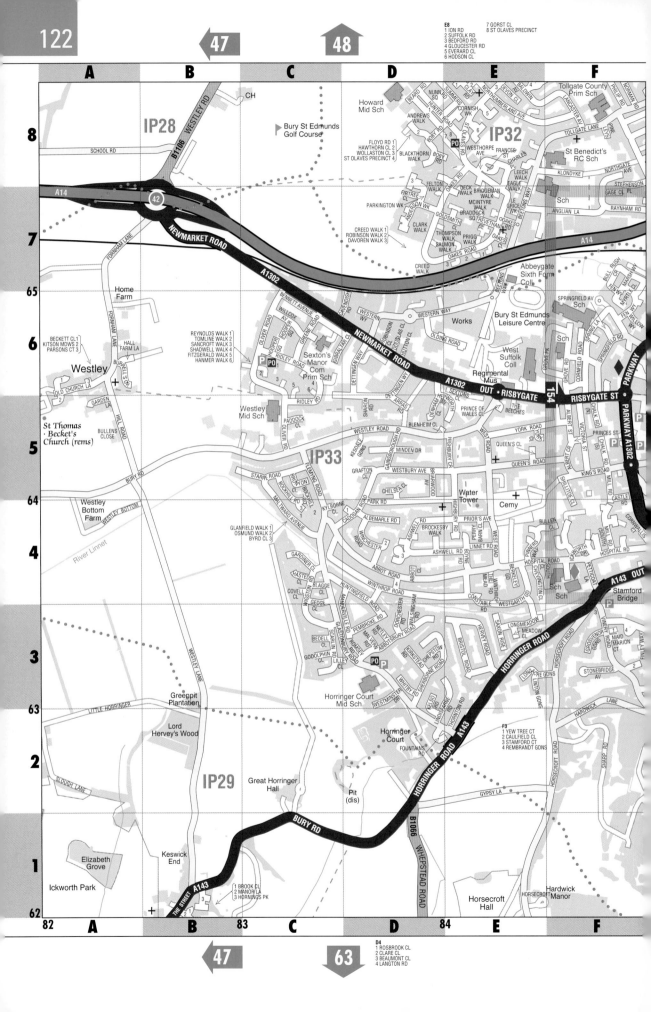

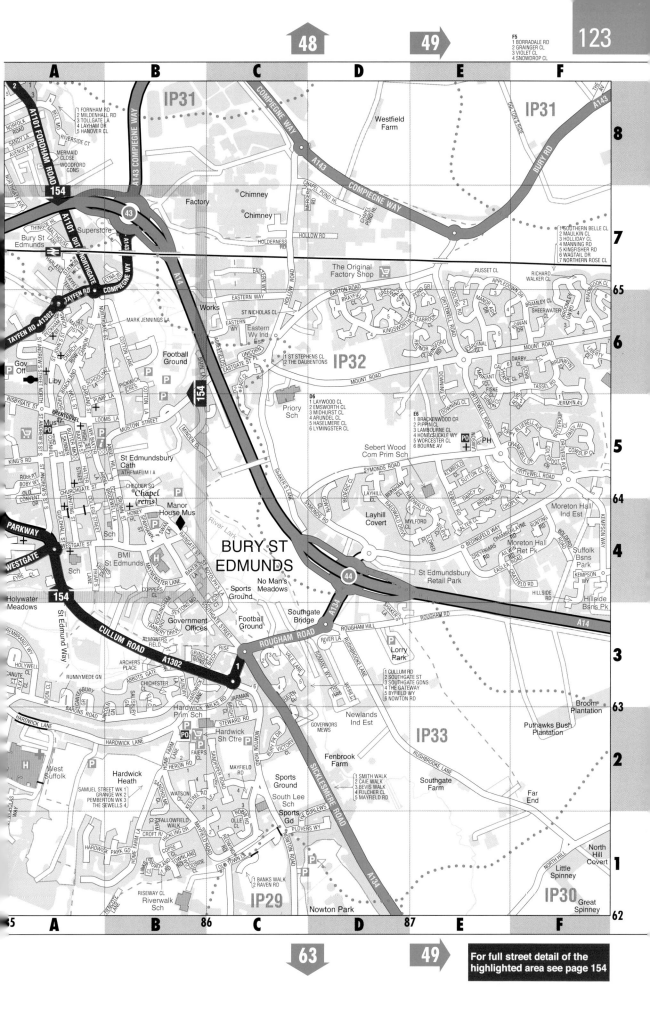

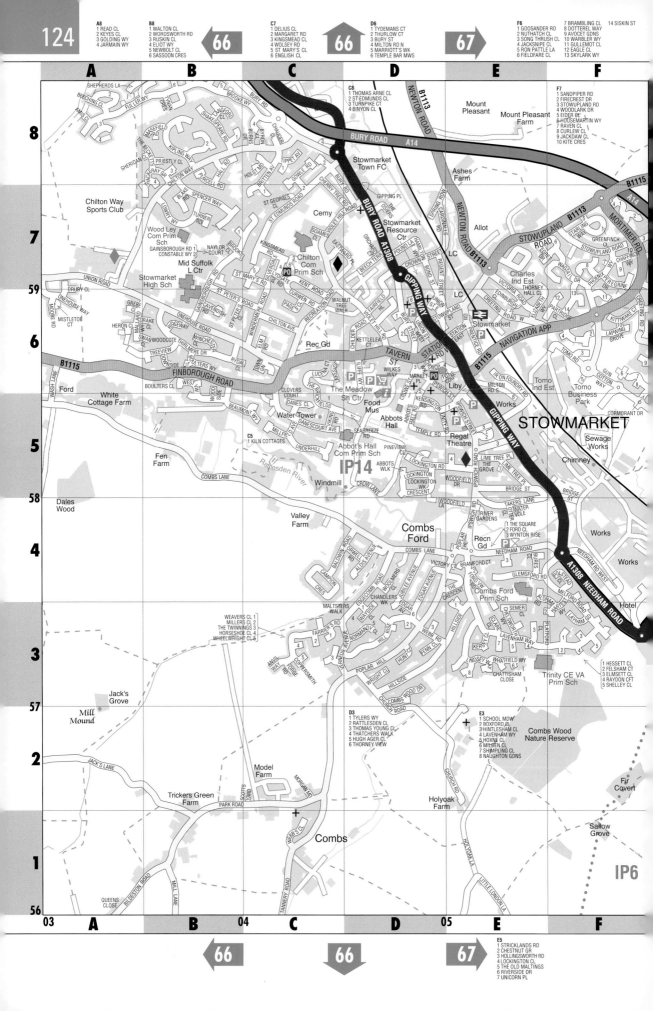

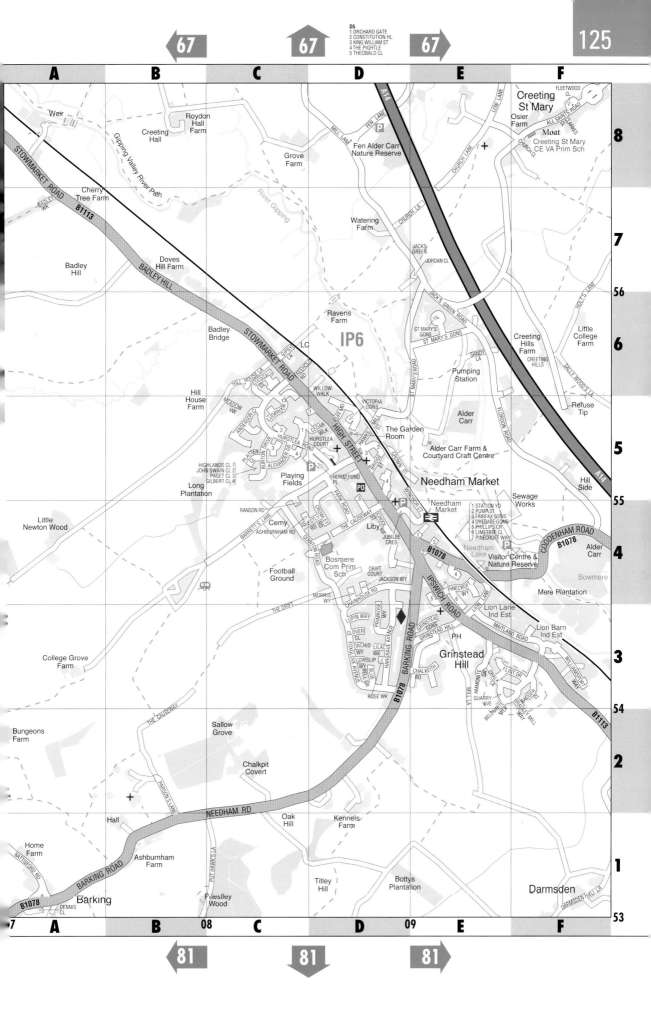

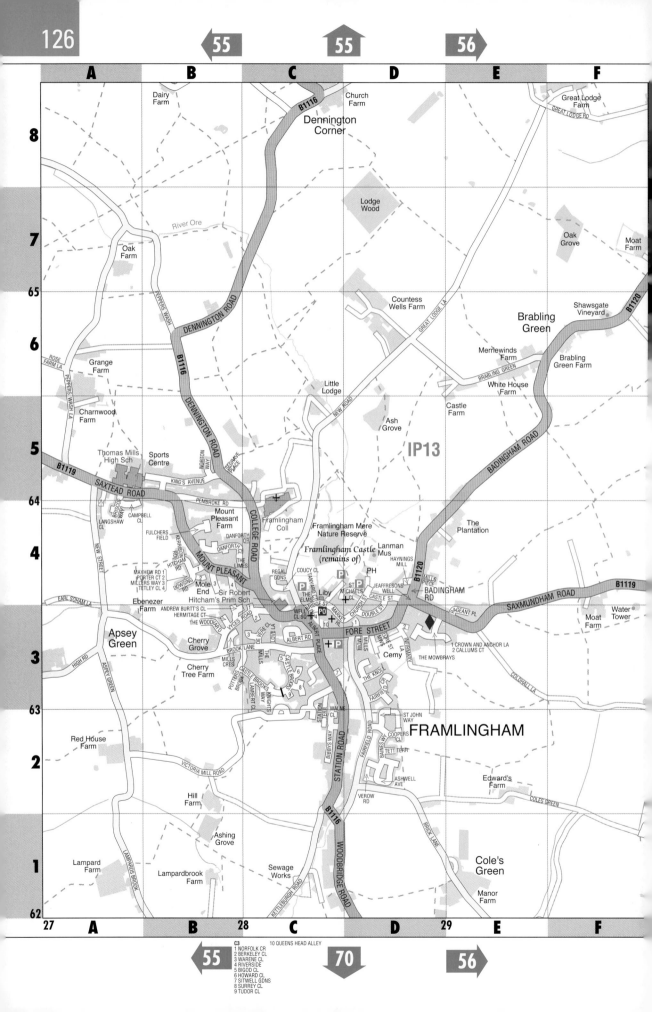

A B C D E F

8

7

65

6

5

64

4

3

63

2

1

62

27 A B 28 C D 29 E F

Dairy Farm

Church Farm

Great Lodge Farm

GREAT LODGE RD

Dennington Corner

B1116

Lodge Wood

Oak Grove

Moat Farm

River Ore

Oak Farm

Countess Wells Farm

DENNINGTON ROAD

PEPPERS WASH

B1116

Great Lodge La

Brabling Green

Shawsgate Vineyard

B1120

ROSE FARM LA

Grange Farm

Merriewinds Farm

Brabling Green Farm

PEPPERS WASH LA

Charnwood Farm

Little Lodge

NEW ROAD

White House Farm

BRABLING GREEN

Castle Farm

Thomas Mills High Sch

Sports Centre

IP13

Ash Grove

BADINGHAM ROAD

B1119

SAXTEAD ROAD

KING'S AVENUE

NORTON WAY

The Plantation

Pembroke Rd

Mount Pleasant Farm

Framlingham Coll

Framlingham Mere Nature Reserve

Lanman Mus

BRISCOE WAY

LANGSHAW CL

CAMPBELL CL

FULCHERS FIELD

DANFORTH DR

THE LIMES

Framlingham Castle (remains of)

HAYNINGS MILL

B1120

SAXMUNDHAM ROAD

B1119

MAYHEW RD 1
PORTER CT 2
MILLERS WAY 3
TETLEY CL 4

KERRISON RD

HITCHAM RD

DOWSING RD

Mole End

DANFORTH DR

REGAL GDNS

COUCY CL

PH

MILLS PIECE

BADINGHAM RD

Water Tower

NEW STREET

MOUNT PLEASANT

COLLEGE ROAD

Sir Robert Hitcham's Prim Sch

THE ELMS

Liby

ST MICHAELS CL

JEAFFRESONS WELL

CASTLE ST

Moat Farm

EARL SOHAM LA

Ebenezer Farm

ANDREW BURTT'S CL

HERMITAGE CT

THE WOODYARD

WYLES ROAD

COLLEGE CL

BRIDGE ST

WELL CL SQ

PO

MARKET

CHURCH ST

DOUBLE ST

PAGEANT PL

HIGH RD

Apsey Green

Cherry Grove

BROOK LANE

MILLS CRES

ALBERT RD

ALBERT PLACE

FORE STREET

MILLS

Cemy

CASTLE ST LA

THE MOWBRAYS

COLDHALL LA

Cherry Tree Farm

POTTERS BROOK

CASTLE BROOK

KNIGHTS WAY

LAMBERT CL

THE MILLS

CASTLE BROOK

STATION RD

WALNE CL

THE KNOLL

FAIRFIELD CR

1 CROWN AND ANCHOR LA
2 CALLUMS CT

St John Way

FRAMLINGHAM

Red House Farm

ASPEY GREEN

VICTORIA MILL ROAD

BIBB'S WAY

STATION ROAD

FAIRFIELD ROAD

COOPERS CL

BAINES W

TETT TERR

Edward's Farm

COLES GREEN

Hill Farm

LAMPARDS BROOK

ASHWELL AVE

VEROW RD

Ashing Grove

B1116

Cole's Green

Lampard Farm

Lampardbrook Farm

Sewage Works

KETTLEBURGH ROAD

WOODBRIDGE ROAD

BRICK LANE

Manor Farm

C3
10 QUEENS HEAD ALLEY
1 NORFOLK CR
2 BERKELEY CL
3 WARENE CL
4 RIVERSIDE
5 BIGOD CL
6 HOWARD CL
7 SITWELL GDNS
8 SURREY CL
9 TUDOR CL

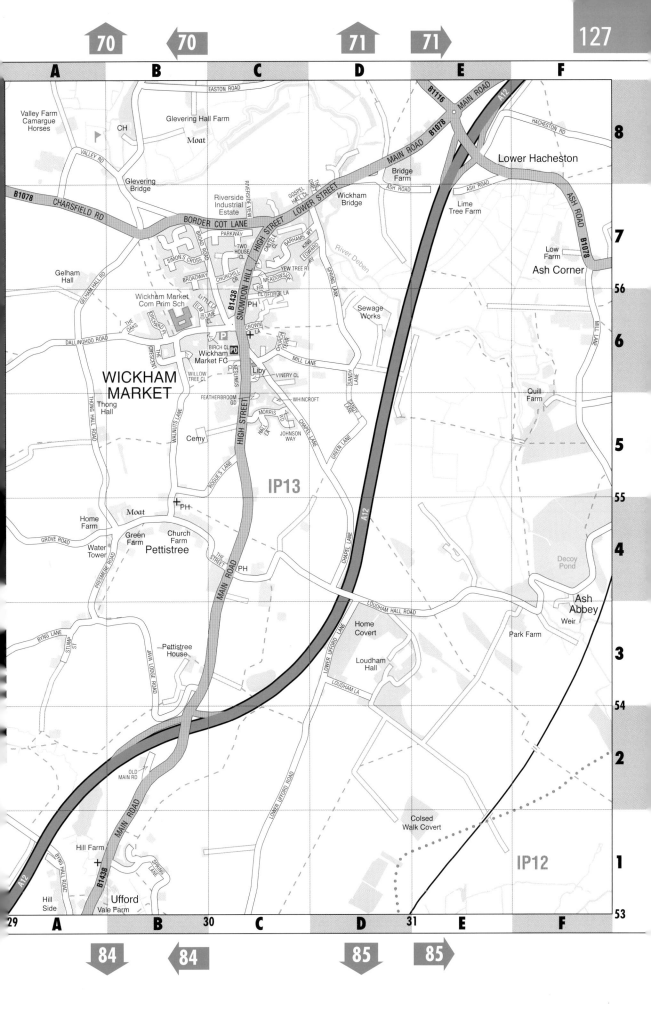

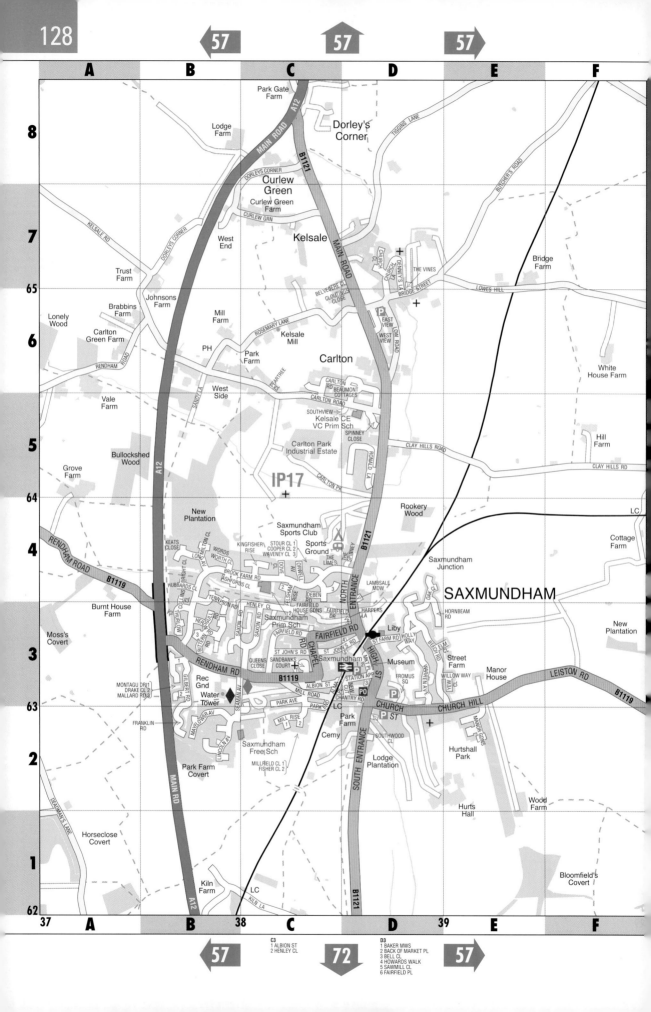

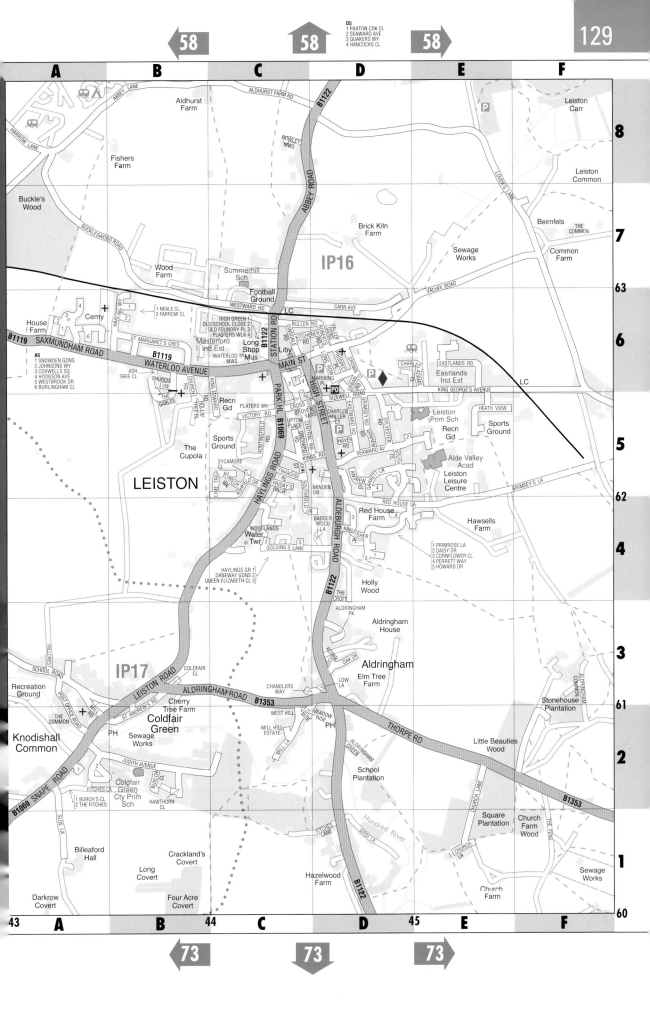

D5
1 PAXTON CDK CL
2 SEAWARD AVE
3 QUAKERS WY
4 HANCOCKS CL

8

ABBEY LANE
ALDHURST FARM RD
Aldhurst Farm
ROWLEY MWS
B1122
HARROW LANE
Fishers Farm
Leiston Carr

Buckle's Wood
IP16
Leiston Common

BUCKLESWOOD ROAD
Brick Kiln Farm
Beirnfels
THE COMMON
7

Wood Farm
Summerhill Sch
Sewage Works
Common Farm

Football Ground
VALLEY ROAD
63

WESTWARD HO
CARR AVE
LC
House Farm
Cemy
STATION RD
HIGH GREEN 1
OLD SCHOOL CLOSE 2
OLD FOUNDRY PL 3
PLASTERS WLK 4
BULLER RD
KITCHENER RD
Eastlands Ind Est
LC
6

B1119 SAXMUNDHAM ROAD
ST MARGARET'S CRES
B1122
Masterford Ind Est
Long Shop Mus
Liby
Eastlands Rd

A6
1 SNOWDEN GDNS
2 JOHNSONS WY
3 COXWELLS SQ
4 HODGSON AVE
5 WESTBROOK DR
6 BURLINGHAM CL
WATERLOO AVENUE
ASH TREE CL
MAIN ST
WATERLOO MWS
PO
CHARLES ADAMS
KING GEORGE'S AVENUE
HEATH VIEW
Eastlands Ind Est

CHURCH VW
THE GABLES
Recn Gd
MAFEKING PL
SIZEWELL ROAD
Leiston Prim Sch
Recn Gd
Sports Ground
5

The Cupola
PLATERS WK
VICTORY RD
CROSS ST
UPTON PLACE
ORCHARD
HAVEN
CHARLES MILLER CT
Alde Valley Acad
Leiston Leisure Centre

LEISTON
Sports Ground
SYCAMORE CL
PARADISE
KINGS RD
SEAWARD AV
SOUTH RD
Red House La
62

LIME TREE AV
BEECH
ASHFIELD DR
FRIDAY'S ORCH
MINDEN DR
BADGER WOOD LA
Red House Farm
Hawsells Farm

HAYLINGS ROAD
Water Twr
GOLDING'S LANE
KINGFISHER
1 PRIMROSE LA
2 DAISY DR
3 CORNFLOWER CL
4 PERRETT WAY
5 HOWARD DR
4

HAYLINGS GR 1
DANEWAY GDNS 2
QUEEN ELIZABETH CL 3
ALDEBURGH ROAD
Holly Wood

B1122
THE CROFT
Aldringham PK
Aldringham House
3

IP17
COLDFAIR CL
ACHIM CL
OAK DR
Aldringham
School Road
LEISTON ROAD
CHANDLERS WAY
LOW LA
Elm Tree Farm
Stonehouse Plantation

Recreation Ground
ALDRINGHAM ROAD
B1353
WEST HILL
MILL HILL
MEADOW RISE
PH
THORPE RD
61

THE COMMON
POST OFFICE ROAD
MILL RD
ST ANDREW'S RD
Cherry Tree Farm
Coldfair Green
MILL HILL ESTATE
MILL LA
ALDRINGHAM GREEN
Little Beauties Wood
2

Knodishall Common
PH
Sewage Works
JUDITH AVENUE
BUXLOW CL
School Plantation
Square Plantation
Church Farm Wood

B1069 SNAPE ROAD
SLOE LA
FITCHES LA
1 BURCH'S CL
2 THE FITCHES
Coldfair Green Cty Prim Sch
HAWTHORN CL
Hundred River
GIPSY LA
CHURCH LANE
B1353
THE FENS

Billeaford Hall
Crackland's Covert
FITCHES LANE
CHURCH LA
Sewage Works
1

Darkrow Covert
Long Covert
Four Acre Covert
Hazelwood Farm
B1122
Church Farm
60

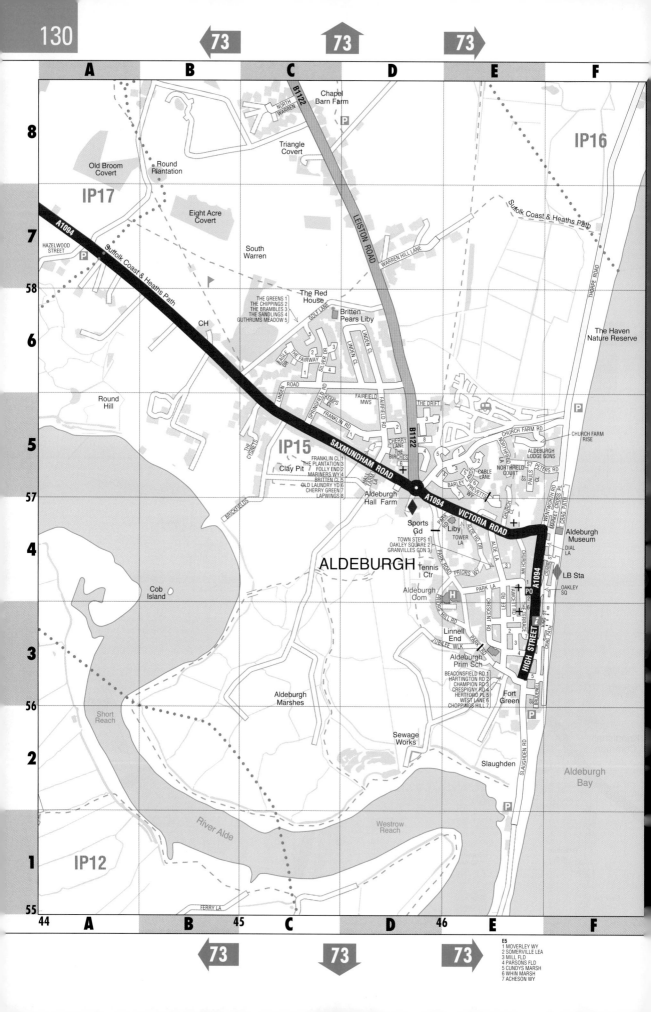

73 73 73

A B C D E F

8

IP16

Chapel
Barn Farm

North
Warren

Triangle
Covert

Old Broom
Covert

Round
Plantation

IP17

Eight Acre
Covert

Suffolk Coast & Heaths Path

7

Hazelwood
Street

A1094

Suffolk Coast & Heaths Path

Warren Hill Lane

LEISTON ROAD

58

South
Warren

The Red
House

The Haven
Nature Reserve

CH

THE GREENS 1
THE CHIPPINGS 2
THE BRAMBLES 3
THE SANDLINGS 4
GUTHRUMS MEADOW 5

Golf Lane

Britten
Pears Liby

6

EAGLE DR

THE FAIRWAY

SILVER DR

LINDEN CL

LINDEN CL

Round
Hill

LINDEN ROAD

FAIRFIELD
MWS

FAIRFIELD RD

THE DRIFT

SPRINGFIELD RD

KEMPS RD

FRANKLIN RD

5

IP15

THE CYGNETS

Clay Pit

FRANKLIN CL 1
THE PLANTATION 3
FOLLY END 2
MARINERS WY 4
BRITTEN CL 5
OLD LAUNDRY YD 6
CHERRY GREEN 7
LAPWINGS 8

SAXMUNDHAM ROAD

CHERRY
LANE

THE
BIRCHES

B1122

CHURCH FARM RD

CHURCH FARM
RISE

ALDEBURGH
LODGE GDNS

NORTHFIELD RD

ST PAULS CL

NORTHFIELD
COURT

ST PETERS RD

BARLEY LANDS

PRIORS WY

CABLE
LANE

57

BRICKFIELDS

Aldeburgh
Hall Farm

A1094

VICTORIA ROAD

WENTWORTH RD

MARKET CROSS PL

CRAG PATH

Aldeburgh
Museum

4

Cob
Island

Sports
Gd

Liby

TOWER
LA

TOWN STEPS 1
OAKLEY SQUARE 2
GRANVILLES GDN 3

ALDEBURGH

Tennis
Ctr

Aldeburgh
Com

H

PARK ROAD

PRIORS WY

ALDE LA

PARK LA

CHURCH ST

DIAL
LA

A1094

LB Sta

OAKLEY
SQ

PO

3

Aldeburgh
Marshes

Linnell
End

JUBILEE WLK

Aldeburgh
Prim Sch

BEACONSFIELD RD 1
HARTINGTON RD 2
CHAMPION RD 3
CRESPIGNY RD 4
HERTFORD PL 5
WEST LANE 6
CHOPPINGS HILL 7

PARK HILL RD

CRESCENT RD

FAWCETT RD

THE TERRACE

KING ST

HIGH STREET

CRAG PATH

Fort
Green

ST BRUDENELL

56

Short
Reach

Sewage
Works

Slaughden

River Alde

Westrow
Reach

Aldeburgh
Bay

2

IP12

1

55

44 A B 45 C D 46 E F

73 73 73

E5
1 MOVERLEY WY
2 SOMERVILLE LEA
3 MILL FLD
4 PARSONS FLD
5 CUNDYS MARSH
6 WHIN MARSH
7 ACHESON WY

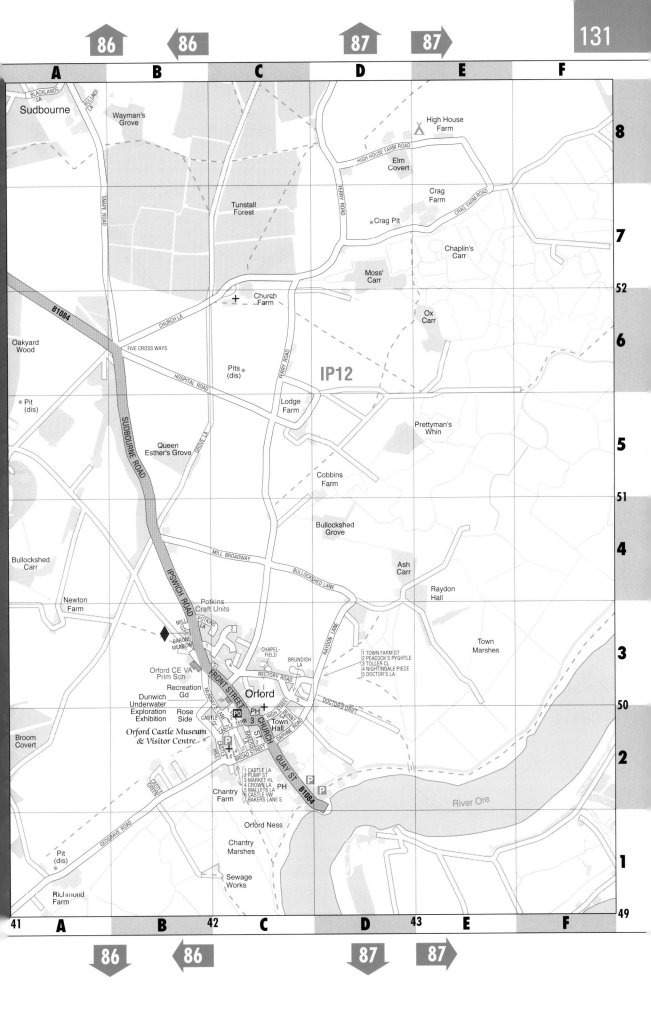

A B C D E F

8

7

52

6

5

51

4

3

50

2

1

49

Blacklands La
Sudbourne
Bullage La
Wayman's Grove
Snape Road
Tunstall Forest
High House Farm Road
Ferry Road
High House Farm
Elm Covert
Crag Farm
Crag Farm Road
Crag Pit
Chaplin's Carr
Moss' Carr
B1084
Oakyard Wood
Church La
Church Farm
Five Cross Ways
Ferry Road
Ox Carr
IP12
Hospital Road
Pits (dis)
Pit (dis)
Lodge Farm
Prettyman's Whin
Sudbourne Road
Grove La
Queen Esther's Grove
Cobbins Farm
Mill Broadway
Bullockshed Grove
Bullockshed Carr
Bullockshed Lane
Ash Carr
Raydon Hall
Town Marshes
Newton Farm
Ipswich Road
Potkins Craft Units
Mill Cl
Potkins La
Barons Meadow
Chapel-Field
Brundish La
Raydon Lane
1 TOWN FARM ST
2 PEACOCK'S PYGHTLE
3 TOLLER CL
4 NIGHTINGALE PIECE
5 DOCTOR'S LA
Orford CE VA Prim Sch
Front Street
Mundy's Lane
Orford
PH
Recreation Gd
Rectory Road
Doctor's Drift
Dunwich Underwater Exploration Exhibition
Rose Side
Castle Cl
Castle Terr
PO
Church St
Town Hall
High Street
Burn La
Daphne Road
Orford Castle Museum & Visitor Centre
Castle Hill
Bakers La
Broad Street
Quay St
B1084
PH
Castle Green
1 CASTLE LA
2 PUMP ST
3 MARKET HL
4 CROWN LA
5 MALLETS LA
6 CASTLE VW
7 BAKERS LANE S
Broom Covert
Chantry Farm
Gedgrave Road
Orford Ness
Chantry Marshes
River Ore
Pit (dis)
Sewage Works
Richmond Farm

41 A B 42 C D 43 E F 49

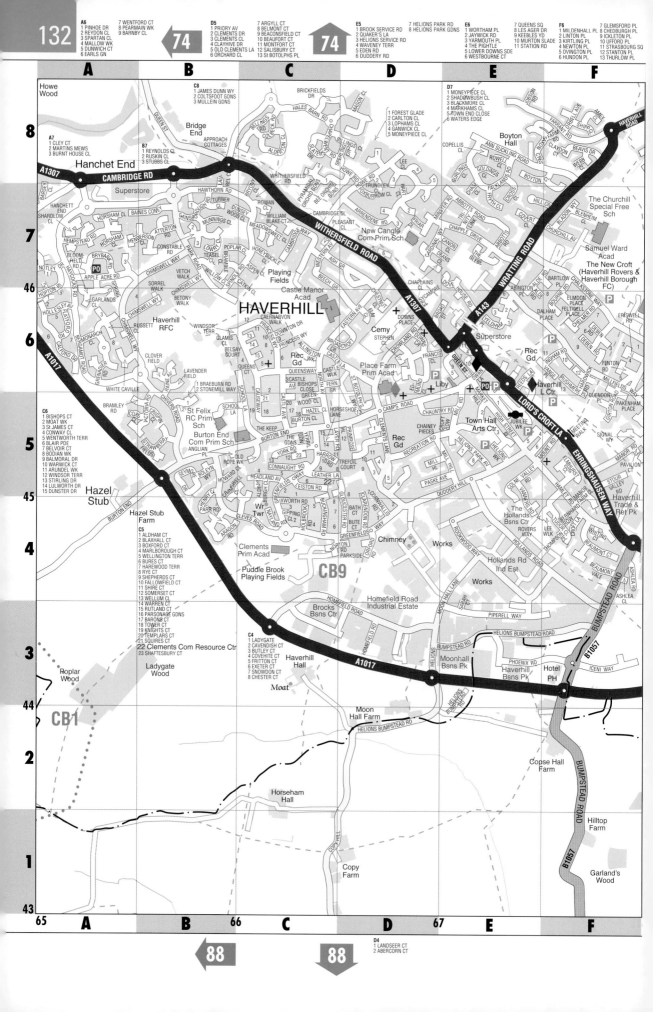

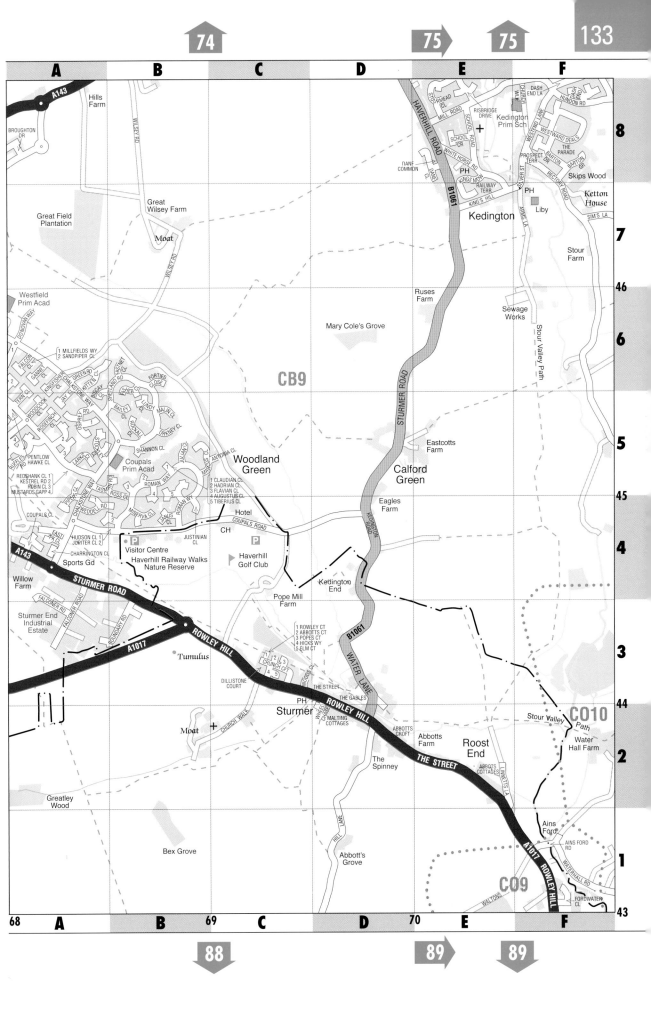

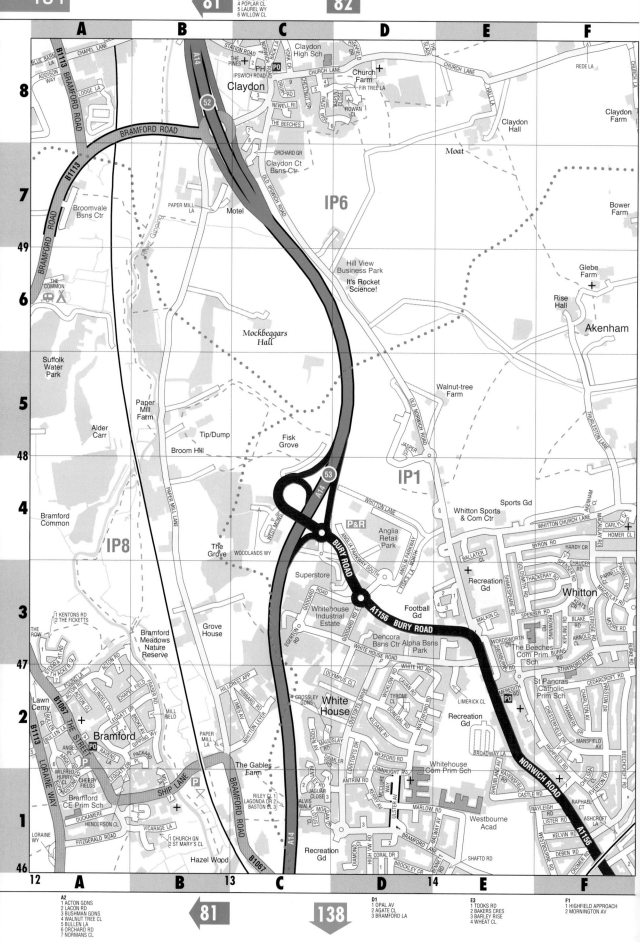

C8
1 ST PETER'S AV
2 QUOITS FIELD
3 MORGAN CT
4 POPLAR CL
5 LAUREL WY
6 WILLOW CL

7 LIMEKILN CL
8 OLD PAPER MILL LA
9 ALASDAIR PL

A2
1 ACTON GDNS
2 LACON RD
3 BUSHMAN GDNS
4 WALNUT TREE CL
5 BULLEN LA
6 ORCHARD RD
7 NORMANS CL

D1
1 OPAL AV
2 AGATE CL
3 BRAMFORD LA

E3
1 TOOKS RD
2 BAKERS CRES
3 BARLEY RISE
4 WHEAT CL

F1
1 HIGHFIELD APPROACH
2 MORNINGTON AV

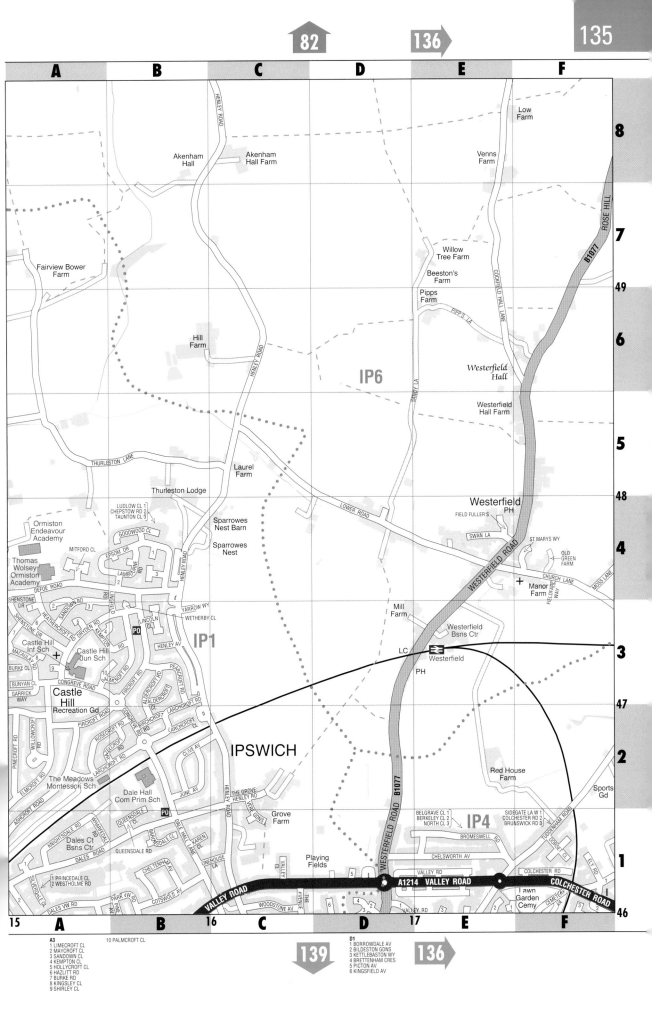

A B C D E F

Low Farm
Akenham Hall
Akenham Hall Farm
Venns Farm
HENLEY ROAD
ROSE HILL
B1077
Willow Tree Farm
Fairview Bower Farm
Beeston's Farm
Pipps Farm
COCKFIELD HALL LANE
Hill Farm
PIPP'S LA
IP6
Westerfield Hall
SANDY LA
Westerfield Hall Farm
THURLESTON LANE
Laurel Farm
Thurleston Lodge
LOWER ROAD
Westerfield PH
FIELD FULLER'S
SWAN LA
ST MARYS WY
LUDLOW CL 1
CHEPSTOW RD 2
TAUNTON CL 3
Ormiston Endeavour Academy
GOODWOOD CL
Sparrowes Nest Barn
Sparrowes Nest
OLD GREEN FARM
MITFORD CL
EPSOM DR
CRNE
Thomas Wolsey Ormiston Academy
LAMBO
DEFOE ROAD
YARROW WY
WETHERBY CL
WESTERFIELD ROAD
CHURCH LANE
MOSS LANE
Manor Farm
FIELD/FREE WAY
SHENSTONE DR
SANDOWN RD
HEATHERCROFT RD
DRYDEN RD
LINGFIELD RD
KEMPTON RD
HENLEY AV
LINCOLN CL
PO
IP1
Mill Farm
Westerfield Bsns Ctr
Castle Hill Inf Sch
Castle Hill Jun Sch
MACAULY CL
PALMCROFT RD
PEASCROFT RD
ALDERCROFT RD
LC
Westerfield
BURKE CL
BUNYAN CL
CONGREVE ROAD
Castle Hill Recreation Gd
BIRCHCROFT
LARCHCROFT RD
PH
GARRICK WAY
FIRCROFT ROAD
ROSECROFT RD
LARCHCROFT CL
PINECROFT RD
WILLOWCROFT
ELMCROFT RD
ASHCROFT ROAD
CLIVE AV
IPSWICH
Red House Farm
Sports Gd
SILVERDALE RD
The Meadows Montessori Sch
JUNE AV
Dale Hall Com Prim Sch
HENLEY RD
THE GROVE, Henley Rd
VERE GDNS
Grove Farm
BELGRAVE CL 1
BERKELEY CL 2
NORTH CL 3
IP4
SIDEGATE LA W 1
COLCHESTER RD 2
BRUNSWICK RD 3
KNIGHTSDALE RD
WHITEFOALS
WINFIELD
Dales Ct Bsns Ctr
DALE HALL LANE
BARRY CL
KAREN CL
ONEHOUSE LA
PO
QUEENSDALE RD
CHELTENHAM WY
BROMESWELL RD
B1077
WESTERFIELD ROAD
TUDDENHAM ROAD
GORSE RD
ELY RD
COLCHESTER RD
DALES VW RD
PARK VW RD
PINE
COTSWOLD AV
WOODSTONE AV
Playing Fields
VALLEY CL
THE AVENUE
A1214 VALLEY ROAD
VALLEY RD
CHELSWORTH AV
COLCHESTER RD
CEMETERY
Lawn Garden Cemy
1 PRINCEDALE CL
2 WESTHOLME RD
VALLEY ROAD

A3
1 LIMECROFT CL
2 MAYCROFT CL
3 SANDOWN CL
4 KEMPTON CL
5 HOLLYCROFT CL
6 HAZLITT RD
7 BURKE RD
8 KINGSLEY CL
9 SHIRLEY CL

10 PALMCROFT CL

D1
1 BORROWDALE AV
2 BILDESTON GDNS
3 KETTLEBASTON WY
4 BRETTENHAM CRES
5 PICTON AV
6 KINGSFIELD AV

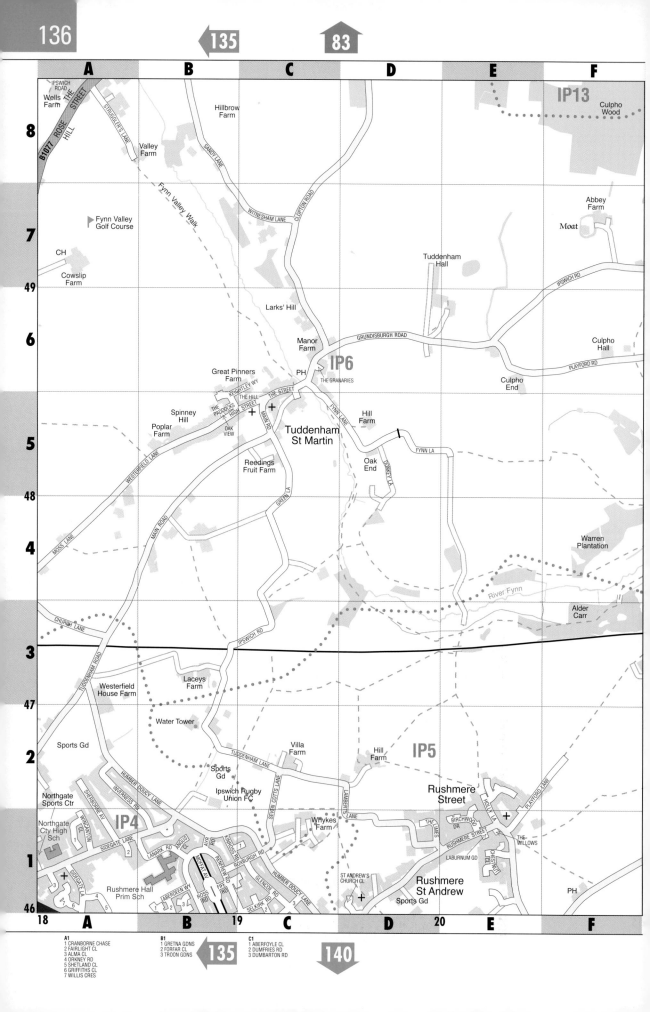

135
83

A B C D E F

8

7

49

6

5

48

4

3

47

2

1

46

18 A B 19 C D 20 E F

Ipswich Road
Wells Farm
THE STREET
B1077 ROSE HILL
Valley Farm
Struggler's Lane
Hillbrow Farm
Sandy Lane
Witnesham Lane
Clopton Road
IP13
Culpho Wood
Abbey Farm
Moat
Fynn Valley Walk
Fynn Valley Golf Course
CH
Cowslip Farm
Larks' Hill
Tuddenham Hall
Ipswich Rd
Manor Farm
Grundisburgh Road
Culpho Hall
IP6
PH
THE GRANARIES
Playford Rd
Great Pinners Farm
Knightley Wy
The Hill
High Street
The Street
Culpho End
Spinney Hill
The Paddocks
Main Rd
Oak View
Fynn Lane
Hill Farm
Poplar Farm
Tuddenham St Martin
Westerfield Lane
Reedings Fruit Farm
Green La
Fynn La
Oak End
Donkey La
Warren Plantation
Moss Lane
Main Road
Ipswich Rd
River Fynn
Alder Carr
Church Lane
Tuddenham Road
Westerfield House Farm
Laceys Farm
Water Tower
Villa Farm
Hill Farm
IP5
Sports Gd
Tuddenham Lane
Sports Gd
Rushmere Street
Northgate Sports Ctr
Humber Doucy Lane
Inverness Rd
Ipswich Rugby Union FC
Seven Cotts Lane
Whykes Farm
Lambert's Lane
Birchwood Dr
Holly La
Playford Lane
Northgate Cty High Sch
IP4
Sherborne Av
Wincanton Cl
Sidegate Lane
Lanark Rd
Angus Cl
Ayr Rd
Moffat Av
Kinross Rd
Roxburgh Rd
Humber Doucy Lane
St Andrew's Church Cl
The Limes
Rushmere Street
Laburnum Gd
Chestnut Cl
The Willows
Rushmere Hall Prim Sch
Aberdeen Wy
Ross Rd
Fife Rd
Glencoe Rd
Selkirk Rd
Renfrew Rd
Rushmere St Andrew
Sports Gd
PH
Sidegate La

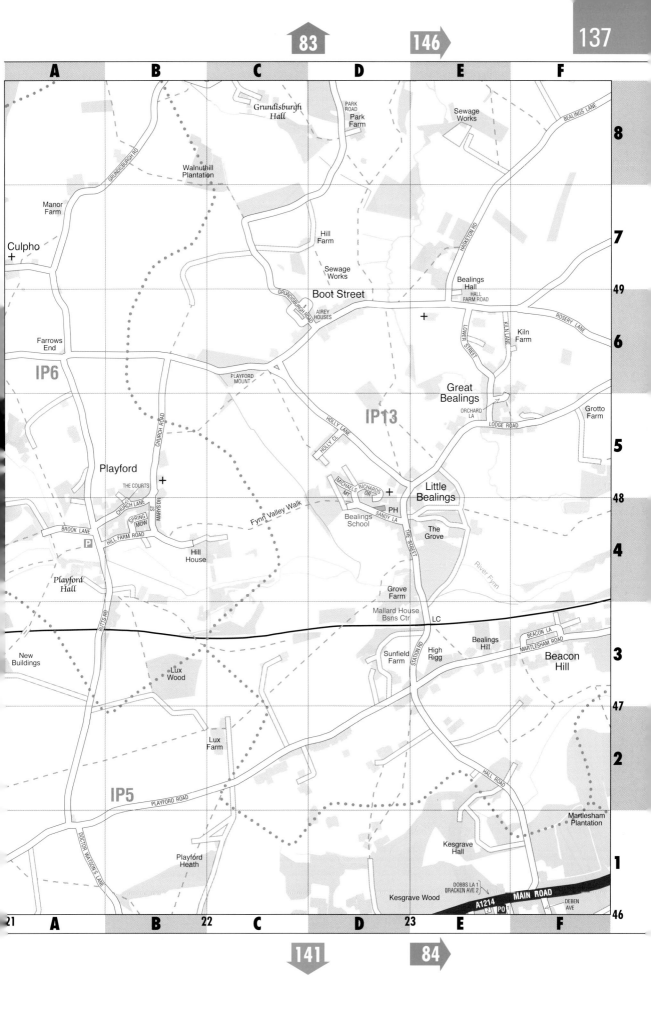

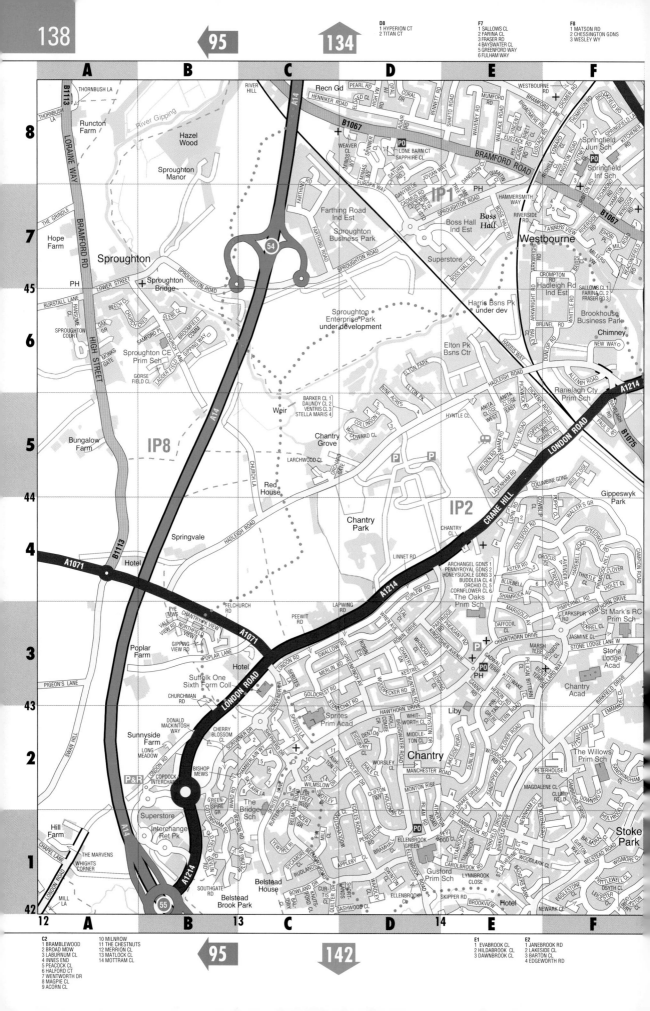

IPSWICH

IP4

IP1

IP3

IP2

Stoke

Maidenhall

Greenwich

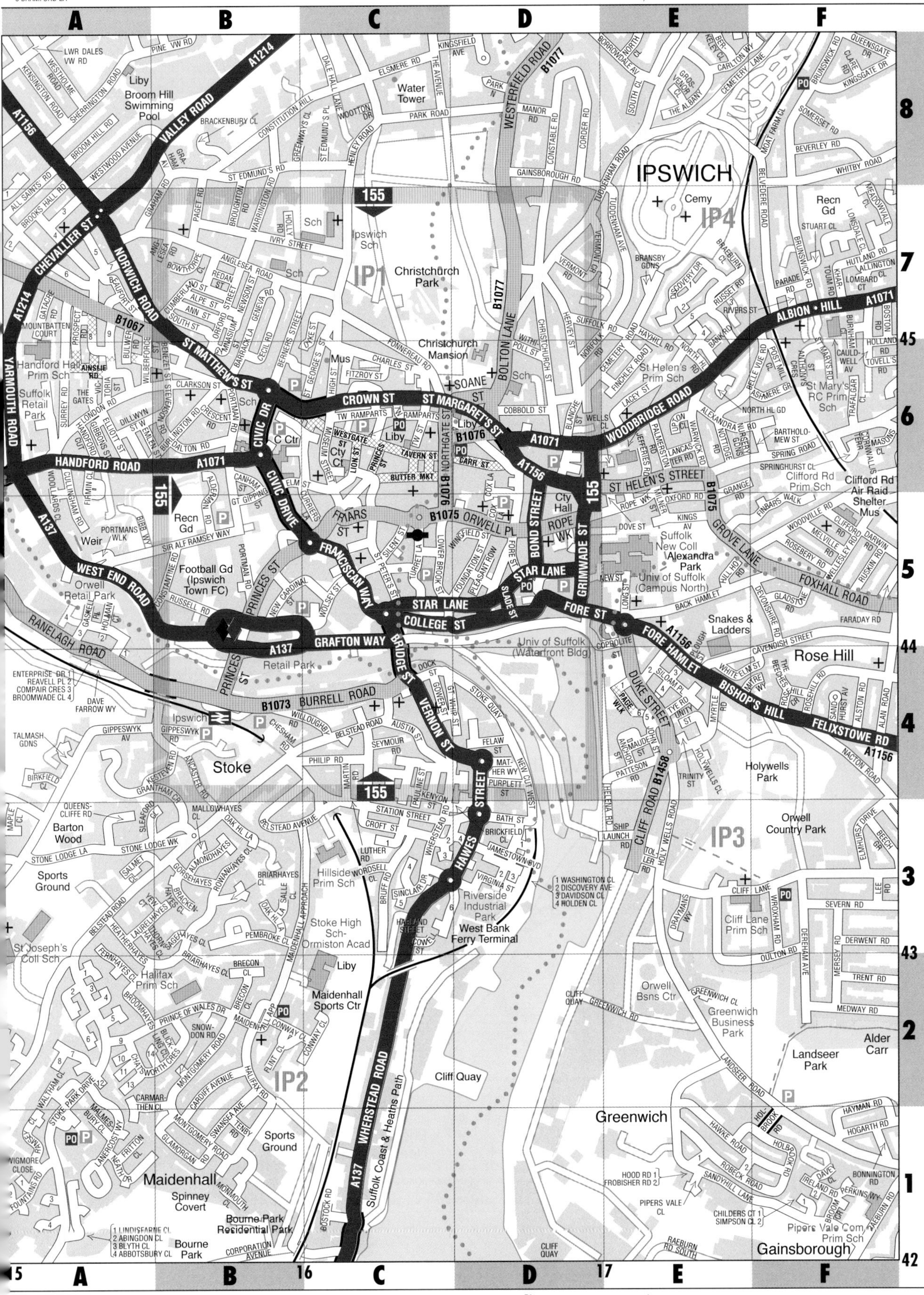

Gainsborough

Rose Hill

155

For full street detail of the highlighted area see page 155

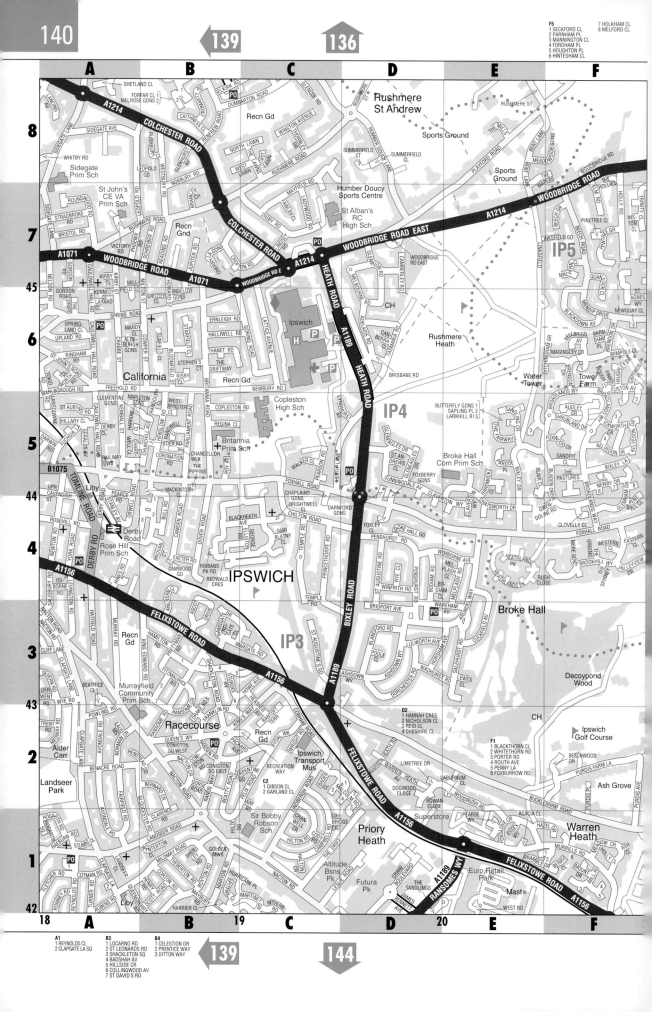

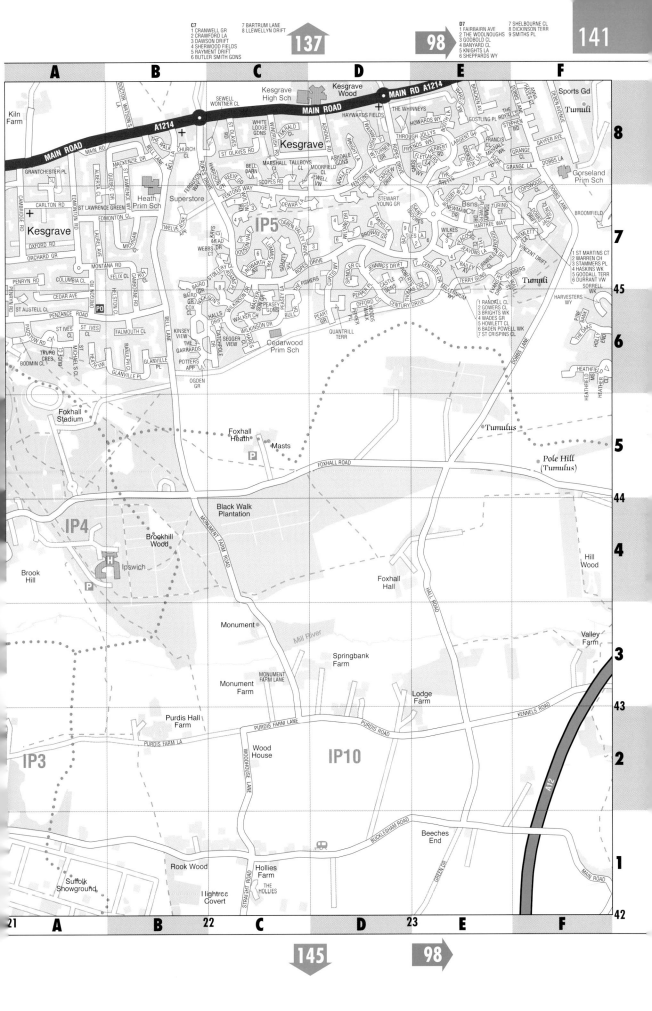

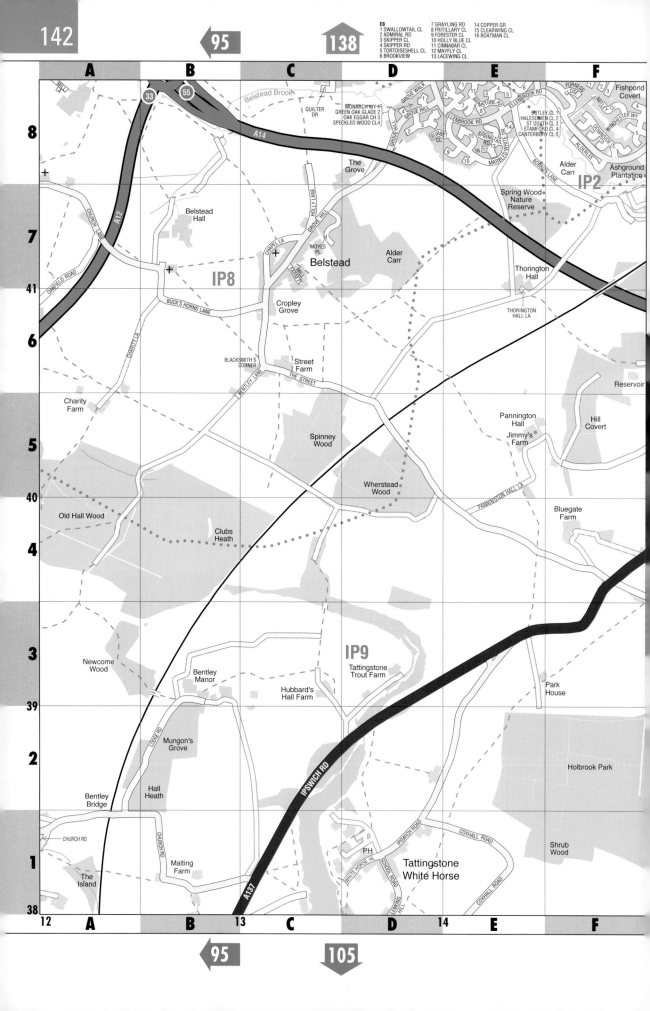

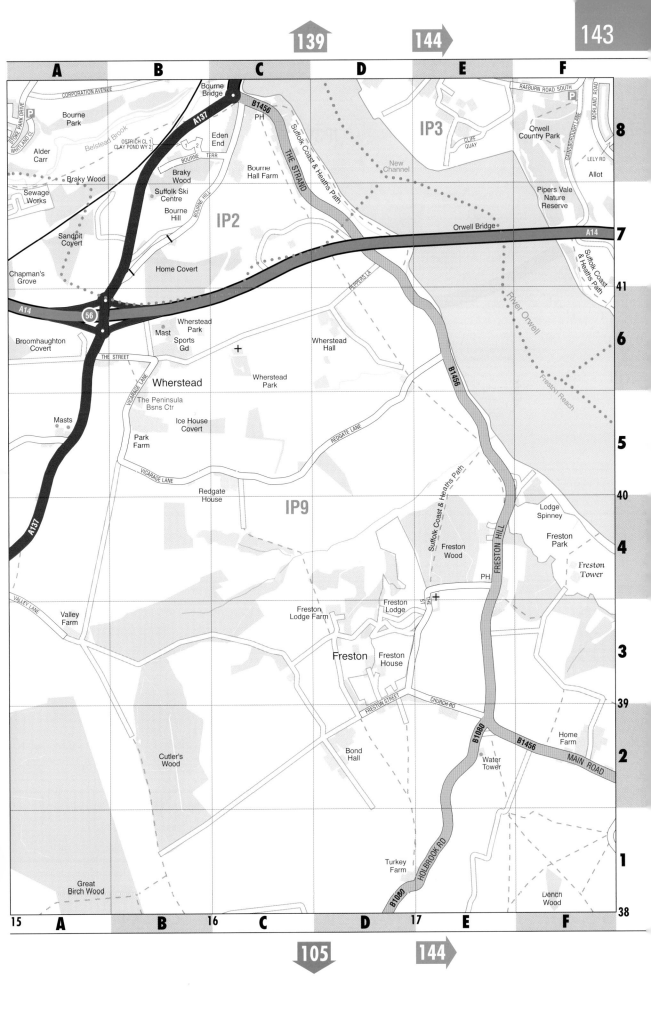

144

A8		7 VANDYCK RD
1 MORLAND RD		8 LEIGHTON SQ
2 REYNOLDS AV		9 FISHBANE CL
3 CHESAPEAKE RD		
4 SHANNON RD		
5 NIGHTINGALE SQ		
6 LOWRY GDNS		

C8		7 LACKFORD PL
1 FIREFLY WY		8 CHASER CL
2 HUNTER RD		
3 LYSANDER DR		
4 DARTER CL		
5 DAMSELFLY RD		
6 PASHFORD PL		

D8		D7
1 ALNESBOURN CR		1 MANSBROOK BD
2 TITCHWELL DR		2 HAVERGATE RD
3 HAVERGATE RD		

143   140

B8
1 QUEENSBERRY RD
2 NASH GDNS
3 SWATCHWAY CL

C7
1 DOWNHAM BD
2 CRANBERRY SQ
3 MULBERRY RD
4 LOGANBERRY RD
5 MANSBROOK BD
6 ELDERBERRY RD
7 HUCKLEBERRY CRES

IP3

Sports Centre

Ipswich Acad
Gainsborough

Morland CE VA Prim Sch

Brazier's Wood

Ravenswood Community Prim Sch

Pond Hall Farm

Bridge Wood Nature Reserve

Orwell Country Park

Mulberry Middle

Alnesbourne Priory

CH

Alnesbourn Priory

IP10

Deals Carr

Watercress Carr

Fox's Carr

Foxes Farm

Goldsmith's Covert

Mansbrook Grove

Robert's Grove

Airport Farm

Hotel

Bluebird Lodge

Mansbrook BLVD

Alnesbourn Cres

Ransomes Europark

Nacton Heath

Yale Business Park

Round Plantation

Downham Reach

River Orwell

Potter's Reach

Freston Park

Toweralder Carr

Whinnyfield Wood

Corners House

Woolverstone

Kennels Wood

Woolverstone Marina

Cathouse Point

Cat House

Hall Pt

IP9

Ipswich High Sch for Girls

Water Tower

MAIN ROAD

Woolverstone Park

Sewage Works

RICHARDSONS LA

Suffolk Coast & Heaths Path

Park Farm

Orwell Park

Orwell Park House

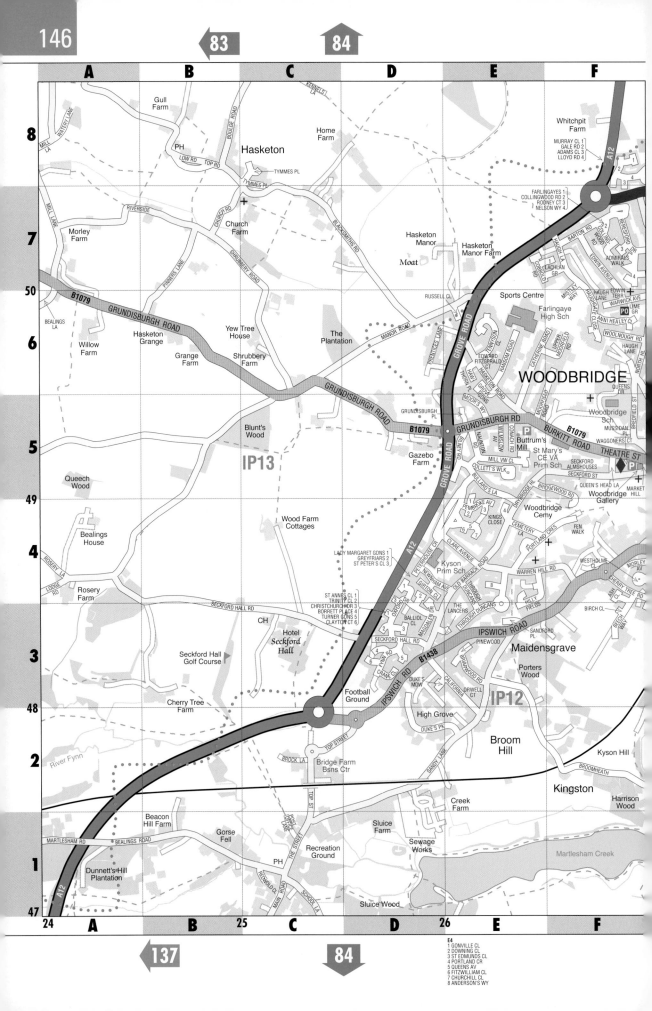

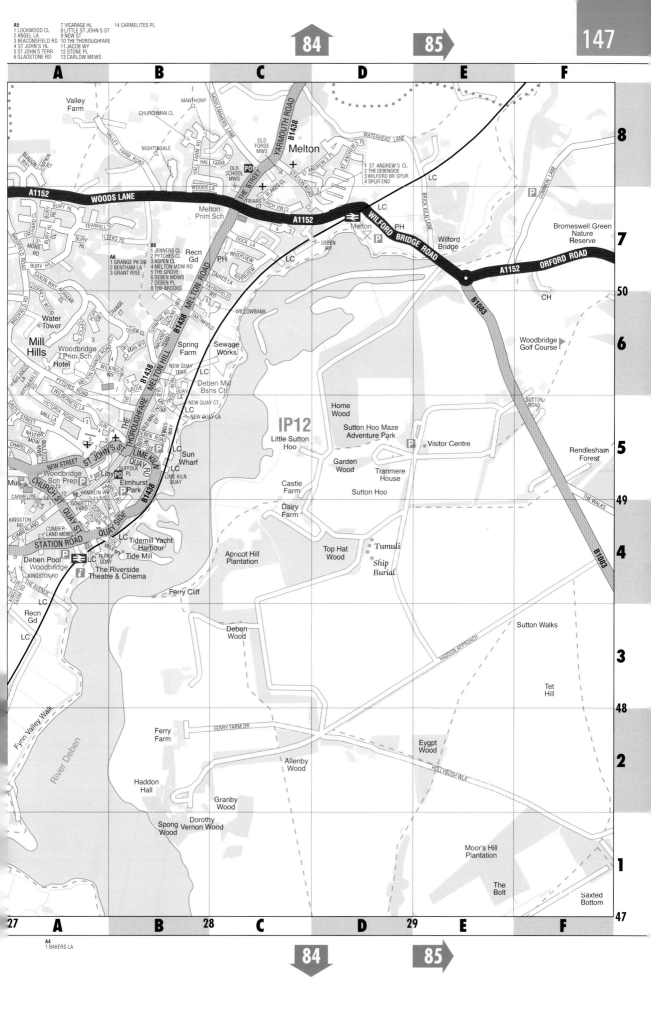

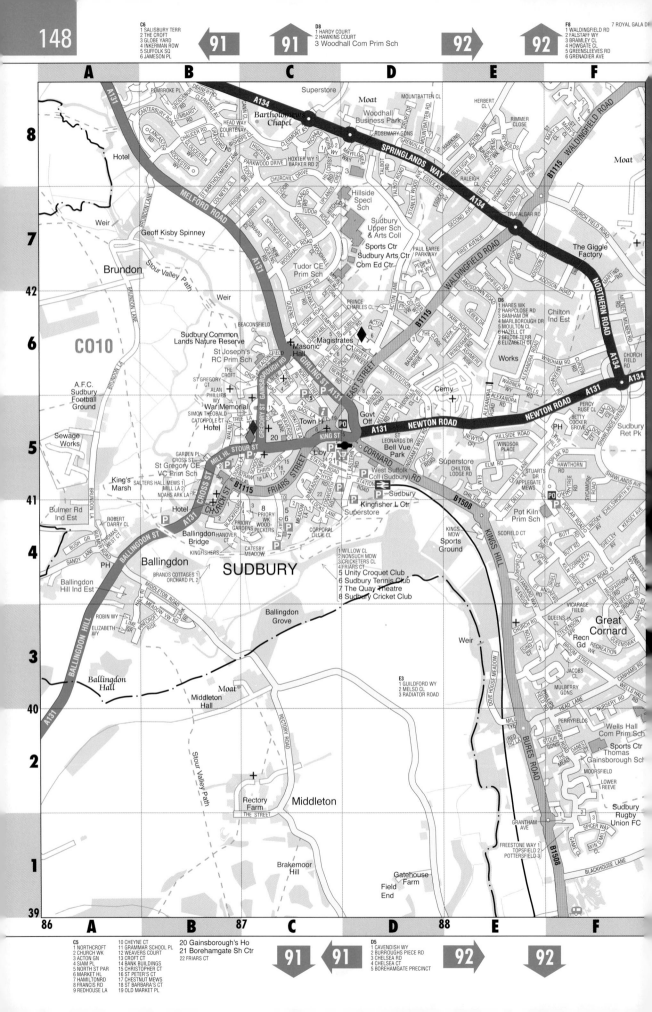

← 94   94 →   94 →

D5
1 CHURCH ST
2 SILK MILL CL
3 TOPPESFIELD CL
4 TAYLER CL
5 GAELL CR

D6
1 THREADNEEDLE ST
2 WEAVERS CL
3 INKERMAN TR
4 INKERMAN CL
5 SPOONERS LA
6 QUEEN ST

E6
1 DRAPERS CL
2 FULLERS CL
3 BARNES CL
4 MURIEL CL
5 WOOLNER CL
6 ROUSIES CL

7 BOURCHIER CL
8 ALABASTER CL

F7
1 EMMA GIRLING CL
2 ALICE PARKINS CL
3 ANN STRUTT CL
4 PAINTER CL
5 HARRISON DR
6 CARDMAN DR
7 HUDSON WY
8 KEELE CL

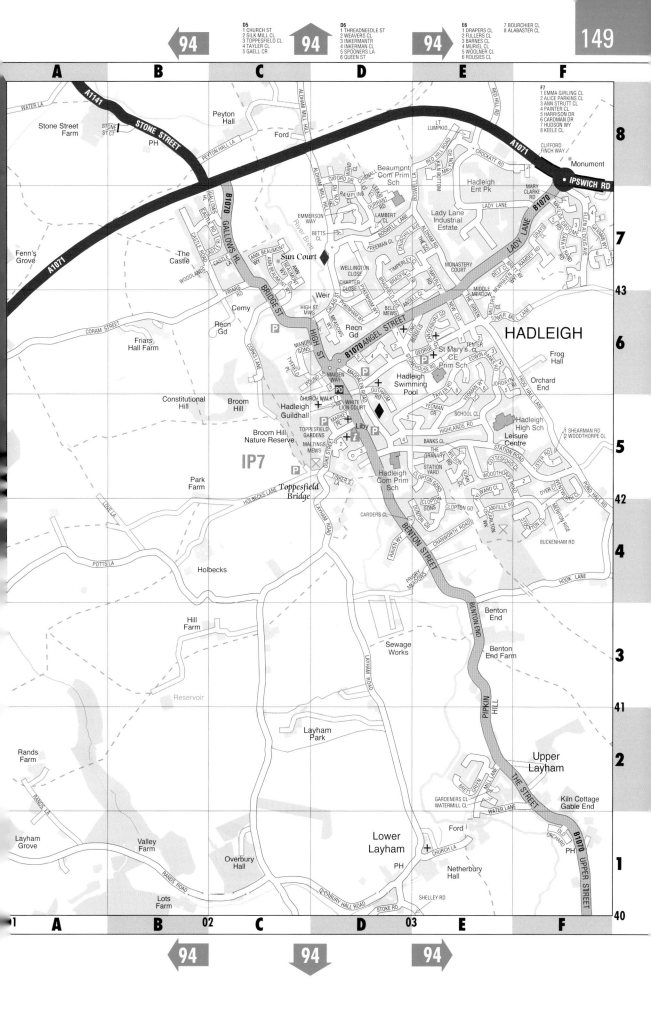

A   B   C   D   E   F

8

Moat

Vauxhall
Farm

Brimlin
Wood

Rookery
Farm

WENHAM ROAD

Cottage
Farm

The Grange
Farm

7

BOTTLE BRIDGE RD

Wenham
Grange

Wenham
Thicks

40

Green
Fields

CO7

IP8

6

Park House

Clay
Hall

5

Lodge
Farm

Binny's
Wood

Little Wenham

HILL LA

WENHAM RD

Wenham
Castle

Grove
Farm

Jermyns
Farm

GROVE LA

39

CASTLE FARM LA

RAYDON ROAD

CHURCH LA

Binny's
Wood

Brook
Farm

IP9

4

PH

Gipsy
Row

THE ROW

BROOK LANE

Churchford
Hall

Churchford
Farm

Mushroom
Farm

ROE DEER DR

1 BADGER SETT CL
2 FOX EARTH CL
3 PIPISTRELLE WY

DOVE CL

DAWES CL

ASH GR

THORNEY RD

HAWBRIDGE 1
RYLANDS 2
THE SQUIRRELS 3

BROOM WY

LINGFIELD RD

1 GLEBE END
2 TWO ACRES
3 ROUNDRIDGE RD
4 FARTHINGS WENT
5 THE QUEECH
6 JERMYNS CL
7 DAISY CL
8 BLUEBELL DR
9 SNOWDROP DR

THE
PIGHTLE

PENN
CL

LITTLE FTS

GREAT
TUFTS

BOUNDARY
OAKS

Capel St Mary

Corner
Farm

WENHAM RD

Priory
Farm

CHURCH LA

CHURCH LA

Great
Wenham

Wenham
Place

Sewage
Works

WENHAM LANE

Wenham
Hill

MILL HILL

WINDMILL
HL

MILL
CL

DAYS GREEN

DAYS ROAD

CEDARS LA

Driftway
End

THE DRIFT

AISTHORPE 1
LITTLE GULLS 2
COOMBERS 3
RED SLEEVE 4

Springhill

POUND LANE

THE STREET

PLOUGH

CATESBY

OLD RECTORY
WALK

SNOWCROFT

CL

WOOD

MANOR
CL

CAPEL

LETTICE RD

LITTLE GR

SAWYERS
CL

Capel St Mary
CE Prim Sch

BUSHEY

REMBROW RD

VINE
WALK

BOYLANDS

PO

ELM
CL

WHITE HORSE

PLAYFIELD

BARNFIELD

GARROSS

HOMEFIELD

LONG PERRY

LONG
PERRY

LONDON ROAD

THE OLD
PH

MOWLANDS

FRIARS

Liby

A12

3

38

Capelgrove

Mast

2

Capelgrove
Farm

CAPEL GR

Bush Farm

Great Gilberts
Farm

Dovefield
Farm

BLUEGATE LANE

Bluegate
Farm

Boynton
Hall

1

POUND
LA

A12

Boydland
Farm

Manor
House

OLD LONDON ROAD

Bradfield
Farm

37

07   A   B   08   C   D   09   E   F

E3
1 SCHOOL CL
2 CROTCHETS CL
3 PENNY MDW
4 PETER'S GR
5 WINDING PIECE
6 TOLL GATE RD
7 CHALKNERS CL
8 STOCKMERS END
9 SMITHERS CL

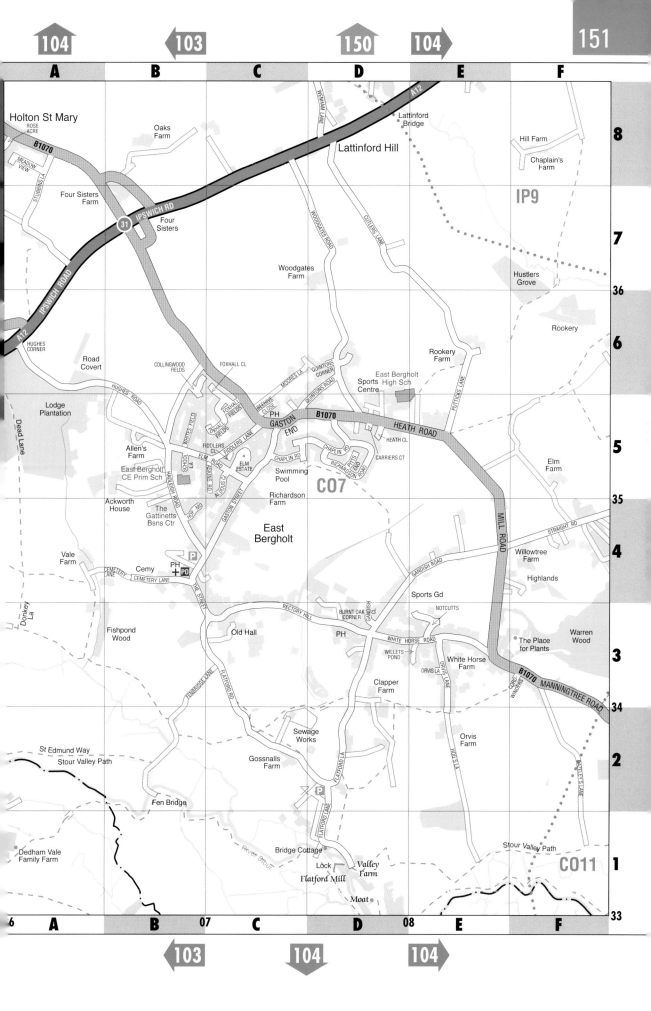

107
107
107

D5
1 KILN FIELD
2 CHILDERS FLD
3 FEATHERS FLD
4 REEDLAND WY
5 WINSTON CL
6 OTLEY CT

7 BREDFIELD CL
8 BRACKLEY CL
9 LARKHILL WY
10 EYNOLDS CT
11 WILLIAM BOOTH WY
12 GENERALS MEWS
13 ALDRINGHAM MEWS

14 SUDBOURNE RD
15 RENDLESHAM RD
16 MICKFIELD MEWS
17 WESTLETON WY
18 MELLIS CT
19 DARSHAM CL

E5
1 HALL FLD
2 GARDEN FLD
3 CROSSGATE FLD
4 BEACON FLD
5 BROOM FLD
6 HAMILTON ST

7 JAMES BODEN CL

	A	B	C	D	E	F

Great Street Farm
WOODLANDS AVE
MARINERS WAY
THURMANS LA
Egypt Wood
Hill House Farm
Gandlet Farm
Gulpher Business Park

Trimley St Mary
Trimley St Mary Prim Sch

60

CANDLET ROAD

Cowpasture Farm

1 LANGSTONS
2 THE KEMPSTERS
3 SPRITES END
4 EASTLAND CT

Trimley

LC

Chapman's Grove

Searsons Farm Bsns Units

Clickett Hill

BLOOMFIELD RD

Felixstowe Sch

Causton Jun Sch

1 LONGCROFT
2 GROSS ST

1 ST MARY'S CR
2 ROGERS CL
3 TAUNTON RD

Recreation Gd

Garden Wood

IP11

1 BARNFIELD
2 LONGFIELD

Walton

Maidstone Inf Sch

FELIXSTOWE

Christmasyards Wood

Trinity Distribution Park

Trinity Distribution Park

61

Superstore

Grange Com Prim Sch

Cemy

A14

Dock Gate 2

A154

WALTON AVENUE

TRINITY AVENUE A154

PORT OF FELIXSTOWE ROAD

1 CLONCURRY GDNS
2 NEWBOURNE GDNS
3 LARKSWAY

UNDERCLIFF RD W

B1082

Felixstowe L Ctr

GARRISON LANE

ORWELL ROAD

Container Park

62

Felixstowe Beach Holiday Park

Langer Park

Langer Prim Acad

Manning's Amusement Park

The Port of Felixstowe

1 SHOTLEY CL
2 HOLBROOK CR
3 PARSONAGE CL

SILVER BIRCH WLK 1
CHESTNUT CL 2
WILLOW RISE 3
LIMETREE AVE 4

Summit Bsns Pk

1 BEACH STATION RD
2 NACTON RD
3 PRETYMAN RD

Martello Tower

Jetty

Carr Rd Bsns Ctr

STONEGROVE RD

LC

LANGER ROAD

A154

CARR RD

27	A		B	28	C		D	29	E		F

107
107

C3
1 NAYLAND RD
2 ICKWORTH CT

C4
1 LIDGATE CT
2 WICKHAMBROOK CT
3 SUDBURY RD
4 EUSTON CT
5 KENTFORD RD
6 THURSTON CT
7 BOXFORD CT

D4
1 SHOTLEY CL
2 HOLBROOK CR
3 PARSONAGE CL

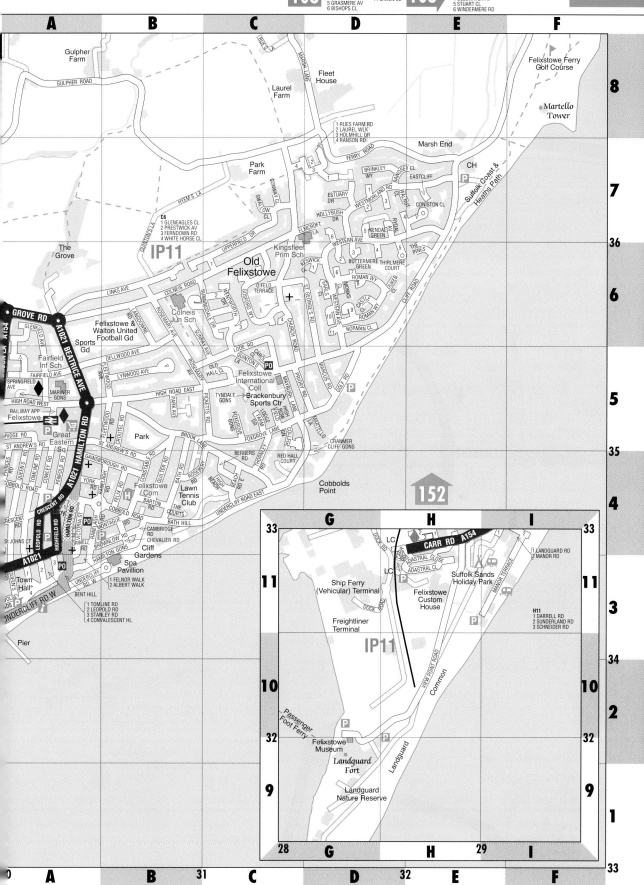

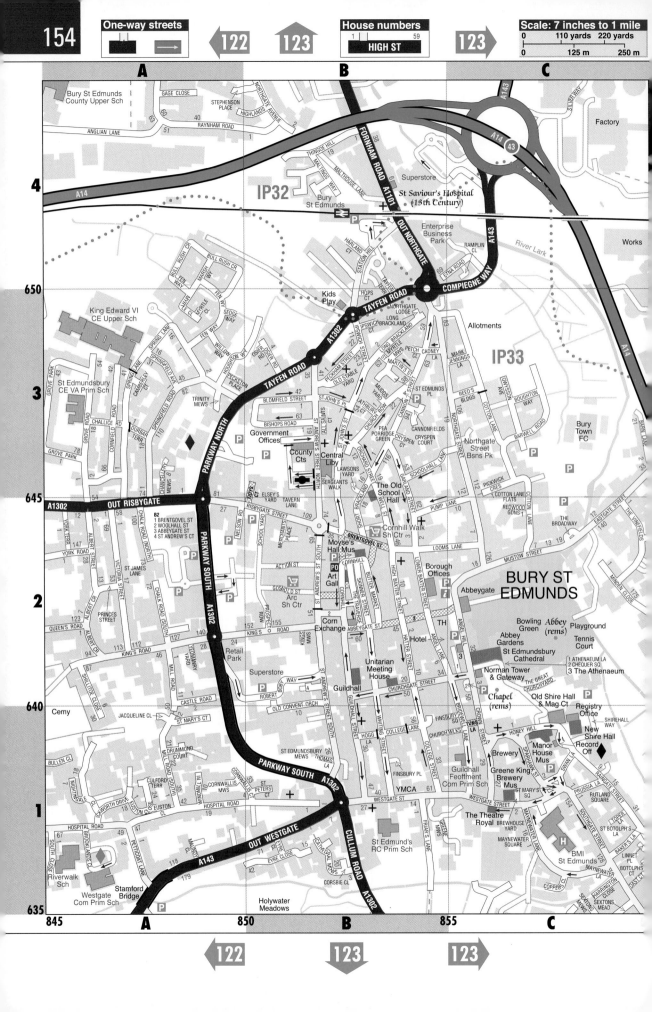

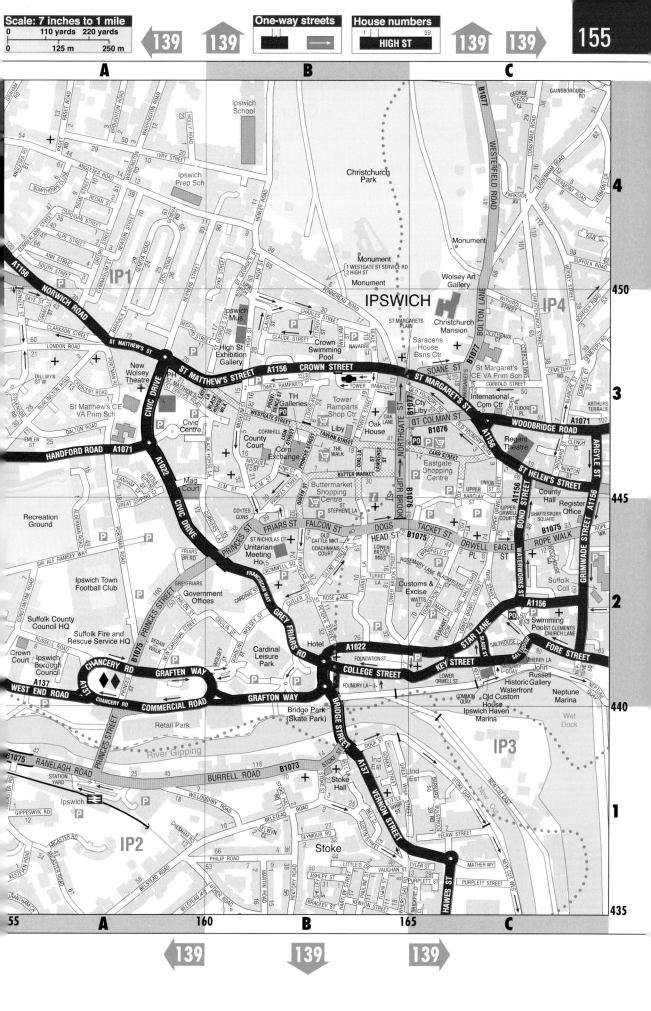

Index

Place name May be abbreviated on the map

Location number Present when a number indicates the place's position in a crowded area of mapping

Locality, town or village Shown when more than one place has the same name

Postcode district District for the indexed place

Page and grid square Page number and grid reference for the standard mapping

Church Rd 6 Beckenham BR2..........**53** C6

Cities, towns and villages are listed in CAPITAL LETTERS

Public and commercial buildings are highlighted in **magenta**   **Places of interest** are highlighted in blue with a star ★

Abbreviations used in the index

Acad	**Academy**	Comm	**Common**	Gd	**Ground**	L	**Leisure**	Prom	**Promenade**
App	**Approach**	Cott	**Cottage**	Gdn	**Garden**	La	**Lane**	Rd	**Road**
Arc	**Arcade**	Cres	**Crescent**	Gn	**Green**	Liby	**Library**	Recn	**Recreation**
Ave	**Avenue**	Cswy	**Causeway**	Gr	**Grove**	Mdw	**Meadow**	Ret	**Retail**
Bglw	**Bungalow**	Ct	**Court**	H	**Hall**	Meml	**Memorial**	Sh	**Shopping**
Bldg	**Building**	Ctr	**Centre**	Ho	**House**	Mkt	**Market**	Sq	**Square**
Bsns, Bus	**Business**	Ctry	**Country**	Hospl	**Hospital**	Mus	**Museum**	St	**Street**
Bvd	**Boulevard**	Cty	**County**	HQ	**Headquarters**	Orch	**Orchard**	Sta	**Station**
Cath	**Cathedral**	Dr	**Drive**	Hts	**Heights**	Pal	**Palace**	Terr	**Terrace**
Cir	**Circus**	Dro	**Drove**	Ind	**Industrial**	Par	**Parade**	TH	**Town Hall**
Cl	**Close**	Ed	**Education**	Inst	**Institute**	Pas	**Passage**	Univ	**University**
Cnr	**Corner**	Emb	**Embankment**	Int	**International**	Pk	**Park**	Wk, Wlk	**Walk**
Coll	**College**	Est	**Estate**	Intc	**Interchange**	Pl	**Place**	Wr	**Water**
Com	**Community**	Ex	**Exhibition**	Junc	**Junction**	Prec	**Precinct**	Yd	**Yard**

Index of towns, villages, streets, hospitals, industrial estates, railway stations, schools, shopping centres, universities and places of interest

100–All

100th Bomb Group Meml
Mus The★ IP21.... 21 D4
95th Bomb Group
Museum★ IP21 .... 38 D3

A

Abbey Cl
🔟 Burwell CB5........44 A5
🔟 Ixworth IP31......34 B1
Rendlesham IP12......85 D7
Abbeydale NR32 .... 114 E2
Abbey Farm La IP12...86 B4
Abbeyfields IP33 .. 123 C6
Abbey Fields IP14....66 D8
Abbeygate Sixth Form
Coll IP32............ 122 E7
Abbeygate St 3
IP33................154 B2
Abbey Gdns IP13......71 C2
Abbey Hill IP21........38 C7
Abbey La IP31......129 B8
Abbey Pl 14 CB7 ....29 A1
Abbey Rd
Capel Green IP12......86 B4
Earsham Street IP21 ...22 C1
Flixton NR35 ....7 E1
Flixton NR35..........23 F8
Leiston IP16 .... 129 C7
St Peter South Elmham
NR35 ....24 A7
Sibton IP17...........57 A8
Sudbury CO10....... 148 C7
Abbitts Place 12 CO10 77 A3
Abbot Cl IP33........ 122 D4
Abbot Rd IP30........ 122 D4
Abbotsbury Cl IP2 .. 139 A1
Abbotsbury Rd IP33. 122 D3
Abbots Cotts CB9 ...133 E2
Abbots Gate IP33 ...123 B3
Abbots Hall★ IP14.. 124 D5
Abbot's Hall Com Prim
Sch IP14........... 124 C5
Abbot's Hall Drift
CO10 ....78 E2
Abbot's Hall Rd IP14 124 D5
Abbots Wlk IP14.... 124 D5
Abbots Way IP22......36 B7
Abbott Cl CO10 ....91 F8

Abbott Rd CO12......106 F1
Abbotts Croft CB9... 133 D2
Abbotts Ct CB9 .... 133 C3
Abbotts Green Acad
IP32 .... 49 A3
Abbotts Meadow
Redlingfield IP23 ....38 C2
8 Woolpit IP30......50 D1
Abbotts Rd CB9......132 E7
Abbott Way IP9.....105 F8
Abdy Ave 5 CO12...106 F1
Abercorn Ct 2 CB9 .132 D4
Aberdeen Way IP4...136 B1
Aberfoyle Cl 1 IP4 .136 C1
Abingdon Cl IP2 ...139 A1
Abington Pl CB9 ...132 E7
Ablett Cl IP21........22 E2
Ablitts Meadow IP13..83 E6
Abrey Cl IP28........47 D5
Acacia Ave IP32......48 C5
Acacia Cl
Ipswich IP3 ....140 E1
11 Red Lodge IP28 ...30 C1
Acacia Rd CO7.......95 A1
Acer Gr IP8.........138 C1
Acer Rd IP12........85 D8
Acer Way 21 IP28 ...30 C1
Acheson Way 7
IP15...............130 E5
Acorn Cl
Aldringham IP16.... 129 D3
9 Ipswich IP8.......138 C2
Acorn Rise IP12 ....100 A8
Acorns The IP30......49 E3
Acorn Way IP5......98 B8
Acorn Way
9 Herringswell IP28...30 C1
15 Stowmarket IP14 ...67 A6
Acre Cl IP6.........83 A6
Acre Rd CB8........74 B8
Acres Wlk 8 IP28....30 C8
Action St IP33 .....154 B2
ACTON..............92 B7
Acton CE Prim Sch
CO10...............92 B7
Acton Cl
Bramford IP8 ....134 A2
Sudbury CO10.......148 D6
Acton Gdns 1 IP8 ..134 A2
Acton Gn 3 CO10 ...148 C5
Acton La
Acton CO10..........92 A6
Sudbury CO10.......148 D6
Airfield Rd
Bury St Edmunds IP32 ..49 A3

ACTON PLACE........92 B8
Acton Pl Ind Est CO10 92 A8
Acton Rd
Acton CO10..........92 C7
Bramford IP8 ....134 A2
Lowestoft NR33 ....115 B4
Adair Rd IP1........138 D8
Adams Cl
9 Haughley IP14.....51 C1
Woodbridge IP12 ...146 F8
Adam's La IP18.......43 C5
Adamson Rd IP18....119 B8
Adams Pl IP5........141 C7
Adastral Cl
Felixstowe IP11 ....153 H11
Newmarket CB8 ....120 E4
Adastral Pk IP5 .....98 B8
Adders La 5 IP26.....5 A3
Addington Rd IP11.. 152 C7
Addison Cl IP26.......4 F5
Addison Rd CO10 ...148 E7
Addison Way IP8 ...134 A8
Adeane Meadow
IP26................6 A8
Adelaide Cl 17 CB7...28 D4
Adelaide Rd IP4 ....140 D6
Adelaide St 1 CO12..106 F3
Admiral Rd 2 IP8 ..142 E8
Admirals' Acad 2
IP24 .... 16 C7
Admirals Wlk
11 Thorpeness IP16....73 F6
12 Woodbridge IP12 ..146 F7
Adnams Brewery★ 22
IP18 ....119 D5
Adrian Rd 6 NR32 ..113 D2
Adventure Island Play
Park★ NR33........ 114 F2
Africa Alive!★ NR33.. 11 A1
Agate Cl 2 IP1 .....134 D1
Aggas Acre IP23......37 A5
Ailmar Cl NR32 ....113 A5
Ailwin Rd IP32......123 E4
Ainger Rd 30 CO12 ..106 F1
Ains Ford Rd CO9 ...133 F1
Ainslie Rd IP1 .....139 A6
Airedale NR33 ......114 E2
Airey Cl
Lowestoft NR32 ....112 F5
Newton CO10........92 E3
Airey Houses IP13 ..137 D6
Airfield Rd

Airfield Rd continued
Fersfield NR16 ....19 E7
Tilbury Green CO9 ....89 F4
Airstation La IP21.....21 E6
Air Station Rd
NR34 ....26 F4
Aisthorpe IP9 ......150 D3
AKENHAM 134 F6
Akenham Cl IP1 ....134 F4
Akethorpe Way
NR32 ....113 A3
Alabaster Cl 8 IP7...149 E6
Alandale Dr 25 NR33 .11 C5
Alan Hutchinson Way
NR34 ....111 C5
Alan Phillips Way
CO10 ....148 B5
Alan Rd IP3.........139 F4
Alasdair Pl 9 IP6...134 C8
Alban Sq 2 IP12.....84 A1
Albany Rd 1 NR32 ..113 E2
Albany The IP4 .....139 E8
Albemarle Rd IP33.. 122 D4
Albemarle St 6
CO12...............107 B3
Alberta Cl IP5 .....141 A8
Albert Cres IP33 ....154 A2
Albert Pl IP13 ......126 C3
Albert Pye Com Sch The
NR34..............111 B4
Albert Rd IP13......126 C3
Albert Rolph Dr
IP27..............109 E4
Albert St IP33 .....154 A2
Albert Wlk IP11.....153 B3
Albion Hill IP4......139 F7
Albion Rd NR35 ....110 D3
Albion St
Saxmundham IP17 ...128 C3
1 Saxmundham IP17 128 C3
ALBURGH............7 A1
Alburgh with Denton
CE Prim Sch IP20 ...7 A1
Alconbury IP27......14 A2
ALDEBURGH 130 D4
Aldeburgh Cl CB9...132 C5
Aldeburgh Community
Hospl IP15........130 D4
Aldeburgh Gdns IP4 141 A6
Aldeburgh Lodge Gdns
IP15...............130 E5
Aldeburgh Mus★
IP15 .... 130 F4

Aldeburgh Prim Sch
IP15 .... 130 E3
Aldeburgh Rd
Friston IP17........72 F7
Leiston IP16 ......129 D4
Aldeburgh Rd
(Remembrance Rd)
IP16................73 F6
Aldecar La IP17......72 C7
Alde House Dr IP15 .130 E4
Alde La IP15........130 E4
Alder Carr Farm & Cyd
Craft Ctr★ IP6 ...125 E5
Alder Cl IP17.......72 C8
Alder Covert 6 IP24 .16 D6
Aldercroft Cl IP1 ...135 B3
Aldercroft Rd IP1 ...135 B3
Alde Rd CB9........132 E7
Alder Dr 2 NR33....114 C4
Aldergrove Cl IP19.. 118 A3
Alderlee IP2........142 F8
Alderman Rd IP1 ...155 A2
Aldershot Ave IP12 ..85 C3
ALDERTON...........99 E4
Alderton Cl CB9.....132 C8
Alderton Rd
Hollesley IP12......99 E6
Shottisham IP12......99 B6
Alder Way CO10..... 148 D6
Alde Valley Acad
IP16 ....129 E6
ALDHAM.............94 E8
Aldham Ct 1 CB9 ...132 C5
Aldham Gdns IP14 ..124 E4
Aldham Mill Hill IP7 149 E6
Aldham Rd IP7 .....149 E7
Aldhurst Farm Rd
IP16..............129 C8
Aldis Ave IP14 .....124 D4
Aldon Cl 14 CO12...106 E1
Aldous Cl CO7 .....151 C5
Aldous Corner IP19...24 D4
Aldous Ct 13 IP14 ...53 F2
Aldrich Way 6 IP22...20 C3
Aldridge La 2 IP28...48 B6
ALDRINGHAM 129 D3
Aldringham Mews 13
IP11...............152 D5
Aldringham Pk IP16. 129 D3
Aldringham Rd IP17 .129 B3
Aldwyck Way NR33. 114 F4
Aletha Farm Pl CO9 ..89 E3

Alexander Cl NR34 .. 111 C2
Alexander Dr
Finningham IP14 .....52 A8
8 Great Waldingfield
CO10 ....92 C6
Needham Market IP6 125 C5
Alexander Way
Risby IP28 ....47 E5
Scole IP21 ....21 A1
Alexandra Rd
Beccles NR34 .....111 B5
Felixstowe IP11 ....152 E6
Ipswich IP4 ....139 E6
Lowestoft NR32 ....113 D1
Sudbury CO10......148 E5
Alexandra St 8
CO12 ....107 B3
Alfred Corry Mus★
IP18 ....119 C2
Algar Dr CB8 ....59 F4
Algar Rd IP22........19 B8
Algars Farm La IP22 .20 D3
Alice Driver Rd 9
IP13................83 E5
Alice Parkins Cl 2
IP7................149 F7
Alicia Ct IP33 ......123 C3
Allenby Rd IP2.......138 F4
Allen Rd
Hadleigh IP7....... 149 E6
Lowestoft NR32 ... 112 D1
Alley Rd IP10........98 D2
Allfields 3 CO12.... 107 A1
Allington Cl IP4...... 139 F7
Allington Rd 7 IP19 118 A3
Allington-Smith Cl
NR32 ....112 E5
Allington Wlk CB9 .. 132 C6
Allotment La IP6......69 A1
All Saints IP27........63 E1
All Saints CE Prim Sch
IP29 ....63 E1
All Saints' CEVA Prim Sch
CB8............... 121 B3
All Saints CE VA Prim
Sch IP22 ....20 C8
All Saints' CE VA Prim
Sch
Harwich CO12...... 106 F2
Laxfield IP13.........40 A3
All Saints Cl
Gazeley CB8 ....46 C3
Wetheringsett IP14 ..53 A5

Column 1

All Saints Ct IP33 .....154 B3
All Saints Dr NR34... 111 C3
All Saints Gn 6
NR34 ....111 F4
All Saints Rd
Creeting St Mary
IP6 ....125 F8
Newmarket CB8 .....121 B3
All Saints' Rd
Ipswich IP1 ....139 A7
Lowestoft NR33 .....115 B4
ALL SAINTS SOUTH
ELMHAM 24 B5
All Saints Wlk IP28....30 B4
Allthorpe Rd 12 IP20 ..22 D6
ALLWOOD GREEN......36 A2
Alma Cl 3 IP4......136 A1
Alma Pl IP17 ....128 D3
Alma Rd NR32 ......113 C1
Almond Dr IP28.......30 C2
Almond Gr IP24......16 A4
Almondhayes IP2....139 B3
Almoners Field IP33 .123 B3
Almshouse Rd IP30 ..49 C1
Alnesbourn Cres
1 Gainsborough
IP2 ....144 D8
Ipswich IP3 ....144 D7
Alnesbourne Priory
IP10..............144 C6
Alpe St IP1 ....155 B4
Alpha Bsns Pk IP1..134 D3
Alphamstone Rd
CO8 ....101 A6
ALPHETON 78 A5
Alston Cl CO10......92 D3
Alston Rd IP3.......139 F4
Altitude Bsns Pk IP3 140 C1
Alton Hall La IP9....105 C6
Alton Wr Sports Ctr
IP9 ....105 C6
Alvis Cl IP32........123 F5
Alvis Wlk IP1 ....134 C1
Alycidon Mws CB8 ..120 E2
Amber Dr 21 NR33 ....11 B1
Amberfield Dr IP10 ..145 C6
Amberley Cl IP19 ....42 F6
Amberley Ct 3
NR32 ....112 F4
Amber Mus The★
IP18 ....119 D5
Ambleside Gdns 11
NR32 ....113 A4
America Hill IP6......83 A6
Amey Cl CB9........132 F8
Amis Cl IP14........124 A8
Amis Ct IP27........109 D4
Ammonite Dr IP6....125 E3
Amos Hill CO10 ......91 D1
AMPTON.............33 A2
Ampton Rd IP31.....33 B3
Amy Johnson Ct 6
IP28..............116 B5
Ancaster Rd IP2 ....155 A1
Ancells Cl 4 IP29....63 D1
Anchor End 2 CO11. 105 A2
Anchor La
Burwell CB5........44 A6
Dedham CO7......104 A2
Lakenheath IP27 ...109 C6
1 Mistley CO11....105 A2
Anchor St
Ipswich IP3 ....139 E4
Lowestoft NR33 ....115 C6
Anchor Way NR33...114 B4
Ancient House Museum
of Thetford Life★
IP24 ....16 C6
Anderson Cl IP6 ....125 C5
Anderson's Way 8
IP12..............146 E4
Anderson Wlk IP32 .122 D7
Andrew Burtt's Cl
IP13..............126 B3
Andrew Cl
Felixstowe IP11 ....152 E3
Leiston IP16 ......129 D5
Andrew Johnston Way
IP19..............118 B3
Andrew Rd CB8.....120 E5
Andrews Cl 9 IP14...53 F2
Andrews Wlk IP32 ..122 D8
Andrew Way NR33 ..114 D6
Andros Cl IP3.......144 A7
Angela Cl IP12......84 A1
Angelgate Espl 4
CO12 ....107 C2
Angel Hill
Bury St Edmunds
IP33 ....154 C2
Stonham Earl IP14...67 F5
Angel La
Blythburgh IP19 .....42 F6
Bury St Edmunds IP33 154 B2
Glemsford CO10......77 A2
Ipswich IP4 ....155 C2
2 Woodbridge IP12..147 A5
Angel Link IP19.....118 B3
Angel Meadows 13
CO10 ....77 A2
Angel Pl IP8........134 A2
Angel Rd IP8 ....134 A2
Angel St IP7........149 D6
Angerstein Cl IP27....5 E4
Anglesea Rd IP1 ....155 A3
Anglian La IP32.....154 A4
Anglian Pl CB9......132 B5

Column 2

Anglian Way NR31 .....3 B7
Anglia Parkway N
IP1...............134 D4
Anglia Parkway S
IP1...............134 D3
Anglia Ret Pk IP1..134 D4
Anglo Saxon Way IP30 49 B3
Angus Cl IP4........136 B1
Animal Health Trust
Visitor Ctr★ CB8 ...45 F5
Anita Cl E IP2......138 E5
Anita Cl W IP2......138 E5
Anna Gurney Cl IP24..16 C7
Anna Hayes Ct IP15 .141 F8
Annandale Dr NR34 . 111 C4
Ann Beaumont Way
IP7...............149 C7
Annbrook Rd IP2....138 E1
Ann Coles Cl CB8...28 E3
Annes Cl 3 CB8....120 B8
Anne St IP11 ....152 F2
Anni Healey Cl IP12..146 F6
ANNIS HILL.........110 E3
Annis Hill IP6......110 E3
Annis Hill La 2
NR35..............110 D3
Annis Hill Rd NR35..110 D3
Annison Ct NR33....115 B5
Ann St IP1..........155 A4
Ann Strutt Cl 3 IP7..149 F7
Ann Suckling Rd
CB9 ....132 E8
Ansell Cl IP7.......149 D6
Anselm Ave 9 IP32..48 C5
Anson Rd 7 IP5......98 A8
Anson Way NR34.....10 A3
Antonia Cl IP9......133 C5
Antrim Rd IP1 ......134 D1
Anvil Acre IP14......80 C8
Anvil Way CB8.......46 A5
Anvil Way IP14......124 C3
Anzani Ave IP11 ....152 C4
Apple Acre Rd CB9..132 A7
Appleby Cl IP19.....138 C1
Apple Cl 28 IP27....13 F2
Appledore Dr NR33 .114 D4
Appledown Dr IP30 .123 E7
Applegate Mews
CO10 ....148 E5
Apple Gr IP14.......51 A2
Apple Tree Cl IP13..115 B6
Appletree Gr 2 CB5..44 A6
Appletree La 3 IP22..20 C3
Apple Tree Mws 11
CO8 ....101 C5
Applewood Cl NR33 .114 A3
Approach Cotts CB9.132 B8
APSEY GREEN......126 A3
Aragon Ct 8 CO10....90 A7
Aragon Rd CB9.....132 B4
Arbor Cl CB5........44 A7
Arbor La NR33......115 A2
Arcade St IP1.......155 B3
Archangel Gdns IP2..138 E4
Archbishop Sancroft
High Sch IP20......22 C6
Archers' Ave 3 IP26...4 D5
Archers Cl CB7......28 D3
Archers Place IP33 .123 B3
Arc Sh Ctr IP33....154 B2
Arderne Cl 8 CO12..106 F1
Ardleigh Heath...103 F1
Ardleigh Rd CO7...103 E2
Argent Place CB8...121 A6
Arger Fen CO8......101 E5
Arger Fen Nature
Reserve★ CO10...101 F6
Argyle St IP4........155 C3
Argyll Ct 7 CB9.....132 D5
Ark Cl 7 NR33.......11 B1
Arkle Ct IP5........141 D7
Arkwright Rd IP2 ...138 E6
Arlington Way IP24...16 C5
Arms La CB9........133 F7
Armstrong Cl
Hundon CO9........90 A1
Newmarket CB8 ....121 B3
Armstrong Way
Great Yeldham CO9...90 A1
12 Thetford IP24 ...16 D7
Arnhem Ct NR32....113 C4
Arnhem Rd IP16.....129 D5
Arnold Cl IP1.......134 F3
Arnold St 3 NR33...113 E1
Arras Rd IP33.......122 D5
Arrendene Rd IP8....28 D3
Arrowhead Dr IP27 .109 C7
Artesian Cl CO10....78 C3
Arthurs Terr IP4....155 C3
Arthurs Way CB7....29 A2
Artillery Dr 7 CO12 .106 E1
Artillery Way 11
NR32 ....113 E2
Artiss Cl IP7........79 F4
Arundel Cl 4 IP32...123 C7
Arundel Way
Ipswich IP3 ....140 E3
2 Lowestoft NR33..114 D4
Arwela Rd IP11.....152 E5
Ascot Cl 2 CB8......120 B8
Ascot Dr
Felixstowe IP11 ....152 E6

Column 3

Ascot Dr continued
Ipswich IP3 ....140 B3
ASH ABBEY 127 F3
Ash Ave 1 IP7......80 D6
ASHBOCKING........69 A1
Ashbocking Rd
Ashbocking IP6......69 A2
Coddenham IP6......68 D2
Henley IP6 ....82 E6
Swilland IP6 ....82 B8
Ashbourne Ct CB8 ..121 B3
Ashburnham Rd IP6 125 C4
Ashburnham Way
NR33 ....114 D4
Ashby Rd NR32 .....113 C1
Ash Cl
Bacton IP14........51 F6
10 Lakenheath IP27 ..13 F2
7 Lowestoft NR33...114 D5
Thetford IP24......16 A4
Warren Heath IP3 ..140 F1
Woodbridge IP12 ..146 F4
ASH CORNER 127 F7
Ashcroft La IP1.....134 F1
Ashcroft Rd IP1....135 A1
Ash Ct 22 IP28......30 C1
Ashdale Dr NR34 ....111 E4
Ashdale Gdns IP5...141 D8
Ashdale Pk IP27.....14 E8
Ashdown Way IP3 ..140 D3
Ash Dr IP23.........117 D3
Ashen Cl CO10......89 E5
Ashen Hill CO10......89 E5
Ashen La CO10......89 E6
Ashen Rd
Ashen CO10 ....89 F5
Ashen CO10 ....90 A7
Ridgewell CO9......89 D4
Ashe Rd
Marlesford IP13.....71 C4
Tunstall IP12.......71 F2
Ashe Row IP13......71 C2
Ashes Fm La IP22....19 A6
Ashes The IP14......54 D1
ASHFIELD...........54 D2
Ashfield Cres NR33..114 F7
ASHFIELD CUM
THORPE..........54 C1
Ashfield Dr IP16 ...129 C5
Ashfield Gdns
17 Isleham CB7.....29 C5
Norton Little Green
IP31 ....50 D5
ASHFIELD GREEN
Stradbroke 39 D4
Wickhambrook 62 A2
Wickhambrook CB8 ..61 F2
Ashfield Hill IP31....50 F6
Ashfield Rd
Elmswell IP30......50 F3
Norton IP31.......50 C4
Norton Little Green
IP31 ....50 E5
Peats Corner IP14...69 B8
Wetherden IP14....51 A2
Ashford Cl NR34.....9 B6
Ashfords Cl IP17....128 B4
Ash Gd Cl
3 Brantham CO11...104 E4
10 Felixstowe IP11..107 D8
Ash Gr
17 Burwell CB5....44 A5
Capel St Mary IP9...150 E3
Haverhill CB9......132 C7
4 Sudbury CO10...92 B3
Ash La IP30.........50 B2
Ashlea Cl CB9......132 F4
Ashlea Rd CB9.....132 F4
ASHLEY..............60 F8
Ashley Cl IP30......50 B3
5 Risby IP28.......47 E5
Woodbridge IP12 ..147 A4
Ashley Downs NR32. 113 C3
Ashley Heath CB8....45 D2
Ashley Rd
Cheveley CB8.......60 E8
Harwich CO12......107 A2
Newmarket CB8 ....121 B2
Ashley Sch Acad The
NR32 ....113 C4
Ashley St 7 IP7.....155 B1
Ashman's Rd NR34..111 A4
Ashmere Gr IP4.....139 F6
Ashmere Rise CO10 .148 E6
Ashness Cl 2 NR32 .113 A4
Ash Plough IP21.....39 A5
Ash Rd
Burgate IP22.......36 F6
Campsey Ash IP12...71 C1
Hacheston IP13 ....127 F7
Onehouse IP14.....66 C6
Rendlesham IP12....85 C7
Ash Rise 8 CO6.....102 C5
Ash St 4 CO10......93 C3
ASH STREET.........80 A1
Ashton Cl
Ipswich IP2 ....138 C2
11 Rendlesham IP12 .85 D8
Ashton Rd IP23.....117 C3
Ash Tree Cl
Beccles NR34 ......9 F4
Felixstowe IP11 ....152 E2
7 Fessingfield IP21...39 D8
9 Occold IP23......37 F1
Ashtree Gdns NR33 .114 D3
Ashurst Pl 5 NR33...115 B4
Ashwell Ave IP13 ...126 D2

Column 4

Ashwell Rd IP33 .....122 D4
Ash Wlk CB8.......75 C7
Askins Rd CO7 .....151 C5
Aspal Cl 5 IP28......30 B8
Aspal Close Nature
Reserve★ IP28......30 B7
Aspal Hall Rd IP28 ..30 B8
ASPALL..............53 C6
Aspall Rd IP14......30 B8
Aspall Rd 14 IP14....53 F3
Aspall Pk IP28......30 B8
Aspal Pl 11 IP28.....30 B8
Aspel Est IP28......13 D1
Aspen Cl
Claydon IP6.......134 D8
Great Barton IP31...49 B6
Haverhill CB9......132 C7
4 Ipswich IP6......81 F5
3 Woodbridge IP12 .147 B6
Aspen Coppice 6
NR32 ....112 F5
Aspen Ct IP12......85 D8
Aspen Way
24 Herringswell IP28..46 A8
48 Red Lodge IP28...30 C1
48 Red Lodge IP28...30 C1
Soham CB7 ....28 C5
Aspey Green IP31...126 A3
Aspinall Cl 4 NR33 .114 F4
ASSINGTON..........92 F1
ASSINGTON GREEN ..76 B6
Assington La CO6....93 A1
Assington Rd
Bures Green CO8...101 C8
Newton CO10......92 D3
Astbury Rd 6 NR32 .113 B5
Aster Cl 7 IP28......45 F8
Aster Rd IP2........138 E4
Aston Cl IP1........134 C1
Ataka Rd IP11.......152 F6
ATHELINGTON.......38 E2
Athelington Rd IP21 ..38 E2
Athenaeum La IP33 .154 C2
Athenaeum The★
IP33 ....154 C2
Atherton Rd IP2 ....138 D2
Atterton Rd CB9 ....132 B7
ATTLETON GREEN....61 D1
Aubretia Cl 3 NR33..114 F7
Auction Yd 10 IP14...51 C1
Audley Cl IP22......20 E6
AUDLEY END
Burston and
Shimpling 20 E5
Lawshall 77 D8
Audley End IP21.....20 F5
Audley Gr IP4.......140 E7
Augusta Cl IP10.....144 E7
Augustus Cl CB9 ....133 B5
Aureole Wlk CB8....120 E8
Austin Cl IP31.......50 E7
Austin St IP2........155 B1
Aveley Hall La CO10 ..93 A2
Aveley La IP29......77 D6
Aveling Way NR33 ..114 B4
Avenue App IP32 ...123 A8
Avenue Rd IP27.....109 E4
Avenue The
Brome & Oakley
IP23..............117 E8
3 Burwell CB5.....44 B6
Copdock & Washbrook
IP8 ....95 F4
Felixstowe IP11 ....152 B7
Great Barton IP31...123 F8
Halesworth IP19 ...118 B5
Ipswich IP1 ....135 C1
4 Kessingland NR33...11 B1
Lowestoft NR33 ....115 B5
Newmarket CB8 ....121 A3
Risby IP28.........47 E5
5 Risby IP28.......47 E5
Ufford IP13........84 F7
Woodbridge IP12 ..147 A4
Aves Cl CB7........29 C5
Avocet Cl NR33 ....114 D5
Avocet Gdns 9 IP14 .124 F6
Avocet Gr 12 CB7....28 D5
Avocet La 28 IP5....98 A8
Avocet Mews 13
IP12..............85 D8
Avondale Rd
Ipswich IP3 ....140 A2
Lowestoft NR32 ....113 C1
Aylmer Cl IP28......47 D5
Aylward Cl IP7......149 E4
Ayr Rd IP4.........136 B1

Column 5 (B)

B

Babb's La IP14......52 F2
BABEL GREEN.......75 D3
Babergh Cl 9 CO10..92 B7
Babington Dr IP19 ..118 B2
Baby La IP30........65 D4
Back Hamlet IP3....139 E5
Back Heywood Rd
IP22..............20 D7
Back Hill IP9.......105 F6
Back Hills IP22......36 A7
Back La
Badwell Ash IP31....50 F8
Baylham IP6........81 D6
Boyland Common IP22 ..20 B7
Burrough Green CB8...59 F2
Claydon IP6.......134 C8
Conyers Green IP31...49 B8

Column 6

Back La continued
Copdock & Washbrook
IP8 ....95 F5
Diss IP22.........20 D7
Falkenham IP10 ....98 F1
Felixstowe IP11 ....152 F5
Fritton NR31.......2 C8
Harwich CO12......106 D1
Kettlebaston IP7....79 C5
Little Blakenham IP8 ..81 F2
Long Melford CO10...91 E7
Lound NR32 ....2 F6
Mendlesham Green
IP14..............52 C1
Monks Eleigh IP7...79 C2
St Mary, South Elmham
otherwise Homersfield
IP20..............23 C8
Scole IP21.........21 A5
Shimpling IP21.....21 A6
Smallworth IP22....18 D4
Snape IP17........72 C6
Tattingstone IP9 ...105 B7
Wicken CB7 ....28 A1
Wrentham NR34....27 A6
Back Of Market Pl 2
IP17..............128 D3
Back Rd
Brockdish IP21.....21 A4
Burstall IP8........95 A7
Eastbridge IP16....58 D5
Middleton IP17.....58 B6
Rattlesden IP30....65 E6
Trimley St Martin IP10 .98 D2
Wenhaston with Mells
Hamlet IP19.......42 C6
Back St
Garboldisham IP22...18 D5
Gislingham IP23....36 B1
Lakenheath IP27 ...109 D6
BACK STREET.......61 E5
Bacon Rd 7 IP6.....82 B5
Bacon's Gn Rd IP19 .25 D3
Bacons Green CO7..103 F8
BACTON............51 E6
Bacton Com Prim Sch
IP14..............51 F6
BACTON GREEN....51 E4
Bacton Rd IP11.....152 F3
Baden Powell Wlk
IP5...............141 E7
Bader Cl 3 IP12.....140 C2
Bader Ct 26 IP5.....98 A8
Badger Cl IP6.......125 F3
Badgers Bank IP2...138 E1
Badger Sett CI IP7 ..150 D4
Badgers Gr CO6....102 D1
Badger's Holt 10
NR33 ....115 B5
Badgerwood Cl
NR33 ....115 B5
Badger Wood La
BADINGHAM........56 A6
Badingham IP13.....56 A4
Capon's Green IP13 ..55 F6
Framlingham IP13 ..126 D4
Framlingham IP13 ..126 E5
Badley Hill IP6.....125 D8
Badley La IP14......67 A2
Badley Rd CO10....92 A3
Badleys Cl 6 CO10...92 C6
Badley Wlk IP6.....125 A4
Badlingham Rd CB7 ..46 E8
Badshah Ave 4 IP3 .140 E3
BADWELL ASH.......50 F8
BADWELL GREEN....51 B8
Badwell Rd
Walsham le Willows
IP31..............35 B1
Wyverstone IP14....51 C6
Bagsham La IP28....30 A6
Bahram Cl CB8.....120 E4
Bailey Ave IP5......141 E7
Bailey Cl
Haverhill CB9......133 B5
Ipswich IP2 ....138 E6
Bailey La CO10......90 B8
Baileypool La IP31...49 F8
Baileypool Rd IP31...49 F7
Baines Coney CB9...132 A7
Baines Way IP13 ...126 D2
Baird Cl IP2........138 F7
Baird Gr IP5........141 B6
Bakehouse Hill CB8 ..59 F4
Baker Dr 4 CB5......44 B6
Baker Mws 1 IP17...128 D3
Baker Rd 2 IP4......107 A4
Baker's Cnr IP14....80 E6
Bakers Cres 2 IP1...134 E3
Baker's Hill IP18....58 C4
Bakers La
Ditchingham NR35...110 B8
Hightown Green IP30 ..65 D3
Orford IP12........131 C2
Wincton IP14.......68 E8
1 Woodbridge IP12..147 A4
Baker's La
Bury St Edmunds
IP33 ....154 C1
Thorndon IP23.....53 C6
Westleton IP17......58 C8
Bakers La S IP12....131 C2
Bakers Mill 10 IP30..50 E2
Baker's Rd CO10.....90 D5

Column 7

All – Bar 157

Bakers Row CB8 ....121 A4
Baker's Score 1 NR32 .3 D4
Bakers Way 1 IP28...30 F2
Balaton Pl CB8......121 A6
Baldry Cl IP8........138 C1
Baldrys Wlk NR35...110 B7
Baldwin Dr 3 IP32 ..122 E8
Baldwin Rd IP14....124 C4
Baldwin Way IP3 ...117 C5
Ballast Wharf Wlk 6
IP3...............139 E4
Ballater Cl IP1......134 E4
BALLINGDON........148 B4
Ballingdon Hill IP28 148 A3
Ballingdon Hill Ind Est
CO10..............148 A4
Ballingdon St CO10..148 A4
Balliol Cl IP12......146 D3
Ball's Chace CO6....101 C1
Balls Hill IP7........79 D5
Ball's Way IP14......67 D6
Ballygate NR34 .....111 A5
Balmoral Cl IP2.....138 F1
Balmoral Dr 9 CB9 .132 C6
Balsham Rd CB8.....59 D2
Balton Way 7 CO12 .106 F1
Bancroft Drove CB7...28 D6
Bancroft La CB7.....28 D5
Bangor Rd IP27......13 F2
Banham Mws 16 CB9 .74 A1
Banham Rd NR34 ...111 C2
Banham's La CB9.....7 B6
Banhams Yard 2
IP29..............77 B7
Bank Alley 8 IP18 ..119 D5
Bank Bldgs 14 CO10 .148 C5
Bank Mws IP4......26 F6
Bank Rd IP4........139 E6
Banks Cl IP7.......149 E5
Banks' La IP19......24 C3
Banks Wlk IP33.....123 C1
Bannocks La
Cransford IP13.....56 B3
Cransford IP13.....56 B4
Banstockfield CB9 ..88 D4
Banters La NR34 .....8 F2
Bantoft Terr IP3 ...140 C2
Banyard Cl 4 IP5...141 D7
BANYARD'S GREEN...40 C4
Barbara Stradbroke Ave
CB8 ....120 D1
Barber Cl 3 NR33...11 B1
Barbers La CB8......61 F5
Barber's La NR35.....7 B6
Barber'S La IP31....50 D8
Barbrook Green
IP18..............119 B8
Barcham Rd CB7....28 C7
Bar Cl 24 IP18......49 E4
Bardolph Rd NR35..110 B3
BARDWELL..........34 C4
Bardwell CE VC Prim Sch
IP31 ....34 C5
Bardwell Rd IP31....33 F5
Bardwell Windmill★
IP31..............34 B4
Bargate La
Beck Row, Holywell Row &
Kenny Hill IP28.....29 F5
Dedham CO7......104 A2
Bargate Rd IP28.....30 A6
BARHAM............82 C6
Barham Picnic Site
Visitor Ctr★ IP6...82 A6
Barhams Way IP13 .127 C7
Barker Cl
Ipswich IP2 ....138 D5
6 Manningtree CO11 104 D2
3 Steeple Bumpstead
CB9..............88 D3
Barker Rd CO10.....148 C8
Barkers Field Cl 1
IP30..............65 D8
BARKING...........125 A1
Barking Rd
Barking IP6........125 A1
Willisham IP8......81 A5
BARKING TYE........81 A7
Barkis Meadow NR32 ..3 A4
Barkways 3 CB5.....44 B5
Barley Cl
2 Newmarket CB8 ..121 B4
Thorney Green IP14..67 A7
Barleycorn Way 16
IP28..............30 A8
Barleyfields 14 IP31 .49 E4
BARLEY GREEN
39 C5
Ashfield Green IP21...39 D4
Barley Lands IP15...130 E5
Barley Meadow 5
IP19..............118 A3
Barley Rise 3 IP1 ...134 E3
Barley Way NR33....114 F2
Barlings CT CB8....121 A4
Barnaby Gn IP18...119 C5
BARNABY GREEN....26 C2
BARNARDISTON......75 B3
Barnardiston Hall Prep
Sch CB9 ....75 A5
Barnardiston Rd CB9..75 C4
Barnard Sq IP3.....155 C1
Barnards Way NR32 .113 B1

BARNBY 10 B5
Barnby Cl 9 CB9. . . . 132 A6
Barnby & N Cove Prim
  Sch NR34. . . . . 10 C4
Barnby & North Cove
  Community Prim Sch
  NR34. . . . . 10 C4
Barn Cl
  2 Hopton on Sea
    NR31. . . . . .3 C7
  Lowestoft NR33 . . . . . 114 D5
  Southwold IP18 . . . . . .119 B8
  Swingleton Green IP7. . .79 C2
Barnes Cl
  Brandon IP27. . . . . .14 E8
  3 Hadleigh IP7 . . . . 149 E6
Barnfield
  Capel St Mary IP9. . . . .150 F3
  Felixstowe IP11 . . . . . 152 D6
  26 Manningtree CO11 . .104 E2
Barn Field 2 IP29 . . . . .62 C6
BARNHAM. 16 C2
Barnham CE Prim Sch
  IP24. . . . . .16 B1
Barnham Pl IP5. . . . . .140 F6
Barnham Rd
  Barnham IP24. . . . . . . .16 E2
  Elveden IP24 . . . . .15 D2
BARNINGHAM. 34 F7
Barningham CE VC Prim
  Sch IP31. . . . . .34 F7
Barningham Rd IP31. . .34 E5
Barn La
  Bury St Edmunds
    IP33. . . . . 154 C3
  Preston St Mary CO10 . .79 A6
Barn Meadow IP29. . . . .77 F7
Barn Owl Cl 21 NR31. . . .3 B6
Barn St 12 CO10. . . . . . .78 D4
Barons Cl
  9 Felixstowe IP11. . . .153 D6
  Halesworth IP19 . . . . .118 A2
Barons Ct 17 CB9 . . . . 132 C5
Baronsdale Cl IP1 . . . .135 B1
Barons Meadow
  IP12. . . . . .131 B3
Barons Rd IP33 . . . . . 123 A2
Baron Way CO9 . . . . . . .89 F1
Barrack La
  Harwich CO12. . . . . . . 107 C2
  Ipswich IP1 . . . . 155 A3
  Ufford IP13. . . . . .84 F7
Barrack Sq IP5 . . . . . . .98 A8
Barracks Rd CO10. . . . .101 F8
Barr Dr IP27 . . . . 109 D7
Barrell's Rd IP31. . . . . .49 F3
Barrett's La IP6. . . . . . 125 C4
Barric La IP23 . . . . . . .37 F1
BARROW. 47 A2
Barrow CE VC Prim Sch
  IP29 . . . . 47 A3
Barrow Hill
  Acton CO10. . . . . .92 B8
  Barrow CO29. . . . . .47 A2
Barrow Rd
  Bird's End IP29. . . . . . .62 B8
  Denham IP29 . . . . .46 F1
  Little Saxham IP29. . . . .47 D2
Barrow's Cnr IP24. . . . .32 C8
Barry Lynham Dr
  CB8. . . . . .121 B2
Barsey Cl CB9. . . . . . . 132 A7
BARSHAM. 9 A4
Bartholomew Gn
  IP18. . . . . 119 D5
Bartholomew's La
  IP19. . . . . .42 B6
Bartholomew St IP4 . . .139 F6
Bartlet Hospl IP11. . . .153 C4
Bartlow Pl CB9 . . . . . .132 F7
Barton Bottom IP31. . . .48 E7
Barton Cl 3 IP2 . . . . .138 E2
Barton Crossing IP30 .49 C3
Barton Dr CB9 . . . . . .133 F8
Barton Gr CB9 . . . . . .133 F8
Barton Hamlet IP31. . . .49 C6
Barton Hill IP31. . . . . . .48 D5
BARTON MILLS 116 D2
Barton Rd
  Bury St Edmunds
    IP32. . . . . 123 D6
  Conyers Green IP31. . . .49 B8
  Felixstowe IP11 . . . . . 153 B4
  Great Livermere IP31. . .33 D1
  Thurston IP31. . . . . . . .49 D4
  Woodbridge IP12. . . . .146 F7
Bartons Pl CB8. . . . . . 120 E5
Bartram Cl IP31. . . . . . .49 D7
Bartrum La 7 IP5 . . . . 141 D7
Bartrums Mews 8
  IP22. . . . . .20 D2
Barway Rd CB7 . . . . . . .28 A6
Barwell Rd IP33 . . . . . 154 C3
Barwick Ave IP32. . . . . .48 C5
Base Bsns Pk IP12. . . . .85 E8
BASE GREEN. 51 B2
Base Green Rd IP14. . . .51 B1
Basepoint Bsns Ctr
  IP3 . . . . .145 A2
Basil Brown Cl 1
  IP22. . . . . .36 A6
Bassingbourn 4 IP27 13 F2
Bastings Hall Rd IP14 .69 C4
Bates La IP22. . . . . . . .19 D6
Bath Ct CB9 . . . . 132 D4

Bath Hill IP11. . . . . . .153 B4
Bath Hills Rd NR35. . . . .7 E4
Bath Rd IP11 . . . . .153 B4
BATH SIDE. 107 B3
Bath St IP2. . . . . 139 D3
Battery Gn 7 NR32. . . .113 E1
Battery Gn Rd 5
  NR32. . . . . .113 E1
Battery La 10 IP9 . . . . 107 A4
BATTISFORD. 66 F1
Battisford Rd
  Barking IP6. . . . . 125 A1
  Wattisham IP7 . . . . . . .80 A8
BATTISFORD TYE 66 C1
Battlesea Green 39 A6
Battlesea Green Cl
  Battlesea Green IP21. . .39 A6
  Battlesea Green IP21. . .39 A6
Battlesea Hill IP21 . . . .39 A6
Battles La IP5 . . . . 141 D7
BATTLIES GREEN 49 C3
BAWDSEY. 99 E3
Bawdsey CE Prim Sch
  IP12. . . . . .99 E2
Bawdsey Cl IP11. . . . . 153 D7
Bawdsey Manor
  Workshops★ IP12 . . .108 D8
Bawdsey Radar Sta★
  IP12. . . . . .99 E1
Bayberry Cl 34 IP28. . . .30 C1
Bayfield Dr H CB5 . . . .44 B5
BAYLHAM. 81 E6
Baylham House Rare
  Breeds Farm★ IP6 . .81 F7
Baynard's La IP22. . . . . .20 A3
Bay Rd 11 CO12 . . . . . . 107 B2
Bayswater Cl 4 IP1. . .138 F7
BAYTHORNE END 89 C5
Baytree Way IP9 . . . . . 105 D5
Beachams La CO6. . . . 102 D7
Beach Farm Rd 14
  IP16. . . . . .73 F6
Beach La
  Alderton IP12. . . . . .99 E4
  Bawdsey IP12. . . . . .99 F3
Beach Mews 6
  NR32. . . . . .115 D8
Beach Rd
  Covehithe NR34 . . . . . .27 A4
  Dunwich IP17. . . . . .43 B1
  1 Harwich CO12. . . . . 107 B1
  Hopton on Sea NR31. . . .3 C6
  Kessingland NR33 . . . . .27 C8
  Lowestoft NR32. . . . . 115 D8
Beach Rd E IP11 . . . . . 153 C4
Beach Rd W IP11 . . . . .152 F2
Beach Sta Rd IP11 . . . .152 E1
Beacon Field 4
  IP11. . . . . 152 E5
BEACON HILL. 137 F3
Beacon Hill Ave
  CO12 . . . . 107 C2
Beacon Hill La IP16 . . .73 F7
Beacon La IP13. . . . . . .137 F3
Beacon Rally Karts★
  IP5 . . . . 84 A2
Beaconsfield Cl
  Halesworth IP19 . . . . .118 A3
  Isleham CB7. . . . . .29 B5
  11 Lakenheath IP27 . . .13 F2
  Sproughton IP8 . . . . . .138 A6
Beaconsfield Ct 9
  CB9 . . . . .132 D5
Beaconsfield Rd
  Aldeburgh IP15 . . . . . .130 B3
  Ipswich IP1 . . . . 138 F7
  21 Kessingland NR33 . .11 C1
  Lowestoft NR33 . . . . . 115 C6
  Sudbury CO10. . . . . . .148 C6
  3 Woodbridge IP12 . . . 147 A8
Beadon Way IP12. . . . .147 A8
Beaker Pl 13 IP30. . . . . .50 D1
Beale Cl 12 IP32. . . . . . .49 A3
Beale Rd 16 IP29. . . . . .47 A2
Beales Dr IP30. . . . . . .79 B8
Bealings La IP13. . . . . .137 F8
Bealings Rd IP12 . . . . 146 A1
Bealings Sch IP13 . . . .137 D8
Bean's La IP22. . . . . . .36 F7
Beardmore Pk 10 IP5 .98 A8
Beard Rd
  Bury St Edmunds
    IP32. . . . . 122 D8
  2 Fornham All Saints
    IP32. . . . . .48 B5
Bear Meadow 5 IP30 49 F2
Bear's La CO10. . . . . . .78 D3
Bear St CO6 . . . . 102 C5
Beatrice Ave IP11. . . .153 A5
Beatrice Cl IP3 . . . . . .140 A3
Beatty Rd
  Ipswich IP3 . . . . 140 B2
  Sudbury CO10. . . . . . .148 E7
Beaufort Rd IP31. . . . .32 F1
Beaufort Ct 10 CB9 . . 132 D5
Beaufort St IP1. . . . . . 139 A7
Beaumont Cl 3
  IP33. . . . . 122 D4
Beaumont Com Prim Sch
  IP7 . . . . 149 D8
Beaumont Cotts
  IP17. . . . . 128 C6
Beaumont Ct CB9 . . . .132 F4
Beaumont Rd NR33 . . .114 B2
Beaumont Vale CB9 . . .132 F4
Beaumont Way IP14 . .124 B5
Beaverbrook Rd CB8 121 A5
Beavis Dr IP30. . . . . . .79 A8
BECCLES. 111 D5
Beccles Bsns Pk
  NR34. . . . . .10 A3

Beccles & District Mus★
  NR34. . . . . .111 A5
Beccles & District War
  Meml Hospl The
  NR34. . . . . .111 B4
Beccles Free Sch
  NR34. . . . . .111 C4
Beccles Gall★ 10
  NR34. . . . . .111 B5
Becclesgate 1
  NR34 . . . . .111 B6
Beccles Rd
  Aldeby NR34. . . . . 9 F8
  Aldeby/Wheatacre/Burgh St
    Peter NR34. . . . . .10 B8
  Blyford IP19 . . . . .25 C1
  Bungay NR35. . . . . .8 D5
  Bungay NR35. . . . . . . 110 C4
  Carlton Colville NR33 . .114 A4
  Fritton & St Olaves NR31 . .2 C7
  Holton IP19. . . . . .118 F4
  Lowestoft NR33. . . . . 114 D7
  Mutford NR34. . . . . . . .10 C3
  Redisham NR34 . . . . . .25 C7
  Wrentham NR34. . . . . .26 D6
Beccles Sports Ctr
  NR34. . . . . .111 A3
Beccles Sta NR34. . . . 111 C5
Beck Cl 5 IP12. . . . . . .85 D8
Beckers View IP19. . . .42 C6
Beckett Cl IP33. . . . . . 122 A6
Becketts La IP7. . . . . . .94 B1
Becketts The IP14 . . . .124 B8
Beckford Rd 17
  CO11. . . . . 105 A2
Beckham Rd NR32. . . . 113 C1
BECK ROW 30 A8
Beck Row Prim Sch
  IP28 . . . . .30 B8
Becks Gn La NR34. . . . .24 F8
Beck's Green Bsns Ctr
  NR34. . . . . .24 F7
Beck St IP22. . . . . .35 A7
Beck The IP26. . . . . . . 4 E5
Beck View 3 IP20 . . . .22 D6
Bedell Cl IP33 . . . . . . 122 C3
Bederic Cl IP32. . . . . . 123 D4
BEDFIELD. 54 E5
Bedfield CE Prim Sch
  IP13 . . . . 54 D5
Bedfield Rd
  Bedfield IP13 . . . . .54 E4
  Earl Soham IP13. . . . . .55 A3
Bedford Rd 8 IP32 . . .122 E8
Bedford St IP1. . . . . . .155 A3
Bedingfeld Way
  IP32. . . . . .123 E4
BEDINGFIELD. 53 F7
Bedingfield Cres
  IP19. . . . . 118 A1
Bedingfield Rd
  Lowestoft NR32. . . . . .112 E3
  Rishangles IP23 . . . . . .53 E7
BEDINGHAM GREEN. . . .7 B7
Beech Circus 5 IP7. . .80 D6
Beech Cl
  Halesworth IP19 . . . . .118 A3
  Isleham CB7. . . . . .29 B5
  11 Lakenheath IP27 . . .13 F2
  Sproughton IP8 . . . . . .138 A6
Beechcroft IP29. . . . . .64 A3
Beech Croft
  Brinkley CB8. . . . . .59 E1
  South Lopham IP22. . . .19 B4
Beechcroft Rd IP1. . . .134 F2
Beech Dr 5 CB8. . . . . .46 A8
Beeches Cl
  11 Ixworth IP31. . . . . .34 B1
  Weston Ditch IP28 . . . .29 F7
Beeches La IP21. . . . . .21 F7
Beeches Rd IP28. . . . . .29 F7
Beeches The
  5 Benhall Green
    IP17. . . . . .72 C8
  Claydon IP6 . . . . .134 C8
  Horringer IP29 . . . . . . .63 A8
  Ipswich IP3 . . . . .139 F4
  31 Ipswich CO11 . . . .104 E2
  Little Blakenham IP8 . . .81 E3
Beech Gr
  Haverhill CB9 . . . . . . .132 C7
  Ipswich IP3 . . . . .139 F3
Beeching Cl IP14 . . . .124 A8
Beeching Dr NR32 . . . .113 D4
Beech La 2 IP14 . . . . . 51 A1
Beech Paddocks 4
  IP30. . . . . .64 F8
Beech Pk IP31. . . . . . .49 B6
Beech Rd
  Ipswich IP5 . . . . .140 F7
  Lowestoft NR33 . . . . . 114 D3
  Saxmundham IP17 . . . .128 D3
  Sudbury CO10. . . . . . .148 F4
Beech Rise IP33 . . . . . 123 C3
Beech Row CB8. . . . . . .46 C1
Beech Terr IP14 . . . . .124 D7
Beech Tree Cl NR34. . .111 B4
Beech Tree Way 9
  NR35 . . . . 7 F4
Beech Way
  Dickleburgh IP21 . . . . .21 C5
  Woodbridge IP12. . . . .146 F3
Beech Wlk IP16. . . . . . 129 C5
Beechwood Cl CB8. . . 120 C8
Beechwood Dr IP3. . . .140 F2
Beechwood Gdns
  NR33. . . . . .115 A6

Beehive Cl CO7 . . . . . 151 C5
Bee Orchid Gdns
  CB9. . . . . .132 C7
Beetons Way IP32 . . . .122 C7
Beevors Gdn NR35 . . . .110 B7
Belaugh Ave NR33 . . . .114 F5
Belchamp Hall★
  CO10. . . . . 91 A3
BELCHAMP OTTEN . . .90 E4
Belchamp Rd
  Clare CO10 . . . . .90 C7
  Tilbury Juxta Clare CO9 .90 A3
BELCHAMP ST PAUL . .90 D5
Belchamp St Paul CE
  Prim Sch CO10. . . . . .90 D5
BELCHAMP WALTER . .90 F3
Belcher Gn IP18 . . . . . 119 C8
Belemnite Wlk IP6. . . .125 C3
Belfry Rd IP3 . . . . .144 F7
Belgrave Cl IP4. . . . . .135 C1
Bellands Way IP23 . . . .117 C3
Bell Barn La IP5 . . . . . 141 C8
Bell Cl
  Ipswich IP2 . . . . 155 B1
  3 Saxmundham IP17 128 D3
Bell Corner CO10 . . . .78 E1
Belle Vue Rd
  Ipswich IP4 . . . . 139 F6
  Sudbury CO10. . . . . . .148 D5
Bellflower Cres 18
  IP28. . . . . .30 C1
Bell Gdns 13 CB7. . . . . .28 D4
Bell Gn IP19 . . . . .40 C6
Bell Hill CO8. . . . . . . .101 B6
Bellings Rd CB9. . . . . .132 C8
Bell La
  Barton Mills IP28 . . . . 116 D2
  Ipswich IP2 . . . . 155 B1
  Marlesford IP13. . . . . .71 C4
  Worlington IP28. . . . . . .30 B4
Bell Meadow IP32 . . . .123 A8
Bell Mews IP7. . . . . . .149 D6
Bellrope La 8 IP27. . . .20 A3
Bell's Corner 102 F8
BELL'S CROSS. 82 D7
Bell's Cross IP14. . . . . .67 C6
Bell's Cross Rd IP6. . . .82 C7
Bells Hill CO8. . . . . . . 101 D2
Bells La
  Glemsford CO10. . . . . .77 A3
  Hinderclay IP22 . . . . . .35 E8
Bell's La
  Hawstead IP29. . . . . . .63 E5
  Stowupland IP14 . . . . .67 C7
Bells Meadow 3 IP7. .94 F1
Bells Rd CO10. . . . . . .90 F3
Bell St IP26. . . . . 4 E5
Bell Trees IP27 . . . . . 109 D4
Bellwell La
  Debenham IP14 . . . . . .53 F4
  Kenton IP14 . . . . .54 A4
Belmont Ct
  8 Haverhill CB9. . . . . 132 D5
  Newmarket CB8. . . . . 120 F3
Belmont Gdns NR32. . .113 B3
Belmont Rd IP8. . . . . .138 C1
Belsay Ct CB9. . . . . . .132 B6
Belseybridge Rd NR35. .7 F7
BELSTEAD. 142 C7
Belstead Ave IP1 . . . . 155 A1
Belstead Rd IP2 . . . . . 155 A1
Belstead Sch IP2 . . . . 155 A1
Belt The CB8. . . . . . . .61 B4
Belvedere Cl IP17. . . .128 C7
Belvedere Dr 23
  NR33 . . . . .36 F2
Belvedere La IP26 . . . . .5 C4
Belvedere Rd
  Ipswich IP4 . . . . 139 F8
  Lowestoft NR33 . . . . . 115 C7
Belvoir Ct 7 CB9 . . . .132 C6
BENACRE. 27 A7
Benacre National Nature
  Reserve★ NR34. . . . .27 B6
Benacre Rd
  Ellough NR34 . . . . .111 F1
  Henstead with Hulver Street
    NR34. . . . . .26 E8
  Ipswich IP3 . . . . 140 A2
Ben Curley Dr 6
  IP24. . . . . .16 C6
Bendalls Ct 39 CO11. .104 E2
Benefield Rd 1 CB8. . .45 F3
Benezet St IP1. . . . . . 155 A3
BENHALL GREEN. 72 C8
Benhall St Mary's CE
  VC Prim Sch IP17. . . 72 C8
BENHALL STREET. . . .71 F8
Benjamin Britten High
  Sch NR32 . . . . .113 A5
Bennett Ave
  Bury St Edmunds
    IP33. . . . . 122 C6
  Elmswell IP30. . . . . . . .50 F2
Bennett Cl IP31. . . . . .49 D5
Bennett Rd
  Ipswich IP1 . . . . .134 C1
  5 Red Lodge IP28 . . . .30 C1
Benouville 10 NR33 . . .114 F3
Bensly's Drift IP19 . . .118 C4
Bentham La IP12. . . . .147 A6
Bent Hill IP11. . . . . . . .153 A3
Bent La IP4. . . . . .140 E8
BENTLEY. 104 F8
Bentley CE VC Prim Sch
  IP9. . . . . .104 F8
Bentley Dr NR32 . . . . .113 A6
Bentley Hall Rd IP9 . . .95 E1

Bentley La
  Belstead IP8. . . . . . . .142 C5
  Stutton IP9. . . . . .105 B6
Bentley Rd IP1. . . . . . .134 C2
Benton End IP7. . . . . .149 E3
Benton La IP7. . . . . . . .65 C1
Benton St IP7 . . . . . . .149 D4
Benton Way IP19 . . . . .118 B4
Bentwaters 6 IP27 . . . .13 F2
Bentwaters Airfield
  (disused) IP12 . . . . .85 E8
Bentwaters Bsns Pk
  IP12. . . . . .85 E8
Bentwaters Cold War
  Museum★ IP12. . . . .85 F8
Benwell Cl IP29. . . . . . .62 D4
Benyon Gdns IP30. . . . .32 D1
Berberis Dr 1 IP28 . . . .45 F8
Bere Rd 15 IP30. . . . . .50 F2
Beresford Dr IP12 . . . .146 F7
Beresford Rd NR32. . . .113 D2
Bergamot Cl 12 IP28 . .30 C1
Bergamot Rd CB9. . . . .132 A6
Berghersh Dr IP3. . . . . .83 A7
Berghersh La IP6. . . . . .82 E7
Bergholt Rd
  Bentley IP9. . . . . .104 E7
  Brantham CO11 . . . . . 104 D4
Berkeley Cl
  2 Framlingham
    IP13. . . . . 126 C3
  Ipswich IP4 . . . . 135 C1
Berkeley Gdns
  Bury St Edmunds
    IP33. . . . . 122 C4
  Lowestoft NR32. . . . . 113 A4
Bermuda Rd IP10. . . . .144 D7
Bernard Cres IP3 . . . . .140 B2
Bernard Mws 11
  IP6. . . . . .83 A8
Bernard Rooke Pottery &
  Gall★ IP6. . . . . . . .83 A8
Bernards Cl IP28. . . . . .29 F7
Berners Field IP9. . . . .105 F7
Berners Rd 10 IP28. . .153 C4
Berners St IP1. . . . . . .155 A3
Bernes Cl IP32. . . . . . 123 D5
Bernhard Row CB9. . . .132 F4
Berry Cl
  Ipswich IP3 . . . . .140 F1
  Lowestoft NR32. . . . . 112 E1
Berrycroft 11 CB7. . . . .28 D4
Bertuna Cl IP31. . . . . . .49 B5
Berwick Rd IP3. . . . . .144 F7
Beryl Rd 8 CO12. . . . .106 E1
Bessies Orchard IP23 .37 D1
Bethel Dr 24 NR33. . . .11 C1
Betjeman Cl IP24 . . . . .16 C7
Betony Wlk CB9. . . . . .132 B6
Betts Ave IP5. . . . . . . .98 A8
Betts Cl IP7. . . . . .149 D7
Betty Cocker Gr
  CO10 . . . . .148 F5
Bevan St E 3 NR32. . . .115 D8
Bevan St W NR32. . . . .113 C1
Beverley Cl NR33 . . . . 114 C2
Beverley Rd IP4 . . . . .139 F8
Beversham Rd IP13. . . .71 F5
Bevis Wlk IP33. . . . . . .123 D2
Bewicks Mead 10 CB5. 44 B5
Bexley Ave 16 CO12 . .106 F1
Bexley Dr IP4 . . . . . . .140 E5
Bexley La IP4 . . . . . . .140 F5
Bixley Rd
  Ipswich IP3 . . . . .140 D3
  2 Lowestoft NR33. . . . 115 C6
Black Barn Cl 6 IP8 . .81 C3
Black Barns IP11. . . . .152 C7
Black Bear Cl CB8. . . .120 F3
Black Bear La CB8. . . .120 F3
Blackberry La
  Soham CB7. . . . . .28 B5
  12 Soham CB7 . . . . . . .28 B5
Blackberry Way
  Lowestoft NR32. . . . . .112 E2
  3 Red Lodge IP28 . . . .30 C1
Blackbird Ave IP27. . . .6 A1
Blackbird Cl 16 IP31 .49 C6
Blackbird Dr
  9 Bury St Edmunds
    IP31. . . . . .49 A4
  4 Bury St Edmunds
    IP31. . . . . .49 A3
Blackbird Rd 3 IP28. .13 B1
Blackbird Way
  18 Harleston IP20 . . . .22 D5
  10 Stowmarket IP14 . .67 A3
Blackbourne Rd IP30 .50 F3
Black Boy La CO11 . . .106 A2
Black Boy Meadow
  NR34. . . . . .111 B4
Blackdike Dro IP26 . . . .4 A2
Blackdown Ave IP5 . . .140 F6
Blackdyke Cl 9 IP26. . . .4 D5
Blackdyke Cres 13
  IP26. . . . . .4 D5
Black Dyke Rd IP26 . . . .4 A2
Blackfriars CO10. . . . .148 B4
Blackfriars Ct IP4. . . .155 C2
Black Gr La CO10 . . . . .75 E4
Black Grove La CO10 . .76 A4
BLACKHEATH. 42 C5
Blackheath Ave IP3 . . .140 C4
Blackheath Rd
  Lowestoft NR33 . . . . . 115 A5
  Wenhaston with Mells
    Hamlet IP19. . . . . . .42 C5

Birch Cl continued
  Wickham Market IP13 .127 C6
  Woodbridge IP12. . . . .146 F3
Birch Covert IP24. . . . .16 D6
Birch Cres IP27. . . . . .109 D7
Birchcroft Rd IP1 . . . .135 B2
Birch Dr 8 CO11. . . . .104 C5
Birches The
  4 Kennett IP28 . . . . . .46 A8
  Soham CB7. . . . . .28 C5
Birch Fall 7 CO6. . . . .102 C5
Birch Gdns IP31 . . . . . .50 F7
Birch Gr IP5. . . . . .98 A7
Birchgrove IP23. . . . . .52 F7
Birchinhill Dro IP28. . .12 F2
Birch Rd
  Onehouse IP14. . . . . . .66 C6
  10 Thurstow IP31. . . . .49 E4
Birch's La CO10. . . . . . .93 C3
Birch St CO6. . . . . 102 D5
Birch Wlk 24 IP27 . . . .13 F2
Birchwood Dr IP5. . . . .136 C1
Birchwood Primary Sch
  IP5. . . . . .98 A8
Birchwood Rd CO7. . . .103 D2
BIRDBROOK. 89 A4
Birdbrook 3 IP29 . . . .63 A1
Birdbrook Rd
  Birdbrook CO9. . . . . . .89 C3
  Stambourne CO9. . . . . .89 A2
Birdcage Wlk CB8. . . . 120 F2
Birds Croft IP31. . . . . .33 C2
BIRDS END. 62 B7
Birds Gn IP30. . . . . . . .65 E5
Birds Hill IP13 . . . . . . .83 D8
Birds La
  Framsden IP14. . . . . . .69 D5
  Lowestoft NR33 . . . . . .115 B6
Bird's La IP30 . . . . .64 D2
Birds Meare IP6 . . . . . .69 C2
Bird's Rd IP31 . . . . .49 F3
BIRD STREET. 80 A7
Bird View Sq 1 IP26 . . .4 E5
Birkdale Ave IP28. . . . .116 B5
Birkdale Ct 10 IP28. . . .48 C6
Birkfield Cl IP2 . . . . . .139 A4
Birkfield Dr IP2. . . . . .138 E1
Biscay Cl CB9. . . . . . .133 A5
Bishop Mews IP8 . . . . .138 B2
Bishop's CE Prim Sch The
  IP24. . . . . .16 B6
Bishops Cft IP31. . . . . .34 E8
Bishops Cl
  6 Felixstowe IP11. . . .153 D6
  Haverhill CB9 . . . . . . .132 C6
  Sudbury CO10. . . . . . .148 C8
Bishops Ct 1 CB9. . . . 132 C6
Bishops Field CB7. . . . .29 A2
Bishop's Hill IP3 . . . . .139 E4
Bishops Rd IP33 . . . . .154 B3
Bishops Way IP21. . . . .39 A4
Bishops Wlk
  10 Hopton on Sea
    NR31. . . . . .3 B7
  Lowestoft NR32. . . . . 113 D5
Bittern
  Ipswich IP2 . . . . .138 E3
  Thetford IP24. . . . . . . .16 C4
Bittern Cres 27 IP14. . .67 A5
Bittern Gn NR33 . . . . .114 D4
Bittern Grove CB7. . . . .28 C5
Bittern Rd IP17. . . . . .128 B3
Bixley Dr IP4 . . . . .140 E5
Bixley La IP4 . . . . .140 F5
Bixley Rd
  Ipswich IP3 . . . . .140 D3
  2 Lowestoft NR33. . . . 115 C6
Black Barn Cl 6 IP8 . .81 C3
Black Barns IP11. . . . .152 C7
Black Bear Cl CB8. . . .120 F3
Black Bear La CB8. . . .120 F3
Blackberry La
  Soham CB7. . . . . .28 B5
  12 Soham CB7 . . . . . . .28 B5
Blackberry Way
  Lowestoft NR32. . . . . .112 E2
  3 Red Lodge IP28 . . . .30 C1
Blackbird Ave IP27. . . .6 A1
Blackbird Cl 16 IP31 .49 C6
Blackbird Dr
  9 Bury St Edmunds
    IP31. . . . . .49 A4
  4 Bury St Edmunds
    IP31. . . . . .49 A3
Blackbird Rd 3 IP28. .13 B1
Blackbird Way
  18 Harleston IP20 . . . .22 D5
  10 Stowmarket IP14 . .67 A3
Blackbourne Rd IP30 .50 F3
Black Boy La CO11 . . .106 A2
Black Boy Meadow
  NR34. . . . . .111 B4
Blackdike Dro IP26 . . . .4 A2
Blackdown Ave IP5 . . .140 F6
Blackdyke Cl 9 IP26. . . .4 D5
Blackdyke Cres 13
  IP26. . . . . .4 D5
Black Dyke Rd IP26 . . . .4 A2
Blackfriars CO10. . . . .148 B4
Blackfriars Ct IP4. . . .155 C2
Black Gr La CO10 . . . . .75 E4
Black Grove La CO10 . .76 A4
BLACKHEATH. 42 C5
Blackheath Ave IP3 . . .140 C4
Blackheath Rd
  Lowestoft NR33 . . . . . 115 A5
  Wenhaston with Mells
    Hamlet IP19. . . . . . .42 C5

Black Hill (Tumulus)★
  IP31 . . . . 33 C5
Black Horse La
  Ditchingham NR35 . . . 110 C7
  Ipswich IP1 . . . . 155 A3
Black Horse Wlk
  IP1 . . . . 155 B3
Blackhouse La CO10 .148 F1
Blacklands La IP12. . 131 A8
Black Mill Rd IP18 . . 119 C5
Blackmore Cl **8**
  CB9 . . . . 132 C7
Blackshore IP18 . . . 119 B4
Black Slough IP17 . . . 58 B7
Blacksmith Cl
  Newton CO10 . . . . .92 D3
  Wangford NR34 . . . . . . 26 B2
Blacksmith La
  Barnham IP24 . . . . .16 B2
  Thorpe Morieux IP30 . . .78 F7
Blacksmith Rd
  Bacton IP14 . . . . .52 A6
  Rede IP29 . . . . .62 E2
Blacksmith's Cnr
  IP8 . . . . 142 C6
BLACKSMITH'S
  GREEN 53 C5
Blacksmiths Hill
  CO10 . . . . .89 D6
Blacksmiths La
  Bulmer CO10 . . . . .91 C1
  Coddenham IP6 . . . . . . .68 B1
  Forward Green IP14. . . .67 D7
  Stonham Earl IP14 . . . .67 D6
Blacksmiths Loke
  NR32 . . . . .2 D4
Blacksmith's Loke
  NR32 . . . . 2 F6
Blacksmiths Rd IP13 146 C7
Blacksmiths Way
  IP30 . . . . .50 F3
Black St NR33. . . . . . . 10 F1
Blackstock Crossing Rd
  IP13. . . . . .71 D3
BLACK STREET 11 A2
Blackthorn Cl
  4 Diss IP22. . . . . 20 D3
  14 Herringswell IP28. .46 A8
  1 Ipswich IP1 . . . . . . 138 C5
Blackthorn Ct CB7 . . . 28 C5
Blackthorn Way CO6 .102 B7
Blackthorn Wlk
  IP32 . . . . 122 D8
BLACKTHORPE 49 C2
Blackthorpe Barn★
  IP30 . . . . 49 C2
Blacktiles La IP12. . . .84 A1
Bladen Dr IP4 . . . . . 140 F5
Bladon Way CB9 . . . 132 F7
Blagge Cl IP33. . . . . 122 C4
Blair Cl IP4. . . . . 140 E5
Blair Par **6** CB9 . . . 132 C6
Blake Ave **4** IP9 . . . 107 A5
Blake Cl **7** CO11. . . 104 D2
Blakenham Cl **4**
  NR32 . . . . 112 F4
Blakenham Woodland
  Gdn★ IP6 . . . . .81 F4
Blake Rd
  Ipswich IP1 . . . . 134 F3
  Stowmarket IP14 . . . . 124 B7
Blakes Cl IP12 . . . . . 147 C2
Blakes La IP13. . . . . . .70 C2
Blanche St IP4. . . . . 155 C3
Blandford Rd IP3 . . . 140 D3
Blands Farm Cl **8**
  IP22. . . . . .20 C1
BLAXHALL 72 B4
Blaxhall Church Rd
  IP12. . . . . .71 F2
Blaxhall Ct **2** CB9. . 132 C5
Blaxhall Heath Nature
  Reserve★ IP12 . . . . 72 C3
BLEACH GREEN. 39 A8
Blenheim Cl
  10 Brantham CO11. . 104 E5
  Bury St Edmunds
  IP33 . . . . 122 D5
  Haverhill CB9 . . . . . . 132 F7
  Weston Ditch IP28 . . . .29 F7
Blenheim Dr IP7 . . . .80 C6
Blenheim Meadow
  IP7 . . . . .80 B4
Blenheim Rd **3** IP1 . 139 A7
Blenheim Way **2**
  IP22. . . . . .20 A3
Blenheim Wlk **37**
  CO11 . . . . 104 D2
Blickling Cl IP2 . . . . 139 B2
Blinco Rd NR32 . . . . 112 C1
Blind La
  Blythburgh IP19 . . . . . . .42 F5
  Hartest IP29. . . . . .77 B6
Blocka Rd NR32. . . . . .2 C6
Blockmoor Rd CB7. . . .28 A6
Block Rd CB7. . . . . . .28 E1
Block'S La NR34 . . . . .26 A4
Blofield Rd IP11 . . . . 152 B4
Blois Rd CB9. . . . . . . .88 F4
Blomfield St IP33 . . . 154 B3
BLO' NORTON 18 E2
Blo' Norton Rd
  Blo' Norton IP22. . . . . .18 F3
  Garboldisham IP22. . . .19 A4
Blood Hill IP8 . . . . . . .81 B3
BLOODMAN'S
  CORNER. 3 A6
BLOODMOOR HILL . .114 E2

Bloodmoor La **2**
  NR33 . . . . .114 E3
Bloodmoor Rd **1**
  NR33 . . . . .114 E3
Bloomfield Cl IP31. . . .33 F5
Bloomfield Ct **12**
  CO10 . . . . .90 A8
Bloomfield La NR34. . . .26 C3
Bloomfield Rd IP11 . 152 D6
Bloomfield St 140 B6
Bloomfield Way
  Debenham IP14 . . . . . . .53 E1
  7 Lowestoft NR33 . . 114 E3
Bloomsbury Cl NR32 112 E4
Blooms Ct IP28 . . . . 116 D5
Bloomsfield **8** CB5 . . 44 B5
Blooms Hall La CO10 . .77 D5
Blossom Cl **18** CB5. . . 44 A6
Blower's La NR33 . . . . .10 E2
Blue Barn Cl **13**
  IP1 . . . . 107 D8
Blue Barn La IP8. . . . 134 A8
Bluebell Ave IP32 . . 123 F5
Bluebell Cl
  Ipswich IP2 . . . . 138 E4
  7 Lowestoft NR33 . . . 114 E3
Bluebell Dr IP9 . . . . 150 F3
Bluebell Gdns IP27 . 109 D6
Bluebell Gr IP6 . . . . 125 D3
Bluebell Rd CB7 . . . . .29 C8
Bluebell Rise **45** IP28 . 30 C1
Bluebell Wlk **2** CB7. . 28 D4
Bluebell Way
  15 Barrow IP29 . . . . .47 A2
  Felixstowe IP11 . . . . . 152 F6
Bluebird Lodge IP10 144 D7
Bluegate La IP9 . . . . 150 F1
Blue House La IP14 . . .52 F3
Bluestem Rd IP3 . . . 144 D8
Blunden Cl CO10 . . . . .91 D7
Blundens The CO6 . . 102 E7
Blunders Corner
  CO6 . . . . 102 E7
BLUNDESTON. 3 A4
Blundeston CE VC Prim
  Sch NR32 . . . . .3 A4
Blundeston Marsh La
  NR32 . . . . .112 B7
Blundeston Rd
  Corton NR32 . . . . 112 F8
  Somerleyton, Ashby &
    Herringfleet NR32 . . .112 B8
Blyburgate **2** NR34 . 111 C4
BLYFORD 42 C7
Blyford La
  Blyford IP19 . . . . .42 B8
  Holton IP19 . . . . 118 E3
  Wenhaston with Mells
    Hamlet IP19 . . . . .42 C6
Blyford Rd NR32 . . . 113 A5
Blyford Way IP11 . . . 152 C4
BLYTHBURGH 42 C7
Blythburgh Rd IP17. .58 C8
Blyth Cl
  Ipswich IP2 . . . . 139 A1
  Wenhaston IP19. . . . . .42 C6
Blythe Cl **12** CO10 . . 92 E7
Blyth Mws IP19 . . . . 118 B4
Blyth Rd
  Halesworth IP19 . . . . 118 C2
  Southwold IP18 . . . . . 119 B5
Blyth Road Ind Est
  IP19 . . . . 118 B2
Blyth View IP19 . . . . .42 E2
BMI St Edmunds Hospl
  (Private) IP33 . . . . . 154 C1
Boarded Barn Rd IP7. .80 D2
Boathouse La
  Carlton Colville
    NR32 . . . . 114 B8
  Lowestoft NR32 . . . . . 112 B1
Boatman Ct **16** IP8 . . 142 E8
Bobbits La
  Pinewood IP9 . . . . 142 E8
  Wherstead IP9 . . . . . . 143 A7
BOBBY HILL 35 C5
Bobbys Way IP31 . . . .34 F4
Boby Rd IP32 . . . . . . 122 D8
Bockhill Rd IP33 . . . 122 C5
Bodiam Cl IP3 . . . . . 140 D4
Bodiam Rd IP3 . . . . . 140 D4
Bodiam Way **8**
  NR33 . . . . .114 D4
Bodian Wlk **8** CB9 . 132 C6
Bodmin Cl IP5 . . . . . 141 A6
Boeing Way IP28 . . . 116 B5
Bohemia Pl CB7 . . . . .29 B6
Boldero Rd IP32 . . . 123 F4
Boleyn Way CB9 . . . 132 B5
Boleyn Wlk CB8. . . . 121 C3
Bollard Way NR33. . . 114 E5
Bolton Cl **2** CB5. . . . .44 A5
Bolton La IP1. . . . . . 155 C3
Bolton St **10** CO10 . . .78 D4
Bombose La CO8. . . 101 B5
Bond Cl IP21 . . . . . . .21 F8
Bonds Meadow
  NP32 . . . . .112 F2
Bond's Rd NR15. . . . . .5 F1
Bond St
  Ipswich IP4 . . . . 155 C2
  Stowmarket IP14 . . . . 124 D7
Bon Marche **7**
  NR32 . . . . .115 D8
Bonnington Rd IP3 . 139 F1
Bonny Cres IP3 . . . . 144 C8
Bonsey Gdns NR34 . . .26 E5

Boon Cl IP33 . . . . . . 123 A3
Boon Dr NR33. . . . . . .114 E6
Boons Heath NR34 . . . .10 B7
Boons Rd NR34 . . . . . .10 B7
Boons Turn NR34 . . . .10 B8
Boot Drift IP9 . . . . . 106 E7
Booth La IP5 . . . . . . 141 E8
BOOT STREET 137 D6
Border Cot La IP13. . 127 B7
Border La NR32 . . . . . .2 E6
Borderham gate Prec **5**
  CO10 . . . . 148 D5
Borderham gate Sh Ctr **21**
  CO10. . . . . 148 C5
Boreham Pl CO9 . . . . .89 A5
BORLEY 91 C5
Borley Cl IP31. . . . . . .33 F5
Borley Cres **2** IP30 . . .50 F2
BORLEY GN IP30 . . . .65 F7
Borley Gn
  Borley. 91 A4
  Woolpit. 65 E7
Borley La CB9. . . . . . . .75 B4
Borley Mill CO10 . . . .91 D5
Borley Rd
  Belchamp St Paul
    CO10 . . . . .90 F5
  Long Melford CO10. . . .91 D6
Borough End **3**
  NR34 . . . . 111 C3
Borough La IP14 . . . . .66 A3
Borradale Ct **5** CB9. . .88 D3
Borradale Rd IP32 . . 123 F5
Borrett Pl IP12 . . . . 146 D3
Borretts Farm La
  IP13. . . . . .70 D6
Borrow Cl NR33. . . . 114 C3
Borrowdale Ave **1**
  IP4. . . . . 135 D1
Borrow Rd NR32 . . . 112 C1
Bosmere Com Prim Sch
  IP6 . . . . 125 D4
Bosquet Cl **1** NR32 . 112 F5
Boss Hall Ind Est
  IP1 . . . . 138 E7
Boss Hall Rd IP1. . . . 138 E7
Bostock Rd IP2 . . . . 139 C1
Boston End **6** IP24 . . .16 A5
Boston Rd
  Ipswich IP4 . . . . 139 F7
  Lowestoft NR32 . . . . . 113 D2
Boswell La IP7 . . . . . 149 D7
Botany Farm Dr IP17 . .72 B6
Botany Farm Rd
  IP13. . . . . .70 D4
Botany La IP17 . . . . . .71 E7
BOTESDALE. 36 B6
Bothy Cl IP23 . . . . . . 117 C4
Botolphs Ct IP33 . . . 154 C1
Bottle Bridge Rd
  IP8. . . . . 150 A7
Bouchain Ct **1** IP19. 118 A3
Boughton Way IP33. 154 C3
Boulevard The NR32 114 D8
Boulge Rd
  Burgh IP13 . . . . .83 F6
  Hasketon IP13 . . . . . . 146 B8
Boulters Cl IP14 . . . 124 B6
Boulters Way IP14 . . 124 B6
Boundary Cl IP20 . . . . .4 D3
Boundary La NR34 . . . .9 D8
Boundary Oaks IP9 . 150 F4
Boundary Rd
  Haverhill CB9 . . . . . . 133 B3
  1 Hockwold cum Wilton
    IP26. . . . . .5 A3
  Red Lodge IP28 . . . . . . 30 C1
Bourchier Cl **7** IP7. 149 E6
Bourne Ave **6** IP32 . 123 E6
Bourne Hill IP2 . . . . . .143 B7
Bourne Pk Residential
  Park IP2. . . . . 139 B1
Bourne Rd
  Haverhill NR32 . . . . . 132 F6
  Lowestoft NR32 . . . . . 113 B3
Bourne Terr IP2 . . . . 143 B8
Bovingdon IP27 . . . . . .14 A8
BOWBECK 34 C6
Bowdens La CO6. . . . 101 F3
Bower Hall La CO10 . . .90 D7
BOWER HOUSE TYE . . .93 E3
Bower's La **7** CB7 . . .29 C5
Bowland Dr IP8. . . . . 138 C1
Bowl Corner IP14 . . . .66 C1
Bowl Meadow IP14 . . .66 C1
Bowl Rd IP14 . . . . . . .66 C1
Bowman's La IP17 . . . .42 D1
Bowthorpe Cl IP11. . 155 A4
Bowyer Cl **8** IP6. . . . .82 A6
Box Bush La IP13 . . . .55 D5
BOXFORD 93 C3
Boxford CE VC Prim Sch
  CO10. . . . . .93 C3
Boxford Cl **2** IP14 . . 124 C3
Boxford La CO10 . . . .93 A3
Boxford Rd
  Kersey Upland IP7 . . . .93 F6
  Milden IP7 . . . . .93 B8
Box Hall La IP12 . . . . .99 D7
Boxhouse La CO7 . . . 103 D3
BOXTED
  Colchester. 77 A6
  Glemsford 102 F4

Boxted Church Rd
  CO6 . . . . 102 E2
BOXTED CROSS. . . . 103 A3
Boxted Rd CO6. . . . . 102 D2
Boxted Straight Rd
  CO4 . . . . 103 A2
Boyden Cl **1** CB8 . . . .61 E2
Boyden Ct CB7. . . . . . .29 A7
BOYDEN END
  61 D2
  Wickhambrook CB8 . . . .61 E2
Boydlands IP9 . . . . . 150 E3
Boyne Rd IP33 . . . . . 122 E4
Boyscott La **1** NR35. 110 B3
Boys Grave Rd CB8. . . .45 E5
BOYTON 86 B2
Boyton Cl CB9 . . . . . 132 E8
BOYTON END. 89 B7
Boyton La NR31. . . . . . .3 B6
Boyton Rd
  Hollesley IP12 . . . . . . .86 A1
  Ipswich IP3 . . . . 140 B1
Boyton's La CB10 . . . .88 A1
Boyton Vineyard★
  CO9. . . . . .89 B7
BRABLING GREEN. . . 126 E6
Braces La NR35 . . . . . .8 E7
Bracken Ave IP5. . . . 137 E1
Brackenbury Cl IP1 . 139 B8
Brackenbury Sports Ctr
  IP11 . . . . 153 C5
Bracken Farm La
  IP12. . . . . .72 B1
Bracken Rise IP20 . . . . .6 A8
Bracken Row **6** IP31. .49 D4
Brackenwood Cres **1**
  IP32 . . . . 123 E6
Brackley Cl **8** IP11 . 152 D5
Bracks Drove CB7. . . .28 C2
Bradbrook Cl IP32 . . 123 F6
Braddock Sq IP32. . . 122 E7
BRADFIELD 105 C1
BRADFIELD
  COMBUST 64 A4
Bradfield Cres IP7 . . 149 D7
Bradfield Prim Sch
  CO11. . . . . 105 C1
Bradfield Rd IP30 . . . .64 D3
BRADFIELD ST
  CLARE 64 C4
BRADFIELD ST
  GEORGE. 64 D7
Bradfield St George Rd
  IP30. . . . . .64 D5
Bradfield Woods National
  Nature Reserve★
  IP30 . . . . .64 F4
Bradford Ct IP5. . . . . .98 A4
Bradley Hill CO10 . . . .90 A6
Bradley Mill Way
  IP6 . . . . 125 F3
Bradley Rd
  Burrough Green CB8. . . .59 F3
  Cowlinge CB8 . . . . .60 F1
  Great Bradley CB8 . . . . .74 F8
  Kirtling CB8. . . . . .60 F2
  Stetchworth CB8. . . . . .60 A1
Bradley St IP2 . . . . . 155 B1
Braeburn Cl IP4 . . . . 139 E7
Braeburn Rd CB9 . . . 132 B5
Braggon's Hill IP29 . . .77 A5
Braiseworth IP23 . . . .37 D2
BRAISEWORTH 37 D2
Braiseworth La IP23 . .37 C3
Braiseworth Rd
  Braiseworth IP23. . . . . .37 D2
  Eye IP23. . . . . 117 A1
Braithwaite Dr **7**
  CO10 . . . . .92 C6
Braithwaite Rd CO10 . .91 F8
Bramble Cl
  Haverhill CB9 . . . . . . 132 B7
  8 Laxfield IP13 . . . . .40 B3
Bramble Dr IP3. . . . . 140 E1
Bramble Gn NR32 . . . 113 B3
Brambles The IP15. . 130 C6
Bramble Tye **20**
  CO12 . . . . 106 E1
Bramble Walk **6** CB8 .46 A8
Bramble Way CO6. . . 102 B7
Bramble Wlk **17** IP28. . 30 B8
Bramblewood **1**
  IP8. . . . . 138 C2
Bramblewood Way
  IP19. . . . . 118 C4
Brambling Cl
  12 Stowmarket IP14 . .67 A3
  7 Stowmarket IP14 . . 124 B7
Brames La IP20 . . . . . .23 D3
BRAMFIELD 41 E4
Bramfield CE Prim Sch
  IP19 . . . . .42 A4
Bramfield House Sch
  IP19 . . . . .41 E4
Bramfield Rd
  Halesworth IP19 . . . . 118 A7
  Lowestoft NR32 . . . . . 113 A3
  Walpole IP19 . . . . .41 C5
  Wenhaston with Mells
    Hamlet IP19 . . . . .42 B5
BRAMFORD 134 A2
Bramford CE Prim Sch
  IP8 . . . . 134 A1
Bramford Ct **1** IP14. 124 E4
Bramford La **6** IP1 . 139 A7

Bramford Meadows
  Nature Reserve★
  IP1 . . . . 134 B3
Bramford Rd
  Bramford IP8 . . . . 134 B1
  Claydon IP8 . . . . 134 A7
  Great Blakenham IP6 . 134 A8
  Ipswich IP1 . . . . 138 E8
  Sproughton IP8 . . . . . 138 A7
Bramhall Cl IP2. . . . . 138 D1
Bramley Chase IP4 . 140 B7
Bramley Cl
  Bury St Edmunds
    IP32 . . . . 123 D6
  3 Sudbury CO10 . . . 148 B8
Bramley Rise
  Diss IP22 . . . . .20 B3
  Haverhill CB9 . . . . . . 132 A5
Bramley Rise NR34. . 111 C3
BRAMPTON 25 C5
Brampton CE Prim Sch
  NR34. . . . . .25 C5
Brampton Gr **9**
  NR32 . . . . 112 F4
Brampton Sta NR34. . 25 C6
BRAMPTON STREET. . .25 C4
BRANDESTON 70 B7
Brandeston Cl **10**
  CO10 . . . . .92 C6
Brandeston Hall
  Framlingham Coll Prep
  Sch IP13 . . . . 70 A7
Brandeston Rd
  Brandeston IP13 . . . . . .70 A7
  Cretingham IP13 . . . . . .69 E7
  Cretingham IP13 . . . . . .69 F8
  Earl Soham IP13 . . . . . .54 F1
BRANDON. 6 A1
Brandon Bsns Ctr
  IP27 . . . . .14 E8
Brandon Ctry Pk Visitor
  Ctr★ IP27 . . . . 14 E8
Brandon Fields IP27 . .14 C8
Brandon Her Ctr★
  IP27 . . . . .5 F1
Brandon Rd
  Brandon IP27 . . . . .14 D7
  Felixstowe IP11 . . . . . 152 C4
  Hockwold cum Wilton
    IP26. . . . . .5 B3
  Lakenheath IP27 . . . . . .14 C4
  Methwold IP26 . . . . .5 B8
  Mildenhall IP28 . . . . . 116 E5
  Thetford IP24 . . . . .15 F6
  Weeting IP27 . . . . .5 D3
  Wordwell IP28 . . . . .32 C3
Brandon St IP27 . . . 109 F1
Brandon Sta IP27. . . . .5 F2
Brand Rd IP31. . . . . . .49 C7
Brandreth Cl IP21. . . .21 B5
Brands Cl **12** CO10 . . .92 B3
Brands La IP29 . . . . . .63 D3
Bransby Gdns IP4. . . 139 E7
BRANTHAM 104 F4
Brantham Hill CO11. . 104 E4
Brantham Rd CO11. . 104 D3
Braybrooke Cl **12**
  IP14. . . . . .52 E4
Brayfield Cl IP32. . . . 123 D6
Braziers La IP31 . . . . .51 B6
Brazier's Wood Rd
  IP3. . . . . 144 B8
Brazilian Terr CB8 . . 120 F3
Breach Dro IP28 . . . . .13 C1
Breck Gdns IP27 . . . 109 D6
Breckland Ave IP27 . 109 D7
Brecklands **5** IP26 . . .6 B8
Breckland Way
  Lowestoft NR32 . . . . . 113 A3
  Mildenhall IP28 . . . . . 116 C5
Brecon Cl IP2 . . . . . 139 B2
BREDFIELD. 84 C7
Bredfield Cl **7** IP11. 152 D5
Bredfield Rd
  Bredfield IP13 . . . . .84 C8
  Woodbridge IP12 . . . . 147 A7
Bredfield St IP12 . . . 146 F5
Breed Fen Drove CB7 .28 A1
Brendon Cl IP14 . . . . 124 E4
Brendon Dr IP5. . . . . 140 F6
Brent Cl IP28 . . . . . . 116 D4
Brent Eleigh Rd
  Lavenham CO10 . . . . . .78 D3
  Monks Eleigh IP7 . . . . .79 B2
Brentgovel St **1**
  IP33. . . . . 154 B2
Brent Mill Dr CO10 . . .79 A2
BRESSINGHAM 19 F4
BRESSINGHAM
  COMMON 19 F5
Bressingham Prim Sch
  IP22 . . . . .19 F4
Bressingham Rd IP22 .19 F4
Bressingham Steam Mus
  & Gdns★ IP22. . . . . .19 F4
Brett Ave IP7 . . . . . . 149 E7
Brett Cl IP1. . . . . 138 E8
BRETTENHAM
  Stowmarket 79 C8
  Thetford 17 B6
Brettenham Cres **4**
  IP1 . . . . 135 D1
Brettenham Rd
  Buxhall IP14 . . . . .65 F4
  Felsham IP30 . . . . .65 B3
  Hitcham IP7 . . . . .79 D8
  Poystreet Green IP30. . .65 C5

Brettenham Rd continued
  Shadwell IP24. . . . . . . .17 C6
Brett Gn IP7. . . . . . . 149 E2
Brett Rise IP30 . . . . . .78 C8
Bretts The IP5 . . . . . 141 E8
Brewers Cl IP27 . . . . 109 C6
Brewers Gn La IP22 . .20 B3
BREWERS GREEN 20 B3
Brewers La CB8. . . . . 121 A4
Brewhouse La **19** CB7 .28 D4
Breydon Way
  Gainsborough IP3. . . . 144 C7
  Lowestoft NR33 . . . . . 114 F6
Briar Cl
  Halesworth IP19 . . . . 118 C4
  Lowestoft NR32 . . . . . 113 B5
Briardale Ave **4**
  CO12 . . . . 106 F2
Briarhayes Cl IP2 . . . 139 B3
Briar Hill IP30 . . . . . . .50 D1
Briar La IP22 . . . . .35 F5
Briar Rd **39** IP20 . . . . .22 D6
Briarwood Ave IP33. 122 D5
Briarwood Rd
  Lowestoft NR33 . . . . . 114 F5
  Woodbridge IP12 . . . . 146 B3
Brices Way IP7 . . . . . .77 A3
Bricett Bsns Pk IP7. . .80 E6
Brick Dr **28** IP6 . . . . . .82 A5
Brickfield Cl IP2 . . . . 155 C1
Brickfields IP15 . . . . 130 B4
Brickfields Ave CB8 . 120 D7
Brickfields Bsns Pk
  IP30 . . . . 50 D1
Brickfields Dr CB9 . . 132 C8
Brickfields The IP14 124 C6
Brick Kiln Ave NR34 . 111 C4
Brick Kiln Cl **15**
  IP11. . . . . 107 D8
Brick Kiln Farm Rd
  IP19. . . . . 118 C1
Brick Kiln Hill CO6 . . . .93 C2
Brickkiln La IP22 . . . . .19 C3
Brick Kiln La
  Huntingfield IP19 . . . . .40 F4
  Melton IP12 . . . . 147 E7
Brick Kiln Rd
  Ellingham NR35 . . . . . . .8 C3
  Harkstead IP9 . . . . . . 106 B6
  Mildenhall IP28 . . . . . 116 D5
Brick La
  Framlingham IP13 . . . 126 D1
  Parham IP13. . . . . .71 A7
Brickman's Hill CO11 105 B2
Brickwork La NR33. . . .11 B3
Bridewell Cl IP28 . . . 116 B4
Bridewell La
  Botesdale IP22. . . . . . . .36 A6
  Bury St Edmunds IP33 154 C2
Bridewell St CO10. . . .90 B8
Bridge Cl **16** IP29 . . . .22 D6
Bridge Cottage★
  CO7. . . . . 151 D1
Bridge End Rd IP28 . . .30 B1
Bridge Farm Barns (Craft
  Ctr)★ IP2 . . . . 79 D2
Bridge Farm Bsns Pk
  IP12 . . . . 146 C2
Bridge Farm Ct IP28 .116 B3
Bridge Foot Cnr
  IP18. . . . . 119 C7
BRIDGE GREEN 20 F6
Bridge La IP19. . . . . . 118 E2
Bridgeman Wlk IP32 122 F7
Bridge Pk (Skate Park)★
  IP1 . . . . 155 B1
Bridge Pl **13** CO11. . 104 E4
Bridge Rd
  Bromeswell IP12 . . . . . .85 A6
  Burston & Shimpling
    IP22 . . . . .20 E7
  Felixstowe IP11 . . . . . 153 A5
  Levington IP10 . . . . . . 145 E4
  Lowestoft NR32 . . . . . 112 E1
  Reydon IP18 . . . . 119 C7
  6 Scole IP21 . . . . . . .20 F1
  Snape IP17 . . . . .72 D4
Bridge St Rd CO10 . . . .79 A2
Bridge Sch The IP8. . 138 C2
Bridge St
  Beccles NR34 . . . . . . 111 A7
  Brandon IP27 . . . . .5 F2
  Bungay NR35 . . . . 110 B4
  4 Bures Hamlet CO8. 101 C5
  Carlton IP17 . . . . 128 D6
  Framlingham IP13 . . . 126 C3
  Hadleigh IP7 . . . . 149 C7
  Halesworth IP19 . . . . 118 B4
  Huntingfield IP19 . . . . .41 A4
  Ipswich IP1 . . . . 155 B2
  Moulton CB8. . . . . .45 F3
  Needham Market IP6. . 125 D5
  Renndham IP17 . . . . . . .56 F3
  Stowmarket IP14 . . . . 124 F5
  Thetford IP24 . . . . .16 B5
BRIDGE STREET 77 F4
Bridge Terr **7** CO10. 148 F6
Bridge Trad Est IP6. . .82 A5
Bridge Wlk IP14 . . . . .66 D8
Bridge Wood Nature
  Reserve★ IP3 . . . . 144 B6
Bridgewood Rd IP12 146 F5
Bridgham La NR16 . . . .17 F8
Bridgwater Rd IP2 . . 138 D2
Bridlemere Ct CB8 . . 120 F3

Bridles The **4** NR34..**111** F4
Bridport Ave IP3.... **140** D3
Brier La IP31 ...... **17** E1
Bright Cl
　Bury St Edmunds
　　IP33 .... **123** C3
　Saxmundham IP17 ... **128** B4
Brighton St IP27..... **14** A3
Bright's La CO10 ..... **78** C4
Brights Wlk IP5...... **141** E7
BRIGHTWELL **98** A6
Brightwell Cl
　Felixstowe IP11 .... **152** C4
　Ipswich IP3 .... **140** C4
Brightwell St IP10 ... **98** A5
Brimstone Rd IP8.... **142** E8
Brindles The 7
　NR33 .... **114** E4
BRINKLEY **59** E2
Brinkley Rd
　Brinkley CB8....... **59** E1
　Carlton CB8 .... **74** A8
　Dullingham CB8 .... **59** F4
Brinkley Way IP11 ... **153** D7
Brisbane Rd IP4 ..... **140** D6
Briscoe Way
　Framlingham IP13 .. **126** A4
　Lakenheath IP27 ... **109** C8
Bristol Hill IP9...... **107** A4
Bristol Rd
　Bury St Edmunds
　　IP33 .... **122** B3
　Ipswich IP4 .... **140** A7
Bristol St IP27 ...... **14** A2
Britannia Prim Sch
　IP4 .... **140** B5
Britannia Rd IP4..... **140** B6
Britten Ave IP14 .... **124** C7
Britten Cl IP15 ..... **130** D5
Britten Ctr The
　NR32............ **113** D1
Britten Rd NR33..... **115** A6
Brittons Cres 3 IP29..**47** A2
Brittons Rd 8 IP29..**47** A2
Brize Norton **17** IP27 ..**13** F2
Broadcorner Drove
　IP27............. **13** C3
Broadcroft Cres CB9 **132** C6
Broadfields Rd
　5 Gislingham IP23 ..**36** D2
　7 Gislingham IP23 ..**36** D2
Broad Fleet Cl 2
　NR32............ **112** E4
Broad Gn Cl **4** IP29..**62** C6
BROADGRASS
　GREEN.......... **50** C1
Broadgrass Green
　IP30............. **50** C2
BROAD GREEN
　Cheveley **60** F6
　Chevington **62** B6
　Creeting St Peter or West
　　Creeting......... **67** C6
　Steeple Bumpstead CB9 **88** F5
Broad Green Rd IP14..**67** C6
Broadhill Drove CB7 ..**28** D7
Broad La CO6........ **102** E1
Broadland Cl
　Beccles NR34....... **111** E4
　Lowestoft NR33 .... **114** C7
Broadland Rd IP33... **123** B1
Broadlands Hall Sch
　CB9.............. **74** E2
Broadlands Way IP4 **140** F5
Broad Meadow
　2 Ipswich IP8..... **138** C2
　2 Walsham le Willows
　　IP31........... **35** C2
Broadmere Rd IP11.. **138** E8
Broadoak Cl 4
　NR33............. **114** C4
Broad Oaks CO6 ..... **102** B8
Broad Piece CB7..... **28** C5
Broad Rd
　Cotton IP14........ **52** A6
　Little Thurlow CB9.... **74** F6
　Lowestoft NR32 ..... **112** D1
　Wickham Market IP13 **127** B7
Broads Rd CB5....... **44** B8
Broads Rd Bsns Pk
　CB5.............. **44** B7
Broad St
　Boxford CO10....... **93** C3
　Bungay NR35....... **110** A5
　Eye IP23 .... **117** D2
　20 Harleston IP20....**22** D6
　Haverhill CB9 ...... **132** D6
　Orford IP12 .... **131** C2
BROAD STREET.... **52** A2
Broad View Rd NR32 **114** C8
Broadwater Gdns 6
　IP9.............. **107** A4
Broadwaters Rd
　NR33............. **114** C5
BROADWAY **118** C6
Broadway
　6 Fressingfield IP21.. **39** E8
　11 Glemsford CO10 .. **77** A3
　Pakenham IP31 ..... **49** F8
　Wickham Market IP13 **127** B7
Broad Way
　Dickleburgh & Rushall
　　IP21........... **21** A4
　Shimpling IP21...... **21** B4
　Smallworth IP22...... **18** C5
Broadway Dr IP19 ... **118** C6
Broadway La
　Ipswich IP1........ **134** E2
　Smallworth IP22...... **18** D4
　Smallworth IP22...... **18** D4
Broadway The
　Badwell Ash IP31.... **50** F8
　Wickham Skeith IP23 ..**52** D8
BROCKDISH **21** F2
Brockdish Prim Sch
　IP21 .... **22** A2
Brockesby Wlk IP33. **122** D4
BROCKFORD GREEN ..**53** A4
Brockford Rd IP14 ... **53** A4
BROCKFORD STREET..**52** F5
Brock La IP13 ...... **146** C2
BROCKLEY CORNER..**32** D2
Brockley Cres IP1... **134** D1
BROCKLEY GREEN
　Hartest............ **63** A1
　Hundon............ **75** C2
Brockley Green Rd
　CO10............. **75** D2
Brockley La IP29..... **46** F2
Brockley Rd
　Hartest IP29........ **77** A8
　Whepstead IP29...... **63** B4
Brocks Bsns Ctr CB9 **132** C3
Broke Ave IP8 .... **134** B2
BROKE HALL **140** E3
Broke Hall Com Prim Sch
　IP4 .... **140** E5
Broke Hall Gdns IP9 **140** E5
Broke Hall Pk IP10.. **145** C3
BROME............ **117** B7
Brome Ave IP23 ..... **117** B8
Brome Hall La IP23 .. **117** A7
Brome Ind Est IP23. **117** A6
Brome Link Rd IP23. **117** A7
Brome Rd IP21 ..... **117** A7
BROME STREET **117** E8
BROMESWELL...... **85** A5
Bromeswell Gn Nature
　Reserve★ IP12 ..... **147** F7
Bromeswell Rd IP4 . **135** E1
Bromley Cl **4** IP29 ... **139** C3
Bromley Rd CO11 .... **104** D1
Bronyon Cl IP33 .... **122** C5
Brook Cl
　Horringer IP29...... **122** B1
　Hundon CO10....... **75** D3
　Lowestoft NR33 .... **114** D4
　Stowmarket IP14 ... **124** B7
Brook Dam La **22** CB7 ..**28** D4
Brook Dr 3 IP17..... **56** F8
Brooke Bsns & Ind Pk
　NR33............. **1** B6
Brookes Corner IP29.. **62** E6
Brookes UK Independent
　Sch IP28 .... **47** E7
Brooke Way IP14 .... **124** B8
Brook Farm La
　Grundisburgh IP13...**83** D5
　4 Holbrook IP9 .... **105** E7
Brook Farm Rd
　Badwell Ash IP31.... **50** E7
　Saxmundham IP17 ... **128** B4
Brook Field **6** CB8... **60** E7
Brookfield Rd
　Ipswich IP1........ **138** F8
　Mount Bures CO6 ... **101** A1
Brookfields Cl CB8... **121** B5
BROOK GREEN **63** C5
Brook Hall Rd CO10 ..**93** C3
Brookhill Way IP4... **140** F4
Brookhouse Bsns Pk
　IP2.............. **138** F6
Brook House Rd IP14 **52** B6
Brook La
　Burgate IP22....... **36** E6
　Burgate IP22....... **36** E6
　Capel St Mary IP9... **150** C4
　Felixstowe IP11 .... **153** B5
　Framlingham IP13 .. **126** B3
　Lawford CO11....... **104** C2
　Mickfield IP14...... **53** A2
　Needham IP20....... **22** B4
　Playford IP6 .... **137** A4
　St Margaret, Ilketshall
　　NR35........... **24** C7
　Trimley St Martin IP10 ..**98** E1
Brooklands Cl IP33 . **154** A1
Brooklands Prim Sch
　CO11............. **104** E4
Brooklands Rd CO11 **104** E4
Brooklands Rise
　CO11............. **104** E4
Brooklyn Ct 30 CO12..**107** B2
Brooklyn Rd 14
　CO12............. **107** B2
Brook Pk IP22....... **35** F5
Brook Rd NR34 ...... **10** B4
Brook Service Rd 1
　CB9.............. **132** C7
Brooksfield **1** IP7 ... **79** F4
Brooks Hall Rd IP1... **139** A7
Brookside
　Dalham CB8........ **61** C8
　Moulton CB8........ **45** F3
　Newmarket CB8 .... **120** C8
Brooks Malting 33
　CO11............. **104** E2
Brook St
　Dedham CO7........ **103** E4
　Glemsford CO10..... **77** A3
　Soham CB7......... **28** D3
　Upsher Green CO10.. **92** C4

Brook St continued
　Woodbridge IP12 ... **147** A5
　Yoxford IP17....... **57** D7
BROOK STREET **77** A3
Brooksview **14** IP7 ... **79** F4
BROOK THE **36** E7
Brookview
　6 Ipswich IP2...... **142** E8
　Pinewood IP2....... **142** E8
Brook Way **8** IP8..... **81** C3
Broom Cres IP3 ..... **139** F1
BROOME **110** D7
BROOME HEATH **110** D7
Broomfield
　Martlesham IP5 ..... **141** F7
　17 Martlesham Heath
　　IP5............ **98** A8
Broomfield Comm
　IP8.............. **138** B6
Broomfield Mews 18
　IP5.............. **98** A8
Broomhayes IP3 ..... **139** A2
Broomheath IP12 ... **146** F2
Broomhill IP9 .... **105** E7
Broomhill Cl **2** IP28 ..**30** C1
Broomhill La IP30.... **50** C1
Broom Hill La
　Fakenham Magna
　　IP24........... **33** E7
　Kirton IP10 .... **98** D4
Broom Hill Nature
　Reserve★ IP7 ..... **149** C5
Broom Hill Rd IP1... **139** A8
Broom Hill Swimming
　Pool IP1.......... **139** A8
Broom Knoll **1**
　CO11............. **104** E5
Broomley Gn Rd
　IP32............. **123** F6
Broom Pin IP28...... **46** E6
Broom Rd
　Lakenheath IP27 ... **109** E5
　2 Lowestoft NR32... **113** B2
Broom Rd Cl IP27 ... **109** E5
BROOM'S BARN **46** F4
Broomspath Rd IP14..**67** A6
Broom St CO10 ..... **148** F3
Broomvale Bsns Ctr
　IP8.............. **134** A7
Broomwade Cl IP2.. **139** A5
Broom Way IP9...... **150** E4
Broom Wlk **9** IP28.... **30** B8
Brotherton Ave IP11 **152** B8
Brotherton Way 11
　NR31............. **3** B6
Broughton Dr CB9 ... **133** A8
Broughton Rd IP1 .. **155** A4
Browning Rd
　10 Brantham CO11...**104** E4
　Ipswich IP1........ **134** F3
Brownlow Rd IP11 .. **153** A4
Browns Cl
　5 Acton CO10...... **92** B7
　Hitcham IP7........ **79** E6
　5 Wickhambrook CB8 ..**61** E2
Browns Gr IP5...... **141** D7
Brown St IP14 ...... **52** A2
Browse Cl IP32 ..... **123** E4
BROWSTON GREEN ..**2** E8
Browston La NR32... **2** E7
Broxtead Cl IP12..... **85** C2
Broxtead Estate Rd
　IP12............. **99** A8
Bruce St NR33 ...... **115** C7
Brudenell St IP15.... **130** E3
Bruff Rd IP7 .... **139** C3
Bruges Cl **14** CO12 ... **107** A1
BRUISYARD **56** C3
Bruisyard Rd IP13.... **56** C3
Bruisyard Vineyard★
　IP17 .... **56** C5
BRUNDISH **40** A7
Brundish La IP12 ... **131** C3
Brundish Rd
　Brundish Street IP13 ..**39** F2
　Wingfield IP21...... **39** C2
BRUNDISH STREET ..**39** F2
BRUNDON **148** A7
Brundon La CO10 ... **148** A5
Brunel Rd IP2 ...... **138** E6
Brunel Way IP24..... **16** B7
Brunel Way Ind Est
　IP24............. **16** B7
Brunswick Gdns **22**
　CO11............. **105** A2
Brunswick House Cut 13
　CO11............. **105** A2
Brunswick Rd IP4.... **135** F1
Bruntingthorpe **18**
　IP27............. **13** F2
Brunwyn Cl IP32.... **123** F6
Brushmakers St **11**
　NR35............. **110** C3
Bryant Cl
　Haverhill CB9 ...... **132** C7
　6 Lowestoft NR33... **114** F3
Buccaneer Rd IP31... **33** D5
Buckanay La IP12.... **99** E5
Buckenham Ct **17**
　IP18............. **119** D5

Buckenham Rd IP7 ..**149** D4
Buckfast Cl **4** IP2 .... **139** A2
Buckingham Cl 4
　IP12............. **84** A1
Buckingham Rd CB9 **132** C4
Buckingham's Hill
　IP21............. **39** E8
Buck La IP23 .... **117** E8
Buckles Field **8** IP31 ..**34** E4
BUCKLESHAM **98** A5
Bucklesham Hall Dr
　IP10............. **98** B5
Bucklesham Prim Sch
　IP10............. **98** B4
Bucklesham Rd
　Ipswich IP3 .... **140** E2
　Kirton IP10 .... **98** D3
Buckleswood Rd
　IP16............. **129** A7
Bucknam Cl **14** NR33 ..**11** C1
Bucks Green IP23.... **53** F6
Buck's Head La IP6 .. **67** F2
Buckshorn La IP23.. **117** D2
Buck's Horns La IP8 **142** B6
Buckthorn Way **25**
　IP28............. **46** A8
Buddleia Cl IP22.... **138** E4
Bude Cl IP5 .... **141** A6
Buggs Hole La IP22 ..**18** D2
Bugg's La
　Brettenham IP7 ..... **65** C1
　Hitcham IP7........ **79** D8
Bugg's Rd IP22 ...... **36** D6
Bugsby Way IP5 .... **141** E7
BULCAMP **42** D7
Bulcamp Drift IP19 ..**43** A7
Bullace La IP12 ..... **131** A8
Bullard's La IP12 ... **146** E5
Bull Dr IP5 .... **141** C6
Bullen Cl
　Bramford IP8 ...... **134** A2
　Bury St Edmunds IP33 **154** A1
Bullen La **5** IP8 ..... **134** A2
Bullens Cl IP33 ..... **122** A5
Buller Rd IP16 ...... **129** C6
Bullfinch Cl **24** CO12..**106** F1
Bull Hall La IP6...... **83** A5
Bullion's La NR34 ... **26** B2
Bull La
　Acton CO10......... **78** A1
　Hawstead IP29...... **63** C5
　Long Melford CO10.. **91** E8
　Rickinghall Superior
　　IP22........... **36** B4
Bull Lane Ind Est
　CO10............. **92** A8
Bullock Fair Cl **14**
　IP20............. **22** B6
Bullocked La IP12 ... **131** C4
Bullocks La CO10 ... **148** C5
Bull Rd
　Ipswich IP3 .... **140** B4
　Pakenham IP31 ..... **49** F6
　Thornham Parva IP23..**37** B3
Bullride Mws IP12 .. **147** A5
Bull Rush Cres IP33. **154** A4
Bull's Ash Cnr IP7 ... **80** F5
Bull's Rd IP6 .... **82** C7
Bullswood La
　Cockfield IP30 ...... **64** D1
　Saxstead Green IP13.. **54** F4
Bull's Wood Nature
　Reserve★ IP30..... **64** C1
BULMER........... **91** C3
Bulmer La CO10...... **93** C4
Bulmer Rd CO10 ... **148** A4
Bulmer Rd Ind Est
　CO10............. **148** A4
Bulmer St Andrews CE
　Prim Sch CO10 ... **91** C2
Bulmer St
　Bulmer CO10....... **91** C3
　Foxearth CO10 ..... **91** B7
BULMER TYE **91** D1
Bulstrode Rd IP2 ... **155** C1
Bulwer Rd IP1...... **139** A6
Bumblebee Gdns
　NR34............. **111** B2
Bumpstead Rd CB9.. **132** F3
Bunbury Ave
　1 Great Barton IP31..**49** A5
　Mildenhall IP28 .... **116** C5
Bunbury Rd **8** IP32.. **48** C5
Bunbury Terr **9**
　CB8.............. **121** A3
Bungalow Rd NR34...**26** C2
BUNGAY.......... **110** B3
Bungay Castle (rems)★
　NR35............. **110** A4
Bungay High Sch
　NR35............. **110** C2
Bungay Mus★ NR35 **110** B4
Bungay Prim Sch
　NR35............. **110** C3
Bungay Rd
　Alburgh IP20....... **7** B1
　Barsham NR34...... **9** B4
　Beccles NR34....... **111** A4
　Bungay NR35....... **8** A8
　Dickleburgh & Rushall
　　IP21........... **21** B1
　Ellingham NR35 .... **8** C8
　Halesworth IP19 ... **118** B4
　Halesworth IP19 ... **118** C7
　Redenhall IP20...... **22** F7
　Scole IP21 .... **21** A1

Bungay Rd continued
　Stockton NR34 ..... **8** F8
Bunker La NR33 .... **115 A5
Bunkers Hill
　Bramfield IP19...... **41** F3
　Lawshall Green IP29 ..**77** F7
Bunn's La IP21...... **22** C6
Bunters Rd CB8..... **61** E2
Bunting Rd
　Bury St Edmunds
　　IP32 .... **123** F4
　Ipswich IP2 .... **138** D3
Buntings Cres **15** CB5 **44** A8
Buntings La IP5...... **24** D2
Buntings Path CB5... **44** A6
Buntings The **19** IP14 **67** A5
Buntry La CO10...... **75** C2
Bunyan Cl IP1 ...... **135** A3
Burch's Cl IP17 ..... **129** A2
Burdock La IP26..... **4** C3
Burdock Rd IP28..... **46** A8
Buregate Rd IP11.... **152** F2
BURES............ **101** C5
Bures CE VC Prim Sch
　CO8.............. **101** C4
Bures Cl IP14 ...... **124** E4
Bures Ct **6** CB9..... **132** C5
BURES GREEN **101** D6
Bures Rd
　Lamarsh CO8....... **101** B6
　Little Cornard CO10 **101** A8
　Mount Bures CO6 ... **101** A2
　Nayland-with-Wissington
　　CO6 .... **101** D1
　Rose Green CO10 ... **101** E8
　Sudbury CO10...... **148** A3
Bures Sta CO8 ..... **101** C4
BURGATE **36** E6
Burgate Rd
　Gislingham IP23 .... **36** D3
　Higham IP28....... **46** E3
Burgess Cl **5** NR32 .. **112** F2
Burgess Pl **22** IP5 ... **98** A8
BURGH **83** F6
Burghley Cl **14** IP29 .. **139** A2
Burghley Rise **5** CB5..**44** B5
Burgh Rd
　Burgh St Peter NR34.. **2** C1
　Burgh St Peter NR34.. **10** D8
BURGH ST PETER ... **10** B8
Burke Cl IP1........ **135** A3
Burke Rd **7** IP1 ..... **135** A3
Burkitt Rd IP12 ..... **146** E5
Burkitts La IP12 ..... **148** D6
Burlingham Cl 6
　IP16............. **129** A6
Burlingham Dr NR33 **114** B3
Burlington Rd IP1 .. **155** A3
Burling Way **4** CB5... **45** A4
Burnet Cl IP8 ...... **142** D8
Burnham Cl
　Felixstowe IP11 .... **152** C7
　Ipswich IP4 .... **139** F7
Burnham Way NR33 **115** A4
Burns Cl IP23....... **37** B5
Burns Dr IP14 ...... **124** C8
Burns Rd IP1 .... **134** E3
Burnt Dick Hill CO4 **102** E4
Burnt Fen Turnpike
　IP28............. **12** C6
Burnt Hill La NR33 .. **114** B7
Burnt Hill Way NR33. **114** D5
Burnt House Cl 3
　CB9.............. **132** A7
Burnthouse La
　Battisford IP14...... **66** D1
　Needham IP20 ..... **22** B8
Burnt House La IP10 **98** D2
Burnt La IP21 ...... **131** C2
Burnt Oak Cnr CO7.. **151** D3
Burntoak La IP20 ... **22** E8
Burr Cl
　17 Harwich CO12...**106** C1
　16 Stowmarket IP14..**67** A6
Burrell Cres IP28 ... **116** D2
Burrell Rd IP2 ..... **155** B1
Burrell's Orch IP33. **122** A6
Burrell Way IP24.... **16** A5
BURROUGH END.... **59** E2
Burrough Gn CE Prim
　Sch CB8........... **59** F2
BURROUGH GREEN..**59** F2
Burroughs Piece Rd **2**
　CO10............. **148** D5
Burrow Dr IP27 .... **109** C8
Burrows Cl CO11 ... **104** D2
Burrows Gn NR34.... **2** A1
Burrows Rd **7** IP12.. **84** E6
BURSTALL **95** D7
Burstall Hall La IP8.. **95** E7
BURSTALLHILL **95** C8
Burstall Hill IP8 .... **95** C8
Burstall La IP8...... **95** E7
Burstall Rd IP8...... **95** E8
BURSTON **20** E6
Burston Com Prim Sch
　IP22............. **20** E6
Burston Rd
　Dickleburgh & Rushall
　　IP21........... **20** F4
　Diss IP22......... **20** D4
　Gissing IP22....... **20** F7
　Scole IP21 .... **21** B5
BURTHORPE **47** B3
Burton Cl
　11 Diss IP22....... **20** B3

Burton Cl continued
　Haverhill CB9 ...... **132** C5
Burton Dr IP6 ...... **125** C2
Burton End
　Haverhill CB9 ...... **132** A4
　Haverhill CB9 ...... **132** C5
Burton End Com Prim
　Sch CB9........... **132** B5
Burton Green CB9 ... **74** B3
Burton Hill CB9 ..... **74** B3
Burton St NR32 .... **113** C2
Burtonwood IP27 ... **14** A2
Burwash **1** IP6...... **83** A5
BURWELL **44** B5
Burwell Mus★ CB5 ..**44** B5
Burwell Rd
　Exning CB8 .... **120** A8
　Exning CB8 .... **120** A8
Burwell Village Coll Prim
　Sch CB5.......... **44** A6
Burwood Pl
　7 Lowestoft NR32...**113** B6
　Trimley St Mary IP11 **152** C8
Bury Bottom IP27.... **15** A5
Bury Drift IP31 ..... **48** C6
Bury Hill IP12....... **147** A7
Bury Hill Cl IP12 ... **147** A7
Bury La
　Barnham IP24....... **16** E1
　Lidgate CB8 .... **61** C4
　Moulton CB8........ **45** F3
　Stanton IP31........ **34** E3
　Wickhambrook CB8 .. **61** E4
Bury Pk Dr IP33..... **123** C2
Bury Rd
　Alpheton CO10...... **78** A5
　Barnardiston CB9.... **75** A5
　Barrow IP29........ **47** A2
　Beyton IP30........ **49** E2
　Bradfield St Clare IP30 ..**64** C4
　Brandon IP27 ...... **14** F8
　Brettenham IP7 ..... **79** C7
　Brockley IP29....... **63** A2
　Bury St Edmunds IP29 **122** C1
　Bury St Edmunds IP31 **123** F8
　Bury St Edmunds IP33 **122** A5
　Chedburgh IP29 .... **62** D4
　Cockfield IP30 ...... **64** C1
　Felsham IP30....... **65** A4
　Flempton IP28 ..... **47** F8
　Fornham All Saints
　　IP28........... **48** B8
　Fornham St Martin
　　IP31........... **48** E5
　Great Barton IP31... **49** A5
　Great Livermere IP31..**33** C1
　Great Thurlow CB9 ..**74** F5
　Great Whelnetham
　　IP30........... **63** F4
　Haughley IP14 ..... **66** D3
　Hengrave IP28...... **48** A7
　Hepworth IP22...... **35** A4
　Ipswich IP1 .... **134** D4
　Kentford CB8 ...... **46** B5
　Lady's Green CB8 .... **61** F6
　Lavenham CO10..... **78** C5
　Lawshall IP29....... **63** D2
　Little Saxham IP29... **47** E2
　Market Weston IP22...**18** B1
　Mildenhall IP28 .... **116** E4
　Moulton CB8........ **45** D4
　Newmarket CB8 .... **121** C5
　Rickinghall Inferior
　　IP22........... **35** F5
　Sicklesmere IP30.... **63** F7
　Stanton IP31........ **34** F4
　Stowmarket IP14 ... **124** C8
　Thetford IP24....... **16** B3
　Thorpe Morieux IP30 ..**64** E7
　Timworth Green IP31 ..**48** D7
　Wickhambrook CB8 ..**61** F1
　Wortham IP22...... **36** E8
BURY ST
　EDMUNDS........ **154** C2
Bury St Edmunds
　Abbey★ IP33 ...... **154** C2
Bury St Edmunds Abbey
　Gdns★ IP33....... **154** C2
Bury St Edmunds Art
　Gall★ IP33........ **154** B2
Bury St Edmunds County
　Upper Sch IP32 ... **154** A4
Bury St Edmunds Leisure
　Ctr IP33.......... **122** C3
Bury St Edmunds Sta
　IP32............. **154** B4
Bury St **3** IP14 ..... **124** C4
Bush Cnr IP14 ...... **53** E1
Bushel La CB7 ...... **28** D4
Bushey Cl IP9 ..... **150** E3
Bush Gr CO10 ..... **148** A4
BUSH GREEN **64** C4
Bush La IP13 ...... **54** C1
Bushman Gdns 3
　IP8.............. **134** A2
Bushy La IP12 ...... **99** E7
Bussock La IP12 .... **99** D7
Buston Rd **5** IP22 ... **20** B2
Butchers La IP9 .... **150** F3
Butcher's La CO10 ... **93** C4
Butcher's Rd IP17... **128** E7
Bute Ct IP9......... **132** D4
Butfield CO10....... **78** D3
Butchers Rd IP12 ... **147** A7
Butler's La CO11 ... **105** F1
Butler Smith Gdns 6
　IP5.............. **141** C7
Butlers Way CO9.... **90** A1

BUTLEY 86 B5
Butley Cl IP2 . . . . . .142 F8
Butley Ct **8** CB9 . . . .132 C3
Butley Dr **3** NR32 . .112 F3
BUTLEY HIGH
  CORNER 86 C4
BUTLEY LOW
  CORNER 86 C4
Butley Pottery ★ IP12 .86 B6
Butley Rd IP11 . . . . . .152 E3
Buttenhaugh Green
  IP30 . . . . .50 F4
Buttercup Cl
  Bury St Edmunds
   IP32 . . . . .123 F5
  Ipswich IP8 . . . . . . .138 C1
  Isleham CB7 . . . . . . .29 C4
  3 Lowestoft NR33 . .114 C4
Butterfly Dr NR34 . . . 114 A2
Butterfly Gdns IP4 . .140 E5
  IP1 . . . . .155 B3
Buttermarket Sh Ctr
  IP1 . . . . .155 B3
Buttermere Gn IP11. 153 D6
Buttermere Way
  NR33 . . . . .114 D2
Butter Mkt
  Bury St Edmunds
   IP33 . . . . .154 B2
  Ipswich IP1 . . . . . . .155 B3
Butt La IP24 . . . . .33 E7
BUTTON HAUGH
  GREEN 50 F4
Buttons Cl CO10 . . . . .91 D6
BUTTON'S GREEN . . .78 E8
Buttons Hill IP13. . . . .55 C5
Button's Rd IP13. . . . .71 D6
Butt Rd
  Stoke-by-Nayland
   CO6 . . . . .102 E7
  Sudbury CO10 . . . . .148 F4
Buttrum's Mill ★
  IP12 . . . . .146 E5
Butts Cl **10** CB7 . . . . .28 D3
Butts La CB7 . . . . .28 B1
Butts Rd IP6 . . . . . . .137 A3
Butt's Rd
  Holton IP19 . . . . . . .118 D8
  Spexhall IP19 . . . . . . .25 A4
Butts The
  Debenham IP14 . . . . .53 E2
  Soham CB7 . . . . .28 D3
BUXHALL 66 A4
BUXHALL FEN
  STREET 66 A6
Buxhall Rd
  Cook's Green IP7 . . . .79 E8
  World's End IP7 . . . . .65 C5
Buxlow Cl IP17 . . . . .129 B2
Buxton Way IP19 . . . .118 C4
Buzzard Cl **20** NR31 . . .3 B6
Buzzard Rise **23** IP14. .67 A5
Byerley Cl **4** CB8 . . . . .45 F5
Byfield Way IP33 . . . .123 C3
Byford Rd CO10 . . . . .148 E7
Bylam La IP9 . . . . . . .106 A7
Byland Cl **6** IP2 . . . . .139 A2
Byng Hall Rd
  Pettistree IP13. . . . . .84 E8
  Ufford IP13. . . . . . . .127 A1
Byng La IP13 . . . . . . .127 A3
Byrd Cl IP33 . . . . . . .122 C4
Byron Cl IP14 . . . . . .124 C8
Byron Rd IP1 . . . . . .134 E4

C

Cabin Cl NR33 . . . . . .114 B4
Cable La IP15. . . . . . .130 E5
Caddie's Wlk NR33 . .115 A5
Cadenham Rd CB5 . . . .44 A1
Cadiz Way **1** NR31 . . . .3 C6
Cadmus Rd IP1 . . . . .138 D7
Cadney La IP33 . . . . .154 B3
Cadogan Rd IP33 . . . .122 D4
Cadwall Way CB7 . . . .28 C5
Caernarvon Wlk CB9 .132 C6
Cage La
  Boxted CO4. . . . . . . .103 A3
  Felixstowe IP11. . . . .152 E5
Cages Way **1** IP14. . . .84 E6
Cagman's La IP14. . . . .65 F3
Caithness Cl IP4 . . . .140 B8
Caie Wlk IP33 . . . . . .123 D2
Cakebridge La IP7 . . . .79 D3
Cake St Cl **21** IP28. . . .30 B8
Cake St IP13. . . . . . . .39 F4
Calais St
  Boxford CO10 . . . . . .93 D3
  Hadleigh IP7 . . . . . . .149 D6
CALAIS STREET 93 D2
Caldecott Rd NR32 . .112 D1
Calder Rd **6** IP12. . . . .84 E6
Caledonia Rd **8** IP9 .107 A4
Calfe Fen Cl **3** CB7 . . .28 D5
Calfe Fen Dro CB7 . . . .28 D5
Calford Dr CB9. . . . . .132 A6
CALFORD GREEN . . .133 D5
CALIFORNIA 140 B6
California IP12 . . . . .146 D3
California La IP8. . . . . .95 B4
California Rd **14**
  CO11 . . . . .105 A2
Calkewood La IP22 . . . .35 E5
Calledge Drove IP27 . .13 F7
Callendars Houses
  NR34 . . . . .9 A4
Callis St **5** CO10 . . . .90 A8

Callisto Ct IP1 . . . . . .138 D7
Callow Balk CB7 . . . . .28 D2
Callowhill La IP31 . . . .33 D2
Callums Ct IP13. . . . .126 D3
Calthorpe Cl IP32 . . .123 E6
Calvers La NR34 . . . . .24 D7
Calves La CO6 . . . . . .102 D8
Camberley Ct IP33 . .154 A3
Camberley Rd IP4 . . .140 D7
Camborne Rd IP5. . . .141 B7
Cambria Cl **9** CO11 .105 A2
Cambrian Cres **2**
  NR32 . . . . .112 D2
Cambridge Cl CB9 . . .132 C7
Cambridge Dr
  Ipswich IP2 . . . . .138 F2
  38 Lawford CO11 . . .104 D2
Cambridge Rd
  Dullingham CB8 . . . . .59 C7
  Felixstowe IP11 . . . . .153 B4
  Haverhill CB9 . . . . . .132 A8
  Ipswich IP5 . . . . .141 A7
  Lowestoft NR32 . . . . .113 D3
Cambridge Way
  9 Bures CO8 . . . . . .101 C4
  Mildenhall IP28 . . . . .132 C7
Camden Rd IP3 . . . . .140 B4
Camden St **5** NR32 . .113 E3
Camelot Rd **3** NR31. . .3 A8
Cameron Cl CO10 . . . .91 E7
Campbell Cl
  Framlingham IP13 . . .126 A4
  1 Mildenhall IP28 . .116 B5
Campbell Rd IP3. . . . .140 C1
Camp Cl **2** IP26 . . . . .4 D5
Campion Cl CB7 . . . . .28 C5
Campion Cres IP14 . .124 C4
Campion La CO6 . . . .102 B6
Campion Rd IP2 . . . .138 F4
Campions Hill CO6. . .102 B7
Campion Way CO6 . . .102 B7
Camp Rd
  Lowestoft NR32 . . . . .113 D1
  15 Thorpeness IP16 . . .73 F6
CAMPSEA ASHE 71 C3
CAMPS HEATH 112 D3
Camps Rd
  Haverhill CB9 . . . . . .132 D5
  Helions Bumpstead
   CB9. . . . . .88 A5
Camwood Gdns IP3 .140 B4
Canaletto Cl **4**
  NR32 . . . . .113 B6
Canberra Cl
  Ipswich IP4 . . . . .140 D6
  2 Mildenhall IP28 . . . .30 A8
Candler's La **18** IP20 . .22 D6
Candle St IP22. . . . . . .35 F5
CANDLE STREET 35 F5
Candlet Farm La
  IP11. . . . . .152 F8
Candlet Gr IP11. . . . . .152 F5
Candlet Rd IP11 . . . . .152 E7
Cangles La IP30 . . . . . .49 F1
Canhams Farm Rd
  CO10 . . . . .89 E8
CANHAM'S GREEN . . .51 F4
Canhams Rd CO10 . . .148 F3
Canham St IP1 . . . . . .155 A3
Cann Cl CO10 . . . . . .148 C8
Canning Rd NR33 . . . .115 B8
Canning St **10** CO12 . .107 B3
Cannonfields IP33 . . .154 B3
Cannon St IP33. . . . . .154 B3
Canon Cl CB9 . . . . . .132 D7
Canon Pugh Dr **6**
  CO10 . . . . .92 B7
Canterbury Cl IP2. . .142 F8
Canterbury Gdns
  IP7. . . . . .149 E6
Canterbury Gn IP33 .123 A3
Canterbury Rd CO10 .148 B8
Canterbury Way IP24 .16 B6
Canute Ct IP33 . . . . .123 A3
Capel Cl
  4 Felixstowe IP11. . .107 D8
  Troston IP31. . . . . .33 D3
Capel Dr IP11. . . . . . .152 C4
CAPEL GREEN 86 A4
Capel Grove IP9 . . . .150 E2
Capel Hall La IP11 . . .107 E8
Capel Wlk **2** IP31. . . .34 E4
Capel Rd IP9 . . . . . . .104 E8
CAPEL ST ANDREW . .86 B3
Capel St Andrew Rd
  IP12. . . . . .86 A1
CAPEL ST MARY 150 E4
Capel St Mary CE Prim
  Sch
  Capel St Mary IP9. . . .150 E3
  Copdock IP7 . . . . .95 F4
CAPON'S GREEN 55 E6
Capon's Green IP13. . .55 E6
Capps La IP19 . . . . . . .23 F5
Capstan Way NR33 . .114 B4
Captain's La IP14 . . . . .51 A2
Caraway Rd IP24. . . . .16 D6
Carbonels **12** CO10 . . .92 C6
Cardew Drift IP5. . . . .141 D8
Cardigan St
  Ipswich IP1 . . . . .155 A4
  Newmarket CB8 . . . . .121 A3
Cardinal Cl IP32 . . . .123 E6
Cardinalls Rd IP14 . .124 D7
Cardinal Pk IP1 . . . . .155 B2
Cardinal Rd IP1 . . . . .155 B2

Cardinal Way CB9. . .132 D7
Cardington Rd **10** IP26 . .4 D5
Cardman Dr **6** IP7. . .149 F7
Carey Dr IP19. . . . . . .118 D4
Cargo La **14** IP32. . . . .48 B5
Carlford Cl **14** IP5. . . .98 A8
Carlow Mews **13**
  IP12. . . . . .147 A5
CARLTON
  Carlton 74 A8
  Kelsale cum Carlton . . 128 C6
Carlton Cl
  Great Yeldham CO9. . . .90 A1
  Haverhill CB9 . . . . . .132 D8
CARLTON
  COLVILLE 114 C2
Carlton Colville Prim Sch
  NR33. . . . . .114 C1
Carlton Cross NR33 . .114 C2
Carlton Gn Rd CB8 . . .74 A7
CARLTON GREEN 74 A6
Carlton La IP17. . . . . .57 A4
Carlton Rd
  Brinkley CB8. . . . . . . .59 F1
  Carlton IP17. . . . . . . .128 C5
  Ipswich IP5 . . . . .141 A7
  Lowestoft NR33 . . . . .115 B6
Carlton Sq IP31 . . . . .114 C2
Carlton Way IP4 . . . .139 E8
Carlton Wlk IP7 . . . . .149 E4
Carlyle Cl IP1. . . . . . .134 F4
Carmarthen Cl IP2. . .139 A2
Carmelite Pl **14** IP2 .147 A5
Carnation Way **2**
  IP28. . . . . .46 A8
Carnoustie Dr
  13 Fornham St Martin
   IP28. . . . . .48 C6
  1 Lowestoft NR33. . . .114 F4
Carol Ave **9** IP12 . . . .84 A1
Carolbrook Rd IP2. . .138 E1
Carol Cl IP11 . . . . . . .153 C5
Carpenters Cl CB8 . . .46 C3
Carpenters Yd IP21 . . .39 D8
Carr Ave IP6 . . . . . . .129 D6
Carriage Cl IP11 . . . .152 C8
Carriers Ct CO7 . . . . .151 D5
Carr La
  Bardwell IP31. . . . . . . .34 A3
  Kirton IP11. . . . . .98 B1
Carrops The CB8. . . . . .46 A7
Carr Rd IP11. . . . . . . .152 E1
Carr Road Bsns Ctr
  IP11 . . . . .152 D1
Carrs Hill IP13. . . . . . .56 B6
Carr St IP1 . . . . .155 C3
Carsons Dr **6** CO10 . . .92 B3
Carson Wlk CB8 . . . . .120 F6
Carter Rd CB5 . . . . . . .44 A6
Carters Hill CO4 . . . .103 A3
Carters La IP14 . . . . . .80 E6
Carter St CB7. . . . . . . .29 B1
Carters Teapot Pottery ★
  IP14 . . . . .53 F1
Carters Vineyard ★
  CO4. . . . . .102 F3
Cart Score IP14 . . . . .113 E3
Carver Way **15** IP20 . . .22 D5
Casburn La **13** CB5 . . .44 A6
Case La IP9. . . . . .104 E8
Casey Jones Cl **20**
  IP31. . . . . .49 A3
Castell Cl
  Stradbroke IP21. . . . . .39 A5
  Wickham Market IP13 .127 C7
Castle Ave CB9 . . . . .132 C6
Castle Brooks IP13. . .126 C3
Castle Cl
  Felixstowe IP11 . . . . .153 D6
  Orford IP12 . . . . .131 B2
  Weeting-with-Broomhill
   IP27 . . . . .5 E3
Castle East Sch
  NR35. . . . . .110 D3
Castle Farm La CO7 . .150 B4
Castle Gdns IP5 . . . . .141 E7
CASTLE HILL 135 A3
Castle Hill
  Beccles NR34. . . . . . .111 C4
  Dedham CO7. . . . . . .103 F2
  Eye IP23 . . . . .117 D2
  Eyke IP12 . . . . .85 B6
  Halesworth IP19 . . . .118 C3
  Orford IP12 . . . . .131 C2
  Thorndon IP23 . . . . . .37 E1
Castle Hill Inf Sch
  IP1 . . . . .135 A3
Castle Hill Jun Sch
  IP1 . . . . .135 A3
Castle La
  Bungay NR35 . . . . . .110 A4
  Hadleigh IP7 . . . . . . .149 C7
  Haverhill CB9 . . . . . .132 C6
  Offton IP8. . . . . .81 A4
  Orford IP12 . . . . .131 C2
  Thetford IP24. . . . . . . .16 C5
Castle Manor Acad
  CB9. . . . . .132 C6
Castle Meadow IP8 . . .81 A4
Castle Orch NR35 . . .110 B4
Castle Rd
  Bury St Edmunds
   IP33 . . . . .154 A1

Castle Rd continued
  Hadleigh IP7. . . . . . . .149 B7
  Ipswich IP1 . . . . .134 E1
  Mettingham NR35. . . .110 F2
  Offton IP8. . . . . .81 A4
Castle Rise
  Hadleigh IP7. . . . . . . .149 B7
  2 Haughley IP14. . . . .51 C1
Castle St
  Eye IP23 . . . . .117 D2
  Framlingham IP13 . . .126 D4
  Thetford IP24. . . . . . . .16 C5
  Woodbridge IP12 . . . .147 A5
Castle Terr IP12 . . . . .131 C2
Castleton Ave NR33 .114 B4
Castleton Cl **5**
  NR32 . . . . .113 B4
Castleton Way
  Eye IP23 . . . . .117 B3
  Yaxley IP23. . . . . .37 C5
Castle View IP12 . . . .131 C2
Castle Wlk CB9 . . . . .132 C6
CASTLING'S HEATH . .93 D6
Catchpole Cl **19** NR33 .11 B1
Catchpole Ct CO10 . .148 B5
Catchpole Dr IP5 . . . .141 C6
Catchpole Way **10**
  IP31. . . . . .34 E4
Catchpole Wlk IP21. . .21 C5
Caters Rd IP13. . . . . . .84 C8
Catesbray IP9 . . . . . .150 D3
Catesby Meadow
  CO10 . . . . .148 B4
Cathcart Ct **8** NR32. .113 D2
Cathedral Meadows
  IP33. . . . . .154 B1
Catherine Rd IP12 . . .146 E6
Catherines Hill **4** IP6 .68 B1
Cat House La IP9 . . . .144 C2
Catkin Cl IP3 . . . . . . .132 B7
Catshill IP6. . . . . .81 E6
Cat's La CO10 . . . . . .148 E5
CATTAWADE 104 E4
Cattawade St **12**
  CO11 . . . . .104 E4
Cattlegate IP30 . . . . . .50 F3
Catts Cl IP30 . . . . . . .105 C5
Cattsfield IP9 . . . . . . .105 C5
Caudle Ave IP27 . . . . .109 E4
Caudlehole Drove
  CB7 . . . . .29 B5
Cauldwell Ave IP4 . . .139 F6
Cauldwell Hall Rd
  IP4. . . . . .140 A5
Caulfield Cl **2** IP33 . .122 F3
Causeway
  Haverhill CB9 . . . . . .132 C5
  Lakenheath IP27 . . . .109 B5
  Lowestoft NR33 . . . . .115 B4
Causeway Cl
  Brockdish IP21. . . . . . .21 F2
  8 Glemsford CO10 . . . .77 B3
Causeway End CO11. .104 D3
Causeway Est IP12. . . .79 F7
Causeway The
  Barking IP6. . . . . .125 B2
  Boxford CO10 . . . . . .93 C3
  Burwell CB5 . . . . .44 A5
  Earl Soham IP13. . . . . .54 F2
  Great Horkesley CO6 . .102 D1
  Hitcham IP7 . . . . .79 E6
  Isleham CB7. . . . . . . .29 C5
  Middleton IP17 . . . . . .58 A4
  Needham Market IP6 .125 D4
  4 Occold IP23. . . . . . .37 F1
  Ridgewell CO9 . . . . . .89 C4
  Soham CB7 . . . . .28 D3
  Walsham le Willows
   IP31. . . . . .35 B2
  Westhall IP19 . . . . . . .25 C4
Causton Jun Sch
  IP11 . . . . .152 E6
Caustons Cl **9** CO10 . .92 B3
Cautley Rd IP18. . . . .119 D6
Cavan Rd IP1 . . . . . . .134 D2
Cavell Cl IP12. . . . . . . .99 E3
CAVENDISH 76 D1
Cavendish CE Prim Sch
  CO10. . . . . .76 E1
Cavendish Cl
  7 Lowestoft NR32. . . .113 A3
  Mildenhall IP28 . . . . .116 D6
  12 Thurstow IP31. . . . .34 B1
Cavendish Ct **2** CB9 .132 C4
Cavendish Dr **21**
  CO11 . . . . .104 D2
Cavendish Gdns **16**
  IP11. . . . . .107 D8
Cavendish La CO10. . . .76 F2
Cavendish Rd
  Bury St Edmunds
   IP33 . . . . .122 C6
  Clare CO10 . . . . .90 B8
  Felixstowe IP11 . . . . .152 F3
  Stowmarket IP14 . . . .124 B6
Cavendish St IP3 . . . .139 F4
  CO10 . . . . .148 D5
Cavendish Way **1** . . . .
CAVENHAM 47 A8
Cavenham Heath
  National Nature
  Reserve ★ IP28 . . . . .31 C3
Cavenham Rd
  Risby IP28 . . . . .47 C6
  Tuddenham IP28. . . . . .31 A1
Cawley Rd CO6 . . . . .102 A7
Cawseyhorn Drove
  IP27. . . . . .14 A6

Caxton Mews **4**
  NR34 . . . . .111 B6
Caxton Rd NR34. . . . .111 B6
Caxton Way Ind Est
  IP24 . . . . .16 A5
CAY HILL. 52 C2
Cecilia St IP1. . . . . . .155 B2
Cecil Lodge Cl CB8. . .120 F3
Cecil Rd IP1 . . . . .155 A4
Cedar Ave IP5 . . . . . .141 A6
Cedar Cl
  Bacton IP14 . . . . .51 F6
  7 Brantham CO11. . . .104 E5
  8 Great Bricett IP7. . . .80 D6
  22 Herringswell IP28. . .46 A8
  32 Lakenheath IP27 . . .12 F2
  Occold IP23 . . . . .37 F2
  Stradbroke IP21. . . . . .39 B4
Cedar Cres
  13 Barrow IP29. . . . . .47 A2
  30 Manningtree CO11 .104 E2
Cedarcroft Rd IP4 . . .134 F2
Cedar Ct
  Alderton IP12. . . . . . . .99 E5
  10 Beck Row, Holywell Row
   & Kenny Hill IP28 . . .13 B1
Cedar Dr
  Lowestoft NR33 . . . . .114 C5
  Worlingham NR34. . . .111 F3
Cedar Farm Cl **27** IP6. .82 A5
Cedar Rd
  1 Barrow IP29 . . . . . .47 A2
  2 Bentwaters Airfield
   IP12. . . . . .85 E8
  9 Thetford IP24. . . . . .16 D7
Cedars Hill IP14 . . . . .53 A5
Cedars La IP9 . . . . . .150 D3
Cedars Pk Com Prim Sch
  IP4 . . . . .67 A5
Cedars Rise IP23 . . . . .37 F1
Cedars The IP27 . . . . .109 E5
Cedar Wlk IP6 . . . . . .125 D5
Cedarwood Prim Sch
  IP5 . . . . .141 C6
Celandine Cl
  Lowestoft NR33 . . . . .114 C5
  7 Thorney Green IP14. .67 B7
Celandine View **1**
  CB7 . . . . .28 E3
Celestion Dr **1** IP3 . .140 B4
Cely Rd **4** IP31. . . . . .49 A4
Cemetery Hill CB8 . . .120 F7
Cemetery La
  East Bergholt CO7 . . .151 A4
  Ipswich IP4 . . . . .135 F1
  Woodbridge IP12 . . . .146 E4
Cemetery Rd
  Bedfield IP13 . . . . . . .54 E4
  Eastbridge IP16 . . . . .58 C5
  Ipswich IP4 . . . . .155 C3
  Lakenheath IP27 . . . .109 D6
  Wickhambrook CB8 . . .61 E2
Central Ave IP3 . . . . .144 D8
Central Rd IP16. . . . . .129 C5
Central Rd South
  IP11. . . . . .152 B2
Centre Academy East
  Anglia The IP7 . . . . . .65 C1
Centre Cl NR34 . . . . .111 C3
Centre Dr CB8 . . . . . .121 D2
Centre Rd CB7 . . . . . .28 E2
Century Dr IP5 . . . . .141 E7
Century Rd IP23 . . . .117 C4
Chadacre Rd IP29. . . . .77 B7
Chaffinch Dr **14**
  CO12 . . . . .106 F7
Chaffinch Mws **17**
  IP20. . . . . .22 D5
Chaffinch Rd **1** IP32. .49 A3
Chaffinch Way IP14. .124 F7
Chaffinch Wlk **9**
  IP18. . . . . .30 C8
Chainey Pieces CB9. .132 D5
Chainhouse Rd IP6 . .125 D3
Chalfont Dr **1** IP17 . . .72 C8
Chalk Cl **3** IP24 . . . . .16 C6
Chalkeith Rd IP6. . . . .125 E3
Chalk Hill La IP6. . . . . .81 F5
Chalk Hill Rise **11** IP6 .81 F5
Chalk La
  Culford IP31. . . . . . . .32 E5
  2 Ixworth IP31. . . . . .34 B1
  Needham Market IP6 .125 E3
Chalkners Ct **7** IP9 . .150 E3
Chalk Rd IP27 . . . . . . .5 D1
Chalk Rd (North)
  IP33. . . . . .154 A2
Chalk Rd (South)
  IP33. . . . . .154 A2
Chalkstone Way CB9 .133 A6
Challice Rd IP33. . . . .154 A3
Chalon St IP1. . . . . . .155 A2
Chamberlain Way
  IP8. . . . . .138 C2
Chamberlayne Rd
  IP32. . . . . .123 E4
Chamberlin Cl **2** IP7 .79 F4
Chambers Cl IP13. . . . .54 D5
Chamomile Cl
  6 Red Lodge CB8. . . . .46 A8
  4 Thorney Green IP14. .67 B7
Champion Rd IP15. . .130 E3
Champney'S Dr **19**
  IP22. . . . . .20 D2
Chancellery Mews
  IP33. . . . . .154 A3
Chancellor Wlk IP4 . .140 B5
Chancery La **5** IP14 . .53 F7

But–Cha 161

Chancery Rd IP1. . . .155 A2
Chandlers Ct **8** CB5 . .44 A6
Chandlers Way IP16 .129 C3
Chandlers Wlk IP14 .124 D4
Chandos Ct **8** IP12. . .84 A1
Chandos Dr **5** IP12 . .84 A1
Channel The IP8. . . . . .81 C1
Chantala Cl IP21. . . . . .39 B4
CHANTRY 138 D2
Chantry Acad **2** 138 F3
Chantry Cl
  Campsey Ash IP13 . . . .71 C2
  Ipswich IP2 . . . . .138 E4
Chantry Dr IP06 . . . . .101 F2
Chantry Gn IP2 . . . . .138 D3
Chantry Pk View IP8 .138 B3
Chantry Rd IP17 . . . .128 C3
Chapel Cl
  Capel St Mary IP9 . . . .150 E3
  4 Fressingfield IP21. . . .39 E8
  Garboldisham IP22. . . .18 D4
  4 Great Waldingfield
   CO10 . . . . .92 C6
  Mill Green IP14. . . . . .65 F4
  Wootten Green IP21. . .39 B4
Chapel Ct **10** NR32 . .113 D2
Chapel Cut **16** CO11 .105 A2
Chapel End Way CO9. .89 A1
Chapel Farm Cl IP23 . .36 C2
Chapel Farm La
  Bildeston IP7. . . . . . . .79 D4
  Thornham Parva IP23. . .37 A4
Chapelfield IP12. . . . .131 C3
Chapel Field IP8. . . . . .19 A2
Chapel Fields IP9. . . .106 F5
Chapel Green
  Gipping IP14. . . . . . . .52 A1
  15 Long Melford CO10 . .91 E8
Chapel Hill
  Belchamp Walter
   CO10 . . . . .90 B1
  Framsden IP14. . . . . . .69 B7
  Thorpe Morieux IP30. . .79 A8
Chapel La
  Belstead IP8. . . . . . . .142 C7
  Botesdale IP22. . . . . . .36 A6
  Boxted CO4. . . . . . . .103 A2
  Broad Green IP14. . . . .67 D6
  4 Brockley IP29 . . . . . .63 A1
  Claydon IP6 . . . . .134 A8
  Copdock & Washbrook
   IP8. . . . . .138 A1
  Drinkstone IP30 . . . . . .65 B7
  Great Glemham IP17 . . .56 D1
  13 Grundisburgh IP13 . .83 E5
  Horham IP21. . . . . . . .38 F2
  Hulver Street NR34. . . .10 C1
  Kirby Row NR35 . . . . .8 E7
  Kirtling CB8. . . . . .60 E3
  Little Cornard CO10 . . .92 B1
  2 Somersham IP8. . . . .81 C4
  Stoke-by-Nayland CO6 .103 B7
  17 Stowmarket IP14 . . .67 A6
  Tuddenham IP28. . . . . .30 F2
  Wenhaston with Mells
   Hamlet IP19. . . . . . . .42 C6
  Wicken CB7 . . . . .28 B1
  Wickham Market IP13 .127 C5
  Wortham IP22 . . . . . . .36 D7
Chapel Meadow **7**
  NR34 . . . . .8 E7
Chapel Pond Hill
  IP32. . . . . .123 C8
Chapel Rd
  Beck Row, Holywell Row &
   Kenny Hill IP28. . . . . .29 F6
  Bedingham NR35 . . . . .7 C8
  Blythburgh IP19 . . . . .42 F6
  Boxted CO4. . . . . . . .103 A2
  Bradfield Combust with
   Stanningfield IP29 . . . .64 A3
  Bucklesham IP10. . . . . .98 B4
  Cockfield IP30 . . . . . .64 F6
  Grundisburgh IP13. . . .83 E5
  Lady's Green CB8 . . . . .61 F5
  Langham CO4 . . . . . .103 B2
  Lowestoft NR33 . . . . .114 B3
  Mendlesham IP14 . . . .52 E5
  Mutford NR34. . . . . . .10 D3
  Old Newton with Dagworth
   IP14. . . . . .52 A1
  Otley IP6. . . . . .69 D3
  Rendham IP17 . . . . . .56 E3
  Ridgewell CO9 . . . . . .89 D4
  St Andrew, Ilketshall
   NR34 . . . . .8 F2
  Saxmundham IP17 . . .128 C3
  Saxtead IP13 . . . . .55 A4
  Stoke Ash IP23 . . . . . .37 B2
  Stratford St Andrew
   IP17. . . . . .71 F6
  Theberton IP16 . . . . . .58 C8
  Thorpe Street IP22. . . .35 E7
  Wattisfield IP22 . . . . . .35 E4
  Wrentham NR34. . . . . .26 D5
Chapel Row
  8 Ashley CB8 . . . . . . .60 F8
  11 Wickhambrook CB8 . .61 E2
Chapel St
  5 Bildeston IP7. . . . . . .79 F4
  Diss IP22. . . . . .20 C2
  Exning CB8 . . . . .120 B8
  9 Lowestoft NR32. . . .113 D2
  Peasenhall IP17 . . . . . .56 F8
  Steeple Bumpstead CB9 .88 E4

Chapel St *continued*
Stoke-by-Clare CO9 89 C6
Woodbridge IP12 147 A5
Chapelwent Rd CB9 132 C8
Chaplains Cl CB9 132 D7
Chaplains Gdns IP3 140 C5
Chaplin Rd CO7 151 C5
Chaplin Wlk 16 CO10 92 B3
Chappel Rd CO6 101 C2
Chapple Dr CB9 132 E7
Chare La IP31 34 D5
Chare Rd IP31 34 D5
Charity La
Bedfield IP13 54 D6
Ipswich IP8 142 A6
Swilland IP6 83 C8
Charity William Way
IP31 34 F4
Charles Adams Cl
IP16 129 D6
Charles Ave 8 IP13 83 E5
Charles Cl CB8 120 E3
Charles Ind Est IP14 124 E7
Charles Melrose Cl 1
IP28 116 B4
Charles Miller Ct
IP16 129 D5
Charles Pl IP32 122 E8
Charles Rd IP11 152 E3
Charles St IP1 155 B3
CHARLES TYE 80 C7
Charlock Rd 5 IP24 16 D7
Charlotte Cl IP11 152 D3
Charlotte's IP8 95 F5
Charlton Ave IP1 134 F2
Charrington Cl CB9 133 A4
CHARSFIELD 70 B3
Charsfield CE Prim Sch
IP13 70 B3
Charsfield Rd
Charsfield IP13 70 D3
Clopton Corner IP13 69 E1
Wickham Market IP13 127 A7
Charter Cl IP7 149 D7
Charter Way 6
NR33 114 C5
Chartres Piece NR34 25 E7
Chartwell Cl IP4 140 A5
Chase Ave 17 IP28 30 B1
Chase Cl CB9 132 E7
Chase Ct 36 CO12 106 F1
Chase La 6 CO12 106 F1
Chase Lane Prim Sch
CO12 106 F1
Chaser Cl 8 IP3 144 C8
Chase Rd IP28 48 C5
Chase's La IP17 72 F6
Chase The
Beccles NR34 111 E5
Brandon IP27 6 A1
Brantham CO11 104 F5
Dedham CO7 104 A2
Felixstowe IP11 152 F4
Foxearth CO10 91 B7
27 Manningtree CO11 104 E2
20 Martlesham Heath
IP5 98 A8
5 Stanton IP31 34 E4
Steeple Bumpstead
CB9 88 D4
Chatsworth Cl 5
NR32 113 A3
Chatsworth Cres
Felixstowe IP11 152 C7
Ipswich IP2 139 A2
Chatsworth Dr IP4 140 E4
Chatten Cl NR34 26 E5
CHATTISHAM 95 C5
Chattisham Cl IP10 124 E3
Chattisham La IP8 95 C6
Chattisham Rd IP8 95 E4
Chaucer Cl IP14 124 C8
Chaucer Rd
Felixstowe IP11 152 F3
Ipswich IP1 134 F3
Sudbury CO10 148 B8
Chaucer St NR35 110 A4
Chaukers Cres NR33 114 C5
Chauntry Rd CB9 132 D5
CHEDBURGH 62 C4
Chedburgh Pl 8
CB9 132 F6
Chedburgh Rd
Chevington IP29 62 C5
Whepstead IP29 62 F5
Chedgrave Rd NR33 114 F5
CHEDISTON 41 C8
CHEDISTON GREEN 24 C1
Chediston Green
Chediston IP19 41 B8
Chediston Green IP19 24 B1
Chediston Pottery★
IP19 24 B1
Chediston Rd IP19 24 B2
Chediston St
Chediston IP19 41 D8
Halesworth IP19 118 A3
Chedworth Pl IP9 105 B8
Chelmer Rd CB9 132 F6
CHELMONDISTON 106 C8
Chelmondiston CE VC
Prim Sch IP9 106 B8
Chelsea Cl
Bury St Edmunds
IP33 122 D5

Chelsea Cl *continued*
Ipswich IP1 134 F1
Chelsea Ct 4 CO10 148 D5
Chelsea Rd 3 CO10 148 D5
CHELSWORTH 79 E3
Chelsworth Ave
Ipswich IP4 135 E1
Sudbury CO10 148 F4
CHELSWORTH
COMMON 79 E2
Chelsworth Rd IP11 152 D3
Chelsworth Way
IP14 124 E3
Cheltenham Ave IP1 135 B1
Chenerys Loke NR34 111 D1
Chepstow Rd
Bury St Edmunds
IP33 122 D3
Felixstowe IP11 152 F5
Ipswich IP1 135 B4
Chequer Field IP12 85 C2
Chequers La
Bressingham IP22 19 E3
Burston & Shimpling
IP22 20 E8
Crackthorn Corner IP22 19 A2
Glemsford CO10 77 B3
Chequers Pk IP7 80 F1
Chequer Sq IP33 154 C2
Chequers Rd CO11 104 E1
Chequers Rise 1 IP6 81 F5
Chequers Row IP17 72 F7
Cherry Blossom Cl
IP8 138 B2
Cherry Cl IP19 118 B1
Cherry Ct 35 IP28 30 C1
Cherryfields IP8 134 A1
Cherry Green IP15 130 D5
Cherry Hill
Barton Mills IP28 30 E3
Mildenhall IP28 116 D1
Cherry Hill Cl 1
NR34 111 F4
Cherry La
Aldeburgh IP15 130 D5
Belton with Browston
NR31 2 E8
Lakenheath IP27 13 F2
Cherry La Gdns IP4 140 B7
Cherry Tree Cl
Debenham IP14 53 F1
Mundford IP26 6 A8
North Lopham IP22 19 A6
3 The Marsh IP22 36 E8
Yaxley IP23 37 B5
Cherry Tree Gdns
IP28 13 A1
Cherrytree La
Rickinghall Inferior
IP22 36 A7
Soham CB7 28 D3
Cherry Tree La IP14 53 F1
Cherrytree Rd CO10 148 F5
Cherry Tree Rd
Stowmarket IP14 124 C8
Woodbridge IP12 146 F4
Cherry Tree Rise IP30 65 B7
Cherry Tree Row 3
IP31 35 C2
Cherrywood 10 IP20 22 D5
Chervil Wlk 3 IP24 16 D6
Chesapeake Cl 8
IP9 106 C8
Chesapeake Rd 3
IP3 144 A8
Chesham Rd IP2 155 A1
Cheshire Cl 4 IP3 140 D2
Chessington Gdns 2
IP1 138 F8
Chester Ct 8 CB9 132 C4
Chesterfield Dr IP1 134 F2
Chester Gr 35 CO11 104 D2
Chester Pl 5 IP31 49 A5
Chester Rd
Felixstowe IP11 152 F5
6 Southwold IP18 119 D5
Chester St IP27 14 A3
Chesterton Cl IP2 138 F1
Chestnut Ave
Great Bricett IP7 80 D6
Lowestoft NR32 112 E2
Chestnut Cl
4 Beccles NR34 111 E3
6 Bentwaters Airfield
IP12 85 E8
Felixstowe IP11 152 D2
Felixstowe IP11 152 E4
1 Fornham All Saints
IP28 48 B6
Great Barton IP31 49 B6
10 Great Blakenham
IP6 81 F5
3 Great Waldingfield
CO10 92 C6
Haverhill CB9 132 D6
1 Mildenhall IP28 116 D4
Rushmere St Andrew
IP5 136 E1
4 Stowupland IP14 67 A6
Chestnut Cres
Chedburgh IP29 62 D4
6 Lowestoft NR33 114 C3
Chestnut Dr
Claydon IP6 134 C8
6 Soham CB7 28 D4
Chestnut Gr 2 IP14 124 E5
Chestnut Mews 17
CO10 148 C5

Chestnut Rd
Dickleburgh IP21 21 C5
Glemsford CO10 77 A3
Pulham St Mary IP21 21 F8
Stradishall CB8 75 C6
Chestnut Rise
1 Burwell CB5 44 A6
5 Witnesham IP6 83 A5
Chestnuts The
5 Great Finborough
IP14 66 B4
11 Ipswich IP2 138 C2
Rickinghall Superior
IP22 36 A6
Wrentham NR34 26 E5
Chestnut Way 21 IP27 13 F2
Chevalier Rd IP11 153 B4
Chevallier St IP1 139 A7
CHEVELEY 60 E7
Cheveley CE Prim Sch
CB8 60 E7
Cheveley Rd
Moulton CB8 45 F2
Newmarket CB8 121 C3
Woodditton CB8 60 E6
CHEVINGTON 62 C6
Chevington Cl IP33 122 E4
Chevington Rd
Chedburgh IP29 62 C5
Hargrave IP29 62 B6
Horringer IP29 63 A7
Cheviot Rd 3 NR32 112 D2
Chevy Ct 3 CO12 106 E1
Cheyne Ct 10 CO10 148 C5
Cheyney Green IP17 42 B1
Chicheley Cl CB7 28 D5
Chichester Cl IP33 123 B3
Chichester Dr NR33 114 D6
Chichester Rd IP19 118 A5
CHICKERING 38 F7
Chickering Rd
Chickering IP21 28 E7
Hoxne IP21 38 D6
Childer Rd IP14 124 D6
Childers Cl 1 IP9 107 A5
Childers Ct IP3 139 F1
Childers Field 2
IP11 152 D5
CHILLESFORD 86 C7
Chilli Company The★
IP14 52 F3
Chiltern Cres NR32 112 E2
CHILTON 92 B5
Chilton Ave IP14 124 C6
Chilton Com Prim Sch
IP14 124 C7
Chilton Ct CO10 148 E5
Chilton Ind Est CO10 148 F6
Chilton Lodge Rd
CO10 148 E5
Chilton Rd
Chilton Street CO10 76 A1
Ipswich IP3 140 C4
CHILTON ST CO10 75 F2
CHILTON STREET 75 F1
Chilton Way IP14 124 B7
Chilton Way Sports Club
IP14 124 A7
Chimers La IP13 69 F4
Chimer's La IP13 70 A4
Chimney Mill Galleries★
IP19 24 C1
Chimney Mills IP28 32 C1
Chimney Pot La IP13 84 A6
CHIMNEY STREET 75 C3
Chimswell Way CB9 132 A6
CHIPPENHALL
GREEN 40 A6
CHIPPENHAM 45 C8
Chippenham Fen
National Nature
Reserve★ CB7 45 A8
Chippenham Rd
Chippenham IP28 29 E2
Fordham CB7 29 C1
Moulton CB8 45 F3
Chipperfield Rd 20
NR33 11 C1
Chippings The IP15 130 C6
Chislehurst Rd 5
NR33 114 C4
Chisnall Cl IP7 149 D8
Chiswick Ave IP28 116 C6
Chivers Rd CB9 132 B5
Choppings Hill IP15 130 E3
Christchurch Dr
IP12 146 D3
Christchurch Mansion★
IP1 155 C3
Christ Church Sq
NR32 113 E1
Christchurch St IP4 155 C3
Christmas La
Lowestoft NR32 112 C1
Metfield IP20 23 D3
Christopher Ct 15
CO10 148 C5
Christopher La CO10 148 C5
Church Ave NR32 112 C2
Church Cl
Aldeburgh IP15 130 E4
19 Beck Row IP28 30 B8
Bucklesham IP10 98 A5
Carlton IP17 128 D7
4 Cavendish CO10 76 E1
Creeting St Mary IP6 125 F8
Dullingham CB8 59 F4
Exning CB8 120 C8

Church Cl *continued*
Fornham St Martin
IP28 48 D5
Great Wenham CO7 150 A3
Hepworth IP22 35 A5
Ipswich IP5 141 B8
Kenton IP14 54 B4
Pulham St Mary IP21 22 A8
Rede IP29 62 E3
Risby IP28 47 E5
1 Roydon IP22 20 A3
Somersham IP8 81 D3
15 Stanton IP31 34 E4
Wangford NR34 26 B2
Wilby IP21 39 C3
Wortwell IP20 22 F7
Church Cres IP8 138 A6
Church Dr IP13 71 E5
CHURCH END 106 F7
Church Farm Cl
Candle Street IP22 35 F6
Horham IP21 38 F3
3 Palgrave IP22 20 C1
Church Farm Green
IP21 39 D8
Church Farm La
3 Halesworth IP19 118 A3
Whatfield IP7 80 C1
Church Farm Rd
Aldeburgh IP15 130 E5
Bramfield IP19 41 F4
Church Farm Way
IP27 109 C6
Church Field
Kettleburgh IP13 70 C7
Monks Eleigh IP7 79 C2
Walberswick IP18 119 A2
Church Field Rd
CO10 148 F7
Churchfields Dr 1
CB9 88 D3
Church Fm Rise
IP15 130 F5
Churchgate CO10 77 B3
Churchgate St
Bury St Edmunds
IP33 154 B2
15 Soham CB7 28 D4
Church Gdns
1 Barningham IP31 34 E7
6 Beck Row, Holywell Row
& Kenny Hill IP28 29 F6
Church Gn
Bramford IP8 134 B1
Normanston NR32 113 C3
Church Green
Finningham IP14 52 A8
Hitcham IP7 79 E6
Little Yeldham CO9 90 B2
Stoven NR34 25 F4
Church Green La
IP22 35 D5
Church Hall Ct 23
CB7 28 D4
Church Hill
Alburgh IP20 7 B1
Benhall IP17 72 C8
Burstall IP8 95 D7
Coney Weston IP31 17 F2
Cookley IP19 41 C5
Helions Bumpstead
CB9 88 B4
Hoxne IP21 38 C8
Kersey IP7 94 A6
Lawford CO11 104 C2
Lidgate CB8 61 C5
Monks Eleigh IP7 79 C2
Pakenham IP31 49 E6
Ramsey & Parkeston
CO12 106 D1
Saxmundham IP17 128 D2
Starston IP20 22 C7
Westhall IP19 25 D3
Whepstead IP29 63 B5
Wyverstone IP14 51 E6
Churchill Ave
Hadleigh IP7 149 D7
Haverhill CB9 132 F7
Ipswich IP4 140 B5
Newmarket CB8 120 D5
Churchill Cl
3 Lawshall IP29 63 D1
Lowestoft NR32 113 C4
7 Woodbridge IP12 146 E4
Churchill Cres IP13 127 C7
Churchill Ct CB8 120 F3
Churchill Dr
Mildenhall IP28 116 B5
Sudbury CO10 148 C8
Churchill Rd
Halesworth IP19 118 B5
5 Southwold IP18 119 C8
Thetford IP24 16 C6
Church Knoll IP6 81 E6
Church La
Aldeby/Wheatacre/Burgh
St Peter NR34 2 B1
Aldham IP7 94 D7
Aldringham cum Thorpe
IP16 129 E1
Alpheton CO10 77 F5
Arwarton IP9 106 E5
Barnardiston CB9 75 B3
Barnham IP24 16 C2
Barrow IP29 46 F3
Barsham NR34 9 A4
Barton Mills IP28 116 D1
Baylham IP6 81 E6

Church La *continued*
Beck Row, Holywell Row &
Kenny Hill IP28 29 F6
Bedfield IP13 54 E5
Birds End IP29 62 A7
Blo' Norton IP22 18 E2
Blythburgh IP19 42 F6
Boxted CO4 102 F4
Brantham CO11 104 F5
Bressingham IP22 19 E3
Brockdish IP21 21 F2
Bromeswell IP12 85 A5
Broome NR35 8 B7
Brundish IP13 55 C8
Bucklesham IP10 98 A5
Burgh St Peter NR34 10 E8
Burrough Green CB8 59 F2
15 Burwell CB5 44 A5
Capel Green IP12 86 A4
Carlton IP17 128 D7
Chelmondiston IP9 106 C8
1 Cheveley CB8 60 E7
Claydon IP6 134 E8
Clopton IP13 83 E8
Cockfield IP30 64 C1
Copdock & Washbrook
IP8 142 A7
Corton NR32 3 C4
Creeting St Mary IP6 125 D7
Dalham CB8 46 C1
Ditchingham NR35 7 F7
Dullingham CB8 59 F4
Earl Soham IP13 55 A2
Exning CB8 120 B8
Felixstowe IP11 152 E6
Finningham IP14 52 A8
Freckenham IP28 29 E2
Fritton & St Olaves
NR31 2 C7
Frostenden NR34 26 C4
Gissing IP22 20 F8
Great Wenham CO7 150 A3
Harkstead IP9 106 B6
Hemingstone IP6 82 C8
Hemley IP12 98 E5
Henley IP6 82 E5
Hepworth IP22 35 A5
Hitcham IP7 79 E6
Hockwold cum Wilton
IP26 5 A2
Hoo IP13 70 B6
Iken IP12 72 F3
Kennett CB8 45 F6
Kenton IP14 54 A4
Kirton IP10 98 E2
Levington IP10 145 E3
Little Wenham CO7 150 C4
Lower Layham IP7 149 E1
Lowestoft NR33 114 B2
Martlesham IP12 84 B1
Mistley CO11 104 F2
3 Mundford IP26 6 B8
Nayland CO6 102 D5
Newmarket CB8 121 A3
Norton IP31 50 C4
2 Occold IP23 37 F1
Orford IP12 131 B6
Ovington CO10 90 A5
Playford IP6 137 B4
Preston St Mary CO10 79 A5
Redenhall with Harleston
IP20 22 E7
Rendlesham IP12 85 C7
Rickinghall Superior
IP22 36 A5
Ridgewell CO9 89 D3
Rushford IP24 17 B3
St James, South Elmham
IP19 23 F4
St Mary, South Elmham
otherwise Homersfield
IP20 23 B8
Santon Downham IP27 6 D2
Semer IP7 79 F1
Shottisham IP12 99 C7
Somersham IP8 81 D3
Spexhall IP19 24 F3
Sproughton IP8 138 B6
Stetchworth CB8 60 A5
Stoke Ash IP23 37 B1
Stoke-by-Nayland CO6 102 E7
Stonham Earl IP14 67 E6
Stuston IP21 37 D8
Swilland IP6 83 A7
Thelnetham IP22 18 E1
Thwaite IP23 52 F7
Timworth IP31 48 E8
Troston IP31 33 E3
9 Ufford IP13 84 F7
Walberswick IP18 43 C5
Wenhaston with Mells
Hamlet IP19 42 C6
Westerfield IP6 135 F4
Westhall IP19 25 D3
Westley Waterless CB8 59 D3
Weston NR34 9 E2
Wickham Skeith IP23 52 D7
Winfarthing IP22 20 B8
Wixoe CO10 89 B5
Worlington IP28 30 B4
Yaxley IP23 37 C4
Yoxford IP17 57 D7
Church La Cl IP28 116 D2
Churchman Cl IP12 147 B8
Churchman Rd IP8 138 B3
Church Meadow
Barton Mills IP28 116 D2
Bulmer CO10 91 C2

Church Meadow *continued*
Rickinghall Inferior
IP22 35 F6
Church Meadows
1 Henley IP6 82 D6
Waldringfield IP12 98 D7
Church Pk CO10 89 E6
Church Rd
Alburgh IP20 7 A2
Ashbocking IP6 68 E1
Bacton IP14 51 F6
Bardwell IP31 34 B4
Barningham IP31 34 E7
Barrow IP29 47 A3
Battisford IP14 66 E1
Bedfield IP13 54 E5
Bentley IP9 142 A1
Beyton IP30 49 F1
6 Bildeston IP7 79 F4
Blaxhall IP12 71 F4
Blundeston NR32 3 A4
Blythburgh IP19 42 F6
Borley Green CO10 91 A4
Boxted CO4 102 F3
Bradfield Combust with
Stanningfield IP29 63 F3
Bradfield St George
IP30 64 D6
Brandon IP27 5 E1
Brettenham IP7 65 C1
Brockdish IP21 21 F2
Bruisyard IP17 56 C5
Bulmer CO10 91 C2
Burgh St Peter NR34 10 B8
Butley IP12 86 B5
Carlton CB8 74 A8
Charsfield IP13 70 B3
Chediston IP19 41 B8
1 Chelmondiston IP9 106 C8
Chelmondiston IP9 106 D8
Chevington IP29 62 C6
Coddenham IP6 68 B1
Combs IP14 124 E2
Cotton IP14 52 B5
Cratfield IP19 40 D5
Crowfield IP6 68 C4
Dallinghoo IP13 70 C1
Denham IP21 38 C5
Dickleburgh & Rushall
IP21 20 F3
Earl Soham IP13 54 D3
Earsham NR35 7 F3
Ellingham NR35 8 D7
Ellough NR34 111 F1
Elmswell IP30 50 E2
Felixstowe IP11 153 C6
Felsham IP30 65 A4
Flixton NR35 7 E1
Freston IP9 143 E3
Friston IP17 72 F7
Garboldisham IP22 18 D4
Gillingham NR34 9 C7
Gisleham NR33 11 A3
Great Barton IP31 49 A5
1 Great Finborough
IP14 66 B4
Great Glemham IP17 71 D8
Great Livermere IP31 33 C2
Great Yeldham CO9 89 F1
Hasketon IP13 146 B7
Hedenham NR35 7 E8
Henstead with Hulver Street
NR34 26 E8
Heveningham IP19 40 E3
Holbrook IP9 105 F6
Honington IP31 33 F5
Hulver Street NR34 10 A1
Kessingland NR33 11 B1
Kettleburgh IP13 70 C7
Kirby Cane NR35 8 E8
Knodishall IP17 58 A1
Leiston IP16 129 B6
Lindsey IP7 93 D7
Little Glemham IP13 71 E5
Little Thurlow CB9 74 D6
Little Waldingfield
CO10 92 E8
Lowestoft NR32 113 C3
Lowestoft NR33 114 F1
Market Weston IP22 18 C1
Marlesford IP13 71 C5
Mendlesham IP14 52 E4
Milden IP7 79 B1
Monewden IP13 69 F5
5 Moulton CB8 45 F3
Mount Bures CO8 101 C3
Mutford NR34 10 D3
Nacton IP10 145 B4
Newton CO10 92 D3
North Lopham IP22 19 A5
Nowton IP29 62 E7
Old Newton with Dagworth
IP14 51 F1
Otley IP6 69 C1
Pettaugh IP14 68 E6
Playford IP6 137 B5
Ramsholt IP12 99 B5
Redlingfield IP23 38 C1
Ringsfield Corner NR34 9 B2
Rushbrooke with Rougham
IP30 49 C1
St Peter South Elmham
NR35 24 A7
Saxstead IP13 55 C4
Shelfanger IP22 20 B6
Snape IP17 72 D5
Stambourne CO9 89 B1
Stowmarket IP14 67 B8

Church Rd *continued*
Stowmarket IP14 . . . . .**124** D3
Stowupland IP14 . . . . . .**67** B7
Stutton IP9 . . . .**105** D5
Sudbury CO10. . . . . . .**148** E3
Sutton IP12. . . . .**85** A1
Tattingstone IP9. . . . . .**105** B7
Theberton IP16 . . . .**58** B4
Thistley Green IP28 . . . .**29** F6
6 Thorpeness IP16 . . . .**73** F6
Thurston IP31. . . . .**49** E4
Tostock IP30. . . . .**50** B2
Uggeshall NR34 . . . . . .**26** A3
Weybread IP21. . . . .**22** D2
Wheatacre NR34 . . . .**2** A1
Wicken CB7 . . . .**28** B1
Wickhambrook CB8 . . . .**61** F1
Wilby IP21. . . . .**39** C3
Wingfield IP21 . . . .**39** A7
Woodton NR35 . . . .**7** C8
Worlingworth IP13. . . . .**54** E7
Wormingford CO6. . . . .**101** F2
Wortham IP22 . . . .**19** F1
Wrabness CO11 . . . . . .**105** F2
Church Rd N IP21. . . . .**21** F3
Church Rise CB9. . . . . .**88** B4
Church Row
Bury St Edmunds
IP33 . . . .**154** B3
Framsden IP14. . . . .**69** C6
Church Score NR34 . .**111** B6
Church Sq 4 CO8. . .**101** C4
Church St
2 Ashley CB8 . . . .**60** F8
Belchamp Otten CO10. . .**90** D5
1 Boxford CO10 . . . . . .**93** C3
Boxted CO4. . . . .**103** A4
6 Clare CO10 . . . .**90** A8
Diss IP22 . . . .**20** C2
Exning CB8 . . . .**120** C8
Eye IP23 . . . .**117** D2
Fordham CB7 . . . .**29** B1
Framlingham IP13 . . . .**126** D3
2 Fressingfield IP21. . . .**39** E8
Gestingthorpe CO9. . . . .**90** F1
Groton CO10. . . . .**93** C5
1 Hadleigh IP7 . . . . . .**149** D5
23 Harleston IP20 . . . . .**22** D6
3 Harwich CO12. . . . .**107** B3
5 Harwich CO12. . . . .**107** C3
Hundon CO10 . . . .**75** D3
10 Isleham CB7 . . . . . .**29** C5
Lavenham CO10 . . . . . .**78** D3
Occold IP23 . . . .**37** F1
Orford IP12 . . . .**131** C2
Peasenhall IP17 . . . .**56** F8
Saxmundham IP17 . . . .**128** D3
12 Southwold IP18. . . .**119** D5
Steeple Bumpstead
CB9. . . . .**88** D4
Stoke-by-Nayland CO6 .**102** E6
Stradbroke IP21. . . . . . .**39** B4
Sudbury CO10. . . . . . .**148** B4
Wangford NR34 . . . .**26** B2
Wetherden IP14. . . . . . .**51** A1
Wetheringsett-cum-
Brockford IP14. . . . . .**53** A6
Withersfield IP21 . . . . . .**74** A2
Woodbridge IP12 . . . . .**147** A5
11 Woolpit IP30 . . . . . .**50** D1
Worlingworth IP13. . . . .**54** F7
CHURCH STREET **90** D6
Church Terr
4 Cheveley CB8. . . . . .**60** E7
Wickham Market IP13 .**127** C6
Church View
6 Elmsett IP7 . . . .**80** F1
Halesworth IP19 . . . . .**118** E4
Harleston IP20. . . . .**22** E6
1 Haughley IP14 . . . . . .**51** C1
31 Lawford CO11 . . . . .**104** D2
Leiston IP16 . . . .**129** B6
Stowlangtoft IP31. . . . . .**50** B7
Wixoe CO10 . . . .**89** B6
Wyverstone IP14 . . . . . .**51** E6
Church View CI IP12 **147** C7
Church Walks IP33. . .**154** C1
Churchway 3 IP22 . . .**36** A8
Church Wlk
Aldeburgh IP15 . . . . . .**130** E4
Hadleigh IP7. . . . .**149** C5
Haverhill CB9 . . . .**133** F8
3 Laxfield IP13 . . . .**40** B3
Long Melford CO10. . . . .**77** E1
Mildenhall IP28 . . . . . .**116** B4
Shelfanger IP22 . . . .**20** B6
Shotley IP9 . . . .**106** E7
Stowmarket IP14 . . . . .**124** D6
Sturmer CB9. . . . .**133** C2
2 Sudbury CO10 . . . .**148** C5
Wetherden IP14. . . . . . .**51** A1
Church Wood IP19. . .**118** E4
Churchyard
Bury St Edmunds
IP33 . . . .**154** C2
Mildenhall IP28 . . . . . .**116** B4
Cinnabar CI 11 IP8 . .**142** E8
Circular Rd IP6. . . . . .**81** D5
Civic Dr IP1 . . . .**155** A2
Clacton Rd CO11. . . .**104** E1
Clapgate La IP3. . . . .**140** A1
Clapgate La Sq 2
IP3. . . . .**140** A1
Clapham Rd Central 3
NR32 . . . .**113** D1
Clapham Rd S NR32 .**113** D1
Clapstile CO10. . . . . . .**78** A5
CLARE. **90** B8

Clare Ancient House
Mus★ CO10 . . . .**90** A8
Clare Ave IP12. . . . . .**146** E4
Clare Castle Ctry Pk★
CO10. . . . .**90** B8
Clare Castle (remains
of)★ CO10 . . . .**90** A8
Clare CI
2 Bury St Edmunds
IP33 . . . .**122** D4
Mildenhall IP28 . . . . . .**116** D5
Stowmarket IP14 . . . . .**124** E3
Clare Com Prim Sch
CO10. . . . .**90** A8
Claremont Pier
NR33. . . . .**115** D6
Claremont Rd 1
NR33 . . . .**115** C6
Clarence Rd
7 Clare CO10 . . . .**76** A1
Ipswich IP3 . . . .**140** B1
1 Lowestoft NR33. . . .**113** D2
Sudbury CO10. . . . . . .**148** C6
Clarendale Est CB9. . .**74** C7
Clarendon Rd CB9 . . .**132** D5
Clare PI CB8 . . . .**121** B2
Clarke CI IP22 . . . .**20** C1
Clarkes CI IP6 . . . . . .**125** F8
Clarkes La NR34. . . . . .**8** F3
Clarke's Rd 3 CO12. .**106** F2
Clark Rd NR35 . . . . . .**110** C7
Clark's Dro CB7. . . . . .**28** B4
Clarkson Rd NR32. . .**112** D1
Clarkson St IP1. . . . .**155** A3
Clark Wlk IP32. . . . . .**122** D7
Claude Oliver CI
CO11 . . . .**104** D1
Claude St IP1. . . . . . .**155** A3
Claudian CI CB9 . . . . .**133** B5
Claverton Way IP4 . .**140** D5
CLAY COMMON. **26** B4
Clay Common La
NR34 . . . .**26** B4
CLAYDON. **134** C8
Claydon Bsns Pk IP6 **82** A5
Claydon Court Bsns Ctr
IP6 . . . .**134** C7
Claydon Ct CB9 . . . . .**132** F8
Claydon Dr NR32. . . .**112** F3
Claydon High Sch
IP6 . . . .**134** C8
Claydon Prim Sch IP6**82** B5
Clay Drift IP31. . . . . . .**48** F6
Clayhall La CO10 . . . . .**92** C7
Clayhall PI CO10 . . . . .**92** C7
Clay Hill
Dennington IP13. . . . . . .**55** F5
Hadleigh IP7. . . . .**94** D7
Hintlesham IP8. . . . .**95** B5
Monks Eleigh IP7 . . . . . .**79** D2
Ubbeston IP19 . . . .**40** E3
Clayhill La
Hitcham IP7 . . . .**79** F6
Wattisham IP7 . . . .**80** A6
Clay Hill La CO10. . . . .**78** E4
Clay Hills Rd IP17. . . .**128** F5
Clayhive Dr 4 CB9. . .**132** D5
Clay La
Bacton IP14. . . . .**51** F6
Hadleigh IP7. . . . .**94** F4
Henley IP6 . . . .**82** E7
Hepworth IP22. . . . .**35** B5
Honington IP31. . . . .**33** F3
Ixworth IP31. . . . .**34** A2
Stoke Ash IP23. . . . .**37** B1
Claypit CI 14 IP30 . . . .**50** D1
CLAYPITS. **109** B4
Claypits Ave 1 CO8. .**101** D4
Claypits La CO10 . . . . .**91** B7
Clay Pond Way IP2. . .**143** B3
Clay Rd
20 Bury St Edmunds
IP32 . . . .**48** C5
Bury St Edmunds IP32 .**122** E8
1 Fornham All Saints
IP32 . . . .**48** B5
Clay St
Soham CB7 . . . .**28** D4
Thornham Magna IP23. .**36** F1
Walsham le Willows
IP31 . . . .**35** D2
CLAY STREET. **35** D2
Clayton CI IP12 . . . . . .**146** D3
Clayton Rd 2 CO12 . .**106** E1
Clearwing CI 15 IP8 .**142** E8
Clematis CI
4 Red Lodge IP28 . . . .**30** B1
Westleton IP17. . . . .**58** B8
Clemence St NR33 . . .**113** C1
Clementine Gdns
IP4. . . . .**140** C6
Clement Rd NR33 . . . .**115** B6
Clements CI
4 Haverhill CB9. . . . .**132** D5
8 Scole IP21 . . . .**20** F1
Clements Dr 2 CB9 . .**132** D5
Clements La CB9 . . . .**132** D5

Clements Prim Acad
CB9. . . . .**132** C4
Clement Sq NR33 . . . .**115** B6
Clements Rd 4 IP12 . .**84** E6
Clement's Way 11
IP28. . . . .**30** B8
Clench CI IP4. . . . . . .**155** C3
Clench Rd IP9 . . . . . .**105** E8
Clerk's Piece NR34. . .**111** D3
Clermont Ave CO10 . .**148** C8
Cleveland Rd NR33. . .**115** C7
Cleves Rd CB9 . . . . . .**132** A8
Cley Ct 1 CB9 . . . . . .**132** A7
Clicket Hill CO8. . . . .**101** D4
Clicket Hill Rd IP11 . .**152** C4
Cliff Farm La NR33 . . . .**11** B2
Cliff La
Great Yarmouth NR31. . . .**3** B8
Ipswich IP3 . . . .**139** E3
Cliff La Prim Sch
IP3 . . . .**139** E3
Clifford Dr NR33 . . . .**114** E5
Clifford Finch Way
IP7. . . . .**149** F8
Clifford Rd IP4 . . . . . .**139** F5
Clifford Rd Air Raid
Shelter Mus★ IP4 . .**139** F5
Clifford Rd Prim Sch
IP4 . . . .**139** F6
Cliff Quay
Greenwich IP3 . . . .**139** D2
Ipswich IP3 . . . .**143** E8
Cliff Rd
Felixstowe IP11 . . . . . .**153** D6
Harwich CO12. . . . .**107** B2
Ipswich IP3 . . . .**139** E3
Lowestoft NR33. . . . . . .**115** C6
Waldringfield IP12 . . . . .**98** E7
Cliff Rise NR32. . . . . .**113** D4
Cliffs The NR33 . . . . . .**115** B2
Cliff View NR32 . . . . .**113** D4
Clifton Dr 8 IP24 . . . . .**16** D7
Clifton Mws CB8 . . . . .**46** B5
Clifton Rd NR33. . . . . .**115** C7
Cliftons Farm Dr 14
CO10. . . . .**90** A8
Cliftonville NR33. . . . .**115** B2
Cliftonville Rd NR33. .**115** B3
Clifton Way IP2. . . . . .**138** D2
Clifton Wood 2 IP9. .**105** E7
Clingos Way IP26. . . . . .**4** F3
Clink The IP19 . . . .**41** C5
Clint Hill IP31. . . . .**33** F6
Clint Rd IP21 . . . .**37** D1
Clive Ave IP1 . . . .**135** B2
Cloak La CB8 . . . .**61** E1
Clockhall La CO10. . . . .**75** D3
Clockhouse La IP14. . .**67** F7
Cloncurry Gdns
IP11. . . . .**152** D3
CLOPTON CORNER. . . .**69** E1
Clopton Dr 2 CO10 . . .**91** E7
Clopton Gdns IP7 . . . .**149** E4
CLOPTON GREEN
Wickhambrook **62** A1
Woolpit. **65** D7
Clopton Pk CB8 . . . . . .**62** A1
Clopton Rd
Burgh IP13 . . . .**83** F7
Otley IP13. . . . .**69** E4
Tuddenham St Martin
IP6 . . . .**136** C7
Clopton Yard CB8. . . . .**62** A1
Close The
Corton NR32 . . . .**3** D4
9 Harwich CO12. . . . .**107** A2
Kennett CB8 . . . .**45** F7
North Lopham NR22. . . . .**19** A6
Sudbury CO10. . . . .**148** D6
3 Tattingstone IP9 . . .**105** B8
Clough Dr 10 IP26. . . . . .**4** E5
Cloutings CI IP17 . . . .**128** C6
Clovelly CI IP4. . . . . . .**140** F4
Clovelly Rise NR32. . .**113** B3
Clover CI
Ipswich IP2 . . . .**138** F4
Needham Market IP6 . . .**125** D3
8 Thorney Green IP14. .**67** B7
Clover Ct IP14 . . . .**53** F1
Clover Field CB9 . . . . .**132** B6
Cloverfield Dr CB7 . . . .**28** C5
Cloverfields 2 IP31. . . .**49** E4
Clovers Ct IP14 . . . . . .**124** C6
Clover Way
Lowestoft NR32 . . . . . .**113** C5
1 Red Lodge IP28 . . . .**30** C1
Clowes Ct NR34. . . . .**111** B5
Clowes's Cnr IP14 . . . .**54** D2
Cluanie Orch CO10. . . .**76** F1
Clubs La 9 CO10. . . . . .**93** C3
Clump Field IP2 . . . . .**138** F2
Clumps The IP12. . . . . .**86** A4
Clunch CI IP27 . . . . . .**109** C6
Clyde Dr 13 IP24 . . . . .**16** D7
Coach La CB8 . . . .**60** E7
Coachmans Ct IP1 . . .**155** B2
Coachman's Paddock 3
IP9. . . . .**105** E7
Coakers La IP13 . . . . . .**70** A1
Coalpit La IP29 . . . .**46** F4
Coastguard La 22
NR33 . . . .**11** C1
Coast Guards The 8
IP16. . . . .**73** F6
Coast Rd NR32 . . . .**3** C5
Coates Dro 1 CB7 . . . .**29** C5
Cobb CI IP32 . . . .**123** F6
Cobbler's Cnr IP8. . . . .**95** B5

COBBLER'S GREEN. **7** C6
Cobbold CI
Combs IP14 . . . .**66** C1
2 The Marsh IP22 . . . .**36** E8
Cobbold Mews IP4. .**155** C3
Cobbold Rd
Felixstowe IP11 . . . . . .**153** A4
Woodbridge IP12 . . . . .**146** E7
Cobbold St
Diss IP22 . . . .**20** B2
Ipswich IP4 . . . .**155** C3
Cobbs Hall La IP29 . . . .**62** D8
Cobbs Hall Rd IP29 . . .**47** C1
Cobbs Place IP14 . . . . .**51** C3
Cobden PI IP4. . . . . . .**155** C3
Cobham Rd IP3. . . . . .**140** C2
Coblers Way 3 CO10. .**92** B7
Cock & Bel La CO10 . . .**91** E8
COCK & END. **75** C8
COCKFIELD. **64** C1
Cockfield CE Prim Sch
IP30. . . . .**64** C1
Cockfield Hall La
IP6. . . . .**135** E7
Cockfield Rd
Alpheton IP29. . . . .**78** A8
Felsham IP30 . . . .**65** A3
Little Welnetham IP30 . . .**64** B5
Cock Hill CB9. . . . . . .**133** F7
Cock La
Brent Eleigh CO10. . . . . .**78** F2
Hundon CO10 . . . .**75** D5
Cockpen Rd CB7 . . . . .**28** F1
Cock Rd IP14 . . . .**52** A6
Cockrell's Rd CO6. . . .**102** A2
Cocks Gn La IP30 . . . . .**64** C5
Cock's Rd IP23 . . . . . .**117** F1
COCK STREET. **102** C7
CODDENHAM. **68** C1
CODDENHAM GREEN. . .**67** F2
Coddenham Rd IP6. . . .**67** E1
Coddington Way 8
IP31. . . . .**34** B1
Codling Rd IP32 . . . . .**123** E6
Codlins La NR34 . . . . .**111** E4
Cody Rd IP3 . . . .**140** C1
Coggeshall Rd
Dedham CO7. . . . .**104** A2
Foxash Estate CO7 . . . .**103** F1
Coke St 11 CO12. . . . .**107** B3
Colbeck Rd CB9. . . . . .**132** C8
COLCHESTER GREEN. .**64** E2
Colchester Rd
Bures CO8. . . . .**101** C4
Bures CO8. . . . .**101** D3
Dedham CO7. . . . .**103** E2
Ipswich IP4 . . . .**135** F1
10 Manningtree CO11 .**104** E2
Wormingford CO6. . . . .**102** A1
Coldfair CI IP17. . . . . .**129** B3
COLDFAIR GREEN. . . .**129** B2
Coldfair Green County
Prim Sch IP17. . . . .**129** B2
Coldhall La IP13 . . . . .**126** E3
Coldham Hall La
IP29. . . . .**63** D3
Coldham La IP23. . . . . .**36** D2
Cold Store Rd IP11. . .**152** B2
Coleman CI IP22 . . . . . .**20** C1
Cole Ness Rd IP3 . . . .**144** A8
Coleridge Rd
17 Diss IP22 . . . .**20** D2
Ipswich IP1 . . . .**134** F3
Coles Croft IP19 . . . . .**42** C6
COLES GREEN. **95** D4
Coles Green IP13 . . . .**126** E2
COLE'S GREEN. **126** E1
Coles Hill IP19. . . . . . .**42** C7
Coles La CB8 . . . .**59** E1
Coles Oak La CO7 . . . .**103** E3
Cole St
Wilby IP21. . . . .**39** B2
Worlingworth IP13. . . . .**54** F8
Coles View IP19 . . . . . .**42** C6
Colethorpe La IP29 . . . .**46** F3
Colin Law Way NR33 .**115** B8
College CI
8 Horringer IP29 . . . . .**63** A8
11 Soham CB7 . . . .**28** D3
College Ct 38 CO11. . .**104** E2
College Gn IP11 . . . . .**153** C5
College Heath Rd
IP28. . . . .**116** D6
College La
Bury St Edmunds
IP33 . . . .**154** B1
Worlingham NR34. . . . .**111** F2
College Meadows 2
NR32 . . . .**113** A3
College Mws IP32. . . . .**48** C5
College Rd
Bruisyard IP17 . . . .**56** D6
Framlingham IP13 . . . .**126** C4
Hockwold cum Wilton
IP26. . . . .**4** F3
Lowestoft NR33. . . . . . .**115** C6
2 Soham CB7 . . . .**28** D3
College St
Bury St Edmunds
IP33 . . . .**154** B1
Ipswich IP3 . . . .**155** B2
Collett Rd IP11 . . . . . .**152** D6
Colletts Chase CO6. .**101** F2
Collett's Wlk IP14 . . .**146** E5
Collge Rd IP14. . . . .**51** D6
Collimer CI 2 IP9 . . . .**106** C8
Collings PI CB8 . . . . . .**120** E5

Collingwood Ave 6
IP3. . . . .**140** B3
Collingwood Fields
CO7 . . . .**151** B6
Collingwood Rd
IP12. . . . .**146** F7
Collins CI IP17. . . . . . .**128** B3
Collin's Hill CB7 . . . . . .**29** B1
Collinson's IP2 . . . . . .**138** D5
Colman Rd 4 NR32 . . . .**3** D4
Colneis Jun Sch
IP11. . . . .**153** B6
Colneis Rd IP11. . . . . .**153** B6
Colne Rd CO8. . . . . . .**101** C4
Colne Springs CO9. . . .**89** D4
Colne Valley Rd CB9 .**132** E5
Colneys CI CO10 . . . . .**148** B7
Colony Rd IP12. . . . . .**100** A7
Colsterdale NR33. . . . .**114** D3
Coltishall 7 IP27. . . . . .**13** F2
COLTON. **48** F5
Colton's Ride IP31. . . .**123** B8
Colton's Ride IP31. . . . .**48** F5
Coltsfoot CI
7 Ixworth IP31. . . . . . .**34** B1
8 Lowestoft NR33. . . .**114** F3
7 Wickhambrook CB8 . .**61** E2
Coltsfoot Gdns 2
CB9 . . . .**132** C8
Coltsfoot Rd IP22 . . . .**138** E4
Colts Hall Rd CO10 . . . .**76** D1
Columbia CI IP5 . . . . .**141** A7
Columbine CI 7
NR33 . . . .**114** C5
Columbine Gdns IP22**138** E5
Columbines The
CO10 . . . .**76** F1
Columbine Way 3
IP23. . . . .**36** D2
Columbyne CI IP14 . . . .**67** A7
Colville Rd NR33. . . . .**114** E6
Colville Way NR33. . . .**114** C3
Comber CI IP21. . . . . . .**21** A2
Combers The IP5 . . . . .**141** E7
COMBS. **124** C1
COMBS FORD. **124** D4
Combs Ford Prim Sch
IP14. . . . .**124** E4
Combs Gn IP14 . . . . . .**66** D2
Combs La IP14. . . . . . .**124** D4
Combs Wood Dr
IP14. . . . .**124** D3
Combs Wood Nature
Reserve★ IP14 . . . .**124** E2
Comet Way IP28 . . . . .**116** B5
Comfrey Rd IP14. . . . . .**67** A7
Comfrey Way IP24 . . . .**16** D6
Commerce Way 3
CO11 . . . .**104** E3
Commercial Rd
Ipswich IP1 . . . .**155** A1
Lowestoft NR32 . . . . . .**113** D6
Commister 14 IP31 . .**34** B1
Commodore Rd
NR32 . . . .**112** C1
Common Drove
Lakenheath IP27 . . . .**14** B6
Lakenheath IP27 . . . . . .**109** A2
Common Gate Dro
CB7 . . . .**29** A5
Common La
Beccles NR34 . . . .**9** F8
Beccles NR34 . . . .**111** C5
Bromeswell IP12 . . . . .**147** F7
Lakenheath IP27 . . . . . .**109** D1
Langham IP31. . . . .**50** D8
Ridgewell CO9 . . . .**89** D3
Syleham IP21. . . . .**22** A4
Troston IP31. . . . .**33** E3
Common La Ind Est
NR34. . . . .**111** C6
Common La N NR34. .**111** B6
Common Quay IP4. . .**155** C2
Common Rd
Aldeby NR34. . . . .**10** B7
Botesdale IP22. . . . .**36** B5
Bressingham IP22 . . . . .**19** F4
Brinkley CB8. . . . .**59** F1
Hopton IP22. . . . .**18** C2
Metfield IP19 . . . .**23** D2
St James, South Elmham
IP19 . . . .**23** D4
Scole IP21 . . . .**21** B4
Shelfanger IP22 . . . .**19** F7
Stetchworth CB8. . . . . . .**60** A1
Stubbing's Green IP22 . .**36** B5
Common St 3 CO10. . . .**90** A8
COMMON THE. **81** F3
Common The
Beccles NR34 . . . .**111** E5
Claydon IP8 . . . .**134** A6
1 Framsden IP14 . . . . .**22** D5
Knodishall Common
IP17 . . . .**129** A1
Leiston IP16 . . . .**129** F7
Southwold IP18 . . . . . .**119** C5
Compair Cres IP22 . . .**139** A5
Compass CI IP27. . . . .**109** D4
Compass St NR32 . . . .**113** E2
Compiegne Way
IP33 . . . .**154** B3
Conach Rd IP12. . . . . .**146** E5
Coney CI IP24 . . . .**16** A2
Coney Hill NR34. . . . . .**111** D3
CONEY WESTON. **17** E1

Coney Weston Rd
Coney Weston IP31 . . . . .**34** D8
Fakenham Magna IP31. .**33** F6
Sapiston IP31. . . . .**34** A6
Coney Wlk 25 IP31. . . .**34** D4
Congreve Rd IP1. . . . .**135** A3
Conifer CI IP28 . . . . . .**116** D6
Coningsby 33 IP27. . . .**13** F2
Coniston CI IP11. . . . .**153** E7
Coniston Rd IP3 . . . . .**140** B2
Coniston Sq E IP3. . . .**140** B2
Coniston Sq W IP3. . . .**140** B2
Coniston Wlk 12
NR32 . . . .**113** A4
Connaught Rd
Haverhill CB9 . . . .**132** C5
Ipswich IP1 . . . .**134** D2
Conrad CI NR33 . . . . .**114** D6
Conrad Rd NR33 . . . . .**114** D6
Consent La IP7 . . . .**79** E4
Constable CI
Brockford Street IP14 . . .**52** F5
Halesworth IP19 . . . . . .**118** A2
Lowestoft NR32 . . . . . .**112** F1
3 Manningtree CO11 .**104** D2
Nayland-with-Wissington
CO6 . . . .**102** A5
Constable Ct 15 IP20 . .**22** D6
Constable Rd
Bury St Edmunds
IP33 . . . .**122** E4
Felixstowe IP11 . . . . . .**153** B4
Haverhill CB9 . . . .**132** B7
Ipswich IP4 . . . .**155** C4
Sudbury CO10. . . . . . .**148** C6
Constable Way IP14. .**124** B7
Constantine Rd IP1 . .**155** A2
Constitution Hill
Ipswich IP1 . . . .**139** B8
2 Needham Market
IP6. . . . .**125** D5
Southwold IP18 . . . . . .**119** D4
Sudbury CO10. . . . . . .**148** D6
Convalescent Hill
IP11. . . . .**153** A3
Conway CI
Felixstowe IP11 . . . . . .**153** C7
4 Haverhill CB9. . . . .**132** C6
Ipswich IP2 . . . .**139** B2
Conway Rd 2 IP32. . . .**48** C5
CONYERS GREEN. **49** B7
Conyers Way IP31 . . . .**49** A6
Cooke CI NR33 . . . . . .**114** F2
Cooke Rd NR33 . . . . . .**114** F2
COOKLEY. **41** A6
COOKLEY GREEN. **40** F6
Cookley La IP23 . . . . . .**38** B5
Cookley Rd IP23 . . . . . .**38** A5
Cook Mws IP31. . . . . . .**49** D5
Cooks CI IP5 . . . .**141** E8
Cook's Dro IP28 . . . . . .**12** C2
COOK'S GREEN. **79** D8
Cooks Green La CO8 .**101** A5
Cooks Hill
Boxted CO4. . . . .**103** A4
Letheringham IP13 . . . . .**70** D4
Cook's La IP20. . . . .**22** F6
Cooks Rd IP30. . . . .**50** E2
Cook's Rd IP29 . . . .**62** E1
Coombers IP9 . . . . . .**150** D3
Coombes Hill IP7 . . . . .**79** B2
Cooper CI 2 IP17. . . . .**128** C4
Cooper La IP29 . . . .**63** E8
Cooper Rd IP6. . . . .**68** C1
Coopers CI
Framlingham IP13 . . . .**126** D2
Witnesham IP6. . . . .**83** A6
Cooper's CI CB8 . . . . . .**60** A5
Coopers Dr 27 NR33. . .**11** C1
Coopersfield 6 IP14. .**53** F2
Coopers La. **11** B1
Cooper's La CO7 . . . . . .**103** F2
Cooper's Rd 30 IP5 . . .**98** A8
Cooper's Rd IP6. . . . . . .**82** C6
Coopers Way 4 IP6. . .**82** A1
COPDOCK. **95** F4
Copdock Intc IP2 . . . .**138** B2
Copdock Prim Sch
IP8 . . . .**95** F4
Copellis CI CB9 . . . . . .**132** B5
Copeman Rd 3 IP22 . . .**20** A3
Copland Way NR34. . . .**10** A3
Copleston High Sch
IP4 . . . .**140** C5
Copleston Rd IP4 . . . .**140** B5
Coplow Dale 12
NR33 . . . .**114** E3
Copper Beech Dr 5
NR33 . . . .**114** D4
Copper CI IP23 . . . . . .**117** C3
Copper Ct 28 IP31. . . . .**34** B1
Copperfield Rd IP2 . .**138** E5
Copperfields 7 IP30. .**49** F2
Copperfield Way 11
CB5 . . . .**44** B5
Copper Gr 14 IP8 . . . .**142** E8
Coppers CI IP33 . . . . .**154** C1
Coppersmith IP14 . . .**124** C3
Copperwheat Ave
IP18. . . . .**119** B8
Coppice CI
Lowestoft NR32 . . . . . .**112** F2
Woodbridge IP12 . . . . .**147** A6
Coppice Rd NR33. . . . .**115** A6

Coppice The IP31......49 A6
Copplestone Cl [12]
  NR34.............9 F4
Coppy Meadow [3]
  IP29..............77 B7
Coprolite St IP3...139 E5
Copse Cl
  Bury St Edmunds
  IP33............123 B1
  Martlesham Heath IP5 ...98 B8
Copswood Cl IP5....141 F7
Copy Hill CB9......132 C1
Coral Dr IP1.......134 D1
Coram St IP7......149 A6
Cordell Pl CO10......91 E8
Cordell Rd CO10.....91 E8
Corder Rd IP4......139 D8
Cordwainer Cl CB9....75 A2
Cordwinders CO7....151 F5
Cordy's La IP11......152 B6
Cordys Meadow IP13 .54 D7
Coriander Dr IP24.....16 D6
Corinth Cl IP28......29 F6
Corks La IP7.......149 C6
Corkway Dro IP26......4 A4
Cormorant Dr IP14...124 F5
Cornard Rd CO10....148 D5
CORNARD TYE......92 C4
Corn Cl [14] CO10.....92 B7
Cornerth Cres CO10..148 F4
Cornfield Ave IP27...109 D7
Cornfield Cres [5]
  NR32..............3 D4
Cornfield Rd IP33...154 A3
Cornfields
  [12] Burwell CB5.......44 B5
  Dickleburgh IP21....21 B5
Cornflower Cl
  Ipswich IP2.......138 E4
  Leiston IP16......129 D4
  [6] Thorney Green IP14..67 B7
Cornford Way [13]
  CO11............104 D2
Corn Hatches La IP7...80 E1
Cornhill
  Bury St Edmunds
  IP33............154 B2
  Ipswich IP1......155 B3
Cornhill Wlk Sh Ctr
  IP33............154 B2
Cornish Hall End Rd
  CO9..............89 A1
Cornish Wlk IP32....122 E8
Cornmill Gn [9] IP30...50 D1
Cornmills Rd CB7.....28 E2
Cornwall Cl [25] CO11..104 D2
Cornwallis Cl IP28....32 C1
Cornwallis Ct IP33...154 A1
Cornwallis Mws
  IP33............154 A1
Cornwallis Rd CB9...132 D4
Cornwallis Terr IP4...139 F6
Cornwall Rd IP11....152 F5
Cornwell Cl
  Isleham CB7.......29 B4
  Soham CB7.......28 C4
Coronation Ave IP9...129 D6
Coronation Dr IP11...152 D3
Coronation Rd IP14...140 B5
Coronation Rise [1]
  CO10..............92 C6
Corporal Lillie Cl
  CO10............148 C4
Corporation Ave IP2 .139 B1
Corrance Cl IP13......71 A7
Corsbie Cl IP33.....154 B1
Corsican Pine Cl
  CB8.............120 F5
CORTON...........3 C4
Corton CE Prim Sch
  NR32.............141 B8
Corton Long La
  NR32............113 B8
Corton Rd
  Ipswich IP3......140 B1
  Lowestoft NR32......113 D6
Cory Dr NR32......112 D3
Cosford Rd IP7......94 C7
Cossie Cl [8] IP32....48 B5
Cotes The CB7......28 B6
Cotman Ave [8]
  CO11............104 D2
Cotman Cl
  [5] Diss IP22.......20 C2
  [3] Lowestoft NR32...113 B6
Cotman Rd IP1......140 A1
Cotmer Rd NR33....114 F7
Cotswold Ave IP1....135 B1
Cotswold Dr [1] CO10..91 E7
Cotswold Way NR32...112 A6
Cottage Gdns IP27...109 D6
Cottesford Cl IP7....149 E5
Cottingham Rd IP8...138 B2
COTTON...........66 E8
Cotton End Rd CB8..120 C8
Cotton Hall La CO10...89 B7
Cotton La
  Bury St Edmunds
  IP33............154 C3
  Cotton IP14.......52 A6
  Wickham Skeith IP23 ..52 E8
Cotton La Flats IP33 154 C3
Cotton Rd IP14......52 C5
Cotton Way [32] IP14...67 A5
Coucy Cl IP13......126 C4

Coulson La [1] IP27.....5 F1
Coupals Cl CB9.....133 A4
Coupals Primary Acad
  CB9.............133 B5
Coupals Rd CB9.....133 C4
Courier Cl IP28......116 C3
Courtenay Cl CO10..148 B8
Court Farm Bsns Ctr
  CO11............105 A5
Court Knoll
  (Earthworks)★
  CO6.............102 D4
Court St CO6.......102 D5
Courts The
  Felixstowe IP11....153 B4
  Playford IP6.......137 B5
COVE BOTTOM
  26 E3
  Cove Bottom NR34....26 E2
Cove Dam NR34......10 B5
Covehite Ct [4] CB9...132 C4
COVEHITHE........27 B4
Covell Cl CB9......132 E7
Coverdale [6] NR33...114 E3
Covert Cl CB9......132 E7
Covert Rd IP18......119 C8
Covert Sycamore [5]
  IP24..............16 D6
Covey Dr IP27......109 E6
Covey Way IP27....109 E6
Cow and Sheep Dro
  IP28..............29 E7
Cowell St IP22......139 C3
Cow Fair [7] IP30......50 D1
Cowfen La IP22......35 F8
COW GREEN.......51 F4
Cow La IP9 CO12....107 C3
Cowle's Dro IP26......4 D1
Cowles Drove IP26.....4 F2
Cowley Rd IP11.....153 A4
COWLINGE........61 B1
Cowlinge La CB8......61 C4
Cowlinge Rd CB8......60 F3
Cowpasture Pl IP11..152 F6
Cowpasture La IP23...36 F4
Cowper St IP4......140 B6
Cowslip Cl
  Bury St Edmunds
  IP32............123 F5
  Ipswich IP2......138 E4
Cowslip Cres NR33...114 C5
Cowslip Dr [10] IP8...81 C3
Cowslip Way IP6....125 D3
Cox Cl IP5........141 B6
COX COMMON
  25 A5
  Cox Common IP19.....25 B5
Coxhall Rd IP9......142 E1
Cox Hill CO10........93 C3
Cox La
  Great Barton IP31....49 B6
  Ipswich IP4......155 C2
Coxs Cl CB9.......132 A5
Cox's Cl NR34......111 C3
Cox's Hill CO11.....104 D2
Cox's La IP18......119 C8
Coxwells Sq [3] IP16..129 A6
Coytes Gdns IP1.....155 B2
Crabbe's Cl [8] IP26.....4 E5
Crabbe St
  Aldeburgh IP15....130 F4
  Ipswich IP4......140 A6
Crabtree Cl IP19....118 B2
Crabtree La
  Aldeby NR34........9 F8
  Little Horkesley CO6..102 B1
Crabtree Meadow [5]
  IP30..............50 F2
Crabtree Rise IP21...21 F2
Cracks La IP12.......85 C6
CRACKTHORN
  CORNER.........19 A1
Crag Farm Rd IP12...131 E7
Crag Path IP15.....130 F3
Craig Cl [7] IP11.....107 D8
Craig's Hill CO8.....101 C3
Craig's La CO8.....101 B3
Cramswell Cl CB9...132 B4
Cranberry Sq [2] IP3 .144 C7
Cranborne Chase [1]
  IP4.............136 A1
Cranbrook La CO10..177 C1
Crane Boulevard
  IP3.............140 D1
Crane Cl IP12......146 D3
Crane Hill London Rd
  IP2.............138 E4
Cranesbill Dr IP32...123 E5
Cranesbill Rd NR33..114 E3
Cranesbill Way IP7...67 A7
Cranes Meadow [31]
  IP20..............22 D6
Cranfield Cl [4] NR33 115 A3
Cranfield Pk IP8.......95 D7
Cranleigh Rd NR33...114 F3
CRANLEY..........37 F3
Cranley La IP23.....117 F1
Cranley Rd IP23.....117 D2
Cranmer Cliff Gdns
  IP11............153 D5
CRANMER GREEN...35 E2
Cranmoregreen La
  CO10..............77 C1
CRANSFORD.......56 B3
Cransford Rd
  North Green IP13.....56 B1
  Rendham IP17.......56 E3
Cranwell Cres IP3...140 C1

Cranwell Gr [1] IP5...141 C7
Cranwich Heath Rd
  IP26...............5 E8
Cranworth Gdns [1]
  NR32............112 F4
Cranworth Rd IP7...149 E4
CRATFIELD.........40 D6
Cratfield La IP19......40 C4
Cratfield Rd
  Bury St Edmunds
  IP32............123 E4
  Cookley IP19.......41 A6
  Fressingfield IP21....39 E8
  Fressingfield IP21....39 F8
  Huntingfield IP19....40 E5
  Ubbeston IP19......40 E4
Craven Way IP18....120 E6
Crawford Ave IP14....66 D8
Crawford Cl [5] IP5...51 A1
Crawford La [2] IP5...141 C7
Crawford's CE VC Prim
  Sch IP14........51 C1
Crayford Rd CO10...148 B8
Creed Wlk IP32.....122 D7
CREETING BOTTOMS..67 F5
Creeting Hills IP6....125 F6
Creeting La IP14......67 B7
Creeting Rd W IP14...124 E6
Creeting Rise [20] IP14 .67 A5
Creeting Road IP14....67 A5
Creeting Road E
  IP14............124 F6
Creeting Road East
  IP14..............67 A5
CREETING ST
  MARY..........125 F8
Creeting St Mary CE VA
  Prim Sch IP6......125 F8
CREETING ST PETER .67 C5
Crepping Hall Dr
  IP9.............105 C5
Crepping Hall Rd
  CO6.............101 C1
Crescent Rd
  Aldeburgh IP15....130 E4
  Felixstowe IP11....153 A4
  Ipswich IP1......155 A2
Crescents The IP18 .119 B8
Crescent The
  Dullingham CB8......59 D5
  East Harling NR16....18 C8
  Great Horkesley CO6 .102 D1
  [6] Soham CB7......28 D3
  Stowmarket IP14...124 D4
  Wicken CB7........28 B1
  Wickham Market IP13 .127 B6
Cresmedow Way IP30 .50 F2
Crespigny Rd IP15...130 E3
Cresslands La IP29...76 D8
Crestland Bsns Pk
  CO10..............92 A8
Crestview Dr NR32...113 A4
CRETINGHAM......69 F7
Cretingham La
  Brandeston IP13.....70 A7
  Cretingham IP13.....69 E6
Cretingham Rd IP14...69 D7
Cricketers Cl CO10..148 C4
Cricket Field Rd CB8 .121 B2
Cricket Hill Rd IP11..152 D5
Cricket Meadow CB8 ..75 F7
Cricket View CB8.....116 B7
Crick's Rd
  Beck Row, Holywell Row &
    Kenny Hill IP28......30 A6
  Thistley Green IP28...29 F6
Crimbold's La IP30....64 D1
Crimp Cramp La NR34 .10 B8
Crisp Cl [3] NR32....113 B4
Crispin Cl IP29.....132 B5
Crisp Rd NR35........8 E7
Crockatt Rd IP7.....149 E8
Crockfords Rd CB8...121 A1
Crocus Cl
  [15] Gislingham IP23...36 D2
  Ipswich IP2......138 E4
  [33] Red Lodge IP28....30 C1
Croft Cl
  Beccles NR34.......111 C4
  Diss IP22..........20 C2
  [10] Harleston IP20.....22 D6
  [3] Wickhambrook CB8 ..61 E2
Croft Ct [13] CO10....148 C5
Croft House Dr [1] IP26 .4 F6
Croft La
  Chelsworth Common
    IP7...............79 E2
  Diss IP22...........20 C2
  Haverhill CB9.......132 F4
  Trimley St Martin IP10 .98 B2
Croft Lea CO10.......92 E8
Croft Pl IP28.......116 C4
Croft Rd
  [15] Isleham CB7......29 C5
  Newmarket CB8.....120 F5
  Sudbury CO10.....148 C6
Croft Rise IP33.....123 B1
Croft Row CB9......132 E5
Croftside [8] CO8.....101 C5
Croft St IP7.........139 C3
Croft The
  Bardwell IP31.......34 C4
  [6] Bures CO8......101 C5
  [1] Glemsford CO10....77 A2
  Great Yeldham CO9....90 A1

Croft The continued
  [1] Lowestoft NR32...113 C1
  [2] Sudbury CO10...148 C6
Cromarty Rd IP4....140 B8
Cromer Rd IP1......134 F1
Crome Wlk NR32....113 B6
Crompton Rd
  Ipswich IP2......138 F7
  Lowestoft NR33....114 E7
Cromwell Ave NR34 .111 B3
Cromwell Cl
  Beccles NR34......111 B3
  [8] Weeting IP27......5 E4
Cromwell Ct NR33...114 D2
Cromwell Rd
  Ringsfield NR34......9 C2
  Weeting IP27........5 E4
  Weston NR34......111 B1
Cromwell Sq IP1....155 B2
Crooked Creek Rd [10]
  IP22..............85 E8
Crooked House Gall
  The★ CO10.......78 D4
Cropley Cl IP32.....123 E4
Crossbill Rd [24] IP14...67 A5
Cross Cl CB9.......132 E7
Cross Cottages CO4 .103 A3
Cross Drove IP26......4 D2
Crossfields CO6.....102 E7
Cross Field Way
  CO4.............103 A3
Crossgate Field [3]
  IP11............152 E5
CROSS GREEN
  Cockfield...........64 B2
  Dullingham CB8......59 F4
  Hartest............77 A7
  Hitcham............79 E7
Cross Green
  Debenham IP14......53 F2
  Old Newton IP14.....51 F1
  Wicken CB7........28 B1
Crossing Rd IP22.....20 C1
Cross La Cl IP27....109 C6
Crossley Gdns IP1...134 C2
Cross Rd IP20........22 C6
Cross St
  [1] Bungay NR35....110 B4
  Drinkstone IP30......65 C7
  Elmswell IP30.......50 E2
  Eye IP23..........117 C2
  Felixstowe IP11....152 E6
  Hoxne IP21.........38 C7
  Leiston IP16......129 C5
  Sudbury CO10.....148 B4
  Sudbury CO10.....148 B4
CROSS STREET......38 C7
Cross The IP23......117 C2
Cross Ways IP30......50 E2
Crotchets Cl [2] IP9..150 E3
Croutel Rd IP11.....153 B5
Crowbrook Pl IP30....78 C8
Crowcroft Glebe IP7...80 B5
Crowcroft Rd IP7.....80 B5
Crowcroft Road Ind Est
  IP7...............80 B5
Crowfield Rd
  Coddenham IP6......68 C2
  Stonham Aspal IP14...68 C6
Crowfoot Cl [9] IP14...67 B7
Crowfoot Com Prim Sch
  NR34............111 D4
Crowfoot Gdns [7]
  NR34............111 B5
Crowhurst Cl [4]
  NR33............114 D4
Crow La IP14......124 D5
Crowland Cl [1] IP2 .139 A2
Crowland Rd CB9....132 D6
Crowley Rd IP6.....125 D4
Crown And Anchor La
  IP13............126 D3
Crown Cl
  Dickleburgh IP21....21 B5
  [10] Martlesham IP12...84 A1
Crown Cnr IP6........68 B1
CROWN CORNER.....39 D1
Crown Cres IP31.....34 B1
Crownfield Rd [8]
  CO10..............77 A3
Crownfields [2] IP13...84 F7
Crown Gn IP22.......20 E6
Crown La
  Coney Weston IP31....17 E1
  Ixworth IP31........34 B1
  Orford IP12.......131 C2
  Wickham Market IP13 127 C6
Crown Meadow Wlk [3]
  NR32............113 C2
Crown Mill [3] IP30....50 F2
Crown Pl IP12......147 A4
Crown Rd IP26........6 B8
Crown St E [5] NR32 .113 E2
Crown St W NR32...113 D2
Crown Score NR32...113 E2
Crown St
  Brandon IP27........14 E8
  Bury St Edmunds IP33 154 C1
  Dedham CO7......103 F3
  Felixstowe IP11....152 E5
  Ipswich IP1......155 B3
  Leiston IP16......129 D6
  Needham Market IP6 .125 D5

Crown St continued
  Stowmarket IP14...124 D7
Crown Swimming Pool
  IP1.............155 B3
Crown Wlk CB8.....121 A4
Crows Hall Rd IP14...53 F1
Crow St IP31........34 D8
Crowswell Ct [6]
  IP11............107 D8
Croxton Cl IP10......98 E2
Croxton Rd IP24......16 C7
Crozier Cl IP4......140 B6
Crunch Croft CB9...133 C3
Cryspen Ct IP33....154 B3
Ct Barns CB8........60 A6
Cuckfield Ave IP3...140 E3
CUCKOLD'S GREEN ...5 C4
Cuckoo Cl IP23......37 C4
CUCKOO GREEN......3 A6
Cuckoo Grn NR32......3 A6
Cuckoo Hill CO8.....101 C5
Cuckoo Hill (Tumulus)★
  IP28..............47 C8
Cuckoo La IP20......22 F6
CUCKOO TYE.......92 A7
Cucumber La NR34...111 D1
CULFORD...........32 D1
CULFORDHEATH.....32 F5
Culford Heath IP31...32 D6
Culford Rd
  Bury St Edmunds
  IP28..............48 C6
  Ingham IP31........32 F1
Culford Sch IP28.....32 D1
Culford Terr IP33....154 A1
Culford Wlk IP11....152 C3
Culingford Rd IP13....40 B3
Cullcott Cl IP17......57 D7
Culley Way [2] NR31...3 B6
Cullingham Rd IP1...139 A6
Cullum Rd IP33.....154 B1
CULPHO...........137 A7
Culphs La IP7........93 F5
Culvers Meadow [4]
  IP31..............34 E4
Culzean Gdns [1]
  NR32............113 A4
Cumberland Ave [23]
  IP32..............48 C5
Cumberland Cl
  [4] Felixstowe IP11...153 D6
  [5] Southwold IP18...119 D5
Cumberland Mews
  IP12............147 A4
Cumberland Pl [13]
  NR32............113 E2
Cumberland Rd
  IP18............119 D5
Cumberland St
  Ipswich IP1......155 A4
  Woodbridge IP12...147 A4
Cumbria Way NR32 .113 A6
Cumby Way [4] NR31...3 B6
Cundle Gn La IP17....72 C5
Cundys Marsh [5]
  IP15............130 E5
Cunningham Way
  NR33............115 B3
Curlew Cl
  Lakenheath IP27....109 D5
  [8] Stowmarket IP14 .124 F7
Curlew Gn NR32....112 C1
CURLEW GREEN....128 C7
Curlew Grn IP17....128 C7
Curlew Rd IP22.....138 D4
Curlew Rd IP32......113 E2
Curlews The IP33....123 C1
Currents La [12] CO12 107 C3
Curriers' La IP1.....155 A2
Curtis Cl IP8.......138 C1
Curtis Dr [1] IP26......4 D5
Curtis Rd [27] IP32....48 C5
Curtis Way IP5.....141 D7
Curwen Rd IP14.....124 C6
Curzon Rd CO10....148 F6
Cutcheys Fields IP31...51 B7
Cuthbert Cl [2] IP24...16 D6
Cutler Rd [5] NR32...112 D2
Cutlers La CO7......151 D7
Cutler's La IP14......66 A6
Cutler St IP1.......155 B2
Cutters Cl [14] IP28....30 A8
Cutter's La IP31......49 E8
Cuttings Cl [9] IP14...52 E4
Cutting's Rd IP21......21 E4
Cutts La CO10.......77 B2
Cygnet Rd [28] IP14...67 A5
Cypress Cl IP28.....116 C6
Cypress Way [4]
  NR33............114 F7
Cyprian Rust Way [12]
  CB7..............28 D5

D

Dace Dr [11] CB7......28 E3
Dad's Army Mus★
  IP24..............16 C6
Daffodil Cl
  Ipswich IP2......138 E3
  [3] Thorney Green IP14 .67 B7
Daffodil Wlk NR33....114 C5
Daffodil Way [17] IP28 .46 A8
DAGWORTH........66 E8
Dagworth La IP14.....66 D8
Daimler Rd IP1.....134 C2
Dains Pl IP11......152 C7
Daires La IP12......147 C7

Dairy Barn Mws [33]
  CO11............104 D2
Dairy Cl IP12........99 F8
Dairy Dr
  [13] Beck Row IP28....30 A8
  [4] Fornham All Saints
    IP28..............27 A8
Dairy Farm Rd IP22...37 C8
Dairy Hill IP19.....118 B4
Dairy La
  Ixworth IP31........34 A2
  Mutford NR34......10 C3
Dairy Rd IP7........80 A1
Dairy Row IP13......39 E2
Daisy Ave IP32.....123 F5
Daisy Cl IP9.......150 F4
Daisy Ct [27] IP28....30 C1
Daisy Dr
  Isleham CB7........29 C4
  Leiston IP16......129 D4
Daisy Gn La IP23....52 D7
DAISY GREEN
  Great Ashfield......51 A6
  Wickham Skeith......52 D7
Daisy Green CO10....93 B6
Daisy Hill IP21......39 F8
Daisy Way Tulip Cl
  NR34...............9 B7
Daisy Way [2] IP14....67 B7
Daking Ave CO10....93 B3
Daking's Drift [6]
  IP19............118 A3
Dakota Rd [6] IP28....30 A8
Dale End NR33.....114 E2
Dale Hall Com Prim Sch
  IP1.............135 B2
Dale Hall La IP1.....135 B1
Dale Haven IP33....114 D3
Dale Hill IP14.......53 A6
Dale Rd
  Cook's Green IP7.....79 D7
  Stanton IP31........34 D8
Dales Ct Bsns Ctr
  IP1.............135 A1
Dales Rd
  Fressingfield IP21....22 D1
  Ipswich IP1......135 A1
Dales View IP8......95 F4
Dales View Rd IP1...135 A1
Dale Tree Rd [11] IP29 .47 A2
DALHAM...........61 C8
Dalham Pl CB9......132 F6
Dalham Rd
  Ashley CB8.........61 B8
  Gazeley CB8........46 B2
  Moulton CB8.......45 F2
DALLINGHOO........70 D1
Dallinghoo Rd
  Bredfield IP13......84 C8
  Wickham Market IP13 127 A6
Dalton Rd IP1......155 A3
Damask Cl [5] NR33...114 C4
DAM GREEN.......19 C8
Dam La
  Burgate IP22.......36 E7
  Kessingland NR33....11 A1
Damselfly Rd [5] IP3 .144 C6
Dams La IP22.......37 A7
Damson Cl [28] IP29...30 C1
Dandalan Cl IP1.....138 E8
Dandelion Cres [19]
  IP28..............46 A8
DANDY CORNER.....52 B6
Dane Comm CB9....133 D8
Dane Hill Rd CB8.....45 E7
Danes Cl IP14......124 C5
Danescourt Ave
  IP14............124 C5
Danes Ct CO10.....148 F2
Daneway Gdns IP16 .129 C4
Danforth Cl IP13....126 B4
Danforth Dr IP13....126 C4
Daniel Gdns IP23...117 C3
Daniels Cl [8] CO10...92 B7
Daphne Rd IP12.....131 C2
Darby Cl IP32......123 F6
Darby Rd NR34......111 B3
Darcy Cl IP32......123 E4
Darkings La IP30.....64 F2
Dark La
  Dickleburgh & Rushall
    IP21.............20 E2
  Easton IP13........70 E7
  Monks Eleigh IP7.....79 C3
DARMSDEN........125 F1
Darmsden Hall La
  IP6.............125 F1
Darnford Gdns IP3..140 D1
Darrell Rd [1] IP11...153 H11
Darrow Gn Rd IP20...2 A4
Darrow La IP22.......20 A4
Darrow Wood La
  IP22..............20 A5
DARSHAM..........42 C1
Darsham Cl [19] IP11 .152 C5
Darsham Marshes Nature
  Reserve★ IP17.....57 F8
Darsham Rd
  Darsham IP17.......42 D2
  Westleton IP17......58 B8
Darsham Sta IP17....57 E8
Darsham Vale [8]
  NR32............112 F4
Darter Cl [4] IP3....144 C6
Darwin Cl IP28.....116 C6
Darwin Pl CB8......121 B1

Darwin Rd IP4 . . . . . . .139 F5
Darwin Wlk 10 CB9. . . .74 A1
Dash End CB5. . . . . . . .133 F8
Dash End La
  Kedington CB9 . . . . .75 A2
  Kedington CB9. . . . . . .133 F8
Dashwood Cl IP8 . . . .138 C1
Daundy Cl IP2 . . . . . . .138 D5
Davall Cl 16 CO12 . . . .106 E1
Dave Farrow Way
  IP2. . . . . 139 A4
Davey Cl
  Bungay NR35 . . . . . . .110 E4
  Ipswich IP3 . . . . .139 F1
Davey La IP13 . . . . . . .70 B4
Davey's La IP31. . . . . .34 C4
Davidson Cl
  Ipswich IP2 . . . . .139 D3
  Sudbury CO10. . . . . . .92 B2
Davoren Wlk IP32. . . .122 D7
Dawes Cl IP9 . . . . . . .150 D4
Dawnbrook Cl 3
  IP2. . . . . .138 E1
Dawn Pointon Pl
  NR32 . . . . 113 D3
Dawson Dr IP11 . . . . .152 C8
Dawson Drift 3 IP5. . .141 C7
Dawson Mews NR32. . .113 A6
Dawson's La IP9 . . . . .106 B4
Daw St CO9. . . . . .89 A3
Days Gn IP9 . . . . .150 D3
Day's La IP31. . . . . . . .34 E8
Days Rd IP9 . . . . .150 D3
Dazeley's La CO7 . . . . .151 F2
Deacon Ct 8 IP11 . . . .153 D6
Deacon's Cl 2 CO10 . .78 D4
Dead La
  Alpheton IP29. . . . . . .78 B7
  Ardleigh CO7. . . . . . . .103 E1
  Bures St Mary CO8 . . .101 F5
  Lawford CO11. . . . . . .104 E1
Deadman's La
  Benhall IP17. . . . . . . .128 A2
  Combs IP14 . . . . .66 E1
  Rendham IP17 . . . . . . .57 A3
  Stoke Ash IP23. . . . . . .53 A8
  Woolpit IP30. . . . . . . .50 C1
Deanery Cl CO10. . . . .148 B8
Deane's Cl 1 CO12. . . .107 A1
Deane'S La CO12. . . . .106 F1
Deans Cl CB9 . . . . . . .132 E7
DEBACH 70 A1
Debach Airfield Mus★
  IP13 . . . . .69 F1
Debach Rd IP13 . . . . . .84 A8
Deben Ave
  Ipswich IP5 . . . . .141 E4
  Martlesham IP5 . . . . . .137 F1
Deben Dr CO10 . . . . . .148 E6
DEBENHAM 53 E2
Debenham CE High Sch
  IP14 . . . . .53 E2
Debenham La IP14. . . .67 C8
Debenham Rd
  Bedingfield IP23. . . . . .53 E6
  Crowfield IP6 . . . . . . .68 E5
  Kenton IP14. . . . . .54 A3
  Middlewood Green IP14 67 F8
  Mill Green IP14. . . . . . .68 C7
  Winston IP14 . . . . .53 F1
Debenham Sports Ctr
  IP14 . . . . .53 E2
Deben La
  Waldringfield IP12 . . . .98 E7
  6 Woodbridge Airfield
  IP12 . . . . .85 B3
Deben Mdws 6
  IP12. . . . . .147 B6
Deben Mill Bsns Ctr
  IP12 . . . . 147 B6
Deben Pl 7 IP12. . . . .147 B6
Deben Pool IP12 . . . . .147 A4
Deben Rd
  Haverhill CB9 . . . . . . .132 F6
  Ipswich IP1 . . . . .134 F1
  Saxmundham IP17 . . . .128 C4
  Woodbridge IP12. . . . .147 B5
Deben Rise IP14 . . . . . .53 F1
Debenside The IP12 . . .147 C7
Deben Valley Dr IP5 . . .141 C7
Deben Way IP11. . . . . .152 E3
Deben Way IP12 . . . . .147 D7
De Burgh Pl 6 CO10 . .76 A1
Deck Wlk IP32. . . . . . .122 E7
Decoy Rd IP27. . . . . . .12 F8
DEDHAM. 103 F4
Dedham CE VC Prim Sch
  CO11. . . . . .104 A3
Dedham Dr 4 NR32. . .112 F3
DEDHAM HEATH. 103 F2
Dedham Meade CO7 .103 F2
Dedham Rd
  Ardleigh CO7 . . . . . . .103 E1
  Boxted CO4. . . . . .103 A3
  Hornestreet CO4 . . . . .103 C4
  Lawford CO11. . . . . . .104 C2
Dedham Vale Family
  Farm★ CO7 . . . . .151 A1
Deepdale NR33. . . . . .114 F2
Deepdale Rd 6
  CO12. . . . . 107 A2
Deer Row NR35. . . . . . .8 D5
Defoe Rd IP1. . . . . . . .135 A4
Degas Gdns 1 NR32. . .113 B6
De Greys Cl 8 CO10. . .92 B3
De Havilland Ct 7
  IP28. . . . . .116 B5
Delbrig Dro CB7. . . . . .29 A5

Delf Cl IP7. . . . . .149 E7
Delius Cl
  Lowestoft NR33 . . . . .115 A6
  1 Stowmarket IP14 . .124 C7
Dell Ct NR33. . . . . . . .114 E7
Dell Prim Sch NR33. .114 E7
Dell Rd NR33 . . . . . . .114 E7
Dell Rd E NR33. . . . . .114 F7
Dellview NR33 . . . . . .114 D6
Dellwood Ave IP11. . .153 B5
Delph Dro IP28 . . . . . .12 D1
Delph Rd IP27 . . . . . . .109 D2
De Lucy Cl 10 IP22. . . .20 C3
Demesne Gdns 6
  IP5. . . . . .98 A8
De Morley Cl 5 IP22. . .20 B3
Dencora Bsns Ctr
  IP1. . . . . .134 D3
Dene Rd NR32 . . . . . .113 D4
DENHAM
  Denham 61 F8
  Hoxne. 38 D5
Denham Cl IP33 . . . . .122 D5
Denham Cnr IP21. . . . .38 D3
DENHAM END 46 F2
Denham La IP29 . . . . . .47 A2
Denham Low Rd IP21 .38 C5
Denham Rd
  Dalham CB8. . . . . .61 C8
  Denham IP29 . . . . .47 A1
  Hoxne IP21. . . . . .38 D6
Denmark Ct 10 IP22. . .20 C1
Denmark Gdns 1
  IP9. . . . . .105 E7
Denmark Hill IP22 . . . .20 C2
Denmark La 6 IP22. . . .20 B2
Denmark Rd
  Beccles NR34 . . . . . . .111 B6
  9 Lowestoft NR32 . . .115 D8
Denmark Rise 1
  IP22. . . . . .20 C2
Denmark St IP22. . . . . .20 C2
Denney's La IP17 . . . . .128 D7
DENNINGTON 55 E5
Dennington CE Prim Sch
  IP13 . . . . 55 D6
DENNINGTON
  CORNER. 126 C8
Dennington Rd
  Brundish IP13. . . . . . . .55 D8
  Dennington IP13. . . . . .55 F8
  Framlingham IP13. . . .126 B5
  Laxfield IP13. . . . . .40 B1
  Tannington IP13. . . . . .55 B6
Dennis Cl IP6. . . . . . . .125 A1
Denny Ave IP14. . . . . . .66 F8
Denny's Hill IP20 . . . . .23 A6
DENSTON. 76 A7
DENTON 7 A3
Denton Cl IP2. . . . . . .138 D2
Denton Dr NR33 . . . . .114 F5
Denton Rd IP20. . . . . . .7 C2
DEPDEN 62 B3
DEPDEN GREEN 62 B4
Depden La IP29. . . . . . .62 C5
Depot Rd CB8. . . . . . .120 E6
Derby Cl IP4. . . . . . . .140 A5
Derby Pl 8 IP31 . . . . . .49 A5
Derby Rd IP3 . . . . . . .140 A4
Derby Rd Sta IP3. . . . .140 A4
Dereham Ave IP3 . . . .139 F3
Derrick Hill IP8. . . . . . .81 B4
Derry Brook La 1
  IP14 . . . . .53 F2
Derwent Gdns 5
  NR32 . . . . 113 A4
Derwent Rd
  16 Bury St Edmunds
  IP32 . . . . .48 C5
  Ipswich IP3 . . . . .139 F3
De Saumarez Dr 3
  IP6. . . . . .82 A6
Desmond Cl 9
  NR32 . . . . 112 D2
Dettingen Way
  IP33. . . . . .122 D5
Devereaux Ct IP4 . . . .155 C3
De Vere Cl IP31. . . . . .124 C2
De Vere Way 32 CO12 106 F1
Devils Dyke Nature
  Reserve★ CB5. . . . . . . 44 A3
Devil's La IP17 . . . . . . .42 C1
Devlin Rd IP8. . . . . . . .138 B1
Devon Cl IP32. . . . . . .122 E8
Devon Rd
  Felixstowe IP11 . . . . .152 F5
  7 Stowupland IP14. . . .67 A6
Devonshire Rd IP3. . . .139 F5
Devon Way 10 CO12 . .106 E1
Dewar La IP5. . . . . . . .141 C7
Dewarrene Dr IP27 . . . .5 E3
Dewberry View 1
  IP14. . . . . .67 B7
Dhobi Pl IP1. . . . . . . .138 F7
Dial La
  Aldeburgh IP15 . . . . . .130 F4
  Ipswich IP1. . . . . .155 B3
  Saxstead Green IP13 . .55 B2
Diamond Academy 7
  IP24 . . . . .16 B5
Diamond Cl IP21 . . . . .134 D1
Diamond Jubilee Cl 26
  CB7 . . . . .28 D4
Diary Farm Rd IP14 . . .53 D4
Diary La IP31. . . . . .48 D8
Dickens Ct 6 NR32 . . . .3 A4
Dickens Rd IP2. . . . . .138 E6

Dickinson Terr 8
  IP5. . . . . .141 D7
DICKLEBURGH. 21 B5
DICKLEBURGH
  MOOR. 21 D6
Dickleburgh Prim Sch
  IP21. . . . . .21 B5
Dickleburgh Rd IP21. .21 A5
Dick Perryman Ct 1
  CB8 . . . . .121 B3
Dicks Mount NR34. . . .10 D7
Dicky Hill IP20. . . . . . .22 D7
Didsbury Cl IP2 . . . . .138 D2
Digby Cl 5 IP5 . . . . . . .98 A7
Digby Rd IP4 . . . . . . .140 C7
Dillistone Ct CB8. . . . .133 C3
Dillwyn St W IP1. . . . .155 A3
Dingle Hill IP17. . . . . . .43 B2
Dinsdale Rd IP16 . . . .129 C6
Diomed Dr IP31. . . . . .49 A5
Diprose Dr NR32 . . . . .113 A6
Dip The CB8 . . . . .121 D2
Dirty La IP21 . . . . .21 F7
Discovery Ave IP2 . . .139 D3
Discovery Dr IP4. . . . .139 E7
DISS. 20 C4
Diss CE Jun Acad
  IP22 . . . . .20 C3
Diss High Sch IP22 . . .20 D3
Diss Mus★ IP22 . . . . . .20 C3
Diss Rd
  Botesdale IP22. . . . . . .36 B7
  Burston & Shimpling
  IP22. . . . . .20 E5
  Garboldisham IP22. . . .18 D4
  Rickinghall IP22 . . . . . .36 A6
  3 Scole IP21. . . . . .20 F1
  South Lopham IP22. . . .19 C4
  Wattisfield IP22 . . . . . .35 D5
Diss Sta IP22. . . . . . . .20 D2
DITCHINGHAM 110 C7
Ditchingham CE Prim
  Acad NR35 . . . . 110 C7
Ditchingham Dam
  NR35. . . . . .110 B5
Ditchingham Gr IP4. .100 F6
Ditton Cl CB8. . . . . . . .121 A1
Ditton Gn CB8 . . . . . . .60 B5
DITTON GREEN 60 B4
Ditton Lodge Prim Sch
  CB8. . . . . .121 B2
Ditton Way 3 IP3. . . .140 B4
Dixon Cl 11 CO11. . . . .104 C2
Dixon Dr NR33. . . . . .114 E7
Dobbs Drift IP5. . . . . .141 F7
Dobbs La IP5. . . . . . . .137 E1
Dobede Way CB7 . . . . .28 C3
Dobson Way NR34 . . .111 C5
DOCKENEY. 8 F6
Dock Farm Rd
  Capel St Andrew IP12. .86 C2
  Snape IP12. . . . . .72 C4
Dockfield Ave 5
  CO12. . . . . 106 F2
Docking Drove IP27. . .13 F7
Dockings La 11 CB7. . .29 C5
Dock La IP12 . . . . .147 C7
Dock Rd
  Felixstowe IP11 . . . . .152 C1
  Ramsholt IP12 . . . . . . .99 B4
Dock St IP2. . . . . .155 B1
Doctor'S Drift IP12 . . .131 D3
Doctors La IP21. . . . . . .39 B4
Doctor's La
  Ashen CO10. . . . . .89 E5
  Orford IP12 . . . . .131 C3
  Pulham St Mary IP21 . .22 A6
Doctor Watson's La
  IP5. . . . . .137 A1
Docuras Farm Rd
  CO4 . . . . .103 C4
Dodmans IP9. . . . . . . .150 D3
Dodson Vale IP5. . . . .141 C7
Does Field IP22. . . . . . .68 C6
Dog La
  Kirton IP10 . . . . .98 F1
  Shelfanger IP22. . . . . .20 A8
  Tannington IP13. . . . . .55 A4
Dogs Head St IP4 . . . .155 B2
Dogs La NR34. . . . . . . .9 C7
Dogwood Cl IP3 . . . . .140 D2
Dogwood Wlk 31 IP27 13 F2
Doit La IP22 . . . . .20 A3
Doit The IP22. . . . . . . .19 F2
Dolphin Cl
  3 Lowestoft NR33. . . .115 B4
  18 Thorpeness IP16. . .73 F6
Dolvers View IP28 . . . .30 C8
Dombey Rd IP2. . . . . .138 E5
Dome Leisure Ctr
  IP28 . . . . .116 E4
Donald Mackintosh Way
  IP8. . . . . .138 B2
Donegal Rd IP1. . . . . .134 D2
Donkey La
  Bradfield Combust with
  Stanningfield IP29 . . . .63 F2
  Friston IP17. . . . . .72 F7
  Ipswich IP6 . . . . .136 D5
Donovan Way CB9 . . .133 A6
Dooley Rd IP11. . . . . .152 C3
Dorchester Rd
  Bury St Edmunds
  IP33. . . . . .122 D3
  Ipswich IP3 . . . . .140 D3
Doric Pl IP12 . . . . . . .147 A4
Doris St CB8. . . . . . . .120 F3

Dorking Rd NR32. . . . . .3 A6
DORKING TYE 101 D7
Dorley Dale NR33 . . . .114 E3
Dorleys Corner IP17 . .128 A7
DORLEY'S CORNER . . .128 B8
Dorothy Hodgkin Ct
  NR34 . . . . .111 B2
Dorset Cl IP4 . . . . . . .135 F1
Dorset Sq 35 CO11 . . .104 D2
Dotterel Way 8
  IP14. . . . . .124 F6
Doubleday Cl IP22 . . . .20 C2
Double Rd IP31. . . . . .49 D4
Double St IP13. . . . . .126 D3
Doughty Wylie Cres
  IP16. . . . . .58 B4
Douglas Cl
  Halesworth IP19 . . . . .118 C5
  Lowestoft NR33 . . . . .114 D3
Douglas Rd 11 CO12. .107 A2
Doug Smith Cl CB8. . .120 F6
Doune Way 9 IP20 . . . .22 D6
Dove Cl
  Capel St Mary IP9. . . .150 D4
  15 Debenham IP14. . . .53 F2
  9 Harleston IP20 . . . . .22 D5
  Lakenheath IP27 . . . . .109 D6
  Saxmundham IP17 . . . .128 C4
Dove Cres 9 CO12 . . . .106 E1
Dovedale
  Felixstowe IP11 . . . . .152 D3
  2 Lowestoft NR33. . . .114 F3
Dovedale Cl IP31. . . . .50 E7
Dove Gdns 2 IP14 . . . .67 A5
Dovehouse Hill IP29 . .77 D7
Dove House Meadow
  CO10 . . . . .148 E3
Dove House Rd CB9 . .132 E7
Dove La
  Eye IP23 . . . . .117 D2
  Wickham Skeith IP23 . .52 D8
DOVERCOURT. 107 B2
Dovercourt Sta
  CO12. . . . . 107 B2
Dovercourt Swimming
  Pool CO12. . . . . .107 B1
Dove Rd IP18. . . . . . . .119 B7
Dover Rd IP3. . . . . . . .140 B4
Dove St
  Ipswich IP4 . . . . .139 E5
  Lowestoft NR32 . . . . .113 D2
  Stowmarket IP14 . . . .124 A6
Dowes Hill La NR34. . .111 B2
Dowling Rd CO8 . . . . .101 C2
DOWN FIELD 29 C4
Down Field Windmill★
  CB7. . . . . .28 F2
Downham Bvd IP3 . . .144 C7
Downham Way IP27 . . .6 A1
Downing Cl
  Bury St Edmunds
  IP32 . . . . .123 E5
  Ipswich IP2 . . . . .138 F2
  Mildenhall IP28 . . . . . .116 D5
  Newmarket CB8 . . . . .121 B2
  2 Woodbridge IP12. . .146 E4
Downing Dr 4 IP31. . .49 A6
Downlands 4 IP7 . . . .80 F1
Downs Cres CB9 . . . . .132 D6
Downs Farm La IP20. .23 B7
Downside IP14 . . . . . .124 B6
Downside Cl IP2 . . . . .142 F8
Downs Pl CB9. . . . . . .132 D6
Downs The
  Felixstowe IP11 . . . . .152 D5
  Rushbrooke with Rougham
  IP30. . . . . .49 C2
Downton Dr CB9. . . . .132 C6
Dowsing Rd IP13 . . . .126 B4
Dowson Dr 2 NR33 . . .11 B1
Drabs La IP13 . . . . .69 F1
Drab's La IP13. . . . . . .83 E7
Dragonfly Cl NR34 . . .111 B3
Drake Cl
  Saxmundham IP17 . . . .128 B3
  Stowmarket IP14 . . . .124 A6
Drake Primary School 3
  IP24 . . . . .16 C7
Drake Rd CO10. . . . . .148 E7
Drake's Heath NR32. .113 B2
Drake Sq S IP3 . . . . . .140 B2
DRAKESTONE
  GREEN 93 E8
Drapers Cl 1 IP7 . . . .149 E6
Drapers Green CB9 . . .88 A5
Drapers Hill IP21 . . . . .39 B5
Drapers La
  Ditchingham NR35 . . . .8 A7
  Helions Bumpstead
  CB9. . . . . .88 A5
Drapery Comm 3
  CO10 . . . . .77 A2
Draycott Rise 4 IP22 .20 C1
Draymans Way IP3. . . .139 E3
Drays The CO10. . . . . .91 D7
Drift Ct IP6. . . . . .125 D4
Drift Rd IP27 . . . . .109 C8
Drift The
  Botesdale IP22. . . . . . .36 A7
  Coney Weston IP31 . . .17 E1
  2 East Bergholt
  CO11. . . . . .104 E5
  Exning CB8 . . . . .120 A8
  Fornham St Martin
  IP31. . . . . .48 D5
  Holbrook IP9 . . . . . . .105 E5
  Ipswich IP3 . . . . .140 C1

Drift The continued
  Ipswich IP4 . . . . .140 A6
  Levington IP10 . . . . . .145 E3
  24 Martlesham Heath
  IP5. . . . . .98 A8
  Middleton IP17. . . . . . .58 B6
  Polstead CO6 . . . . . . .93 D2
  Sudbury CO10. . . . . . .92 B3
  Tostock IP30. . . . . .50 B2
  Wickham Market
  IP13. . . . . .127 D8
Driftway The
  15 Grundisburgh
  IP13 . . . . .83 E5
  Ipswich IP4 . . . . .140 B6
Drings Rd IP13 . . . . . . .56 A2
DRINKSTONE 65 C8
DRINKSTONE GREEN. .65 B7
Drinkstone Mills★
  IP30 . . . . .50 C1
Drinkstone Rd
  Beyton IP30. . . . . .49 F2
  Gedding IP30 . . . . .65 B5
  Rattlesden IP30 . . . . . .65 C6
Drinkwater Cl CB8 . . .120 E4
Drive The
  Harwich CO12. . . . . . .107 A5
  Heveningham IP19 . . . .41 B3
  Hitcham IP7 . . . . .80 A8
  Lowestoft NR32 . . . . .112 F2
  Martlesham Heath IP5 .98 B8
  Rushbrooke with Rougham
  IP30. . . . . .64 B8
  Southwold IP18 . . . . . .119 B7
Dross La IP22. . . . . . . .38 B8
Drout's La IP31 . . . . . . .34 E7
Drove La
  Wetherden IP14 . . . . . .51 A3
  Wicken CB7 . . . . .28 B2
Drovers Dr NR32 . . . . .123 F5
Drover's Ct IP11 . . . . .152 B8
Drovers Rise IP31 . . . . .34 F3
Drovers Yard IP16 . . . .129 D5
Drove The IP27. . . . . . .14 D8
Druids Cl 10 IP28. . . . . .30 C8
Druids La IP22 . . . . . . .20 B6
Druids' La IP22 . . . . . . .20 A7
Drum Field 5 CO7 . . . .103 E5
Drummond Ct IP13 . . .154 A1
Drunkards La IP10 . . . .98 E2
Drury Cl
  Blackthorpe IP30. . . . . .49 C2
  19 Kessingland NR33. . .11 C1
  Stowmarket IP14 . . . .124 A6
Drury Dr CO10 . . . . . .148 D8
Drury La
  Mellis Green IP23. . . . .36 F6
  Milden IP7. . . . . .79 B1
  Ridgewell CO9 . . . . . . .89 D3
  Wicken CB7. . . . . .28 B1
Drury Pk IP17. . . . . . . .72 D5
Drury Rd IP6. . . . . . . .134 C8
Drybridge Hill IP12 . . .146 E4
Drydale Bottom IP12. .86 A7
Dryden Rd IP1. . . . . . .135 A3
DUBLIN. 53 E8
Dublin Rd IP23 . . . . . . .53 E8
Duchess Dr
  Newmarket CB8 . . . . .121 D2
  Woodditton CB8 . . . . . .60 C8
Duckamere IP8. . . . . .134 A1
Duck Dro CB7. . . . . . . .12 A6
Duck Drove CB7 . . . . .12 B7
Duck La
  Dedham Heath CO7 . . .103 F2
  Tunstall IP12. . . . . .71 F2
Ducksen Rd 1 IP14. . . .52 E4
Ducks Hall La CO10 . . .76 F2
Ducks La CB8 . . . . . . .120 C7
Duddery Hill CB9 . . . .132 E6
Duddery Rd 6 CB9. . .132 E6
Dudley St IP27. . . . . . .109 F1
Duffs Hill CO10. . . . . . .77 A4
Dukes Cl IP11 . . . . . . .153 D6
Dukes Dr 11 IP8 . . . . . .81 C3
Duke's Dr IP19 . . . . . .118 A2
Dukes Head St 6
  NR32. . . . . .113 E2
Duke'S La IP12 . . . . . . .99 B3
Dukes Meadow
  1 Beccles NR34 . . . . .111 C4
  Cockfield IP30. . . . . . . .64 D3
Duke's Meadow
  IP12. . . . . .146 D3
Duke's Pk IP12 . . . . . .146 D2
Duke's Rd NR35. . . . . .110 C2
Dukes Ride
  Barnham IP24 . . . . . . .16 C1
  Euston IP24 . . . . .16 F1
Duke's Ride IP24 . . . . .32 B8
Duke St
  Beccles NR34 . . . . . . .111 D3
  4 Bildeston IP7. . . . . .79 F4
  Hadleigh IP7. . . . . . . .149 D5
  Haughley IP14 . . . . . . .51 C1
  Hintlesham IP8. . . . . . .95 C5
  Ipswich IP3 . . . . .139 E4
  7 Stanton IP31 . . . . . .34 E4
DUKE STREET 95 B5
Dukesway 1 NR35. . . . .7 F6
Dulgate Rd NR35. . . . . .7 F7
DULLINGHAM 59 F5
DULLINGHAM LEY 60 D3
Dullingham Ley CB8. . .59 F4
Dullingham Rd
  Newmarket CB8 . . . . .120 F1
  Woodditton CB8 . . . . . .59 F7
Dullingham Sta CB8. .59 D7

Dar–Eas 165

Dulls Rd NR35 . . . . .8 C8
Dumbarton Rd 3
  IP4. . . . . .136 C1
Dumfries Rd 2 IP4 . . .136 C1
Dumplingbridge La
  IP27. . . . . .109 C6
Dunburgh Rd NR34. . . . .9 A6
Duncan Rise CO9 . . . . .89 F1
Dunche's La IP6 . . . . . .67 E4
Dun Cow Rd NR34. . . .10 B8
Dunhill La
  Hepworth IP22. . . . . . .35 B5
  Hepworth IP22. . . . . . .35 B7
Dunlin Rd IP2 . . . . . . .138 E2
Dunlop Rd IP2. . . . . . .138 F6
Dunn Cl IP7 . . . . .149 E5
Dunnell Way IP32. . . . .48 B5
Dunningham Dr 2
  IP7. . . . . .94 F1
Dunnock Cl 18 IP14 . . .67 A5
Dunsey Wood Cl
  CB9 . . . . .132 C7
Dunstall Gn Rd CB8 . . .61 E6
DUNSTALL GREEN 61 E7
Dunster Dr 5 CB9 . . . .132 C6
Dunston Dr NR32 . . . .112 E4
Dunston's Cnr IP6 . . . .82 B8
Dunton Gr IP7. . . . . . .149 E4
DUNWICH. 43 B1
Dunwich Cl IP3 . . . . . .144 C7
Dunwich Ct 5 CB9. . . .132 A6
Dunwich Heath Nature
  Reserve★ IP17 . . . . . .58 F7
Dunwich La IP17. . . . . .41 A2
Dunwich Mus★ IP17. .43 B1
Dunwich Pl 2 IP31. . . .49 A5
Dunwich Rd
  Blythburgh IP19 . . . . . .42 F5
  4 Southwold IP18. . . .119 D5
  Westleton IP17. . . . . . .58 D8
Dunwich Underwater
  Exploration Ex★
  IP12. . . . . .131 B3
Dunwich Way 11
  NR32. . . . . .112 F4
Durban Cl IP19 . . . . . .118 B2
Durban Rd NR33 . . . . .115 B7
Durbar Terr IP33 . . . . .154 B3
Durbidge's Hill IP22. . .20 E5
Durham Cl 2 IP32. . . . .48 C5
Durham Rd IP27 . . . . . .14 A3
Durham Way CB8 . . . .120 E5
Durinda Green IP10 . . .98 F2
Durrant Rd IP/. . . . . . .149 D/
Durrant's Cl 8 NR33 . .11 C1
Durrant View IP11. . . .141 E7
Dutchman Ct NR33. . .114 D7
Dux St IP7. . . . . .65 B1
Dyehouse Meadow La
  CO10 . . . . .91 D8
Dyer Ct IP7. . . . . .149 F5
Dyers La CO10 . . . . . . .92 E2
Dyers Rd CO9. . . . . . . .89 C1
Dyke St IP1. . . . . .155 B3
Dyson's Dro CB5. . . . . .44 A7

E

Eades Farm Rd NR33 . .10 E5
Eades Wlk NR33 . . . . .114 C5
Eagle Cl
  20 Red Lodge IP28. . . .30 B1
  12 Stowmarket IP14 . .124 F6
Eagle Ct NR34 . . . . . . .26 E5
Eagle Dr IP15. . . . . . . .130 C6
Eagle La CB8 . . . . .59 E5
Eagle Pl 22 IP28 . . . . .30 B8
Eagles Cl IP11 . . . . . . .152 F4
Eagle St IP4. . . . . .155 C2
Eagle Way IP5 . . . . . . .98 A8
Eagle Wlk IP32 . . . . . .122 E8
Earlhams Cl 25 CO12 .106 F1
Earlsbrook 1 IP11. . . . .51 E6
Earls Cl IP11. . . . . . . .153 D6
Earl's Cl IP19 . . . . .118 A2
Earlsfield IP27. . . . . . .13 F2
Earlsford Rd
  Mellis IP23 . . . . .36 F5
  Thornham Parva IP23. .37 A4
Earls Gn 6 CB9 . . . . . .132 A6
EARL'S GREEN. 51 D5
Earls Green Rd IP14 . . .51 E5
Earls Hall Rd IP30. . . . .78 D8
EARL SOHAM 54 E2
Earl Soham Bsns Ctr
  IP13 . . . . .54 F2
Earl Soham Comm Prim
  Sch IP13. . . . . .54 F2
Earl Soham La IP13. . .126 A4
Earl Soham Rd IP13. . .69 F8
EARL STONEHAM 7 E4
EARSHAM. 7 E4
Earsham CE Prim Sch
  NR35. . . . . .7 F4
Earsham Dam NR35 . .110 A4
Earsham Rd NR35 . . . . .7 E6
Earsham St NR35 . . . .110 A4
EARSHAM STREET. . . .22 C1
Earth La NR32 . . . . .2 F5
Easdale NR33. . . . . . .114 E2
Easlea Rd IP32. . . . . . .123 E4
East Anglia Transport
  Mus★ NR33 . . . . .114 A3
EAST BARTON. 49 C4

East Barton Rd
Great Barton IP31 . . . . . .**49** B5
Great Barton IP31 . . . . .**49** B5
EAST BERGHOLT. . . . **151** C4
East Bergholt CE Prim
Sch C07 . . . . **151** B6
East Bergholt High Sch
C07. . . . . **151** B6
EASTBRIDGE. **58** D4
Eastbridge Rd IP16 . . . .**58** D3
East Church St NR16 . .**19** B8
East Cl IP33 . . . . **123** C6
Eastcliff IP11. . . . . **153** E7
East Cliff IP18 . . . . **119** E5
East Dock Rd CO12 . . . **106** F3
EAST END
East Bergholt **104** E6
Stonham Aspal **68** D6
East End La
Burgh St Peter NR34. . . .**10** B6
East Bergholt CO7 . . . . .**104** E6
East End Rd IP14. . . . . . .**68** C6
Easten Greene CO6 . . .**101** D7
Eastern Ave
Haverhill CB9 . . . . **132** D6
18 Soham CB7 . . . .**28** D4
Eastern Cl IP4 . . . . **140** F4
Eastern Way
Bury St Edmunds
IP32 . . . . **123** C6
Elmswell IP30. . . . .**50** F2
Lowestoft NR32 . . . . . . **113** B1
Eastern Way Ind Est
IP32 . . . . **123** C6
Eastfen Dro IP26. . . . . . .**5** B2
East Fen Dro CB7 . . . . . .**28** F4
East Fen Rd CB7 . . . .**29** D5
Eastfield Gdns 3
NR33. . . . . **114** E4
Eastgate Sh Ctr IP4 **155** C3
Eastgate St IP33 . . . . . **154** C2
East Gn IP18. . . . . **119** D5
EAST GREEN
Great Bradley. **74** B4
Kelsale cum Carlton **57** E4
East Harling Rd NR16. .**18** F8
East La
Bawdsey IP12. . . . .**99** F2
Dedham CO7. . . . . **104** A2
Middleton IP17. . . . .**58** B6
Thurston End IP29 . . . . .**76** D6
Ufford IP13. . . . .**85** A7
Eastland Ct IP11. . . . . **152** D7
Eastlands IP21. . . . .**39** B4
Eastlands Ind Est
IP16 . . . . **129** C6
Eastlands La IP23 . . . . . **52** B8
Eastlands Rd IP16. . . . **129** E6
East Lawn IP4 . . . . **140** C8
Eastlowhill Rd IP30 . . .**64** B8
Eastlow Hill (Tumulus) *
IP30 . . . .**64** C8
EASTON. **70** E5
Easton Farm Pk *
IP13 . . . .**70** D5
Easton La
Hacheston IP13 . . . .**70** F5
Reydon IP18. . . . .**27** A1
Easton Prim Sch
IP13 . . . .**70** E5
Easton Rd
Easton IP13 . . . .**70** C6
Hacheston IP13 . . . .**71** A4
Lampardbrook IP13 . . . .**70** E8
Woodbridge Airfield
IP12 . . . .**85** B3
East Pk Cl CB9 . . . . . . **133** A4
East Point Academy
NR33. . . . . **115** A6
East Point Pavilion
Visitor Ctr * NR33 . **115** D8
East Rd CB7 . . . .**29** C5
East Side CO4. . . . . . . **103** A2
East St
6 Harwich CO12 . . . . **107** B2
Southwold IP18 . . . . . . **119** D5
Sudbury CO10. . . . . . . **148** D5
East View
All Saints South Elmham
IP19 . . . .**24** B5
Carlton IP17. . . . . **128** D6
Freckenham IP28. . . . . . .**29** E3
Eastward Ho IP16. . . . **129** D5
Eastward Pl IP14 . . . . . **124** C6
Eastwood Ave NR33. . .**114** F6
East Wretham Rd IP27 . .**6** F4
Eaton Cl IP11. . . . . **152** C7
Eaton Ct 32 CO11. . . . **104** D2
Eaton Gdns IP11. . . . . **152** E2
Eccles Rd IP2. . . . . **138** D2
Economy Rd IP4 . . . . . **115** C7
Eddies The NR33. . . . . **114** E4
Eddowes Rd IP6 . . . .**82** B5
Edelweiss Cl 1
NR33. . . . . **114** C4
Edendale NR32 . . . . . . **112** D2
Eden Rd
5 Haverhill CB9. . . . . . **132** E5
Ipswich IP4 . . . . **140** B5
Edes Paddock 9
IP31. . . . .**49** A6
Edgar Ave IP14 . . . . . . **124** B7
Edgar Sewter Com Prim
Sch IP19 . . . . **118** B5

Edgeborough Cl 1
CB8. . . . .**46** A5
Edgecomb Rd IP14. . **124** D3
Edgefield Ave 15
CO11 . . . . **104** D2
Edgerton Rd NR33 . . **115** A7
Edgeworth Rd 4
IP2. . . . . **138** E2
Edies La CO6 . . . . **102** B7
Edinburgh Cl
6 Barnham IP24 . . . . . **16** C2
Stowmarket IP14 . . . . **124** B7
Edinburgh Gdns IP6 . .**82** B5
Edinburgh Rd
Lowestoft NR32 . . . . . **113** D3
Newmarket CB8. . . . . **120** E4
Edison Cl IP10. . . . . . . **145** A8
Edith Cavell Way CB9 . **88** E3
Edith Cook Way IP3. . **144** D8
Edmonton Cl IP5 . . . . **141** A7
Edmonton Rd IP5. . . . **141** A7
Edmund Cl CB9 . . . . . **132** D6
Edmund de Moundeford
VC Prim Sch IP26 . . . .**4** D5
Edmund Moundford Rd
11 IP26 . . . .**4** E5
Edmund Rd IP27. . . . . . **14** D8
Edmunds Rd IP14. . . . . .**65** F4
Edward Cl IP1 . . . . **138** F8
Edward Fitzgerald Ct
IP12. . . . . **146** E6
Edwards La IP19. . . . . . **41** F5
Edward St 6 CO12. . . **106** F3
EDWARDSTONE. **93** A5
Edwin Ave IP12 . . . . . **146** C7
Edwin Panks Rd IP7. . **149** E6
Edwin Terr IP12 . . . . . **146** F6
Egerton Rd IP1 . . . . . . **134** C3
Egglestone Cl IP2. . . . **138** F1
Eggshell La CO9 . . . . . . **88** E1
Eglantine Way 2
CO6 . . . . **102** A7
Egremont Rd 8 IP22. . **20** C3
Egremont St CO10 . . . . .**77** A2
Egret Dr IP14. . . . . **124** C7
Ehringshausen Way
CB9 . . . . **132** F5
Eider Cl 5 IP14. . . . . **124** C7
Eider Terr IP2 . . . . **138** E3
El Alamein Rd NR32 . **113** A4
Elderberry Rd
8 Herringswell IP28. . .**30** C1
6 Ipswich IP3. . . . . . **144** C7
Elder Crescen 2 IP7. .**80** D6
Elders The IP27. . . . . . **109** E5
Elderstub La IP30 . . . . . .**49** B1
Eldith Ave CB7. . . . .**29** C1
Eldo Gdns 8 IP28. . . . . .**29** F6
Eldon La IP28. . . . .**30** D8
Eldo Rd IP28. . . . .**29** F6
Eldred Cl
Bury St Edmunds
IP32 . . . . **123** E4
Westbourne IP1. . . . . **138** D8
Eldred Dr CO10 . . . .**92** B2
Eleanor Pl 6 IP41 . . . . . **49** A6
Electric Picture Palace *
IP18 . . . . **119** C5
Elevenways IP28. . . . .**30** A4
Eley's Cnr IP7 . . . .**94** E8
Elgar Cl NR33. . . . . **115** A6
Elim Terr 11 NR32. . . . . **113** D2
Eliot Way 4 IP14 . . . . **124** B7
Elizabeth Ave CB8. . .**120** E5
Elizabeth Bonhote Cl 3
NR35 . . . . **110** C2
Elizabeth Ct
20 Red Row IP28 . . . . .**30** B8
8 Sudbury CO10 . . . . **148** D6
Elizabeth Dr IP29 . . . . .**62** D5
Elizabeth Par CB8. . . . . .**45** F5
Elizabeth Rd
Brandon IP27 . . . .**5** F1
15 Harwich CO12 . . . **107** A2
Elizabeth Way
Burrough Green CB8. . . .**59** F2
Eye IP23 . . . . **117** C3
Felixstowe IP11 . . . . . . **152** D3
Stowmarket IP14 . . . . **124** E6
Sudbury CO10. . . . . . . **148** A3
Elizabeth Wlk 27 IP20 .**22** D6
Ellen Aldous Ave
IP7. . . . . **149** F7
Ellenbrook Cl IP2. . . . **138** D1
Ellenbrook Gn IP2 . . . **138** D1
Ellenbrook Rd
Ipswich IP2 . . . . **138** D1
Pinewood IP9 . . . . **142** E8
ELLINGHAM. **8** D7
Ellingham Mill Rd
NR35. . . . .**8** D6
Ellingham Prim Sch
NR35. . . . .**8** D7
Ellington Rd IP24 . . . . **16** C2
Elliott Ave IP18 . . . . . . **119** C8
Elliott Cl CB8 . . . . **121** A6
Elliott St IP1 . . . . **139** A6
Ellis Gdns 5 CB5 . . . . . .**45** A4
Ellisons Cres 1 IP4. . **139** C7
Ellis Rd CO4 . . . . **102** F2
Ellis St CO10. . . . .**93** C3
Elliston Cl 4 IP30. . . . . .**50** F7
ELLOUGH. **9** E6
ELLOUGH HILL. **111** D3
Ellough Ind Est NR34 **10** A3

Ellough Rd
Beccles NR34 . . . . **111** D4
Worlingham NR34 . . . . **111** F2
Ellwood Cl NR34 . . . . **111** B7
Ellwoods Cl 2 CB7. . . . .**29** C5
Elm Cl
10 Bentwaters Airfield
IP12 . . . .**85** E8
6 Brantham CO11. . . . **104** E5
Dullingham CB8 . . . .**59** E5
9 Great Blakenham
IP6. . . . .**81** F5
Haverhill CB9 . . . . **132** D6
Lakenheath IP27 . . . . . **109** C7
Lowestoft NR33 . . . . . **114** C3
12 Martlesham IP12. . .**84** A1
Saxmundham IP17 . . . **128** D3
Elm Coppice 6
NR33. . . . . **114** E4
Elmcroft NR33. . . . . . . **114** E4
Elmcroft Cl 12 IP28 . . . .**30** A8
Elmcroft La IP11. . . . . **153** C7
Elmcroft Rd IP1 . . . . . . **135** A2
Elm Ct CB9 . . . . **133** C3
Elmdale Dr
Lowestoft NR33 . . . . . **114** D4
29 Mistley CO11. . . . **104** E2
Elmdon Pl CB9. . . . . . . **132** F6
Elm Dr
9 Fordham CB7. . . . . . **29** A1
22 Harwich CO12 . . . **107** B2
Hessett IP30 . . . .**49** F1
6 Walsham Le Willows
IP31. . . . .**35** C2
Elmers La IP5 . . . . **141** D7
Elm Est CO7 . . . . **151** C5
Elm Gn
Garboldisham IP22. . . . . **18** D4
6 Nayland CO6 . . . . . **102** C5
Elm Green La IP30 . . . . .**64** D3
Elmham Dr IP10 . . . . . **145** B8
Elmhurst Ave NR32. . . **112** C1
Elmhurst Cl CB9 . . . . . **132** F5
Elmhurst Dr IP3 . . . . . **139** F3
Elmhurst Rd 17
CO12 . . . . **107** B2
Elm La
Capel St Mary IP9. . . . . **150** E3
Copdock & Washbrook
IP8 . . . .**95** F4
Elm Lodge Rd 7 IP13 .**40** B3
Elm Rd
East Bergholt CO7 . . . . **151** B5
Ipswich IP5 . . . . **140** F7
Stowmarket IP14 . . . . **124** C6
Sudbury CO10. . . . . . . **148** E5
Thetford IP24 . . . .**16** B4
Wickham Market IP13 . **127** B6
Elms Cl
6 Earsham NR35. . . . . .**7** F4
Great Barton IP31 . . . . . .**49** B6
Elmsett CE Prim Sch
IP7 . . . .**80** F1
Elmsett Cl IP14 . . . . . . **124** F3
Elmsett Rd
Burstallhill IP8 . . . .**95** B8
Somersham IP8 . . . .**81** B3
Whatfield IP7 . . . .**80** D1
Elms La NR34 . . . .**26** B2
Elmsley Way IP17 . . . . . .**57** C8
Elms Rd
Beccles NR34 . . . .**9** E8
Cowlinge CB8 . . . .**75** B7
Freckenham IP28 . . . .**29** F2
Elm St IP1 . . . . **155** B3
Elms The
Framlingham IP6 . . . . . **126** C4
4 Horringer IP29 . . . . **63** A8
ELMSWELL. **50** E2
Elmswella Cres IP30 . . .**50** E3
Elmswell Com Prim Sch
IP30 . . . .**50** F2
Elmswell Rd
Great Ashfield IP31 . . . . .**50** F6
Wetherden IP14. . . . .**51** A1
Woolpit IP30. . . . .**50** D1
Elmswell Sta IP30 . . . . . .**50** E3
Elmtree Bsns Pk
IP30 . . . .**50** E3
Elm Tree Cl 1 IP14 . . . .**51** E1
Elm Tree Farm La
IP13. . . . . **83** D5
Elm Tree La 5 CO6 . . . **102** A2
Elm Tree Prim Sch
NR33. . . . . **114** E5
Elm Tree Rd
Lowestoft NR33 . . . . . **114** E4
Lowestoft NR33 . . . . . **114** E5
Elm Tree Rd W NR33 . **114** E5
Elm Way IP14. . . . . **51** F6
Elm Wlk 30 IP27 . . . . . .**13** F2
Elsey's Yd IP33 . . . . **154** B3
Elsmere Rd IP1 . . . . **139** C8
Elswick Rd 11 IP24. . . . .**16** D7
Elton Park Bsns Ctr
IP2 . . . . **138** E6
Elton Pk IP2. . . . . **138** D6
ELVEDEN. **15** D3
Elveden CE Prim Acad
IP24 . . . .**15** C2
Elveden Rd IP24 . . . . . . **15** F2
Elvedon Cl IP28 . . . . **15** F7
Elvedon Rd IP3 . . . . . . **144** B7
Elvedon Way CB8 . . . . **120** E5
Elwes Cl CO10 . . . .**89** E6
Ely Cl IP33. . . . . **123** B3
Ely Ct IP28 . . . . **116** C4

Ely Rd
5 Claydon IP6. . . . .**82** B5
Ipswich IP4 . . . . **135** F1
Soham CB7 . . . .**28** B6
Embry Cres 10 IP7 . . . .**80** D6
Emerald Cl IP5 . . . . **141** C8
Emerald Way CB7 . . . . . **28** E3
Emily Frost Cl 4 CB8. .**61** E2
Emlen St IP1 . . . . **155** A3
Emma Girling Cl 1
IP7. . . . . **149** F7
Emmanuel Cl
Ipswich IP2 . . . . **138** F2
Mildenhall IP28 . . . . . . **116** D5
Emmerson Way IP7. . . **149** D7
Emperor Circ IP3 . . . . **144** C8
Empire Rd 32 CO12. . **107** B2
Emsworth Cl 2
IP32. . . . . **123** D6
Endway The CB9 . . . . . .**88** E4
Englehard Rd CB8 . . . **121** A4
Engine Rd CB7. . . . .**28** B5
English Cl IP14 . . . . **124** C7
Englishes La NR34 . . . . . .**8** C1
Ennerdale Cl
2 Felixstowe IP11. . . . **153** D6
Lowestoft NR32 . . . . . **113** A5
Diss IP22 . . . .**20** B3
Ennion Cl 13 CB7. . . . . .**28** D3
Ensign Way 2 IP22 . . . .**20** E2
Enstone Rd IP33 . . . . . **115** B6
Enterprise Bsns Pk
IP33 . . . . **154** C4
Enterprise Dr IP2 . . . . **139** B4
Enterprise Way 12 CB9 **74** A1
Entry The IP23. . . . .**52** D8
Epsom Dr IP1. . . . . **135** A4
Erbury Pl CO10. . . . .**90** A8
ERISWELL. **13** F1
Eriswell Dr IP27 . . . . . . **109** D5
Eriswell Rd
Beck Row, Holywell Row &
Kenny Hill IP28. . . . . .**13** C1
Haverhill CB9 . . . . **132** F6
Lakenheath IP27 . . . . . **109** D4
Ernest Nunn Rd IP14. . .**66** A3
Ernest Seaman Cl 8
IP21. . . . .**20** F1
Ernleigh Rd IP4. . . . . . . **140** B6
Erratts Hill CB8 . . . .**61** B1
Errington Way IP30 . . . . .**50** B2
Erskine Way 14 CO11 . **104** E2
ERWARTON. **106** D5
Erwarton Wlk IP9. . . . . **106** E6
Eskdale Way NR32 . . . . **113** A4
Esky Rd 13 IP31. . . . . . . **49** A3
Esplanade NR33 . . . . . **115** D7
Essex Ave CO10 . . . . . . **148** D2
Essex Rd NR32 . . . . **113** B1
Essex Way IP3 . . . . **140** E1
Estuary Cres 5 IP9. . . **107** A4
Estuary Dr IP11. . . . . . . **153** D7
Estuary Rd 7 IP9. . . . . **107** A4
Ethel Mann Rd 5
NR35 . . . . **110** C2
Ethel Rd NR32 . . . . **113** D1
Ethelreda Dr 1 IP24. . .**16** D7
Etna Rd IP33 . . . . **154** B4
Europa Rd NR32 . . . . . . **113** C4
Europa Way
9 Harwich CO12 . . . . . **106** F2
Ipswich IP1 . . . . **138** D8
Eurscope * NR32 . . . . **113** E2
Eustace Rd IP1 . . . . **138** E8
EUSTON. **16** F1
Euston Ave IP4 . . . . **140** F6
Euston Cl IP33. . . . . **154** A1
Euston Ct 4 IP11. . . . . **152** C4
Euston Hall * IP24. . . . . **16** E1
Euston Rd
Barnham IP24 . . . .**16** D2
Rushford IP24 . . . .**17** B3
Thetford IP24. . . . .**16** D4
Evabrook Cl 1 IP2. . . . **138** E1
Evans Cl IP18. . . . . **119** C7
Evans Dr NR32 . . . . **113** B2
Evans Drift IP5 . . . . **141** E7
Evans' Heath CO10 . . . . .**93** F4
Eve Balfour Way
IP14. . . . .**66** D8
Evelyn Cl IP21 . . . .**38** C7
Everard Cl 5 IP32 . . . . **122** E8
Evergreen Cl IP6 . . . .**68** D4
Evergreen La CB8. . . . . . .**74** C8
Evergreen Rd NR32 . . . **113** B2
Evergreen Way IP28 . . **116** D6
Everitt Rd NR33 . . . . . . **114** D6
Everton Cres IP1. . . . . . **134** F1
Eves Ct 12 CO12. . . . . . **106** E1
Evesham Cl 7 IP2 . . . . **139** A2
Excalibur Rd 2 NR31. . .**3** A8
Exchange Sq 6
NR34 . . . . **111** B5
Exchange St 32 IP20 . . .**22** D6
Exeter Cres IP27. . . . . . **109** F1
Exeter Ct 6 CB9 . . . . . **132** C4
Exeter Rd
5 Claydon IP6. . . . .**82** B5
Felixstowe IP11 . . . . . . **152** F5
Ipswich IP3 . . . . **140** B4
Newmarket CB8 . . . . . **121** A4
Exeter Way IP24 . . . . . . **16** A6
Exmoor Rd IP11 . . . . . . **152** F6
EXNING. **120** B8
Exning Prim Sch
CB8. . . . . **120** B8
Exning Rd CB8 . . . . **120** F6
EYE. **117** D3

Eye Airfield Ind Est
IP23. . . . . **117** A6
Eye Castle * IP23. . . . . **117** D2
Eye Hill Dro CB7 . . . .**28** B7
Eye Ind Est IP23 . . . . . **117** A5
Eye Rd
Brome IP23 . . . . **117** B7
Kenton IP14 . . . .**54** B5
Occold IP23 . . . .**37** F2
Rishangles IP23 . . . .**53** D7
South Green IP23 . . . . . .**38** B6
Yaxley IP23 . . . .**37** C5
EYKE. **85** B6
Eyke CE Prim Sch
IP12 . . . .**85** B6
Eyke Rd
Bromeswell IP12 . . . .**85** A5
Campsea Ashe IP13 . . . .**71** C2
Eyre Cl IP33 . . . . **154** B1

F

Factory La
Brantham CO11. . . . . . **104** E4
Chevington IP29. . . . . . .**62** C5
Diss IP22 . . . .**20** B3
Factory St NR32. . . . . . **113** D2
Fagbury Rd IP11. . . . . . **152** A4
Faiers Cl IP33 . . . . **123** B3
Fairbairn Ave 1 IP5 **141** D7
Fair Cl
Beccles NR34 . . . . **111** B5
14 Feltwell IP26. . . . . . .**4** E5
Fairey Fox Dr 2
IP28. . . . . **116** B5
Fairfax Cl NR34 . . . . . . **111** B3
Fairfax Dr IP27 . . . .**5** E4
Fairfax Gdns IP6 . . . . . **125** E4
Fairfield Ave IP11. . . . . **153** A5
Fairfield Cres IP13. . . . **126** D3
Fairfield Dr
Lowestoft NR33 . . . . . **114** D6
Saxmundham IP17 . . . **128** C3
Fairfield Hill IP14. . . . . **124** D5
Fairfield House Gdns
IP17 . . . . **128** C3
Fairfield Inf Sch
IP11 . . . . **153** A5
Fairfield Mws IP15. . . . **130** D5
Fairfield Pl 6 IP17. . . . **128** C3
Fairfield Rd
Aldeburgh IP15 . . . . . . **130** D5
Bungay NR35 . . . . **110** C2
Framlingham IP13 . . . . **126** D2
Ipswich IP3 . . . . **140** A2
Lowestoft NR33 . . . . . **114** D6
Reydon IP18. . . . . **119** C8
Saxmundham IP17 . . . **128** C3
Fairfields IP24. . . . .**16** C7
Fairfield Way 12 IP26 . .**4** E5
Fair Green
14 Brook Street CO10. . .**77** A3
4 Diss IP22 . . . . **20** C2
Fairhaven Way IP30 . . . .**50** B2
Fairhead Loke NR33 . . **114** A1
Fairlawns Rd CB8 . . . . **120** F4
Fairlight Cl 2 IP4. . . . **136** A1
Fairmead IP30. . . . .**50** F3
Fairmile Cl 2 NR32 . . . **113** A4
Fairstead Farm La
IP19. . . . . **118** B8
Fairstead House Sch
CB8. . . . . **121** B4
Fairstead The IP22. . . . . .**36** A7
Fair View Rd IP19 . . . . . **118** C5
Fairways IP22. . . . .**20** E1
Fairways The IP4 . . . . . **140** E5
Fairway The
Aldeburgh IP15 . . . . . . **130** C6
1 Great Yarmouth NR31. .**3** B8
Lowestoft NR33 . . . . . **114** F5
Fakenham Hill IP31. . . . .**33** F5
FAKENHAM MAGNA. . . .**33** E7
Fakenham Road Ride
IP24. . . . .**17** B1
Falcon Ave IP22 . . . . **20** D3
Falcon Cl
Haverhill CB9 . . . . **133** A6
18 Hopton on Sea NR31. .**3** B6
Falcon Dr IP22 . . . .**20** A1
Falconer Ave 3 IP14. . . .**51** E1
Falconer Rd
Haverhill CB9 . . . . **133** A3
19 Red Lodge IP28 . . . . .**30** B1
Falcon Gr 1 IP14 . . . . . .**67** A6
Falcon Inn Rd
Wrentham NR34. . . . .**26** C7
Wrentham NR34. . . . .**26** D5
Falcon La NR33 . . . . **110** B5
Falcon Rd 15 IP26. . . . . . .**4** E5
Falcon St
Felixstowe IP11 . . . . . . **152** E6
Ipswich IP1 . . . . **155** B2
Falcon Way IP28. . . . . . . **13** B1
FALKENHAM. **98** E2
Falkenham Rd IP10 . . . . .**98** E2
FALKENHAM SINK. **98** F2
Falklands Dr 21
CO11 . . . . **104** E2
Falklands Rd CB9 . . . . **132** E7
Fallowfield 7 IP30 . . . . . .**49** F2
Fallowfield Ct 10
CB9 . . . . **132** C5
Fallowfields NR32. . . . . **112** F5
Fallowfield Wlk
IP33. . . . . **123** D1
Falmouth Ave CB8. . . . **120** F3

Falmouth Cl IP5 . . . . . **141** B6
Falmouth Gdns CB8. . **121** A6
Falmouth St CB8. . . . . **120** F3
Falstaff Way 2 CO10 **148** F8
Famona Rd NR33. . . . . **114** C2
Faraday Rd IP3 . . . . **139** F5
Farford Field 5 CO10 . .**92** B3
Farina Cl 2 IP1. . . . . . . **138** F7
FARLEY GREEN. **75** D3
Farlingaye High Sch
IP12 . . . . **146** E6
Farlingayes IP12. . . . . . **146** F7
Farm Cl
Bungay NR35 . . . . **110** B2
Bury St Edmunds IP33 **123** B1
5 Lowestoft NR33. . . . **114** D5
Wissett IP19. . . . .**24** C2
Farm Ct St IP20. . . . .**23** A5
Farmerie Rd CO10 . . . . . .**75** D3
Farmers View 23 IP28 . **30** B8
Farmland Cl IP18. . . . . **119** D8
Farm Meadow 9
IP30. . . . .**50** E2
Farm Rd CB9 . . . . **132** F4
FARNHAM. **72** A7
Farnham Rd
Blaxhall IP12 . . . .**71** F5
Snape IP17. . . . .**72** D6
Farrant Rd CB9 . . . . . . **132** E8
Farrer Rd NR32 . . . . **112** E3
Farrier Mws 3 CB8 . . . .**45** F5
Farriers Cl
15 Martlesham Heath
IP5 . . . .**98** A8
Stradbroke IP21. . . . .**39** B4
Farrier's Rd IP14 . . . . . **124** C3
Farriers Went IP11. . . . **152** D7
Farrow Cl IP16. . . . . **129** B6
Farthing Dro
Beck Row, Holywell Row &
Kenny Hill IP27. . . . . .**12** C6
Lakenheath IP27 . . . . . .**13** A6
Farthing Hall Rd
CO6 . . . . **102** A6
Farthingland 19 IP30. .**50** F2
Farthing Rd IP1. . . . . . . **138** C7
Farthing Rd Ind Est
IP1 . . . . **138** C7
Farthings The IP28. . . . . **31** D3
Farthings Went IP9. . . . **150** F4
Fastnet CB9 . . . . **133** B6
Fastolf Cl 4 NR32. . . . . **113** A3
Fastolff Way IP11 . . . . **152** C7
Faversham Ct NR33 . . **115** A4
Fawcett Rd IP15 . . . . . . **130** E4
Fawley Cl IP4. . . . . **140** C7
Fayrefield Rd IP12. . . . **147** B7
Feast Cl 7 CB7 . . . .**29** A1
Featherbroom Gdns
IP13. . . . . **127** C5
Feathers Field 3
IP11. . . . . **152** C5
Feilden Way CB8. . . . . **120** E5
Felaw St IP2. . . . . **155** C1
Felchurch Rd IP2. . . . . **138** B3
Felgate Cl IP33 . . . .**40** B3
Felgate Way 18 IP13 . . **83** E5
Felix Cl IP5 . . . . **141** B7
Felix Rd
Felixstowe IP11 . . . . . . **153** B4
Ipswich IP3 . . . . **140** C2
5 Stowupland IP14. . . . **67** A6
Felix Sq IP7 . . . . **140** B1
FELIXSTOWE. **152** E4
Felixstowe Com Hospl
IP11 . . . . **153** B6
FELIXSTOWE
FERRY. **108** C3
Felixstowe International
Coll IP11. . . . . **153** C5
Felixstowe Leisure Ctr
IP11 . . . . **152** F3
Felixstowe Mus *
IP11. . . . . **107** E2
Felixstowe Rd
Ipswich IP3 . . . . **139** F1
Kirton IP11. . . . .**98** B1
8 Martlesham IP5. . . . . .**98** A8
Felixstowe Sch IP11 **153** B6
Felixstowe Sta IP11 **153** A5
Fellbrigg Ave IP5 . . . . . **140** F6
Fellows Cl IP21. . . . .**21** A1
Fell Rd CO9. . . . .**89** A4
Felnor Wlk IP11 . . . . . . **153** B3
FELSHAM. **65** A3
Felsham Chase CB5 . . . .**44** B5
Felsham Ct IP14 . . . . . . **124** F3
Felsham Rd
Bradfield St Clare
IP30 . . . .**64** D4
Button's Green IP30. . . . .**78** E7
Rattlesden IP30. . . . .**65** C5
Felsham Rise IP7 . . . . . **128** C3
Feltons 6 CB7. . . . .**29** A1
Felton Wlk IP32 . . . . . . **122** D8
FELTWELL. **4** D5
Feltwell Pl CB9 . . . . . . **132** F6
Feltwell Rd IP26 . . . .**4** F1
Fen Alder Carr Nature
Reserve * IP6 . . . . . **125** D8
Fen Bank CB7. . . . .**29** C6
Fen Bank Rd CB7 . . . .**29** B8
Fenbridge La CO7. . . . . **151** B3
Fen Bright Circle
IP3. . . . . **144** C2
Fen Ct NR33 . . . . **115** A6

Fen Farm Rd IP30 . . . . .65 D2
Fengate Dro IP27 . . . . .5 E2
Fen La
  Ardleigh CO7 . . . . . .103 E1
  Beccles NR34 . . . . . . .111 B7
  Beck Row, Holywell Row &
   Kenny Hill IP28 . . . . .13 D1
  Braiseworth IP23 . . . . . .37 D3
  Creeting St Peter or
   West Creeting IP6 . .125 D8
  Ditchingham NR35 . . . . . .7 E7
  Garboldisham IP22 . . . .18 D3
  Hitcham IP7 . . . . .79 E5
  Holywell Row IP28 . . . .30 C8
  Rickinghall Inferior
   IP22 . . . . .36 A6
  Roydon IP22 . . . . .19 F3
  Stonham Earl IP6 . . . . .67 D4
  Thelnetham IP22 . . . . . .18 E1
Fenlands Cres NR33 . .114 F6
Fen Meadow
  Felixstowe IP11 . . . . .152 C8
  Shottisham IP12 . . . . . .99 A8
Fenn Cl
  Halesworth IP19 . . . .118 A5
  Stowmarket IP14 . . . .124 D3
Fennel Dr 20 IP28 . . . .30 C1
Fenn La IP12 . . . . .98 D6
Fenn St IP14 . . . . .53 F1
Fen Rd
  Blo' Norton IP22 . . . . .18 F2
  Grimstone End IP31 . . . .49 F8
  Pakenham IP31 . . . . . .49 F6
Fen St
  7 Boxford CO10 . . . . . .93 C3
  Hinderclay IP22 . . . . . .18 F1
  Nayland CO6 . . . . . . .102 D5
  Rattlesden IP30 . . . . . .65 F6
FENSTEAD END 76 E5
FEN STREET
  Hopton 18 B2
  Redgrave 19 C2
Fenstreet Rd IP17 . . . . .58 A7
Fenton Rd CB9 . . . . . .132 F6
Fentons Way IP5 . . . . .141 C7
Fen View
  Copdock & Washbrook
   IP8 . . . . .95 F4
  Thorndon IP23 . . . . . . .53 B8
Fen Way IP33 . . . . . . .154 A8
Fen Wlk IP12 . . . . .146 F4
Feoffee Farm Dr
  IP6. . . . . .69 A1
Ferguson Way IP5 . . .141 B8
Ferini Gdns NR33 . . . .115 B3
Fern Ave NR32 . . . . . .112 D2
Ferndale Cl CB8 . . . . .121 B6
Ferndown Rd 3
  IP11. . . . . .153 C6
Ferneley Cres CB8 . . .121 A4
Fern Gn Cl 1 NR32 . . .112 E4
Fern Gr CB9 . . . . .132 C6
Fernhayes Cl IP2 . . . .139 A3
FERN HILL 77 B4
Fern Hill CO10 . . . . . . .77 A4
Fernhill Cl IP12 . . . . . .147 A7
Fernlea Rd 4 CO12 . .107 B3
Fern Way 8 IP28 . . . . .30 C1
Ferriers La CO8 . . . . .101 B4
Ferry Drove CB7 . . . . .29 D5
Ferry Farm Dr IP12 . .147 C2
Ferry La
  Aldeburgh IP12 . . . . . .73 C1
  Aldeburgh IP12 . . . . .130 B1
  Beck Row, Holywell Row &
   Kenny Hill IP28 . . . . .29 F5
  Felixstowe IP11 . . . . .152 C3
Ferry Quay IP12 . . . . .147 A4
Ferry Rd
  Bawdsey IP12. . . . . . . .99 D1
  Felixstowe IP11 . . . . .153 D7
  Southwold IP18 . . . . .119 C3
  Sudbourne IP12 . . . . .131 C6
  Walberswick IP18 . . . .119 B2
FERSFIELD 19 D6
Fersfield Rd IP22 . . . . .19 C4
Festival Cl 4 IP17 . . . .72 C8
Festival Rd 14 CB7 . . . .29 C5
Feveryears Yd 4
  IP21. . . . . .39 D8
Fiddlers Cl CO7 . . . . .151 C5
Fiddlers La CO7 . . . . .151 C5
Fiddler's La IP23. . . . .117 F2
Field Barn Rd IP31 . . . .33 F3
Field Cl 3 IP30 . . . . . .49 F2
Fieldfare 3 IP28 . . . . .30 C4
Fieldfare Cl 6 IP14 . .124 F6
Fieldfare Way IP6 . . .135 F4
Field Fuller's IP6 . . . .135 E4
Field Grange NR32 . .112 F5
Field House Gdns
  IP22. . . . . .20 D2
Field La
  Kessingland NR33 . . . .11 B1
  Stanton Chare IP31 . . . .34 F5
Field Maple Cl 15
  IP28. . . . . .46 A8
Field Rd IP20 . . . . . . .116 C5
Field Stile Rd 2
  IP18. . . . . .119 D5
Fields View CO10 . . . .148 D6
Field Terr Rd CB8 . . . .120 F5
Field View
  Bucklesham IP10 . . . . . .98 A4
  8 Thurstow IP31. . . . . .49 E4
Fieldview Dr NR32 . . .113 A1

Field View Gdns
  NR34 . . . . .111 D3
Field Vw 13 CB5. . . . . .44 B5
Field Way
  Debenham IP14 . . . . . .53 F1
  18 Stanton IP31. . . . . . .34 E4
Field Wlk IP28 . . . . . .116 C5
Fife Rd IP4 . . . . .136 B1
Fillisters Mws NR32 . .113 C1
Finbars Wlk IP4 . . . . .139 F5
Finborough Cl IP4 . . . .140 F6
Finborough Rd IP14 . .124 B6
Finborough Sch IP14 .66 B5
Fincham Rd IP28 . . . .116 B5
Finch Cl 7 IP14 . . . . . .67 A5
Finch Hill CO10 . . . . . .91 D4
Finchfield Rd CB10. . . .88 C1
Finchingfield Rd
  Stambourne CO9 . . . . .89 B1
  Steeple Bumpstead CB9 88 E3
Finchley Ave IP28. . . .116 B6
Finchley Rd IP4. . . . . .139 E6
Findley Cl IP9 . . . . . . .105 C5
Fingal St IP13 . . . . . . .39 A1
FINKLE GREEN 89 A2
Finley Way IP33 . . . . .122 F3
Finney's Drift IP10 . . .145 C5
FINNINGHAM 52 B8
Finningham Rd
  Gislingham IP23 . . . . . .36 D1
  Old Newton with Dagworth
   IP14 . . . . .51 F2
  Rickinghall Superior
   IP22 . . . . .36 A4
  Walsham le Willows
   IP31. . . . . .35 D2
  Wickham Skeith IP23 . .52 C8
Finsbury Pl IP33 . . . . .154 B1
Finsbury Sq IP33. . . . .154 C1
Fir Cl
  Barnby NR34. . . . . . . .10 C4
  Mundford IP26. . . . . . . .6 B8
  Wickham Market IP13 127 C6
Fircroft Rd IP1 . . . . . .135 A2
Firebrass La IP12 . . . . .85 C2
Firebronds Rd 7
  IP9. . . . . .105 E7
Firecrest Dr 2 IP14 . .124 F7
Firefly Cl 15 CO11 . . . .105 A2
Firefly Way 1 IP3 . . .144 C8
Firfield Cl NR34. . . . . .111 B3
Fir La NR32 . . . . .113 A2
Firmin Cl IP1 . . . . . . .139 A6
Fir Rd IP24 . . . . .16 B4
First Ave
  4 Glemsford CO10 . . . .77 B3
  1 Harwich CO12 . . . . .107 B2
  Sudbury CO10. . . . . . .148 C5
First Dro
  Burwell CB5 . . . . .44 B8
  Lakenheath IP27 . . . . .109 A8
First Drove IP27 . . . . .109 B6
Firs The
  Beccles NR34 . . . . . . .111 F4
  Lakenheath IP27 . . . . .109 E6
  Lowestoft NR33 . . . . .114 C3
  Southwold IP18 . . . . .119 B8
  St Mary, South Elmham
   otherwise Homersfield
   IP20 . . . . .23 B8
  Somerleyton, Ashby &
   Herringfleet NR32 . . . .2 F4
Firtree Cl IP32. . . . . . .122 D7
Fir Tree Cl
  Mildenhall IP28 . . . . .116 D6
  Weybread IP21. . . . . . .22 D2
Fir Tree Hill IP9 . . . . .105 F7
Fir Tree La
  Claydon IP6 . . . . .134 D8
  Haughley IP14 . . . . . . .51 C3
Fir Tree Rise IP8. . . . .138 C2
Fir Wlk 25 IP17 . . . . . .13 F2
Fishbane Cl 9 IP3 . . .144 A8
Fisher Cl
  Haverhill CB9 . . . . . . .133 B5
  10 Laxfield IP13 . . . . . .40 B3
  2 Saxmundham IP17 .128 C2
Fisherman's Way 13
  NR33 . . . . .11 C1
Fisher Rd IP22. . . . . . . .20 D2
Fisher Row
  Carlton Colville
   NR32 . . . . .114 B8
  Lowestoft NR32 . . . . .112 B1
Fishers Dr IP28 . . . . . .47 E5
Fisher's Dro IP28 . . . . .12 D3
Fisher's La
  East Bergholt CO7 . . . .104 E6
  Hoxne IP21. . . . . .38 C8
Fishers The IP5. . . . . .141 C7
Fisher Theatre ★
  NR35. . . . . .110 B4
Fish Pond Hill IP9. . . .106 B6
Fishpond La IP31 . . . . .35 C3
Fishpond Rd IP12. . . . .98 D7
Fishponds Hill CO6. . .102 C3
Fishponds La IP9 . . . .105 F7
Fishponds Way IP14 . .66 C8
Fiske Cl IP32 . . . . .123 E6
Fisk's La IP1. . . . . . . .134 D3
Fison Way IP24 . . . . . .16 B7
Fison Way Ind Est
  IP24 . . . . .16 B7
Fitchœ La
  Aldringham IP16. . . . . .129 D1
  Leiston IP17 . . . . .129 A2
Fitches The IP17 . . . . .129 A2
Fitzeral Meadow 8
  CO10 . . . . .93 C3
Fitzgerald Cl 4
  CO11 . . . . .104 D2
Fitzgerald Rd
  Bramford IP8 . . . . . . .134 A1

Fitzgerald Rd continued
  Woodbridge IP12 . . . . .147 A6
Fitzgerald Wlk IP33. . .122 B6
Fitzmaurice Rd IP3 . .140 B3
Fitzroy St
  Ipswich IP1 . . . . .155 B3
  Newmarket CB8 . . . . .121 A1
Fitzwalter Rd 18 IP22 .20 D2
Fitzwilliam Cl
  Ipswich IP2 . . . . .138 F2
  Newmarket CB8 . . . . .121 B1
  6 Woodbridge IP12 . . .146 E4
Five Acre La NR35. . . . . .7 E3
Five Acres 12 IP9 . . . .105 E7
Five Cross Ways
  Butley IP12. . . . . .86 B4
  Sudbourne IP12 . . . . .131 B6
  Wetheringsett-cum-
   Brockford IP23. . . . . .53 A7
Fiveways IP28 . . . . . . .116 F3
Flaggy Pond View
  CO6. . . . . .93 F1
Flash Corner IP16. . . . .58 C4
Flatford Cl IP14. . . . . .124 E3
Flatford La CO7 . . . . .151 D1
Flatford Mill ★ CO7 . .151 D1
Flatford Rd
  East Bergholt CO7 . . .151 C3
  Haverhill CB9 . . . . . . .132 A6
Flatts La IP30. . . . . . . .50 B2
Flavian Cl CB9 . . . . . .133 B5
Flax La CO10 . . . . .77 B2
Fleet Dyke Rd NR33 . .114 E5
Fleetwood Ave IP11. .153 B5
Fleetwood Cl IP6 . . . .125 F8
Fleetwood Rd IP11. . .153 B5
Fleming Ave IP28 . . . .116 C5
Flemington Cl IP28 . .116 B5
Fleming Way 6 CB9 . .74 A1
Flemish Ave 12 IP32. . .48 B5
FLEMPTON 47 F8
Flempton Bridge Carr
  IP28. . . . . .32 B1
Flempton Rd
  Risby IP28 . . . . .47 D5
  West Stow IP28 . . . . . .32 B1
Flemyng Rd IP33. . . . .122 C5
Fletcher Cl 3 IP6. . . . . .82 A5
Fletcher Rd IP33. . . . .140 A1
Fletchers La IP5 . . . . .141 E8
Fletcher's La IP17 . . . .58 B6
Flindell Dr IP8. . . . . . .134 A2
Flint Cl IP2 . . . . .139 B2
Flint Dr IP6. . . . . .125 E3
Flint Way IP27 . . . . . .109 C7
Flint Way 13 CO10. . . . .92 B7
FLIXTON 7 D1
Flixton Marsh La
  NR32 . . . . .112 B6
Flixton Rd
  Blundeston NR32 . . . .112 C8
  Bungay NR35. . . . . . .110 A1
  Flixton NR35. . . . . .7 C1
  Flixton NR35. . . . . .7 E2
  Lowestoft NR32 . . . . .112 D7
  St Mary, South Elmham
   otherwise Homersfield
   IP20 . . . . .23 B8
Flixton View NR32 . . .112 E5
Floral Loke NR32. . . . . .2 D4
Flora Rd NR33 . . . . . .115 A3
Flordon Rd IP6 . . . . . .125 E5
Florence Barclay Cl
  IP24. . . . . .16 C7
Florence Gdns 34
  CO11 . . . . .104 D2
Florence Rd NR33. . . .115 B3
Florence Way NR35 . . .8 D7
Flowerday Cl 4 NR31 . .3 B7
Flowerden Mdw IP21 .21 A2
FLOWTON. 81 C1
Flowton Rd
  Elmsett IP7. . . . . .81 A1
  Flowton IP8 . . . . .95 B8
  Somersham IP8 . . . . . .81 C3
Floyd Rd IP32 . . . . . . .122 D8
Foal's Gn Rd IP21 . . . .39 D2
FOALS GREEN 39 D2
Fodderfen Dro
  Beck Row, Holywell Row &
   Kenny Hill IP28. . . . . .12 C1
  Feltwell PE38 . . . . .4 A3
Foden Ave IP1. . . . . . .134 C2
Folly End IP15 . . . . . .130 D5
Folly La
  Bressingham IP22 . . . . .19 F4
  Copdock & Washbrook
   IP8 . . . . .95 E2
  Lawshall IP29 . . . . .63 C3
Folly Rd
  Capel St Mary IP8. . . . .150 C8
  Chapel St Mary IP8. . . .95 C4
  Chilton St CO10. . . . . . .75 F2
  Great Waldingfield
   CO10 . . . . .92 C6
  Hundon CO10 . . . . . . .75 F3
  Mildenhall IP28 . . . . .116 A7
Folly The
  Harleston IP14. . . . . . . .66 C8
  Haughley IP14 . . . . . . .51 C1
Fonnereau Rd IP1 . . . .155 B3
Food Mus ★ IP14 . . . .124 D5
Forbes Dr NR34 . . . . .111 B3
Ford Cl
  Beck Row, Holywell Row &
   Kenny Hill IP28. . . . . .29 F7

Ford Cl continued
  Stowmarket IP14 . . . .124 C4
FORDHAM 29 B1
Fordham CE Prim Sch
  CB7. . . . . .29 B1
Fordham Pl
  4 Ipswich IP4. . . . . . .140 F5
  24 Ixworth IP31. . . . . . .34 E1
Fordham Rd
  Fordham CB8 . . . . . . .44 F7
  Freckenham IP28 . . . . .29 D2
  Mount Bures CO6 . . . .101 C1
  Newmarket CB8 . . . . .120 F7
  Snailwell CB8 . . . . . . .45 A7
  7 Soham CB7. . . . . . . .28 D3
  Soham CB7. . . . . .28 F2
  Wormingford CO6. . . .101 E2
Fordhams Cl 21 IP31 . .34 E4
Ford Hill IP12. . . . . . . .99 B7
Fordley Rd IP17 . . . . . .57 F6
Ford Rd IP13 . . . . .71 C5
Fordson Way NR33. . .114 C3
Ford View Rd IP14 . . .124 E4
Fordwater Cl CO9 . . . .133 C1
Fore Hamlet IP3 . . . . .139 E5
Fore St Mws IP13 . . . .126 D3
Fore St
  Framlingham IP13 . . . .126 D3
  Ipswich IP4 . . . . .155 C2
Forest Community Prim
  Sch IP27. . . . . .5 F1
Forest End CB8 . . . . . .46 A7
Forester Cl 9 IP8. . . .142 E8
Foresters Wlk 6 IP6. .82 A5
Forest Gdns 9 IP21. . . .85 D8
Forest Glade CB9 . . . .132 D8
Forest La
  Dunwich IP17 . . . . .42 F2
  3 Martlesham Heath
   IP5. . . . . .98 A7
Forest Mount NR31 . . .2 B7
Forest Rd IP14. . . . . . .66 B6
Forest Ret Pk IP24 . . .16 A5
Forest Way IP28 . . . .116 E4
Forfar Cl
  2 Ipswich IP4. . . . . . .136 B1
  Ipswich IP4 . . . . .140 B8
Forge Cl
  2 Benhall IP17 . . . . . .72 C8
  Bucklesham IP10 . . . . .98 A5
  Palgrave IP22. . . . . . . .20 C1
Forge End IP28 . . . . . .48 B6
Forge Gr NR34 . . . . . . .9 B6
Forge Rd IP14 . . . . . .124 C3
Forge St CO7 . . . . . . .104 A3
Forge Way
  Garboldisham IP22. . . . .18 D4
  Garboldisham IP22. . . . .18 D4
Formula Dr CB8. . . . . .120 E6
FORNHAM ALL
  SAINTS. 48 B6
Fornham House Cl
  IP28. . . . . .48 D6
Fornham La IP33 . . . .122 A7
Fornham Rd
  Bury St Edmunds
   IP32 . . . . .154 B4
  Fornham St Martin
   IP31 . . . . .48 D5
  Great Barton IP31 . . . . .49 A5
FORNHAM ST
  GENEVIEVE 48 C6
FORNHAM ST
  MARTIN. 48 C6
Forrester Rd 21
  CO11 . . . . .105 A2
Forties Cl IP9 . . . . . . .133 B6
Fortress Fields 16
  CO10 . . . . .92 C6
Fortress Rd NR33 . . . .114 B3
Fortress Way IP31. . . . .49 A2
Forum Cl 8 IP6 . . . . . .81 F5
Fosse Meadow IP14. . .51 F1
Foster Cl 4 IP18. . . . .119 D6
Foster Rd 7 CO12 . . .106 F3
Foster's Drove IP26. . . .4 A1
Foundation St IP4. . . .155 B2
Foundry Cl 11 CO10 . . .77 B3
Foundry La IP1. . . . . .155 B2
Fountain La CB7 . . . . .28 D4
Fountain Rd 4 IP12. . .85 D8
Fountain's La NR34 . . .10 C4
Fountains Rd
  Bury St Edmunds
   IP33 . . . . .122 D2
  Ipswich IP2 . . . . .139 A1
Fountain Way IP18. . .119 C8
FOUR ASHES 35 C5
Four Ash Hill CO9 . . . .89 C4
Fourth Ave 5 CO10 . . .77 A3
Four Wheel Dr IP30. . .49 B2
Fowe's La CO10 . . . . . .90 D4
Fowler's Cres 2 NR32. .3 D4
Fox And Pin La IP29. . .63 A7
FOXASH ESTATE 104 B1
Foxberry Gdns IP3 . . .140 D5
Foxborough Rd
  NR32 . . . . .113 A4
Foxburrow Cl CB9. . . .132 D7
Foxburrow Farm Nature
  Reserve ★ IP12 . . . . .84 D6
Foxburrow Hill NR32 .113 A6
Foxburrow Rd 6
  IP3. . . . . .140 F1
Foxburrow Wood Nature
  Reserve ★ NR32. . . . .113 B6
Fox Ct IP14 . . . . .124 D6

FOXEARTH 91 B7
Fox Earth Cl IP9 . . . . .150 C4
Foxearth Rd
  Long Melford CO10. . . . .91 D7
  Pentlow Street CO10 . . .91 A8
Foxes La
  Ashen CO10 . . . . .89 E5
  Mendham IP20 . . . . . .23 B4
Foxes Rd CO10. . . . . . .89 E5
Foxes Wlk NR32. . . . . .113 A6
Foxglade NR32 . . . . . .112 C2
Foxglove Ave IP6 . . . .125 D3
Foxglove Cl
  Lowestoft NR33 . . . . .115 A2
  1 Worlingham NR34 . .111 E3
Foxglove Cres IP3 . . . .140 E1
Foxglove Rd IP24 . . . . .16 D6
Foxgrove Gdns IP11. . .153 C5
Foxgrove La IP11 . . . .153 C5
Foxhall Cl CO7. . . . . . .151 C6
Foxhall Fields CO7 . . .151 C5
Foxhall Rd
  Foxhall IP10 . . . . .98 A8
  Ipswich IP3 . . . . .139 F5
Foxhall Stadium IP4 141 A5
Fox Hill
  Hollesley IP12 . . . . . . .99 F7
  St Cross, South Elmham
   IP20. . . . . .23 C7
Fox La IP17. . . . . .42 B1
Fox Lea IP5. . . . . .141 E8
Foxley Cl IP3 . . . . .140 D4
Fox'S La IP22. . . . . .35 D7
Foxtail Rd IP3 . . . . . . .144 D8
Foxwood Cl CO11 . . . .104 B1
Foxwood Cres IP4 . . .140 F5
Fox Wood N 7 CB7 . . . .28 D5
Fox Wood S 11 CB7. . . .28 D5
Fox Yd IP18 . . . . .119 D5
Foysters Hall IP7 . . . . .79 D2
FRAMLINGHAM 126 D2
Framlingham Cl 4
  IP12. . . . . .85 B3
Framlingham Coll
  IP13 . . . . .126 C6
Framlingham Mere
  Nature Reserve ★
   IP13 . . . . .126 C6
Framlingham Rd
  Dennington IP13. . . . . . .39 F2
  Dennington IP13. . . . . . .55 E5
  Earl Soham IP13. . . . . . .54 F2
  Easton IP13 . . . . .70 E5
  Kettleburgh IP13 . . . . . .70 D7
  Laxfield IP13. . . . . .40 A2
Frampton Cl CB8. . . . .121 A5
Frampton Rd IP3 . . . .144 A8
FRAMSDEN 69 B6
Framsden La IP13 . . . . .69 D4
Framsden Rd
  Framsden IP14. . . . . . . .69 C7
  Pettaugh IP14 . . . . .68 F7
Framsden Windmill ★
  IP14 . . . . .69 B6
Frances St IP32. . . . . .122 E8
Franciscan Way IP1. . .155 B2
Francis Cl
  Haverhill CB9 . . . . . . .132 D6
  Ipswich IP5 . . . . .141 E8
Francis Rd
  13 Kessingland NR33 . .11 B1
  3 Sudbury CO10 . . . . .148 C5
Frank Bridges Cl 4
  CB7. . . . . .28 D3
Franklin Cl IP15 . . . . .130 D5
Franklin Rd
  Aldeburgh IP15 . . . . . .130 C5
  Ipswich IP3 . . . . .140 B2
  Saxmundham IP17 . . . .128 B2
Frank Wheeler Way 21
  CO12 . . . . .107 A2
Frary Place NR35 . . . .110 D4
Fraser Rd
  Bramford IP8 . . . . . . .134 B2
  3 Ipswich IP1. . . . . . .138 F7
FRECKENHAM 29 F3
Freckenham Rd
  Freckenham CB7. . . . . .29 E2
  West Row IP28 . . . . . . .29 F4
  Worlington IP28 . . . . . .30 A3
Fred Archer Way
  CB8 . . . . .121 A3
Fred Castle Way IP30 .49 B3
Fred Dannatt Rd
  IP28. . . . . .116 A6
Fredericks Cl IP9 . . . .105 A7
Frederick's Rd 3
  NR34 . . . . .111 C4
Frederick Talbot Cl 14
  CB7 . . . . .28 D4
Freehold Rd
  Ipswich IP4 . . . . .140 A6
  Needham Market IP6. .125 C6
Free La NR35. . . . . . . .110 A8
Freelands 5 IP14. . . . . .52 E4
Freeman Ave 4 IP6. . .82 D6
Freeman Cl IP7 . . . . . .149 D7
Freeman Com Prim Sch
  IP14 . . . . .59 C6
Freemantle Rd NR33 .115 C7
Freestone Way CO10 .148 F1
Freewood St IP30. . . . .64 D6
Freezes Barns CB9. . . . .88 D4

Frenesi Cres 26 IP31 . . .49 A3
FRENZE. 20 F3
Frenze Hall La IP22. . . .20 D3
Frenze Rd IP22 . . . . . . .20 D2
Frere Cnr 7 IP22 . . . . .20 A3
Frere Rd 30 IP20 . . . . .22 C6
Freshfields
  17 Harwich CO12 . . . .106 F1
  Newmarket CB8 . . . . .120 F4
Freshfields Rd CO12 .106 F3
FRESSINGFIELD 39 D8
Fressingfield CE VC Prim
  Sch IP21 . . . . .39 D8
Fressingfield Rd
  Metfield IP20 . . . . .23 C1
  Withersdale Street
   IP20. . . . . .22 F3
FRESTON 143 D3
Freston Hill IP9. . . . . .143 E4
Freston St IP9 . . . . . . .143 E4
Freston Twr ★ IP9. . . .143 F4
Friar Cl CB9 . . . . .132 D7
Friars IP9 . . . . .150 F2
Friars Bridge Rd IP1 155 A2
Friars Cl 7 IP11 . . . . .153 D6
Friars Croft IP21. . . . . .22 D3
Friars Ct
  Melton IP12 . . . . .147 C7
  22 Sudbury CO10 . . . .148 C4
Friar's La IP33. . . . . . .154 B1
Friars Meadow IP21 . .22 D3
Friars Rd IP7 . . . . .149 C6
Friars St
  Ipswich IP1 . . . . .155 B2
  Sudbury CO10. . . . . . .148 C5
Friary Meadow IP28. .148 D5
Friday's Orch IP16. . . .129 C5
Friday St
  Beck Row, Holywell Row &
   Kenny Hill IP28. . . . . .29 F6
  Cretingham IP13 . . . . . .69 F6
  Rendlesham IP12. . . . . .85 D7
FRIDAY STREET
  Benhall 72 B7
  Brandeston. 70 A6
  Rendlesham. 85 D7
Friday Street Farm ★
  IP17 . . . . .72 B7
Friends Field 7
  CO8 . . . . .101 C5
Friends Wlk IP5 . . . . .141 D8
Friesian Cl 15 IP28. . . .30 A8
Frigmore Dr 19 IP31 . .49 A3
FRISTON. 72 F7
Fristonmoor La
  Knodishall IP17 . . . . . . .57 E1
  Sternfield IP17 . . . . . . .72 E8
Friston Rd IP12. . . . . . .85 C2
Fritillary Cl 8 IP8 . . . .142 E8
FRITTON 2 B7
Fritton Cl
  Ipswich IP2 . . . . .139 A1
  12 Oulton NR32 . . . . .112 F4
Fritton Ct 5 CB9. . . . .132 C4
Fritton Lake & Visitor
  Ctr ★ NR31 . . . . .2 C6
FRIZZELER'S GREEN . .47 C1
Frobisher Rd
  21 Harwich CO12 . . . .106 F1
  Ipswich IP3 . . . . .139 E1
Frog Hall La IP7 . . . . .149 F6
Frogmore CB8. . . . . . .120 B7
Frogs Alley IP9 . . . . . .106 F6
Frogs Alley Vineyard ★
  IP9 . . . . .106 F7
Frogs Hall Rd CO10. . . .78 D5
Frogs Hole NR32. . . . . .2 C5
Fromus Sq IP17. . . . . .128 D3
Fronk's Ave 3 CO12 .107 B1
Fronk's Rd CO12 . . . . .107 A1
Front Rd IP3. . . . . . . .144 D8
Front St
  Mendlesham IP14 . . . . .52 E4
  Orford IP12 . . . . .131 B3
  Ousden CB8 . . . . .61 E6
FROSTENDEN 26 C4
FROSTENDEN
  CORNER. 26 D3
Frostenden Cres 1
  NR32 . . . . .113 B4
Frostley Bridge Rd
  IP13. . . . . .55 E7
Frowd Cl CB7. . . . . . . .29 B1
Fryatt Ave 7 CO12 . . .107 A2
Fryatt Hospl CO12 . . .107 A2
Fryth Cl IP7 . . . . .132 E7
Fuchsia La IP4 . . . . . .140 A5
Fulcher Cl IP33 . . . . . .123 D2
Fulchers Field IP13 . .126 B4
Fulford Cl 8 IP28. . . . . .48 C6
Fulham Way 6 IP1 . . .138 F7
Fuller Cl NR32 . . . . . .112 D2
Fuller Rd IP20. . . . . . . .22 D5
Fullers Cl 3 IP7 . . . . . .149 E6
Fullers Mill ★ IP28. . . .32 A2
Fullers Teasle NR33 . .114 A3
Fuller Way IP14. . . . . .124 A8
Fulmar Way NR33. . . .114 D5
Fulmerston Rd IP24. . . .16 B4
Furlong Cl 18 IP30 . . . .50 F2
Furness Cl IP2 . . . . . .142 F8
Further St CO10. . . . . .92 E2
Furthest Dro IP27. . . . . .4 D1
Furthest Drove IP27 .109 A5
Furze Cl 4 IP31 . . . . . .49 D4

Furze Way IP22........36 D5
Futura Pk IP3.......140 D1
Fyffe Way 12 NR33. 115 D8
Fynn La IP6......136 C5
Fynn Rd IP12......146 D3
Fyson's La IP22.......19 A4

G

Gables The CB9.....133 D3
Gadwall Terr IP2....138 E3
Gaell Cres 5 IP7..149 D5
Gage Cl IP32......154 A4
Gage's Rd CO10.....90 C4
Gaines Hall Rd CB8...61 E2
GAINSBOROUGH....144 B8
Gainsborough Ave 6
 IP22.............20 C2
Gainsborough Ctr
 IP3..........144 B8
Gainsborough Dr
 Halesworth IP19....118 A2
 Lowestoft NR32.....113 B6
 Manningtree IP19...104 D2
Gainsborough La
 IP3.............143 F8
Gainsborough Rd
 Bury St Edmunds
 IP33............122 D5
 Felixstowe IP11....153 A4
 Haverhill CB9......132 B7
 Ipswich IP4.......155 C4
 Stowmarket IP14....124 B6
 Sudbury CO10......148 C5
Gainsborough's House★
 20 CO10.........148 C5
Gainsborough St
 CO10...........148 C5
Gale Rd IP12.......146 F8
Gallery La CO10......75 D3
Galley Cl NR33.....114 B4
Galley Rd CO10......75 D3
Gallow La IP30......78 C7
Gallows Hill IP7....149 B7
Gallows La IP14.....66 C7
Galway Ave IP1.....134 E1
Game Cl CO10......148 F1
Gandish Cl CO7.....151 D3
Gandish Rd CO7....151 E4
Ganges Rd 1 IP9...107 A4
Gannet Cl CB9......133 A6
Gannet Rd IP27......46 A8
Gants Meadow IP7....80 B4
Ganwick Cl CB9....132 D8
Ganymede Rd IP2...138 D7
Gaol La
 Beccles NR34.....111 B5
 Sudbury CO10......148 C5
Gap The NR33......114 F6
GARBOLDISHAM....18 B4
Garboldisham Church
 Prim Sch IP22.....18 D4
Garboldisham Rd
 Harling NR16......18 C7
 Kenninghall NR16...18 F7
Garden City CO11...104 C1
Garden Cl
 Bungay NR35.......110 C3
 5 Great Barton IP31..49 A6
 Normanston NR32...113 B2
 Shotley IP9.........106 F6
Garden Ct 2 CB5....44 B6
Gardeners Cl IP7...149 E4
Gardeners La 21 CB7..28 D4
Gardeners Rd IP14...53 F1
Gardeners Wlk 3
 IP30.............50 E2
Garden Field 2
 IP11............152 E5
Garden Fields IP31...33 D2
Gardenhouse La IP22.36 A6
Garden House La
 IP30.............65 C6
Gardenia Cl IP12....85 D8
Garden La
 Beccles NR34......111 F4
 Westley IP33.......122 A5
Garden Pl CO10....148 B5
Garden Room The★
 IP6.............125 D5
Garden Sq 1 IP12...85 D8
Gardens The
 4 Beyton IP30......49 F2
 Lowestoft NR33....114 C2
Gardiner Cl IP33...122 C4
Gardner Rd IP18....119 D5
Garfield Cl IP11....152 F3
Garfield Rd IP11....152 F3
Garland Cl 2 IP3...140 C2
Garland Rd 5 CO12..106 F3
Garland Rd South 10
 CO12...........106 F3
Garlands Cl IP31....132 A6
Garland St IP33....154 B3
Garlic St IP21.......22 A6
GARLIC STREET......22 A6
Garman Way IP7...149 F7
Garnons Chase 3
 CO6............101 F2
Garrard Pl 17 IP31...34 B1
Garrards Rd 3 IP7...80 F1
Garrards The IP5...141 B6
Garrett Cl IP17......72 D5
Garrett Cres IP16..129 D5

Garrick Way IP1....135 A3
Garrison La
 Felixstowe IP11....152 F4
 5 Great Waldingfield
 CO10...........92 C6
Garrod App IP12.....84 E7
Garrods IP9........150 F3
Garrods End IP29....62 C5
Gascoigne Dr 3 IP6..82 D6
Gashouse Dro IP27....5 F1
Gaskell Pl IP1......139 A5
Gassock Dr 7 IP22...20 C1
GASTHORPE.........18 A4
Gaston End CO7....151 C5
Gaston St CO7.....151 C4
Gas Works Rd NR32.113 C2
Gatacre Rd IP1.....139 A7
Gate Farm Rd 2
 IP9.............107 A5
Gatekeeper Cl 20
 IP31.............49 E4
Gatesbury's La IP29..62 C2
Gates Cl IP31.......49 D4
Gateway The IP33...123 C3
Gattinetts Bsns Ctr The
 CO7............151 B4
Gavell St IP19......24 D5
Gawdy Cl 2 IP20....22 D6
Gaye Cres IP23....117 B3
Gaye St IP1.......155 A3
Gayfer Ave IP5.....141 F8
Gayford Sq IP7......80 C6
Gayford Terr IP9...106 E6
Gaymers La IP11....152 B8
GAZELEY...........46 B3
Gazeley Gate CO8..101 F6
Gazeley Rd
 Ashley CB8.........46 A1
 Higham CB8........46 D4
 Kentford CB8.......46 A5
Gdn Meadow View
 IP14..............52 A6
GEDDING............65 A5
Gedding Hill IP30....65 A6
Gedding Rd IP30.....65 B7
Gedge Cl IP33.....122 C4
Gedgrave Rd IP12..131 A1
GELDESTON...........8 F7
Geldeston Hill NR34...8 F6
Geldeston Rd
 Ellingham NR35......8 F7
 Geldeston NR34......9 B6
Gelham Hall Rd
 IP13.............127 A7
General Castle Way
 IP30..............49 B2
Generals Mews 12
 IP11............152 D5
GENESIS GREEN......61 F4
Genesta Dr 2 IP31...49 D4
Geneva Ave IP5......98 B8
Geneva Gdns 4 NR31..3 C6
Geneva Rd IP1.....155 A4
Genevyll Cl 7 CO10..76 E1
Gentle Ct 3 IP27.....5 F1
Gentle Rise IP27...109 C7
Gents La IP29.......77 F7
George Baldry Way 2
 NR35............110 C2
George Brown Way
 NR34............111 C3
George Cl NR32....112 E1
George Davey Cl
 NR34............111 D2
George Elliston Rd
 IP3.............140 C4
George Frost Cl IP4.155 C4
George Gent Cl 7
 CB9..............88 D3
George Gibson Cl
 CB8............120 C8
George Hill IP31.....34 E4
George La
 3 Glemsford CO10...77 B2
 Stanton Chare IP31...34 E5
 Wickham Market IP13 127 C6
George Lambton Ave
 CB8............120 F5
George Rd
 Leiston IP16........58 B3
 3 Thetford IP24....16 D6
George St
 Brandon IP27.......5 F1
 Hadleigh IP7......149 E6
 2 Harwich CO12...107 B3
 Hintlesham IP8......95 C8
George Westwood Way
 NR34............111 C4
Geralds Ave IP4....140 A5
GESTINGTHORPE.....90 F1
Gestingthorpe Rd
 CO10.............90 F2
Ghent Field Circle
 IP31.............49 D4
Ghent Field Wlk IP31..49 D5
Gibbon Cl IP32....123 E5
Gibbons St IP1.....139 A6
Gibraltar Cl IP33...122 C6
Gibraltar Rd IP6....69 E8
Gibson Cl 1 IP3...140 C2
Gidney La 12 CB7...28 D3
Gifford Cl 6 IP9...105 E7
Giffords La
 Clopton Green CB8....62 A4
 Denston CB8........76 B8
Giffords Pl IP4.....140 F6
Giggle Factory The★
 IP7............148 F7

Gilbert Cl IP6......125 C5
Gilbert Rd
 2 Clare CO10......90 A8
 Saxmundham IP17..128 B3
 Stanton IP31........34 F3
Giles Way
 Risby IP28.........47 E5
 4 Witnesham IP6....83 A5
Gilletts Rd IP19.....41 D5
GILLINGHAM..........9 C6
Gillingham Rd NR34...9 A6
Gillingham St Michael's
 CE Prim Acad NR34...9 B6
Gillingham Dam
 NR34............111 A7
Gillyflower Way 20
 IP28..............46 A8
Gilpin Rd NR32....112 D1
Gilray Rd IP27......20 D2
Gilstrap Rd IP31....48 D5
Gimbert Rd 7 CB7...28 D4
Gin La IP13.........40 C2
Gippeswyk Ave IP2..139 A4
Gippeswyk Rd IP2..155 A1
GIPPING...........52 B2
Gipping Cl IP9.....132 C4
Gipping Pl IP14....124 D7
Gipping Rd
 Claydon IP6........82 A5
 Gipping IP14.......52 A1
 Stowupland IP14....67 A7
Gippingstone Rd
 IP8.............134 A1
Gipping View Rd
 IP8.............138 B3
Gipping Way
 Bramford IP8.......134 B2
 Sproughton IP8....138 B6
 Stowmarket IP14...124 D7
Gipsies La IP31......50 A4
Gipsy La
 Aldringham cum Thorpe
 IP16............129 D1
 Frostenden NR34....26 D4
 Hopton IP22........18 D1
 Needham Market IP6. 125 C6
GIPSY ROW.........150 A4
Girling St CO10....148 C6
Girling Way IP28....13 C1
Girton Cl
 Mildenhall IP28....116 C6
 Woodbridge IP12...146 D4
 Woodditton CB8....121 B1
Girton Rd CB9.....132 F5
Girton Way IP1.....138 F1
GISLEHAM..........11 A3
Gisleham Rd
 Gisleham NR33......11 A3
 Lowestoft NR33....114 B3
GISLINGHAM........36 D2
Gislingham CE Prim Sch
 IP23............36 C2
Gislingham Rd
 Finningham IP14....36 C1
 Gislingham IP23.....36 D3
GISSING...........20 F8
Gissing Rd
 Burston & Shimpling
 IP22............20 F6
 Gissing NR15.......21 B8
Glades The IP22...112 D2
Glade The IP24......16 C7
Gladstone Rd
 1 Corton NR32......3 C4
 Ipswich IP3......139 F5
 6 Woodbridge IP12.147 A5
Glamis Cl IP9......132 B6
Glamis Ct 28 IP20...22 D6
Glamorgan Rd IP2..139 A3
Glanely Gdns CB8...120 C8
Glanfield Wlk IP33..122 C4
Glanville Pl IP5....141 B6
Glanville Rd IP7...149 E4
Glassfield Rd IP31...34 D4
Glastonbury Cl IP2..138 F1
Glastonbury Rd IP33 122 C3
Glebe Cl
 Bayham IP6.........81 E6
 Horringer IP29......63 A4
 Ingham IP31........32 F1
 Lowestoft NR32....113 C5
 Sproughton IP8....138 B6
 1 Tattingstone IP9..105 B8
 2 Thetford IP24....16 C6
Glebe Dr CB8......120 A8
Glebe End IP9.....150 F4
Glebe La IP9.......144 B1
Glebe Meadow IP13..54 F2
Glebe Rd
 Bredfield IP13......84 C7
 Gissing IP21.........21 A8
 Weeting IP27.........5 E3
Glebe Rd E 15 NR33..11 B1
Glebe Rd W 18 NR33..11 B1
Glebes The IP17.....72 D5
Glebe The
 Haverhill CB9.....132 E7
 Lavenham CO10.....78 D3
Glebe View NR34...111 C3
Glebe Way
 1 Claydon IP6......82 B5
 Mendlesham IP14....52 E4
Glemham Dr IP4....140 F4
Glemham Hall★ IP13.71 E6
Glemham House Drive
 IP17..............71 E8
Glemham Rd IP17....56 E2
GLEMSFORD........77 B2

Glemsford Cl IP11..152 D3
Glemsford Com Prim Sch
 CO10.............77 A3
Glemsford Pl 7 CB9.132 F6
Glemsford Rd
 Fenstead End IP29...76 E5
 Lowestoft NR32....112 F4
 Stowmarket IP14...124 E4
Glenare Ct 2 CB7...28 E3
Glenavon Rd IP4...140 D7
Glenbourne Wlk 2
 NR33...........114 C3
Glencoe Rd IP4....136 C1
Gleneagles Cl
 4 Bury St Edmunds
 IP28.............48 C6
 1 Felixstowe IP11..153 C6
Gleneagles Dr IP4..140 D5
Glenfield Ave IP11..153 A6
Glenhurst Ave IP4..140 B8
Glenside CO10.....148 E4
Glenwood Ct CB8..120 F3
Glenwood Dr NR34.111 E4
Global Ct IP18.....119 D8
Globe Cl IP28......116 C5
Globe Yd 3 CO10...148 C6
Gloster Rd IP5......98 A8
Gloucester Ave
 NR32...........112 F3
Gloucester Pl 4
 CO10.............76 A7
Gloucester Rd
 4 Bury St Edmunds
 IP32............122 E8
 Haverhill CB9......132 D5
 Ipswich IP3......140 A2
Gloucester Way
 CO10...........148 B8
Go Ape★ IP27......15 C8
Gobbets La IP22.....35 E7
Gobbetts La IP22....35 E8
Gobbitts Yd IP12....147 A4
Godbold Cl 3 IP5...141 D7
Goddard Pl IP14.....66 B7
Goddard Rd IP1....134 C3
Goddard Rd E IP1..134 D3
Goddard St 6 IP3...82 A5
GODDARD'S CORNER .55 E7
Goddard St 2 IP3...82 A5
Godetia Cl 6 NR32..113 B4
Godfreys Cl IP29....63 A7
Godfrey's Ct 12
 NR32...........113 D2
Godfrey's Hill IP19...40 F8
Godfrey's Wood
 IP12............147 A7
Godolphin Cl IP33...122 C3
Godyll Rd IP18.....119 C5
Goldbrook IP21......38 C7
Goldcrest Rd IP2...138 C3
Golden La IP29......63 C2
Golden Lion La 5
 CO12...........107 B3
Goldenlond CO10...102 E7
Golden Miller Cl
 CB8............120 D7
Golden Mws IP3....140 D1
Golden Sq IP21......39 D8
Golden Sq La NR34...26 E4
Goldings Cl CB9....132 E8
Golding's La IP16...129 C4
Golding Way 1 CO10.77 A2
Golding Way IP14...124 A8
Goldsmith Cl IP32..122 D7
Goldsmith Rd IP1..134 E3
Goldsmiths 12 IP13..84 F7
Goldsmith Way
 Pulham St Mary IP21..21 F8
 Upthorpe IP31......34 F4
Golf La IP15.......130 C6
Golf Links Rd
 Barton Mills IP28...30 C3
 Worlington IP28....116 A1
Golf Rd IP11.......153 D5
Gondree NR34......114 E3
Gonville Cl
 Mildenhall IP28....116 D6
 1 Woodbridge IP12.146 E4
Goodall Terr IP5...141 E8
Goodchilds Gdns 8
 CB7.............29 C5
Goodchild Way CO9..90 A1
Goodlake Cl 9 CO12.106 F1
Goodlands CO10.....93 B3
Goodman Gr IP5...141 E7
Goodrich Cl IP14....52 B6
Goodwood Cl IP1...135 B4
Goosander Rd 1
 IP14............124 F6
Goose Gn E NR34...111 C5
Goose Gn W NR34..111 C5
Gorams Mill La IP13..40 B3
Gordon Rd
 California IP4......140 A6
 5 Harwich CO12...107 A1
 Ipswich IP4.......140 A7
 Lowestoft NR32....113 D1
Gordon Richards Cl
 CB8............120 F6
Goring Rd IP4......140 C6
Gorleston Rd
 Blundeston NR32...112 F8
 Corton NR32........3 B4
Gorse Cl
 Lakenheath IP27...109 E4
 5 Red Lodge IP28...30 C1
Gorse Fell IP8......138 B6
Gorse Gn NR32.....113 B3
Gorsehayes IP2....139 B3

Gorse Ind Est IP24...16 A3
Gorse La IP18.....119 C7
Gorseland Prim Sch
 IP5.............141 F8
Gorselands IP12.....99 F7
Gorse Rd
 Ipswich IP3.......140 B2
 Southwold IP18....119 C6
Gorse View IP17.....58 C8
Gorst Cl 7 IP32....122 E8
GOSBECK...........68 D2
Gosbeck Rd
 Coddenham IP14....68 F2
 Crowfield IP6........68 D4
Gosford Cl 4 CO10...90 A8
Gosford Rd NR34...111 C5
Gosford Way IP11..153 C6
Goshawk Dr 22 NR31..3 B6
Goshawk Way IP24...16 C4
GOSLAND GREEN.....76 A5
GOSLING GREEN.....93 C5
Gosling Way 18 IP11 107 D8
Gosnold St IP33....154 B2
Gospel Hall Rd IP13..127 C7
Gostling Cl 2 IP22....20 B2
Gostling Pl IP5....141 E8
Gothic 2 IP20.......22 D5
Gotsfield Cl 1 CO10...92 B7
Gough Pl 9 IP31....34 B1
Goulders Farm La
 IP21.............39 A8
Governors Mews
 IP33............123 C2
Gowers Cl IP5.....141 E7
Gowers End 6 CO10..77 B3
Gower St IP21.....155 B1
Gowle Rd IP11.....124 C8
Goyfield Ave IP11..152 F4
Gracechurch St IP14..53 E2
Grace Farrant Rd 19
 CO10.............92 B3
Graften Way IP1...155 A2
Grafton Cl IP33....122 D5
Grafton Rd 2 CO12.107 B2
Grafton Way IP1...155 B2
Graham Ave IP1...139 B8
Graham Rd
 Felixstowe IP11....152 F5
 Ipswich IP1.......155 A4
Grainger Cl IP32...123 F5
Grainge Way 3 IP14..51 C1
Grammar Sch Pl 11
 CO10............148 C5
Grampian Way NR32 112 D2
Granaries The IP6...136 C6
Granary Crafts★ IP14 66 A5
Granary Rd CB8....121 B2
Granary The
 1 Clare CO10......90 A7
 Hadleigh IP7......149 E5
Granby St IP33....121 B3
Grand Ave NR33....115 B3
Grange Bsns Ctr IP5 141 E7
Grange Cl
 Felixstowe IP11....152 E5
 Ipswich IP5.......141 F8
Grange Com Prim Sch
 IP11............152 D4
Grange Ct IP12....147 B6
Grange Dr IP8.......95 D7
Grange Farm Ave
 IP11............152 D5
Grange Farm La IP17..56 E4
Grange La
 Barton Mills IP28...116 D2
 Ipswich IP5.......141 E8
 Ridgewell CO9......89 B1
Grange Meadows 23
 IP30..............50 D4
Grange Mill 3 IP29...62 C6
Grange Pk Dr 1
 IP12............147 A6
Granger Cl 9 IP31...35 C2
Grange Rd
 Ashfield cum Thorpe
 IP14.............54 A1
 Beccles NR34......111 A4
 Flixton NR35.........7 E1
 Flixton NR35.......23 E8
 Halesworth IP19...118 C1
 16 Harwich CO12...107 A2
 Ipswich IP4.......139 E6
 Lawford CO11.....104 C1
 Lowestoft NR32....112 D2
 Walpole IP19........41 E6
 Wickham Skeith IP23.52 D7
 Winston IP14.......69 A8
Grange View IP17....58 B7
Grange Wlk IP33....122 E8
Grantchester Pl IP5.141 A8
Grantchester Rise
 CB5.............44 A7
Grantham Ave CO10.148 F1
Grantham Cres IP2.155 A1
Grant Rise 3 IP12...147 A6
Granville Cl IP6......68 D1
Granville Gdns 3
 IP28.............116 A4
Granville Rd IP11..152 F3
Granvilles Gd IP15..130 C4
Granville St IP1....155 A3
Granworth Cl IP13...83 E6
Grasmere Ave 5
 IP11............153 D6
Grasmere Dr 10
 NR32...........113 A4
GRASS GREEN......89 D1

Grassy La IP30......65 E8
Gratton Dale NR33..114 E2
Gravel Dam NR32...112 B2
Gravel Dro IP28......29 E6
Gravel Hill CO6....102 D5
Gravel Hill Way
 CO12...........106 F1
Gravel Pit La
 Brantham CO11....104 F5
 Mundford IP26........6 F5
Grayling Rd 7 IP8..142 E8
Graylings The 10
 NR33...........114 E4
Grays Cl
 3 Gislingham IP23...36 D2
 Hadleigh IP7......149 F7
Grays La IP17.......72 C8
Gray's La IP19......24 D4
Grayson Ave NR33...115 A3
Grayson Dr NR33...115 A2
Gray's Orch IP10....98 E2
Grays Rd NR34......10 C7
GREAT ASHFIELD....50 F6
Great Back La 4 IP14.53 F2
GREAT BARTON......49 A6
Great Barton CE Prim
 Sch IP31..........49 B6
GREAT BEALINGS...137 E6
GREAT BLAKENHAM..82 A5
GREAT BRADLEY.....74 C7
GREAT BRICETT.....80 E5
Great Colman St
 IP1............155 C3
Great Comm La NR34..8 E1
GREAT COMMON......8 E2
GREAT CORNARD...148 F3
Great Cornard Ctry Pk★
 CO10.............92 B2
Great Cornard Sports Ctr
 CO10............148 F2
Great Eastern Rd
 CO10...........148 D5
Great Eastern Sq
 IP11............153 A5
Great Fen Rd CB7....28 D8
Great Field IP11....152 C8
GREAT FINBOROUGH.66 B4
Great Finborough CE VC
 Prim Sch IP14.....66 A4
Great Gipping St
 IP1............155 A2
GREAT GLEMHAM....71 E7
Great Glemham Rd
 IP17.............71 E7
Great Glen IP31.....49 F4
GREAT GREEN
 Burgate...........36 D7
 Cockfield.........64 D2
 Denton............7 A4
Great Green IP22....36 D7
 Norton IP31........50 A4
 Thrandeston......29 C3
Great Halt Dr 25 IP32..48 C5
Great Harlings IP9...107 A5
Great Heath Acad
 IP28............116 C6
GREAT HORKESLEY..102 E1
GREAT LIVERMERE...33 C2
Great Lodge La IP13 126 D6
Great Lodge Rd
 IP13............126 E6
GREAT OAK CT CO9..90 A1
GREAT SAXHAM.....47 C1
GREAT THURLOW....74 E5
Great Tufts IP9....150 F3
GREAT
 WALDINGFIELD.....92 C6
Great Waldingfield CE VC
 Prim Sch CO10.....92 C6
GREAT WELNETHAM.63 F6
GREAT WENHAM....150 A3
Great Whelnetham CE
 Prim Sch IP30......63 F6
Great Whip St IP2..155 B1
GREAT WRATTING...74 E4
Great Wratting Rd
 CB9.............75 A4
GREAT YELDHAM....90 A1
Great Yeldham Rd
 CO9.............89 C1
Grebe Cl
 Ipswich IP2......138 E2
 Mildenhall IP28....116 D3
 Stowmarket IP14...124 A4
Green Acre 2 CO10...92 C6
Greenacre Cres 1
 NR32...........113 B2
Greenacres IP14.....51 F1
Greenbank IP19....118 C5
Green Cl IP30.......65 B7
Green Cres IP10.....98 A4
Greencroft 2 IP30...65 D8
Green Dr
 Ipswich IP10......141 E1
 Ipswich IP10......145 D8
 Lound NR32..........2 D7
 Lowestoft NR33....115 A4
Greene King Brewing
 Mus★ IP33......154 C1
Greene Mws IP33...154 B1
Greene Rd IP33....122 C6
Green Farm La 5
 IP29.............47 A2
Green Farm Loke NR32..2 F4
Green Farm Rd IP13..69 F5
Greenfield Rd NR33..114 F6
Greenfields CB8....121 C3

Greenfields Way
CB9 . . . . 132 C5
Greenfinch Ave IP2 . . 138 D3
Greenfinch Cl IP14. . .124 F7
Greenford Way 5
  IP1. . . . . .138 F7
Greengage Cl 4 IP7 . .94 F1
Greenham Common 16
  IP27. . . . . .13 F2
Green Hill IP6 . . . . . . .68 B1
Greenhills CB7. . . . . . .28 E3
Green La
  Barsham NR34 . . . . .9 A4
  Boxted CO4. . . . . . . .102 E3
  Burgh St Peter NR34. . . .10 C8
  Burston IP22 . . . . .20 E6
  Burwell CB5 . . . . .44 B5
  Calais Street CO6 . . . . .93 E2
  Cockfield IP30 . . . . . . .64 D2
  Covehithe NR34 . . . . . .27 A4
  Creeting St Mary IP14 . .67 F5
  Ditchingham NR35 . . . 110 C7
  Eastbridge IP16 . . . . . .58 D5
  6 Feltwell IP26 . . . . .4 E5
  Finningham IP14 . . . . .52 A7
  Frostenden NR34 . . . . .26 C4
  Garboldisham IP22. . . . .18 F5
  Great Barton IP30 . . . . .48 B5
  Great Livermere IP31. . . .33 B4
  10 Herringswell IP28. . .46 A8
  Hundon CO10 . . . . . . .75 D2
  2 Kennett IP28 . . . . . .45 F8
  Kenninghall NR16. . . . .19 C8
  Kessingland NR33 . . . .11 C1
  Lawford CO11. . . . . . .104 F2
  3 Martlesham IP12. . . . .84 A1
  Pettistree IP13. . . . . . 127 D5
  Redenhall with Harleston
    IP20 . . . . .22 E6
  Redlingfield IP23 . . . . .38 D2
  Rennham IP17 . . . . . . .56 F3
  Reydon IP18. . . . . . . .26 E1
  Ridgewell CO9 . . . . . . .89 E4
  Rougham Green IP30 . . .64 C8
  Shipmeadow NR34. . . . .8 F5
  Somerleyton, Ashby &
    Herringfleet NR32 . . . . .2 E4
  Sotterley NR34 . . . . . .26 A6
  Southwold IP18 . . . . .119 B8
  Starston IP20. . . . . . . .22 D8
  Stratford St Mary CO7 .103 A4
  Syleham IP21 . . . . . . .38 E8
  2 Tattingstone IP9 . . .105 B8
  Thelnetham IP22 . . . . .35 C6
  Thetford IP24. . . . . . . .16 C6
  Thrandeston IP21. . . . .37 B6
  Troston IP31. . . . . . . .33 C5
  Tuddenham St Martin
    IP6. . . . . .136 C4
  Westleton IP17. . . . . . .58 C8
  Wetheringsett-cum-
    Brockford IP14. . . . . .53 A6
  Whelp Street CO10. . . . .79 B4
  Yoxford IP17. . . . . . . .57 A7
Green La Cl IP18. . . . .119 B8
Greenlands IP13. . . . . .54 F4
Green Man Way
  IP12. . . . . .147 B6
Green Oak Glade
  IP8. . . . . .142 D8
Green Oaks IP18. . . . .119 B7
Green Pk
  Brinkley CB8. . . . . . . .59 E1
  42 Harleston IP20 . . . . .22 D6
Green Rd
  Brandon IP27. . . . . .6 A1
  Haughley Green IP14. . . .51 C1
  Haverhill CB9 . . . . . .133 A6
  Newmarket CB8 . . . . .121 A2
  Thorpe Morieux IP30 . . .64 F1
  Thorpe Morieux IP30 . . .78 F7
  Woolpit IP30. . . . . . . .50 D1
  Yoxford IP17. . . . . . . .57 A7
Green St The IP22 . . . .36 A8
Greenside IP17 . . . . . . .42 B1
Greensleeves Rd 5
  CO10 . . . . .148 F8
Greensmill 2 CO11 . .104 E3
Greenspire Gr IP8 . . .138 B2
Green St IP21. . . . . . . .38 C8
Greens The
  Aldeburgh IP15 . . . . . 130 C6
  Ipswich IP4 . . . . .140 F4
GREENSTREET
  GREEN. 80 D5
Green The
  4 Ashley CB8 . . . . . . .60 F8
  Beck Row, Holywell Row &
    Kenny Hill IP28. . . . . .29 E7
  Chedburgh IP29 . . . . . .62 C4
  8 Earsham NR35. . . . . . .7 F4
  Fornham All Saints
    IP26 . . . . .48 B6
  1 Grundisburgh IP13 . .83 E5
  Hadleigh IP7. . . . . . . .149 E6
  Hessett IP30 . . . . .64 F8
  Kersey IP7 . . . . .94 A7
  Kirtling CB8. . . . . .60 E3
  Lound NR32 . . . . .2 F6
  Lowestoft NR33 . . . . .114 F6
  Martlesham IP14 . . . . .52 D2
  2 Mistley CO11. . . . . .104 F2
  North Lopham IP22 . . . .19 C2
  Snailwell CB8. . . . . . . .45 A6
  Walberswick IP18 . . . .119 B2
Greenview IP29. . . . . . .77 B7

Green View IP6 . . . . . . .81 E7
Greenway 4 IP31. . . . . .49 A5
Green Way IP6 . . . . . . .68 E4
Greenways IP12 . . . . . .85 C2
Greenways Cl IP1. . . .139 B8
Greenways Cres
  IP32. . . . . .123 D6
Greenway The NR34. . .111 B4
GREENWICH 139 E1
Greenwich Bsns Pk
  IP3 . . . . .139 E2
Greenwich Cl IP3 . . . .139 E2
Greenwich Rd IP3 . . .139 D2
Green Willows CO10 . . .78 C2
Greenwood Cl IP3. . . .132 C5
Greenwood Ct 28
  IP31. . . . . .49 A3
Greenwoods The
  IP31. . . . . .49 E6
Greenwood Way 1
  NR32 . . . . .113 A6
Gregory Rd IP28 . . . . .116 A6
Gregory St CO10 . . . . .148 C5
Grenadier Ave 6
  CO10 . . . . .148 F8
Grenadier Rd CB9. . . . .132 A6
Grenville Rd CO10. . . .148 D8
Gresham Ave NR32. . . .112 F2
Gresham Cl NR32 . . . .112 F2
Gresham Rd NR34. . . .111 C6
Gresley Gdns 3
  IP2. . . . . .139 C3
Gretna Gdns 1 IP4 . .136 B1
Greville Starkey Ave
  CB8 . . . . .121 A5
Greyfriars ★ IP17 . . . .43 B1
Greyfriars
  Ipswich IP1 . . . . .155 A2
  Woodbridge IP12 . . . . .146 D4
Greyfriars Rd IP32 . . .123 E4
Grey Friars Rd IP1 . . .155 B2
Greyhound Hill CO4. . .103 C2
Greyhound La IP22. . . . .18 B1
Greyhound Rd 7
  CO10 . . . . .77 A2
Greys Cl 5 CO10. . . . . .76 E1
Greys Hall Corner
  CO10 . . . . .92 C2
Greys La CB9 . . . . .75 A3
Grice Cl 3 NR33 . . . . .11 C1
Griffin Gdns CB8. . . . .120 F5
Griffin La IP14 . . . . . . .52 F6
Griffith Cl 4 NR33 . . . .11 C1
Griffiths Cl 6 IP4. . . . 136 A1
Grime Drove IP27. . . . .13 E7
Grimsey Rd IP16. . . . .129 D5
Grimsey's La IP16. . . . .129 D5
GRIMSTONE END 49 F8
Grimston La IP11 . . . .107 C8
Grimwade Cl 9
  CO11 . . . . .104 E4
Grimwade St IP4 . . . . .155 C2
Grinder's La IP21. . . . . .22 D4
Grindle Gdns IP33 . . . .123 B3
Grindle The IP8. . . . . . .95 F8
Grinstead Gdns IP6 . .125 E3
GRINSTEAD HILL. 125 E3
Grinstead Hill IP6. . . . .125 E3
GROMFORD 72 C5
Gromford La IP17. . . . . .72 C5
Groomes Cl 5 NR31 . . . .3 B7
Grosvenor Cl IP4 . . . .139 E8
Grosvenor Gdns
  IP33. . . . . .122 F3
Grosvenor House Ct 9
  IP28. . . . . .116 B5
Grosvenor Rd
  Lowestoft NR33 . . . . .115 C7
  Sudbury CO10. . . . . . .148 B8
Grosvenor Yd CB8 . . . .121 A3
GROTON 93 B4
Groton St CO10 . . . . . .93 B5
Groton Wood Nature
  Reserve ★ CO10. . . . .93 D6
Grove Ave CO10. . . . . .92 E8
Grove Cl
  Hepworth IP22 . . . . . .35 A4
  Nayland CO6. . . . . . . .102 C5
Grove End IP21. . . . . . .39 B5
Grove Farm La IP9 . . .105 F8
Grove Farm Rd
  Renndham IP17 . . . . . .56 F3
  Snape IP12. . . . . .72 A4
Grove Gdns
  Carlton Colville
    NR33. . . . . .114 C4
  Fordham CB7 . . . . .29 A2
  Woodbridge IP12 . . . . .146 E2
Grove; Henley Rd The
  IP1. . . . . .135 C2
Grove Hill
  Belstead IP8. . . . . . . .142 C7
  Dedham CO7. . . . . . . .103 E2
  Langham CO4 . . . . . . .103 C3
Grove La
  Ashfield cum Thorpe
    IP14. . . . . .54 C2
  Elmswell IP30. . . . . . . .51 A3
  Eye IP21. . . . . .37 D8
  Harkstead IP9 . . . . . . .106 C7
  Ipswich IP4 . . . . .139 E5
  Little Wenham IP9 . . . .150 D5
  Mendham IP20. . . . . . .23 A2
  Orford IP12 . . . . .131 B5
  Stanton IP31. . . . . . . .34 F4
  Thetford IP24. . . . . . . .16 C6

Grove Mews 4
  NR34. . . . . .111 C4
Grove Pk
  Bury St Edmunds IP33 .154 A3
  Fordham CB7 . . . . .29 A2
  5 Walsham le Willows
    IP31 . . . . .35 C2
Grove Prim Sch
  NR33. . . . . .114 C4
Grove Rd
  Beccles NR34 . . . . . . .111 B5
  Bentley IP9. . . . . .104 F7
  2 Brantham CO11. . . .104 E4
  Brockdish IP21. . . . . . . .21 F3
  Bury St Edmunds IP33 .154 A3
  Gissing IP21. . . . . .21 A8
  Knodishall IP17 . . . . . .72 F7
  Lowestoft NR33 . . . . .114 C4
  Oak Hall IP12. . . . . . .100 A8
  Pettistree IP13. . . . . . 127 A4
  Starston IP20. . . . . . . .22 C6
  Walsham le Willows
    IP31 . . . . .35 C2
  Woodbridge IP13 . . . . .146 E6
Grove Rd N NR33. . . . .114 D5
Grove The
  Great Glemham IP17 . . .56 F1
  12 Martlesham Heath
    IP5 . . . . .98 A8
  Mildenhall IP28 . . . . . .29 F8
  Stowmarket IP14 . . . .124 E5
  5 Woodbridge IP12. . .147 B6
Grove Wlk IP8 . . . . . . .142 D8
Grubbs La CO10. . . . . .78 E6
Grub La IP19 . . . . .24 E5
GRUNDISBURGH. 83 D5
Grundisburgh Pl
  IP12. . . . . .146 E5
Grundisburgh Prim Sch
  IP13. . . . . .83 E5
Grundisburgh Rd
  Clopton IP13. . . . . .83 D8
  Great Bealings IP13 . . .137 C6
  Tuddenham St Martin
    IP6. . . . . .136 D6
  Tuddenham St Martin
    IP6. . . . . .137 B8
Grundle Cl 6 IP31. . . . .34 E4
Guildford Way 1
  CO10 . . . . .148 E3
Guildhall Feoffment Com
  Prim Sch IP33. . . . . .154 C2
Guildhall La NR34. . . . . .26 D5
Guildhall of Corpus
  Christi The ★ CO10. . .78 D4
Guildhall St IP33. . . . .154 B2
Guildings La IP17. . . . . .72 D5
Guineas Cl CB8 . . . . . .120 E6
Guineas Sh Ctr The
  CB8. . . . . .121 A4
Guinevere Rd 4 NR31. . .3 A8
Gules Gn IP21. . . . . . . .22 F1
Gules Green La IP21 . . .23 A1
Gullemot Cl 11 IP14. . .124 F6
Gull Hill IP19 . . . . .25 C3
GULLING GREEN 63 A3
Gull La
  Grundisburgh IP13. . . . .83 D6
  Shipmeadow NR34. . . . .8 F4
  Thornham Magna IP23. . .37 A2
Gull Rd IP17 . . . . .128 B3
Gull's La CO7 . . . . . . .104 A2
Gull St 7 IP21 . . . . . . .39 E8
Gull The IP13 . . . . .70 C2
Gulpher Bsns Pk
  IP11 . . . . .152 F8
Gulpher Rd
  Felixstowe IP11 . . . . . .152 E6
  Felixstowe IP11 . . . . . .152 F8
Gun Cotton Way IP14 124 F6
Gun Hill
  Dedham CO7. . . . . . . .103 D4
  Southwold IP18 . . . . . 119 D4
Gun La NR32. . . . . . . .113 E2
GUNTON 113 C6
Gunton Ave NR32. . . . .113 A7
Gunton Church La
  NR32. . . . . .113 C5
Gunton Cliff NR32. . . . 113 D5
Gunton Com Prim Sch
  NR32. . . . . .113 C5
Gunton Dr NR32. . . . . 113 D5
Gunton Pk Mws
  NR32 . . . . .113 B8
Gunton St Peter's Ave
  NR32 . . . . .113 C5
Guntons Cl 12 CB7 . . . .28 D4
Gunton Warren Nature
  Reserve ★ NR33. . . . .113 C6
Gurdon Rd 5 IP13 . . . .83 E5
Gurling Cl CO10. . . . . . .78 D3
Gurlings Cl CB9. . . . . .132 E8
Gurney Cl 9 NR31 . . . . .3 B6
Guscot Cl NR32 . . . . . 113 A6
Gusford Prim Sch
  IP2 . . . . .138 D1
Guston Gdns IP10. . . . .98 E2
Guthrum Rd IP7 . . . . .149 D6
Guthrums Meadow
  IP15 . . . . .130 C6
Guyatt Ct 6 CB5. . . . . .44 A5
Guy Cook Cl CO10. . . . .92 B2
Gwendoline Rd IP4 . . .140 E4
Gwynne Rd 4 CO12 . . .107 B2
Gymnasium St IP1 . . .155 A3
Gypsy La IP29 . . . . . . .122 E2
Gypsy's Walk CB8. . . . . .60 D8

H

HACHESTON 71 A6
Hacheston Rd
  Easton IP13 . . . . .70 F5
  Wickham Market IP13 .127 F8
Hackney Rd
  Peasenhall IP17 . . . . . .56 E8
  Woodbridge IP12 . . . . .147 B6
Hackney's Cnr IP6. . . . .81 F5
Hackney Terr IP12 . . . .147 B6
Haddiscoe Sta NR31 . . .2 A5
Haddon Approach
  IP12. . . . . .147 E3
Hadenham Rd NR33. . .114 F1
HADLEIGH. 149 F6
Hadleigh Bsns Pk IP7 94 E4
Hadleigh Com Prim
  Sch IP7. . . . . .149 D5
Hadleigh Dr NR32. . . .112 F3
Hadleigh Ent Pk IP7 149 E7
Hadleigh Guildhall ★
  IP7. . . . . .149 D5
HADLEIGH HEATH 93 F4
Hadleigh High Sch
  IP7. . . . . .149 F5
Hadleigh Railway Walk ★
  IP7. . . . . .94 E3
Hadleigh Rd
  Aldham IP7. . . . . .94 E8
  Bildeston IP7. . . . . . . .79 F3
  Boxford CO6 . . . . .93 D2
  East Bergholt CO7 . . . .151 B4
  Elmsett IP7. . . . . .80 F1
  Higham CO7 . . . . . . .103 D7
  Ipswich IP2 . . . . .138 E6
  Kersey IP7 . . . . .94 A7
  Monks Eleigh IP7 . . . . .79 D2
Hadleigh Rd Ind Est
  IP2 . . . . .138 F7
Hadleigh Swimming
  Pool IP7 . . . . .149 D6
Hadrian Cl CB9 . . . . . .133 B5
Haggar La IP23 . . . . . .53 B8
Haggars Mead IP14. . . .67 D7
HAGMORE GREEN. 93 B2
Hague Cl NR33. . . . . .114 C6
Hailes Meadow IP14 . .66 C8
Hakluyt Cl IP14. . . . . . .53 A5
Halcyon Cres NR32. . . 113 C1
Hale Cl IP2 . . . . .138 D2
Hales Barn Rd CB9. . . .132 C8
Halesowen Cl IP2. . . . .142 F8
HALESWORTH. 118 A4
Halesworth Bsns Ctr
  IP19 . . . . .118 C6
Halesworth & District
  Mus ★ IP19. . . . . . . .118 B4
Halesworth Gall ★
  IP19 . . . . .118 B3
Halesworth (Holton)
  Airfield Mus ★
  IP19 . . . . .118 D6
Halesworth Millennium
  Green IP19. . . . . .118 B3
Halesworth Rd
  Brampton with Stoven
    IP19. . . . . .25 E3
  Broadway IP19. . . . . . .24 E1
  Bungay NR34 . . . . .8 D2
  Chediston IP19. . . . . . .41 B8
  Halesworth IP19 . . . . .118 C1
  Heveningham IP19 . . . .40 F3
  Linstead Parva IP19. . . .40 F8
  Reydon IP18. . . . . . . .119 B7
  St Andrew, Ilketshall
    NR34 . . . . .25 A6
  St Lawrence, Ilketshall
    NR34 . . . . .24 E7
  Sibton IP17. . . . . .41 B1
  Uggeshall NR34 . . . . . .25 F3
  Walpole IP19 . . . . .41 C5
  Wenhaston with Mells
    Hamlet IP19. . . . . . . .41 F6
Halesworth Sta
  IP19 . . . . .118 B4
Half Acre Drove
  IP28. . . . . .12 F1
Half Moon Cl IP27. . . . . .9 C1
Halfmoon La IP27. . . . .109 C2
Half Moon La
  6 Grundisburgh
    IP13. . . . . .83 E5
  Redgrave IP22 . . . . . . .36 A8
Half Moon St IP30 . . . .65 D5
Half Moon Yd 13
  CO10 . . . . .90 A8
Halford Ct 6 IP8 . . . . .138 C2
Halford La IP21. . . . . . .19 D3
Halifax Prim Sch
  IP2 . . . . .139 A2
Halifax Rd
  Ipswich IP2 . . . . .139 B2
  9 Mildenhall IP28 . . . .30 A8
Halifax St IP27. . . . . . .109 F1
Halifax Way CB8 . . . . .120 E5
Haling Way IP14 . . . . . .16 A6
Hall Barn Rd CB7. . . . . .29 B5
Hall Cl
  Depden IP29. . . . . .62 B4
  9 Weeting IP27. . . . . . .5 E4
Hall Cl The IP28. . . . . . .31 D4
Hall Dr
  17 Feltwell IP26. . . . . . .4 E5
  Lakenheath IP27 . . . . .109 C7
  Lowestoft NR32 . . . . . 112 C1
  Santon Downham IP27. . .6 C2

Hall Farm Bungalows 9
  IP6. . . . . .82 A6
Hall Farm Cl IP12 . . . .147 B8
Hall Farm La
  Aldeburgh IP15 . . . . . 130 D5
  Bury St Edmunds IP33 122 A6
  Henstead with Hulver Street
    NR34 . . . . .10 E1
  Nowton IP29. . . . . . . .62 E7
Hall Farm Rd
  Boot Street IP13. . . . . .137 C6
  Darsham IP17 . . . . . . .42 B3
  Woodbridge IP12 . . . . .147 B8
Hall Field 1 IP11 . . . .152 E5
Hallfields IP27. . . . . . .109 C7
HALL GREEN 90 C2
Hall Hill 9 IP22. . . . . . .20 C3
Hallifax Pl IP29 . . . . . . .77 F7
Halliwell Rd IP4 . . . . .140 B6
Hall La
  Bacton Green IP14. . . . .51 D4
  Battisford IP14. . . . . . .66 F1
  Blundeston NR32 . . . . . .3 A4
  Bressingham IP22 . . . . .19 D5
  Brinkley CB8. . . . . .59 F1
  Burston & Shimpling
    IP21 . . . . .21 A6
  Burwell CB5 . . . . .44 A5
  Claydon IP6 . . . . .134 E8
  Dallinghoo IP13 . . . . . .70 D1
  Elmswell IP30. . . . . . . .50 E3
  Harwich CO12. . . . . . .107 A1
  Hawkedon CO10 . . . . .76 C7
  Knettishall IP22 . . . . . .17 F4
  Little Wenham IP9 . . . .150 C5
  Mutford NR34 . . . . . . .10 C2
  Otley IP6. . . . . .69 C2
  Otley IP6. . . . . .69 C3
  Oulton NR32 . . . . . . .112 C4
  Redgrave IP22 . . . . . . .36 A8
  Ridgewell CO9 . . . . . . .89 D3
  Risby IP28 . . . . .47 D5
  Roydon IP22 . . . . .20 A3
  Rushall IP21. . . . . .21 C5
  St Nicholas, South Elmham
    IP20 . . . . .23 D6
  Scole IP21. . . . . .21 C4
  Shelfanger IP22. . . . . . .20 B6
  Shop Corner IP9. . . . . .106 C5
  Smallworth IP22. . . . . .18 D2
  Somersham IP8 . . . . . .81 C3
  Spexhall IP19 . . . . .24 E4
  Stratford St Andrew
    IP17 . . . . .71 E7
  Wetheringsett-cum-
    Brockford IP14. . . . . . .53 B4
  3 Witnesham IP6 . . . . .83 A5
  Yaxley IP23 . . . . .37 B4
  Yoxford IP17. . . . . . . .57 E8
Hallmark Cl IP27. . . . .109 D5
Hall Mead IP29 . . . . . . .63 E1
Hall Pond Way IP11 . . .152 D5
Hall Rd
  Alderton IP12. . . . . . . .99 C4
  Athelington IP21. . . . . .38 E1
  Barnardiston CB8. . . . . .75 B5
  Barsham NR34 . . . . . . .8 F3
  Bedingfield IP23. . . . . .54 A7
  Bedingham NR35 . . . . . .7 C3
  Belchamp Walter CO10. . .91 A3
  Blundeston NR32 . . . . .112 C8
  Borley CO10 . . . . .91 C5
  Borley CO10 . . . . .91 D5
  Brandeston IP13 . . . . . .70 A7
  Bredfield IP13 . . . . . . .84 A8
  Bredfield IP13 . . . . . . .84 B7
  Brockdish IP21. . . . . . .22 A3
  Bruisyard IP17 . . . . . . .56 D5
  Burston & Shimpling
    IP22. . . . . .20 C8
  Carlton Colville NR33 . .114 B2
  Charsfield IP13. . . . . . .69 F3
  Cowlinge CB8. . . . . . . .75 A7
  Earsham NR35 . . . . . . .7 E4
  Easton IP13 . . . . .70 E5
  Ellingham NR35 . . . . . . .8 C7
  Foxhall IP10 . . . . .141 E4
  Framsden IP14. . . . . . .69 C6
  Great Bradley CB8 . . . . .74 D8
  7 Hopton on Sea NR31. . .3 B7
  Hundon CO10 . . . . . . .75 E4
  Kenton IP13 . . . . .54 B5
  Kersey IP7 . . . . .94 A7
  Kersey Upland IP7 . . . . .93 F6
  9 Kessingland NR33 . . .11 C1
  Lavenham CO10 . . . . . .78 D4
  Lindsey Tye IP7. . . . . . .93 E8
  Little Bealings IP5 . . . .137 E2
  Lowestoft NR32 . . . . . 112 D1
  Marlesford IP13. . . . . . .71 C5
  Mendham IP20. . . . . . .23 B6
  Mount Bures CO8 . . . . .101 C3
  Parham IP13. . . . . .71 B7
  Preston St Mary CO10 . .79 A5
  Pulham St Mary IP21. . .22 A8
  Stowmarket IP14 . . . .124 B8
  Stratford St Andrew
    IP17. . . . . .71 E7
  Thorndon IP23 . . . . . . .53 C7
  Wenhaston with Mells
    Hamlet IP19. . . . . . . .42 D5
Hall Rise CO10 . . . . . .148 A3
Halls Drift IP5 . . . . . . .141 C6
Hall's La IP31. . . . . . . .50 B5
Hall St
  Long Melford CO10. . . . .91 E8
  Soham CB7 . . . . .28 D4

Hall Wlk IP8 . . . . .81 F1
Hallwong La IP20. . . . . .22 D7
Hallwyck Gdns CB8 . . .120 F2
Halstead Rd
  Long Melford CO10. . . . .91 C7
  Pentlow Street CO10 . . . .91 A8
Halton Cres IP3 . . . . . .140 C1
Hambling's Piece
  NR16. . . . . .18 C8
Hamblin Rd IP12. . . . . 147 A5
Hamblin Wlk IP12. . . . 147 A5
Hambrook Cl IP30 . . . . .63 F7
Hambros The 3 IP31 . .49 D4
Hamilton Gdns
  Felixstowe IP11 . . . . . .153 A4
  8 Fordham CB7. . . . . . .29 A1
Hamilton Rd
  Felixstowe IP11 . . . . . .153 A4
  Ipswich IP3 . . . . .140 B3
  Lowestoft NR32 . . . . . 113 E1
  Newmarket CB8 . . . . .120 D5
  7 Sudbury CO10 . . . . .148 C5
Hamilton St
  6 Felixstowe IP11. . . . .152 E5
  4 Harwich CO12 . . . . .106 F3
Hamiltons The CB8 . . .120 F2
Hamilton Way
  Ditchingham NR35 . . . .110 C8
  Stowmarket IP14 . . . .124 D7
Hamlet Ct 2 CO8 . . . .101 C4
Hamlet Rd CB9 . . . . . .132 F5
Hammers La IP31 . . . . .33 D3
Hammond Cl CB8 . . . .120 E6
Hammond Croft 16
  CO10 . . . . .77 A3
Hammond's Cnr IP14 .67 C6
Hammonds Wlk
  IP19. . . . . .42 C6
Hampstead Ave IP28 116 B6
Hampton Rd IP1. . . . .138 F7
Hanbury Cl IP19 . . . . . .118 A2
Hanbury Paddocks
  IP28. . . . . .47 E5
HANCHET END. 132 A8
Hanchet End CB9 . . . . .74 A1
Hanchett End CB9 . . . . .74 A1
Hancocks Cl 4 IP16 129 D5
Handford Cut IP1. . . . .139 A6
Handford Hall
  Prim Sch IP1. . . . . . . .139 A6
Hankin Ave 13 CO12 .106 E1
Han Lans Dr NR34. . . . .10 A3
Hanmer Ave IP28 . . . . .116 C5
Hanmer Wlk IP12. . . . .124 D7
Hannah Cres 1 IP3. . .140 D2
Hanners Green NR33. . .10 F2
HANNINGFIELDS
  GREEN 63 F1
Hanover Cl
  5 Bury St Edmunds
    IP32. . . . . .123 A8
  Exning CB8 . . . . .120 E6
  Oulton Broad NR33. . . .114 F5
Hanover Ct CO10 . . . . .148 B4
Hantons La IP31. . . . . . .51 A6
Ha'penny Field 8
  IP9. . . . . .105 E7
Ha'penny Pier Visitor
  Ctr ★ CO12 . . . . .107 B3
Harbourage The
  NR34 . . . . .111 C5
Harbour Cres 7
  CO12 . . . . .107 C3
Harbour La IP22 . . . . . .18 D3
Harbour Rd NR32 . . . .112 E1
Harbour Road
  Ind Est NR32. . . . . . . 114 E8
Harcourt Ave 1
  CO12 . . . . .107 A2
Hardfields Ct 8 CB7 . .28 E3
Harding's La IP31. . . . . .50 E4
Hardpiece La IP17 . . . . .58 C7
Hardwick Cl IP4 . . . . .140 E5
Hardwick La IP33 . . . .122 F2
Hardwick Pk Gdns
  IP33. . . . . .123 A1
Hardwick Prim Sch
  IP33 . . . . .123 B2
Hardwick Rd
  Haverhill CB9 . . . . . . .132 F6
  Starston IP20. . . . . . . .22 C7
Hardwick Sh Ctr
  IP33 . . . . .123 F4
Hardy Cl
  8 Brantham CO11. . . .104 C4
  Lowestoft NR33 . . . . .115 A7
Hardy Cres IP1 . . . . . .134 F4
Hardy Ct 1 CO10 . . . .148 D8
Harebell Rd
  16 Herringswell IP28. . .30 C1
  Ipswich IP2 . . . . .138 F4
Harebell Way NR33 . . .114 C5
Hare Drift CO10. . . . . . .77 F1
Harefield CO10 . . . . . . .77 E1
Hare Fields IP9 . . . . . .105 D5
Hare & Hounds Cnr
  IP6. . . . . .82 F8
Hare Rd 30 IP14. . . . . .67 A5
Hares Cl IP19 . . . . . . .141 C6
Hares La IP19 . . . . .25 B4
Hares Rd IP7 . . . . .65 D1
Hares Run CB7. . . . . . .29 B1
Hares Wlk 1 CO10 . . .148 D6

Harewood Terr [7]
CB9 . . . . **132** C5
HARGRAVE **62** B6
Hargrave Ave IP6 . . . **125** D3
Hargrave Rd
  Chevington IP29 . . . .**62** B6
  Little Saxham IP29 . . . . .**47** D1
  Little Saxham IP29 . . . . .**47** D2
HARKSTEAD **106** B5
Harkstead La
  Freston IP9 . . . .**105** F8
  Woolverstone IP9 . . . . .**144** A1
Harkstead Rd [3] IP9 **106** A5
Harland Ct IP32 . . . .**154** B4
Harland St IP7 . . . .**139** C3
HARLESTON
  Harleston **66** B7
  Rendenhall with
   Harleston **22** E5
Harleston CE Prim Sch
  IP20 . . . .**22** D6
Harleston Green IP14 **66** B6
Harleston Hill IP21 . . . .**39** E8
Harleston Mus ★ IP20 **22** D6
Harleston Rd
  Metfield IP20 . . . .**23** B3
  Pulham Market IP21 . . . . .**21** E8
  Scole IP21 . . . .**21** D5
  Weybread IP21 . . . .**22** D4
Harling Dro IP27 . . . .**6** E3
Harling Drove IP27 . . . . .**6** B3
Harling Rd
  Garboldisham IP22 . . . .**18** C6
  Garboldisham IP22 . . . .**18** F7
  North Lopham IP22 . . . . .**18** F7
Harling Way IP16 . . . .**129** B6
Harmer Pl IP22 . . . .**35** C4
Harold Rd NR33 . . . .**115** C6
Harpclose Rd [2]
  CO10 . . . .**148** D6
Harper's East [9] CO6 . .**102** C5
Harper's Hill CO6 . . . . .**102** C5
Harpers La IP17 . . . . . .**128** D3
Harp La CO10 . . . .**90** B7
Harp's Cl Rd NR32 . . . .**113** B3
Harpur's Rd [2] CO10 . . .**77** A2
Harrier Cl IP3 . . . .**140** B1
Harrier Dr NR33 . . . . . .**114** E5
Harriers Wlk [17] NR31 . . .**3** B6
Harriers Wlk IP13 . . . . . .**70** E5
Harrier Way
  [6] Diss IP22 . . . .**20** D3
  [12] Stowmarket IP14 . . .**67** A5
Harrington Ave
  NR32 . . . .**113** C6
Harrington Cl IP33 . . . .**154** C1
Harris Ave NR32 . . . . .**113** C4
Harris Bsns Pk IP2 . .**138** E6
Harris Ct [12] IP14 . . . .**53** F2
Harrison Dr [5] IP7 . . . .**149** F7
Harrison Gn [3] IP18 . .**119** C8
Harrison Gr IP5 . . . . . .**141** C8
Harrison Rd
  Lowestoft NR32 . . . . . .**112** E1
  Lowestoft NR33 . . . . . .**115** C4
Harrisons La IP19 . . . .**118** C5
Harrison Way IP26 . . . . .**4** F3
Harris Way NR34 . . . . .**111** D4
Harrod Cl NR33 . . . .**115** C7
Harrop Dale [10]
  NR33 . . . .**114** E3
Harrow Cl IP4 . . . .**140** A5
Harrow Dr [24] IP20 . . . .**30** B8
Harrow Gn [3] IP29 . . . . .**63** D1
HARROW GREEN **63** D1
Harrow La
  Benhall IP17 . . . .**72** A7
  Farnham IP17 . . . .**71** A7
  Smallworth IP22 . . . .**18** E4
  Theberton IP16 . . . .**129** A8
Harrow Rd CB9 . . . . . .**132** C5
Harrow St CO6 . . . .**102** B8
Harry Carr Cl CB8 . . . .**120** F3
Harry Palmer Cl [1]
  CB7 . . . .**29** A1
Hart Cl CB9 . . . .**132** D8
HARTEST **77** A7
Hartest CE VC Prim Sch
  IP29 . . . .**77** A7
HARTEST HILL **77** C7
Hartest Hill IP29 . . . . . .**77** C6
Hartest La IP29 . . . .**63** C1
Hartest Rd IP29 . . . .**63** A1
Hartest Way
  Stowmarket IP14 . . . . .**124** F3
  Sudbury CO10 . . . .**148** F4
Hartfield Rd CB8 . . . . . .**59** F2
Hartington Rd IP15 . .**130** E3
Hartismere High Sch
  IP23 . . . .**117** B3
Hartismere Hospl
  IP23 . . . .**117** C3
Hartley St IP2 . . . .**155** B1
Hartree Way IP5 . . . . .**141** E7
HART'S GREEN **63** E2
Hartshall La IP31 . . . . . .**35** E1
Harts La [4] IP22 . . . .**36** E8
Hart's La CO7 . . . .**103** E1
Harvard Rd [6] IP26 . . . .**4** D5
Harvest Cl IP14 . . . .**71** D1
Harvest Dr NR33 . . . . .**114** F2
Harvesters Way
  Martlesham IP5 . . . .**141** F6

Harvesters Way continued
  [2] Martlesham Heath
  IP5 . . . .**98** A7
Harvest Way IP20 . . . . .**22** E6
Harvey Adam Ent Ctr
  IP27 . . . .**14** E8
Harvey Cl [7] CO11 . . . .**104** E2
Harvey La IP21 . . . .**21** C5
Harvey's La IP6 . . . .**82** C6
Harvey Wlk [9] CB9 . . . .**74** A1
Harvey Way IP12 . . . . . .**85** D8
HARWICH **107** A3
Harwich Community
  Prim Sch CO12 . . . . . .**107** C2
Harwich & Dovecourt
  High Sch CO12 . . . .**107** A1
Harwich Int Port
  CO12 . . . .**106** F3
Harwich Rd
  Foxash Estate CO11 . . .**104** A1
  Mistley CO11 . . . .**105** A2
  Ramsey & Parkeston
   CO11 . . . .**106** A1
  Wrabness CO11 . . . .**105** F1
Harwich Town Sta
  CO12 . . . .**107** B3
Harwood Ave IP24 . . . . .**16** C7
Harwood Pl CO10 . . . . . .**78** C3
Hascot Hill
  Barking IP6 . . . .**125** A1
  Battisford IP14 . . . .**81** A8
Haselmere Cl [5]
  IP32 . . . .**123** D6
HASKETON **146** C8
Hasketon Rd
  Boot Street IP13 . . . . . .**137** E7
  Burgh IP13 . . . .**83** F6
Haskins Wlk IP5 . . . . . .**141** E7
Haslemere Dr [4]
  IP4 . . . .**139** E7
Hasse Rd CB7 . . . .**28** E8
Hasted Cl IP33 . . . .**122** C4
Hatchley Cl IP12 . . . .**85** C3
Hatfield Rd IP3 . . . .**140** A3
Hatley Dr CB5 . . . .**44** A6
Hatter St IP33 . . . .**154** B2
Haughgate Cl IP12 . . . .**146** F6
Haugh La
  Great Ashfield IP31 . . . . .**50** F5
  Haughley IP14 . . . .**51** D1
  Woodbridge IP12 . . . . .**146** F6
HAUGHLEY **51** C1
Haughley Dr IP4 . . . . . .**140** F6
Haughley Gn IP14 . . . . . .**51** C2
HAUGHLEY GREEN **51** C3
HAUGHLEY NEW ST
  Dagworth IP14 . . . .**66** B8
  Wetherden IP14 . . . .**51** A1
HAUGHLEY NEW
  STREET **51** B1
Haughley Pk ★ IP14 . . **51** A1
Haughley Rd IP14 . . . . . .**66** B7
Hauliers Rd IP11 . . . . . .**152** D2
Haven Ave NR32 . . . . . .**113** B3
Haven Cl
  Bury St Edmunds
  IP33 . . . .**123** C3
  Felixstowe IP11 . . . .**152** D4
Haven Exchange
  IP11 . . . .**152** D2
Haven Exchange South
  IP11 . . . .**152** D2
Haven Nature Reserve
  The ★ IP16 . . . .**130** F6
Haven Rd IP16 . . . .**129** D5
Havens The IP10 . . . . . .**144** E7
Haven The IP16 . . . .**73** F6
Havergate Island
  National Nature
  Reserve ★ IP12 . . . .**86** F2
Havergate Rd [3]
  IP3 . . . .**144** D8
HAVERHILL **132** C6
Haverhill Arts Ctr ★
  CB9 . . . .**132** E5
Haverhill Bsns Pk
  CB9 . . . .**132** E5
Haverhill & District Local
  History Ctr ★ CB9 . .**132** E5
Haverhill Leisure Ctr
  CB9 . . . .**132** F6
Haverhill Railway Walks
  Nature Reserve ★
  CB9 . . . .**133** B4
Haverhill Rd
  Haverhill CB9 . . . .**132** F8
  Helions Bumpstead CB9 **88** B5
  Kedington CB9 . . . .**133** E8
  Sowley Green CB8 . . . . . .**75** B6
  Steeple Bumpstead
   CB9 . . . .**88** D5
Haverhill Research Pk
  CB9 . . . .**74** A1
Haverhill Trade & Retail
  Pk CB9 . . . .**132** F4
Haward St NR32 . . . . . .**113** C1
Hawbridge IP9 . . . .**150** E4
Hawbush Rd CB8 . . . . . .**75** C8
Hawe's La
  Norton IP31 . . . .**50** B4
  Wicken CB7 . . . .**28** A2
Hawes St IP2 . . . .**155** C1
Hawk Cres [3] IP22 . . . .**20** D3
HAWKEDON **76** D7
Hawkedon Rd
  Hawkedon IP29 . . . .**76** C8
  Rede IP29 . . . .**62** E2
Hawk End La [2] IP30 . .**50** E2

Hawke Rd IP3 . . . .**139** E1
Hawker Dr
  Martlesham Heath
  IP5 . . . .**98** A8
  Soham CB7 . . . .**28** E3
Hawker'S La IP30 . . . . . .**64** A7
Hawkers St [18] IP28 . . . .**30** B1
Hawkes La IP11 . . . .**152** D6
Hawkins Ct [2] CO10 . .**148** D8
Hawkins Rd CO10 . . . . .**148** E8
Hawk's La IP29 . . . .**63** A2
Hawks Mill St IP6 . . . . .**125** D5
HAWSTEAD **63** D6
Hawstead Green **63** E5
Hawstead La IP29 . . . . . .**63** E6
Hawstead Rd IP29 . . . . . .**62** E7
Hawthorn Ave NR33 . .**115** A7
Hawthorn Cl
  Beccles NR34 . . . .**111** E4
  Bury St Edmunds
  IP32 . . . .**122** D8
  [23] Diss IP22 . . . .**20** D2
  Knodishall IP17 . . . .**129** B2
  [8] Stowupland IP14 . . . . .**67** A6
Hawthorn Dr
  [9] Horringer IP29 . . . . . .**63** A8
  Ipswich IP7 . . . .**138** D2
Hawthorne Cl [19] IP28 . .**30** C1
Hawthorne Way CB8 . . .**75** C7
Hawthorn La [25] IP27 . .**13** F2
Hawthorn Pl IP12 . . . . .**146** E6
Hawthorn Rd
  Haverhill CB9 . . . .**132** B7
  Middleton IP17 . . . .**58** A5
  Sudbury CO10 . . . .**148** F5
  Theberton IP16 . . . .**57** F4
Hawthorns The [8]
  IP31 . . . .**49** D4
Hawthorn Way CB5 . . . .**44** B6
Hawthorn Wlk [10]
  IP28 . . . .**30** B8
Hawthorn Way [9]
  CO6 . . . .**102** A7
Hay Barn Meadow [2]
  IP30 . . . .**50** D1
Haycocks Rd CB9 . . . . .**132** A7
Haycroft La CB5 . . . .**44** C6
Haygate IP23 . . . .**117** C3
Hayhill Rd IP4 . . . .**139** E7
Hayland Dro IP28 . . . . . .**29** D7
Haylings Gr IP16 . . . . . .**129** C4
Haylings Rd IP16 . . . . . .**129** C4
Hayman Rd IP3 . . . .**139** F1
Haynings Mill IP13 . . . .**126** D4
Haythill La IP26 . . . .**4** D6
Hayward Cl IP23 . . . . . .**117** D2
Haywards Fields
  IP5 . . . .**141** D8
Haywood Dr [16] CO10 . .**91** E8
Hazel Cl
  [9] Bentwaters Airfield
  IP12 . . . .**85** E8
  Haverhill CB9 . . . .**132** C5
  Mildenhall IP28 . . . .**116** E4
Hazel Covert [4] IP24 . .**16** C6
Hazelcroft Rd IP1 . . . . .**135** B2
Hazel Ct [6] CO10 . . . . .**148** D6
Hazel Dr
  [10] Horringer IP29 . . . . .**63** A8
  Ipswich IP3 . . . .**140** E1
Hazel Rd [22] IP31 . . . . . .**49** A3
Hazel Rise IP6 . . . .**134** C8
Hazels La IP17 . . . .**42** D5
HAZEL STUB **132** A5
Hazelville Cl [11]
  CO12 . . . .**106** F1
Hazelwood [1] IP7 . . . . .**80** F1
Hazelwood Cl IP31 . . . .**49** D4
Hazelwood Marshes
  Nature Reserve ★
  IP15 . . . .**73** B4
Hazelwood St IP17 . . . .**130** A7
Hazlitt Rd [6] IP1 . . . . .**135** A3
Headingham Cl [13]
  IP2 . . . .**139** A2
Head La CO10 . . . .**148** F2
Headland Ave CB9 . . . .**132** C5
Headland Dro IP26 . . . . .**4** A1
Head Way CO10 . . . . . .**148** B8
Healey Cl NR32 . . . .**113** A5
Heasman Cl CB8 . . . . . .**120** F5
Heathbell Rd CB8 . . . . .**121** C3
Heath Cl
  East Bergholt CO7 . . . .**151** D5
  Hessett IP30 . . . .**64** F8
  Polstead CO6 . . . .**93** F3
Heath Cottages La
  IP12 . . . .**72** D1
Heath Ct
  [16] Beck Row IP28 . . . . . .**30** B8
  [12] Felixstowe IP11 . . . . .**107** D8
  [20] Thurston IP31 . . . .**49** D4
Heath Dr IP12 . . . .**99** C7
Heather Ave IP3 . . . . . .**140** C2
Heather Cl
  [1] Great Barton IP31 . . .**49** D4
  Martlesham Heath
  IP5 . . . .**141** F6
Heathercroft Rd IP1 . .**135** A3
Heather Ct [15] IP28 . . . .**30** B8
Heatherhayes IP27 . . . .**139** A3
Heather Rd NR32 . . . . .**113** D4
Heatherset Way IP28 . .**30** C1
Heather Way
  Brandon IP27 . . . .**6** A1
  Worlingham NR34 . . . . .**111** F3
Heath Estate [17] CO10 .**92** C6
Heather Ct [15] IP28 . . . .**30** B8
Heath Farm Rd IP28 . . .**30** B1

Heathfield IP5 . . . .**141** F6
Heathfield Mews
  IP5 . . . .**141** F6
Heathfield Rd [9]
  IP9 . . . .**105** E7
Heathfields IP11 . . . .**98** D1
Heathgate Piece
  IP11 . . . .**152** C8
Heath Gdns IP30 . . . . . .**65** B8
Heath La
  Blundeston NR32 . . . .**3** A4
  Honington IP31 . . . .**33** F3
  Ipswich IP4 . . . .**140** C5
  Pakenham IP31 . . . .**49** D8
Heathlands
  [11] Beck Row IP28 . . . . . .**30** C8
  [7] Honey Tye CO6 . . . . .**102** A7
Heathlands Pk IP4 . . . .**140** E4
Heathland Way IP28 . .**116** D6
Heath Prim Sch IP5 . .**141** B7
Heath Rd
  Burwell CB5 . . . .**44** C2
  Dullingham CB8 . . . .**59** A5
  East Bergholt CO7 . . . .**151** D5
  Exning CB8 . . . .**120** A4
  Fritton & St Olaves NR31 . .**2** B5
  Geldeston NR34 . . . .**9** A7
  Halesworth IP19 . . . . . .**118** E2
  Hessett IP30 . . . .**64** F8
  Ipswich IP4 . . . .**140** C7
  Ixworth IP31 . . . .**33** E2
  Kenninghall NR16 . . . . . .**19** A7
  Knettishall IP22 . . . .**17** E3
  Lowestoft NR33 . . . .**114** F8
  Mildenhall IP28 . . . .**116** C5
  Mistley CO11 . . . .**105** A2
  Newmarket CB8 . . . . . .**121** C3
  Norton IP31 . . . .**50** B4
  Polstead CO6 . . . .**93** F2
  Sapiston IP31 . . . .**34** B7
  Sutton IP12 . . . .**85** E1
  Swaffham Prior CB5 . . . . .**44** A1
  Thurston IP31 . . . .**49** D4
  Troston IP31 . . . .**33** D3
  Troston IP31 . . . .**33** D5
  Wenhaston with Mells
   Hamlet IP19 . . . .**42** B7
  Woodbridge Walk IP12 . .**99** E8
  Woolpit IP30 . . . .**50** D1
HEATH THE **105** A7
Heath The
  Dedham CO7 . . . .**104** A2
  Great Waldingfield
   CO10 . . . .**92** C6
  Woolpit IP30 . . . .**65** F8
Heath View
  Ipswich IP5 . . . .**141** A6
  Leiston IP16 . . . .**129** C5
  Westleton IP17 . . . .**58** C8
Heath Way CO10 . . . . . .**92** C6
Heath Wlk IP12 . . . .**72** A4
Hebe Gdns CO11 . . . . . .**104** D1
HECKFIELD GREEN **38** D7
HEDENHAM **7** E8
Hedgerows IP29 . . . .**63** A1
Hedge Sparrow Rd [25]
  IP14 . . . .**67** A5
Hedley La NR33 . . . . . .**114** A3
Heigham Dr NR33 . . . .**114** F5
Heighams La IP22 . . . . . .**35** D7
Heights The NR34 . . . .**111** C4
Heldhaw Rd IP32 . . . . .**123** E5
Helena Rd IP3 . . . .**139** E4
Helens Cl [2] IP22 . . . . . .**36** A8
HELIONS
  BUMPSTEAD **88** B4
Helions Bumpstead Rd
  CB9 . . . .**132** D3
Helions Pk Ave CB9 . .**132** C5
Helions Pk Gdns [8]
  CB9 . . . .**132** C5
Helions Pk Rd [7]
  CB9 . . . .**132** C5
Helions Rd CB9 . . . .**88** D4
Helions Service Rd [3]
  CB9 . . . .**132** C5
Helions Wlk CB9 . . . . . .**132** C5
HELMINGHAM **69** B6
Helmingham Hall &
  Gdns ★ IP14 . . . .**69** A4
Helmingham Prim Sch
  IP14 . . . .**69** B6
Helmingham Rd
  Coddenham IP6 . . . .**68** D2
  Framsden IP14 . . . .**69** B6
  Otley IP6 . . . .**69** C2
Helston Cl IP5 . . . .**141** B7
HEMINGSTONE **82** C8
HEMLEY **99** F7
Hemmant Way NR34 . . . .**9** B7
HEMP GREEN **57** C8
Hemplands The [2]
  NR32 . . . .**113** D2
Hempnall Rd NR35 . . . . .**7** A8
Hempstead Rd CB9 . . .**132** A7
Hencote La
  Horringer IP29 . . . .**63** C8
  Nowton IP33 . . . .**123** B1
Henderson Cl
  Bramford IP8 . . . .**134** A1
  Haverhill CB9 . . . .**132** A7
HENGRAVE **48** A7
Hengrave Hall [1] ★ IP2 .**139** A2
Hengrave Hall ★ IP28 **48** A7
Henham Park ★ NR34 **25** F1
Henham Rd NR32 . . . **113** A5
Henhan Green NR34 . . **25** F1

Hening Ave IP3 . . . . . .**144** D8
HENLEY **82** D6
Henley Ave IP1 . . . . . .**135** B3
Henley Cl
  Saxmundham IP17 . . .**128** C3
  [2] Saxmundham IP17 .**128** C3
Henley Prim Sch IP6 .**82** E6
Henley Rd
  Henley IP6 . . . .**82** D5
  Ipswich IP1 . . . .**155** B4
  Newbourne IP12 . . . .**98** D6
Henniker Rd
  [3] Debenham IP14 . . . . .**53** F2
  Ipswich IP1 . . . .**138** C8
Henny Rd CO8 . . . .**101** A7
Henny St CO10 . . . .**101** A8
HENNY STREET **91** F1
Henry Cl CB9 . . . .**132** B4
Henry Rd IP3 . . . .**140** B1
Henry St IP14 . . . .**53** E2
Henry Ward Rd [1]
  IP20 . . . .**22** D6
Henry Watson's
  Potteries ★
  IP22 . . . .**35** D5
Henslow Rd IP4 . . . . . .**140** B5
HENSTEAD **26** E8
Henstead Arts & Crafts
  Ctr ★ NR34 . . . .**10** F1
Henstead Exotic Gdn ★
  NR34 . . . .**26** E8
Henstead Gdns IP3 . . .**140** A2
Henstead La NR34 . . . . .**26** C7
HEPWORTH **35** A6
Hepworth Ave IP33 . . .**122** D5
Hepworth Rd
  Barningham IP31 . . . .**34** F7
  Hepworth IP22 . . . .**35** A7
  Stanton IP31 . . . .**34** E4
  Thelnetham IP22 . . . .**35** B7
Herbert Cl CO10 . . . . . .**148** E8
Herbert Human Cl [3]
  CB7 . . . .**28** D4
Herbert Rd IP5 . . . .**141** E8
Hercules Rd [12] IP12 . .**85** E8
Hereford Dr [14] IP6 . . . .**82** B5
Hereward Ave IP28 . . .**116** C5
Hereward Way
  [5] Feltwell IP26 . . . .**4** D5
  Littleport CB7 . . . .**12** B7
  Weeting-with-Broomhill
   IP27 . . . .**5** E3
Heritage Gn [6] NR33 . .**11** B5
Heritage Workshop Ctr ★
  NR32 . . . .**113** B3
Herivan Cl NR32 . . . . . .**112** E4
Herivan Gdns [6]
  NR32 . . . .**112** E4
Herkstean La CM7 . . . . .**88** E1
Hermitage Ct IP13 . . . .**126** B3
Hermitage Meadows
  CO10 . . . .**76** B1
Hernsey Wood Rd
  IP17 . . . .**56** D6
Herolf Way [11] IP20 . . . .**22** D6
Heron Cl
  [5] Mildenhall IP28 . . . . . .**13** B1
  Stowmarket IP14 . . . . . .**124** A6
Heron Ct CB7 . . . .**28** C5
Heron Hill IP14 . . . .**66** C6
Heron Rd
  Bury St Edmunds
  IP33 . . . .**123** B2
  Ipswich IP2 . . . .**138** E3
  Saxmundham IP17 . . . .**128** B3
Herons Cl IP32 . . . .**123** B2
Heron Way [23] CO12 . .**107** B2
Herring Fishery Score [2]
  NR32 . . . .**113** C1
HERRINGFLEET **2** D4
Herringfleet Drainage
  Mill ★ NR32 . . . .**2** B4
Herringfleet Rd NR31 . .**2** B5
Herring Mkt [14]
  NR32 . . . .**115** D8
HERRINGSWELL **46** C8
Herringswell Rd
  Herringswell IP28 . . . . . .**30** D2
  Kentford CB8 . . . .**46** A6
Hertford Gn [19] IP32 . . .**48** C5
Hertford Pl IP15 . . . . . .**130** E3
Hertford Rd [5] CO10 . . .**76** A1
Hertfords Pl IP12 . . . . . .**86** D7
Hervey Cl [6] IP9 . . . . .**107** A5
Hervey Rd IP33 . . . . . .**122** E3
Hervey St
  Ipswich IP4 . . . .**155** C4
  Lowestoft NR32 . . . . . .**115** C8
HESSETT **64** F8
Hessett Cl IP14 . . . .**124** F3
Hessett Rd IP30 . . . .**64** E7
HESTLEY GREEN
  IP23 . . . .**53** D6
Hethersett Cl CB8 . . . .**120** E8
HEVENINGHAM **40** F3
Heveningham Long La
  IP17 . . . .**41** A1
Heveningham Rd
  IP19 . . . .**40** C5
Hewitt Rd
  [15] Ramsey CO12 . . . . .**106** E1
  [19] Ramsey CO12 . . . . .**106** E1
Hexham Cl [3] IP2 . . . . .**139** A2
Heycroft Way [4]
  CO6 . . . .**102** C5
Heyford Ct [8] IP28 . . . .**116** B5

Heywood Ave IP22 . . . . .**20** C3
Heywood Cl IP2 . . . . . .**138** D1
Heywood Rd IP22 . . . . . .**20** C4
Hibbard Rd IP8 . . . .**134** C2
Hibbs Green IP29 . . . . . .**77** F8
Hibbs Rd IP19 . . . .**41** C4
Hicfield Rd [1] IP28 . . . . .**30** C8
HICKFORD HILL **90** C7
Hickford Hill CO10 . . . . .**90** B7
Hickling Dr IP33 . . . . . .**123** B1
Hick's Drove CB7 . . . . . .**28** E7
Hicks La CO10 . . . .**101** E8
Hicks Way CB9 . . . .**133** C3
Higdon Cl IP22 . . . .**20** E6
HIGHAM
  Bury St Edmunds **46** E4
  Stratford St Mary **103** D6
Higham Hill IP7 . . . .**103** D8
Higham Race Course
  CO7 . . . .**103** D7
Higham Rd
  Hadleigh IP7 . . . .**94** D2
  Higham CO7 . . . .**103** D6
  Tuddenham IP28 . . . .**31** A1
Highbank Meadow
  IP14 . . . .**52** A8
High Baxter St IP33 . .**154** B2
High Beach IP11 . . . . . .**153** C4
High Beech NR32 . . . . .**113** B2
Highbridge Gravel Dro
  IP27 . . . .**109** B7
Highbury Cres IP33 . . .**122** E5
Highbury Rd IP33 . . . . .**122** E5
Highbury Way CO10 . .**148** F5
Highclere Cl CB8 . . . . .**120** D8
High Comm Rd IP22 . . .**18** F5
High Ct IP20 . . . .**22** E6
Higher Dr NR32 . . . . . .**112** F2
High Farm La IP13 . . . .**70** D1
Highfield
  Blythburgh IP19 . . . .**42** F6
  Clare CO10 . . . .**90** B8
  Eye IP23 . . . .**117** C3
Highfield App [1] IP1 . .**134** F1
Highfield Ave CO12 . . .**107** A2
Highfield Cl
  Gisleham NR33 . . . .**114** B1
  [20] Lavenham CO10 . . . . .**78** D4
Highfield Dr IP6 . . . . . .**134** D8
Highfield La IP14 . . . . . .**18** F6
Highfield Rd
  Felixstowe IP11 . . . .**153** A4
  Halesworth IP19 . . . . . .**118** B2
  Ipswich IP1 . . . .**134** F2
  [6] Stowupland IP14 . . . . .**67** A6
  Sudbury CO10 . . . .**148** E7
Highfields
  Bentley IP9 . . . .**104** F7
  Great Yeldham CO9 . . . . .**90** A1
  Lakenheath IP27 . . . . . .**109** E6
Highfields County Prim
  Sch CO11 . . . .**104** E2
Highfields Dr IP27 . . . .**109** D6
Highgate La IP13 . . . . . .**70** B2
High Gn IP16 . . . .**129** C6
HIGH GREEN **63** D7
High Green IP20 . . . .**7** C4
Highgrove Cl NR32 . . . .**113** A3
High Hall Cl [2] IP11 . . .**107** D8
High Hall Rd IP8 . . . .**81** C6
High House Dr IP13 . . . .**56** C7
High House Farm Rd
  IP12 . . . .**131** B8
High House La IP7 . . . . .**79** B5
High House Rd IP6 . . . . .**69** C1
High La IP14 . . . .**53** B6
Highland Dr NR34 . . . .**111** E4
Highlands
  Bury St Edmunds
  IP32 . . . .**154** B4
  Lakenheath IP27 . . . . . .**109** E6
  [1] Thetford IP24 . . . .**16** C6
Highlands Cl IP6 . . . . . .**125** C5
Highlands La IP12 . . . .**147** A6
Highlands Rd
  Hadleigh IP7 . . . .**149** E5
  Monks Eleigh IP7 . . . . . .**79** F4
Highlands The CB8 . . . .**120** D8
Highland Way NR33 . . .**114** F6
High Leas NR34 . . . .**111** C3
High Leas Cl [2]
  NR34 . . . .**111** C3
High Lighthouse Wireless
  Mus ★ CO12 . . . .**107** C3
High Lodge Forest Ctr
  Thetford Forest Pk ★
  IP27 . . . .**15** C7
High London La IP22 . .**20** A8
High Rd
  Badingham IP13 . . . .**56** C6
  Bressingham IP22 . . . . . .**19** F4
  Felixstowe IP11 . . . .**152** B8
  Framlingham IP13 . . . . .**126** A3
  Great Finborough IP14 . . .**66** A2
  Kettleburgh IP13 . . . .**55** B2
  Leavenheath CO6 . . . . .**102** A7
  Needham IP20 . . . .**22** B3
  Redenhall IP20 . . . .**22** F7
  Roydon IP22 . . . .**20** A3
  Swilland IP6 . . . .**83** A7
  Trimley St Martin IP11 . . .**98** C1
  Wortwell IP20 . . . .**23** A7
High Rd E IP11 . . . .**153** B5
High Rd W IP11 . . . . . .**152** F5
HIGH ROUGHAM
  49 E1
  Rougham IP30 . . . .**64** D8
High Row Field IP11 **153** C5

High St Ex Gall★
  IP1 . . . . 155 B3
High St Mws IP7 . . . . 149 D6
High St
  Acton CO10 . . . . 92 B7
  Aldeburgh IP15 . . . . 130 E3
  Ashley CB8 . . . . 60 F8
  Brandon IP27 . . . . 5 F1
  Brinkley CB8 . . . . 59 F1
  5 Bures CO8 . . . . 101 C5
  Burwell CB5 . . . . 44 A5
  Cavendish CO10 . . . . 76 E1
  Cheveley CB8 . . . . 60 E8
  Chippenham CB7 . . . . . . 45 C8
  Clare CO10 . . . . 90 A8
  Debenham IP14 . . . . 53 F2
  Dedham CO7. . . . . 103 F3
  Dunwich IP17. . . . . 43 B1
  Felixstowe IP11 . . . . . . 152 E6
  Feltwell IP26 . . . . 4 E5
  Flowton IP8 . . . . 81 C1
  Gislingham IP23 . . . . . . 36 D2
  Great Yeldham CO9 . . . . 90 A1
  Hadleigh IP7. . . . . 149 D6
  Harwich CO12 . . . . 107 B2
  Haverhill CB9 . . . . 132 E5
  Hemingstone IP6 . . . . . . 68 C1
  Hitcham IP7 . . . . 79 F4
  Hopton IP22 . . . . 18 C2
  Ipswich IP1 . . . . 155 B3
  Ixworth IP31 . . . . 34 B1
  Kessingland NR33 . . . . . 11 B1
  Lakenheath IP27 . . . . . 109 C6
  Langham CO4 . . . . 103 B2
  Lavenham CO10 . . . . . . 78 D4
  Laxfield IP13. . . . . 40 B3
  Leiston IP16 . . . . 129 C6
  Little Waldingfield CO10 92 F7
  Long Melford CO10 . . . . 77 E1
  Long Melford CO10 . . . . 77 E1
  7 Lowestoft NR32 . . . . 113 E2
  Manningtree CO11 . . . . 104 E2
  Mildenhall IP28 . . . . . . 116 C4
  Nayland CO6 . . . . 102 D5
  Needham Market IP6 . . 125 D5
  Newmarket CB8 . . . . . . 120 F2
  Orford IP12 . . . . 131 C2
  Pettistree IP13 . . . . . . 127 C5
  Rattlesden IP30 . . . . . . 65 D6
  St Margaret, Ilketshall
    NR35 . . . . 24 D7
  Saxmundham IP17 . . . 128 D3
  Soham CB7 . . . . 28 D4
  Southwold IP18 . . . . . 119 D5
  Sproughton IP8 . . . . . 138 A6
  Stansfield CO10 . . . . . . 76 C6
  Stetchworth CB8. . . . . 60 A5
  Thelnetham IP22 . . . . . 18 E1
  Thorndon IP23 . . . . 53 C8
  Tuddenham IP28. . . . . . 30 F2
  Tuddenham St Martin
    IP6 . . . . 136 B5
  Wangford with Henham
    NR34 . . . . 26 B2
  Wicken CB7 . . . . 28 A1
  Wickham Market IP13 127 C7
  Wrentham NR34. . . . . . 26 E5
  Yoxford IP17. . . . . 57 D8
HIGH STREET
  Darsham. 42 B1
  Iken 73 B2
  St Margaret, Ilketshall . 24 D7
HIGH STREET
  GREEN 66 A2
High Town Gn IP30 . . . 65 D3
HIGHTOWN GREEN. . . . 65 D3
Highview Cl CO10 . . . 148 C8
High View Rd IP1 . . . 134 D1
Highwood Cres CB8. . . 46 B2
Highwood La CO10. . . . 92 E5
Highwood Rd CB8. . . . 46 B2
Hildabrook Cl 2
  IP2. . . . . 138 E4
Hildesley Ct NR33. . . 115 B4
Hillary Cl IP4 . . . . . . 140 A5
Hill Cl
  6 Long Melford
    CO10 . . . . 91 E8
  Newmarket CB8 . . . . . 120 E3
Hill Cres CB9 . . . . . . 132 E7
Hillcrest
  Friston IP17 . . . . 72 F7
  Knodishall IP17 . . . . . 129 A3
Hillcrest App IP8 . . . 134 D7
Hillcrest Cl 3 NR34 . . 111 E3
Hillcrest Ct 29 CO12 . 107 B2
Hillcrest Dr NR32 . . . 113 B4
Hillcrest Gdns NR32. . 113 B3
Hillcrest Rd
  Beccles NR34 . . . . . 111 B4
  Sudbury CO10. . . . . . 148 C8
Hill Farm Barns IP6. . 82 E7
Hill Farm Chase CO10 92 F1
Hill Farm La
  9 Chelmondiston
    IP9 . . . . 106 C8
  Drinkstone IP30 . . . . . 65 C8
  Gestingthorpe CO9. . . 90 F1
Hill Farm Rd
  Friday Street IP17 . . . 72 A6
  Grundisburgh IP13. . . 83 D6
  Halesworth IP19 . . . . 118 C3
  Laxfield IP13. . . . . . . 40 B3
  Playford IP6 . . . . . . 137 B4
  Tunstall IP12. . . . . . . 72 F2
Hill Farm View CB8 . . 59 D5
Hill Farm Way CO4 . . 103 A3

Hillfield Ct IP18. . . . 119 C7
Hill Green CO10. . . . . 78 D6
Hill House Farm Rd
  CO10 . . . . 78 F5
Hill House Gdns
  Lowestoft NR33 . . . . 115 C5
  Wrentham NR34. . . . . 26 E5
Hill House La IP6 . . . 125 C6
Hill House Rd IP4 . . . 139 E5
Hilling Gdns 2 IP22 . . 20 C1
Hill La
  Barking IP14. . . . . . . 81 A8
  Sturmer CB9. . . . . . . 133 D1
Hill of Health (Tumulus)★
  IP28 . . . . 32 D2
Hill Rd
  27 Harwich CO12 . . . 107 B2
  Lowestoft NR32 . . . . 113 C1
  Southwold IP18 . . . . 119 C6
  Wangford with Henham
    NR34 . . . . 26 B1
  Westley IP33 . . . . . . 122 A5
Hill Rise IP14 . . . . . . 124 D3
Hillrise Cl NR34. . . . . 111 E3
Hillside
  Brandon IP27 . . . . . . 14 D8
  Poslingford CO10 . . . . 76 B3
  Stowmarket IP14 . . . . 124 D3
  Westleton IP17 . . . . . 111 E4
Hillside Ave NR34. . . 111 E4
Hillside Bsns Pk
  IP32 . . . . 123 F3
Hillside Cres 5 IP3 . . 140 B3
Hillside Ct 1 NR35 . . 110 C2
Hillside Meadow
  Candle Street IP22. . . . 35 F5
  Fordham CB7 . . . . . . 29 B1
Hillside Prim Sch
  IP2 . . . . 139 C3
Hillside Rd
  Bury St Edmunds
    IP32 . . . . 123 F4
  Southwold IP18 . . . . 119 C7
  Sudbury CO10. . . . . . 148 B5
Hillside Rd E NR35 . . 110 D3
Hillside Rd W NR35. . 110 B2
Hillside Specl Sch
  CO10. . . . . 148 C8
Hillside Way IP19 . . . 118 B5
Hill St 20 IP26 . . . . . . 4 E5
Hill The
  North Cove NR34 . . . . 10 C4
  Shipmeadow NR34 . . . . 8 F4
  Tuddenham St Martin
    IP6 . . . . 136 C5
  Westleton IP17. . . . . . 58 C8
Hill Top IP31 . . . . 34 E5
Hilltop Gn IP31 . . . . . 34 E5
Hilltop Rise 2 NR34. . 111 E3
Hilltop Way IP31. . . . . 34 E5
Hill View CB8 . . . . 61 C4
Hill View Bsns Pk
  IP6 . . . . 134 D6
Hilly Cl IP31 . . . . 33 F5
Hilly Fields IP12 . . . 146 E4
Hilton Cl 15 CO11 . . . 104 E2
Hilton Cl
  Ipswich IP3 . . . . . . 140 C1
  Martlesham Heath IP5. . 98 A8
HINDERCLAY. 35 E7
Hinderclay Rd
  Redgrave IP22 . . . . . 19 A1
  Rickinghall Inferior
    IP22. . . . . 35 F6
Hines Rd IP3 . . . . . . 140 A4
Hintesham Cl 6 IP4 . 140 F5
HINTLESHAM. 95 C6
Hintlesham & Chattisham
  Prim Sch IP8 . . . . . . 95 C6
Hintlesham Cl 3
  IP14. . . . . 124 E3
Hintlesham Dr IP11 . . 152 D4
Hinton Corner IP17 . . 42 E2
Hinton Lodge Rd
  IP17. . . . . 42 E4
Hinton Rd
  Darsham IP17 . . . . . . 42 B2
  Darsham IP17 . . . . . . 42 B2
Hipperson Cl NR34. . 111 D4
Histon Cl IP5 . . . . . . 140 F7
HITCHAM. 79 E6
Hitcham Rd
  2 Debenham IP14. . . . 53 F2
  Framlingham IP13 . . . 126 B4
  Kettlebaston IP7 . . . . 79 C5
  Wattisham IP7 . . . . . . 80 B6
Hitcham's La NR34 . . . 26 E4
Hitchcock Pl CO10 . . 148 C7
HMS Ganges Mus★
  IP9 . . . . 107 B4
Hobart Cl NR32. . . . . 112 E3
Hobart Way NR32 . . . 112 E3
Hobbies La IP14 . . . . . 52 D4
HOBBLES GREEN 75 A8
Hobbs Cl NR32. . . . . . 112 D3
Hobbs Dr CO4 . . . . . 103 A3
Hobbs La CO10. . . . . . 77 B2
Hobbs Warren CB8. . . 60 E6
Hobbs Way 15 NR31 . . 3 B6
Hobland La NR32 . . . . 2 F8
Hobland Rd
  Belton with Browston
    NR31. . . . . 2 F8
  Bradwell NR31 . . . . . . 3 A8
Hocket Cres IP12. . . . 71 F2
Hockey Hill IP14. . . . 53 A5
Hockley Hole La
  CO10. . . . . 93 C2
Hockney Gdns IP3 . . 144 A8

HOCKWOLD CUM
  WILTON 5 A3
Hockwold Rd IP27 . . . . 5 D3
Hodgkinson Rd IP11 . 152 C3
Hodgson Ave 4
  IP16. . . . . 129 A6
Hodson Cl
  6 Bury St Edmunds
    IP32 . . . . 122 E8
  Soham CB7 . . . . 28 D4
Hoe La CO10 . . . . 90 F8
Hogarth Rd IP3 . . . . 139 F1
Hogarth Sq IP3 . . . . 140 A1
Hogarth Wlk NR32 . . 113 B6
HOGGARD'S GREEN . . 64 A3
Hoggars Rd IP14. . . . . 52 C4
Hogg La
  Bury St Edmunds
    IP33 . . . . 154 B1
  Earsham NR35 . . . . . . 7 C5
Hog Hill La IP17 . . . . 57 C7
Hog La
  St Lawrence, Ilketshall
    NR34 . . . . 24 F6
  Wenhaston with Mells
    Hamlet IP19. . . . . . . 42 C5
  Westhall NR34 . . . . . . 25 A6
Hog's La CO7 . . . . . . 151 E2
Hogsty La IP21 . . . . . 22 A5
Holbecks La IP7 . . . . 149 C4
Holbein Way 2
  NR32. . . . . 113 B6
Holborn Ave IP28 . . . 116 B6
HOLBROOK 105 E7
Holbrook Acad IP9 . . 105 E8
Holbrook Barn Rd 6
  CO10 . . . . 93 C3
Holbrook Cl 11 CO10 . 92 C6
Holbrook Cres 2
  IP11. . . . . 152 D4
Holbrook Prim Sch
  IP9 . . . . 105 E7
Holbrook Rd
  Freston IP9. . . . . . . 143 E1
  Haverhill CB9 . . . . . . 132 C4
  Holbrook IP9 . . . . . . 106 A5
  Ipswich IP3 . . . . . . 139 F1
  Lowestoft NR32 . . . . 112 F4
  Stutton IP9. . . . . . . 105 D5
Holcombe Cres IP2 . . 138 D2
Holdans La IP17 . . . . 56 D2
Holdans Meadow
  IP17. . . . . 56 E2
Holden Cl
  Ipswich IP2 . . . . . . 139 D3
  Lowestoft NR32 . . . . 112 C1
Holden Rd IP28 . . . . . 31 F1
Holderness Rd IP32. . 123 C7
Holdsworth Cl 12
  CO10 . . . . 77 A2
Holeywall La IP31. . . . 35 A1
Holfen Cl IP12 . . . . . . 84 B1
Holkham Cl 7 IP4 . . . 140 F5
Holkham Mead 1
  CB5 . . . . 44 B5
Holland Pk CB8 . . . . . 60 E8
Holland Rd
  Felixstowe IP11 . . . . 152 F3
  Ipswich IP4 . . . . . . 139 F6
Holland Rise IP19. . . . 41 A4
Hollands Bsns Ctr The
  CB9. . . . . 132 E4
Holland's La NR35 . . . 7 C7
Hollands CB9 . . . . . . 132 E4
Hollands Rd Ind Est
  CB9. . . . . 132 E4
HOLLESLEY 99 E7
Hollesley Ave IP3. . . 132 A6
Hollesley Prim Sch
  IP12 . . . . 99 F7
Hollesley Rd
  Capel St Andrew IP12. . 86 B2
  Hollesley IP12 . . . . . 99 D7
  Rendlesham IP12 . . . . 85 D7
Holliday Cl IP32 . . . . 123 F7
Hollingsworth Rd
  Lowestoft NR33 . . . . 113 C3
  3 Stowmarket IP14 . . 124 E5
Holllow La IP13. . . . . . 71 C5
Hollowell Cl 3
  NR32. . . . . 112 E4
Hollow Gr Way NR33 114 C4
Hollow Hill CB9 . . . . 74 A2
Hollow Hill Rd NR35. 110 B7
Hollow La
  Badingham IP13. . . . . 56 C6
  Barningham IP31 . . . . 34 F8
  Bures St Mary CO8 . . 101 C6
  Carlton Colville NR33 . . 114 C4
  6 Chelmondiston IP9 106 C8
  Coney Weston IP31 . . . 18 A1
  Dickleburgh IP21 . . . . 21 D4
  Earl Soham IP13 . . . . . 54 F3
  Mendham IP20 . . . . . . 23 A4
  Saxstead Green IP13 . . 55 A4
  Sibton IP17. . . . . 57 B8
  Thurston IP31 . . . . . . 49 F3
  Tostock IP30. . . . . . . 50 A2
Hollow Rd
  Ashen CO10 . . . . 89 F6
  Bury St Edmunds IP32 123 C6
  Bury St Edmunds IP32 123 C7
  Copdock & Washbrook
    IP8. . . . . 95 E4
  Fornham St Martin
    IP31. . . . . 48 E5
Hollows The IP6 . . . . . 67 F2
Hollow Way Hill NR34 . . 9 D8

Holly Blue Cl 10 IP8 . 142 E8
Holly Blue Way 16
  IP31. . . . . 49 E4
Holly Bush Cnr IP7 . . 103 E7
HOLLYBUSH
  CORNER. 64 D6
Hollybush Dr IP11 . . 153 D7
Hollybush La
  Bradfield St George
    IP30 . . . . 64 D6
  Hightown Green IP30 . . 65 C4
Hollybush Wlk IP12 . 147 E2
Holly Cl
  Beccles NR34 . . . . . 111 E3
  5 Horringer IP29 . . . 63 A8
  Little Bealings IP13 . . 137 D5
  6 Red Lodge IP28 . . . 30 B1
  Warren Heath IP3 . . . 140 F1
Hollycroft Cl 5 IP1 . . 135 A3
Holly Ct 34 IP20. . . . . 22 D6
Hollydene Cl 4
  NR32. . . . . 112 D2
Holly End IP5. . . . . . . 141 F6
Holly Gr NR34. . . . . . 111 C4
HOLLY HILL 110 B8
Holly Hill NR32. . . . . 112 C3
Holly La
  Belstead IP8. . . . . . . 142 C4
  Bucklesham IP10 . . . . 98 B4
  Great Horkesley CO6 . . 102 E2
  Hadleigh IP7. . . . . . . 94 D7
  Lakenheath IP27 . . . . 109 D5
  Little Bealings IP13 . . 137 D5
  Mutford NR34. . . . . . 10 E3
  Rushmere St Andrew
    IP5 . . . . 136 E2
  Stutton IP9. . . . . . . 105 C6
Holly Oaks 2 CO6. . . 101 F2
Holly Rd
  4 Great Bricett IP7. . . 80 D6
  Ipswich IP1 . . . . . . 155 A4
  Lowestoft NR32 . . . . 112 E1
  Willisham IP8. . . . . . 81 A5
Holly Tree Cl IP16. . . 129 B5
Holly Way IP17 . . . . . 128 D3
Holly Wlk 8 IP28 . . . . 30 B8
Holman Cl IP2. . . . . . 139 A5
Holm Cl 4 NR34. . . . . . 9 F4
Holme Cl IP22 . . . . . . 18 C2
Holmere Dr IP19. . . . 118 A3
Holme's Hill IP17 . . . 41 A1
Holmes La 5 CB7. . . . 28 D5
Holmhill Dr IP11. . . . 153 D7
Holmsey Gn
  Beck Row, Holywell Row &
  Kenny Hill IP28. . . . . 13 C1
  Mildenhall IP28 . . . . . 30 B8
Holmsey Gn Gdns 7
  IP28. . . . . 30 B8
Holst Cl NR33 . . . . . . 115 A6
Holst Mead IP14 . . . . 124 C8
HOLTON 118 E4
Holton Ave NR32. . . . 112 F4
Holton Park Bsns Ctr
  IP7 . . . . 103 F7
Holton Rd
  Halesworth IP19 . . . . 118 C3
  Halesworth IP19 . . . . 118 F2
HOLTON ST MARY . . . 151 A8
Holton St Peter
  Postmill★ IP19 . . . . 118 E3
Holton St Peter
  Prim Sch IP19. . . . . 118 E4
Holton Terr IP19. . . . 118 C4
Holt Rd CO6 . . . . 93 E2
Holts Drove CB7 . . . . 28 A6
Holt's La IP6 . . . . . . 125 F6
Holts Meadow IP22 . . 36 B7
Holt's Rd CO6. . . . . . 102 A2
Holyhouse Drift 1
  IP31. . . . . 49 A6
Holyoak La IP14 . . . . 124 E1
Holyrood 4 CO12 . . . 106 F1
Holyrood Cl IP2. . . . . 138 F1
Holystone Way
  NR33 . . . . 114 C4
Holywell Cl IP33 . . . 123 A3
Holywell Dro IP28 . . . 13 C2
Holywell Drove IP27 . 13 C4
HOLYWELL ROW 30 C8
Holywells Cl IP3. . . . 139 E4
Holy Wells Rd IP3 . . . 139 E3
Homechurch IP6 . . . . 81 E6
Home Cl CB9 . . . . 88 E4
Home Farm La IP33 . . 123 B1
Home Farm Lane
  IP19. . . . . 41 A4
Home Farm Rd NR35 . . 8 C7
Homefield
  Boxford CO10. . . . . . 93 C3
  Capel St Mary IP9. . . 150 F3
Home Field 8 IP30 . . . 50 E2
Homefield Ave
  5 Beccles NR34 . . . . 111 B5
  Lowestoft NR33 . . . . 114 F6
Homefield Paddock
  NR34. . . . . 111 B5
Homefield Rd CB9 . . . 132 C4
Homefield Rd Ind Est
  CB9. . . . . 132 D4
Home Meadow
  Cross Green IP30 . . . . 64 B2
  4 Laxfield IP13 . . . . . 40 B3
Home Piece IP22 . . . . 35 A8
Homeport NR32. . . . . 113 E3
Homer Cl IP1. . . . . . 134 F4
HOMERSFIELD 23 B8
Homersfield Rd NR35 . . 7 C1

Homestall Cres CB9 . . 74 A2
Homestead Dr 2
  IP28. . . . . 30 B8
Homestead The
  NR33 . . . . 114 D3
Homey Bridge Rd
  CO6 . . . . 93 E1
Honeyhill IP29. . . . . . 47 E3
Honey Hill IP33 . . . . 154 C1
Honey Mdw CO6. . . . 102 B6
Honeymeade Cl 23
  IP31. . . . . 34 E4
Honeypot La
  Kelsale cum Carlton
    IP17 . . . . 57 E4
  Mendham IP20 . . . . . 23 C4
  Monewden IP13 . . . . . 69 F4
  Wattisfield IP22 . . . . . 35 D4
Honeypot Meadow 2
  NR35 . . . . 110 B3
Honeysuckle Cl
  Haverhill CB9 . . . . . . 132 C7
  8 Lowestoft NR33 . . . 115 A3
  1 Red Lodge IP28 . . . 46 A8
  4 Soham CB7 . . . . . . 28 D4
Honeysuckle Gdns
  IP2. . . . . 138 E4
Honeysuckle Way 4
  IP32. . . . . 123 E6
HONEY TYE 102 B6
Honeywood Grove
  IP31. . . . . 50 C4
HONINGTON. 33 E5
Honington CE VC Prim
  Sch IP31. . . . . 33 F5
Honington Rise IP31 . . 33 F5
HOO. 70 B5
Hood Dr 5 IP6 . . . . . . 81 F5
Hood Rd IP3. . . . . . . 139 F1
Hood's La NR34. . . . . . 25 F4
Hook La IP7 . . . . 149 F4
Hoo La IP12 . . . . 71 E4
Hooper Sq IP33 . . . . 122 C6
Hoo Rd IP13 . . . . 70 B4
Hope Cres IP12 . . . . . 147 A6
Hope Ct 4 IP3. . . . . . 139 E4
Hope Lodge Rd IP13 . . 69 D5
Hopelyn Cl 4 NR32 . . 113 B4
Hop Meadow CO7. . . 151 B4
Hopper'S La IP7 . . . . 80 E2
Hopper Way IP22 . . . . 20 B2
Hops Ct IP32 . . . . . . 154 B3
HOPTON 18 C2
Hopton CE VC Prim Sch
  Hopton IP22. . . . . . . 18 C1
  Hopton on Sea NR31. . . 3 C6
Hopton Gdns NR31 . . . 3 B7
HOPTON ON SEA. 3 C7
Hopton Rd
  Barningham IP31. . . . . 34 F8
  Garboldisham IP22. . . 18 D4
  Hopton IP22. . . . . . . 18 B1
  Thelnetham IP22 . . . . 18 D1
Hopton Rise
  3 Haverhill CB9. . . . . 74 A1
  Haverhill CB9 . . . . . . 132 A6
Hopton St IP22 . . . . . 18 D3
Hopton Yard IP17 . . . . 57 E7
Hopwoods Rd 24 IP32 48 B5
Hopyard La IP14 . . . . 51 B1
Hordle Pl 33 CO12 . . 107 B2
Hordle St 33 CO12. . . 107 B2
HORHAM. 38 E3
Horham Rd
  Athelington IP21 . . . . 38 E1
  Stanway Green IP21. . . 39 B2
Horizon School
  NR35. . . . . 110 D3
Horkesley Hill CO6. . . 102 D4
Horkesley Rd CO6. . . 102 D4
Hornbeam Ave 9
  CB8 . . . . 46 A8
Hornbeam Cl
  Beccles NR34 . . . . . 111 E4
  Great Blakenham IP6 . . 81 F6
  Rosedale Park NR33. . 114 F4
Hornbeam Dr IP29. . . 63 A8
Hornbeam Rd
  Mildenhall IP28 . . . . 116 C5
  Saxmundham IP17 . . 128 C3
  2 Stowupland IP14. . . 67 A6
Hornbill Way NR34. . . . 9 F3
Horner Cl 4 IP22. . . . 20 B3
HORNER'S GREEN . . . 93 C4
HORNESTREET 103 C3
Horn Hill NR33. . . . . 115 C7
Hornings Pk IP29 . . . 122 B1
Horn La CB8 . . . . 60 D3
HORRINGER 63 A8
Horringer Ct Mid Sch
  IP33 . . . . 122 D3
Horringer Rd IP29 . . 122 D2
Horsecroft IP29 . . . . 122 E1
Horsecroft Rd
  Bury St Edmunds
    IP33 . . . . 122 F2
  Horringer IP29. . . . . 63 C8
Horsefair IP30. . . . . . 50 E2
Horsefair Cl 9 IP14. . 52 C4
Horse Fen Dr CB7. . . . 28 C7
Horsefen Drove CB7 . . 28 C1
Horseheath Rd CB9 . . 74 A2
Horsepond Pl IP6 . . . 125 D3
Horseshoe Cl IP14. . . 124 C3
Horseshoe La CB9 . . . 132 C5
Horseshoe Rd 24
  IP31. . . . . 34 E4

Horse Watering La
  NR35 . . . . 8 E6
Horsham Ave IP3 . . . 140 D3
Horsham Cl CB9 . . . . 132 A7
Hose Ave IP22 . . . . . . 20 A3
Hospital Rd
  Bury St Edmunds
    IP33 . . . . 154 A1
  Orford IP12 . . . . . . 131 B6
Hossack Rd IP3. . . . . 144 A8
Hotson Rd IP18. . . . . 119 D6
Houghton Dr
  Hopton on Sea NR31. . . 3 B6
  Oulton NR32 . . . . . . 112 C4
Houghton Pl 5 IP4 . . 140 F5
Houghtons La IP29 . . . 29 D5
Houghton Way IP33. . 154 A3
Houldsworth Terr
  CB8 . . . . 120 F3
Houldsworth Valley Prim
  Acad CB8 . . . . 120 E3
Housemartin Way 6
  IP14. . . . . 124 F7
Howard Ave 33 CO12 . 106 F1
Howard Cl
  6 Framlingham
    IP13. . . . . 126 C3
  Harleston IP20. . . . . . 22 E6
  Haverhill CB9 . . . . . . 132 B5
  Sudbury CO10. . . . . . 148 C7
Howard de Walden Way
  CB8 . . . . 121 A4
Howard De Walden Way
  CB8 . . . . 121 A4
Howard Dr IP3 . . . . . 129 C4
Howard Mid Sch
  Bury St Edmunds IP32 48 B5
  Fornham All Saints
    IP28. . . . . 122 D8
Howard Rd 1 NR35 . . 110 D3
Howards Cl 8 IP23 . . . 36 D2
Howard St IP4. . . . . . 140 B7
Howards Walk 4
  IP17. . . . . 128 D3
Howards Way IP5. . . . 141 D8
Howe Ave IP3 . . . . . . 140 C3
Howe La
  Cockfield IP30 . . . . . . 64 C1
  Thornham Parva IP23. . 37 A3
Howe Rd
  Gosling Street CO10 . . 93 C5
  Haverhill CB9 . . . . . . 132 D4
Howes Ave IP31. . . . . 49 D4
Howgate Cl 4 CO10 . . 148 F8
How Hill (Tumulus)★
  IP27. . . . . 31 B7
Howlem Balk CB5. . . . 44 B7
Howlett Cl IP5. . . . . . 141 E7
Howlett Way
  Thetford IP24. . . . . . . 16 B7
  Trimley St Martin
    IP11. . . . . 107 D8
Howley Gdns NR32. . 113 A6
HOXNE. 38 B8
Hoxne Cl 5 IP14. . . . 124 E3
Hoxne Rd
  Brockdish IP21 . . . . . 21 F1
  Eye IP23 . . . . 117 E2
  Hoxne IP21. . . . . 38 D3
  Syleham IP21 . . . . . . 22 B2
  Upper Weybread IP12 . 22 B2
Hoxter Way CO10 . . . 148 C8
Hoylake Cl 6 IP28 . . . 48 C6
Hubbard's Ave 2
  NR32. . . . . 113 C6
Hubbards Cl IP17 . . . 128 B4
Hubbard's Hill IP17 . . 41 B1
Hubbards La IP22. . . . 18 E2
Hubbard's La IP30 . . . 64 F8
Hubbard's Loke
  NR32. . . . . 113 C6
Huckleberry Cres 7
  IP3. . . . . 144 C7
Hudson Cl
  10 Harwich CO12 . . . 107 A1
  Haverhill CB9 . . . . . . 133 A4
Hudsons La CO6 . . . . 103 A7
Hudson Way 6 IP29 . . 47 A2
Hudson Way 7 IP7 . . 149 F7
Huggins La IP23 . . . . 37 B1
Hugh Ager Cl 5
  IP14. . . . . 124 D3
Hughes Cnr CO7 . . . . 151 A6
Hughes Rd CO7 . . . . 151 B6
Hull St IP27. . . . . . . 109 F1
Hulver La IP17. . . . . . 72 C6
Hulver Rd
  Ellough NR34 . . . . 9 F2
  Hulver Street NR34. . . 10 C5
HULVER STREET 10 C5
Humber Doucy La
  IP4. . . . . 136 A2
Humber Doucy Sports Ctr
  IP4. . . . . 140 D7
HUMBLE GREEN 92 F8
Hummingbird Cl 5
  IP3. . . . . 49 A3
Humphry Rd CO10 . . 148 C6
HUNDON. 75 E3
Hundon Com Prim Sch
  CO10. . . . . 75 D3
Hundon Pl 6 CB9 . . . 132 F6
Hundon Rd
  Barnardiston CB9. . . . 75 B4

Hundon Rd continued
Hundon CO10 . . . . **75** B1
Kedington CB9 . . . .**133** F8
Stoke by Clare CO10 . . . . .**89** E8
Hundred Acres Drove
CB7 . . . .**28** D8
Hundred Acre Way
Herringswell IP28 . . . .**30** C1
11 Herringswell IP28 . . . .**46** A8
Hundred La
Boxted CO4 . . . .**103** B2
Daisy Green IP31 . . . .**51** B6
Old Newton with Dagworth
IP14 . . . .**51** F3
Hungarian Cl IP13 . . . . .**84** E8
Hungate NR34 . . . .**111** B5
Hungate Ct NR34 . . . . . .**111** B5
Hungate La NR34 . . . . . .**111** B5
Hungerdown La
CO11 . . . .**104** B1
Hungry Hall La CO10 . .**77** E3
HUNSTON **50** D7
HUNSTON GREEN **50** C5
Hunston Rd IP31 . . . . . .**50** E7
Hunt Cl
5 Redenhall with
Harleston IP20 . . . . . .**22** D6
Stowmarket IP14 . . . . .**124** D3
Hunter Dr
19 Manningtree
CO11 . . . .**104** D2
18 Thurstow IP31 . . . . .**49** D4
Hunter Gall The★
CO10 . . . .**91** E8
Hunter Rd
Bury St Edmunds
IP32 . . . .**122** D8
2 Ipswich IP3 . . . .**144** C8
Hunter's Chase CO7 . .**103** F1
Hunters Dr 21 IP28 . . . .**30** B1
Hunters End IP11 . . . . .**152** C7
Hunters La
Mendham IP20 . . . .**23** A3
Metfield IP20 . . . .**23** B2
Hunters Ride 21 IP25 . .**98** A8
Huntingdon Cl 9
NR33 . . . .**115** A3
HUNTINGFIELD **41** A5
Huntingfield Rd
Bury St Edmunds
IP33 . . . .**122** C4
Cratfield IP19 . . . .**40** D5
Heveningham IP19 . . . . .**40** F4
Leiston IP16 . . . .**129** C5
Huntley Cres IP19 . . . .**118** C5
Huntley Ct IP19 . . . . . .**118** C5
Hunton Rd NR32 . . . . . .**112** D2
Hunts Hill CO10 . . . .**77** A2
Hurdle Dro IP28 . . . .**29** F8
Hurdle Makers Hill
IP8 . . . .**95** F6
Hurn Crag Rd IP18 . . . .**119** C7
Hurricane Pl IP3 . . . . . .**140** B1
Hurstfen Drove IP28 . .**116** E7
Hurstlea Cl IP6 . . . .**125** D5
Hurstlea Rd IP6 . . . . . .**125** C5
Hurth Way IP24 . . . .**16** C6
Hurts Croft 3 CB7 . . . . .**29** A1
Husseygreen La IP21 . . .**40** A7
Hut Hill (Tumulus)★
IP31 . . . .**17** E3
Hutland Rd IP14 . . . . . .**139** F7
Hutton Cl IP33 . . . .**122** D6
Hutton Ct IP23 . . . .**117** D3
Hyacinth Dr 21
IP28 . . . .**46** A8
Hyams La IP9 . . . .**105** E7
Hyam's La IP9 . . . .**105** C5
Hyde Pk Corner IP12 . . .**86** F8
Hyde Rd
Risby IP28 . . . .**47** F5
Sudbury CO10 . . . .**148** C5
Hydewood Rd CO9 . . . . .**90** A2
Hyem's La IP11 . . . .**153** B7
Hyntle Cl IP27 . . . .**138** C5
Hyperion Cl IP1 . . . . . .**138** C8
Hyperion Way CB8 . . . .**120** D8
Hythe Cl 9 CB5 . . . .**44** A6
Hythe La CB5 . . . .**44** A6
Hythe Rd IP26 . . . .**4** E7

I

Ian Rose Way 20
CO11 . . . .**105** A2
Ice House Quay
NR32 . . . .**114** E8
Iceni Acad Hockwold
IP26 . . . .**5** A2
Iceni Way CB8 . . . .**120** B8
Iceni Way CB9 . . . .**132** F3
Icepits IP31 . . . .**49** C6
Icewell Hill CB8 . . . . . .**121** A4
Ickleton Pl 9 CB9 . . . . .**132** F4
ICKLINGHAM **31** D4
Icklingham Rd
Lackford IP28 . . . .**31** F2
Tuddenham IP28 . . . .**30** A3
West Stow IP28 . . . .**32** B2
Icknield Cl 3 CB8 . . . . .**60** E7
Icknield Way IP26 . . . . . .**16** B5
Ickworth Cres IP4 . . . .**140** F5
Ickworth Ct 2 IP11 . . .**152** C3
Ickworth Dr IP33 . . . . .**154** A1

Ickworth House Pk &
Gdn★ IP29 . . . .**62** F8
Ickworth Pk Prim Sch
IP29 . . . .**63** A8
Ickworth Vineyard★
IP29 . . . .**62** E8
IKEN **72** F2
Iken Cliff Rd IP17 . . . . .**72** D4
Ilex Cl IP33 . . . .**123** A3
Iliffe Way IP14 . . . .**124** D6
ILKETSHALL ST
ANDREW **8** E2
ILKETSHALL ST
LAWRENCE **24** F6
Ilketshall St Lawrence
Sch NR34 . . . .**24** F6
ILKETSHALL ST
MARGARET **24** B8
Imperial Mews NR31 . . . .**3** B6
Impson Way IP28 . . . .**6** A8
Infirmary La IP13 . . . . .**126** D3
Ingate NR34 . . . .**111** C4
Ingelow Gdns IP4 . . . . .**141** B6
Ingestre St 1 CO12 . . .**107** B2
INGHAM **32** F1
Ingham Rd
Haverhill CB9 . . . .**132** E6
West Stow IP28 . . . .**32** C1
Ingram's Rd IP21 . . . . . .**21** F3
Ingram's Well Rd
CO10 . . . .**148** D5
Inkerman Cl 4 IP7 . . . .**149** D6
Inkerman Row 4
CO10 . . . .**148** C6
Inkerman Terr 3
IP7 . . . .**149** D6
Innes End 4 IP8 . . . . . .**138** C2
Innocence La IP10 . . . . . .**98** C2
Interchange Ret Pk
IP8 . . . .**138** B1
International English
Schools Breckland
IP27 . . . .**14** D8
Inverness Rd IP4 . . . . .**136** A2
Inworth La CO6 . . . .**101** B1
Ion Rd 1 IP32 . . . .**122** E8
IPSWICH **155** B3
Ipswich Acad IP3 . . . . .**144** B8
Ipswich Ave 3 IP12 . . .**85** B3
Ipswich Cl 1 IP12 . . . . .**85** B3
Ipswich Cl IP33 . . . . . .**154** B3
Ipswich High Sch for
Girls IP9 . . . .**144** C2
Ipswich Hospl (NHS)
IP4 . . . .**140** C7
Ipswich Hospl (Private)
IP10 . . . .**141** B4
Ipswich Mus★ IP1 . . . .**155** B3
Ipswich Prep Sch
IP1 . . . .**155** B4
Ipswich Rd
Brantham CO11 . . . .**104** E5
Charsfield IP13 . . . .**70** B2
Claydon IP6 . . . .**134** C8
Cretingham IP13 . . . .**69** F6
Dedham CO4 . . . .**103** D3
East Bergholt CO7 . . . . .**151** A6
Elmsett IP7 . . . .**95** A8
Eye IP23 . . . .**117** A6
Gosbeck IP6 . . . .**68** D3
Grundisburgh IP13 . . . . .**83** E5
Hadleigh IP7 . . . .**149** F7
Harkstead IP9 . . . .**106** A6
Helmingham IP6 . . . .**69** A3
Holbrook IP9 . . . .**105** E8
Ipswich IP6 . . . .**136** C3
Lowestoft NR32 . . . .**113** D4
Nacton IP10 . . . .**145** A5
Nedging-with-Naughton
IP7 . . . .**80** C4
Needham Market IP6 . . . .**125** E4
Newbourne IP12 . . . .**98** C6
Orford IP12 . . . .**131** B4
2 Scole IP21 . . . .**20** F1
Scole NR15 . . . .**21** C7
Stowmarket IP14 . . . . . .**124** D6
Stratford St Mary CO7 . .**103** E4
Tattingstone White House
IP9 . . . .**142** D1
Thornham Magna IP23 . .**37** B2
Tuddenham St Martin
IP6 . . . .**136** F7
Waldringfield IP12 . . . . . .**98** D7
Willisham IP8 . . . .**81** B4
Winston IP14 . . . .**53** F1
Witnesham IP6 . . . .**136** A8
Woodbridge IP12 . . . . . .**146** E3
Ipswich Sch IP1 . . . . . .**155** B4
Ipswich St
Bury St Edmunds
IP33 . . . .**154** B3
Lakenheath IP27 . . . . . .**109** F1
Stowmarket IP14 . . . . . .**124** D6
Ipswich Sta IP2 . . . . . .**155** A1
Ipswich Transport Mus★
IP3 . . . .**140** C2
Ipswich Way IP14 . . . . . .**68** E6
Ireland Rd IP3 . . . .**139** F1
Irex Rd NR33 . . . .**115** B3
Iris Cl IP2 . . . .**138** F5
Iris Ct 37 IP28 . . . .**30** C1
Irlam Rd IP24 . . . .**138** D2
Ironbridge Path CB7 . . .**29** A1
Iron Foundry Rd
IP14 . . . .**124** E6
Isaacson Rd CB5 . . . .**44** B4
Isham Pl 3 IP3 . . . .**139** E4

Isinglass Cl CB8 . . . . . .**121** E2
ISLEHAM **29** B5
Isleham CE Prim Sch
CB7 . . . .**29** C5
Isleham Priory★ CB7 **29** C5
Isleham Rd
Fordham CB7 . . . .**29** B2
West Row IP28 . . . .**29** F4
Isleham Rd
Ivan Blatny Cl IP3 . . . .**140** C4
Ivan Garwood Cl 23
CO11 . . . .**105** A2
Ives Cl 15 IP22 . . . .**20** D2
Ives Way 10 NR31 . . . . . .**3** B6
Ivry St IP1 . . . .**155** A4
Ivy Cl IP13 . . . .**54** E7
Ivy La NR33 . . . .**114** C7
Ivy Lodge Rd IP21 . . . . . .**71** D1
Ivy Robyn Way IP20 . . .**23** A8
Ivy Tree La IP7 . . . .**94** C7
Ixer La IP30 . . . .**64** B5
IXWORTH **34** B2
Ixworth Abbey IP31 . . . .**34** A1
Ixworth CE Prim Sch
IP31 . . . .**34** B1
Ixworth Free Sch
IP31 . . . .**34** B1
Ixworth Rd
Great Barton IP31 . . . . . .**49** C6
Haverhill CB9 . . . .**132** C4
Honington IP31 . . . .**33** F5
Stowlangtoft IP31 . . . . . .**50** B6
Thurston IP31 . . . .**49** D5
Troston IP31 . . . .**33** D3
Walsham le Willows
IP31 . . . .**35** A1
IXWORTH THORPE **33** F4
Ixworth Thorpe Rd
IP31 . . . .**34** B4

J

Jackdaw Cl 9 IP14 . .**124** F7
Jack Jarvis Cl 5
CB8 . . . .**121** A3
Jacks Field 6 IP13 . . . . .**83** A5
Jacks Gn IP6 . . . .**125** E7
Jack's Gn Rd IP6 . . . . .**125** E6
Jack's La IP14 . . . .**124** A2
Jacksnipe Cl 4 IP14 . .**124** F6
Jackson Pl 6 IP6 . . . . . .**82** A6
Jackson Rd IP12 . . . . . .**98** C5
Jackson Way IP6 . . . . .**125** D4
Jack Taylor Cl CB8 . . . .**120** F4
Jacob Cl IP31 . . . .**49** D4
Jacobs Cl
14 Stanton IP31 . . . . . .**34** E4
Sudbury CO10 . . . .**148** F3
Jacobs Meadow
IP30 . . . .**65** D5
Jacobs St 7 NR32 . . . . .**113** D2
Jacob Way 11 IP12 . . . .**147** A5
Jacqueline Cl
Bury St Edmunds
IP33 . . . .**154** A1
7 Grundisburgh IP13 . .**83** E5
James Bennett Ave
IP3 . . . .**140** D1
James Boden Cl 7
IP11 . . . .**152** E6
James Carter Rd
IP28 . . . .**116** A6
James Dunn Way 1
CB9 . . . .**132** C8
Jameson Pl 6 CO10 . . .**148** C6
Jamestown Bvd IP2 . . .**139** D3
Jamestown Cl 23
CO12 . . . .**107** A2
Jamie Allen Cl 20
CO10 . . . .**92** B3
Janebrook Rd 1
IP2 . . . .**138** E2
Janet Hadenham Cl 11
NR34 . . . .**9** F4
Jane Walker Pk CO6 . .**102** A5
Janey Rd 8 IP31 . . . .**49** A4
Jankes Green Rd
CO6 . . . .**101** C1
Janus Cl IP3 . . . .**133** B4
Jaques Cl 3 CO10 . . . . . .**77** B3
Jarmain Way 4 IP14 **124** A8
Jarman Cl IP33 . . . .**123** C3
Jarman's La IP28 . . . . . .**29** F7
Jarrett La CO6 . . . .**102** C3
Jarrold Cl 1 IP31 . . . . . .**34** F7
Jarvis Way CB8 . . . . . .**120** C5
Jasmine Cl
9 Felixstowe IP11 . . . .**107** D8
Ipswich IP2 . . . .**138** F3
Jasmine Gn NR32 . . . . .**113** C2
Jasmine Rd 13 IP28 . . . .**46** A8
Jasper Cl IP6 . . . .**134** D5
Java Lodge Rd IP13 . . .**127** B3
Jay Cl CB9 . . . .**133** A5
Jay La NR32 . . . .**3** A6
Jays Croft Rd 2 IP12 . . .**85** E8
Jay's Gn IP20 . . . .**22** E6
Jay's Hill Rd
Ellough NR34 . . . .**10** B2
Willingham St Mary
NR34 . . . .**26** A8
Jay's La CO9 . . . .**90** B3
Jaywick Rd 3 CB9 . . . .**132** E6
Jeaffresons Well
IP6 . . . .**126** D4

Jeannie Mann Ct
NR32 . . . .**113** B3
Jeavons La IP11 . . . . . .**141** E7
Jeddah Way 5 CB8 . . . . .**45** F5
Jefferies Rd IP4 . . . . . .**139** E6
Jellicoe Ave NR33 . . . .**114** D6
Jenkins Gn NR32 . . . . .**113** A5
Jenkins Hill CO11 . . . . .**105** B2
Jenkinsons Pightle
NR35 . . . .**7** B8
Jenner Cl NR35 . . . .**110** C2
Jenners Cl 1 IP12 . . . . .**147** B6
Jennings Drift IP5 . . . .**141** E7
Jennings Way IP22 . . . .**20** C5
Jennings Way 14 IP22 **20** C3
Jermyn Ave IP32 . . . . .**123** F5
Jermyns Cl IP9 . . . .**150** F4
Jermyns Rd IP18 . . . . . .**119** B8
Jermyn Way IP19 . . . . .**118** A2
Jersey Ct 27 IP28 . . . . . .**30** B8
Jersey Meadow 6
CB8 . . . .**46** A5
Jervis Cl 10 IP9 . . . . . .**105** E7
Jervises Croft 17
IP30 . . . .**50** F2
Jewell View IP5 . . . . . .**141** D8
Jew's La IP12 . . . .**84** E6
Jex Way 6 NR31 . . . .**3** B6
Jigsaw Place IP14 . . . . .**68** B7
Jim Mollison Ct 5
IP3 . . . .**140** B1
Jimmy's Farm★ IP9 . .**142** E5
Jimmy's La CO11 . . . . .**104** F5
Job's La IP22 . . . .**20** C1
Jobson Rd CB9 . . . .**132** E8
Jocelyn Cl 16 IP32 . . . . .**48** C5
Jockey's La
Combs IP14 . . . .**66** C2
Framsden IP14 . . . .**69** B7
Joes Rd
Great Cornard CO10 . . . .**92** C3
Page's Green IP14 . . . . .**53** C4
John Archer View
CB9 . . . .**74** D5
John Childs Way
NR35 . . . .**110** C2
John Lawrence Cl
NR34 . . . .**111** B2
John Russell Gall★
IP3 . . . .**155** C2
John Shepherd Rd 1
IP21 . . . .**39** D8
Johnson Cl 5 IP2 . . . . .**139** C3
Johnson Rd 7 IP29 . . . . .**47** A2
Johnsons Way 2
IP16 . . . .**129** A6
Johnson Way
Oulton NR32 . . . .**113** A5
Wickham Market IP13 . .**127** C5
John St
Leiston IP16 . . . .**129** C5
Lowestoft NR33 . . . .**115** C4
Rose Hill IP3 . . . .**139** E4
John Swain Cl
IP6 . . . .**125** C5
John Tibauld Ct 4
CB9 . . . .**88** D3
Jolly's Way 2 IP31 . . . . .**35** C1
Jones La IP19 . . . .**40** B6
Jones Rd CO10 . . . .**76** C3
Jordan Cl IP6 . . . .**125** E7
Jordayn Rise IP7 . . . . .**149** E6
Joshua Ct 3 NR31 . . . . . .**3** B8
Josselyns The IP11 . . .**152** B8
Jovian Way IP1 . . . .**138** E8
Joyce Rd NR35 . . . .**110** D3
Jubilee Ave IP14 . . . . .**124** D4
Jubilee Cl
11 Claydon IP6 . . . . . .**82** B5
11 Felixstowe IP11 . . .**107** D8
10 Harwich CO12 . . . .**106** F1
13 Isleham CB7 . . . . . .**29** C5
2 Laxfield IP13 . . . . . .**40** B3
Norton IP31 . . . .**50** B4
Sweffling IP17 . . . .**56** E2
4 Thetford IP24 . . . . . .**16** B5
Weeting IP27 . . . .**5** E3
Jubilee Cres
Needham Market
IP6 . . . .**125** D4
Stowupland IP14 . . . .**67** A7
Jubilee Ct CB8 . . . .**60** A5
Jubilee Ctr IP28 . . . . . .**116** C3
Jubilee End 5 CO11 . .**104** E3
Jubilee Rd
Bungay NR35 . . . .**110** B2
Lakenheath IP27 . . . . . .**109** C8
Lowestoft NR33 . . . .**115** A2
Sudbury CO10 . . . .**148** D6
Jubilee Terr 10 IP30 . . .**50** F2
Jubilee Way NR32 . . . .**113** E2
Jubilee Wlk
Aldeburgh IP15 . . . .**130** E3
Haverhill CB9 . . . .**132** E5
Judas La IP23 . . . .**37** B5
Judith Ave IP17 . . . . . .**129** B2
Julian Cl CB9 . . . .**133** B5
Julian Way 12 NR31 . . . .**3** B8
Julius Martin La CB7 . .**28** C4
Junction Rd IP28 . . . . .**116** B5
June Ave
Ipswich IP1 . . . .**135** B2
Lowestoft NR32 . . . .**113** B3
Stowmarket IP14 . . . . . .**124** D5
KENTFORD **46** A5
Kentford Paddocks 5
CB8 . . . .**46** A5
Kentford Rd 5 IP11 . . .**152** C4
KENTON **54** B5
KENTON CORNER **54** C4

Jupiter Rd
7 Bury St Edmunds
IP32 . . . .**49** A3
Ipswich IP4 . . . .**140** B7
Justinian Cl CB9 . . . . .**133** B4

K

Kalen Ct NR33 . . . .**114** F1
Karen Cl
Ipswich IP1 . . . .**135** B1
4 Scole IP21 . . . .**20** F1
Kate's La IP14 . . . .**51** A1
Katwijk Way 2
NR32 . . . .**115** D8
Kays Cl IP5 . . . .**141** C7
Kearney Dr NR32 . . . . .**112** D3
Keating Cl 2 CO11 . . . .**104** D2
Keats Cl IP17 . . . .**128** B4
Keats Cres IP1 . . . .**134** F3
Kebbles 9 CO10 . . . .**77** A3
Kedges La IP7 . . . .**93** F7
KEDINGTON **133** E7
Kedington Cl IP30 . . . . .**49** C2
Kedington Hill CO10 . . .**92** A1
Kedington Prim Sch
CB9 . . . .**133** E8
Kedington Rd CB9 . . . .**133** D4
Keeble Rd CO11 . . . . . .**104** F5
Keebles Yd 9 CB9 . . . . .**132** E6
Keel Cl NR33 . . . .**114** B4
Keele Cl 8 IP7 . . . .**149** F7
Keens La IP18 . . . .**119** B7
Keeper's La
Marlesford IP13 . . . .**71** D5
Stoke-by-Nayland CO6 . .**102** C8
Trimley St Mary IP11 . . .**152** A7
Keep Rise 6 NR35 . . . . .**110** B4
Keiffer Ct 13 CO10 . . . . .**92** C6
Keightley Way IP6 . . . .**136** B5
Kell's Acres NR34 . . . . . .**8** F7
Kell's Way NR34 . . . .**8** F7
Kelly-Pain Ct NR32 . . .**113** D3
Kelly Rd IP2 . . . .**138** E5
KELSALE **128** C3
Kelsale CE VC Prim Sch
IP17 . . . .**128** C5
Kelsale Rd
Saxmundham IP17 . . . . . .**57** A4
Saxmundham IP17 . . . . .**128** A7
Kelso Rd IP33 . . . .**122** D2
Kelvedon Dr IP4 . . . . . .**140** F5
Kelvin Dr 7 CB9 . . . .**74** A1
Kelvin Pl IP4 . . . .**16** A4
Kelvin Rd IP1 . . . .**134** F1
Kemball St IP4 . . . .**140** A5
Kembold Cl IP32 . . . . . .**123** C5
Kemps Cl IP15 . . . .**130** C5
Kempshorne Cl
NR32 . . . .**112** E4
Kemps La NR34 . . . .**111** B3
Kempson Dr 7 CO10 . . . .**92** B3
Kempson Way IP30 . . . .**123** F4
Kempsters The IP11 . .**152** D7
Kempton Cl 4 IP1 . . . . .**135** A3
Kempton Cross
NR34 . . . .**111** E4
Kempton Rd IP1 . . . . . .**135** A3
Kemsley Rd IP11 . . . . .**152** F5
Kendal Gn IP11 . . . .**153** D7
Kendall Cl IP32 . . . .**49** A3
Kendall Ct
10 Bury St Edmunds
IP32 . . . .**49** A3
Tuddenham IP28 . . . .**30** F2
Kendal Rd NR33 . . . . . .**115** B5
Kennedy Ave IP19 . . . .**118** A1
Kennedy Cl
Halesworth IP19 . . . . . .**118** B1
Ipswich IP4 . . . .**140** A6
Kennedy Rd 8 CB7 . . . . .**29** C5
Kennedy St IP27 . . . . . .**109** E1
Kennel Loke NR31 . . . . . .**3** B8
Kennels La IP13 . . . . . .**146** C8
Kennels Rd
Brightwell IP10 . . . .**98** A6
Foxhall IP10 . . . .**141** F2
Kennetside CB8 . . . .**61** B1
KENNETT **45** F7
Kennett Com Prim Sch
CB8 . . . .**45** F6
Kennett Pk Cl 10 CB8 . .**46** A5
Kennett Rd IP28 . . . .**46** A8
Kennett Rd or Moulton
CB8 . . . .**45** F3
Kennett Sta CB8 . . . . . .**45** F6
Kenney Cl IP8 . . . .**95** D7
KENNINGHALL **19** B8
Kenninghall Prim Sch
NR16 . . . .**19** A8
Kenninghall Rd
Bressingham Common
IP22 . . . .**19** F6
Kenninghall NR16 . . . . . .**19** A7
Smallworth IP22 . . . .**18** D6
KENNY HILL **12** F2
Kennyhill Dro IP28 . . . . .**13** A3
Kensington Rd
Ipswich IP1 . . . .**139** A8
Lowestoft NR33 . . . .**115** C4
Stowmarket IP14 . . . . . .**124** D5
KENTFORD **46** A5

Kenton Rd
Bedingfield IP23 . . . .**54** A6
Debenham IP14 . . . .**53** F2
Kenton IP14 . . . .**54** A3
Monk Soham Green
IP13 . . . .**54** C5
Kentons Rd IP8 . . . . . .**134** A3
Kent Rd
Lackford IP28 . . . .**31** F1
Lowestoft NR32 . . . .**113** B1
Stowmarket IP14 . . . . . .**124** C7
Kents La
Bungay NR35 . . . .**110** D3
Soham CB7 . . . .**28** D4
Kentwell Cl IP4 . . . . . .**140** F4
Kentwell Hall & Gdns★
CO10 . . . .**77** E2
Kentwell Pl 3 CB5 . . . . .**44** B5
Kenyon Cl 7 CO7 . . . . .**103** E5
Kenyon Dr 7 CO10 . . . . .**92** C6
Keats Cl IP17 . . . .**128** B4
Kenyon St IP2 . . . .**155** B1
Kerridges NR16 . . . .**18** C8
Kerridge's Cut **15**
CO11 . . . .**105** A2
Kerridge Way 29 IP20 . .**22** D6
Kerrison Con Ctr
IP23 . . . .**37** D1
Kerrison Gdns IP23 . . . .**37** D1
Kerrison Rd
Bungay NR35 . . . .**110** D2
Framlingham IP13 . . . . .**126** B4
Kerry Ave IP1 . . . .**134** D1
Kerrys Farm La IP4 . . . .**51** F4
KERSEY **94** A7
Kersey Ave CO10 . . . . .**148** F4
Kersey CE Prim Sch
IP7 . . . .**94** A6
Kersey Cl IP14 . . . .**124** E3
Kersey Pottery★ IP7 . **94** A7
Kersey Rd
Felixstowe IP11 . . . .**152** D4
Kersey IP7 . . . .**93** E7
KERSEY TYE **93** E6
KERSEY UPLAND **93** E5
Kersley Hall La IP21 . . . .**39** A3
Kesdale Gdns IP33 . . . .**122** D5
KESGRAVE **141** E8
Kesgrave High Sch
IP5 . . . .**141** D8
KESSINGLAND **11** C2
KESSINGLAND
BEACH **27** C8
Kessingland CE Prim
Acad NR33 . . . .**11** C2
Kesteven Rd IP2 . . . . . .**155** A1
Kestrel Cl
1 Beck Row, Holywell Row
& Kenny Hill IP28 . . .**13** B1
19 Harleston IP20 . . . .**22** D5
Thetford IP24 . . . .**16** C4
Kestrel Dr IP14 . . . .**67** A5
Kestrel Rd
Bury St Edmunds
IP33 . . . .**123** B2
Haverhill CB9 . . . .**133** A5
Ipswich IP2 . . . .**138** D3
Keswick Cl IP11 . . . . . .**153** C6
KETTLEBASTON **79** C5
Kettlebaston Way 3
IP1 . . . .**135** D1
Kettleborrow Cl 21
IP31 . . . .**34** B1
KETTLEBURGH **70** C7
Kettleburgh Rd
Easton IP13 . . . .**70** D6
Framlingham IP13 . . . . .**126** C1
Kettlefields CB8 . . . .**59** F5
Kettlefields Primary Sch
CB8 . . . .**59** F5
Kettle La
Creeting St Mary IP6 . . . .**67** E1
Feltwell IP26 . . . .**4** C6
Kettlelea Ct IP14 . . . . .**124** D6
Kettles La IP17 . . . .**72** B7
Kevington Dr NR32 . . . .**112** C2
Keyes Cl 2 IP14 . . . . . .**124** A8
Keynes Way 18 CO12 . .**106** F1
Key St
Ipswich IP3 . . . .**155** C2
Ipswich IP4 . . . .**155** C2
Keytes Way 6 IP6 . . . . . .**81** F5
Khartoum Rd IP4 . . . . .**139** F7
Kidds Cl 14 NR31 . . . .**3** B8
Kids Play★ IP32 . . . .**154** B4
Kidz Kingdom★ IP5 . **98** A8
Kilbourn Rd 6 NR33 . . .**115** A3
Kilbrack NR34 . . . .**111** C5
Kilbrack Gdns NR34 . . .**111** C5
Kilby Way 22 CO10 . . . .**92** B3
Kildare Ave IP1 . . . .**134** D2
Killick Cres NR32 . . . . .**114** C4
Kilmaine Rd 22 CO12 . .**106** F1
Kiln Bottom IP7 . . . . . .**149** B8
Kiln Cl
23 Great Blakenham
IP6 . . . .**82** A5
Ipswich IP4 . . . .**155** C4
Kiln Cotts IP14 . . . .**124** C5
Kiln Dr CO10 . . . .**148** E4
Kiln Field 1 IP11 . . . . .**152** D4
Kiln La
Alderton IP12 . . . .**99** E3
Badwell Green IP31 . . . . .**51** B8
Benhall IP17 . . . .**128** C1
Boot Street IP13 . . . .**137** E4

Kiln La continued
Buxhall IP14 . . . . 65 F3
Dickleburgh & Rushall
  IP21 . . . . 21 C2
Elmswell IP30 . . . . 50 E1
Friston IP17 . . . . 72 D7
32 Mistley CO11 . . . . . 104 E2
Needham IP20 . . . . 22 A4
Rede IP29 . . . . 62 E2
Rede IP29 . . . . 62 E4
Stowlangtoft IP31 . . . . . 34 E1
Kiln Rd NR34 . . . . 26 C3
Kiln Rise **6** IP22 . . . . 36 A6
Kilverstone Rd
  Brettenham IP24 . . . . . 17 A6
  Thetford IP24 . . . . 16 F7
Kimberley Rd NR33 . 115 A7
Kimms Belt IP24 . . . . 16 B5
Kingbird Rd **22** IP31 . 49 A3
King Edward Ave
  IP13 . . . . 127 C7
King Edward Rd
  Ipswich IP3 . . . . 140 B3
  Leiston IP16 . . . . 129 C6
King Edward VI CE
  Upper Sch IP33 . . . 154 A3
King Edward VII Dr
  IP9 . . . . 107 A4
King Edward VII Rd
  CB8 . . . . 120 E5
Kingfisher Ave IP2 . 138 D3
Kingfisher Cl
  Haverhill CB9 . . . . . . 133 A6
  Thetford IP24 . . . . . . 16 C4
Kingfisher Cres
  IP18 . . . . 119 A7
Kingfisher Ct NR33 . 114 C6
Kingfisher Dr
  6 Burwell CB5 . . . . . 44 A6
  2 Claydon IP6 . . . . . 81 F5
  13 Harwich CO12 . . . 106 F1
  Soham CB7 . . . . 28 C5
Kingfisher Leisure Ctr
  CO10 . . . . 148 D4
Kingfisher Pl IP16 . . 129 D4
Kingfisher Rd IP32 . . 123 F7
Kingfisher Rise
  IP17 . . . . 128 C4
Kingfishers CO10 . . . 148 B4
Kingfisher Way
  Mildenhall IP28 . . . . 116 D4
  6 Stowmarket IP14 . 67 A5
King George Ave
  CB8 . . . . 120 B8
King George's Ave
  3 Harwich CO12 . . . 107 A2
  Leiston IP16 . . . . 129 C6
King Georges Cl **1**
  IP7 . . . . 94 F1
King James Cl CB7 . . 29 C1
Kings Ave IP4 . . . . . 139 E5
King's Ave IP13 . . . . 126 B5
Kingsbury Rd IP11 . . 152 C7
Kings Cl
  7 Acton CO10 . . . . . 92 B7
  1 Manningtree CO11 104 E2
  Mildenhall IP28 . . . . 116 D5
  3 Rougham IP30 . . . 64 D8
  Woodbridge IP12 . . . 146 E4
Kings Court Bsns Ctr
  CB8 . . . . 120 F7
Kings Ct **1** CB8 . . . 120 B8
King's Dam NR34 . . . 9 B6
Kings Dr CB8 . . . . . . 121 B1
Kingsfield Ave IP1 . . 139 D8
Kingsfleet Prim Sch
  IP11 . . . . 153 C6
Kings Fleet Rd IP11 . 152 E3
Kingsgate Dr IP4 . . . 139 F8
KINGSHALL GREEN . . 64 D7
Kingshall St IP30 . . . 64 D8
KINGSHALL STREET . . 64 D8
Kings Head La IP22 . . 19 A4
King's Head St **2**
  CO12 . . . . 107 C3
Kings Hill CO10 . . . . 148 E4
King's Hill CB9 . . . . 133 C7
King's La
  Blyford IP19 . . . . 42 C8
  Gosbeck IP6 . . . . 68 D3
  Long Melford CO10 . . 92 A7
  Sotherton NR34 . . . . 25 D2
  Tannington IP13 . . . . 55 B7
  Walsham le Willows
    IP31 . . . . 35 C3
  Weston NR34 . . . . . . 9 D1
Kingsland IP9 . . . . . 106 F5
Kingsland La **3**
  CO6 . . . . 102 A7
Kingsley Cl **8** IP1 . 135 A3
Kings Mead CB8 . . . . 60 E8
Kingsmead Cl **3**
  IP14 . . . . 124 C7
Kings Meadow
  Great Cornard CO10 . 148 E4
  Kedington CB9 . . . . . 133 C5
Kingsmead Rd IP14 . 124 C7
Kings Mws IP33 . . . . 154 B2
Kings Parade CB7 . . . 28 C3
King's Path CB7 . . . . 29 C1
Kings Pk IP29 . . . . . . 62 D5
Kings Quay St **9**
  CO12 . . . . 107 C3
Kings Rd
  Bungay NR35 . . . . . . 110 C2
  Glemsford CO10 . . . . 77 A3
  Leiston IP16 . . . . 129 C5
  Thurston IP31 . . . . . . 49 D4

King's Rd
  Bury St Edmunds
    IP33 . . . . 154 A2
  Harwich CO12 . . . . . 107 A2
  Topcroft NR35 . . . . . . 7 A8
King St
  Aldeburgh IP15 . . . . 130 E3
  Felixstowe IP11 . . . . 152 E6
  Ipswich IP1 . . . . 155 B3
  1 Mildenhall IP28 . 116 C4
  Sudbury CO10 . . . . . 148 C5
  Weybread IP21 . . . . . 22 D3
King's Theatre CB8 . 120 F3
KINGSTON 146 F2
Kingston Cl NR33 . . . 115 A3
Kingston Ct NR34 . . . 111 D5
Kingston Dr NR34 . . . 111 C5
Kingston Farm Rd
  IP12 . . . . 147 A4
Kingston Pas **3** CB8 121 A3
Kingston Rd
  Ipswich IP1 . . . . 138 F8
  Woodbridge IP12 . . . 147 A4
Kingsway
  4 Earsham NR35 . . . 7 F4
  9 Harwich CO12 . . . 107 B2
  Mildenhall IP28 . . . . 116 C4
  Newmarket CB8 . . . . 120 F4
  Woodbridge IP12 . . . 147 B5
King's Way IP3 . . . . 140 B2
Kingswood Ave
  NR33 . . . . 114 D4
Kingsworth Rd IP32 . 123 D6
King William St **3**
  IP6 . . . . 125 D5
Kinross Rd IP4 . . . . . 136 B1
Kinsey View IP5 . . . . 141 B6
Kipling Cl **5** NR33 . 111 C1
Kipling Rd IP1 . . . . . 134 F3
Kipling Way IP14 . . . 124 B8
KIRBY CANE 8 E8
Kirby Cane Wlk
  NR32 . . . . 113 A3
Kirby Cl IP4 . . . . 140 A7
Kirby La IP6 . . . . 83 B7
KIRBY ROW 8 E7
Kirby St IP4 . . . . 140 A7
Kirkdale Ct **4** NR33 . 115 B4
Kirkham Cl **2** IP2 . . 139 A2
KIRKLEY 115 B5
Kirkley Cliff Rd
  NR33 . . . . 115 C5
Kirkley Gdns NR33 . . 115 B6
Kirkley Pk Rd NR33 . 115 B6
Kirkley Rise NR33 . . . 115 C7
Kirkley Run NR33 . . . 115 A7
**Kirkley Sports & Fitness
  Ctr** NR33 . . . . 115 B7
Kirksdale Way **4**
  NR33 . . . . 113 A4
Kirkton Cl IP9 . . . . . 107 A5
Kirkwood Dr **1**
  NR33 . . . . 114 C3
KIRTLING 60 E3
KIRTLING GREEN . . . 60 E2
Kirtling Pl **3** CB8 . . 132 F6
Kirtling Rd CB8 . . . . 60 E5
KIRTON 98 E2
Kirton Rd IP11 . . . . . 107 D8
Kismet Cl **6** IP31 . . 49 A4
Kitchener Cl IP27 . . . 109 D7
Kitchener Rd
  Ipswich IP1 . . . . 138 F8
  Leiston IP16 . . . . 129 C6
Kitchener Way **5**
  IP9 . . . . 107 A5
Kitchen Hill CO10 . . . 91 D4
Kite Cres **10** IP14 . . 124 F7
Kitson Meadows
  IP33 . . . . 122 A5
Kitten La CB9 . . . . . . 133 A6
Kittiwake Cl
  Ipswich IP2 . . . . 138 E3
  Lowestoft NR33 . . . . 114 D5
Kittiwake Ct IP14 . . . 124 F6
Klondyke IP32 . . . . . 122 F8
Knaves Acre Dro CB7 . 29 B6
KNAVES GREEN 53 A5
Knaves La NR35 . . . . . 7 C8
KNETTISHALL 17 F3
**Knettishall Heath Ctry
  Pk** ★ IP31 . . . . 17 E3
**Knettishall Heath Nature
  Reserve** ★ IP22 . . . . 17 E3
Knettishall Rd IP22 . . 17 E3
Knight Rd IP12 . . . . . 85 D8
Knights Cl
  7 Debenham IP14 . . . 53 F2
  10 Felixstowe IP11 . 153 D6
  6 Manningtree CO11 104 E2
  4 Old Newton with
    Dagworth IP14 . . . . 51 E1
Knights Ct
  19 Haverhill CB9 . . . 132 C5
  Roman Hill NR32 . . . 113 C1
Knightsdale Rd IP1 . . 135 A6
Knights Farm La IP9 106 D5
Knights La **5** IP5 . . . 141 D7
Knights Way IP11 . . . 126 C2
Knightswood **3**
  NR32 . . . . 113 B5
Knights Yd NR34 . . . 111 B6
KNODISHALL 73 A4
**KNODISHALL
  COMMON** 129 A2
Knoll Cl IP22 . . . . . . 36 A8

Knoll The IP13 . . . . . 126 D3
Knowle The **17** IP31 . 34 E4
KNOWL GREEN 90 C4
Knox La IP31 . . . . 34 C4
Knutsford Cl IP8 . . . . 138 C1
Kreswell Gr **7** CO12 . 107 A1
Kylborne Cl IP33 . . . 122 C4
Kyson Hill ★ IP12 . . . 146 F2
Kyson Prim Sch
  IP12 . . . . 146 D4

L

Laburnham Gdns **17**
  IP12 . . . . 84 A1
Laburnum Ave IP28 . 116 E5
Laburnum Cl
  Ipswich IP3 . . . . 140 D2
  3 Ipswich IP8 . . . . 138 C2
  Red Lodge IP28 . . . . . 30 B1
  Worlingworth IP13 . . . 54 E7
Laburnum Dr IP14 . . . 80 C8
Laburnum Gdns IP5 . 136 E1
Laburnum La **11** CB5 . 44 A6
Laburnum Rd **3**
  NR35 . . . . 110 B3
Laburnum Way **2**
  CO6 . . . . 102 C5
Lacewing Cl **18** IP8 . 142 E8
Lacey's La CB8 . . . . . 120 B7
Lacey St IP7 . . . . 139 E6
Lachlan Gn IP12 . . . . 146 F2
LACKFORD 31 F1
Lackford La IP28 . . . . 47 D6
Lackford Pl IP12 . . . . 80 E1
**Lackford Wildfowl Nature
  Reserve** ★ IP28 . . . . 31 F1
Lacon Rd **2** IP8 . . . . 134 A2
Ladbroke Cl IP7 . . . . 80 E1
Ladbrooke Cl **1** IP22 . 20 C2
Ladbrook Meadow
  IP8 . . . . 95 C5
Ladder Field IP8 . . . . 138 B6
Ladyfield IP14 . . . . . 66 D8
Ladygate **1** CB9 . . . 132 C4
Lady La
  Hadleigh IP7 . . . . . . 149 E7
  Ipswich IP1 . . . . 155 A3
Lady La Ind Est IP7 . 149 E7
Lady Margaret Gdns
  IP12 . . . . 146 D4
Lady Miriam Way
  CB8 . . . . 120 F6
Lady Rd **23** IP31 . . . . 49 E4
LADY'S GREEN 61 F6
Lady's La IP22 . . . . . 19 F5
Lady's Meadow
  NR34 . . . . 111 B6
Lady St **15** CO10 . . . 78 D4
Ladywell Rd IP4 . . . . 51 F7
Ladywood Rd IP4 . . . 140 C7
Lagonda Dr IP1 . . . . 134 C1
La Grange Pl CB8 . . . 120 B8
La Hogue Rd CB7 . . . 45 D7
Lake Ave IP32 . . . . . . 48 C5
Lakeland Dr NR32 . . . 112 F1
Lakelands **3** IP26 . . . 5 A3
LAKENHEATH 109 E7
Lakenheath Airfield
  IP27 . . . . 14 A5
**Lakenheath American
  Elementary Sch**
  IP27 . . . . 14 A3
**Lakenheath Com Prim
  Sch** IP27 . . . . 109 D6
**Lakenheath Fen Nature
  Reserve** ★ IP27 . . . . . 4 F1
Lakenheath Mid Sch
  IP26 . . . . 4 D5
**Lakenheath Senior High
  Sch** IP27 . . . . 109 F1
Lakenheath Sta IP27 . . 4 F1
Lake Side IP14 . . . . . 124 C6
Lakeside Ave IP16 . . . 73 E6
Lakeside Cl
  2 Ipswich IP2 . . . . . 138 E3
  Reydon IP18 . . . . . . 119 B7
Lakeside Pk Dr IP18 . 119 B6
Lakeside Rd IP2 . . . . 138 E2
Lakeside Rise NR32 . 112 C8
Lakes Rd IP21 . . . . . . 21 D5
Lakeview Meadow
  IP22 . . . . 36 B7
Lake View Rd NR33 . 114 E8
Lake View Terr NR33 114 F8
Lakforth **4** CO10 . . . 91 E8
LAMARSH 101 A6
Lamarsh Hill **1** CO8 . 101 C5
Lamarsh Rd CO8 . . . 101 A6
LAMB CORNER 103 E2
Lamb Ct IP28 . . . . . . 116 D2
Lambden Cl NR32 . . . 112 D3
Lambert Cl
  Framlingham IP13 . . . 126 C3
  Hadleigh IP7 . . . . . . 149 D7
  Halesworth IP19 . . . . 118 B3
  Weeting IP27 . . . . 5 E4
Lambert Dr CO10 . . . . 92 B7
Lamberts Cl
  21 Feltwell IP26 . . . . 4 E5
  21 Feltwell IP26 . . . . 4 E5
Lamberts La **5** IP25 . 136 D2
Lambert's La
  Mendlesham IP14 . . . 52 C3
  Sudbourne IP12 . . . . 73 B1
Lambert's Way NR35 110 C6
Lambeth Cl **1** IP1 . . . 139 A7

Lambeth Way IP14 . . . 67 F2
LAMBFAIR GREEN . . . 75 A8
Lamble Cl IP28 . . . . . 30 B8
Lambourne Cl **3**
  IP32 . . . . 123 E6
Lambourne Rd IP1 . . 135 B4
Lambsale Meadow
  IP17 . . . . 128 D4
Lambeth St IP23 . . . . 117 C3
Lambs La IP29 . . . . . . 63 D1
Lamdin Rd IP32 . . . . 48 C5
Lamdin Road Ind Est
  IP32 . . . . 48 C5
Lammas Cl IP31 . . . . . 34 C4
LAMPARDBROOK . . . 70 E8
Lampards Brook
  IP13 . . . . 126 A1
Lanarch Dr **2** CB8 . . 45 F5
Lanark Rd IP4 . . . . . . 136 B1
Lancaster Ave IP32 . . 122 F8
Lancaster Cl IP29 . . . 62 C4
Lancaster Dr **8** IP5 . . 98 A7
Lancaster Rd
  5 Feltwell IP26 . . . . . 4 E5
  Ipswich IP4 . . . . 139 E6
  7 Mildenhall IP28 . . . 30 A8
  Sudbury CO10 . . . . . 148 B8
Lancaster Way
  10 Claydon IP6 . . . . 82 B5
  Stradishall CB8 . . . . 75 C7
Lancelot Rd **1** NR31 . 3 A8
Lancers The IP12 . . . 146 E3
Lancewood Wlk **27**
  IP27 . . . . 13 F2
Lancing Ave IP4 . . . . 140 A8
Landguard Fort ★
  IP11 . . . . 107 E2
**Landguard Nature
  Reserve** ★ IP11 . . . . 107 E2
Landguard Rd IP11 . 153 I11
Landsdown Rd
  CO10 . . . . 148 E2
Landseer Cl IP3 . . . . 140 A1
Landseer Ct **1** CB9 . 132 D4
Landseer Rd IP3 . . . . 139 E2
Landspring La NR33 . 114 E6
LANDWADE 44 D6
Landwade Rd CB8 . . . 44 D6
Lanecroft **3** IP30 . . . 65 D8
Lane End **14** CB9 . . . 74 A1
Lanercost Way IP2 . . 139 A1
Lane The
  Creeting St Peter or West
    Creeting IP6 . . . . . 67 B5
  3 Mistley CO11 . . . 104 F2
  Wrentham NR34 . . . . 26 E5
  Yoxford IP17 . . . . . . 57 C8
Langdale Cl **3** IP11 . 153 D6
Langdale Pk NR31 . . . 2 A1
Langer Prim Acad
  IP11 . . . . 152 E2
Langer Rd IP11 . . . . . 152 E2
Langford Cl IP14 . . . 124 B8
Lang Gate Way NR35 . 7 B6
LANGHAM
  Bury St Edmunds 50 D8
  Stratford St Mary . . . 103 D2
Langham La CO4 . . . 103 B1
Langham Oaks Sch
  CO4 . . . . 103 C2
Langham Pl **6** CO12 106 D1
Langham Prim Sch
  CO4 . . . . 103 C2
Langham Rd
  Blaxhall IP12 . . . . . . 72 B4
  Boxted CO4 . . . . 102 F1
  Hunston IP31 . . . . . . 50 D7
Langham Way **2** CB9 . 74 A1
Langley Ave IP11 . . . 152 E4
Langley Cl
  Felixstowe IP11 . . . . 152 E5
  18 Harwich CO12 . . 107 B2
Langley Gdns NR33 . 114 F5
Langley Hill CO8 . . . . 101 B6
Langley La NR35 . . . . 7 F4
Langmere Rd IP21 . . . 21 C4
Langridge The IP31 . . 34 B2
Langshaw Cl IP13 . . . 126 A4
Langstons IP11 . . . . . 152 D7
LANGTON GREEN . . . 117 D4
Langton Green IP23 . 117 B5
Langton Grove IP23 . 117 C5
Langton Pk IP23 . . . . 117 C5
Langton Rd **4** IP23 . 122 D4
Langwoods IP23 . . . . 37 A1
Lanman Mus ★ IP13 . 126 D4
Lansbury Rd IP19 . . . 118 B3
Lansdowne Rd
  Felixstowe IP11 . . . . 153 B6
  Ipswich IP4 . . . . 140 A5
  Lowestoft NR33 . . . . 114 F3
Lanwades Bsns Pk
  CB8 . . . . 46 A5
Lapwing Cl
  10 Diss IP22 . . . . . . 20 D3
  17 Thurston IP31 . . . 49 D4
Lapwing Ct **4** IP28 . 116 D4
Lapwing Gr IP14 . . . 124 F6
Lapwing Rd IP2 . . . . 138 D3
Lapwings IP15 . . . . . 130 D5
Lapwing Way CB7 . . . 28 C5
Larch Cl IP27 . . . . . . 109 D7
Larchcroft Cl IP1 . . . 135 B2
Larchcroft Rd IP1 . . . 135 A2
Larches The NR34 . . . 26 E5
Larch Gr **6** CO6 . . . 102 C5
Larch Rd NR32 . . . . . 113 B3
Larchwood Cl CB8 . . 138 C5

Larchwood Rd **41**
  IP28 . . . . 30 C1
Larch Way
  7 Red Lodge CB8 . . . 46 A8
  42 Red Lodge IP28 . . 30 C1
Larcoms Lawne IP13 . 70 A7
Largent Gr IP5 . . . . . 141 E8
Lark Bank CB7 . . . . . 12 A5
Lark Cl
  4 Stowmarket IP14 . . 67 A5
  Worlington IP28 . . . . 30 A4
Lark Hall Corner Rd
  CB8 . . . . 59 A1
Larkhall Rd CB7 . . . . 28 F1
Lark Hill CB8 . . . . . . 45 F3
Larkhill Rise IP4 . . . 140 E5
Larkhill Way **9** IP11 . 152 D5
Lark Rd IP28 . . . . . . 116 D4
Lark Rise
  28 Martlesham Heath
    IP5 . . . . 98 A8
  Sudbury CO10 . . . . . 148 B3
Larks Cl CB9 . . . . . . 133 A5
Larksfield Cres **5**
  CO12 . . . . 107 A2
Larksfield Rd IP9 . . . 105 D5
Larks Gate IP28 . . . . 48 C6
Larkspur Cl
  Corton NR32 . . . . . . 113 B8
  1 Red Lodge IP28 . . . 30 B1
Larkspur Rd IP2 . . . . 138 F3
Larks Rise IP19 . . . . 118 C3
Larksway IP11 . . . . . 152 D3
Lark Valley Dr **9**
  IP28 . . . . 48 C6
Larters La IP14 . . . . . 67 D8
La Salle Cl IP2 . . . . . 139 B3
Lathbury Ct IP33 . . . 154 B3
Latimer Cl IP3 . . . . . 144 F8
Lattens Sq **4** NR32 . 113 C2
Lattice Ave IP4 . . . . . 140 C6
LATTINFORD HILL . . 151 D8
Laud Mews IP3 . . . . 140 A2
Laud's Cl IP11 . . . . . 152 B8
Laundry La
  Bury St Edmunds
    IP33 . . . . 123 B3
  Gislingham IP23 . . . . 36 F2
  Huntingfield IP19 . . . 41 A4
Laundry Rd IP12 . . . . 85 F1
Launds Farm La CO10 . 89 E5
Laureate Com Prim Sch
  CB8 . . . . 120 E6
Laureate Gdns CB8 . . 120 E6
Laureate Paddocks
  CB8 . . . . 120 F6
Laureate Sch Rd
  CB8 . . . . 120 E6
Laurel Ave
  1 Harwich CO12 . . . 106 F1
  Ipswich IP5 . . . . 141 A7
Laurel Cl
  Haverhill CB9 . . . . . 132 B7
  7 Holywell Row IP28 . 30 C8
  7 Red Lodge IP28 . . . 30 C1
  Sutton IP9 . . . . 105 D5
  19 Thurstow IP31 . . . 49 D4
Laurel Ct **9** IP30 . . . . 50 F2
Laurel Dr
  13 Claydon IP6 . . . . . 82 A5
  8 Long Melford CO10 . 91 E8
Laurel Farm Rd IP19 . 42 D6
Laurelhayes IP2 . . . . 139 A3
Laurel Rd NR33 . . . . . 115 B6
Laurels The
  8 Hopton on Sea
    NR31 . . . . 3 B7
  Worlingham NR34 . . . 111 F3
Laurel Way **5** IP6 . . . 134 C8
Laurel Wlk IP11 . . . . 153 D7
Lavender Cl
  Lowestoft NR33 . . . . 114 F7
  3 Red Lodge IP28 . . . 30 B1
Lavender Field IP30 . 132 B6
Lavender Hill IP2 . . . 138 F4
LAVENHAM 78 D4
Lavenham Com Prim Sch
  CO10 . . . . 78 D4
**Lavenham Guildhall of
  Corpus Christi** ★
  CO10 . . . . 78 E4
Lavenham Rd
  Button's Green IP30 . . 78 F7
  Great Waldingfield
    CO10 . . . . 78 D1
  Ipswich IP2 . . . . 138 E5
  Lavenham CO10 . . . . 78 F5
Lavenham Studios
  CO10 . . . . 78 E4
Lavenham Way
  5 Lowestoft NR32 . . 112 F4
  4 Stowmarket IP14 . 124 E3
LAWFORD 104 D1
Lawford CE VA Prim Sch
  CO11 . . . . 104 D1
Lawford Pl CO11 . . . 104 D2
Lawn Dr IP30 . . . . . . 50 D3
Lawn Gr NR32 . . . . . 112 F5
Lawns The IP4 . . . . . 140 C8
Lawn Way IP11 . . . . . 152 E5
Lawrence Dr NR32 . . 113 B6
Lawrence Rd **2** IP24 . 16 D7
Law's Drift IP10 . . . . 98 C2
LAWSHALL 63 E1
LAWSHALL GREEN . . . 77 F8
Lawshall Rd
  Hartest IP29 . . . . 77 B8
  Hawstead IP29 . . . . . 63 D4

Kil–Ley **173**

Lawshall Rd continued
  Lawshall Green IP29 . . 78 A8
Lawshall Row IP29 . . 63 D2
Lawson Cl **2** NR33 . . 115 C7
Lawson Pl IP32 . . . . . 123 E5
Lawson Rd NR33 . . . . 115 C7
Lawsons Yard IP33 . . 154 B3
LAXFIELD 40 C3
Laxfield & District Mus ★
  IP13 . . . . 40 B3
Laxfield Rd
  Badingham IP13 . . . . 56 B8
  Dennington IP13 . . . . 55 E6
  Fressingfield IP21 . . . 39 F7
  Goddard's Corner IP13 . 55 E7
  Heveningham IP19 . . . 40 F4
  Laxfield IP13 . . . . . . 40 C1
  Stradbroke IP21 . . . . 39 E4
Laxfield Way NR33 . . 114 F4
Layard Cl IP4 . . . . . . 141 A6
Layer Rd CB9 . . . . . . 132 C5
Layham Dr **4** IP32 . . 123 A8
Layham Gdns IP14 . . 124 F3
Layham Rd
  Hadleigh IP7 . . . . . . 149 D4
  Shelley IP7 . . . . 94 D1
Layhill Rd IP32 . . . . . 123 D5
Laywood Cl **1** IP32 . . 123 D6
Layzell Croft CO10 . . 92 B2
Leabrook Cl IP32 . . . 123 E6
Leader's Way CB8 . . . 120 E4
Leamans La IP14 . . . . 52 A7
Lea Rd **14** IP32 . . . . . 50 F2
Lea's Drift **1** NR33 . . 114 C5
Leas The NR32 . . . . . 112 F5
Lea The IP18 . . . . . . 119 B2
Leather Bottle Hill
  IP8 . . . . 81 E3
Leather La
  Great Yeldham CO9 . . 90 A1
  Haverhill CB9 . . . . . 132 C5
Leathes Hill IP12 . . . 112 F1
**Leathes Ham Nature
  Reserve** ★ NR32 . . . 113 A1
LEAVENHEATH 102 B7
Leech Wlk IP32 . . . . . 122 E8
Lee Cl CB9 . . . . 132 D8
Lee Gdns NR34 . . . . . 111 F4
Leeks Cl IP7 . . . . 149 D7
Leeks Hill IP12 . . . . . 147 A7
Leeper Cl IP23 . . . . . 36 F5
Lee Rd
  Aldeburgh IP15 . . . . 130 E3
  Harwich CO12 . . . . . 107 B2
  Ipswich IP3 . . . . 139 F3
Lees Ct **11** CO10 . . . 77 A2
Lee Wlk CB9 . . . . 132 C5
Leggatt Dr IP8 . . . . . 134 A2
Leggett Wlk NR34 . . 111 D4
Legion Rise IP31 . . . . 34 C4
Le Grice Wlk IP32 . . 122 E7
Leicester Cl IP2 . . . . 138 F1
Leighton Rd IP3 . . . . 144 A8
Leighton Sq **8** IP3 . . 144 A8
LEISTON 129 E5
Leiston Abbey ★ IP16 . 58 C3
Leiston Leisure Ctr
  IP16 . . . . 129 E5
Leiston Prim Sch
  IP16 . . . . 129 E6
Leiston Rd
  Aldeburgh IP15 . . . . 130 D7
  Coldfair Green IP17 . . 129 B3
  Eastbridge IP16 . . . . 58 D4
  Haverhill CB9 . . . . . 132 C5
  4 Lowestoft NR32 . . 113 D1
  Saxmundham IP17 . . . 57 E1
  Saxmundham IP17 . . 128 F3
  Theberton IP16 . . . . . 58 B5
Leisure Way NR32 . . 113 B7
Lely Rd IP3 . . . . 143 F8
Lemons Hill IP9 . . . . 105 B8
Lennox Dr CO11 . . . . 104 D1
Lentins The IP14 . . . . 68 E6
Leona Cres NR33 . . . 114 C2
Leonard Dr **2** NR32 . 113 A6
Leonard's La IP26 . . . . 4 D5
Leopold Gdns IP4 . . . 140 B8
Leopold Rd
  Felixstowe IP11 . . . . 153 A3
  Ipswich IP4 . . . . 140 B7
Les Ager Dr **8** CB9 . . 132 E6
Leslie Rd IP3 . . . . . . 140 C1
Lester Piggott Way
  CB8 . . . . 120 F6
LETHERINGHAM 70 C4
Letton Cl IP9 . . . . . . 150 E3
Levant Cl IP30 . . . . . 50 F3
Leverett's La IP18 . . . 119 C2
LEVINGTON 145 E3
Levington Ct NR33 . . 115 D8
Levington La IP10 . . . 98 A3
Levington Rd
  Felixstowe IP11 . . . . 152 E1
  Ipswich IP3 . . . . 140 A4
  Nacton IP10 . . . . 145 C4
Lewes Cl IP3 . . . . . . 140 E3
Lewis Cl
  Ditchingham NR35 . . 110 C8
  Hopton IP22 . . . . 18 C2
Lewis Dr **7** IP22 . . . . 20 B3
Lewis La IP9 . . . . . . 105 B5
Lewis Wlk NR34 . . . . 111 D4
Ley Rd
  Barrow IP29 . . . . 47 A2

Ley Rd continued
Stetchworth CB8. . . . . . .**60** A5
Leys La IP23 . . . .**37** B5
Leys Rd
Barnardiston CB9 . . . . . .**75** B3
Tostock IP30 . . . .**50** B2
Leyton Ave IP28 . . . . . .**116** B6
Liberator Cl 15 CO10 . . .**92** C6
Liberator Cres 14 IP26 . .**4** B5
Liberty Cl IP32 . . . .**123** F6
LIDGATE **61** C4
Lidgate Ct 1 IP11 . . . **152** C4
Lidgate Rd
Dalham CB8 . . . .**61** C8
Upend CB8 . . . .**61** A5
Lighthouse Score 2
NR32 . . . .**113** E3
Lilac Cl IP27 . . . .**14** D8
Lilac Dr
Lakenheath IP27 . . . . . .**109** D6
Lowestoft NR32 . . . .**113** B3
Lilac Wlk IP6 . . . .**125** D3
Lilley Cl IP33 . . . .**122** C3
Lily La NR34 . . . .**10** A7
Lily Cl 13 IP28 . . . .**30** B1
Lily Way NR33 . . . .**114** C5
Lime Ave
Harwich CO12 . . . .**107** A2
Lowestoft NR32 . . . . . .**112** D2
Lime Cl
Burwell CB5 . . . .**44** B5
7 Harleston IP20 . . . . . .**22** D5
Lakenheath IP27 . . . . . .**109** D5
Mildenhall IP28 . . . . . .**116** E5
14 Red Lodge IP28 . . . .**30** B1
6 Ufford IP13 . . . .**84** F7
Wickham Market IP13 . .**127** B6
Limecroft Cl 1 IP1 . **135** A4
Lime Gr
Sudbury CO10 . . . .**148** A3
Woodbridge IP12 . . . .**146** F6
Limekiln Cl 7 IP6 . . **134** C8
Lime Kiln La 25 IP26 . . .**4** F7
Lime Kiln Quay IP12 . .**147** B5
Lime Kiln Quay Rd
IP12. . . . .**147** B5
Limerick Cl IP1 . . . . . .**134** E2
Limes Cl 9 IP22 . . . .**20** C1
Limes The
Framlingham IP13 . . . . .**126** B4
Halesworth IP19 . . . . . .**118** A3
6 Horringer IP29 . . . . . .**63** A8
Long Melford CO10 . . . .**91** E8
Rushmere St Andrew
IP5 . . . .**136** D1
Limestone Cl
19 Great Blakenham
IP6 . . . .**82** A5
12 Isleham CB7 . . . .**29** C5
Limetree Ave IP11 . . . .**152** D2
Limetree Cl IP8 . . . .**134** C2
Lime Tree Cl 3 IP30 . . .**64** F8
Limetree Dr IP3 . . . . . .**140** D2
Lime Tree Farm La
IP13. . . . .**71** C4
Limetree La IP12 . . . . . .**72** A3
Lime Tree Pl
Ipswich IP1 . . . .**138** E7
Stowmarket IP14 . . . . .**124** E5
Lime Wlk IP30 . . . .**65** A3
Lime Way IP21 . . . .**21** C5
Limmer Ave IP21 . . . . . .**21** C5
Lincoln Ave IP17 . . . . .**128** E2
Lincoln Cl IP1 . . . .**135** B3
Lincoln Ct 1 NR32 . . . . .**3** D4
Lincoln Gdns 8 IP6. . .**82** B5
Lincoln Gn IP33 . . . . . .**123** B2
Lincoln La CO6 . . . .**102** C1
Lincoln Rd 10 IP28 . . . .**30** A8
Lincoln Terr IP11 . . . . .**152** F3
Linda Cl 11 NR32 . . . . . .**3** D4
Lindbergh Rd IP3 . . . . .**140** C1
Linden Cl
Aldeburgh IP15 . . . . . .**130** D6
20 Manningtree CO11 .**104** D2
Linden Dr 44 IP28 . . . .**30** C1
Linden Gr 12 IP22 . . . . .**20** C3
Linden Rd IP15 . . . . . .**130** C5
Linden Wlk 15 IP28 . . .**30** B1
Lindisfarne Cl IP2 . . . .**139** A1
Lindisfarne Rd IP33 . .**122** D2
LINDSEY **93** D7
Lindsey Ave CO10 . . . . .**148** F4
Lindsey Rd
Chelsworth Common
IP7 . . . .**79** E2
Ipswich IP4 . . . .**140** C7
Swingleton Green IP7. . .**79** D1
LINDSEY TYE **93** E8
Lindsey Way IP14 . . . .**124** E3
Linen Post La NR31 . . . .**3** A6
Lines Cl 25 CB7 . . . .**28** D4
Lingfield Rd IP1 . . . . . .**135** B4
Lingheath Rd
Brandon IP27 . . . .**6** A1
Elveden IP27 . . . .**15** A8
Ling Rd
Palgrave IP22. . . . .**20** B2
Wortham IP22 . . . .**19** F2
Lings Field IP19 . . . .**70** C7
Lingside 1 IP5 . . . .**98** A7
Ling's La IP9 . . . .**106** B7
Lingwood Cl IP31 . . . . . .**34** F7

Link La
Baylham IP6 . . . .**81** D5
Bentley IP9 . . . .**104** E7
Link Rd
Capel St Mary IP9 . . . .**150** E3
7 Shotley Gate IP9 . . . .**107** A5
Links Ave IP11 . . . .**153** B6
Links Cl
Bury St Edmunds
IP33 . . . .**123** B1
10 Glemsford CO10 . . . .**77** B3
Lowestoft NR33 . . . . . .**114** F5
Worlington IP28 . . . .**30** B4
Links Ct NR32 . . . .**113** D5
Linksfield IP5 . . . .**140** E7
Linksfield Gdns IP5 . .**140** E7
Links Rd
Great Yarmouth NR31. . . .**3** B8
Lowestoft NR32 . . . . . .**113** D5
Links The
Flempton IP28 . . . .**32** B1
Woodditton CB8 . . . .**59** E8
Links View
Newton CO10 . . . .**92** D3
Newton CO10 . . . .**92** D3
Link The IP9 . . . .**104** E7
Linkwood Rd IP30 . . . . .**64** B7
Linnet Dr 14 IP14 . . . . .**67** A5
Linnet Pl IP33 . . . .**154** C1
Linnet Rd
Bury St Edmunds
IP33 . . . .**122** E4
Ipswich IP2 . . . .**138** D4
Linnetts La CB9 . . . . . .**133** E2
Linstead Farm La
IP19. . . . .**40** C6
LINSTEAD PARVA **40** E8
Linstead Parva Rd
IP19. . . . .**24** A1
Linstead Rd IP19 . . . . . .**40** F5
Linton Cl CB8 . . . .**120** F5
Linton Gdns IP33 . . . .**122** E3
Linton Pl 2 CB9 . . . . . .**132** E6
Lintotts Rd IP17 . . . . . .**56** E6
Linx The IP13 . . . .**40** B3
Lion Barn Ind Est
IP5 . . . .**125** F3
Lionel Hurst Cl 15
CO10 . . . .**92** B3
Lion Green 14 IP29 . . . .**47** A2
Lion La IP6 . . . .**125** E3
Lion Lane Ind Est
IP6 . . . .**125** E4
Lion Meadow CB9 . . . . .**88** D4
Lion Rd
Glemsford CO10 . . . .**77** A3
Palgrave IP22. . . . .**20** B1
Wortham IP22 . . . .**36** F8
Lion St IP1 . . . .**155** B3
Lisburn Rd CB8 . . . . . .**121** B3
Lister Rd
Hadleigh IP7 . . . .**149** F5
Ipswich IP1 . . . .**134** F1
LISTON **91** D7
Liston La CO10 . . . .**91** D7
Litchfield 20 CO12. . . .**106** F1
Litchmere La NR35 . . . . .**8** D8
Lithgo Paddock 8
IP31. . . . .**49** A4
Little Back La IP9 . . . . .**53** E4
Little Bank Drove CB7 .**28** E4
LITTLE BEALINGS **137** E5
LITTLE BLAKENHAM . . .**81** F3
LITTLE BRADLEY **74** E6
Little Chadacre IP29 . .**77** F8
LITTLE CORNARD **92** C2
LITTLE DITTON **59** E5
Little Fen Dro CB5 . . . .**44** A7
LITTLE FINBOROUGH . .**66** B1
Littlegarth Sch CO4. .**102** D4
Little Gipping St 1 IP1 **155** A3
LITTLE GLEMHAM **71** E5
Little Gn
Cheveley CB8 . . . .**60** E6
Earl Soham IP13 . . . .**54** F1
Elmswell IP30 . . . .**50** E2
Little Gn Cl IP23 . . . . . .**36** C3
Little Gr IP9 . . . .**150** E2
LITTLE GREEN
Burgate **36** D5
Burgate IP22 . . . .**36** D6
Gislingham **36** C3
Little Green IP21. . . . . .**37** B7
Little Gulls IP9 . . . . . .**150** E6
Little Hall Mus ★
CO10. . . . .**78** E4
Little Hasse Dro CB7 . .**28** E6
Little Heath Thetford IP24 **16**
Little Hill IP7 . . . .**80** E5
LITTLE HORKESLEY . .**102** B3
Little Horkesley Rd
CO6 . . . .**102** A2
Little Horringer
IP29. . . . .**122** A2
Little Horsey Pk IP13. .**71** C2
Little Hyde Cl CO9 . . . .**90** A1
Little Hyde Rd CO9 . . . .**90** A1
LITTLE KNOWLES
GREEN **62** B5
Little La IP13 . . . .**127** C6
LITTLE LONDON **66** E2
Little London IP27 . . . .**13** F1
Little London Drove
CB7 . . . .**29** B5
Little London Hill
IP14. . . . .**53** E4
Little London La
Isleham CB7 . . . .**29** B5

Little London La continued
Stowmarket IP14 . . . . .**66** E2
Stowmarket IP14 . . . . .**124** E1
Little Lonely Farm Rd
IP13. . . . .**56** B2
Little Lumpkid IP7 . . . .**149** E8
Little Meadows Dr
IP6 . . . .**69** C2
Little Mill La IP29 . . . . .**47** A3
Littlemoor Rd IP17. . . .**57** E6
Little Orchard IP9 . . . .**105** E7
Little Oulsham Dro
IP26. . . . .**4** B6
Little St John's St 8
IP32. . . . .**147** A5
Little St Mary's CO10 . .**91** E7
Little's Cres IP27 . . . .**155** B1
Little St IP17 . . . .**57** C8
LITTLE STONHAM **67** F6
LITTLE THURLOW **74** E5
LITTLE THURLOW
GREEN **74** E6
Little Tufts IP9 . . . . . .**150** F3
LITTLE
WALDINGFIELD **92** B8
LITTLE WELNETHAM .**64** B6
LITTLE WELNETHAM .**64** B6
Little Whip St IP2. . . .**155** B1
LITTLE WHITTINGHAM
GREEN **40** A8
LITTLE WRATTING **74** E2
LITTLE YELDHAM **90** B2
Little Yeldham Rd
CO9 . . . .**90** B2
Littleyfield Drove
IP28. . . . .**13** D2
Livermere Drift IP31 . .**48** E6
Livermere Rd
Great Barton IP31 . . . . .**49** A6
Great Livermere IP31. . .**33** C3
Timworth IP31 . . . .**48** F8
Troston IP31 . . . .**33** D2
Lizards Way 2 IP28. . . .**30** C8
Lizzie's La IP17 . . . .**36** A7
Llewellyn Drift 8
IP5. . . . .**141** C7
Lloyd Rd
3 Shotley Gate IP9 . . .**107** A4
Woodbridge IP12 . . . . .**146** F6
Lloyds Ave
Ipswich IP1 . . . .**155** B3
15 Kessingland NR33 . . .**11** B1
Lloyds The IP5 . . . .**141** C7
Loam Pit La IP18 . . . . .**118** C4
Locarno Rd 1 IP3 . . . .**140** B3
Loch Rannoch Cl 4
IP30. . . . .**50** E2
Lock Cl 14 IP14 . . . .**53** F2
Lockhart Rd NR35 . . . . . .**8** D7
Lockington Cl 4
IP14. . . . .**124** E5
Lockington Cres
IP14. . . . .**124** D5
Lockington Rd IP14. . .**124** D5
Lockington Wlk
IP14. . . . .**124** D5
Locks La
26 Beck Row IP28 . . . . .**30** B8
Pinewood NR35 . . . .**8** F6
Lock's La
6 Leavenheath
CO6 . . . .**102** A7
Shipmeadow NR34 . . . . .**8** F5
Wrentham NR34 . . . .**26** F6
Lock's Rd NR34 . . . .**25** C5
Lockwood Cl 1
IP12. . . . .**147** A5
Loddon Rd
Ditchingham NR35 . . . .**110** C7
Gillingham NR34 . . . .**9** B6
Kirby Cane NR35. . . . . . .**8** F8
Lode Cl 1 CB7 . . . .**28** D3
Lode La CB7 . . . .**28** A1
Lodeside Drove CB5. . . .**44** A6
Lodge
Great Barton IP31 . . . . .**49** B6
Old Newton IP14 . . . . . .**51** E1
21 Thurston IP31 . . . . .**49** E4
Lodge Farm Dr
IP11. . . . .**153** C5
Lodge Farm La
Barsham NR34 . . . .**9** B4
6 Melton IP12. . . . .**84** E6
Lodge Farm Rd
Charsfield IP13. . . . .**70** D3
Glemsford CO10 . . . .**77** B1
Lodge La
Blythburgh IP19 . . . .**42** F5
Claydon IP6 . . . .**134** A8
Riddlesworth IP22 . . . . .**18** A3
Shelfanger IP22 . . . .**20** B5
Troston IP31 . . . .**33** D3
Wissett IP19 . . . .**24** D2
Lodge Rd
Cransford IP13 . . . .**56** C3
Feltwell IP26 . . . .**4** F6
Great Bealings IP13 . . .**137** E5
Hollesley IP12 . . . .**99** D7
Holton IP19 . . . .**118** E5
Ipswich IP9 . . . .**142** B2
St John, Ilketshall NR34
NR35 . . . .**110** F2
1 Ufford IP13 . . . .**84** F7
Walberswick IP18 . . . . . .**19** E2
Lodge Way IP24 . . . .**16** B7
Lofft Cl 11 IP31 . . . .**34** E4
Loftus Ave IP18. . . . . . .**19** D5

Loganberry Rd 4
IP3. . . . .**144** C7
Loggers La IP22 . . . .**18** E1
Loke The
Blundeston NR32 . . . .**3** A4
Ditchingham NR35 . . . .**110** B7
Lombard Ct IP1 . . . . . .**139** F7
Lombardy Rd CO10 . . .**148** B8
Lonbarn Hill CO11. . . .**105** D1
London City Rd IP21 . . .**39** C3
London La
Harleston IP14 . . . .**66** C7
4 Mundford IP26 . . . .**6** B8
London Rd
Beccles NR34 . . . .**111** B2
Blythburgh IP19 . . . .**42** E5
Brampton with Stoven
NR34 . . . .**25** E6
Brandon IP27 . . . .**14** E8
Capel St Mary IP9 . . . .**150** E2
Copdock & Washbrook
IP8 . . . .**138** A1
Elveden IP24 . . . .**15** C2
Elveden IP24 . . . .**15** E3
Great Horkesley CO6 . .**102** C1
Halesworth IP19 . . . . . .**118** A2
Harleston IP20 . . . .**22** D5
Icklingham IP27 . . . .**31** E8
Ipswich IP1 . . . .**155** A3
Kessingland NR33 . . . . .**11** B2
Lowestoft NR33 . . . . . .**115** A2
Pinewood IP8 . . . .**138** B2
Thetford IP24 . . . .**16** A5
Uggeshall NR34 . . . .**25** F3
Westley Waterless CB8 .**59** A4
Weston NR34 . . . .**9** D2
Wrentham NR34 . . . .**26** E4
London Rd N IP26 . . . .**113** D1
London Rd Pakefield
NR33 . . . .**115** C4
London Rd S NR33 . . . .**115** C5
Londs La CO6 . . . .**103** A7
Lone Barn Ct IP1. . . . .**138** D8
Lonely Rd IP21 . . . .**21** C6
Longacre IP17 . . . .**58** C8
Long Acre
Kirtling Green CB8 . . . . .**60** D2
Lowestoft NR33 . . . . . .**115** B3
Southwold IP18 . . . . . .**119** B7
Longacre Gdns IP33 .**122** E3
Long Ave IP17 . . . .**128** B4
Longbeach Dr NR33 . . .**115** C6
Long Bessels IP7 . . . . .**149** D6
Long Brackland
IP33. . . . .**154** B3
Longbrook Cl NR33 . . .**114** E3
Longcroft IP11 . . . .**152** E6
Longden Ave NR32 . . . .**112** F2
Long Dolver Dro CB7 . .**28** D6
Long Dr IP23 . . . .**37** C4
Long Field IP11 . . . . . .**152** D6
Longfield Rd IP9. . . . . .**150** E4
Longfield Way 6
NR32 . . . .**112** D2
Longfulans La NR31 . . . .**3** B6
LONG GREEN **36** D8
Long Green IP13 . . . . . .**54** D5
Long La
Bawdsey IP12 . . . .**99** E3
Burston & Shimpling
IP22 . . . .**20** E8
Clare CO10 . . . .**90** B6
Feltwell IP26 . . . .**4** D5
Heveningham IP19 . . . . .**40** E2
Longmans La IP12 . . . . .**71** F1
Long Marsh Cl IP18 . .**119** C7
Longmeadow IP33 . . . .**122** E3
Long Meadow IP8 . . . .**138** B3
Long Meadow Dr
IP22. . . . .**20** B3
Long Meadows 2
CO12. . . . .**106** F1
Long Meadow Wlk
NR33 . . . .**114** D5
LONG MELFORD **77** D1
Long Melford CE Prim
Sch CO10 . . . .**91** E8
Longmere La
Soham CB7 . . . .**28** C5
Soham CB7 . . . .**28** E5
Soham CB7 . . . .**28** E3
Long Pastures 2
CO10 . . . .**77** B2
Long Perry IP9 . . . .**150** F3
Long Rd
Lowestoft NR33 . . . . . .**114** E3
Lowestoft NR33 . . . . . .**114** E4
Manningtree CO11. . . . .**104** D1
Long Rd E CO7 . . . .**104** A2
Long Rd W CO7 . . . . . .**103** F2
Longrigg Rd NR35. . . .**110** E7
Long Row IP16 . . . .**129** D6
Long Shop Mus ★
IP16 . . . .**129** C6
Long St IP3 . . . .**139** E5
LONG THURLOW **51** B7
Long Thurlow Rd
IP31. . . . .**51** A7
Lonsdale Cl IP4 . . . . . .**139** F7
Looe Rd IP11 . . . .**153** C5
Looms La
Bury St Edmunds
IP33 . . . .**154** B2
Debach IP13 . . . .**70** A1
Lopham Dro
Crackthorn Corner
IP22 . . . .**19** A2
Fersfield IP22. . . . .**19** D5

Lopham Rd continued
Harling NR16 . . . .**18** D8
Lophams Cl CB9 . . . . . .**132** D8
Loraine Way IP8 . . . . . .**134** A1
Lord Rd IP22 . . . .**20** D2
Lord's Croft La CB9 . .**132** E5
Lord's Highway The
IP14. . . . .**67** E5
Lord's La CB8 . . . .**61** E5
Lord's Wlk IP27 . . . .**13** F2
Lorne Pk Rd NR33. . . .**115** C6
Lorne Rd
Lowestoft NR33 . . . . . .**115** A2
Southwold IP18 . . . . . .**119** D5
Lothingland Cl NR33 .**112** F5
Lothing St NR32 . . . . .**112** F1
Lotus Cl IP1 . . . .**134** C1
Loudham Hall Rd
IP13. . . . .**127** D3
Loudham La
Ufford IP13 . . . .**85** A7
Wickham Market
IP13 . . . .**127** D3
Louie's La IP22 . . . .**20** C3
LOUND **2** F5
Lound Dam NR14 . . . .**2** A3
Lound Rd
Belton with Browston
NR31 . . . .**2** E8
Blundeston NR32 . . . .**3** A4
Louse La
Dedham CO7. . . . .**103** C3
Rattlesden IP30 . . . .**65** D3
Louvain Rd 13 CO12 .**107** A1
Lovat Cl IP20 . . . .**22** E6
Love La
Bungay NR35 . . . .**110** B1
6 Burwell CB5. . . . .**45** A4
2 Coddenham IP6. . . . .**68** B1
Framlingham IP13 . . . .**126** C3
Hadleigh IP7 . . . .**149** A4
Kirby Row NR35. . . . .**8** C1
Lowestoft NR33 . . . . . .**114** F4
Thorndon IP23 . . . .**53** B8
Wangford NR34 . . . .**26** A1
Westleton IP17. . . . .**58** C7
Love Rd NR32 . . . .**113** C1
Lovers La IP9 . . . .**106** B6
Lover's La IP16 . . . .**129** E8
Lovers' La IP22 . . . .**18** D4
Lovetofts Dr IP1 . . . . .**134** C1
Lovewell Rd NR33 . . . .**115** C6
Low Comm IP22 . . . .**19** B3
Low Comm La NR34 . . . .**2** A1
Low Comm Rd IP22 . . . .**19** B3
Lower Barn Rd IP8 . . . .**95** D5
Lower Baxter St
IP33. . . . .**154** B2
Lower Brook Mws
IP4. . . . .**155** B2
Lower Brook St IP4 . .**155** B2
Lower Broom Rd
IP30. . . . .**50** C1
Lower Byfield IP7. . . . . .**79** C2
LOWER COMMON **25** B3
Lower Common IP9 . . . .**25** B4
Lower Coney Gr IP8 . . .**81** A4
Lower Cres IP6 . . . .**82** A6
Lower Dales View Rd
IP1. . . . .**139** A8
Lower Downs Slade 5
CB9 . . . .**132** E6
Lower Drag Way IP22 . .**19** A4
LOWER FALKENHAM . . .**98** F1
Lower Farm Dr 27
IP31. . . . .**34** B1
Lower Farm Park Bsns
Ctr IP6. . . . .**82** A5
Lower Farm Rd
Borley CO10 . . . .**91** B5
Boxted CO4. . . . .**103** A4
Hightown Green IP7. . . .**65** C2
Ringshall IP7 . . . .**80** E5
Lower Gn IP30 . . . .**64** B6
LOWER GREEN **46** E4
Lower Green
Denston CB8. . . . .**76** B7
Hawkedon IP29 . . . .**76** D7
Higham IP28. . . . .**46** E4
Mount Bures CO6 . . . . .**101** B3
LOWER
HACHESTON **127** F8
Lower Harlings 4
IP9. . . . .**107** A4
LOWER HOLBROOK . . .**106** A6
Lower House La IP12. . .**98** C5
Lower Houses CO9 . . . .**91** A2
Lower Houses Rd
IP9. . . . .**106** B5
LOWER LAYHAM **149** D1
Lower Marine Par
CO12 . . . .**107** B1
Lower N St CO10 . . . . . .**75** D3
Lower Oakley IP21 . . . . .**37** B8
Lower Olland St
NR35 . . . .**110** B4
Lower Orwell St IP4. .**155** C2
Lower Pk Wlk IP19 . . .**118** E4
LOWER RAYDON **94** D1
Lower Rd
Borley CO10 . . . .**91** D6
Borley Green IP14 . . . . .**65** F7
Coddenham IP6 . . . .**68** B1
Falkenham IP10 . . . .**98** F1
Glemsford CO10 . . . .**77** B1
Grundisburgh IP13 . . . . .**83** E5
Hemingstone IP6 . . . . . .**68** C1
Hundon CO10 . . . .**75** D3

Lower Rd continued
Lavenham CO10 . . . .**78** D4
Little Blakenham IP8 . . .**81** D3
Melton IP12 . . . .**84** F6
Mount Bures CO6 . . . . .**101** D3
Onehouse IP14. . . . .**66** B5
Westerfield IP6 . . . .**135** D4
Wicken CB7 . . . .**28** A2
Lower Reeve CO10 . . . .**148** F2
Lower Rose La IP21 . . . .**20** D1
Lower St
Baylham IP6 . . . .**81** E7
Billingford IP21 . . . .**21** B1
Cavendish CO10 . . . .**76** E1
Fenstead End IP29 . . . . .**76** F6
Great Bealings IP13 . . .**137** E6
Higham CO7 . . . .**103** D6
Rattlesden IP30 . . . .**65** D6
Sproughton IP8 . . . . . .**138** A6
Stansfield CO10 . . . .**76** C6
Stanstead CO10 . . . .**77** C3
Stratford St Mary CO7 .**103** E5
Stutton IP9 . . . .**105** D5
Ufford IP13. . . . .**85** A6
Wickham Market IP13 . .**127** C2
Lower Stoke Rd CO10 . .**89** D7
LOWER STREET
Stansfield **76** C6
Stutton **105** D5
Lower Ufford La
IP13. . . . .**127** D3
Lower Ufford Rd
IP13. . . . .**127** C1
Lowes Hill IP17 . . . . . .**128** E7
LOWESTOFT **113** E3
Lowestoft Coll NR32 .**113** C2
Lowestoft Coll (Lound
Campus) NR32 . . . .**3** A5
Lowestoft Ent Pk
NR33 . . . .**114** F2
Lowestoft Maritime
Mus ★ NR32 . . . .**113** E3
Lowestoft Mus ★
NR33 . . . .**114** D4
Lowestoft Porcelain ★
NR32 . . . .**113** E3
Lowestoft Rd
Beccles NR34 . . . .**111** C4
Blundeston NR32 . . . . .**112** E8
Hopton on Sea NR31. . . .**3** B6
Lowestoft NR33 . . . . . .**114** D3
Reydon IP18 . . . .**119** C8
Worlingham NR34. . . . . .**10** A9
Lowestoft Sixth Form
Coll NR32 . . . .**113** C2
Lowestoft Sta NR32 . .**115** D3
Lowestoft War Meml
Museum ★ NR32. . . .**113** E3
Low Farm Dr NR33 . . .**114** C3
Lowgate St IP23 . . . . . .**117** D2
LOW GREEN **63** E7
Low La
Aldringham IP16 . . . . . .**129** D3
Brandeston IP13 . . . .**70** A7
Creeting St Mary IP6 . .**125** D4
Scole IP21 . . . .**21** A2
Lowlands Cl 17 NR33 . .**11** C1
Low Lift Cottage Rd
CO4 . . . .**103** C3
Low Lighthouse Maritime
Mus ★ CO12 . . . .**107** C3
Low Pk Corner IP28. . . .**45** D8
Low Rd
Alburgh IP20 . . . .**7** A1
Bramfield IP19 . . . .**42** A5
Brampton with Stoven
NR34 . . . .**25** D5
Bressingham IP22 . . . . .**19** E1
Burwell CB5 . . . .**44** A5
Carlton IP17 . . . .**128** D6
Cransford IP17. . . . .**56** C4
Darsham IP17 . . . .**57** F8
Debenham IP14 . . . .**53** E1
Denham IP21 . . . .**38** C2
Denton IP20 . . . .**7** B1
1 Dicklebrugh & Rushall
IP21 . . . .**20** F2
Earl Soham IP13 . . . .**54** E2
Eyke IP12 . . . .**85** B7
Friston IP17 . . . .**72** F5
Goddard's Corner IP13. .**55** F8
Great Glemham IP17 . .**56** C1
Harwich CO12. . . . .**106** F1
Hasketon IP13 . . . .**146** B8
Hedenham NR35. . . . .**7** D8
Heveningham IP19 . . . . .**40** F3
Marlesford IP13. . . . .**71** C5
Mettingham NR35. . . . .**110** D5
Monk Soham IP13. . . . . .**54** D3
Peasenhall IP17 . . . .**56** A4
St John, Ilketshall NR34 . .**8** D2
Stratford St Andrew
IP17 . . . .**71** F7
Swefling IP17. . . . .**56** E5
Ubbeston IP19 . . . .**40** D3
Wenhaston with Mells
Hamlet IP19. . . . .**42** C7
Woodton NR35 . . . .**7** A7
Wortham IP22 . . . .**19** E2
Lowry Cl CB9 . . . .**132** B7
Lowry Gdns 6 IP3. . . .**144** A8
Lowry Way
Lowestoft NR32 . . . . . .**113** C5
Stowmarket IP14 . . . . .**124** B2
Low's La IP22 . . . .**20** C1
Low St
Badingham IP13. . . . . . .**56** A7
Bardwell IP31. . . . .**34** C3

Low St *continued*
Benhall Street IP17 . . . . . . **71** F8
Farnham IP17 . . . . **71** A7
Glemsford CO10 . . . . **77** B3
Hoxne IP21 . . . . **38** B8
Kettleburgh IP13 . . . . **70** B7
Rendham IP17 . . . . **56** F1
St Margaret, Ilketshall
NR35 . . . . **24** B8
Lowther St CB8 . . . . **120** F3
Low Wr La IP22 . . . . **20** A1
Loxley Rd NR33 . . . . **114** E6
Lucas Rd CO10 . . . . **148** D5
Lucena Ct IP14 . . . . **124** C6
Lucerne Cl
Lowestoft NR33 . . . . . . **114** C5
5 Red Lodge IP28 . . . . **30** B1
Lucus Cl **3** CB5 . . . . **45** A4
Ludbrook Cl IP6 . . . . **125** C5
Ludgate Cswy IP23 . . . **117** E2
Ludham **34** IP27 . . . . **13** F2
Ludlow Cl IP1 . . . . **135** B4
Luff Meadow IP6 . . . . . . **125** D5
Luffs La IP14 . . . . **53** C1
Lugano Ave IP12 . . . . **98** B8
Lugs Rd NR35 . . . . **8** C8
Lulworth Ave IP3 . . . . . . **140** D3
Lulworth Dr **14** CB9 . . **132** C6
Lulworth Pk 8
NR32 . . . . **113** A4
Lummis Vale IP5 . . . . . . **141** C7
Lundy Cl CB9 . . . . **133** B5
Lunnish Hill CO12 . . . . . **106** C2
Lupin Cl IP18 . . . . **119** B6
Lupin Rd IP2 . . . . **138** E4
Lupin Way IP6 . . . . **125** D3
Lupton Cl NR32 . . . . **112** D3
Lushington Rd 5
CO11 . . . . **104** E2
Luther Rd IP2 . . . . **155** B1
Lutus Cl **3** CO10 . . . . . . **90** A7
Lydgate Cl
11 Bury St Edmunds
IP32 . . . . **48** C5
14 Lawford CO11 . . . . **104** D2
Lydgate Rd IP14 . . . . . . **124** C7
Lyle Cl
Button Haugh Green
IP30 . . . . **50** F4
Kesgrave IP5 . . . . **141** E7
Lymballs La IP17 . . . . **42** D1
Lymingster Cl 6
IP32 . . . . **123** D6
Lymm Rd NR32 . . . . **113** B5
Lincoln Dr NR32 . . . . . . **112** D3
Lyncroft Rd NR33 . . . . . **115** B3
Lyndhurst Ave IP4 . . . . **140** C5
Lyndhurst Rd NR32 . . **113** D4
LYNFORD **6** C5
Lyngate Ave NR33 . . . . . **114** F5
Lyng La IP22 . . . . **18** F5
Lynnbrook Cl IP22 . . . . **138** E1
Lynn Rd IP26 . . . . **5** C5
Lynn's Hall Cl CO10 . . . . **92** C6
Lynton Gdns NR32 . . . . **113** C3
Lynwood Ave IP11 . . . . . **153** E5
Lynx Bsns Pk CB8 . . . . . . **44** F7
Lyon Cl IP23 . . . . **37** C4
Lysander Dr **3** IP3 . . . . **144** C3
Lytham IP10 . . . . **145** A7

M

MacAulay Rd IP1 . . . . . . **134** F3
Macdonald Way 17
IP29 . . . . **47** A2
MACE GREEN **95** E4
Mace Rd IP28 . . . . **116** F5
MacKenzie Dr IP5 . . . . . **141** B8
MacKenzie Pl IP30 . . . . **78** C8
MacKenzie Rd
IP24 . . . . **16** A5
Mackintosh Cl IP3 . . . . **140** B4
Maconochie Way
NR33 . . . . **115** C7
MacPherson Robertson
Way 3 IP28 . . . . **116** B5
Madge's La IP31 . . . . **51** B8
Mafeking Pl IP16 . . . . . . **129** D6
Magdalen Cl 3
NR32 . . . . **113** A3
Magdalen Ct IP23 . . . . . **117** C2
Magdalen Dr IP12 . . . . **146** D3
Magdalene Cl IP22 . . . . **137** E2
Magdalen Rd IP7 . . . . . **149** D6
Magdalen St IP23 . . . . . **117** C2
Magingley Cres IP4 . . **140** F6
Magnolia Cl
9 Beck Row, Holywell Row
& Kenny Hill IP28 . . . . **13** B1
2 Red Lodge IP28 . . . . **30** B1
Magnolia Ct **3** NR32 . **113** D2
Magnolia Dr
Lakenheath IP27 . . . . **109** D5
7 Rendlesham IP12 . . . **85** D8
Magpie Cl
8 Ipswich IP8 . . . . . . **138** C2
Ramsey CO12 . . . . **106** F1
Magpie Ct **33** IP20 . . . . **22** D6
MAGPIE GREEN **19** E1
Magpie Hill IP22 . . . . **19** E1
Maidenhair Way 15
IP28 . . . . **30** B1
MAIDENHALL **139** B1
Maidenhall App IP2 . . **139** B2

Maidenhall Sports Ctr
IP2 . . . . **139** C2
MAIDENSGRAVE **146** E3
Maiden Way IP7 . . . . . . **149** D6
Maid Marion Ct IP33 . **122** F3
Maids Cross Hill
Lakenheath IP27 . . . . **109** E6
Lakenheath IP27 . . . . **109** E6
Maids Cross Way
IP27 . . . . **109** D6
Maidstone Inf Sch
IP11 . . . . **152** E5
Maidstone Rd
Felixstowe IP11 . . . . . **152** E5
Lowestoft NR32 . . . . . **113** C1
Sutton IP12 . . . . **85** C3
Maine St **4** IP24 . . . . . . **16** A5
Main Rd
Ashfield cum Thorpe
IP13 . . . . **54** D1
Barking Tye IP6 . . . . **81** A6
Benhall IP17 . . . . **72** C8
Bucklesham IP10 . . . . . **141** F1
Chelmondiston IP9 . . . **106** B8
Cross Green IP30 . . . . . . **64** A2
Darsham IP17 . . . . **42** A1
Hacheston IP13 . . . . . . **127** D8
Harwich CO12 . . . . **106** F1
Henley IP6 . . . . **82** D6
Ipswich IP5 . . . . **141** A8
Kelsale cum Carlton
IP17 . . . . **128** C8
Marlesford IP13 . . . . **71** D4
Martlesham IP12 . . . . . **146** C1
Parham IP13 . . . . **70** F8
Peats Corner IP14 . . . . . **69** E8
Pettistree IP13 . . . . . . **127** B3
3 Ramsey & Parkeston
CO12 . . . . **106** D1
Somersham IP8 . . . . **81** C3
The Heath IP9 . . . . **105** A6
Tuddenham St Martin
IP6 . . . . **136** B4
Ufford IP13 . . . . **127** B1
Woolverstone IP9 . . . . **143** F2
Wormingford CO6 . . . **101** F2
Yoxford IP17 . . . . **57** D7
Main St
Hockwold cum Wilton
IP26 . . . . **4** F3
Leiston IP16 . . . . **129** C6
Maisie's Meadow
IP13 . . . . **54** D7
Maitland Rd IP6 . . . . . . **125** E3
Major La IP29 . . . . **37** A2
Major's Cl IP29 . . . . **62** C5
Makins Rd **2** CO12 . . **106** F3
Malcolm Rd IP3 . . . . . . **140** D2
Malcolm Way CB8 . . . . **121** A5
Maldon Ct CO10 . . . . . . **148** F5
Malin Cl CB9 . . . . **133** B5
Malkin Cl IP1 . . . . **134** E3
Mallard House Bsns Ctr
IP13 . . . . **137** E3
Mallard Rd
Saxmundham IP17 . . . **128** B3
Southwold IP18 . . . . . . **119** B7
Mallards The IP27 . . . . . **109** D5
Mallard Way
Brandon IP27 . . . . **6** A1
Hollesley IP12 . . . . **99** F7
Ipswich IP2 . . . . **138** F3
Stowmarket IP14 . . . . **124** A6
Sudbury CO10 . . . . **92** B3
Mallard Way CB8 . . . . . **120** A8
Mallets La IP12 . . . . **131** C2
Mallowhayes Cl
IP2 . . . . **139** B3
Mallow Rd **11** IP24 . . . **16** D6
Mallows'S La IP22 . . . . . **18** E5
Mallow Way NR33 . . . . **114** C4
Mallow Wlk **4** CB9 . . . **132** A6
Malmesbury Cl IP2 . . . **139** A2
Malt Cl
5 Laxfield IP13 . . . . . . **40** B3
Newmarket CB8 . . . . . **121** B3
Malthouse Ct **24** IP20 . **22** D6
Malthouse La
Bury St Edmunds
IP32 . . . . **154** B4
Gissing IP22 . . . . **20** F8
Malthouse Rd **22**
CO11 . . . . **104** E2
Malting Cotts CB9 . . . . **133** D2
MALTING END **61** E1
Malting End CB8 . . . . . . **60** E2
Malting Farm La
CO7 . . . . **103** E1
Malting Field **6** IP30 . **50** E2
Malting La
10 Clare CO10 . . . . . . **90** A8
Isleham CB7 . . . . **29** C5
Malting Row IP31 . . . . . . **33** F5
Maltings IP14 . . . . **52** D3
Maltings Cl
2 Bures Hamlet
CO8 . . . . **101** C5
1 Chevington IP29 . . . **62** C6
5 Diss IP22 . . . . **20** D2
Halesworth IP19 . . . . . **118** B4
Moulton CB8 . . . . **45** F3
Maltings Dr **6** IP20 . . . **22** D6
Maltings Garth **9**
IP31 . . . . **49** D4
Maltings House Rd
CB9 . . . . **88** F4

Maltings La
17 Grundisburgh
IP13 . . . . **83** E5
Ingham IP31 . . . . **32** F1
Maltings Mews IP7 . **149** D5
Maltings The
Beccles NR34 . . . . **111** B7
Bungay NR35 . . . . **110** C4
Maltings Way IP33 . . . **154** B4
Malting Wharf CO11 . **104** E3
Malt Office Ave IP19 . . **24** B4
Malt Office La IP19 . . . . **24** A4
Malt's La IP26 . . . . **4** F3
Maltsters' Way NR32 **114** D8
Maltsters Wlk IP14 . . **124** C3
Maltward Ave IP33 . . . **122** C5
Malvern Cl
Ipswich IP3 . . . . **140** B3
Newmarket CB8 . . . . . **121** B2
Malvern Rd IP3 . . . . **140** B3
Malvern Rise NR32 . . . **113** B3
Malyon Rd IP7 . . . . **149** E8
Manchester Rd IP2 . . **138** D2
Manderston Rd IP33 . **120** E3
Manderville Rd IP33 . **122** C4
Mandrake Dr **31** IP28 . **30** C1
Mandy Cl IP4 . . . . **140** A6
Mannall Wlk IP5 . . . . . . **141** E8
Manners Rd IP31 . . . . . . **48** D5
Manning Rd
Bury St Edmunds
IP32 . . . . **123** F7
Felixstowe IP11 . . . . . . **152** E5
Manning's Amusement
Park ★ IP11 . . . . **152** F1
Mannings La IP9 . . . . . **144** A2
Manning's La IP22 . . . . . **35** D5
Mannington Cl 3
IP4 . . . . **140** F5
MANNINGTREE **104** F2
Manningtree High Sch
CO11 . . . . **104** D2
Manningtree Mus ★
CO11 . . . . **104** E2
Manningtree Rd
Dedham CO7 . . . . **104** A3
East Bergholt CO7 . . . **151** F3
Stutton IP9 . . . . **105** C5
Manningtree Sports Ctr
CO11 . . . . **104** D2
Manningtree Sta
CO11 . . . . **104** D3
Mannock Dr IP32 . . . . . . **48** C5
Manor Ash Dr IP32 . . . **123** E6
Manor Cl
Beccles NR34 . . . . **9** F4
9 Beccles NR34 . . . . . . **9** F4
3 Cavendish CO10 . . . **76** E1
Walberswick IP18 . . . . **119** A2
Manor Farm Cl
Haverhill CB9 . . . . **132** F5
11 Southwold IP18 . . **119** D5
Manor Farm Dr **8**
IP30 . . . . **49** F2
Manor Farm Gdns
IP12 . . . . **99** E3
Manor Farm Rd
St John, Ilketshall
NR34 . . . . **8** D3
Sotherton Corner NR34 **25** F1
1 Thistley Green IP28 . **29** F6
Manor Garth IP31 . . . . . **49** E6
Manor Gdns
Hadleigh IP7 . . . . **149** C6
7 Hopton on Sea NR31 . **3** C6
Saxmundham IP17 . . . **128** C2
Manorhouse La **8**
NR34 . . . . **111** B6
Manor House Mus ★
IP33 . . . . **154** C1
Manor La
Gosbeck IP6 . . . . **68** D2
14 Harwich CO12 . . . **107** A2
Horringer IP29 . . . . **122** B1
Stutton IP9 . . . . **105** C5
Swilland IP6 . . . . **83** A8
Manor Pk Rd
Corton NR32 . . . . **3** C4
5 Southwold IP18 . . . **119** D5
Manor Rd
10 Bildeston IP7 . . . . . **79** F4
Brandon IP27 . . . . **5** E1
Bungay NR35 . . . . **110** B2
Clopton IP13 . . . . **69** E1
Elmsett IP7 . . . . **80** F2
Felixstowe IP11 . . . . . **152** B8
Hasketon IP13 . . . . **146** D6
Haverhill CB9 . . . . **132** F5
Hessett IP30 . . . . **64** F7
Hopton on Sea NR31 . . **3** B6
Ipswich IP1 . . . . **139** D8
11 Martlesham Heath
IP5 . . . . **98** A8
Mildenhall IP28 . . . . . **116** B4
Roydon IP22 . . . . **20** B3
Sudbury CO10 . . . . **148** C7
Trimley St Martin
IP11 . . . . **153** I11
Manor Rise NR33 . . . . . **114** A4
Manor Terr IP11 . . . . . . **107** F3
Manor View IP28 . . . . . **116** D2
Manor Way **10** IP22 . . . **20** B3
Manor Wlk **20** NR33 . . **114** E6
Mansbrook Blvd IP3 **144** D7
Mansbrook Bvd 5
IP3 . . . . **144** C7

MAN'S CROSS **89** F2
Manse La IP19 . . . . **40** C6
Mansell Cl IP23 . . . . **20** B3
Mansfield Ave IP1 . . . . **134** F2
Manthorp Cl IP12 . . . . **147** B8
Manwick Rd IP11 . . . . . **152** E2
Maple Cl
6 Great Bricett IP7 . . . **80** D6
26 Harwich CO12 . . . **107** A2
Ipswich IP2 . . . . **139** A3
12 Lakenheath IP27 . . **13** F2
10 Rendlesham IP12 . . **85** D8
27 Soham CB7 . . . . . . **28** D4
10 Walsham le Willows
IP31 . . . . **35** C2
Yaxley IP23 . . . . **37** B5
Maple Covert 5
NR32 . . . . **112** F5
Maplefields IP31 . . . . . . **49** F3
Maple Gn **3** IP31 . . . . . **49** A6
Maple Gr IP6 . . . . **82** A6
Maple Hill
Clare CO10 . . . . **75** E1
Stoke by Clare CO10 . . **89** E8
Maple Rd
5 Lowestoft NR33 . . . **114** F7
Stowupland IP14 . . . . . . **67** A6
Sudbury CO10 . . . . **148** F3
Maplesden Cl NR32 . . **112** E3
Maples Pk IP17 . . . . **57** A3
Maples The IP5 . . . . **140** E8
Mapleton Gdns IP4 . . **140** A5
Maple Tree Cl IP11 . . . **152** F7
Maple Way
Beccles NR34 . . . . **111** C5
Eye IP23 . . . . **117** D3
Leavenheath CO6 . . . . **102** B7
Maple Way **10** CB7 . . . **29** A1
Marbella La NR33 . . . . **114** E5
Marbled White Dr
IP9 . . . . **142** B8
March Pl **2** CO10 . . . . . **76** A1
Marcus Cl CB9 . . . . **133** B5
Marcus Rd IP11 . . . . . . **153** D5
Mardle Rd
Reydon NR34 . . . . **43** B8
Wangford with Henham
NR34 . . . . **26** C1
Mardle The NR33 . . . . **114** C2
Mare Hill CO10 . . . . **75** D3
Margaret Rd 2
IP14 . . . . **124** C7
Margaret St IP11 . . . . . **152** E5
Margate Rd IP3 . . . . . . **140** B3
Marham Parkway
IP32 . . . . **48** B5
Marham Rd 4
NR32 . . . . **113** B2
Maria St **7** CO12 . . . . **107** B3
Marigold Ave IP2 . . . . **138** E3
Marigold Dr **3** IP28 . . **46** A8
Marina **6** NR32 . . . . . . **113** E1
Marina Gdns IP11 . . . . **152** E2
Marina Theatre ★ **11**
NR32 . . . . **113** D1
Marine Cl **3** NR31 . . . . . **3** B8
Marine Par
12 Harwich CO12 . . . **107** B2
Lowestoft NR33 . . . . . **115** D7
Mariner Gdns IP11 . . . **153** A5
Mariner's Cl **2** NR31 . . **3** B8
Mariners Pk Cl **1**
NR31 . . . . **3** B7
Mariners St NR32 . . . . **113** E2
Mariners Way
Aldeburgh IP15 . . . . . . **130** C5
Felixstowe IP11 . . . . . . **152** B8
Marion Cl **5** NR34 . . . . **111** C3
Markant Cl IP32 . . . . . . **123** E6
Market Cross Pl
IP15 . . . . **130** F4
Market Gr
Great Yeldham CO9 . . . **90** A1
Man's Cross CO9 . . . . . . **89** F2
Market Hill
8 Clare CO10 . . . . **90** A8
Clopton IP13 . . . . **83** D8
Framlingham IP13 . . . **126** C3
Haverhill CB9 . . . . **132** E6
Orford IP12 . . . . **131** C2
6 Sudbury CO10 . . . . **148** C5
Market La
Blundeston NR32 . . . . . . **3** B4
Burston & Shimpling
IP22 . . . . **20** E5
Smallworth IP22 . . . . . . **18** E3
Somerleyton, Ashby &
Herringfleet NR32 . . . . **2** D6
Market Pl
11 Bildeston IP7 . . . . . **79** F4
Hadleigh IP7 . . . . **149** D5
2 Halesworth IP19 . . **118** A3
22 Harleston IP20 . . . **22** D6
8 Kessingland NR33 . . **11** B1
11 Lavenham CO10 . . **78** D4
Saxmundham IP17 . . . **128** D3
Southwold IP18 . . . . . **119** D5
Stowmarket IP14 . . . . **124** D6
Market Row NR34 . . . . **111** B5
Market Sq CB8 . . . . **121** A3
Market St
1 Beccles NR34 . . . . **111** B5
Fordham CB7 . . . . **29** A1
3 Harwich CO12 . . . . **107** C3
Laxfield IP13 . . . . **40** B3
3 Mildenhall IP28 . . **116** C4
2 Newmarket CB8 . . **121** A3
16 Soham CB7 . . . . . . **28** D4

Market Thoroughfare
IP33 . . . . **154** B2
MARKET WESTON **35** A8
Market Weston Rd
Hepworth IP22 . . . . **35** A7
Thorpe Street IP22 . . . . **35** C8
Markhams Cl **4**
CB9 . . . . **132** D7
Mark Jennings La
IP33 . . . . **154** C3
Mark La IP31 . . . . **6** C2
Marlborough Ct
4 Haverhill CB9 . . . . **132** C5
Lowestoft NR32 . . . . . **112** F1
Marlborough Dr **4**
CO10 . . . . **148** D6
Marlborough Rd
Ipswich IP4 . . . . **140** A5
Lowestoft NR32 . . . . . **112** F1
Saxtead IP13 . . . . **55** A4
Southwold IP18 . . . . . . **119** D6
MARLESFORD **71** C5
Marlesford Rd
Campsea Ashe IP13 . . . **71** D3
Hacheston IP13 . . . . **71** B5
Marley Cl IP31 . . . . **49** D4
Marlow Rd IP1 . . . . **134** D1
Marriott's Wlk 5
IP14 . . . . **124** D6
Marsden Cl **5** NR33 . . **115** A3
Marshall Cl IP5 . . . . **141** A8
Marshall Dr **18** CO10 . . **92** B3
Marshalls Gn CO10 . . **102** A8
Marshalls La IP20 . . . . . . **7** B2
Marshalls Meadow 3
NR33 . . . . **67** A6
Marsh Drift IP17 . . . . . . **73** A5
Marsh La
Burgh St Peter NR34 . . **10** A7
Carlton Colville NR33 . **114** A4
3 Earsham NR35 . . . . . **7** F4
Felixstowe IP11 . . . . . **152** F8
Felixstowe IP11 . . . . . **153** C8
Fritton NR31 . . . . **2** C8
Gillingham NR34 . . . . **9** B6
Hulver Street NR34 . . . **10** C2
26 Kessingland NR33 . **11** C1
Kessingland NR33 . . . . . **27** C8
North Cove NR34 . . . . . **10** B5
Reydon IP18 . . . . **26** D2
Rushmere NR34 . . . . . . **10** D1
Worlingham NR34 . . . . . **9** F5
Wortham IP22 . . . . **20** A1
Wrentham NR34 . . . . . . **27** A7
Marsh Rd
Boxford CO10 . . . . **93** C3
Fritton & St Olaves NR31 . 2 B7
Lowestoft NR33 . . . . . **114** D7
Stoke-by-Nayland CO6 **103** F2
Marsh Terr **72** D8
Marsh View NR34 . . . . **111** D5
Marsh Way IP33 . . . . . . **154** A4
Marshy La CO10 . . . . **90** A4
Martello La IP11 . . . . . **153** D5
Martello Rd NR34 . . . . **113** B4
Marten's La CO6 . . . . . . **102** F8
Martin Cl
Brandon IP27 . . . . **6** A1
Lowestoft NR33 . . . . . **114** C3
Mildenhall IP28 . . . . . . **116** D3
8 Soham CB7 . . . . **28** D5
Martinet Gn IP3 . . . . . . **140** C1
Martin Rd
16 Burwell CB5 . . . . . . **44** A6
Harleston IP20 . . . . **22** E6
Ipswich IP2 . . . . **155** B1
Martin's Ave NR33 . . . **115** B6
Martins Ave IP13 . . . . . **69** F2
Martins Meadow 6
IP23 . . . . **36** D2
Martin's Meadow Nature
Reserve ★ IP13 . . . . . **69** E4
Martins Mews 2
CB9 . . . . **132** A7
Martins Rd CO10 . . . . . **148** F5
Martinsyde **9** IP5 . . . . . **98** A8
MARTLESHAM **84** A1
MARTLESHAM
HEATH **98** B7
Martlesham Heath
Control Twr Mus ★ **31**
IP5 . . . . **98** A8
Martlesham Prim Acad
IP12 . . . . **84** A1
Martlesham Rd IP13 . **137** F3
Martyn Cl **1** IP22 . . . . . **20** C1
Martyns Rise **5** CO10 . **91** E7
Marvens The IP8 . . . . . **138** A1
Mary Clarke Rd IP7 . . **149** F7
Mary Day Cl IP6 . . . . **66** D3
Mary La CO10 . . . . **75** C3
Maryon Rd IP3 . . . . **140** B1
Mary's La IP19 . . . . **40** C6
Mary Warner Homes
IP12 . . . . **86** B1
Masefield Rd
Diss IP22 . . . . **20** D2
Stowmarket IP14 . . . . **124** B8
Mashay Rd CO9 . . . . **90** B3
Maskell's La IP7 . . . . **80** E4
Mason Cl CB9 . . . . **132** D8
Mason Ct
1 Claydon IP6 . . . . . . **82** A5
13 Mendlesham IP14 . . **52** E4
Mason Dr **15** IP6 . . . . . . **82** A5

Low – Mea 175

Mason Gdns **2** IP28 . . . **29** F6
Mason Rd CB5 . . . . **44** A7
Masons Cl IP4 . . . . **139** F6
Mason's La **5** IP30 . . . **50** D1
Mast Cl NR33 . . . . **114** B4
Masterlord Ind Est
IP16 . . . . **129** B6
Masterson Gr IP5 . . . . **141** C6
Mat Dawson Cl CB8 . . **120** F6
Mather La IP20 . . . . **22** B5
Mather Way IP2 . . . . . . **155** C1
Matilda Groome Rd
IP7 . . . . **149** F7
Matlock Cl **13** IP8 . . . . **138** C2
Matlock Dale 11
IP3 . . . . **114** E3
Matson Rd **1** IP1 . . . . **138** F8
Matthews Cl CO7 . . . . **103** E5
Matthews La CB8 . . . . . **74** C7
Maude St IP3 . . . . **139** E4
Maudslay Rd IP1 . . . . . **134** C2
Maulkin Cl IP32 . . . . . . **123** F7
Maundy Cl IP3 . . . . **154** A1
Mautby Way NR33 . . . **114** F5
Maxim La **5** CO10 . . . . **90** A7
Maybury Rd IP3 . . . . . . **140** B1
Maybush La IP11 . . . . . **153** C5
Maycroft Cl **2** IP1 . . . **135** A3
Mayes La CO12 . . . . . . **106** D1
Mayes Meadow 7
CB8 . . . . **45** F3
Mayfair Rd NR35 . . . . . **110** C3
Mayfield CO6 . . . . **102** B7
Mayfield Ave **12** NR33 . **11** C1
Mayfield La **7** IP5 . . . . **98** A7
Mayfield Rd
Bury St Edmunds
IP33 . . . . **123** B1
Ipswich IP4 . . . . **140** C7
Lowestoft NR33 . . . . . **114** C4
Mayfields
Lakenheath IP27 . . . . **109** C7
6 Martlesham Heath
IP5 . . . . **98** A7
Mayfield Way IP14 . . . . **52** E5
Mayflower Ave
8 Harwich CO12 . . . **107** C3
Saxmundham IP17 . . . **128** B2
Mayflower Primary Sch
The CO12 . . . . **107** A2
Mayflower Way
14 Harleston IP20 . . . **22** D5
Sudbury CO10 . . . . . . **148** D8
Mayfly Cl **12** IP8 . . . . . **142** E8
May Gdns CB8 . . . . **121** B2
Mayhew Rd
Framlingham IP13 . . . **126** B4
Rendlesham IP12 . . . . . **85** D8
Maynewater La IP33 **154** C1
Maynewater Sq
IP33 . . . . **154** C1
MAYPOLE GREEN
Bradfield St George . . . **64** D6
Dennington **55** D6
Maypole La CB8 . . . . . . **60** C6
Maypole Meadow 5
IP22 . . . . **36** A6
May Rd
Ipswich IP3 . . . . **140** C2
Lowestoft NR32 . . . . . **113** C1
May's La CO7 . . . . **103** F2
McCalmont Way
CB8 . . . . **121** E2
McClure Way IP8 . . . . **134** D1
McIntyre Wlk IP32 . . . **122** E7
McLaren Ct **1** NR34 . . **111** C3
McLean Dr **16** NR33 . . **11** B1
Mead Dr IP5 . . . . **141** C7
Meadow Barn IP14 . . . . **66** C2
Meadow Brown Way 15
IP31 . . . . **49** E4
Meadow Cl
Bury St Edmunds
IP33 . . . . **122** C3
8 Felixstowe IP11 . . . **107** D8
Felsham IP30 . . . . **65** A4
Lavenham CO10 . . . . . . **78** D3
8 Soham CB7 . . . . **28** D3
Westhall IP19 . . . . **25** B4
Meadow Cres IP3 . . . **140** F1
Meadow Ct
4 Great Yarmouth
NR31 . . . . **3** B8
Lavenham CO10 . . . . . . **78** D3
16 Stanton IP31 . . . . . **34** E4
Meadow Dr
Great Blakenham IP6 . . **81** F6
Horringer IP29 . . . . **63** A8
Lakenheath IP27 . . . . **109** D7
MEADOWEND **89** E3
Meadow Fram La
IP12 . . . . **86** B1
Meadow Gdns NR34 . **111** A3
Meadow La
Newmarket CB8 . . . . . **121** D1
North Lopham IP22 . . . **19** A6
Sudbury CO10 . . . . . . **148** C4
Thurston IP31 . . . . **49** E4
Meadowlands
1 Blundeston NR32 . . . **3** A4
11 Burwell CB5 . . . . . . **44** A5
Kirton IP10 . . . . **98** D2
4 Woolpit IP30 . . . . . **50** D1
Wrentham NR34 . . . . . . **26** E5
Meadowlands Cl IP17 **57** C8

Meadow Prim Acad
NR33. . . . . **115** B6
Meadow Rd
8 Barrow IP29. . . . . . .**47** A2
Bungay NR35 . . . . . . **110** D2
Lowestoft NR32. . . . .**112** F4
Meadow Rise IP16 . . **129** D2
Meadow Sh Ctr The
IP14 . . . .**124** D6
Meadowside
Blo' Norton IP22. . . . . .**18** E2
Wickham Market IP13 **127** C7
Meadowside Gdns
IP4. . . . . **140** E8
Meadows Montessori
Sch The IP1 . . . . **135** A2
Meadows The
Drinkstone IP30 . . . . . .**65** B7
Worlington IP28 . . . . . .**30** B4
Meadows Way IP7 . . **149** D6
Meadowsweet Cl
Haverhill CB9 . . . . . . **132** C7
3 Lowestoft NR33. . . **114** D5
Meadowvale Cl
Beccles NR34. . . . . . .**111** B2
Ipswich IP4 . . . . **139** F8
Meadow Valley IP7 . .**80** D5
Meadow View
Bucklesham IP10 . . . . .**98** A4
East Bergholt CO7 . . .**151** A8
Needham Market IP6 . **125** C5
Woolpit IP30. . . . .**65** E8
Meadow View Rd
CO10 . . . . **148** B4
Meadow Way
Assington CO10. . . . . .**92** F1
Lowestoft NR33 . . . . **114** C2
Stradbroke IP21. . . . . .**39** A4
Meadow Wlk **3** IP17 .**72** C8
Meadow Way CO10. . .**89** D4
Mead Rd **9** IP32. . . . . .**49** A3
Meads The NR32 . . . **113** D5
Mead The CO10. . . . .**148** F2
Meadway **2** CO11. . .**104** D2
Mead Way IP14. . . . . .**52** E5
Mear Cl IP12 . . . .**85** C2
Mechanical Music Mus &
Bygones★ IP14. . . . . **52** A4
Meddler Mws CB8 . . . .**46** B5
Medway Rd IP3. . . . . **139** F2
Meekings Rd CO10. . .**148** F6
Meeting Field 10
CO10 . . . .**91** E8
Meeting La
Grundisburgh IP13. . . .**83** E5
Ridgewell CO9 . . . .**89** D4
Meeting Wlk CB9 . . . **132** F5
Melbourne Dr IP28 . .**116** B5
Melbourne Rd
Ipswich IP4 . . . . **140** D7
Lowestoft NR32 . . . . **113** D3
Melford Cl
2 Burwell CB5. . . . . . .**44** B5
8 Ipswich IP4. . . . . . **140** F5
Melford Wlk★ CO10 . .**77** E1
Melford Rd
Acton CO10. . . . .**92** A8
Boxted IP29 . . . .**77** A6
Cavendish CO10 . . . . . .**76** F1
Lavenham CO10 . . . . . .**78** C3
Lawshall IP29. . . . .**63** D1
Stowmarket IP14 . . . . **124** F4
Sudbury CO10. . . . . . **148** B7
Melford Way IP11. . . **152** C3
MELLIS **37** A5
Mellis CE Prim Sch
IP23 . . . .**37** A5
Mellis Cl **1** CB9. . . . . .**74** A1
Mellis Ct **8** IP11. . . . **152** D5
MELLIS GREEN **36** F5
Mellis Rd
Gislingham IP23. . . . . .**36** D3
Thornham Parva IP23. .**37** A3
Thrandeston IP21. . . . .**37** B6
Wortham IP22 . . . .**36** E7
Yaxley IP23. . . . .**37** B5
MELLS **118** E2
Mells Rd IP19. . . . .**41** D6
MELON GREEN **63** C4
Melplash Cl IP3. . . . . **140** E4
Melplash Rd IP3 . . . . **140** E4
Melrose Cl NR32. . . . **112** F5
Melrose Gdns
Ipswich IP4 . . . . **140** B8
Newmarket CB8 . . . . .**120** E4
Melso Cl **2** CO10 . . . **148** E3
MELTON **147** C8
Melton Cl CB8 . . . . . .**121** B2
Melton Grange Rd
IP12. . . . . **147** A6
Melton Hill IP12 . . . . **147** B6
Melton Meadow Rd **4**
IP12. . . . . **147** B6
Melton Prim Sch
IP12 . . . .**147** C7
Melton Rd
Hollesley IP12 . . . .**99** F8
Sutton IP12. . . . .**85** F1
Woodbridge IP12 . . . . **147** B6
Melton Sta IP12. . . . .**147** D7
Melville Rd IP4. . . . . .**139** F5
Melvin Way **15** IP30 . . .**50** F2
MENDHAM. **23** A6
Mendham Cl **36**
IP20. . . . .**22** D6

Mendham La
38 Harleston IP20 . . . . .**22** D6
St Cross, South Elmham
IP20 . . . .**23** C6
Mendham Low Rd
Redenhall with Harleston
IP20. . . . .**22** F5
Starston IP20 . . . .**22** C7
Wortwell IP20 . . . .**23** A7
Mendham Prim Sch
IP20 . . . .**23** A6
Mendham Rd IP20 . . . . .**23** A4
Mendip Dr IP5. . . . . . **140** F6
Mendip Rd NR32. . . . .**112** E2
MENDLESHAM **52** E4
Mendlesham Community
Prim Sch IP14. . . . . **52** D4
**MENDLESHAM
GREEN** **52** D2
Mendlesham Rd IP14 .**52** B5
Mendlesham Road
IP14. . . . .**52** F5
Mercers Rd IP32. . . . **123** D7
Merchant Ave **21** IP32 **48** B5
Merchants Place
IP33. . . . .**154** B2
Mere Cl IP31 . . . .**49** C6
Meredith Rd IP1. . . . .**134** E2
Mere Farm La IP31. . . .**49** C6
Mere Gdns IP4 . . . . . .**140** F4
Mere La
Fornham All Saints
IP28 . . . .**48** A6
Risby IP28 . . . .**47** F6
Mere Manor IP22. . . . .**20** C2
Mere Side CB7. . . . . . .**28** C4
Meridan Rise **2** IP4. .**139** E7
Meridian Gdns CB8 . .**121** C5
Meriton Rise IP7. . . . .**149** F4
Merivale **28** CO11 . . .**104** D2
Merivale Rd 17
CO11 . . . .**104** D2
Merlewood IP21. . . . . .**21** C5
Merlin Park IP28 . . . . .**116** A6
Merlin Rd IP2 . . . . . . **138** C3
Merriam Cl **5** CO11. .**104** E4
Merrifield Rd NR33. . .**114** F3
Merrion Cl **12** IP8. . . **138** C2
Merrylees NR34. . . . . **111** C4
Mersey Rd IP3. . . . . . **139** F2
Merton Farm Rd
IP13. . . . .**70** D2
Merville **9** NR33. . . .**114** E3
Messenger Cl NR35 . .**110** B2
METFIELD. **23** C3
Metfield Hall La IP19 . .**23** C1
Metfield La IP21 . . . . . .**23** B1
Metfield Rd
Metfield IP20. . . . .**23** D3
Metfield IP21. . . . .**23** B1
Metfield St IP20. . . . . . .**23** C3
METHERSGATE. **84** E1
Methersgate Hall Dr
IP12. . . . .**84** E1
Metis Place IP1. . . . . **138** D7
METTINGHAM **8** D4
Meynell Gdns CB8 . . .**121** A5
Micawber Mews 4
NR32. . . . .**3** A4
Michaelhouse Way 12
IP31. . . . .**34** E4
Michaels Mount
IP13. . . . . **137** D5
Michaelstowe Cl
Harwich CO12. . . . . . .**106** E1
1 Ramsey & Parkeston
CO12. . . . .**106** E1
Michigan Cl IP5 . . . . .**141** B7
MICKFIELD. **68** B8
Mickfield Mews 16
IP11. . . . . **152** D5
Mickfield Rd IP14. . . . .**68** B7
Micklegate Rd IP11 . .**152** E2
**Micklemere Nature
Reserve★** IP31. . . . . .**49** F8
Micklesmere Dr 23
IP31. . . . .**34** B1
MICKLEY GREEN. **63** B4
Middle Dro CB7. . . . . . .**28** B4
Middlefield Dr 3
IP14. . . . .**66** B4
Middlefield Rd 10
CO11 . . . .**105** A2
Middle Gn CO6. . . . . .**101** B1
MIDDLE GREEN. **46** E4
MIDDLE HARLING **18** B8
Middle La NR34 . . . . . .**10** D8
Middle Meadow IP7 .**149** E6
Middle Rd
Blo' Norton IP22. . . . . .**18** F2
Earsham IP20. . . . .**7** C4
MIDDLETON
Leiston. **58** B6
Sudbury **148** C2
Middleton Cl
13 Beck Row IP28 . . . . .**30** C8
Ipswich IP2 . . . .**138** D2
MIDDLETON MOOR **58** A6
Middleton Prim Sch
IP17. . . . .**58** B6
Middleton Rd
16 Great Blakenham
IP6. . . . .**82** B5
Sudbury CO10. . . . . . .**148** B4
Yoxford IP17. . . . .**57** E7
Middle Way CO10 . . . . .**91** E8
Middle Wlk NR32 . . . **113** C5

**MIDDLEWOOD
GREEN**. **67** D8
Middy Cl **6** IP14. . . . . .**52** E4
Midhurst Cl **3** IP32. .**123** D6
Midmeadow 4
NR34. . . . .**111** B5
Midnight Meadow
IP21. . . . .**39** E8
Mid Suffolk Bsns Pk
IP23 . . . .**117** B5
Mid Suffolk Leisure Ctr
IP14 . . . .**124** B7
Mights Rd IP18 . . . . .**119** C6
Milano Ave IP12 . . . . . .**98** B8
Milburn Dro CB8. . . . . .**45** F3
MILDEN. **79** B1
Milden Cl **6** IP14 . . . **124** E3
MILDENHALL. **116** D6
Mildenhall Airfield
IP28 . . . .**30** B7
**MILDENHALL COLLEGE
ACADEMY** IP28. . . . . .**116** B4
Mildenhall Coll of Tech
IP28 . . . .**116** C4
Mildenhall Dro IP28 . .**12** F3
Mildenhall Ind Est
IP28 . . . .**116** B6
Mildenhall Mus★
IP28. . . . . **116** C4
Mildenhall Pl **1** CB9 .**132** F6
Mildenhall Rd
Barton Mills IP28 . . . .**116** C2
Beck Row, Holywell Row &
Kenny Hill IP28 . . . . **116** C8
2 Bury St Edmunds
IP32. . . . .**123** A8
Fordham CB7 . . . .**29** C1
Icklingham IP28. . . . . .**31** A5
Littleport CB7. . . . .**12** A8
Mildenhall IP28 . . . . .**116** A2
Mildenhall Stadium
IP28 . . . .**29** D8
Milden Rd
Brent Eleigh CO10. . . . .**79** A2
Ipswich IP2 . . . .**138** E5
Lindsey IP7. . . . .**93** C7
Mildmay Rd IP3 . . . . .**140** B1
MILE END **77** A7
Mile End Rd IP4 . . . . . .**14** E8
Mile End Rd CB7. . . . . .**12** A7
Miles Hawk Way
IP28. . . . . **116** A5
Miles Paddock IP14. . .**52** A6
Milestone La **10** NR35 . .**7** F4
Military Rd CB7. . . . . . .**28** E2
Military Way 5
CO12 . . . .**106** E1
Milking Corner Drove
CB7. . . . .**29** A7
Millbank CB8. . . . .**120** F4
Mill Bank **1** NR32. . .**112** F2
Mill Broadway IP12 . **131** C4
Mill Chase CB9 . . . .**88** E3
Mill Cl
6 Burwell CB5. . . . . . .**44** B5
Capel St Mary IP9. . . .**150** C3
Exning CB8. . . . .**120** B8
Felixstowe IP11 . . . . .**152** D4
28 Harwich CO12. . . .**107** B2
Kirby Row NR35 . . . .**8** E7
Laxfield IP13. . . . .**40** B3
Orford IP12 . . . . **131** B3
The Marsh IP22 . . . . . .**36** D7
1 Walsham le Willows
IP31. . . . .**35** C2
Woolpit IP30. . . . .**50** D1
Mill Cnr CB7. . . . .**28** C3
MILL COMMON
25 C4
Cox Common IP19 . . . .**25** B4
Mill Croft 9 CB7. . . . . .**28** D3
Mill Drift IP26 . . . .**5** A3
Mill Dro CB7. . . . .**28** C3
MILL END **60** F3
Mill End La IP14 . . . . . .**67** C7
Millennium Grandstand
CB8. . . . .**120** C1
Millennium Way
Kesgrave IP5 . . . .**141** E7
Lowestoft NR32 . . . . .**113** A4
Miller Cl
Elmswell IP30. . . . .**50** F2
Lowestoft NR33. . . . . **115** B5
Millers Cl
Bungay NR35 . . . .**110** C3
Hadleigh IP7. . . . . **149** B6
Stowmarket IP14 . . . .**124** C3
Millers Ct **5** IP6. . . . . .**82** A5
Millers Dr IP21. . . . .**21** B5
Millers Gn **44** IP20 . . . .**22** D6
Millers La IP21 . . . .**20** F2
Millers Rise IP27. . . . .**109** D7
Millers View IP1. . . . . **138** F7
Millers Way
Framlingham IP13 . . . .**126** B4
Otley IP6. . . . .**69** C2
Miller'S Way IP22. . . . .**35** D5
Millers Yard IP31 . . . . .**34** E7
Mill Farm Pl IP8 . . . . **142** C7
Millfield IP23. . . . .**117** B3
Mill Field
3 Aldeburgh IP15. . . **130** E5
Bramford IP8. . . . .**134** B2
Pettaugh IP14 . . . .**68** E6
Millfield Ave IP14. . . .**124** C5

Millfield Cl
Ditchingham NR35 . . .**110** C8
1 Saxmundham IP17 **128** C2
Millfield Dr IP14. . . . . .**65** F4
Millfield Gdns IP4 . . .**140** A7
Millfield Rd
2 Barningham IP31 . . .**34** F7
Walberswick IP18 . . . .**119** A2
Millfields
Darsham IP17. . . . .**42** B1
2 Peasenhall IP17. . . .**56** F8
Wangford NR34 . . . . . .**26** B2
Mill Fields IP14. . . . . . .**51** D1
Millfields Way CB9 . .**132** F6
Mill Gdns
Bedingham NR35 . . . . . .**7** B8
12 Elmswell IP30. . . . .**50** F2
Mill Green IP14. . . . . . .**65** F4
MILL GREEN
Burston and
Shimpling **20** E7
Buxhall **65** F4
Edwardstone **93** B5
Parham IP13. . . . .**71** B8
Stoneham Aspal **68** B7
Mill Green CO10. . . . . .**89** C6
Mill Heath La IP19 . . . .**42** B7
MILL HILL. **77** E6
Mill Hill
Burgh IP13. . . . .**83** F6
Capel St Mary IP9. . . .**150** C3
Cotton IP14. . . . .**52** A6
Earl Soham IP13. . . . . .**54** E1
Framsden IP14. . . . .**69** B6
Hadleigh IP7. . . . .**94** B7
Haverhill CB9 . . . .**132** D5
Leiston IP16 . . . .**129** C2
Manningtree CO11. . . .**104** E2
Mettingham NR35. . . . . .**8** D5
Newmarket CB8 . . . . .**121** A4
Peasenhall IP17. . . . . . .**56** F8
Sudbury CO10. . . . . . .**148** B5
Wormingford CO6. . . .**101** F3
Mill Hill Dr IP19. . . . . .**118** A4
Mill Hill Est IP16 . . . .**129** C2
MILL HILLS. **147** A6
Mill Hill (Tumulus)★
NR31. . . . .**2** D1
Mill Hoo IP12. . . . .**99** E4
Mill La
Alderton IP12 . . . .**99** E4
All Saints & St Nicholas,
South Elmham IP20 . .**23** E5
Barnham IP24 . . . .**16** B2
Barnham IP24 . . . .**16** B2
Barrow IP29. . . . .**47** A2
Bayham IP6 . . . .**81** F7
Benhall IP17 . . . .**72** C8
Boxted IP29 . . . .**77** A6
Boyton IP12 . . . .**82** B2
Bradfield CO11. . . . . . .**105** B1
Brandeston IP13 . . . . . .**70** A7
Bruisyard IP17 . . . .**56** C5
3 Bures CO8 . . . .**101** D4
Butley IP12 . . . .**86** B6
Campsey Ash IP13 . . . .**127** F6
Cavendish CO10 . . . . . .**90** D8
Chelmondiston IP9. . . .**106** B8
1 Coddenham IP6. . . .**68** B1
Combs IP14 . . . . **124** B1
Copdock & Washbrook
IP8. . . . .**138** A1
Corton NR32. . . . .**3** D4
Cowlinge CB8. . . . .**75** B8
Creeting St Peter or West
Creeting IP6. . . . . . .**125** D8
Dedham CO7. . . . .**103** F4
Dennington IP13. . . . . .**55** D5
Ellingham NR35 . . . .**8** E7
Exning CB8 . . . .**120** B8
Farley Green CB8 . . . . .**75** E8
Felixstowe IP11. . . . . .**152** F4
Fordham CB7 . . . .**29** B1
Framlingham IP13 . . . .**55** A1
Garboldisham IP22. . . .**18** D3
9 Great Blakenham
IP6. . . . .**82** A5
Great Yeldham CO9. . . .**90** A2
Hart's Green IP29. . . . .**63** F4
31 Harwich CO12. . . .**107** B2
Hasketon IP13 . . . .**146** A7
Henley IP6 . . . .**82** D6
Hintlesham IP8. . . . . . .**95** C5
Hockwold cum Wilton
IP26. . . . .**5** A3
Hoo IP13. . . . .**70** C6
Hopton IP22 . . . .**18** C3
Hundon CO10. . . . .**75** D3
Hunston Green IP31. . . .**50** F6
Layham IP7. . . . .**149** E2
Leiston IP16 . . . .**129** C2
Magpie Green IP22. . . .**19** E1
18 Manningtree CO11 .**104** E2
Marlesford IP13. . . . . .**71** C5
Martlesham IP12 . . . . .**84** B1
Mendham IP20. . . . . . .**23** A6
Metfield IP20 . . . .**23** C3
Mildenhall IP28. . . . . .**116** B3
Nayland CO6. . . . .**102** D5
Newton CO10 . . . .**92** D3
North Cove NR34 . . . . .**10** C4
Polstead CO6 . . . .**102** E8
Poystreet Green IP30. . .**65** C5
Preston St Mary CO10 . .**79** A5
Pulham St Mary IP21 . .**21** F8
1 Redgrave IP22. . . . .**36** A8

Mill La *continued*
St John, Ilketshall NR34 . .**8** E2
Shadingfield NR34 . . . .**25** D7
Somersham IP8 . . . . . .**81** C3
Southwold IP18 . . . . . .**119** D5
Stetchworth CB8. . . . . .**59** F5
Stoke Ash IP23 . . . .**52** F8
Stonham Earl IP14 . . . .**67** D5
Stradbroke IP21. . . . . . .**39** C5
Sudbury CO10. . . . . . .**148** B7
Swingleton Green IP7. . .**79** C2
Thetford IP24 . . . .**16** B5
Thornton IP21 . . . .**53** C8
Thurston IP31. . . . .**49** D5
Tunstall IP12. . . . .**72** B1
Wetherup Street IP14 . .**53** C3
Weybread IP21. . . . .**22** F1
Wickham Market IP13 .**127** C6
Woodbridge IP12 . . . . .**147** A5
Woolpit IP30. . . . .**50** D1
Wrentham NR34. . . . . .**26** F5
Mill Mws CB8. . . . . . .**121** A3
Mill Piece IP10 . . . . . .**145** C6
Mill Pk Gdns IP28 . . . .**116** B3
Mill Pool La NR35. . . . . .**8** D6
Mill Pouch IP11. . . . . .**152** C8
MILL RD
Aldeby/Wheatacre/Burgh
St Peter NR34. . . . .**10** B8
Ashley CB8 . . . .**45** F1
Badingham IP13 . . . . . .**56** A7
Barningham IP31 . . . . . .**34** E7
Battisford IP14. . . . .**80** B8
Beccles NR34. . . . .**111** C2
Birdbrook CO9 . . . .**89** C5
Botesdale IP22. . . . .**36** B6
Boxted CO4. . . . .**102** F2
Brockdish IP21. . . . .**21** E3
Brockley IP29. . . . .**63** A1
Burston & Shimpling
IP22 . . . .**20** E6
Bury St Edmunds IP33 .**154** F1
Buxhall IP14. . . . .**65** F4
Chevington IP29. . . . . .**62** C6
Clare CO10 . . . .**90** B8
Coldfair Green IP17 . . .**129** A2
Cotton IP14 . . . .**52** A6
East Bergholt CO7 . . . .**151** E4
Ellingham NR35 . . . .**8** D7
Foxearth CO10 . . . .**91** B7
Friston IP17 . . . .**72** E6
Gazeley CB8 . . . .**46** B3
Great Barton IP31 . . . . .**49** A6
Great Bricett IP7 . . . . . .**80** C2
Grimstone End IP31. . . .**49** F8
Halesworth IP19 . . . . .**118** E3
Hawkedon IP29 . . . .**62** F4
Haverhill CB9 . . . .**88** B4
Haverhill IP12. . . . .**98** E5
Hengrave IP28 . . . .**48** A7
Honington IP31 . . . .**33** F5
Hundon CO10 . . . .**75** D4
Ipswich IP3 . . . .**140** F1
Kedington CB9 . . . . . .**133** E8
Kirtling CB8 . . . .**60** F3
Lakenheath IP27 . . . . .**109** D6
Laxfield IP13. . . . .**40** B2
Lowestoft NR33 . . . . .**115** C7
4 Mendlesham IP14 . . .**52** D4
Moulton CB8 . . . .**46** A1
Mutford NR34. . . . .**10** C3
Newbourne IP12 . . . . . .**98** D5
Occold IP23 . . . .**37** F1
Peasenhall IP17. . . . . . .**56** F8
Redlingfield IP23 . . . . . .**38** C2
Ridgewell CO9 . . . .**89** D3
Rumburgh IP19 . . . .**24** B4
Saxmundham IP17 . . . .**128** C3
Shotford Heath IP21. . . .**22** C4
Stambourne CO9 . . . . .**89** B2
Swefling IP17. . . . .**56** E3
Thelnetham IP22 . . . . . .**18** E1
Westleton IP17 . . . .**58** C7
Winfarthing IP22 . . . . . .**20** B8
Wissett IP19. . . . .**118** A5
Worlingworth IP13. . . . .**54** D7
Wyverstone IP14 . . . . . .**51** D6
Mill Rd S IP22 . . . .**36** B6
Mill Rd (South) IP33 .**154** A1
Mill Reef Cl CB8 . . . . .**120** D7
Mill Rise
11 Holbrook IP9. . . . . **105** F3
Saxmundham IP17 . . . .**128** C2
Mills Cres IP13 . . . . . .**126** B3
Mills Dr NR32. . . . .**3** D4
Millside IP23 . . . .**37** C4
Mills La CO10. . . . .**91** E6
Mills Meadow IP13 . .**126** D4
Mills Piece IP13 . . . . .**126** D4
Mills Rd CO10. . . . . . .**148** E6
Mill St
Gislingham IP23. . . . . .**36** B2
Gislingham IP23. . . . . .**36** D2
Isleham CB7. . . . .**29** C5
Mildenhall IP17. . . . . . .**58** A6
Mildenhall IP28. . . . . .**116** B3
MILL STREET **102** E8
Mill Terr Rd IP14. . . . . .**52** D2
Mill Tye CO10. . . . . . .**148** E2

Mill View CB8. . . . .**46** B3
Mill View Cl IP12. . . . .**146** E5
Millway NR34 . . . .**10** C4
Millway Ave IP22 . . . . .**20** C2
Millway La
Diss IP22 . . . .**20** D4
Palgrave IP22. . . . .**20** A1
Wortham IP22 . . . .**19** F1
Millwood Rd CO6 . . . . .**94** A3
Milner Rd
Chilton CO10. . . . .**92** B4
Sudbury CO10. . . . . . .**148** F6
Milner St IP4 . . . .**139** E6
Milnes Way NR33. . . .**114** B3
Milnrow **10** IP19. . . . .**138** C2
Milton Cl IP17 . . . .**128** B4
Milton Rd CO11. . . . . .**104** D1
Milton Rd E NR32 . . . .**113** D1
Milton Rd N **4** IP14. .**124** D6
Milton Rd S IP14 . . . .**124** D6
Milton Rd W NR32. . . .**113** D1
Milton St IP4 . . . .**140** B7
Mimas Way IP1. . . . . .**138** D8
Mimosa Wlk NR32 . . .**113** B2
Mincarlo Trawler★
NR33. . . . .**115** D8
Minden Cl IP33 . . . . . .**154** C2
Minden Dr
Bury St Edmunds
IP33 . . . .**122** D5
Leiston IP16 . . . .**129** D5
Minden Rd
Lowestoft NR32 . . . . .**113** C2
Sudbury CO10. . . . . . .**148** D5
Minerva Cl
28 Harwich CO12. . . .**106** F1
Haverhill CB9 . . . .**133** B4
Minks Path IP30 . . . . . .**50** E3
Minos Rd NR32 . . . . . .**113** C4
Minos Way IP1 . . . . . .**138** D8
**Minsmere Nature
Reserve★** IP17. . . . . .**58** E6
Minsmere Rd IP17 . . . .**58** F8
Minsmere Rise IP17. . .**58** A6
Minsmere Way CO10. . .**92** B3
Minster Rd CB9 . . . . . .**132** D7
Minton Ent Pk CB8 . . .**120** E7
Mirbeck's Cl **6** NR34. . . .**9** F4
Misburgh Way NR31. . . .**3** C6
Mission La CO10 . . . . .**104** D6
Mission Rd IP22 . . . . . .**20** D2
Mission Way NR16 . . . .**19** F7
Mistletoe Ct IP14 . . . .**124** A6
MISTLEY **105** A2
Mistley Grove CO11 . .**104** E2
MISTLEY HEATH **105** A1
Mistley Norman CE Prim
Sch CO11 . . . .**105** A2
Mistley Quay 1
CO11. . . . .**104** F2
Mistley Sta CO11. . . . .**104** F2
Mistley Way IP12 . . . .**146** F6
Mistral Cl CB7. . . . .**28** E2
Mitchell Ave IP32. . . . .**48** C5
Mitchery La IP14. . . . . .**65** E4
Mitford Cl IP1 . . . .**135** A4
Mitford Rd IP17. . . . . . .**72** B8
Mitre Cl **6** IP30. . . . . . .**50** D1
Mitre Way IP3 . . . .**139** E4
Mizon Cl CO10. . . . .**75** D3
Moat Farm Cl IP4 . . . .**139** F8
Moat La
Alphamstone CO8. . . .**101** A4
Rushbrooke with Rougham
IP30. . . . .**49** D1
Moat Rd
Birdbrook CO9 . . . .**89** B4
Theberton IP16 . . . .**57** F4
Moat Side **12** IP26. . . . . .**4** D5
Moat Wlk **2** CB9 . . . .**132** C6
Mobbs Way NR32 . . . .**112** E3
Mockbeggars Hall★
IP8. . . . .**134** C6
Moffat Ave IP4 . . . . . .**136** B1
MOLE HILL CB8. . . . . . .**61** E1
Molehill Drove IP26. . . . .**4** D7
Moles La
Ilketshall St Margaret
NR35. . . . .**24** C8
St Lawrence, Ilketshall
NR34. . . . .**8** D1
Moleyns Cl NR32. . . . .**112** E3
Moll's La NR34. . . . .**25** D5
Monarch Cl CB9 . . . . .**132** A6
Monarch Way
Carlton Colville
NR33 . . . .**114** A3
Pinewood IP8. . . . .**142** D8
Monastery Ct IP7. . . . .**149** E7
Monastery Hill IP17. . .**43** B1
Monckton Ave NR32 .**112** F2
Monckton Cres
NR32. . . . .**112** F2
Monet Sq **1** NR32. . . .**113** B5
MONEWDEN **69** F5
Monewden Rd
Charsfield IP13. . . . .**70** A3
Otley IP6. . . . .**69** E3
Moneyhole Cnr CO10. . .**78** C9
Moneypiece Cl 1
CB9 . . . .**132** D7
Moneypot La IP22 . . . . .**19** F6
Monks Cl IP11 . . . .**153** D6
MONKS ELEIGH. **79** B2
Monks Eleigh Rd
Brent Eleigh CO10. . . . .**79** B2
Monks Eleigh IP7 . . . . .**79** C3

Monksgate IP24 . . . . . . 16 B6
Monks Gate IP8 . . . . 138 A6
Monkshood Cl 3
 NR33 . . . . 114 F2
Monk's La C07 . . . . . . 103 E2
Monk'S La IP20 . . . . 22 B5
MONK SOHAM 54 D4
Monk Soham La IP13 . 54 D5
Monk Soham Rd
 Bedfield IP13 . . . . 54 E4
Monk Soham Green
 IP14 . . . . 54 C4
Monmouth Cl IP2 . . . . 139 B1
Montagu Dr
 Saxmundham IP17 . . . 128 B3
 Weeting IP27 . . . . 5 E4
Montague Rd IP11 . . . . 153 A4
Montana Place NR32 113 B1
Montana Rd IP5 . . . . . . 141 A7
Montford Cl CB5 . . . . . . 44 B6
Montfort Ct 11 CB9 . . 132 D5
Montgomery Ave
 NR32 . . . . 113 B4
Montgomery Rd IP2 . 139 B1
Monton Rise IP2 . . . . . 138 D2
Montpelier Dr 1
 IP24 . . . . 16 A5
Monument Farm La
 IP10 . . . . 141 C3
Monument Farm Rd
 IP10 . . . . 141 B4
Moonhall Bsns Pk
 CB9 . . . . 132 C4
Moo Play Farm ★
 NR34 . . . . 25 C5
Moorbridge La IP14 . . 66 B8
Moor Drove IP26 . . . . . . 4 F2
Moor Drove East IP26 . . 4 F2
Mooreland Dr IP31 . . . 49 C6
Moore Rd
 Ipswich IP1 . . . . 134 F3
 Rushbrooke with Rougham
 IP30 . . . . 49 B2
 Stowmarket IP14 . . . . 124 A6
Moore's Cl 17 IP14 . . . . 53 F2
Moores La C07 . . . . . . 151 C6
Moorfield Cl IP5 . . . . . 141 D8
Moorfield Rd IP12 . . . 146 E5
Moor Green Cl 10
 CB8 . . . . 61 E2
Moorhall Cswy IP23 . . 117 C1
Moor Hall Rd C010 . . . 89 E7
Moorhouse Farm La
 IP29 . . . . 77 A6
Moorlands IP12 . . . . . . 99 F8
Moor Pasture Way
 CB9 . . . . 74 D2
Moor Rd
 Burston & Shimpling
 IP21 . . . . 21 B6
 Fordham CB7 . . . . 29 A3
 Langham C04 . . . . 103 B2
 Middleton IP17 . . . . 57 F6
Moorsfield C010 . . . . . 148 F2
Moorside IP18 . . . . 119 A2
Moor's Way IP12 . . . . . 146 E5
Morello Chase 6 CB7 . 28 E3
Moreton Hall Ind Est
 IP32 . . . . 123 F4
Moreton Hall Ret Pk
 IP32 . . . . 123 F4
Morgan Ct 3 IP6 . . . . 134 C8
Morgan Dr IP11 . . . . . 134 C1
Morgan Meadow
 IP14 . . . . 124 C2
Morland CE VA Prim Sch
 IP3 . . . . 144 A8
Morland Rd 1 IP3 . . . . 144 A8
Morley Ave IP12 . . . . . 146 F4
Morley Cl 3 IP28 . . . . . 30 B8
Morleys La IP23 . . . . . . 36 D2
Mormor La IP21 . . . . . . 21 F4
Mornington Ave 2
 IP1 . . . . 134 F1
Morris Rd IP13 . . . . . . 127 C5
Morris Way IP6 . . . . . . 125 D4
Mors End 2 C07 . . . . . 103 E5
Morston Hall Rd IP11 . 98 B1
Mortimer La IP28 . . . . . 29 E3
Mortimer Pl 3 C010 . . 76 A1
Mortimer Rd
 27 Bury St Edmunds
 IP31 . . . . 49 A3
 Great Green IP30 . . . . . 64 D3
 Stowmarket IP14 . . . . 124 F7
Morton Peto Cl NR32 . . 2 D3
Morton Rd NR33 . . . . . 115 B4
Moses Wlk 25 IP6 . . . . 82 A5
Moss La IP6 . . . . 135 F4
Mother Quy's IP24 . . . . 15 C5
Mother Quy's Corner
 IP27 . . . . 15 B5
Mottram Cl 14 IP8 . . . 138 C2
MOULTON 46 D3
Moulton Ave 2 CB8 . . 46 A5
Moulton CE Prim Sch
 CB8 . . . . 45 F3
Moulton Cl 5 C010 . . 148 D6
Moulton Packhorse
 Bridge ★ CB8 . . . . 45 F3
Moulton Paddocks
 CB8 . . . . 121 F7
Moulton Rd
 Cheveley CB8 . . . . 121 D4
 Gazeley CB8 . . . . 46 B3
 Kentford CB8 . . . . 46 A5

Moulton Rd continued
 Moulton CB8 . . . . 45 E1
Mountbatten Cl
 C010 . . . . 148 D8
Mountbatten Ct IP1 . 139 A7
Mountbatten Rd
 Bungay NR35 . . . . 110 B2
 Lowestoft NR32 . . . . . 113 B4
 Sudbury C010 . . . . . . 148 D8
MOUNT BURES 101 C3
Mount Cl 5 IP30 . . . . . 64 F8
Mount Dr IP3 . . . . 140 F1
MOUNT PLEASANT . . . 75 D2
Mount Pleasant
 15 Diss IP22 . . . . 20 C3
 Framlingham IP13 . . . 126 B4
 Halesworth IP19 . . . . . 118 B5
 Lowestoft NR32 . . . . . 113 C3
 1 Peasenhall IP17 . . . 56 F8
 Southwold IP18 . . . . . 119 C8
Mount Rd
 Bury St Edmunds
 IP32 . . . . 123 D6
 Haverhill CB9 . . . . 132 E5
 Rushbrooke with Rougham
 IP30 . . . . 49 A3
Mount St IP22 . . . . 20 C3
Mounts The IP17 . . . . . 56 F8
Mount View C010 . . . . 148 C7
Mouse La IP30 . . . . 49 C2
Moverley Way 1
 IP15 . . . . 130 E5
Mowbrays The IP13 . . 126 D3
Mow Hill IP6 . . . . 83 A5
Mowlands IP9 . . . . 150 F3
Mowness Hall La
 IP14 . . . . 68 A6
Mowness Hall Rd
 IP14 . . . . 68 A6
Moyes Pl IP8 . . . . 142 C7
Moyes Rd NR32 . . . . . . 112 D1
Moyse Ave 4 IP18 . . . 119 C8
Moyse's Hall Mus ★
 IP33 . . . . 154 B2
Muck Heap Rd NR35 . . 8 D5
Mudds Yard IP33 . . . . 154 B3
Mulberry Cl
 Beccles NR34 . . . . 111 C5
 18 Feltwell IP26 . . . . . . 4 E5
 Mildenhall IP28 . . . . . 116 E4
Mulberry Gdns
 11 Claydon IP6 . . . . . . 82 A5
 Sudbury C010 . . . . . . 148 F3
Mulberry Green 47
 IP28 . . . . 30 C1
Mulberry Rd 3 IP3 . . 144 C7
Mullein Gdns 3
 CB9 . . . . 132 C8
Mumford Rd IP1 . . . . . 138 E8
Munday's La IP12 . . . . 131 B3
Munden Cl 4 IP26 . . . . 5 A3
MUNDFORD 6 B8
Mundford CE Prim Sch
 IP26 . . . . 6 A8
Mundford Rd
 Brandon IP27 . . . . 5 F2
 Feltwell IP26 . . . . 5 C7
 Thetford IP24 . . . . 16 B7
 Weeting-with-Broomhill
 IP27 . . . . 6 A4
Mundy's Rd IP20 . . . . . 23 A5
Munnings Cl
 Haverhill CB9 . . . . 132 B7
 3 Lowestoft NR33 . . . 114 C3
 Newmarket CB8 . . . . . 121 A5
Munnings Way C011 . 104 D3
Munson's La IP26 . . . . . 4 E6
Munson's La 1 IP26 . . . 4 E6
Murfitt's La CB7 . . . . . . 29 A2
Muriel Cl 4 IP7 . . . . . 149 E6
Murillo Dr 1 NR32 . . 113 C6
Murray Cl IP12 . . . . . . 146 F8
Murrayfield Community
 Prim Sch IP3 . . . . 140 A3
Murray Rd IP3 . . . . . . 140 A3
Murrills Rd IP3 . . . . . . 140 E1
Murton Cl 10 CB5 . . . . 44 A6
Murton Slade 10
 CB9 . . . . 132 E4
Museum St IP1 . . . . . . 155 B3
Musgrave Cl 22
 C012 . . . . 106 F1
Mussidan Pl IP12 . . . . 146 F5
Mustards Gapp CB9 . . 133 A5
Mustow St IP33 . . . . . 154 C2
MUTFORD 10 D2
Mutford Cl NR32 . . . . 112 F1
Mutford Gn IP27 . . . . 109 C7
Mutford Wood NR33 . 10 D4
Mutfordwood La
 NR33 . . . . 114 A2
Mutimer Cl IP13 . . . . . 54 E7
Mutton La IP13 . . . . . . 70 A8
Mutton Meadow
 IP14 . . . . 51 F1
Mylford Cl IP3 . . . . . . 144 C8
Mylodon Rd NR32 . . . 113 C4
Myrtle Cl
 Bury St Edmunds
 IP33 . . . . 154 A3
 26 Eriswell IP27 . . . . . 13 F2
 Lowestoft NR32 . . . . . 113 B2
Myrtle Dr 17 CB5 . . . . 44 A6
Myrtle La 40 IP28 . . . . 30 C1
Myrtle Mws IP25 . . . . 30 A6
Myrtle Rd IP3 . . . . 139 E4
Myrtlewood Rd 15
 IP32 . . . . 48 B5

N

NACTON 145 C5
Nacton CE VC Prim Sch
 IP10 . . . . 145 C5
Nacton Cl 5 IP12 . . . . . 85 B3
Nacton Cres IP3 . . . . . 140 B2
Nacton La 2 IP31 . . . . 49 A6
Nacton Rd
 Felixstowe IP11 . . . . . 152 E1
 Ipswich IP10 . . . . 144 D7
 Levington IP10 . . . . . . 145 E3
Nan Hazle's La IP22 . . 36 B4
Nansen Rd IP3 . . . . . . 140 B2
Napier Pl IP24 . . . . 16 B5
Naples Cl 5 NR31 . . . . . 3 C6
Narrow Way IP19 . . . . 42 C6
Nash Cl C011 . . . . 104 D3
Nash Gdns IP3 . . . . . . 144 B8
Nassau Dr 17 IP11 . . . 107 D8
Nat Flatman St IP13 . . 121 B3
National Horse Racing
 Mus ★ CB8 . . . . 121 A3
National Stud ★ CB8 . 59 B8
Nato Pl IP27 . . . . 109 F1
NAUGHTON 80 C3
Naughton Gdns 8
 IP14 . . . . 124 E3
Naughton Rd IP7 . . . . . 80 C1
Naunton Rd IP12 . . . . 146 E5
Navarre St IP1 . . . . . . 155 C3
Naverne Meadow
 IP12 . . . . 147 A5
Navigation App IP14 . 124 E6
NAYLAND 102 C5
Nayland Dr IP14 . . . . . 80 C8
Nayland Prim Sch
 C06 . . . . 102 D5
Nayland Rd
 Bures St Mary C08 . . . 101 D4
 1 Felixstowe IP11 . . . 152 C3
 Great Horkesley C06 . 102 D2
 Haverhill CB9 . . . . 132 C4
 Leavenheath C010 . . 102 A7
 Little Horkesley C06 . 102 C3
 Stoke-by-Nayland C06 102 E6
Naylor Ct IP14 . . . . . . 124 B7
Nazer Cl 6 IP26 . . . . . . 6 B8
Neale Cl IP16 . . . . 129 B6
Neale St IP1 . . . . 155 B3
Neath Dr IP2 . . . . 139 A1
Neave Cl IP19 . . . . 41 C5
Neaves La IP21 . . . . . . 39 B4
NEDGING 79 F3
Nedging Rd IP7 . . . . . . 79 F3
NEDGING TYE 80 B4
NEEDHAM 22 B4
Needham La IP7 . . . . . 79 E4
Needham Lake Nature
 Reserve & Visitor Ctr ★
 IP6 . . . . 125 E4
NEEDHAM MARKET . . 125 E5
Needham Mkt Sta
 IP6 . . . . 125 E4
Needham Rd
 Barking IP6 . . . . 125 C1
 Coddenham IP6 . . . . . . 67 F1
 Needham IP20 . . . . 22 C5
 Stowmarket IP14 . . . . 124 E4
Needham Rd W IP14 . 124 F4
NEEDHAM ST CB8 . . . . 46 C4
NEEDHAM STREET . . . 46 B4
Needle Cnr IP9 . . . . . . 106 B5
Nelcon Rd 28 C012 . . 107 B2
Nelson Cl IP6 . . . . 83 A8
Nelson Cres 2 IP24 . . 16 B5
Nelson Rd
 Bury St Edmunds
 IP33 . . . . 154 A2
 Ipswich IP4 . . . . 140 A7
 1 Lowestoft NR33 . . . 115 A3
 Sudbury C010 . . . . . . 148 E7
Nelson's Ave IP9 . . . . 144 B1
Nelson Way
 Beccles NR34 . . . . 111 A4
 Woodbridge IP12 . . . . 146 F7
Nelson Wharf NR33 . . 114 F7
Nene Dr IP3 . . . . 144 D7
Neptune Quay IP4 . . . 155 C2
Neptune Sq IP4 . . . . . 155 C2
Neptune St NR32 . . . . 115 C8
Neslings Cl IP13 . . . . . 127 C6
Ness Rd
 Arwarton IP9 . . . . 106 D5
 Burwell CB5 . . . . 44 B7
Nethergate St
 Bungay NR35 . . . . 110 A5
 Clare C010 . . . . 90 A7
 Hopton IP22 . . . . 18 B2
Netherhall Cl IP14 . . . 52 A1
Nether Hall La IP9 . . . 106 B5
Nether Hall Mus & Gall ★
 C010 . . . . 76 A7
Nether Hill C09 . . . . . . 90 E2
Nether Rd 2 C010 . . . 76 E1
NETHER STREET 64 E8
Netley Cl IP27 . . . . . . 142 F8
Netley Rd IP33 . . . . . . 122 D3
NETTLESTEAD 81 C4
Nettlestead Rd
 Baylham IP6 . . . . 81 D6
 Nettlestead IP8 . . . . . . 81 A4
Nevard La C06 . . . . . . 102 C3
Nevill Rd 2 IP24 . . . . . 16 C2
Newall Rd 2 IP24 . . . . 16 C2
Newark Cl IP2 . . . . . . 138 F1
Newark Rd NR33 . . . . 115 B6

New Barn IP29 . . . . 47 B3
New Barn La
 Lidgate CB8 . . . . 61 B4
 Raydon IP7 . . . . 94 E2
New Bells La IP14 . . . . 51 D3
Newberry Rd 7 IP7 . . 79 F4
Newbolt Cl 5 IP14 . . . 124 B8
NEWBOURNE 98 C5
Newbourne Gdns
 IP11 . . . . 152 D3
Newbourne Rd
 Brightwell IP10 . . . . . . 98 A6
 Martlesham IP12 . . . . . 84 B1
 Waldringfield IP12 . . . 98 C7
Newbourne Springs
 Nature Reserve ★
 IP12 . . . . 98 D6
Newbourn Rd IP10 . . . 98 C4
New Breck Rd 16
 IP30 . . . . 50 F2
Newbury Rd IP4 . . . . . 140 C6
Newby Cl IP19 . . . . . . 118 A3
Newby Dr IP4 . . . . 140 F5
New Cangle Com Prim
 Sch CB9 . . . . 132 D7
New Cardinal St IP1 . 155 A2
New Cheveley Rd
 CB8 . . . . 121 C3
New Cut
 5 Bures C08 . . . . 101 C4
 6 Glemsford C010 . . . 77 A2
 Hadleigh IP7 . . . . 149 E6
 Halesworth IP19 . . . . . 118 B4
 Newmarket CB8 . . . . . 121 A3
 Saxmundham IP17 . . . 128 D3
New Cut E IP3 . . . . . . 155 C1
New Cut W IP2 . . . . . . 155 C1
New Delight Rd IP22 . 35 F2
New Dro
 Beck Row, Holywell Row &
 Kenny Hill IP28 . . . . . 12 E1
 Soham CB7 . . . . 28 A4
Newell Rise IP6 . . . . . 134 C8
NEW ENGLAND 89 A5
New England La CB8 . 61 C3
New England Rd C09 . 89 A5
New England Way 2
 IP24 . . . . 16 A5
Newfen Gravel Dro
 IP27 . . . . 109 A8
Newgate
 Beccles NR34 . . . . 111 B5
 Kirby Row NR35 . . . . . . 8 E7
 Newgate La NR31 . . . . 3 C6
 New Gn Ave 13 IP31 . . 49 E4
New Hampshire Way 5
 IP24 . . . . 16 A5
Newhaven Way IP7 . . 149 E7
New House La C010 . . 76 B3
New La IP9 . . . . 105 F6
Newland Rd NR34 . . . 111 E4
Newlands
 2 Elmsett IP7 . . . . 80 F1
 Otley IP6 . . . . 69 D2
Newlands Cl
 40 Harleston IP20 . . . . 22 D6
 Lowestoft NR33 . . . . . 114 F3
 Stanton IP31 . . . . 34 E3
Newlands Ind Est
 IP33 . . . . 123 D3
Newlands La C06 . . . . 102 D5
New Lea IP13 . . . . 56 A7
Newman Dr IP5 . . . . . 141 E7
Newman'S Drove
 IP27 . . . . 13 C6
NEWMAN'S GREEN . . 92 A6
Newman's Rd C010 . . 148 C6
NEWMARKET 121 B4
Newmarket Bsns Pk
 CB8 . . . . 120 F2
Newmarket Coll
 Newmarket CB8 . . . . . 120 F4
 Newmarket CB8 . . . . . 120 F4
Newmarket Hospl
 CB8 . . . . 120 F5
Newmarket Lawn Tennis
 Club CB8 . . . . 120 E3
Newmarket Leisure Ctr
 CB8 . . . . 120 F4
Newmarket Racecourse
 CB8 . . . . 120 B1
Newmarket Rd
 1 Ashley CB8 . . . . 60 F8
 Barton Mills IP28 . . . . 116 D1
 Burwell CB5 . . . . 44 B5
 Bury St Edmunds
 IP33 . . . . 122 D6
 Cowlinge CB8 . . . . 61 B2
 Fordham CB7 . . . . 44 E8
 Kirtling CB8 . . . . 60 E4
 Moulton CB8 . . . . 45 F3
 Newmarket CB8 . . . . . 121 B8
 Red Lodge IP28 . . . . . . 30 B3
 Red Lodge IP28 . . . . . . 30 C2
 Risby IP28 . . . . 47 C5
 Snailwell CB8 . . . . 45 A5
Newmarket Sports Ctr
 CB8 . . . . 120 F3
Newmarket Sta CB8 . 121 A2
Newmarket Swimming
 Pool CB8 . . . . 120 F3
Newmill La C011 . . . . 105 A5
NEW MISTLEY 105 A2
New Mkt NR34 . . . . . . 111 B5
Newnham Ave IP12 . . 146 D4

Newnham Cl IP28 . . . 116 D5
Newnham Ct IP2 . . . . 138 E1
Newnham Dro CB5 . . . 44 A6
New Path 4 CB7 . . . . . 29 A1
Newport Ave CB7 . . . . 29 C1
Newquay Cl IP5 . . . . . 140 F6
New Quay Cl IP12 . . . 147 B5
New Quay Ct IP12 . . . 147 B5
New Quay La IP12 . . . 147 B6
New Quay Terr IP12 . . 147 B6
New Queens Rd
 C010 . . . . 148 C7
New Rd
 Ampton IP31 . . . . 33 A1
 Aspall IP14 . . . . 53 E4
 Badingham IP13 . . . . . 56 B8
 Barnby NR34 . . . . 10 C4
 Beccles NR34 . . . . 111 F7
 Boxted IP29 . . . . 77 A5
 Brettenham IP24 . . . . . 17 B6
 6 Burwell CB5 . . . . . . 44 A6
 Charsfield IP13 . . . . . . 70 A2
 Chevington IP29 . . . . . 62 C7
 Crown Corner IP13 . . . 39 A1
 Dalham CB8 . . . . 61 C8
 Dickleburgh & Rushall
 IP21 . . . . 21 A4
 Elmswell IP30 . . . . 50 E2
 Exning CB8 . . . . 120 B8
 Felixstowe IP11 . . . . . 152 C3
 Framlingham IP13 . . . 126 C5
 Fritton & St Olaves
 NR31 . . . . 2 B7
 Gissing IP22 . . . . 20 F8
 Great Glemham IP17 . . 71 E8
 Helmingham IP14 . . . . 69 A5
 19 Ixworth IP31 . . . . . 34 B1
 Kessingland Beach
 NR33 . . . . 27 B8
 Little Livermere IP31 . 33 A2
 Long Melford C010 . . . 91 D8
 Manningtree C011 . . . 104 E2
 Marlesford IP13 . . . . . 71 C6
 Melton IP12 . . . . 84 D6
 Mettingham NR35 . . . 110 F2
 Nedging-with-Naughton
 IP7 . . . . 80 C3
 Rumburgh IP19 . . . . . . 24 C4
 Rushbrooke with Rougham
 IP30 . . . . 49 D1
 St Cross, South Elmham
 IP20 . . . . 23 D5
 Sibton IP17 . . . . 41 D1
 Thelnetham IP22 . . . . . 35 B7
 Thrandeston IP21 . . . . 37 C8
 Timworth IP31 . . . . . . 48 E8
 Tivetshall St Mary NR15 21 B8
 Tostock IP30 . . . . 50 B2
 Troston IP31 . . . . 33 D4
 Weston Ditch IP28 . . . 29 F8
 Worlingworth IP13 . . . 54 F8
 Wrentham NR34 . . . . . 26 F6
New Ride IP24 . . . . 17 B1
New River Gn CB8 . . . 120 B8
Newry Ave IP11 . . . . . 152 F4
New St Cl IP21 . . . . . . 39 A4
Newson Ave NR34 . . . 10 C3
Newson's Meadow 1
 NR32 . . . . 113 C2
Newson St IP1 . . . . . . 155 A4
New St
 Chippenham CB7 . . . . . 29 E1
 Framlingham IP13 . . . 126 A4
 Fressingfield IP21 . . . . 39 D8
 Glemsford C010 . . . . . 77 A3
 Ipswich IP1 . . . . 139 E5
 4 Mildenhall IP28 . . . 116 C4
 Stradbroke IP21 . . . . . 39 A4
 Sudbury C010 . . . . . . 148 D5
 Newton St IP1 . . . . . . 155 C3
NEWTOWN 54 D7
New Way IP21 . . . . . . 138 F6
Newthorpe IP30 . . . . . 49 C1
NEWTON 92 D3
Newton Croft C010 . . 148 E5
Newton Ct IP29 . . . . . 63 E8
Newton Hall La IP6 . . 83 B7
Newton Pl 4 CB9 . . . 132 F6
Newton Rd
 17 Harwich C012 . . . . 107 A2
 Ipswich IP3 . . . . 140 A4
 Stowupland IP14 . . . . 124 D8
 Sudbury C010 . . . . . . 148 D5
 Newton St IP1 . . . . . . 155 C3
NEWTOWN 54 D7
New Way IP21 . . . . . . 138 F6
Nicholas Dr IP18 . . . . 119 C7
Nicholas Everitt Pk
 NR33 . . . . 114 D8
Nicholas Rd IP11 . . . . 152 C4
Nicholas's St 2
 IP22 . . . . 20 C2
Nicholls Cl 7 IP13 . . . 84 F7
Nicholls Way 8 IP22 . 20 B3
Nichols Cl IP22 . . . . . . 20 D3
Nicholson Cl 2 C011 . 104 D2
Nicholson Cl 3 IP3 . . 140 C7
Nicholson Dr NR34 . . 111 C2
Nicholsons Cl C010 . . 92 D3
Nicholson Sq 2
 NR32 . . . . 113 C2
Nick's La IP23 . . . . 117 B6
Nidderdale 8 NR33 . . 114 E3
Nigel Way 19 IP1 . . . . 107 D8
Nightall Rd 5 CB7 . . . 28 D5
Nightingale Ave
 IP18 . . . . 119 B7

Nightingale Cl
 Bury St Edmunds
 IP33 . . . . 154 A1
 Halesworth IP19 . . . . . 118 B1
 19 Harwich C012 . . . . 106 F1
 5 Mildenhall IP28 . . . 116 D4
 5 Stowmarket IP14 . . 67 A5
 Woodbridge IP12 . . . . 147 B8
Nightingale Hill C04 . 103 C3
Nightingale La 9 IP26 . 4 E5
Nightingale Piece
 IP12 . . . . 131 C3
Nightingale Rd
 Ipswich IP3 . . . . 144 A8
 Lowestoft NR33 . . . . . 115 B3
 New Mistley C011 . . . 105 F2
Nightingale Sq 5
 IP3 . . . . 144 A8
Nightingale Way 13
 IP12 . . . . 84 A1
Nightjar Cl 9 IP22 . . . 20 D3
Nightjar Gr 16 IP12 . . 84 A1
Nimbus Way CB8 . . . . 120 E8
Nine Acres IP2 . . . . . . 138 D6
Ninfield Cl NR33 . . . . 114 D4
Noahs Ark Pl C010 . . 148 B5
Noahs Dr 5 NR33 . . . . 11 B1
Noaks Rd IP7 . . . . 94 F1
Noble's La IP22 . . . . . . 35 D4
Nock Gdns IP5 . . . . . . 141 C6
No Ditch Balk CB7 . . . 28 D2
Noel Cl NR31 . . . . 3 B7
Noel Murless Dr CB8 . 120 F6
Noel Rd NR32 . . . . . . 112 C1
Noel's Wlk NR34 . . . . 111 B6
Noller's La IP19 . . . . . . 24 F4
No Man's Meadow ★
 IP23 . . . . 123 C4
Nonsuch Meadow 2
 C010 . . . . 148 C4
Norbury Rd IP4 . . . . . 140 B7
Nordalls The 16 NR33 . 7 E4
Nordle Corner IP22 . . 19 F5
Norfolk Ave CB8 . . . . 120 E5
Norfolk Cres 1
 IP13 . . . . 126 C3
Norfolk Rd
 Bury St Edmunds
 IP32 . . . . 123 A8
 6 Honington IP31 . . . . 33 D5
 Ipswich IP1 . . . . 155 C3
 Thetford IP24 . . . . 16 C6
 Wangford NR34 . . . . . 26 B2
Norfolk St NR32 . . . . . 113 B1
Norfolk & Suffolk
 Aviation Mus ★ NR35 . 7 D2
Norgate La IP21 . . . . . 21 B2
Norman Cl
 Felixstowe IP11 . . . . . 153 D6
 Woodbridge IP12 . . . . 147 A7
Norman Cres IP3 . . . . 140 A2
Normandie Way 8
 C08 . . . . 101 C4
Normandy Cl IP14 . . . 124 D3
Normandy Rd NR32 . . 113 B4
Normanhurst Cl
 NR32 . . . . 113 A2
Norman Rd
 6 Bury St Edmunds
 IP32 . . . . 48 C5
 Bury St Edmunds IP32 122 F8
 23 Manningtree C011 104 E2
Normans 21 C010 . . . 78 D4
Normans Cl 7 IP8 . . . 134 A2
NORMANSTON 113 B3
Normanston Dr 5
 NR32 . . . . 113 B2
Norman Way 1 C010 . 78 D4
Nornea La CB7 . . . . . . 28 A8
Norse Ave IP29 . . . . . . 64 A3
Northacre 12 NR33 . . 11 B1
North Acres IP8 . . . . . 81 A6
North Ave CB9 . . . . . . 132 C5
North Cl
 Bacton IP14 . . . . 51 F6
 Ipswich IP4 . . . . 135 E1
 9 Stanton IP31 . . . . . . 34 E4
NORTH COMMON 34 F6
North Cote Dr IP7 . . . 79 C2
NORTH COVE 10 C4
North Cres CB9 . . . . . . 88 D4
Northcroft 1 C010 . . 148 C5
North Dr
 Newmarket CB8 . . . . . 120 F5
 1 Soham CB7 . . . . 28 D5
North East Suffolk Bsns
 Ctr NR33 . . . . 114 E2
NORTH END 90 C2
North End CB8 . . . . . . 120 B8
North End Ave IP16 . . 73 F6
North End Rd C09 . . . . 90 C2
North Entrance IP17 . 128 D7
Northern Rd C010 . . . 148 F7
Northern Rose Cl
 IP32 . . . . 123 F7
Northern Way IP32 . . 48 C5
Northfen Drove IP27 . 14 A7
North Field Cl 3
 NR32 . . . . 112 F5
Northfield Ct IP15 . . . 130 E5
Northfield La IP15 . . . 130 E5
Northfield Pk CB7 . . . 28 C5
Northfield Rd
 Onehouse IP14 . . . . . . 66 C6
 Soham CB7 . . . . 28 C5

Northfield St Nicholas
  Prim Sch NR32 . . . . . 113 C3
Northfield View IP8 . **138** B3
Northfield Windmill★
  CB7 . . . . 28 C6
Northgate
  Beccles NR34 . . . . **111** B6
  11 Harleston IP20 . . . . . . **22** D5
  Lowestoft NR32 . . . . . **113** B2
Northgate Ave
  Bury St Edmunds
  IP32 . . . . **122** F8
  Bury St Edmunds IP32 . **154** B4
Northgate High Sch
  IP4 . . . . 136 A1
Northgate Lodge
  IP33 . . . . **154** B3
Northgate St Bsns Pk
  IP33 . . . . **154** C3
Northgate Sports Ctr
  IP4 . . . . 136 A2
Northgate St
  Bury St Edmunds
  IP33 . . . . **154** C3
  Ipswich IP4 . . . . **155** B3
North Gn IP18 . . . . . . **119** D6
North Gn Rd
  Cratfield IP19 . . . . 40 C7
  Pulham St Mary IP21 . . . **22** A8
NORTH GREEN
  Cratfield 40 C7
  Kelsale cum Carlton 57 D5
  Parham 56 B1
North Green Rd IP13 . **71** B8
North Hill
  Bird's End IP29 . . . . 62 C8
  Bury St Edmunds IP30 . . 49 A1
  Bury St Edmunds IP30 . **123** F1
  Rushbrooke IP30 . . . . . . 64 B8
  Woodbridge IP12 . . . . . **146** F6
North Hill Gdns IP4 . **139** E6
North Hill Rd IP4 . . . **139** E6
North La IP21 . . . . **39** C7
North Lawn IP4 . . . . **140** B8
NORTH LOPHAM **19** A5
North Lopham Rd
  NR16 . . . . **19** A7
North Parade
  Lowestoft NR32 . . . . . **113** D4
  Southwold IP18 . . . . . **119** E5
North Par Gdns IP18 . **119** E4
North Pl IP28 . . . . . . **116** C4
North Quay Ret Pk
  NR32 . . . . **113** B1
North Rd
  Great Yeldham CO9 . . . . **90** A1
  Lakenheath IP27 . . . . . **109** E4
  Southwold IP18 . . . . . . **119** D6
North Rise CO10 . . . . **148** E4
  CO10 . . . . 148 C5
North St Parade 5
  CO12 . . . . **106** F1
North St
  Burwell CB5 . . . . 44 A6
  Freckenham IP28 . . . . . **29** E3
  Hundon CO10 . . . . 75 D4
  11 Manningtree CO11 . **104** E2
  Steeple Bumpstead
  CB9 . . . . **88** D4
  Sudbury CO10 . . . . . . 148 C6
  Wicken CB7 . . . . **28** A1
North Stow IP28 . . . . . **32** B6
North Terr IP28 . . . . . 116 C4
Northumberland Ave
  IP32 . . . . **122** E8
North Warren IP15 . . . 130 C8
Northwarren Nature
  Reserve★ IP15 . . . . . **73** D6
Northwood Cl NR33 . . **114** F6
NORTON 50 B4
Norton CE Prim Sch
  IP31 . . . . 50 B5
NORTON LITTLE
  GREEN 50 D5
Norton Rd
  Haverhill CB9 . . . . 132 C4
  Hunston IP31 . . . . 50 E5
  11 Thurstow IP31 . . . . . 49 D4
  Tostock IP30 . . . . 50 B2
  Woolpit IP30 . . . . 50 C2
Norton Way IP13 . . . **126** B5
Norway Cres 2
  CO12 . . . . **106** F2
Norwich La
  Bardwell IP31 . . . . 34 C8
  Coney Weston IP31 . . . . 17 E2
Norwich Rd
  Barham IP6 . . . . 82 A6
  Claydon IP6 . . . . 134 C8
  Coddenham Green IP6 . . **67** F3
  Denton IP20 . . . . 7 B3
  5 Dickleburgh & Rushall
  IP21 . . . . **20** F1
  Ditchingham NR35 . . . . **110** A8
  Earsham NR35 . . . . 7 E5
  Eye IP23 . . . . 117 A7
  Gillingham NR34 . . . . . 111 A8
  Halesworth IP19 . . . . . 118 C5
  Hedenham NR35 . . . . 7 E7
  Ipswich IP1 . . . . 155 A3
  Lakenheath IP27 . . . . . . 109 E4
  Lowestoft NR32 . . . . . **113** C1
  Mendlesham IP14 . . . . . 52 F2
  Newmarket CB8 . . . . . **121** D6

Norwich Rd continued
  Pulham St Mary IP21 . . . **21** F8
  Scole IP21 . . . . **21** B5
  Stockton NR34 . . . . 9 A8
  Stoke Ash IP23 . . . . 37 B1
  Thetford IP24 . . . . 16 C6
Norwich Road
  Community Primary
  School IP24 . . . . 16 C6
Norwood Rd IP27 . . . **14** E8
NOSTERFIELD END
  CB1 . . . . 88 A7
Notcutts CO7 . . . . **151** E3
Notley Dr
  3 Haverhill CB9 . . . . . 74 A1
  Haverhill CB9 . . . . 132 A7
Notley Ent Pk CO7 . . . **95** A4
Notley Rd NR33 . . . . . 115 A7
Nottidge Rd IP4 . . . . **139** E6
Nova Scotia La IP7 . . . 79 B4
NOWTON 63 E7
Nowton Ctry Pk★
  IP33 . . . . 63 E8
Nowton Pk IP29 . . . . . 123 D1
Nowton Rd
  Bury St Edmunds
  IP33 . . . . 123 C1
  Nowton IP29 . . . . 62 E7
  Nowton IP29 . . . . 63 E8
Noyes Ave IP13 . . . . . . 40 B3
Nunn Cl 1 IP12 . . . . . 84 A1
Nunnery Dr IP24 . . . . . 16 C4
Nunnery Gn 2 CB8 . . . 61 E2
Nunnery Pl IP24 . . . . . 16 C4
Nunn's Hill IP19 . . . . . 24 C3
Nunns La IP19 . . . . . . 23 D2
Nunn's La IP19 . . . . . . 23 E1
Nuns La NR34 . . . . 2 B1
Nuns' Bridges Rd
  IP24 . . . . 16 B5
Nunsgate IP24 . . . . 16 B5
Nuns Wlk CO9 . . . . 89 F1
Nursery Cl
  Isleham CB7 . . . . 29 B4
  Lowestoft NR32 . . . . . **112** F2
  Mildenhall IP28 . . . . . . 116 D4
Nursery Gdns
  Brockford Street IP14 . . 52 F6
  Ipswich IP4 . . . . 139 E6
Nursery La
  Garlic Street IP21 . . . . . 22 A6
  Hockwold cum Wilton
  IP26 . . . . 5 A2
  Rushford IP24 . . . . 17 B4
  11 Ufford IP13 . . . . . . 84 F7
  Woolverstone IP9 . . . . . **144** B1
Nursery Rd CO10 . . . . **148** F2
Nursery Wlk IP11 . . . **152** F4
Nursey Cl NR35 . . . . . . 8 D7
Nuthatch Cl 2 IP14 . . **124** F6
Nuts Pightle IP31 . . . . 49 E4
Nuttery La IP17 . . . . . . 73 B6
Nuttery Vale IP23 . . . . 38 B6
Nutteryvale Cl IP21 . . . 38 C7

O

Oak Ave NR34 . . . . 111 F5
Oak Cl
  Bury St Edmunds
  IP28 . . . . 48 C6
  Felixstowe IP11 . . . . . **152** E4
  4 Great Finborough
  IP14 . . . . 66 B4
  Saxmundham IP17 . . . 128 D4
Oak Corner IP13 . . . . . 69 F7
Oak Cres IP23 . . . . 117 C3
Oakdene IP10 . . . . 98 D2
Oak Dr
  Aldringham IP16 . . . . . 129 D3
  Diss IP22 . . . . 20 E2
  6 Mildenhall IP28 . . . . 30 B8
Oak Eggar Chase
  IP8 . . . . 142 D8
Oakes Cl
  Bury St Edmunds
  IP32 . . . . **122** E7
  11 Laxfield IP13 . . . . . 40 B3
Oakes Rd IP32 . . . . . . **122** E7
Oakey Field Rd 6
  IP31 . . . . 49 E4
Oakey Ley IP30 . . . . . . 64 D6
Oak Farm La IP14 . . . . 52 D6
Oakfield Dr CO4 . . . . . 103 A3
Oakfield Rd
  Bacton IP14 . . . . 52 A6
  Copdock & Washbrook
  IP8 . . . . 142 A6
Oakfields IP13 . . . . 54 C5
Oakfield Wood Nature
  Reserve★ CO11 . . . . . 105 E3
Oak Gn IP19 . . . . **118** B2
Oak Gr
  Fornham St Martin
  IP31 . . . . 48 D5
  Sproughton IP8 . . . . . . 138 A6
OAK HILL 100 A8
Oak Hill Cl NR34 . . . . 26 E5
Oak Hill La IP2 . . . . . 139 B3
Oak La
  Beccles NR34 . . . . 111 D2
  Cheveley CB8 . . . . 60 E6
  Elmswell IP30 . . . . 50 F3
  Ipswich IP1 . . . . 155 A3
  Lakenheath IP27 . . . . . . 13 F2
  Rushbrooke with Rougham
  IP30 . . . . 64 D8

Oak La continued
  Woolpit IP30 . . . . 65 E8
Oakland Rd 15 CO12 . **107** B2
Oaklands
  Felixstowe IP11 . . . . . **152** E2
  Leavenheath CO6 . . . . . 102 B8
Oaklands Dr
  Brandon IP27 . . . . 14 D8
  43 Red Lodge IP28 . . . . 30 C1
OAKLEY 38 A8
Oakley Church La
  IP21 . . . . 37 F8
Oakley Rd 11 CO12 . . 106 E1
Oakley Sq
  Aldeburgh IP15 . . . . . . 130 E4
  Aldeburgh IP15 . . . . . . 130 E4
Oak Meadow Cl IP19 . . 42 C6
Oak Rd
  3 Sudbury CO10 . . . . . 92 B3
  Sudbury CO10 . . . . . . 148 F4
Oaks Bsns Pk CB8 . . . 120 F7
Oaks Com Prim Sch The
  IP2 . . . . 138 E3
Oaks Cl 4 IP16 . . . . . . 73 F6
Oaks Dr CB8 . . . . 120 F7
Oaks Farm La IP19 . . . 40 C3
Oaks La NR34 . . . . 2 B1
Oaksmere Gdns 8
  IP2 . . . . 139 A2
Oak St IP26 . . . . 4 E5
Oaks The
  7 Horringer IP29 . . . . . 63 A8
  Martlesham Heath
  IP5 . . . . 141 F6
  Soham CB7 . . . . 28 D3
  Wattisfield IP22 . . . . . . 35 C5
  Woolpit IP30 . . . . 65 F8
Oak Tree Way 8
  IP20 . . . . 22 D5
Oak View IP6 . . . . 136 B5
Oak Way IP19 . . . . 118 A1
Oak Wlk IP4 . . . . 69 A4
Oakwood Pk IP17 . . . . 57 D7
Oakwood Rd NR33 . . . 114 F5
Oasis Camel Ctr★
  IP19 . . . . 40 C8
Oast Cl IP23 . . . . 154 C1
Oatfields 6 IP21 . . . . . 39 D8
Oatlands Cl 4 NR33 . . 114 E4
Oban St IP1 . . . . 155 A4
Oberman Rd 24 IP31 . . 49 A3
OCCOLD 37 F1
Occold Prim Sch IP23 . 37 F1
Occold Rd IP23 . . . . . . 38 B2
O'feld Terr IP11 . . . . . 153 C6
Offord Cl IP5 . . . . 141 D6
Off Sea View Rd
  IP18 . . . . 119 C7
OFFTON 81 A4
Offton Rd
  Elmsett IP7 . . . . 81 A2
  Great Bricett IP7 . . . . . . 80 F5
Ogden Gr IP5 . . . . 141 B6
Ohio Cl 4 NR33 . . . . . 114 E3
Old Bakery La 6
  IP28 . . . . 116 C4
Old Barningham Rd 1
  IP31 . . . . 34 E4
Old Barn Rd CO8 . . . . 101 C3
Old Barrack Rd IP12 . 146 E4
Old Bell La IP6 . . . . 81 F6
Old Brandon Rd IP26 . . 4 F5
Old Bredfield Rd IP13 . 84 E7
Old Brewery Yd
  IP19 . . . . 118 A3
Old Brew House Ct
  IP23 . . . . 117 D2
Old Bridge Cl IP28 . . . . 30 A4
Old Buckenham Hall Sch
  IP7 . . . . 79 B7
Old Bungay Rd NR35 . . 8 D8
Old Bury Rd
  Alpheton CO10 . . . . . . 78 A6
  Lackford IP28 . . . . 31 F1
  Palgrave IP22 . . . . 37 A8
  Stanton IP31 . . . . 34 E4
  Stuston IP21 . . . . 20 D1
  Woolpit IP30 . . . . 50 F1
  Wortham IP22 . . . . 36 F8
Old Cattle Mkt IP1 . . . 155 B2
Old Church La
  Bulmer CO10 . . . . 91 C1
  Westley IP33 . . . . 122 A6
Old Church Rd
  1 Hopton on Sea
  NR31 . . . . 3 B6
  Melton IP12 . . . . 84 F6
Old Clements La 5
  CB9 . . . . 132 D5
Old Coll Cl NR34 . . . . 111 B5
Old Convent Orch
  IP33 . . . . 154 B1
Old Ct 17 CO10 . . . . . . 91 E8
Old Dairy Bsns Pk
  IP31 . . . . 49 B5
Old Dairy Ct IP28 . . . . 116 B3
Old Farm Rd
  Beccles NR34 . . . . 111 C5
  4 Lowestoft NR33 . . . 114 D5
OLD FELIXSTOWE 153 C6
Old Felixstowe Rd
  IP10 . . . . 98 A2
Oldfield Rd IP8 . . . . . . 138 B1
Old Flixton Rd NR35 . . 23 B8
Old Forge Cl IP22 . . . . 36 D8
Old Forge Ct IP21 . . . . 22 A2
Old Forge Mws IP12 . 147 C8
Old Fort Rd IP11 . . . . . 152 E1

Old Foundry Pl IP16 . 129 C6
Old Foundry Rd IP4 . . 155 C3
Old Gram La NR35 . . . . 110 B3
Old Gravel Way IP27 . 109 B3
Old Green Farm IP6 . . 135 F4
Old Hall Cl
  Felixstowe IP11 . . . . . 153 C5
  2 Henley IP6 . . . . 82 D6
  Steeple Bumpstead CB9 88 E4
OLDHALL GREEN 64 C3
Old Hall La
  Bentley IP9 . . . . 95 F2
  Bury St Edmunds IP28 . 48 D5
  Cockfield IP30 . . . . 64 B3
  Westleton IP17 . . . . 58 B8
Old Hall Meadow
  IP30 . . . . 65 D6
Oldhall Rd IP9 . . . . . . 106 F6
Old Hall Rd
  Badingham IP13 . . . . . . 56 C8
  Steeple Bumpstead
  CB10 . . . . 88 F2
Old Harleston Rd NR35 . 7 E3
Old Haverhill Rd CB9 . 74 F2
Old High Rd
  Roydon IP22 . . . . 20 B3
  Yoxford IP17 . . . . 57 D7
Old Homes Rd 7
  IP16 . . . . 73 F6
Old House La CO4 . . . 103 A1
Old House Rd CO6 . . . 102 D1
Old Hundred La IP14 . 52 D1
Olding Rd IP33 . . . . . . 122 D6
Old Ipswich Rd
  Claydon IP6 . . . . 134 C7
  Yaxley IP23 . . . . 37 B4
Old Kirton Rd IP11 . . 107 D8
Old La
  Bradfield Combust with
  Stanningfield IP29 . . . 63 F3
  Corton NR32 . . . . 113 B8
  Thelnetham IP22 . . . . . 35 C6
Old Laundry Yd
  IP15 . . . . 130 D5
Old Lode Ct CB5 . . . . . 44 A6
Old London Rd IP9 . . . 150 D1
Old Maids' La IP13 . . . 70 A7
Old Main Rd IP13 . . . 127 B2
Old Maltings App
  IP12 . . . . 147 B6
Old Maltings Ct IP12 . 147 B5
Old Methwold Rd IP26 . 4 F6
Old Mill Cl IP13 . . . . . . 54 D7
Old Mill Ct IP31 . . . . . . 34 C4
Old Mill Dr IP21 . . . . . 21 F8
Old Mill La
  Barton Mills IP28 . . . . 116 F2
  Beccles NR34 . . . . 111 B4
  Metfield IP19 . . . . 23 D2
Old Mill Rd CO4 . . . . . 103 B3
Old Mill Terr 2
  NR34 . . . . 111 B6
Old Mkt 6 NR34 . . . . . 111 B6
Old Mkt Pl
  21 Harleston IP20 . . . . 22 D6
  19 Sudbury CO10 . . . . 148 C5
Old Mkt Plain 8
  NR32 . . . . 113 E2
Old Mkt St 2 IP14 . . . 52 E4
Old Nelson St
  Lowestoft NR32 . . . . . 113 E1
  4 Lowestoft NR32 . . . 113 E1
OLD NEWTON 52 A1
Old Newton CE Prim Sch
  IP14 . . . . 52 A1
Old Newton Green
  IP14 . . . . 52 A1
Old Newton Rd IP14 . . 51 F3
Old Norton Rd 11
  IP31 . . . . 49 D4
Old Norwich Rd
  Whitton IP1 . . . . 134 D5
  Yaxley IP23 . . . . 37 C5
Old Orch IP7 . . . . 149 F1
Old Orchard 10 IP14 . . 52 E4
Old Orch Cl IP19 . . . . 118 A2
Old Paper Mill La 8
  IP6 . . . . 134 C8
Old Post Office Cl
  IP31 . . . . 49 E3
Old Post Office La
  Blaxhall IP12 . . . . 72 A4
  Kirby Row NR35 . . . . . . 8 E7
  Sutton IP12 . . . . 99 A8
Old Post Office Rd
  IP29 . . . . 62 C6
Old Rd The CO6 . . . . . 102 B8
Old Rectory Cl
  2 Claydon IP6 . . . . . . 82 B5
  6 Roydon IP22 . . . . . . 20 B3
Old Rectory Gdns 3
  IP23 . . . . 37 F1
Old Rectory La IP29 . . 77 E6
Old Rectory Rd IP13 . . 56 A6
Old Rectory Wlk IP9 . 150 D3
Old Rly Rd
  Alburgh IP20 . . . . 7 B1
  Bungay NR35 . . . . 110 A4
Old Rope Wlk CB9 . . . 132 C5
Old St The IP9 . . . . . . 150 F3
Old Sch Cl
  Brampton with Stoven
  NR34 . . . . 25 E5
  5 Burwell CB5 . . . . . . 44 A5
  Leiston IP16 . . . . 129 C6
  2 Soham CB7 . . . . 28 D5
Old Sch Dr IP28 . . . . . 26 E1

Old Sch Hall The★
  IP33 . . . . 154 B3
Old Sch La CB8 . . . . . . 59 F1
Old School Mws
  IP12 . . . . 147 C8
Old Schools Ct 4
  IP30 . . . . 50 E2
Old Sch The NR34 . . . . 10 E1
Old Silk Mill 12 CO10 . 77 B3
Old St IP14 . . . . 51 C1
Old Stable Ct CB5 . . . . 44 A7
Old Stable Yard
  Bury St Edmunds
  IP33 . . . . 154 B3
  3 Kentford CB8 . . . . . 46 A5
Old Sta La NR35 . . . . . . 8 D6
Old Sta Rd
  Halesworth IP19 . . . . . 118 B5
  Mendlesham IP14 . . . . . 52 E3
  Newmarket CB8 . . . . . 121 B4
Old Station Cl 19
  CO10 . . . . 78 D4
Old Stone Pit Way
  IP30 . . . . 78 C8
Old Stores Cl IP13 . . . . 54 E7
Old Stowmarket Rd
  IP30 . . . . 50 D1
Old Vicarage Dr IP31 . 50 F7
Old Vicarage La IP20 . 23 C4
Old Vicarage Rd 13
  CO12 . . . . 107 A2
Old Woolpit Rd IP30 . . 50 B3
Old Yarmouth Rd NR34 . 9 B7
Olive Cl 2 IP27 . . . . . . 13 F2
Olive Ct
  Lowestoft NR32 . . . . . 113 B3
  Mildenhall IP28 . . . . . 116 D2
Oliver Cl NR33 . . . . . . 114 D2
Oliver Rd IP33 . . . . . . 122 C6
Olivers Cl CO10 . . . . . . 91 E8
Olive Way 16 IP28 . . . . 30 B1
Olland Ct 3 NR35 . . . 110 B3
Olle Cl IP33 . . . . 123 C1
Olympus Cl IP11 . . . . 134 C2
One Eyed La IP21 . . . . 22 D3
ONEHOUSE 66 C6
Onehouse La IP1 . . . . . 135 C1
Onehouse Rd
  Harleston IP14 . . . . 66 B6
  Stowmarket IP14 . . . . . 124 B6
  Onehouse Way IP14 . . . 124 A6
One School Global
  Colchester Campus
  CO6 . . . . 103 E7
Onner's La IP16 . . . . . . 58 C4
Ontario Rd NR33 . . . . 115 C6
Opal Ave
  1 Ipswich IP1 . . . . . . 134 D1
  Ipswich IP1 . . . . 138 D8
Orbell Ave CB9 . . . . . . 132 F8
Orcahrd Gr 1 IP22 . . . 20 B3
Orchard Ave NR33 . . . 114 E6
Orchard Brook 13
  CO10 . . . . 91 E8
Orchard Cl
  Beyton IP30 . . . . 49 F1
  2 Blundeston NR32 . . . . 3 A4
  6 Cavendish CO10 . . . 76 E1
  Elmswell IP30 . . . . 50 F3
  Eye IP23 . . . . 117 C2
  Felsham IP30 . . . . 65 A4
  10 Gislingham IP23 . . . 36 D2
  Great Livermere IP31 . . 33 C2
  6 Haverhill CB9 . . . . . 132 B4
  Lidgate CB8 . . . . 61 C4
  2 Ramsey & Parkeston
  CO12 . . . . 106 D1
  Ridgewell CO9 . . . . 89 D3
  Risby IP28 . . . . 47 D5
  Rushbrooke with Rougham
  IP30 . . . . 64 D8
  Woodbridge IP12 . . . . 147 A7
Orchard Croft 2
  NR33 . . . . 114 E4
Orchard Ct IP14 . . . . . 124 D7
Orchard Dr IP14 . . . . . 65 A4
Orchard End 16 IP13 . . 83 E5
Orchard Farm Barns 2
  IP29 . . . . 47 A2
Orchard Farm Bsns Pk
  CB7 . . . . 28 C7
Orchard Gate
  Ipswich IP2 . . . . 138 C5
  1 Needham Market
  IP6 . . . . 125 D5
Orchard Gdn NR34 . . . 111 C4
Orchard Gr
  Claydon IP6 . . . . 134 C7
  Ipswich IP5 . . . . 141 A7
Orchard La
  3 Blundeston NR32 . . . . 3 A4
  Great Bealings IP13 . . . 137 E5
  Thurston IP31 . . . . 49 E5
Orchard Pl
  9 Kentford CB8 . . . . . 46 A5
  Sudbury CO10 . . . . . . 148 B4
  Wickham Market IP13 . 127 B6
Orchard Rd
  6 Bramford IP8 . . . . . 134 A2
  Leiston IP16 . . . . 129 C5
  Rose Green CO10 . . . . . 101 F8
Orchard Rise
  Badingham IP13 . . . . . . 56 A7
  Beccles NR34 . . . . 111 F4

Orchard Row CB7 . . . . 28 E2
Orchard St
  Bury St Edmunds
  IP33 . . . . 154 B3
  Ipswich IP4 . . . . 155 C3
Orchards The 1 IP13 . 40 B3
Orchard Terr 4
  NR33 . . . . 115 C7
Orchard The
  5 Ashley IP14 . . . . . . 60 F8
  Felsham IP30 . . . . 65 A4
  Redisham NR34 . . . . . . 25 B7
Orchard Valley IP19 . 118 D4
Orchard View CO6 . . . 102 B7
Orchard Way
  Badwell Ash IP31 . . . . . 50 F7
  12 Barrow IP29 . . . . . 47 A2
  4 Burwell CB5 . . . . . . 44 A6
  4 Glemsford CO10 . . . 77 A2
  2 Horringer IP29 . . . . . 63 A8
  Scole IP21 . . . . 21 A2
Orchid Cl
  Halesworth IP19 . . . . 118 C4
  Ipswich IP3 . . . . 140 F2
Orchid Dr 23 IP28 . . . . 30 C1
Orchids Cl NR35 . . . . 110 D3
Orchid Way
  Isleham CB7 . . . . 29 B4
  Needham Market IP6 . . 125 D3
Ore Way 5 NR31 . . . . . 3 B6
Oregon Rd IP5 . . . . . . 141 A6
ORFORD 131 C3
Orford Castle Mus &
  Visitor Ctr★ IP12 . . 131 B2
Orford CE VA Prim Sch
  IP12 . . . . 131 B3
Orford Dr NR32 . . . . . 112 F3
Orford Ness★ IP12 . . 131 C1
Orford Ness National
  Nature Reserve★
  IP12 . . . . 87 C3
Orford Rd
  Bromeswell IP12 . . . . . 147 F7
  Butley IP12 . . . . 86 A6
  Chillesford IP12 . . . . 86 B8
  Felixstowe IP11 . . . . . 152 E1
  Haverhill CB9 . . . . 132 D4
  Tunstall IP12 . . . . 71 F2
Orford St IP1 . . . . 155 A4
Oriel Cl CO10 . . . . 148 F4
Original Factory Shop
  The IP32 . . . . 123 D7
Orion Av IP6 . . . . 81 F4
Orion Bsns Pk IP6 . . . 81 F4
Orkney Cl CB9 . . . . . . 133 B5
Orkney Rd 4 IP4 . . . . 136 A1
Ormiston Denes Acad
  NR32 . . . . 113 D4
Ormiston Endeavour
  Acad IP1 . . . . 135 A4
Ormsby Cl 7 NR31 . . . . 3 B6
Orsler Cl 9 IP30 . . . . . 49 F2
Orttewell Rd IP32 . . . 123 E6
Orvis La CO7 . . . . 151 E3
Orwell Ave IP17 . . . . . 128 C4
Orwell Bsns Ctr Ip3 . 139 E2
Orwell Ct IP11 . . . . . . 146 E3
Orwell Ctry Pk★
  IP3 . . . . 139 F3
Orwell Dr 1 NR32 . . . 112 F3
Orwell Pk Sch IP10 . . 145 B3
Orwell Pl IP4 . . . . 155 C2
Orwell Rd
  Felixstowe IP11 . . . . . 152 F3
  10 Harwich CO12 . . . . 107 B2
  Ipswich IP3 . . . . 140 A4
  Stowmarket IP14 . . . . . 124 D4
Orwell Ret Pk IP2 . . . 139 A4
Orwell Rise 10 IP9 . . . 106 C8
Orwell View Rd IP9 . . 106 F6
Osborne Rd IP3 . . . . . 140 A4
Osborne St 4 NR32 . . 113 E3
Osierbed Rd IP13 . . . . 56 B5
Osier Cl IP12 . . . . 147 B6
Osier Rd IP13 . . . . 154 B3
Osiers The IP14 . . . . . 124 D7
Osier View CO10 . . . . . 78 D3
Osmund Wlk IP33 . . . 122 C4
Osprey Cl 21 IP21 . . . . 49 A3
Osprey Dr IP14 . . . . . . 67 A5
Osprey Gn NR33 . . . . 114 C6
Osprey Rd CB9 . . . . . . 133 A5
Ostrich Cl IP2 . . . . 143 B8
Oswyn Cl IP32 . . . . . . 123 D4
Osyth Cl IP2 . . . . 138 F1
OTLEY 69 C2
Otley Coll of Agriculture
  and Horticulture
  IP6 . . . . 83 C8
Otley Hall★ IP6 . . . . . . 69 C3
Otley Ct 6 IP11 . . . . . 152 D5
Otley Prim Sch IP6 . . . 69 C2
Otley Rd
  Framsden IP14 . . . . 69 D5
  Helmingham IP14 . . . . . 69 B3
  Monewden IP13 . . . . . . 69 E5
  Swilland IP13 . . . . 83 C7
  Woodbridge Airfield
  IP12 . . . . 85 C2
Otten Rd
  Belchamp Otten CO10 . . 90 D5
  Borley CO10 . . . . 91 A3
Otter Cl IP14 . . . . 124 C4
Otter Trust The★ NR35 . 7 E3
OULTON 112 F5
OULTON BROAD 114 C8
Oulton Broad N Sta
  NR32 . . . . 112 F1

Oulton Broad Prim Sch NR32 . . . . 112 C2
Oulton Broad S Sta NR33 . . . . 114 D7
Oulton Broad Wr Sports Ctr NR33 . . . . 114 D7
Oulton Cl 6 CO12 . . . . . 106 F2
Oulton Ct NR32 . . . . . . 112 E4
Oulton Ind Est NR32 112 E3
Oulton Marshes Nature Reserve★ NR32 . . . . . 112 B3
Oulton Rd
 Flixton NR32 . . . . 112 F7
 Ipswich IP3 . . . . 139 F2
 Lowestoft NR32 . . . . . . 113 A4
Oulton Rd N NR32 . . . . 112 F5
Oulton St NR32 . . . . . . 112 F4
Ound Farm Nature Reserve★ IP17 . . . . 56 C1
OUSDEN 61 E6
Ousden Rd
 Hargrave IP29 . . . . 62 A6
 Wickhambrook CB8 . . . . 61 E3
Outney Meadow Cvn Pk NR35 . . . . 110 A4
Outney Rd NR35 . . . . . 110 A4
Out Northgate IP33 . . 154 B4
Out Risbygate
 Bury St Edmunds IP33 . . . . 122 E6
 Bury St Edmunds IP33 . . . . 154 B2
Out Westgate IP33 . . 154 B1
Overbury Hall Rd IP7 . . . . 149 D1
Overgang Rd IP7 . . 94 B8
Overhill La IP14 . . . . 51 D7
Overing Ave 14 CO10 . . 92 C6
OVINGTON 90 A5
Ovington Pl 5 CB9 . . 132 F6
Ovington Rd CO9 . . . . 90 A3
Owdall La NR35 . . . . . 7 C7
Owell The IP31 . . . . . 49 E6
Owen Rd 16 IP22 . . . . 20 D2
Owers Cl IP30 . . . . . . 65 D5
Oxenford Cl 28 CO12 . . 106 F1
Oxer Cl IP30 . . . . 50 F2
Oxford Cl
 Mildenhall IP28 . . . . 116 A4
 Sudbury CO10 . . . . . . 148 E4
Oxford Dr
 Hadleigh IP7 . . . . 149 D8
 Woodbridge IP12 . . . . 146 D3
Oxford Rd
 15 Feltwell IP26 . . . . 4 D5
 4 Feltwell IP26 . . . . . 4 E5
 Ipswich IP4 . . . . 139 E5
 Lowestoft NR32 . . . . . 113 D3
 25 Manningtree CO11 . . 104 E2
Oxford St CB8 . . . . . 120 B8
Oxlip Way 5 IP14 . . . . 67 B7

P

Paccas Cl IP31 . . . . . . 49 E6
Packard Ave IP3 . . . . 140 B2
Packard Pl IP8 . . . . 134 B2
Packards La
 Fordham CO6 . . . . . . 102 A1
 Wormingford CO6 . . . . 101 F1
Packlose La IP31 . . . . 34 F2
Packway La IP31 . . . . 50 A5
Packway The IP20 . . . . 23 A7
Paddock Cl
 Bury St Edmunds IP33 . . . . 122 C5
 25 Harwich CO12 . . . . 107 B2
 Kirton IP10 . . . . 98 D2
Paddock Farm IP31 . . 34 D8
Paddock Gr CO6 . . . . 102 C5
Paddock Hill 2 NR33 . . . . 114 E7
Paddock Rd 13 IP20 . . 22 D6
Paddocks Dr CB8 . . . 121 A2
Paddocks Gn NR34 . . 111 F4
Paddocks Prim Sch CB8 . . . . 120 E4
Paddock St CB7 . . . . 28 C4
Paddocks The
 Ashen CO10 . . . . 89 E5
 Badwell Ash IP31 . . . . 50 F7
 6 Bures CO8 . . . . . 101 C4
 12 Burwell CB5 . . . . 44 A5
 Halesworth IP19 . . . 118 C4
 3 Martlesham Heath IP5 . . . . 98 A8
 Tuddenham St Martin IP6 . . . . 136 B5
 Worlington IP28 . . . . 30 B4
Paddock The 18 IP31 . . 34 B1
Paddock Way
 Chedburgh IP29 . . . . . 62 C4
 Troston IP31 . . . . . 33 D3
Paddock Wood Cl 8 NR33 . . . . 114 C4
Paddock Way 12 IP7 . . 79 F4
Padstow Rd IP5 . . . . 141 A6
Pageant Pl IP13 . . . 126 E3
Page Gdns IP5 . . . . 141 E8
Page's Cl IP14 . . . . 124 C6
PAGE'S GREEN 53 C4
Pages Hill IP12 . . . . 99 D6
Pages Hill Rd IP29 . . 63 B6
Paget Cl IP6 . . . . . 125 C5
Paget Pl CB8 . . . . . 121 A6
Paget Rd IP1 . . . . . 155 A4
Page Wlk IP3 . . . . . 139 E4
Paigle Cl 7 IP30 . . . . 50 E2

Paine Cl 12 IP22 . . . . 20 B8
Pains Cl 2 NR34 . . . . 9 F4
Pains Hill IP14 . . . . . 67 F6
Painter Cl 4 IP7 . . . 149 F7
PAKEFIELD 115 B3
Pakefield High Sch NR33 . . . . 115 A3
Pakefield Prim Sch NR33 . . . . 115 A3
Pakefield Rd NR33 . . 115 C5
Pakefield St NR33 . . 115 B4
PAKENHAM 49 E6
Pakenham Pl CB9 . . . 132 F5
Pakenham Rd
 Pakenham IP31 . . . . . 49 D6
 Thurston IP31 . . . . . 49 E4
Pakenham Watermill★ IP31 . . . . 49 F8
Pakenham Windmill★ IP31 . . . . 49 F8
Palace La CB7 . . . . . . 45 B8
Palace St 4 CB8 . . . 121 A3
PALE GREEN 88 B5
Palfrey Height CO11 . . 104 E4
Palfrey Pl IP19 . . . . 118 C6
PALGRAVE 20 C1
Palgrave Prim Sch IP22 . . . . 20 C1
Palmcroft Cl 10 IP1 . . 135 A3
Palmcroft Rd IP1 . . . 135 A3
Palmer Cl NR32 . . . . 113 B6
Palmer Dr IP27 . . . . 109 C7
Palmers La NR34 . . . . 26 F6
Palmer's La IP18 . . . 119 A2
Palmer St IP31 . . . . . 35 C1
Palmerston Rd IP4 . . . 139 E6
Palmerswent Cl CO10 . . 91 F8
Pamment Cl IP30 . . . . 50 B2
Pamment's La 5 IP28 29 F6
Pannels Cl 5 CO10 . . . 77 A2
Pannington Hall La IP9 . . . . 142 E5
Pantile La 12 CB5 . . . 44 A6
Pantshorne La IP22 . . 19 B4
Papeley Meadow IP29 . . . . 47 B2
Paper Mill La
 Bramford IP8 . . . . . . 134 B4
 Ipswich IP8 . . . . . . 134 B2
Parade Dr 6 CO12 . . . 106 E1
Parade Rd IP4 . . . . . 139 F7
Parade Rd N 13 NR33 . . . . 115 D8
Parade Rd S NR33 . . . 115 D7
Parade The CB9 . . . . 133 F8
Paradise Pl IP16 . . . 129 C5
Pardoe Pl IP4 . . . . . 140 E5
PARHAM 71 A7
Parham Airfield Mus★ IP13 . . . . 71 C7
Parish Bush Dro CB7 . . 12 A1
Park Ave
 Felixstowe IP11 . . . . 153 B5
 3 Fornham St Martin IP28 . . . . 48 C6
 Newmarket CB8 . . . . . 121 B3
 Saxmundham IP17 . . . . 128 C3
Park Cl
 2 Bentwaters Airfield IP12 . . . . 85 D8
 1 Lowestoft NR33 . . . 114 D4
 5 Martlesham Heath IP5 . . . . 98 A8
 4 Moulton CB8 . . . . . 45 F3
 Sudbury CO10 . . . . . . 148 E6
Park Corner CO10 . . . . 93 B5
Park Cottages 7 IP8 . . 81 C3
Park Cotts CB8 . . . . 121 B2
Park Dr
 Beccles NR34 . . . . . . 111 E4
 Homerfield NR35 . . . . 23 C8
Park End IP17 . . . . . 128 C2
Parker Ave IP11 . . . . 152 B4
Parker's Dro 3 IP28 . . 29 F6
Parkers Pl 1 IP5 . . . . 98 A8
Parker's Rd IP14 . . . . 52 A5
Parker's Way CO6 . . . 102 D5
Parkers Wlk CB8 . . . 120 E8
PARKESTON 106 F3
Parkeston Rd
 Felixstowe IP11 . . . . 152 D4
 Harwich CO12 . . . . . 107 A2
Park Farm Bsns Ctr IP28 . . . . 48 D7
Park Farm Dr
 Barton Mills IP28 . . . . 30 C2
 Stanton IP31 . . . . . . 34 E3
Park Farm La
 Euston IP24 . . . . 33 B4
 Hoxne IP21 . . . . 38 E6
 Lawshall Green IP29 . . 77 F7
PARK GATE 61 E3
PARK GREEN 53 B3
Park Hill
 Leiston IP16 . . . . . . 129 C6
 Oulton NR32 . . . . . . 112 F5
Parkhurst Green La CO6 . . . . 101 A1
Parkington Wlk IP32 . . . . 122 D7
Parkington Way IP22 . . 35 D3
Park La
 Aldeburgh IP15 . . . . 130 E4
 Bulmer CO10 . . . . . . 91 C2
 Charsfield IP13 . . . . 70 C3
 Eye IP23 . . . . 37 E3
 Eye IP23 . . . . 117 D1
 Glemsford CO10 . . . . 77 B2

Park La continued
 Hawstead IP29 . . . . . . 63 D7
 Ipswich IP10 . . . . . . 144 F4
 Kirton IP10 . . . . 98 E3
 Langham CO4 . . . . . 103 C2
 Newmarket CB8 . . . . . 121 B3
 North Lopham IP22 . . . 19 B6
 South Lopham IP22 . . . 19 C4
 Southwold IP18 . . . . 119 D4
 Tattingstone IP9 . . . 105 B8
 Thornham Parva IP23 . . 37 A3
Parklands 5 IP13 . . . . 84 F3
Parklands Cl 9 CO10 . . 77 F3
Parklands Gn 2 IP28 . . 48 C6
Parklands The NR33 . . 114 D4
Parklands Way 41 IP20 . . . . 22 D6
Park Meadows NR32 . . 112 F6
Park N IP1 . . . . 139 D8
Park Pl IP17 . . . . . . 57 D7
Park Rd
 Aldeburgh IP15 . . . . 130 D4
 Benhall IP17 . . . . . . 72 A7
 Boot Street IP13 . . . . 137 D8
 Burwell CB5 . . . . 44 A5
 Bury St Edmunds IP33 . . . . 122 D4
 Cheveley CB8 . . . . . . 60 D7
 Combs IP14 . . . . . . 124 B2
 Diss IP22 . . . . 20 C2
 Drinkstone IP30 . . . . 50 B1
 East Bergholt CO7 . . . 104 D5
 Great Horkesley CO6 . . 102 D4
 Grundisburgh IP13 . . . 83 E5
 Halesworth IP19 . . . 118 A5
 3 Harwich CO12 . . . . 107 B2
 Haverhill IP9 . . . . . 132 B7
 Ipswich IP1 . . . . . . 139 C8
 Lavenham CO10 . . . . 78 D4
 Letheringham IP13 . . . 70 D4
 Lowestoft NR32 . . . . . 113 D3
 Needham Market IP6 . . 125 D4
 St Cross, South Elmham IP20 . . . . 23 C7
 Southolt IP23 . . . . . 54 A8
 Stanstead IP29 . . . . . 77 F5
 Stoke-by-Nayland CO6 . . 102 F6
 Sudbury CO10 . . . . . 148 E6
 Wetherden IP14 . . . . 51 A1
Parkside
 Chippenham CB7 . . . . 45 C8
 Haverhill CB9 . . . . . 132 D4
 Mildenhall IP28 . . . . 30 C8
 3 Stanton IP31 . . . . 34 E4
Parkside Ave IP4 . . . . 155 C4
Parkside Ct 3 IP2 . . . 20 C2
Parkside Dr NR32 . . . 113 A2
Park St CO6 . . . . . . 102 E7
Park The
 3 Great Barton IP31 . . 49 A5
 Tannintree CO11 . . . . 104 E2
Parkview 12 IP28 . . . . 30 C8
Park View
 Botesdale IP22 . . . . . 36 B7
 Weeting IP27 . . . . . . 5 E3
 Wetherden IP14 . . . . 51 A1
Park View Rd IP1 . . . 135 B1
Parkway IP13 . . . . . 127 C4
Parkway North IP14 . . 154 A4
Parkway South IP33 154 A2
Park Wlk IP19 . . . . 118 E5
Parkwood Dr CO10 . . 148 C8
Park Yd 28 IP31 . . . . 34 B1
PARLIAMENT HEATH . . 93 C6
Parliament Rd IP4 . . . 140 B5
Parmenter Dr 13 CO10 . . . . 92 B3
Parnell Cl 1 IP21 . . . 134 F3
Parnell La IP30 . . . . 50 D3
Parnell Rd IP1 . . . . 134 F3
PARNEY HEATH 103 D2
Parnham Pl 2 IP4 . . . 140 F5
Parrington Way 26 CO11 . . . . 104 D2
Parr Rd CB9 . . . . . . 132 B4
Parry Cl IP19 . . . . . 118 B5
Parsley Cl 15 IP28 . . 30 C1
Parsonage Cl
 5 Burwell CB5 . . . . . 44 A4
 3 Felixstowe IP11 . . 152 D4
Parsonage Farm La CB8 . . . . 60 C5
Parsonage Gdns 16 CB9 . . . . 132 C5
Parsonage Gr 7 CO8 . . . . 101 C4
Parsonage Green IP30 . . . . 64 D2
Parsonage Hill CO4 . . 103 A4
Parsonage La
 Burwell CB5 . . . . 44 A4
 Chelsworth IP7 . . . . . 79 F8
 Little Welnetham IP30 . . 64 B7
Parsons Cl IP33 . . . . 122 A6
Parsons Field 4 IP15 . . . . 130 E3
Parson's Field CO7 . . 104 A3
Parsons Hill IP12 . . . . 99 F7
Parson's La IP6 . . . 125 B2
Parson'S La IP22 . . . . 18 D4
Parsons Yd 24 CO11 . . 104 E2
Partridge Cl
 Boxford CO10 . . . . . . 93 C4
 Stowmarket IP14 . . 124 F6
 15 Thurstow IP31 . . . 49 D4
Partridge Dr IP24 . . . 16 C4
Partridge Rise IP2 . . . 20 D3

Partridge Rise 7 IP22 . . . . 20 D3
Pascoe Pl IP22 . . . . . 19 E4
Pashford Cl IP27 . . . 109 D6
Pashford Pl 6 IP3 . . . 144 C8
Paske Ave CB9 . . . . 132 D5
Pask Way 4 CO10 . . . 90 A7
Pastures The
 Ipswich IP4 . . . . . . 140 F5
 Oulton NR32 . . . . . . 112 F6
Pasture Way 28 IP28 . . 30 B8
Patricia Cl NR32 . . . 112 D2
Patricks La 24 CO12 . . 107 B2
Patten La NR15 . . . . . 21 B7
Patterdale Gdns 3 NR32 . . . . 113 A4
Pattern Bush Cl 4 CO11 . . . . 104 E4
Patteson Rd IP3 . . . . 139 E4
Patticroft 7 CO10 . . . . 77 A3
Paul Earee Parkway CO10 . . . . 148 D7
Pauline St IP2 . . . . . 155 B1
Paul's Rd IP2 . . . . . 138 F5
Pavilion Ct CB9 . . . . 132 F5
Paxton Chadwick Cl 1 IP16 . . . . 129 D5
Payne's La IP26 . . . . . 4 E5
Payne St NR33 . . . . . 115 C7
Peace Pl 17 IP16 . . . . 73 F6
Peacock Cl
 Hockwold cum Wilton IP26 . . . . 4 F3
 5 Ipswich IP8 . . . . 138 C2
 Lowestoft NR33 . . . . 114 C2
 Wootten Green IP21 . . . 39 B4
Peacock Hall Rd CO10 . . . . 92 C1
Peacock Pl 18 IP31 . . 49 E4
Peacock Rise 18 IP31 . . . . 34 B1
Peacocks Cl 1 CO10 . . 76 E1
Peacock's Pyghtle IP12 . . . . 131 C3
Peacock Rd CO10 . . . . 76 E2
Peacock St IP5 . . . . 141 E7
Peak Dale NR33 . . . . 114 E3
Peakhall La CO10 . . . . 92 C8
Pea Porridge Green IP33 . . . . 154 B3
Pearce Rd
 14 Diss IP22 . . . . . 20 D2
 Ipswich IP3 . . . . . . 140 A4
Pearce's Cl 2 IP26 . . . 5 A3
Pearcroft Rd IP1 . . . 135 B3
Pearl Cl IP6 . . . . . . 69 C2
Pearl Rd IP1 . . . . . 138 D8
Pearmain La 6 IP4 . . 139 E7
Pearmain Rd 2 IP22 . . 20 B3
Pearmain Wlk 8 CB9 . . . . 132 A6
Pearse Way IP3 . . . . 140 E1
Pearson Rd IP4 . . . . 140 C5
Pearsons Cl 10 CO10 . . 77 A2
Pearsons Way IP8 . . . . 95 F5
Peart Gr IP5 . . . . . 141 D6
Peartree Cl IP17 . . . 128 C6
Pear Tree Cl
 14 Glemsford CO10 . . 77 A2
 Troston IP31 . . . . . 33 D3
Peartree Hill CO8 . . . 101 D2
Peartree La IP13 . . . . 55 A6
Peasecroft Rd 3 IP33 . . . . 34 B1
PEASENHALL 56 E8
Peasenhall Cl 2 IP12 . . 85 B3
Peasenhall Rd
 Bruisyard IP17 . . . . . 56 E5
 Walpole IP19 . . . . . . 41 C3
Peasey Gdns IP5 . . . 141 C6
Peasey La IP5 . . . . 141 C6
PEATS CORNER 69 B7
Pebble Cl NR31 . . . . . 3 C6
Pebble View Wlk 8 NR31 . . . . 3 C6
Peckham St IP33 . . . 154 B3
Peckston Pl IP33 . . . 154 A3
Pecockes Cl CO10 . . . 92 B3
Peddars Cl 1 IP31 . . . 34 B1
Peddars La NR34 . . . . 111 B4
Peddars Way NR32 . . . 113 B4
Pedlars La IP12 . . . . 86 C7
Peek Cl CO10 . . . . . . 78 C3
Peel St IP1 . . . . . . 155 B3
Peel Yd 2 IP5 . . . . . 98 A8
Peewit Hill IP11 . . . . 152 B5
Peewit Rd IP2 . . . . 138 C3
Pegasus Mews 1 NR32 . . . . 112 C8
Peggs Farm Rd IP30 . . 65 D6
Pegg's Hill IP20 . . . . 22 F2
Pelham 21 CO12 . . . 106 F1
Pelican Cl IP2 . . . . . 138 E3
Pemberton Rd 6 IP20 . . . . 22 D5
Pemberton Wlk IP33 . . . . 123 A2
Pembroke Ave IP12 . . 146 E4
Pembroke Cl
 Ipswich IP2 . . . . . . 139 B3
 Mildenhall IP28 . . . . 116 C5
 Newmarket CB8 . . . . . 121 B4
Pembroke Pl CO10 . . 148 B3
Pembroke Rd
 Bury St Edmunds IP33 . . . . 122 D3
 Framlingham IP13 . . 126 B4

Pembrooke Way 1 NR32 . . . . 113 A3
Penbry Gdns IP31 . . . 50 F7
Pendleton Rd IP22 . . . 138 D1
Penfold Rd IP1 . . . . 153 A4
Peninsula Bsns Ctr The IP9 . . . . 143 B5
Penn Cl IP9 . . . . . . 150 F4
Pennine Way NR32 . . . 124 F7
Pennings Nature Reserve The★ IP23 . . 117 C3
Pennycress Dr 4 IP24 . . . . 16 D7
Pennyfields NR35 . . . 110 B2
Pennygate Dr NR33 . . 114 E6
Penny La
 5 Ipswich IP3 . . . . 140 F1
 Lowestoft NR32 . . . . . 112 E3
Penny Meadow 3 IP9 . . . . 150 E3
Pennypot CO7 . . . . 103 F4
Pennyroyal Gdns IP2 . . . . 138 E3
Pennywort 3 CB7 . . . 28 E3
Penryn Rd IP5 . . . . 141 A7
Penshurst Rd IP3 . . . 140 D4
Pentland Wlk 9 NR32 . . . . 113 A4
PENTLOW 76 E1
Pentlow Hawke Cl CB9 . . . . 133 A5
Pentlow Hill CO10 . . . 91 A8
Pentlow La
 Cavendish CO10 . . . . . 76 F1
 Clare CO10 . . . . 90 F7
Pentlow Ridge CO10 . . 90 F7
PENTLOW STREET 91 A8
Penzance Rd IP5 . . . 141 A6
People Pk Way CO10 148 D7
Peppercorn Way 2 IP2 . . . . 139 C3
Pepper La IP31 . . . . . 49 E3
Peppermint Wlk 29 IP28 . . . . 30 C1
Pepper Pl IP5 . . . . . 141 D6
Peppers Cl IP27 . . . . 5 E3
Peppers High Hill IP27 . 5 F3
Peppers La IP9 . . . . 143 D7
Pepper's Rd CO10 . . . 102 F1
Peppers Wash IP13 . . 126 B6
Peppers Wash La IP13 . . . . 126 A6
Pepys Ave 1 NR34 . . . 9 F4
Perch Chase 10 CB7 . . 28 E3
Percy Ruse CO10 . . . 148 F5
Peregrine Cl 5 IP22 . . 20 D3
Peregrine Dr IP14 . . . 124 F7
Peregrine Way 18 NR33 . . . . 11 C1
Periman Cl CB8 . . . . 121 A5
Periwinkle Cl 8 NR33 . . . . 114 C5
Perkins Rd IP30 . . . . 49 B2
Perkins Way
 Ipswich IP3 . . . . . . 139 F1
 Tostock IP30 . . . . . . 50 B3
Perrett Way IP16 . . . 129 D4
Perry Barn Cl IP33 . . 122 E4
Perrydown La IP30 . . 64 C1
Perryfields CO10 . . . 148 F2
Perry La CO4 . . . . . 103 C2
Persimmon Wlk CB8 120 E7
Pesthouse La IP6 . . . . 82 A6
Petch Cl IP33 . . . . . 154 B3
Peter Dodd Mws CO10 . . . . 92 B3
Peter Dr 3 IP21 . . . . 16 C7
Peterfen Drove IP28 . . 13 D2
Peterhouse Cl
 Ipswich IP2 . . . . . . 138 F2
 Mildenhall IP28 . . . . 116 D4
Peterhouse Cres IP12 . . . . 146 D4
Peterhouse Dr CB8 . . 121 A2
Peter's Gr 4 IP9 . . . 150 E3
Petingo Cl CB8 . . . . 120 D7
Petit Couronne Way NR34 . . . . 111 D3
Peto Way NR32 . . . . 113 A1
Pets Cnr★ NR33 . . . . 114 D7
PETTAUGH 68 E6
Pettaugh La IP6 . . . . 68 E2
Petticoat La
 9 Barrow IP29 . . . . 47 A2
 Bury St Edmunds IP33 154 A1
 Genesis Green CB8 . . . 61 F4
PETTISTREE 127 B4
Pettits Dr IP32 . . . . . 48 B5
Pettits La IP21 . . . . . 20 F3
Pettwood Gdns IP9 . . 105 F7
Pettyfield La CO9 . . . 89 C2
Petunia Way IP27 . . . 14 E8
Peyton Hall La IP7 . . 149 C8
Peyton Hall Rd CO8 . . 101 A4
Pheasant Cl 14 IP31 . . 49 D4
Pheasant Dr 8 IP22 . . 20 D3
Pheasant Rd IP2 . . . 138 E3
Pheasant Rise IP8 . . . 95 F4
Pheasant Way IP27 . . . 6 A1
Pheasants Wlk NR35 . . 7 E4
Philip Ave IP11 . . . . 152 E3
Philipps Cl CB8 . . . 120 D4
Philip Rd
 Bury St Edmunds IP32 . . . . 122 F8
 Ipswich IP2 . . . . . . 155 B1
Phillipps Rd 3 IP6 . . . 82 B5
Phillips Cres IP6 . . . 125 E4

Phillips Field Rd CO10 . . . . 148 E3
Phoenix Rd
 Ipswich IP4 . . . . . . 140 A7
 Lowestoft NR33 . . . . 114 F4
Phoenix Way IP14 . . . 124 F7
Phoenix Yd CB9 . . . . 132 E3
Pickard'S La IP29 . . . . 62 D2
Picketts Rd IP1 . . . . 153 C5
Pickwick Cres IP33 . . 154 C3
Pickwick Dr 5 NR32 . . 3 A4
Pickwick Rd IP2 . . . 138 E6
Picton Ave 5 IP1 . . . 135 D1
Pier Ave IP18 . . . . . 119 D6
Pier Terr NR33 . . . . 115 D8
Pigeon La IP28 . . . . . 48 B6
Pigeons La IP17 . . . . 57 D8
Pigeon's La IP8 . . . . 138 A3
Pightle Cl IP30 . . . . . 50 E2
Pightle Gr IP30 . . . . 65 D5
Pightles La IP12 . . . . 99 F3
Pightle The
 Capel St Mary IP9 . . . 150 F4
 4 Haverhill CB9 . . . 132 E6
 4 Needham Market IP6 . . . . 125 D5
 North Cove NR34 . . . . 10 B4
Pig La
 Beccles NR34 . . . . . 111 B6
 Thorpe Street IP22 . . . 35 C7
Pikes Marsh 10 CO8 . . 101 C5
Pilgrim Ct 6 CB8 . . . 45 F5
Pilgrims Way
 Beccles NR34 . . . . . . 9 C4
 Bungay NR35 . . . . . . 110 C3
 6 Great Finborough IP14 . . . . 66 B4
 1 Thorpeness IP16 . . 73 F6
Pilgrim's Way 7 IP20 22 D6
Pilgrims Way IP27 . . . 5 E3
Pimpernel Rd IP22 . . 138 F3
Pinbush Cl NR33 . . . 114 F2
Pinbush Rd NR33 . . . 114 F2
Pine Ave
 Ipswich IP1 . . . . . . 135 B1
 Landwade CB8 . . . . . 44 E7
Pine Bank IP5 . . . . . 141 F6
Pine Banks NR32 . . . 113 A2
Pine Cl
 1 Brantham CO11 . . 104 E4
 Eye IP23 . . . . 117 D3
 4 Harleston IP20 . . . 22 D5
 9 Lakenheath IP27 . . 13 F2
 Rendlesham IP12 . . . . 85 D8
Pinecroft Rd IP1 . . . 135 A2
Pinecroft Rise CO10 . . 148 B3
Pinecroft Way Needham Market IP6 . . 125 E4
Pine Gr 14 IP13 . . . . 83 F3
Pine Leys IP32 . . . . 122 F8
Pine Ridge 13 IP28 . . 30 B8
Pine Sq IP7 . . . . . . 80 C8
Pines The
 Claydon IP6 . . . . . . 134 C8
 Felixstowe IP11 . . . . 153 E6
Pinetree Cl IP5 . . . . 140 F7
Pine Tree Cl
 Beccles NR34 . . . . . 111 F4
 Halesworth IP19 . . . 118 E4
Pine Tree Ct IP22 . . . 18 C2
Pinetrees NR31 . . . . . 2 B7
Pine Trees Ave IP28 . . 116 E4
Pine View IP14 . . . . . 52 A6
Pineview Cl IP14 . . . 124 D5
Pine View Rd IP1 . . . 139 B8
Pineway Cl 1 IP29 . . . 63 A1
Pinewood IP12 . . . . 146 E3
Pinewood Ave NR33 . . 114 F6
Pinewood Dr IP27 . . . 14 F8
Pinewood Gdns NR34 . 10 B4
PINFORD END 63 D6
Pinhoe Dr 1 CB9 . . . 132 D6
Pinkney's La 19 IP18 119 D5
Pinkuah La CO10 . . . . 90 F7
Pin Mill Cl IP8 . . . . 138 C1
Pin Mill Cliff★ IP9 . . 106 D8
Pinmill Rd IP2 . . . . 106 C8
Pinners La IP13 . . . . 146 B7
Pinners Way IP33 . . . 122 E4
Pintail Cl IP2 . . . . . 138 E3
Pintail Rd 22 IP14 . . . 67 A5
Pinza Cl CB8 . . . . . 120 E8
Pioneer Way 17 CO11 104 E4
Piperell Way IP7 . . . 149 C8
Pipers Cl CB9 . . . . . 133 A4
Pipers Meadow IP13 . . 54 E7
Pipers Vale Cl IP3 . . . 139 E1
Pipers Vale Com Prim Sch IP3 . . . . 139 F1
Pipers Vale Nature Reserve★ IP3 . . . . 143 F7
Pipistrelle Way
 Capel St Mary IP9 . . . 150 D4
 Sicklesmere IP30 . . . . 63 F7
Pipkin Hill IP7 . . . . 149 E2
Pipney Hill IP17 . . . . 56 F4
Pippin Cl
 2 Bury St Edmunds IP32 . . . . 123 E6
 Rose Green CO10 . . . 101 F8
Pippin Ct 17 IP28 . . . 30 C1

Pippin Dr CO4 . . . . . **103** A3
Pippin Post Cl CO10. . . .**76** C6
Pippins The
　Blundeston NR32. . . . .**3** A4
　Glemsford CO10. . . . .**77** B2
Pipp's La IP6. . . . .**135** E6
Pirnhow St NR35. . . **110** D5
Pitcairn Rd IP1. . . . . . .**138** E8
PITCHER'S GREEN **64** D5
PITMAN'S CORNER. . . . **53** C5
Pit La IP23. . . . .**38** A6
Pitmer Rd IP17 . . . .**56** F5
Pitmire La CO8 . . . . . .**101** A7
Pits The CB7. . . . .**29** C4
Pitts End CO7. . . . .**151** D5
Pk Farm Dr NR34. . . . . .**42** F8
Pk La IP31. . . . .**50** B7
Pk Rd CB8 . . . .**61** A2
Pk View IP11. . . . .**152** B8
Place Farm Prim Acad
　CB9. . . . .**132** D6
Place for Plants The★
　CO7. . . . .**151** F3
Plains Rd IP31. . . . .**33** B1
Plampin Cl CO10. . . . . .**92** D3
Plantation The IP15. **130** D6
Plantation Way IP14 . .**66** C1
Plantation Way **32**
　IP28. . . . .**30** C1
Planters Gr **3** NR33. . .**114** F7
Plash Rd IP23 . . . .**53** F7
Plashwood Rd IP14 . . .**51** B1
Plasters Wlk IP16. . . .**129** C6
Platers Wlk IP16. . . . .**129** C5
Platinum Dr IP31 . . . . .**50** F7
Platten Cl IP6 . . . .**125** C5
Platters Cl IP3. . . . . . .**144** A7
Platters Cl IP11. . . . . .**152** E2
Playfield Rd IP9 . . . . . .**150** F3
PLAYFORD. **137** B5
Playford La IP5. . . . . .**136** E2
Playford Mount
　IP13. . . . .**137** B5
Playford Rd
　Ipswich IP4. . . . .**140** E8
　Playford IP5 . . . .**137** B2
　Tuddenham St Martin
　IP6. . . . .**136** F4
Pleasant Cl IP28. . . . .**132** C7
Pleasant Pl NR34. . . . .**111** B3
Pleasant Row IP4. . . .**155** C2
Pleasurewood Cl **5**
　NR32 . . . .**113** B5
Pleasurewood Hill
　NR32 . . . .**113** A7
Pleasurewood Hills
Leisure Pk★ NR32 .**113** C8
Plough Hill CO10. . . . . .**76** C7
Plough La
　Leavenheath CO6 . . . .**102** B7
　Sudbury CO10. . . . . . .**148** B5
Ploughman's Dro IP26 . **4** B5
Plough Rd
　Capel St Mary IP9. . . .**150** D3
　Woolpit IP30. . . . .**50** D1
Plough St IP3 . . . .**139** E4
Plover Cl
　4 Mildenhall IP28. . . . .**13** B1
　11 Stowmarket IP14 . .**67** A5
　Thetford IP24. . . . .**16** C4
Plover Pl CB8. . . . .**120** A8
Plover Rd IP2. . . . .**138** E2
Plovers Way
　Bury St Edmunds
　IP33. . . . .**123** C1
　Hockwold cum Wilton
　IP26. . . . .**4** F3
　Lowestoft NR33 . . . . .**114** D5
Plumbers Arms Cl
　IP31. . . . .**50** B4
Plumbers' Yard IP17. .**56** E8
Plummer Rd **22** IP31. . .**34** B1
Plummers Dell **10**
　IP6. . . . .**82** A5
Plumpton Ave IP28 .**116** C5
Plum St CO10. . . . .**77** A3
Plum Tree Rise **3**
　IP7. . . . .**80** D6
Plumtrees **8** NR32. . .**112** D2
Plymouth Rd
　Felixstowe IP11. . . . . .**152** F6
　2 Troston IP31. . . . . . .**33** D5
Poachers Cl IP19 . . . . .**40** D6
Pockthorpe La IP20. . . .**7** A3
Pokeriage Gdns IP31. .**49** E3
Pole Hill (Tumulus)★
　IP10. . . . .**141** F5
Police Sta Rd **5**
　NR32 . . . .**113** D1
Pollard Piece NR33 .**114** C5
Pollards La IP28. . . . . . .**29** F7
Polls La NR34. . . . .**9** C2
POLSTEAD. **93** F1
Polstead Cl IP14. . . . .**124** F4
Polstead Green CO6. . .**93** F1
POLSTEAD HEATH **93** F2
Polstead Hill CO6 . . . . .**93** F1
Polstead Rd
　Calais Street CO6. . . . .**93** D2
　HADLEIGH IP7. . . . . . .**94** A2
Polstead St CO6 . . . .**102** E7
Pond Cl IP11. . . . .**152** D5
Pond Cottage IP31. . . .**33** A2

Pond End IP6. . . . .**82** E6
Pond Farm IP23 . . . . . .**53** B8
Pond Gn CB7. . . . .**28** A1
Pond Gr Cl IP32. . . . . .**123** E6
Pond Hall Ind Est IP7 **94** E5
Pond Hall Rd IP7. . . . .**149** F5
Pond La
　Halesworth IP19 . . . . .**118** C7
　Heckfield Green IP21. .**38** C6
Pond Piece IP13. . . . . . .**70** A7
Ponds End La IP22. . . . .**35** A8
Poole Cl IP3. . . . .**140** D3
Poole St CO10. . . . .**76** E1
Pooley St IP22. . . . .**19** C3
POOLEY STREET **19** D4
Popes Ct CB9. . . . .**133** C3
Pope's Gn La IP7 . . . . . .**94** B2
Popes Green La IP7. . . .**94** C2
Poplar Ave
　Felixstowe IP11. . . . . .**152** E2
　11 Fordham CB7. . . . . . .**29** A1
Poplar Cl
　1 Barrow IP29. . . . .**47** A2
　4 Claydon IP6. . . . . .**134** C8
　Haverhill IP9. . . . .**132** B7
　11 Honington IP31. . . .**33** D5
　Mildenhall IP28. . . . . .**116** C6
Poplar Farm La
　Swilland IP6. . . . .**83** B8
　Thurston IP31. . . . .**49** E5
Poplar Gr IP30. . . . . . .**145** D6
Poplar Hill IP14. . . . . .**124** E4
Poplar La IP8. . . . .**138** A2
Poplar Meadow IP30. . .**64** B8
Poplar Rd
　Lowestoft NR33 . . . . .**114** D3
　Sudbury CO10. . . . . . .**148** F5
Poplars Cl **1** CB5. . . . . .**44** A5
Poplars CP Sch The
　NR32 . . . .**113** D3
Poplars The
　Beck Row, Holywell Row &
　Kenny Hill IP28. . . . . . .**13** D1
　3 Brantham CO11. . . .**104** E5
　Spexhall IP19 . . . .**24** F5
Poplar Wlk CB8. . . . . . .**75** C6
Poppy Cl
　Bury St Edmunds
　IP32. . . . .**123** E5
　Ditchingham NR35. . .**110** B7
　13 Herringswell IP28. . .**30** C1
　Ipswich IP2 . . . .**138** F5
　Worlingham NR34. . . .**111** F3
Poppy Fields **9** CB7 . .**28** D5
Poppy Gr IP3. . . . .**21** C5
Poppy Way **14** IP29. . . .**47** A2
Pops Bridge Rd CO6. .**102** D4
Popson St NR35. . . . . .**110** A4
Popular Rd **22** IP6 . . . . .**82** A5
Portal Ave IP5. . . . .**84** A1
Portal Cl
　4 Barnham IP24. . . . . .**16** C2
　7 Feltwell IP26. . . . .**4** D5
Porter Ct IP13 . . . .**126** B4
Porter Rd **3** IP3 . . . .**140** F1
Porters Farm Track
　NR34. . . . .**27** A3
Porthole CI NR33 . . . .**114** B4
Port La IP23. . . . .**37** C3
Portland Ave **16**
　CO12. . . . .**107** B2
Portland Cres
　35 Harwich CO12. . . . .**107** B2
　4 Woodbridge IP12. . .**146** E4
Portland Gn CB8. . . . .**120** E3
Portland Rd CB8. . . . .**120** E3
Portland Way **17** IP6 . .**82** A5
Portlight Cl **3** CO11. .**105** A2
Portman Rd IP1 . . . . . .**155** A2
Portmans Wlk IP1 . . . .**139** A5
Portman's Wlk IP1. . .**139** A5
Port of Felixstowe Rd
　IP11. . . . .**152** C3
PORT OF FELIXSTOWE
　THE. **152** C1
Portsch Rd NR33. . . . .**114** E3
Portsmouth Rd **1**
　IP31. . . . .**33** D5
POSLINGFORD **76** A3
Posters La IP31. . . . . . .**50** B7
Post House Rd NR34 . .**26** A2
Post Mill Cl
　21 Grundisburgh
　IP13. . . . .**83** E5
　Ipswich IP4 . . . .**139** F6
Post Mill Cres **12**
　IP13. . . . .**83** E5
Postmill Gdns **11**
　IP31. . . . .**35** C2
Post Mill Gdns **10**
　IP13. . . . .**83** E5
Post Mill Orchard **20**
　IP13. . . . .**83** E5
Post Office Hill CB8 . . .**61** E1
Post Office La
　Glemsford CO10. . . . . .**77** A3
　Martlesham IP12. . . . .**146** C1
Post Office Rd IP17. . .**129** A3
POTASH. **104** F8
Potash Farm Rd IP13. .**70** C2
Potash Fen IP22. . . . . . .**20** B2
Potash La
　Bentley IP9. . . . .**104** F8
　Eye IP23. . . . .**117** B5
　Polstead CO6. . . . .**93** F4
　Wyverstone IP14. . . . .**51** D7
Potkiln Chase CO9. . . .**90** F1

Pot Kiln Chase CO9 . . . .**90** F1
Pot Kiln Prim Sch
　IP13. . . . .**148** E4
Pot Kiln Rd CO10. . . . .**148** F4
Pot Kilns The CO10. . . .**92** B3
Potkin's Craft Units
　IP12. . . . .**131** B3
Potkins La IP12. . . . . .**131** B3
Potland La **15** CO10. . .**78** D4
Potters App IP5 . . . . . .**141** B6
Potters Brook IP6 . . . .**126** B3
Potters Dr NR31 . . . .**3** B7
Pottersfield CO10. . . .**148** F1
Potters La IP14. . . . . . .**52** C5
Potter's La
　Rickinghall Superior
　IP22. . . . .**36** B5
　Stanton IP31. . . . .**34** E4
Potter's St IP16. . . . . . .**58** C4
Potters Vale IP22. . . . . .**35** E7
Pottery Hill IP22. . . . . .**35** D5
Pott Hall Rd IP28. . . . . .**30** A6
Potts La
　Brundish Street IP13. . .**39** F2
　Hadleigh IP7. . . . .**149** A4
Pouch Mill IP11. . . . . .**152** B8
Poulter's La IP29. . . . . .**62** F6
Poultry Rd
　Lakenheath IP27. . . . . .**12** F7
　Lakenheath IP27. . . . . .**13** A7
Pound Cl
　8 Burwell CB5. . . . . . .**44** A5
　Halesworth IP19 . . . . .**118** B8
　4 Harleston IP20 . . . . .**22** D6
　4 Walsham le Willows
　IP31. . . . .**35** C2
Pound Corner
　Barningham IP31. . . . . .**34** E8
　Easton IP13. . . . .**70** D5
Pound Farm Dr
　8 Harwich CO12. . . . .**107** A2
　Lowestoft NR33. . . . . .**114** D5
Pound Farm Parade **7**
　NR32 . . . .**112** F4
Pound Fm Nature
Reserve★ IP17. . . . . .**56** C1
Pound Gn Rd IP13 . . . .**56** C7
POUND GREEN **61** B1
Pound Hill
　Bacton IP14. . . . .**51** F6
　Dallinghoo IP13. . . . . .**70** C1
Pound Hill Cl IP14 . . . .**51** F6
Pound La
　Athelington IP21. . . . . .**38** E2
　Blundeston NR32. . . . . .**3** A4
　Bramford IP8. . . . .**81** F3
　Capel St Mary IP9. . . .**150** D1
　Dallinghoo IP13. . . . . .**70** C1
　Ditchingham NR35 . . . . .**7** E6
　Garboldisham IP22. . . .**18** F5
　Hadleigh IP7. . . . .**149** C6
　Ipswich IP8. . . . .**134** A2
　Isleham CB7. . . . .**29** C5
　Marlesford IP13. . . . . . .**71** B5
　Stowmarket IP14. . . . .**124** D7
　Wattisfield IP22 . . . . . .**35** D4
　Woodbridge IP13. . . . . .**84** C8
Pound Meadow **3**
　IP28. . . . .**48** B6
Pound Meadow Ct
　IP28. . . . .**116** C4
Pound Pl NR34. . . . . . .**111** B6
Pound Rd
　3 Beccles NR34 . . . . .**111** B6
　Creeting St Peter or West
　Creeting IP6. . . . .**67** B4
　Sotterley NR34 . . . .**26** A7
Pound Wlk NR34. . . . .**111** B6
Pouy St IP17. . . . .**41** B1
Powell Cl NR16 . . . .**19** A8
Powling Rd IP3 . . . . . .**140** A2
Pownall Rd **2** IP3 . . . .**139** E4
Powney St IP7. . . . .**93** B8
Poy St Gn IP30. . . . .**65** E5
POYSTREET GREEN. . . .**65** E5
Pratt's La IP9. . . . .**144** A2
Pratt St CB7. . . . .**28** D4
Prentice Rd IP14. . . . .**124** E6
Prentices La IP13 . . . .**146** D6
Prentice St **8** CO10. . .**76** D4
Prentice Way **2** IP3 . .**140** B4
Prescott Dr **11** IP30 . .**50** F2
Presland Ct IP27. . . . .**109** B7
Presmere Rd IP13. . . . .**83** D5
Preston Cl **5** IP31. . . . .**49** A4
Preston Dr IP1 . . . .**134** F2
Preston Rd
　Kettlebaston IP7 . . . . . .**79** C4
　Lavenham CO10 . . . . . .**78** C4
PRESTON ST MARY **79** A5
Prestwick Ave **2**
　IP11. . . . .**153** C6
Pretty Dr IP21 . . . .**21** A2
Pretty Rd IP16. . . . .**58** A4
Pretyman Ave IP14. . . .**51** F6
Pretyman Rd
　Felixstowe IP11. . . . . .**152** E1
　Ipswich IP3. . . . .**140** B3
Prevetts Way IP15 . . .**130** E5
Prickwillow Rd CB7 . . .**12** A2
Priestly Cl IP14. . . . . .**124** B8
Priestly Rd IP6 . . . . . .**125** D4
Prigg Wlk IP32. . . . . . .**122** E7
Primack Rd IP32. . . . . .**49** A3
Primes La
　Blyford IP19. . . . .**42** B8
　Holton IP19. . . . .**118** F5
Primrose Alley IP18. .**119** D4

Primrose Cl
　Isleham CB7. . . . .**29** C4
　Lowestoft NR33. . . . . .**114** F7
Primrose Dr **23** IP28 . .**46** A8
Primrose Hill
　Haverhill CB9 . . . .**132** D5
　Ipswich IP7. . . . .**138** F4
　Royal Hospital School
　IP9. . . . .**105** E6
Primrose La
　Beccles NR34 . . . .**111** A2
　Frostenden NR34. . . . . .**26** B4
　Lavenham CO10 . . . . . .**78** C2
　Leiston IP16. . . . .**129** D4
　Ramsey & Parkeston
　CO11. . . . .**106** A1
　10 Soham CB7. . . . . . .**28** D5
　South Lopham IP22. . . .**19** B4
Primrose Rise NR34. .**111** E3
Primrose Way IP6 . . .**125** D3
Prince Charles Ave **17**
　IP32. . . . .**48** C5
Prince Charles Cl
　CO10. . . . .**148** D6
Prince Cl CB8. . . . .**120** B8
Princedale Cl IP1. . . .**135** A1
Princel La CO7. . . . . . .**103** F4
Princel Mws CO7 . . . .**103** F4
Prince of Wales Cl
　IP33. . . . .**122** E5
Prince of Wales Dr **9**
　IP2. . . . .**139** A2
Princes Gdns IP11. . . .**152** F4
Princes' Gdns **5** IP8. .**81** C3
Princes Gn IP19 . . . . .**118** A2
Princes Rd
　Felixstowe IP11. . . . . .**152** F4
　13 Harwich CO12 . . . .**107** A2
　Lowestoft NR32 . . . . .**113** C2
Prince's Rd IP11. . . . .**152** F4
Princess Rd **2** IP18. .**119** D8
Princess St **11** CO12 .**106** F3
Princes St
　Bury St Edmunds
　IP33. . . . .**154** A2
　Ipswich IP2. . . . .**155** A1
Princess Way
　5 Earsham NR35. . . . . .**7** F4
　Haverhill CB9 . . . .**132** B6
　Newmarket CB8 . . . . .**120** E4
Prince St CO10. . . . . . .**148** C6
Princes Wlk NR32. . . .**113** A2
Princethorpe Rd
　IP3. . . . .**140** C4
Prince William Way
　IP22. . . . .**20** E3
Prior's Ave IP33. . . . . .**122** E4
Priors Cl
　Lowestoft NR32 . . . . .**113** C3
　Rushbrooke with Rougham
　IP30. . . . .**64** D8
Priors' Hill Rd IP15 . .**130** D3
Prior Stephen Way
　IP24. . . . .**16** B5
Priors Way IP15 . . . . .**130** E4
Priory Ave **1** CB9 . .**132** D5
Priory Cl
　7 Burwell CB5. . . . . . .**44** A5
　Ingham IP31. . . . .**32** F1
　Palgrave IP22. . . . .**20** C1
　St Olaves NR31. . . . .**2** A6
　Stradbroke IP21. . . . . .**39** B4
Priory Cres IP21 . . . . . .**39** D8
Priory Gdns
　Isleham CB7. . . . .**29** C5
　St Olaves NR31. . . . .**2** A6
　Sudbury CO10. . . . . . .**148** B4
PRIORY GREEN **92** F6
PRIORY HEATH **140** D1
Priory Hill IP7 . . . .**93** F7
Priory La
　Bungay NR35 . . . .**110** A4
　Carlton Colville NR33 . .**114** A2
　Darsham IP17 . . . .**42** B1
　Debenham IP14 . . . . . .**53** F2
Priory Mdws IP7. . . . .**149** E4
Priory Pk IP10 . . . . . .**144** C6
Priory Rd
　Aldham IP7. . . . .**94** F8
　Beccles NR34 . . . .**111** B4
　Blythburgh IP19 . . . . . .**42** F6
　Burstall IP8 . . . .**95** B7
　Felixstowe IP11. . . . . .**153** C5
　Fressingfield IP21 . . . . .**39** D7
　Fritton & St Olaves NR31 . .**2** A6
　Great Green IP22. . . . . .**37** B8
　Palgrave IP22. . . . .**20** C1
　Snape IP17. . . . .**72** E5
　Sudbury CO10. . . . . . .**148** B7
　Wrentham NR34. . . . . .**26** E5
Priory Sch IP32 . . . . . .**123** C5
Priory Stadium
　CO10. . . . .**148** C4
Priory Wlk CO10 . . . .**148** C4
Pritchard Cl NR32. . . .**112** D3
Prittlewell Cl IP7. . . .**138** F1
Private Rd
　Earsham NR35. . . . .**7** D4
　Mutford NR34. . . . .**10** B2
　4 Oulton Broad
　NR33. . . . .**114** E7
Privet Gn NR33 . . . . . .**115** A4
Privet Way **36** IP28. . .**30** C1
Procession Way **18**
　IP30. . . . .**50** F2
Progress Way IP23. . .**117** B5
Promenade CO12 . . . .**107** A1
Propino Way **18** CO11 **105** A2

Prospect Hill CO10 . . .**92** B2
Prospect Pl
　Leiston IP16. . . . .**129** D6
　Lowestoft NR33 . . . . .**115** B3
Prospect Rd
　Ipswich IP1. . . . .**139** A6
　Lowestoft NR32 . . . . .**112** C1
　Norton IP31. . . . .**50** C4
Prospect Row IP33 . . .**154** B2
Prospect Terr CB9 . . .**133** F8
Provan Ct **2** IP3. . . . .**140** B4
Providence La **5**
　IP1. . . . .**139** A7
Providence Stree
　IP1. . . . .**155** B3
Provost Rd IP26. . . . . . .**4** D5
Prussia La IP33 . . . . . .**154** C1
Pryers Gdns **24** IP26. . .**4** E5
Pryor Cl IP17 . . . .**72** D5
Puddingmoor NR34. .**111** A5
Puddleduck La NR34.**111** F3
Pug St IP21. . . . .**21** A6
Pulham Rd IP21 . . . . . .**21** F6
PULHAM ST MARY **21** F8
Pump Cl IP13. . . . .**84** C7
Pump Ct IP33. . . . .**78** D4
Pump House La IP17. . .**57** A8
Pump La
　Bury St Edmunds
　IP33. . . . .**154** B2
　Laxfield IP13. . . . .**40** B3
Pump St
　Needham Market
　IP6. . . . .**125** C8
　Orford IP12. . . . .**131** C2
Punchard Way IP11. . .**152** C8
Purcell Rd IP14. . . . . .**124** B8
Purdis Ave IP3. . . . . . .**140** F2
Purdis Farm La
　Foxhall IP10. . . . .**141** C2
　Ipswich IP3. . . . .**140** F2
　Purdis Farm IP10 . . . .**141** B2
Purdis Pl IP3. . . . .**140** F2
Purdis Rd IP10. . . . . . .**141** D2
Purplett St **17** IP2 . . .**155** C1
Pursehouse Cl **12**
　IP23. . . . .**36** D2
Pursehouse Way **13**
　IP22. . . . .**20** D2
Put Hawk'S La IP6 . . .**125** C1
Putney Cl
　Brandon IP27. . . . .**14** E8
　Ipswich IP1. . . . .**138** E8
Putticks La CO7. . . . . .**151** E5
PUTTOCK END **90** E3
Pye Mws IP8 . . . .**138** B3
Pyes Cl **8** IP31. . . . . . .**35** C2
Pye's La IP22. . . . .**36** B3
Pyes Meadow **1** IP30 **50** F2
Pykenham Way IP7 . .**149** D6
Pyramidal Orchid Gdns
　CB9. . . . .**132** C7
Pytches Cl **2** IP12. . .**147** B6
Pytches Rd IP12 . . . . .**147** A6

Q

Quadling St IP1. . . . . .**155** B2
Quail Cl **9** IP14. . . . . . .**67** A6
Quaker La
　Bardwell IP31. . . . .**34** C4
　Beyton IP30 . . . .**49** F1
Quaker's La **2** CB9. .**132** E5
Quakers' Rd IP28 . . . .**116** F5
Quakers Way **3**
　IP16. . . . .**129** D5
Quantock Cl IP5 . . . . .**140** F7
Quantrill Terr IP5. . . .**141** D6
Quarries Cross IP14. . .**66** C8
Quarry Ave IP6 . . . . . .**125** E3
Quaves La NR35. . . . . .**110** B4
Quay La
　Reydon IP18. . . . .**26** D1
　Sudbury CO10. . . . . . .**148** C4
Quay Side IP12. . . . . .**147** A4
Quayside CB7 . . . .**109** C2
Quay's Rd IP28 . . . .**47** C5
Quay St
　Halesworth IP19 . . . . .**118** A4
　13 Manningtree CO11 .**104** E2
　Orford IP12. . . . .**131** C2
　Woodbridge IP12. . . . .**147** A4
Quay The **1** CO12. . . .**107** B3
Quay Theatre The★
　CO10. . . . .**148** C4
Quay View NR32. . . . .**113** A4
Quay View Bsns Pk
　NR32. . . . .**113** A4
Quebec Dr IP5. . . . . . .**141** B8
Queech La IP9. . . . .**105** A4
Queech The IP9 . . . . . .**150** F4
Queech Wood Cl **10**
　IP6. . . . .**82** A6
Queen Edith Dr CB9. . .**88** D3
Queen Elizabeth Cl
　IP16. . . . .**129** C4
Queen Elizabeth Dr
　NR34. . . . .**111** D3
Queen Elizabeth's Wlk
　IP28. . . . .**48** A6
Queens Ave **12** IP2 . .**146** E4
Queensberry Rd
　1 Ipswich IP3. . . . . . .**144** B8
　Newmarket CB8 . . . . .**121** A3
Queens Cl
　Beck Row IP28. . . . . . .**30** C8
　Combs IP14 . . . .**124** A1

Queens Cl *continued*
　Halesworth IP19 . . . .**118** A2
　Saxmundham IP17 . . .**128** C3
　Sudbury CO10. . . . . . .**148** C6
　Sudbury CO10. . . . . . .**148** F3
Queen's Cl IP33. . . . . .**122** E5
Queenscliffe Rd IP2. **139** B3
Queens Dr CB9 . . . . . .**132** C6
Queensdale Cl IP1. . .**135** B1
Queensdale Rd IP1 . .**135** B1
Queens Dr
　Halesworth IP19 . . . .**118** A2
　Woodbridge IP12. . . .**146** F6
Queen's Dr IP28 . . . . .**116** B4
Queensgate Dr IP4 . .**139** F8
Queens Head Alley **10**
　IP13. . . . .**126** C3
Queen's Head La
　IP12. . . . .**146** F5
Queen's Head Rd
　CO4 . . . .**102** F1
Queen's Highway
　NR32. . . . .**112** C2
Queens La IP29. . . . . . .**62** D5
Queensland IP9 . . . . .**106** F5
Queens Rd
　Brandon IP27. . . . .**14** E8
　Erwarton IP9 . . . .**106** D5
　1 Southwold IP18. . . .**119** C8
　Sudbury CO10. . . . . . .**148** C6
Queen's Rd
　Beccles NR34 . . . .**111** A4
　Bungay NR35 . . . .**110** B2
　Bury St Edmunds
　IP33. . . . .**154** A2
　Felixstowe IP11. . . . . .**153** A3
　Lowestoft NR32 . . . . .**113** D3
　Southwold IP18 . . . . .**119** C4
Queens Sq **7** CB9. . . .**132** E6
Queens St CB9. . . . . . .**74** B2
Queen St
　Cowlinge CB8. . . . .**61** B1
　Felixstowe IP11. . . . . .**152** E5
　6 Hadleigh IP7 . . . . .**149** D6
　Haverhill CB9 . . . .**132** B8
　Haverhill CB9 . . . .**132** C6
　Ipswich IP1. . . . .**155** B2
　Newmarket CB8 . . . . .**121** B3
　Southwold IP18 . . . . .**119** D5
　Stradbroke IP21. . . . . .**39** B5
Queens View CB8 . . . .**120** A8
Queensway
　4 Acton CO10. . . . . . .**92** B7
　2 Diss IP22. . . . .**20** B3
　7 Earsham NR35. . . . . .**7** F4
　Exning CB8 . . . .**120** B8
　Haverhill CB9 . . . .**132** C6
　3 Manningtree CO11 .**104** E2
　2 Mildenhall IP28. . . .**116** B4
　8 Soham CB7. . . . .**28** D4
　Sudbury CO10. . . . . . .**148** F3
　Thetford IP24. . . . .**16** B5
Queen's Way IP3 . . . .**140** B4
Queensway Inf Acad
　IP24. . . . .**16** B5
Quendon Pl CB9 . . . . .**132** C6
Quentin Cl IP1. . . . . . .**138** E8
Quilter Dr
　Ipswich IP8. . . . .**138** C1
　Pinewood IP8. . . . . . .**142** C8
Quilter Rd
　Felixstowe IP11. . . . . .**153** B4
　Lavenham CO10 . . . . . .**78** D3
Quince Cl IP1 . . . .**104** C5
Quinnell Way **5**
　NR32 . . . .**113** A6
Quinton Rd IP6 . . . . . .**125** C4
Quintons Cnr CO7. . . .**151** D6
Quinton'S La IP11. . . .**153** B7
Quinton's La IP11. . . .**153** C5
Quintons Rd CO7. . . . .**151** C5
Quoits Field **2** IP6. .**134** C8
Quoits Meadow IP14. .**68** B6
Quys Farm La CO9 . . . .**89** C1

R

RACECOURSE **140** D5
Rackham Cl **1** NR31 . . .**3** B7
Radcliffe Dr IP2. . . . .**138** D2
Radcliffe Rd IP27. . . . .**14** A2
Radford Dr **9** CO10 . . .**77** A7
Radiator Rd **3** CO10 .**148** E3
Radleys La CO6 . . . . . .**102** B6
Radnor Cl IP32 . . . . . .**123** C3
Raeburn Rd IP3. . . . . .**139** F1
Raeburn Rd S IP3. . . .**139** F1
Raedwald Dr IP32. . . .**123** D6
Raedwald Way IP11. . .**53** F1
Raglan Rd **2** NR32. . .**113** D1
Raglan St NR32 . . . . . .**113** D1
Rag's La IP30. . . . .**50** D1
Raile Wlk CO10 . . . .**91** E8
Railway App IP11. . . . .**153** A5
Railway Cl **2** CB5. . . . .**44** A4
Railway Hill IP20. . . . . .**22** C6
Railway Mws IP3 . . . .**140** A5
Railway St **19** CO11. .**104** E2
Railway Terr CB9 . . . .**133** E7
Raine Ave CB9 . . . . . .**132** B6
Rainey Ct **37** IP20. . . .**22** D6
Raingate St IP33 . . . . .**154** C1
Raleigh Cl CO10. . . . . .**148** E8
Raleigh Inf Sch **1**
　IP24. . . . .**16** C7
Raleigh Rd CO10 . . . . .**148** E8

Ralph Knight Way 22 CO12 107 A2
Ram La NR15 21 C8
Rampart Way IP24 16 C5
Ramplin Cl IP33 154 C4
Rampling Cl IP7 149 D7
RAMSEY 106 C1
Ramsey Cl IP2 139 A1
Ramsey Rd
Hadleigh IP7 149 F7
Harwich CO12 106 D1
Ramsgate Dr IP3 140 B3
RAMSHOLT 99 A4
Ramsholt Rd
Alderton IP12 99 C4
Shottisham IP12 99 B6
Randall Cl
2 Hopton on Sea NR31 3 B7
Ipswich IP5 141 E7
Randolph Cl IP4 140 B5
Rands La Hadleigh IP7 149
Rands Rd IP7 149 B1
Rands Way IP3 140 B2
Randwell Cl IP4 140 B5
Ranelagh County Prim Sch IP2 138 F5
Ranelagh Rd
Felixstowe IP11 153 A4
Ipswich IP2 155 A1
Ransome Ave IP21 21 A2
Ransome Cl IP8 138 A6
Ransome Cres IP3 140 B2
Ransome Rd IP3 140 B2
Ransomes Europark IP10 144 E8
Ransomes Way IP3 140 D1
Ransom Rd IP12 146 E6
Ranson La CO10 78 D3
Ranson Rd
Felixstowe IP11 153 C7
Needham Market IP6 125 C4
Rant Score NR32 113 E2
Ranulf Rd 11 CO10 92 B7
Ranulph Cl IP5 141 B6
Ranville NR33 114 E3
Ranworth Ave NR33 114 E5
Raphael Ct IP1 134 F1
Raphael Wlk 10 NR32 113 B6
Rapier St 6 IP2 139 C3
Rapsy Tapesy La IP23 117 A2
Rat Hill IP9 106 C5
Rattla Cnr IP16 58 C5
Rattlerow Hill IP21 39 B6
Rattler's Rd IP27 5 F1
RATTLESDEN 65 E6
Rattlesden Cl 2 IP14 124 D3
Rattlesden Prim Sch IP30 65 D6
Rattlesden Rd
Clopton Green IP30 65 D7
Drinkstone IP30 65 C6
Felsham IP30 65 B3
Gedding IP30 65 B5
Raven Cl
Mildenhall IP28 116 D3
7 Stowmarket IP14 124 F7
Raveningham Rd NR34 9 C8
Raven Rd IP33 122 D5
Ravensfield Rd IP1 134 E1
Ravens La IP8 134 A2
Ravensmere
Beccles NR34 9 D5
Beccles NR34 111 B6
Ravensmere E NR34 111 B6
Ravensmere Inf Sch NR34 111 B7
Ravens Way 6 IP12 84 A1
Ravenswood Ave IP3 144 B8
Ravenswood Com Prim Sch IP3 144 C8
Ravenward Dr CB5 44 B6
Raven Way IP7 149 D4
Ravenwood Mews NR33 115 A5
Rawlings Way 22 IP26 4 E5
Rawlings Way 22 IP26 4 E5
Ray Ave CO12 107 A2
RAYDON 94 E1
Raydon Croft IP14 124 F3
Raydon La IP12 131 D3
Raydon Rd
Chapel St Mary CO7 95 A2
Chapel St Mary IP8 95 B4
Little Wenham CO7 150 A4
Raydon Way CO10 92 B3
Rayes La CB8 121 A4
Ray La 8 CO12 106 F3
Rayleigh Rd IP1 134 E1
Rayment Drift 5 IP5 141 C7
Rayner's La NR35 8 D8
Raynham Rd IP32 154 A4
Raynsford Rd IP30 63 F7
Reach Rd CB5 44 A5
Read Cl 1 IP14 124 A8
Reade Rd 5 IP9 105 E7
Reading Gn IP21 38 D4
READING GREEN 38 E5
Reading Rd IP4 140 B7
Reading Room Yard IP21 22 A2
Reading's La IP31 35 A2
Reavell Pl IP2 139 A5
Rebow Rd 9 CO12 107 A1
Reckford Rd IP17 58 B6
Recreation La IP11 152 F6
Recreation Rd
Haverhill CB9 132 D5
Stowmarket IP14 124 C6
Recreation Way
Ipswich IP3 140 C2
Mildenhall IP28 116 C4
Recreation Wlk CO10 148 F3
Rectory Cl
Beccles NR34 111 F4
3 Glemsford CO10 77 A3
Ousden CB8 61 E6
Raydon IP7 94 F1
Rectory Corner 6 IP29 63 D1
Rectory Farm La IP21 37 C7
Rectory Field 4 IP9 106 C8
Rectory Gdns
Beyton IP30 49 F1
Bradfield CO11 105 C1
Long Melford CO10 77 E1
22 Thurston IP31 49 E4
Rectory Gn IP19 118 A4
Rectory Gr IP29 63 B5
Rectory Green 6 IP22 36 A8
Rectory Hill
Botesdale IP22 35 F6
East Bergholt CO7 151 C3
Polstead CO6 102 E8
Rickinghall Superior IP22 36 A5
Rectory La
Beccles NR34 9 F4
Brantham CO11 104 F5
Hedenham NR35 7 D8
Hintlesham IP8 95 C6
Kettlebaston IP7 79 B5
Kirton IP10 98 D2
Mettingham NR35 110 F3
4 Ramsey & Parkeston CO12 106 D1
Scole IP21 21 C5
Stuston IP21 37 D8
Weeting IP27 5 E3
3 Woolpit IP30 50 D1
Rectory Meadow 5 IP28 48 B6
Rectory Pk 3 CO10 93 C3
Rectory Pl IP29 47 A1
Rectory Rd
Aldeby/Wheatacre/Burgh St Peter NR34 10 A8
Bacton IP14 51 E5
Badingham IP13 56 B7
Blaxhall IP12 71 F4
Brome & Oakley IP23 117 B7
Broome NR35 8 B7
Burston & Shimpling IP22 20 E6
Dickleburgh IP21 21 B5
Framlingham IP13 55 C1
Gillingham NR34 9 B7
Gissing IP22 20 F8
Great Waldingfield CO10 92 D6
Harkstead IP9 106 B6
Hemingstone IP6 68 C1
Hollesley IP12 99 F7
Ipswich IP2 155 B1
Kedington CB9 133 F8
Kettleburgh IP13 70 C8
Langham CO4 103 C3
7 Lowestoft NR33 115 C6
Mellis IP23 36 F5
Middleton CO10 148 C2
Newton CO10 92 D2
Orford IP12 131 C3
Shelfanger IP22 20 B6
Sotterley NR34 26 A7
Sweffing IP17 56 E2
Tivetshall St Mary NR15 21 C8
Whatfield IP7 80 C1
Whepstead IP29 63 B4
Wortham IP22 19 F1
Wrabness CO11 106 A2
Wyverstone IP14 51 D6
Rectory St IP19 118 B4
Red Admiral Heights 17 IP31 49 E4
Redan St IP1 155 A4
Red Barn Dr 4 CO6 102 A7
Redbarn La IP17 72 D7
Red Barn Piece 11 IP13 83 E5
Redcastle Family Sch 6 IP24 16 B5
Reddells Cl CO10 148 D5
Red Dock La CB8 61 C1
REDE 62 E2
Rede La IP6 134 F8
REDENHALL 22 E7
Redenhall Rd IP20 22 D6
Rede Rd
Hawkedon IP29 76 E8
Rede IP29 62 E1
Whepstead IP29 62 F4
Rede Way CO10 92 B3
Rede Wood Nature Reserve★ IP6 82 D5
Redgate IP24 16 C6
Redgate La IP9 143 D5
REDGRAVE 36 A8
Redgrave Bsns Ctr IP22 19 B1
Redgrave & Lopham Fen National Nature Reserve★ IP22 19 C2
Redgrave & Lopham Fen Visitor Ctr★ IP22 19 C3
Redgrave Rd IP22 19 B3
Red Hall Ct IP11 153 C4
Red Hill IP7 94 D7
Redhill Cl IP1 138 F8
Red Hill Rd IP7 149 E8
Red House Cl
3 Felixstowe IP11 107 D8
Lowestoft NR32 112 F5
Newton CO10 92 D3
Redhouse Farm La IP13 56 B3
Redhouse Farm Rd IP23 38 B6
Red House Farm Rd
Aldeburgh IP12 73 C1
Orford IP12 87 A8
Redhouse Gdns 5 CB7 28 D3
Redhouse La
Bawdsey IP12 99 E3
Boxted CO4 102 E1
9 Sudbury CO10 148 C5
Red House La
Chediston Green IP19 24 E2
Leiston IP16 129 D4
Sudbury CO10 148 E2
Redhouse Rd IP13 56 B8
Red Houses CB8 59 A4
Red House The★ IP15 130 C6
Red House Wlk IP10 145 E4
REDISHAM 25 B7
Redisham Cl NR32 113 A5
Redisham Corner NR34 25 B7
Redisham Rd
Redisham NR34 25 B6
Weston NR34 9 C1
Redit La CB7 28 A1
Red La IP17 72 D8
REDLINGFIELD 38 D2
Redlingfield Rd
Horham IP21 38 D2
Occold IP23 37 F2
Red Lion Cl IP21 38 C7
Red Lion La NR16 19 A8
RED LODGE 30 B1
REDMERE CB7 12 D8
Red Oak Prim Sch NR33 115 B6
Red Rose Cl IP12 99 E4
Redshank Cl CB9 133 A5
Red Sleeve IP9 150 D3
Redwald Cres IP3 140 B4
Redwald Rd IP12 85 E8
Redwing Cl IP2 138 D3
Redwing Dr 13 IP14 67 A6
Redwing Rd IP33 123 C1
Redwings Horse Sanctuary (Caldecott)★ NR31 2 C8
Redwold Cl IP12 146 C1
Redwood Dr IP32 48 B5
Redwood Gdns IP33 154 C2
Redwood La 23 IP27 13 F2
Redwood Terraces 10 IP13 84 F7
Reed La 18 IP28 46 A8
Reedland Way 4 IP11 152 D5
Reed's Bldgs IP33 154 C3
Reeds La
Haverhill CB9 132 E6
St Olaves NR32 2 A6
Reeds Way IP14 67 A7
Reet 1 NR32 115 D8
Reeve Cl
12 Bury St Edmunds IP32 48 C5
25 Ixworth IP31 34 B1
Scole IP21 21 A2
Tuddenham IP28 30 F2
Reeve Gdns IP5 141 C8
Reeve's Cl NR35 110 C3
Reeves La IP26 5 A3
Reeve St NR32 113 D2
Refinery Rd CO12 106 F3
Regal Dr CB7 28 E3
Regal Gdns IP13 126 C4
Regal La CB7 28 E3
Regal Lane Ind Est CB7 28 E3
Regal Mws 4 CB8 46 A5
Regal Theatre★ IP14 124 E5
Regan Cl NR32 113 A5
Regent Pl 3 CB7 28 D3
Regent Rd NR32 113 D1
Regents Ct 8 CB8 121 A4
Regent St
20 Manningtree CO11 104 E2
Stowmarket IP14 124 D7
Regent Theatre★ IP4 155 C3
Regimental Mus★ IP33 122 E6
Regimental Way 18 CO12 106 E1
Regina Cl IP4 140 B5
Reid Cl 3 IP3 140 D2
Reigate Cl IP3 140 B3
Rembrandt Cl 3 NR32 113 C6
Rembrandt Gdns 4 IP33 122 F3
Rembrandt Way IP33 123 A3
Rembrow Rd IP9 150 E3
Remembrance Rd IP16 73 F6
Remercie Rd 7 CO11 105 A2
Rendall La IP14 67 A8
Rendell Cres
3 Fornham St Martin IP32 48 B5
20 Fornham St Martin IP32 48 B5
RENDHAM 56 E3
Rendham Hall Farm La IP17 56 F4
Rendham Hill IP17 56 F7
Rendham Rd
Bruisyard IP17 56 D4
Kelsale cum Carlton IP17 128 A6
Peasenhall IP17 56 F7
RENDLESHAM 85 C8
Rendlesham Com Prim Sch IP12 85 D8
Rendlesham Est★ IP12 85 D6
Rendlesham Forest Ctr★ IP12 85 F3
Rendlesham La IP13 71 C1
Rendlesham Mews Bsns Ctr IP12 85 D7
Rendlesham Rd
15 Felixstowe IP11 152 D5
9 Ipswich IP1 139 A7
Renfrew Rd IP4 136 B1
Renoir Pl 2 NR32 113 B5
Renson Cl 6 IP30 64 F8
REYDON 119 C7
Reydon Bsns Pk IP18 119 D8
Reydon Cl 2 CB9 132 A6
Reydon La IP18 26 D1
Reydon Mews NR32 113 A6
Reydon Prim Sch IP18 119 C8
Reydon Rd IP18 43 A7
REYDON SMEAR 26 F1
Reydon Wood Nature Reserve★ IP34 26 C2
Reynolds Ave 2 IP3 144 A8
Reynolds Cl
1 Haverhill CB9 132 B7
1 Ipswich IP3 140 A1
Reynolds Ct 10 IP11 152 D5
Reynolds Rd IP3 140 A1
Reynolds Way CO10 148 E8
Reynolds Wlk
Bury St Edmunds IP33 122 B6
Gunton NR32 113 B6
Ribbans Pk Rd IP3 140 B4
Ribblesdale NR33 114 E3
Riby Rd IP11 152 F4
Richard Burn Way CO10 148 C8
Richard Crampton Rd NR34 111 B3
Richard Easter Rd IP24 16 C7
Richards Dr IP13 137 D5
Richardson Rd CO7 151 D5
Richardsons La
Chelmondiston IP9 106 B8
Woolverstone IP9 144 E1
Richards's Cl NR33 114 E6
Richard Walker Cl IP32 123 F7
Richer Cl IP31 50 E7
Richer Rd IP31 50 F7
Richmond Cres 8 CO12 107 A1
Richmond Pl 8 NR33 115 C6
Richmond Rd
Brandon IP27 14 E8
Ipswich IP1 138 F7
Lowestoft NR33 115 C6
RICKINGHALL 36 A6
Rickinghall Bsns Ctr IP22 36 B3
Rickinghall Rd
Allwood Green IP23 36 B2
Clay Street IP31 35 E3
Hinderclay IP22 35 E7
Riddlesworth Hall Sch IP22 17 F4
Rider Haggard La 7 NR33 11 C1
Rider Haggard Way NR35 110 C7
Ridgeville 9 NR33 114 F3
Ridgeway IP14 124 B6
Ridgeways The NR33 114 D5
Ridgeway The 10 CO12 107 A2
RIDGEWELL 89 D4
Ridgewell CE VA Prim Sch CO9 89 D3
Ridgewell Rd CO10 89 D5
Ridings The
3 Beccles NR34 111 F4
Ridings The *continued*
Leavenheath CO6 102 B8
Ridley Rd IP33 122 C6
Rigbourne Hill NR34 111 C3
Rigbourne Hill La 6 NR34 111 C2
Rigby Ave CO11 105 A2
Riley Cl IP1 134 C1
Rimmer Cl CO10 148 E8
Ringham Rd IP4 140 A6
RINGSFIELD 9 B3
Ringsfield CE Prim Sch NR34 9 B2
RINGSFIELD CORNER 9 B2
Ringsfield Rd
Beccles NR34 111 A4
6 Lowestoft NR32 113 A3
Ringsfield NR34 9 A1
RINGSHALL 80 E7
Ringshall County Prim Sch IP14 80 E6
Ringshall Rd IP7 80 E5
RINGSHALL STOCKS 80 F6
Rio Cl 2 NR33 114 C5
Ripon Rd IP12 85 C3
Risbridge Dr CB9 133 E8
RISBY 47 D5
Risby Barn Antique & Craft Ctr★ IP28 47 D5
Risby CE VC Prim Sch IP28 47 D5
Risby Cl IP4 140 B6
Risby Rd IP28 47 E7
Riseway Cl IP33 123 B1
RISHANGLES 53 D7
Rishangles Rd IP23 53 C8
Rishton Rd 7 NR32 113 D1
Rising Sun Hill IP30 65 D5
Rissemere La E IP18 119 C8
Ritabrook Rd IP2 138 E1
Rivendale 4 NR33 114 D3
Riverbank Cl CO10 90 B8
River Gdns IP14 124 E4
River Hill IP8 138 C8
River La
Bury St Edmunds IP33 123 D3
Fordham CB7 29 A1
Halesworth IP19 118 B3
Riverside
4 Framlingham IP13 126 C3
Gillingham NR34 9 A6
Hasketon IP13 146 A7
Palgrave IP22 20 B2
Riverside Ave E 6 CO11 104 E3
Riverside Ave W 4 CO11 104 E3
Riverside Bsns Ctr NR33 115 C8
Riverside Cl IP28 116 B4
Riverside Ct IP32 123 A8
Riverside Dr 6 IP14 124 E5
Riverside Ind Est IP13 127 C7
Riverside Ind Pk IP2 139 D3
Riverside Maltings 4 IP22 20 D2
Riverside Rd
Ipswich IP1 138 E7
Ipswich IP1 138 F7
Lowestoft NR33 115 B8
Riverside Theatre The★ IP12 147 A4
Riverside View IP13 127 C8
Riverside Way IP27 5 F2
Riverside Wlk CB8 45 F3
Rivers St IP4 139 F7
Riverview
Lawford CO11 104 E3
Woodbridge IP12 147 C7
River View NR34 111 B7
River View Rd 1 IP9 106 A5
Riverwalk Sch
Bury St Edmunds IP33 154 A1
Nowton IP33 123 B1
River Way 21 IP6 82 A5
Rivett Cl IP10 98 D3
Rivetts Loke NR34 111 B4
Rivish La CO10 91 E8
Rixon Cres 3 IP12 84 E6
Roamwood Gn La IP14 53 E3
Robeck Rd IP3 139 E1
Robert Boby Way IP33 154 B2
Robert Darry Cl CO10 148 A4
Robertsbridge Wlk
Lowestoft NR33 114 D3
6 Lowestoft NR33 114 D4
Roberts Cl IP5 141 D7
Robert's Hill CO8 101 C2
Roberts Rd IP16 129 D6
Robert Suckling Ct CB9 88 D3
Robin Ave 16 IP20 22 D5
Robin Cl
Haverhill CB9 133 A5
Mildenhall IP28 116 D4
15 Stowmarket IP14 67 A5
12 Thurston IP31 49 D4
Robin Dr IP2 138 D3
Robin Hatch CB8 121 A1
Robin Hill NR32 113 A2
Robin Rd IP33 123 C1
Robins Cl 16 CB7 29 C5
Robinson Cl
Bury St Edmunds IP33 122 D6
8 Haughley IP14 51 C1
Robinson Rd 7 IP21 20 F1
Robinson Wlk IP32 122 D7
Robin Way CO10 148 A3
Robletts IP13 84 D7
Robletts Way 1 CO6 101 F2
Robsons Cl IP23 36 F5
Robsons Mill IP23 36 F5
Rochdale 3 NR33 114 F3
Rochester Rd 1 NR33 115 B4
Rochester Way CO10 148 B8
Rochfort Ave CB8 120 E5
Rockall CB8 61 E6
Rockall Cl CB9 133 B5
Rockalls Rd CO6 93 F1
Rockingham Rd IP33 123 B3
Rock Rd NR32 112 D1
Rockstone La IP19 41 C7
Rodber Way NR32 113 A6
RODBRIDGE CORNER 91 E6
Rodbridge Hill CO10 91 D6
Rodney Ct IP12 146 F7
Rodwell Cl IP9 105 F8
Roebuck Dr IP27 109 E4
Roebuck The IP27 109 E1
Roe Deer Dr IP9 150 D4
Rogeron Cl CO10 75 D3
Rogers Cl IP11 152 F6
Roger's Cl NR31 3 B7
Rogers La IP29 77 A7
Roger's La CO10 92 F4
Rogue's La IP13 127 C5
Rokewood Pl IP29 64 A3
Rolfe Cl IP28 29 E7
Roma Ave IP5 98 B8
Roman Cl
3 Burwell CB5 44 A5
7 Great Blakenham IP6 81 F5
ROMAN HILL 113 C1
Roman Hill Prim Sch NR32 113 C1
Roman La CO10 92 C6
Roman Rd
Ashfield cum Thorpe IP13 54 D1
Lowestoft NR32 113 C1
Smallworth IP22 18 B6
Roman Way
Felixstowe IP11 153 D6
Halesworth IP19 118 A3
Haverhill CB9 133 B4
Long Melford CO10 91 E7
Stoke Ash IP23 37 B1
Romany La NR33 11 B3
Romany Rd NR32 114 C8
Romany Way IP33 123 D3
Romney Pl 6 NR32 113 B6
Romney Rd IP3 140 A1
Romsey Rd IP33 122 D3
Ronald La IP17 128 D5
Ronden Cl NR34 111 B2
Ron Pattle La 5 IP14 124 F6
Rookery Chase CO7 103 F1
Rookery Cl NR33 114 F7
Rookery Dr IP31 50 C4
Rookery Dro 2 IP28 13 B1
Rookery Farm La IP17 56 F3
Rookery Farm Rd IP13 56 A2
Rookery La
Battlesea Green IP21 39 A6
St James, South Elmham IP19 23 F4
Walsham Le Willows IP31 35 C2
Rookery Rd
Elmsett IP7 80 E2
Monewden IP13 69 F5
Rookery Sh Ctr CB8 121 A4
Rookery The
Brandon IP27 5 D1
Eye IP23 117 D2
4 Manningtree CO11 104 E2
Newmarket CB8 121 B3
Rookery Way IP14 51 F1
Rookery Wlk IP27 109 B7
ROOKSEY GREEN 78 E6
Rook's La 7 NR34 111 B5
Rooks Mead IP31 49 F3
Rookwood La CO10 78 F6
Rookwood Way CB9 132 E4
Roosevelt Wlk 5 NR33 114 C5
ROOST END 133 E2
Roper's Ct 3 CO10 78 D4
Ropers Gdns IP30 50 F3
Ropers La CO10 91 D7
Ropes Dr IP5 141 B8
Rope Wlk
Carlton Colville NR33 114 B4
Ipswich IP4 155 C2
Rosbrook Cl 1 IP33 122 D4
Rose Acre CO7 103 F7

Rose And Crown Ct
IP31. . . . . .34 D4
Rosebank 24 CO12 . . . 107 A2
Rosebay Gdns 1 CB7 .28 D4
Rosebery Rd
Felixstowe IP11 . . . . . .153 B4
Ipswich IP4 . . . . .139 F5
Rosebery Way CB8 . .120 E5
Rosecroft Rd IP1 . . . .153 A2
Rosecroft Way IP24. . . .16 D6
Rose Ct
Lowestoft NR32. . . . . . .113 B2
26 Red Lodge IP28. . . .30 C1
Shotley IP9. . . . . .106 F6
Rosedale Cl NR33. . . .114 E4
Rosedale Gdns 9
NR33. . . . . .114 E4
ROSEDALE PARK 114 E4
Rose Farm La
Framlingham IP13 . . . .126 A6
Saxstead Green IP13 . .55 C3
Shotley IP9. . . . . .106 F5
Rose Fields CO11 . . . .104 D1
Rosefinch Cl CB9. . . .133 A5
Rose Gn CO10. . . . . . .101 F8
Rose Gn La 4 IP28. . . .30 B8
ROSE GREEN
Assington 101 E9
Lindsey. 93 D7
Rose Green Rd IP7. . . .93 D7
Rose Hall Gdns
NR35. . . . . .110 B3
ROSE HILL 139 F4
Rose Hill
Grundisburgh IP13 . . . . .83 E5
Withersfield CB9 . . . . . .74 B3
Witnesham IP6. . . . . . .135 F7
Rosehill Cres IP3 . . . .139 F4
Rose Hill Prim Sch
IP3 . . . . .140 A4
Rosehill Rd IP3 . . . . .139 F4
Rosehip Ave 10 IP28 . .30 C1
Rose La
Botesdale IP22. . . . . . . .36 A7
Bungay NR35. . . . . . . .110 B3
Diss IP22 . . . . .20 D1
Elmswell IP30. . . . . .50 E2
Ipswich IP4 . . . . .155 B2
Wickham Skeith IP23 . . .52 D8
Rose La Cl IP22 . . . . . . .20 C1
Rosemary Ave IP11 . .153 B5
Rosemary Cl 4 IP28 . .30 C1
Rosemary Gdns
CO10 . . . . .148 D8
Rosemary La
Ipswich IP4 . . . . .155 B2
Kelsale cum Carlton
IP17. . . . . .128 C6
Wingfield IP21 . . . . .39 B8
Rosemary Rd IP32. .48 C5
Rosery La IP13. . . . . .137 F6
Rose Wlk
Needham Market
IP6 . . . . .125 D3
Ridgewell CO9 . . . . .89 D3
Rosewood NR33 . . . . .115 A5
Rosewood Cl 22 IP27. .13 F2
Ross Cl CB9. . . . . .133 B5
Ross Peers Sports Ctr
CB7. . . . . .28 D3
Ross Rd IP4. . . . . .136 B1
Rosyth Rd 3 IP31. . . . .33 D5
ROTCHFORDS. 101 F1
Rotheram Rd 9 IP7. . .79 F4
Rotten Row CO10 . . . . .92 D2
Rotterdam Rd NR32. .113 B1
ROUGHAM. 64 C8
Rougham CE Prim Sch
IP30 . . . . .49 D1
Rougham Control Twr
Museum★ IP30 . . . . .49 B2
ROUGHAM GREEN. . . .64 C8
Rougham Hill IP33. . .123 D3
Rougham Ind Est
IP30. . . . . .49 B2
Rougham Rd
Bradfield St George
IP30. . . . . .64 D7
Bury St Edmunds IP33 123 C2
Bury St Edmunds IP33 .123 E3
Rougham Tower Ave
IP30. . . . . .49 B3
Roughlands IP27 . . . .109 D6
Round House Hill IP20 . .7 B1
Roundridge Rd IP9 . .150 F4
Roundwood Rd
Dullingham CB8 . . . . . .59 F5
Ipswich IP4 . . . . .140 A7
Rousies Cl 6 IP7 . . . .149 E6
Rous Meml Ct CB8 . . .121 B3
Rous Rd CB8. . . . . . . .121 B3
Routh Ave 4 IP3 . . . .140 F1
Rovers Way CB9 . . . .132 F4
Rowan Cl
Claydon IP6 . . . . .134 D8
25 Harwich CO12 . . . .107 A2
Haverhill IP28 . . . . . . .132 C7
Priory Heath IP3. . . . . .140 D2
Rowan Dr
Brandon IP27 . . . . .14 F8
Bury St Edmunds IP32 .123 F6
Rowan Gn 7 IP32. . . . .123 F6
Rowanhayes Cl IP2 . .139 B3
Rowans Cres IP11 . . .152 E2
Rowans Way 1 CO6. .102 A7

Rowan Way
Beccles NR34 . . . . . . .111 E3
Lowestoft NR33 . . . . . .114 D6
5 Thurstow IP31. . . . . .49 D4
Rowan Wlk IP28 . . . . .116 E5
Rowarth Ave IP5. . . . .141 C7
Rowell Cl CB9 . . . . . . .132 E8
Rowell's La IP14 . . . . . .51 D4
Rowe's Hill IP13 . . . . . .40 C2
Rowlands Yard 35
CO12 . . . . .106 F1
Rowley Cl 7 CO11 . . .104 E4
Rowley Ct
Newmarket CB8 . . . . . .120 E3
Sturmer CB9. . . . . .133 C3
Rowley Dr CB8. . . . . . .120 F3
Rowley Hill
Haverhill CO9 . . . . .133 F1
Sturmer CB9. . . . . .133 B3
Rowley Mws IP16. . . .129 C8
Rowntree Cl 6
NR32 . . . . .113 A6
Rows The CB8 . . . . . . .120 E3
Row The
Bramford IP8 . . . . .134 A2
Gipsy Row CO7 . . . . . . .50 D4
Stratford St Mary CO7 .103 E5
Roxburgh Rd IP4. . . . .136 B1
Roxbury Dr NR16. . . . . .18 C8
Royal Ave NR32. . . . . .113 D3
Royal Gala Dr 7
CO10 . . . . .148 F8
Royal Hospl Sch IP9 105 E6
Royal Naval Patrol
Service Mus★
NR32. . . . . .113 E3
Royal Pal Cl CB8 . . . .120 D7
Royal Plain NR33. . . .115 D8
Royal Terr NR33 . . . . .115 D7
Roy Ave IP4 . . . . .140 B5
Roy Cl IP5. . . . . .141 B7
ROYDON. 20 A3
Roydon Drift CO10 . . . .77 F1
Roydon Fen IP22. . . . . .20 B2
Roydon Prim Sch
IP22. . . . . .20 B3
Roydon Rd IP22. . . . . . .20 C3
Roydon Way 10
NR32. . . . . .112 F4
Roylands La CO10. . . . .93 D3
Roynon Cl 28 NR33 . . . .11 C1
Royston Dr
Ipswich IP2 . . . . .138 D2
Thurston IP31. . . . . .49 D3
Rozel Ct IP28. . . . . .30 C8
Rozlyne Cl 8 NR33. . . .114 E4
Rubens Rd IP3. . . . . . .140 A1
Rubens Wlk
Gunton NR33 . . . . .113 B6
Sudbury CO10. . . . . . . .148 E8
Rubin Cl 18 IP31 . . . . . .49 A3
Ruby Cl 9 NR32 . . . . . . .3 D4
Rudlands IP8 . . . . .138 C1
Rudlands Cl 6 CB7 . . .29 C5
Rues Farm Rd IP11. . .153 D7
Rue's La IP11 . . . . .153 C8
Ruffles Rd CB9. . . . . . .133 A5
Rugby Rd CO10 . . . . . .148 F2
Rule Gdns CB7. . . . . . . .29 A2
Rules Yd 10 CO10 . . . . .93 C3
RUMBURGH. 24 D6
Rumburgh La NR35 . . .24 D6
Rumburgh Rd
All Saints South Elmham
IP19 . . . . .24 D5
Lowestoft NR32 . . . . . .113 B5
Rumburgh IP19 . . . . . . .24 B3
Runce's La NR33. . . . .114 C3
Run Meadow NR33. . . .114 C6
Runnacles Way IP14 152 D5
Runnymede Gn IP33 123 A3
Run The NR34 . . . . .26 A7
RUSHALL. 21 F5
Rushall Rd IP20. . . . . . .22 B6
RUSHBROOKE. 64 B8
Rushbrooke La IP33 123 D3
Rushbury Cl IP14 . . . .140 B8
Rush Cl IP4. . . . . .140 E4
Rushes Farm La IP7. . .94 A7
RUSHFORD. 17 B4
Rushford Rd
Coney Weston IP31 . . . .17 E1
Euston IP24. . . . . .16 E2
Rushford IP24 . . . . .17 B4
Rushlake Way 7
NR33 . . . . .114 D4
Rushmeadow Way 1
IP11. . . . . .153 D7
RUSHMERE. 10 D1
Rushmere Hall Prim Sch
IP4. . . . . .136 A1
Rushmere Pl CB9 . . . .132 F6
Rushmere Rd
Gisleham NR33. . . . . . .114 B1
Ipswich IP4 . . . . .140 A7
Rushmere NR33. . . . . . .10 F3
RUSHMERE ST
ANDREW. 136 E1
Rushmere St IP5. . . . .136 E1
RUSHMERE STREET. . .136 E1
Rushton Dr NR33. . . . .114 B3
Ruskin Cl
1 Haverhill CB9. . . . . .132 B7
3 Stowmarket IP14 . .124 B8
Ruskin Rd IP4 . . . . . . .129 F4
Russel Green IP21 . . . .39 D3
Russell Baron Rd
IP31. . . . . .48 D5

Russell Cl
Sibton IP17. . . . . .56 F8
Woodbridge IP12 . . . . .146 E6
Russell Rd
Felixstowe IP11 . . . . . .152 F2
Ipswich IP1 . . . . .155 A3
Russell's Gn NR34. . . . .9 C2
RUSSEL'S GREEN 39 C3
Russet Cl
4 Beccles NR34 . . . .111 C3
Finningham IP14 . . . . . .52 A8
Great Barton IP32 . . . .123 E7
Russet Dr 10 IP28. . . . .30 C1
Russet Rd IP4 . . . . . . .139 E7
Russett Cl IP33. . . . . . .132 A6
Russset Rd 7 IP22. . . . .20 C3
Rutherford Pl 11
CB9. . . . . .74 A1
Rutland Cl 15 CB9. . . .132 C5
Rutland Sq IP33 . . . . .154 C1
Rutter Cl NR35. . . . . . .110 B6
Rydal Ave IP11. . . . . . .155 C3
Rydal Cl IP14 . . . . .124 B6
Rydal Wlk IP3 . . . . . . .140 C2
Ryders Way 2 IP22. . . .36 A6
Rydwar Cl NR32. . . . . .112 D3
Ryeburn Cl 1 NR33. . . .11 B1
Rye Cl
Ipswich IP3 . . . . .140 D4
3 Lowestoft NR33. . .114 D4
Rye Ct CB9 . . . . .132 C5
Ryedale 1 NR33. . . . . .114 F3
Ryefields IP31 . . . . . . .49 E4
Rye Hill CO10 . . . . .148 F5
Ryes La CO10 . . . . .91 D1
Rylands IP9 . . . . .150 E4
Rylands Cl 1 IP31. . . . .49 E4
Rymer Cl IP31 . . . . .33 F5
Rymer La IP31 . . . . .33 A5

S

SACKERS GREEN 92 D2
Sackville St CB8 . . . . .121 B4
Sackvylle St IP14 . . . . .53 E1
Saddlemakers La
IP12. . . . . .147 C8
Saddler'S La IP29. . . . .63 A3
Saddlers Meadow 2
IP13. . . . . .83 E5
Saddlers Pl IP15 . . . . . .95 A8
Saddlers Yd 17 IP31. . . .34 B1
Saffron Cl 16 IP23. . . . . .36 D2
Saffrons Cl 12 IP30. . . .50 D1
Saffron Sq NR33 . . . . .115 A2
Sage Ct 39 IP28. . . . . . .30 C1
Sagehayes Cl IP2. . . . .139 B3
Sages End Rd CB9. . . . .88 A4
Sailor's Path IP17. . . . .73 B5
Sailor's Path IP17 . . . .72 E5
St Agnes Way IP5. . . . .140 F6
St Albans CB8 . . . . . . .121 A6
St Alban's RC High Sch
. . . . .140 D7
St Andrew 2 CB8. . . . .121 A4
St Andrew Cl 1 NR31 . . .3 C7
St Andrew's CE
Prim Sch IP22. . . . . .19 A5
St Andrew's CE
Prim Sch IP27 . . . . . .28 D3
St Andrew's CE VC Prim
Sch CO9. . . . . .89 F1
St Andrew's Church La
IP5. . . . . .136 D1
St Andrews Cl
2 Barningham IP31 . . .34 E7
2 Great Finborough
IP14 . . . . .66 B4
Ipswich IP4 . . . . .140 D5
3 Isleham CB7 . . . . . .29 C5
Walberswick IP18 . . . . .43 C5
St Andrew's Cl IP12. . .147 D7
St Andrew's Ct 4
IP33. . . . . .154 B2
St Andrews Dr 7
IP28. . . . . .48 C6
St Andrew's Dr 3
IP9. . . . . .106 C8
St Andrews Mead
IP14. . . . . .68 B8
St Andrews Park 24
CB7. . . . . .28 D4
St Andrew's Pl IP12. . .147 D8
St Andrews Rd
Scole IP21 . . . . .21 A1
Sudbury CO10. . . . . . . .148 E4
St Andrew's Rd
Beccles NR34 . . . . . . .111 C2
Coldfair Green IP17 . . .129 B2
Felixstowe IP11 . . . . . .153 A5
St Andrew's Rise
CO10 . . . . .91 C3
St Andrew's St N
IP33. . . . . .154 B3
St Andrew's St S
IP33. . . . . .154 B2
St Andrew's St IP28. . .116 C4
St Annes Cl IP12. . . . . .146 D3
St Anne's Cl NR34. . . . .111 C4
St Anne's Dr IP28. . . . .116 C4
St Anne's Rd NR34 . . . .111 C4
St Anthony 3 CB8. . . . .121 A4
St Anthonys Cres
IP4. . . . . .139 F7
St Aubyns Rd IP4 . . . .140 A5
St Aubyn's Rd 6
NR33 . . . . .115 C6

St Audrys Pk Rd 5
IP12. . . . . .84 E6
St Audrys Rd IP12. . . . .84 E6
St Augustine Rd IP3. 140 D4
St Augustine's Gdns
IP3. . . . . .140 C3
St Austell Cl IP5 . . . . .141 A6
St Austin's La 1
CO12 . . . . .107 C2
St Barbara's Ct 18
CO10 . . . . .148 C5
St Bartholomews La
CO10 . . . . .148 B7
St Benedict's RC Sch
IP32. . . . . .122 F8
St Benedicts Rd IP27. . .6 A1
St Benedict's Rd
NR34 . . . . .111 B6
St Benet's Dr NR34 . . .111 C3
St Benet's RC Minst
NR34. . . . . .111 A4
St Benet's RC Prim Sch
NR34. . . . . .111 A5
St Botolph's CE Prim Sch
IP22. . . . . .36 B7
St Botolph's La IP33 154 C1
St Botolphs Pl 13
CB9 . . . . .132 D5
St Botolph's Way
CB9. . . . . .132 D6
St Catherines Cl
IP28. . . . . .116 C6
St Catherine's Cl
NR33. . . . . .114 E4
St Catherine's Ct
IP2. . . . . .138 E1
St Catherine's Rd 11
CO10 . . . . .91 E8
St Christopher's CE VC
Prim Sch IP28. . . . .30 C1
St Clare Ct 15 NR31. . . . .3 B7
St Clare Hall Rd IP30 .64 D4
St Clement Mews
. . . . .3 B7
St Clements Church La
IP4. . . . . .155 C2
St Crispins Cl IP5 . . . .141 E7
St Cross Rd IP20. . . . . .23 B8
ST CROSS SOUTH
ELMHAM. 23 D7
St David CB8 . . . . .121 A4
St David's Cl 5
NR34 . . . . .111 C2
St Davids La IP12 . . . .100 A8
St David's Rd 7 IP3. . .140 B3
St Denis Cl 11 CO12 . .107 A1
St Denys 5 CB8. . . . . . .121 A4
St Domonic's Dr IP27 . .6 A1
St Edmund Cl 5 IP31 . .34 B1
St Edmund Rd IP27 . . . .5 E4
St Edmundsbury Cath★
IP33 . . . . .154 B3
St Edmundsbury CE VA
Prim Sch IP33. . . . .154 A3
St Edmundsbury Mews
IP33. . . . . .154 A3
St Edmundsbury Ret Pk
IP32. . . . . .123 E4
St Edmunds Cl
Assington CO10 . . . . . .92 F1
2 Beccles NR34 . . . .111 C2
12 Harwich CO12 . . . .107 A1
2 Stowmarket IP14 . .124 C8
3 Woodbridge IP12. . .146 E4
St Edmund's Cl 1
IP12. . . . . .85 A5
St Edmunds Cres 1
NR33. . . . . .11 C1
St Edmund's Dr IP30 . .50 F3
St Edmund's Farm Rd
IP13. . . . . .39 E1
St Edmunds Gate 8
IP31. . . . . .33 D5
St Edmund's Hill
CO10 . . . . .101 B7
St Edmunds La CO8 . .101 D5
St Edmunds Pl IP33 . .154 B3
St Edmund's Pl IP13 . .139 C3
St Edmund's Prim Sch
IP21 . . . . .38 C6
St Edmunds RC Prim Sch
NR35. . . . . .110 B4
St Edmund's RC Prim Sch
IP33 . . . . .154 B1
St Edmunds Rd IP14 124 C7
St Edmund's Rd
Felixstowe IP11 . . . . . .152 E2
Ipswich IP1 . . . . .139 B8
Southwold IP18 . . . . . .119 D6
St Edmunds Sq 7
IP31. . . . . .33 D5
St Etienne IP14 . . . . . . .69 B6
St Fabians Cl CB8 . . . .120 F5
St Farm Cl
Bucklesham IP10 . . . . . .98 A4
5 Holywell Row IP28 . .30 C8
Tunstall IP12. . . . . .71 F2
St Farm Gdns 11
IP23. . . . . .36 D2
St Felix Cl 2 CB7 . . . . . .28 D5
St Felix Prim Sch
CB9. . . . . .132 B5
St Felix Rise NR35. . . . .7 E1
St Felix Sch IP18. . . . .119 A6
St George's Ave 2
CO12 . . . . .107 B1
St Georges Cl IP14 . . .124 C7

St Georges Dr 4
IP22. . . . . .36 A6
St George's Rd
Beccles NR34 . . . . . . .111 B4
Felixstowe IP11 . . . . . .153 C6
Lowestoft NR33 . . . . . .115 B4
Stowlangtoft IP31. . . . .49 C7
St Georges Sq IP18 . .119 A7
St George's St IP1 . . . .155 B3
St Gotthards Ave
IP12. . . . . .98 B8
St Gregory Ct CO10. . .148 B6
St Gregorys CE VC Prim
Sch CO10 . . . . .148 B5
St Gregorys Cl 1
IP12. . . . . .85 E8
St Helena IP17. . . . . . . .43 B3
St Helena Wlk IP28 . . .116 C6
St Helen's Primary Sch
IP4 . . . . .139 E6
St Helen's St 4 IP4. . .155 C3
St Helens Way IP24. . . .16 B7
St Isidores IP5. . . . . . .141 E7
St Ives Cl IP5 . . . . .141 A6
St James 6 CB8. . . . . .121 A4
St James Cl 3 CB9. . . .132 C6
St James' Gn 7
IP18. . . . . .119 D5
St James La IP33 . . . . .154 A2
St James' La
Chediston IP19. . . . . . .24 A3
St James, South Elmham
IP19 . . . . .23 F4
St James Rd
All Saints & St Nicholas,
South Elmham IP19 . .24 A1
St James, South Elmham
IP19 . . . . .23 F4
ST JAMES SOUTH
ELMHAM. 23 F4
St James's St IP17 . . . .43 B1
St Johns Ave IP33 . . . .121 A1
St John's CE VA Prim Sch
IP4 . . . . .140 A7
St Johns Cl IP30 . . . . . .50 E2
St Johns Cl IP28. . . . . .116 D6
St Johns Ct IP11 . . . . .153 A4
St John's Hill
Bungay NR35 . . . . .110 C2
4 Woodbridge IP12. . .147 A5
St Johns Meadow
IP20. . . . . .23 C3
St John's Pl IP33. . . . .154 B3
St John's Rd
Bungay NR35 . . . . .110 B3
Ipswich IP4 . . . . .140 A6
Lowestoft NR33 . . . . . .115 D7
Saxmundham IP17 . . . .128 C3
St Johns Row IP14 . . . .69 B6
St John's St
Beck Row, Holywell Row &
Kenny Hill IP28. . . . .30 C8
Bury St Edmunds IP33 .154 B3
Woodbridge IP12 . . . . .147 A5
St John's Terr 5
IP12. . . . . .147 A5
St John's Way
13 Feltwell IP26 . . . . . .4 E5
Thetford IP24. . . . . . . .16 A5
St John Way IP13 . . . .126 D2
St Joseph's Coll Sch
IP2 . . . . .138 F8
St Joseph's RC Prim Sch
Harwich CO12. . . . . . .107 A1
Sudbury CO10. . . . . . . .148 B6
St Laurence View
CO9 . . . . .89 C4
St Lawrence Cl
NR34 . . . . .111 C2
St Lawrence Gn IP5. . .141 A7
St Lawrence St IP1. . .155 B3
St Lawrence Way
IP5. . . . . .141 B8
St Leger Cl IP33 . . . . .120 F7
St Leonards Cl IP21 . . .21 A1
St Leonards Dr
CO10 . . . . .148 D5
St Leonards Rd 2
IP3. . . . . .140 B3
St Leonard's Rd 1
NR33. . . . . .115 C7
St Leonards St IP26 . . . .6 B8
St Louis RC Prim Sch
CB8. . . . . .121 A4
St Margaret's CE VA Prim
Sch IP4. . . . . .155 C3
St Margaret's Cres
Leiston IP16 . . . . .129 B6
3 Thetford IP24 . . . . .16 B5
St Margarets Ct
IP18. . . . . .119 B8
St Margarets Gn
IP4. . . . . .155 C3
ST MARGARET SOUTH
ELMHAM. 23 E6
St Margaret's Pl CB8 . .75 E7
St Margarets Plain
IP4. . . . . .155 C3
St Margarets Rd
All Saints South Elmham
NR35 . . . . .24 C1
St. Margaret, South Elmham
IP19 . . . . .24 A6
St Margaret's Rd
Bungay NR35 . . . . .110 B1
3 Lowestoft NR32. . . .113 E3
St Margaret's St IP4 153 C3

St Margaret's Way 3
NR31 . . . . .3 B7
St Mark's RC Prim Sch
IP2 . . . . .138 F3
St Martin's Cl CB8. . . .120 C7
St Martins Cl IP1. . . . . .51 E1
St Martins Gn 14
IP11. . . . . .107 D8
St Martin's La IP24. . . . .16 B2
St Martins Meadow
IP24. . . . . .16 B2
St Martin's St IP33. . . .154 B3
St Martin's Way IP24. .116 C5
St Mary's Ave 5 IP14 .51 C1
St Mary's CE Acad
IP28 . . . . .116 C5
St Mary's CE Prim Sch
IP7 . . . . .149 E6
St Mary's CE VA Prim Sch
IP12 . . . . .146 E5
St Marys Cl
1 Gislingham IP23 . . .36 D2
Offton IP8. . . . . .81 A4
St Mary's Cl
Bacton IP14. . . . . .51 F6
Bramford IP8 . . . . .134 B1
Felixstowe IP11 . . . . . .152 B7
Flixton NR35. . . . . .7 E1
Harleston IP20. . . . . . . .22 E6
Horham IP21. . . . . .38 F3
Mildenhall IP28 . . . . . .116 C5
3 Stowmarket IP14 . .124 C7
Sudbury CO10. . . . . . . .148 F8
St Mary'S Cl IP21 . . . . .39 B2
St Marys Cres
Badwell Ash IP31. . . . . .50 E7
Felixstowe IP11 . . . . . .152 F6
St Mary'S Ct IP33 . . . .154 A1
St Mary's Dr IP6. . . . . .137 B4
St Mary'S Dr 21 IP22 . .20 D2
St Marys Gdns 11
IP14. . . . . .52 E4
St Mary's Gdns IP6. . .125 E6
St Marys La
9 Bures CO8 . . . . . . .101 C5
36 Lawford CO11 . . . .104 E2
St Marys Mws
15 Burwell CB5. . . . . .44 B5
Lakenheath IP27 . . . . .109 C6
St Marys Pk IP10. . . . . .98 A4
St Marys RC Prim Sch
NR33 . . . . .115 C5
St Mary's RC Prim Sch
IP4 . . . . .139 F6
St Marys Rd IP4 . . . . .139 F6
St Mary's Rd
Aldeby NR34. . . . . .10 A7
Beccles NR34 . . . . . . .111 A5
Creeting St Mary IP6 .125 E5
St Mary's Rd 6 CB8. . .46 A5
St Marys Rd IP14 . . . .124 B7
St Marys Sq 9 CB8. . .121 A4
St Mary's Sq IP33 . . . .154 C1
St Mary's St
2 Bungay NR35. . . . .110 B4
26 Feltwell IP26 . . . . . .4 E5
St Marys View
Otley IP6. . . . . .69 C2
Pakenham IP31. . . . . . .49 E6
St Marys Way IP6 . . . .135 F4
St Mary's Wlk CB9 . .88 D3
St Mathew's St Service
Rd IP1. . . . . .155 A3
St Matthew's Ave 3
NR34 . . . . .111 C2
St Matthew's CE VA Prim
Sch IP1. . . . . .155 A3
St Matthew's St IP1. .155 B3
St Michaels Cl IP6 . . .126 C4
St Michael's Cl
1 Beccles NR34 . . . .111 C3
Ipswich IP5 . . . . .141 A6
Lowestoft NR32 . . . . . .112 C1
Thetford IP24. . . . . . . .16 C5
St Michaels Ct 16
CO11 . . . . .104 E2
St Michaels Green
NR35. . . . . .24 B6
ST MICHAEL SOUTH
ELMHAM. 24 A6
St Michaels Rd
High Street NR35 . . . . .24 C6
35 Lawford CO11 . . . .104 E2
St Michael's Rd 4
CO12 . . . . .107 B3
St Michael's Way
IP19. . . . . .42 C6
St Nicholas Cl
Bury St Edmunds
IP32 . . . . .123 C6
Kennett CB7 . . . . .45 D7
Rattlesden IP30. . . . . . .65 D5
St Nicholas Ct IP1 . . .155 B2
St Nicholas Dr
23 Feltwell IP26. . . . . . .4 E5
23 Feltwell IP26. . . . . . .4 E5
ST NICHOLAS SOUTH
ELMHAM. 23 E6
St Nicholas St IP1. . . .155 B2
St Nicholas Way
IP33. . . . . .123 A1
ST OLAVES. 2 A6
St Olaves Prec IP32 . .122 D8
St Olaves Precinct
IP32. . . . . .122 E8
St Olaves Rd
Bury St Edmunds
IP32. . . . . .122 E8

St Olaves Rd *continued*
Herring Fleet NR32. . . . . . . .2 D4
Ipswich IP5 . . . . .141 C8
St Osyth Cl IP2. . . . . . . .142 F8
St Pancras RC Prim Sch
IP1. . . . . .134 F2
St Patrick ⑦ CB8 . . . . .121 A4
St Pauls IP15. . . . . .130 E5
St Paul's Cl
④ Beccles NR34 . . . . .111 C2
Brockdish IP21. . . . . .21 F2
St Peters IP7. . . . . .79 C2
St Peters Ave CB8. . . . .45 F2
St Peter's Ave ①
IP6. . . . . .134 C8
St Peter's Brewery &
Visitor Ctr★ NR35 . .24 A8
St Peters Cl
Charsfield IP13. . . . . .70 B3
⑥ Moulton CB8. . . . . . . .45 F3
St Peter's Cl
Brockdish IP21. . . . . .21 F2
⑧ Claydon IP6. . . . . .82 A5
Stowmarket IP14. . . . . .124 B6
Woodbridge IP12. . . . . .146 D4
St Peters Ct
Bury St Edmunds
IP33. . . . . .154 B1
⑪ Clare CO10 . . . . .90 A8
⑮ Great Blakenham
IP6. . . . . .82 B5
St Peter's Ct ⑯
CO10 . . . . .148 C5
St Peter's Hall★ NR35 24 A8
ST PETER SOUTH
ELMHAM. 24 A7
St Peters Path IP19 . .118 E4
St Peters Pl CB7 . . . . . .29 E1
St Peters Rd
Aldeburgh IP15 . . . . . . .130 E5
Lowestoft NR33. . . . . . . .114 C3
St Peter's Rd
Lowestoft NR33. . . . . . . .115 C6
Stowmarket IP14. . . . . . .124 B6
St Peter's St
Ipswich IP4. . . . . .155 B2
④ Lowestoft NR32. . . .113 D2
St Peters Way ⑪
IP31. . . . . .49 E4
St Peter's Wlk IP26 . . . .4 F3
St Philips Rd CB8. . . . .120 F5
St Quinton's Ct NR33 115 B5
St Saviour's Hospital
(13th-Century)★
IP32. . . . . .154 B4
St Stephens Cl IP33. . .123 C6
St Stephens La IP1. . . .155 B2
St Vincent Wlk ⑭
NR31. . . . . .3 B7
St Wendred's Way
CB8. . . . . .120 B7
Salehurst Rd IP3. . . . . .140 E3
Salisbury Ct ⑫ CB9 . .132 D5
Salisbury Gn IP33. . . . .123 B3
Salisbury Rd
Ipswich IP3 . . . . .140 A3
Lowestoft NR33. . . . . . . .115 C7
① Southwold IP18. . . . .119 D5
Salisbury Terr ①
CO10 . . . . .148 C6
Sallows Cl ① IP1 . . . . .138 F7
Sally Cl ⑦ IP31. . . . . . .49 A4
Sally Wood's La IP6. .125 F6
Salmet Cl IP2. . . . . . . .139 A3
Salmond Dr ⑤ IP24. . . .16 C2
Salmon Wlk IP32 . . . . .122 D7
Salter Cl IP32. . . . . . . .123 E4
Salters Gdns ④ IP13 . .83 C5
Salters Hall Mews
CO10 . . . . .148 B5
Salters La IP19 . . . . .41 D6
Saltgate ⑤ NR34. . . . . .111 B6
Salthouse La IP4. . . . . .155 C2
Salthouse St IP4. . . . . .155 C2
Saltman Rd ⑯ IP31 . .49 A3
Saltwater Way NR33 .114 B4
Sam Alper Ct CB8 . . . .120 F6
Samford Cl IP9 . . . . . . .105 E8
Samford Ct ⑤ NR34. .111 F4
Samford Pl IP8 . . . . . . .138 B6
Sampson Dr ⑤ CO10. .91 E8
Samson Cl ⑭ IP32 . . . .122 C3
Samson's La IP22. . . . . .19 F4
Samuel Ct IP21. . . . . . . .39 D8
Samuel St Wlk IP33. . .123 A2
Samuel Vince Rd ②
IP21. . . . . .39 D8
Samuel Ward Acad
CB9. . . . . .132 F7
Sancroft Way
⑤ Fressingfield IP21. . .39 D8
Wortwell IP20. . . . . .23 A7
Sancroft Wlk IP33. . . . .122 B6
Sanctuary Bridge Rd
IP13. . . . . .70 D5
Sanctuary Gdns ④
NR32. . . . . .112 F5
Sanctuary La IP13. . . . .70 C5
Sanctuary The ⑫
IP16. . . . . .73 F6
Sanctuary Way ⑨
NR33. . . . . .11 B1
Sand Acre Cl IP28. . . .116 D5
Sandbank Rd ①
NR33. . . . . .114 E4
Sandbanks Ct IP17. . .128 C3

Sanderling Cl ③
IP28. . . . . .116 D4
Sanderling Dr ⑭
IP14. . . . . .67 A6
Sanders Cl ② NR32 . .112 F4
Sandford Pl IP12. . . . . .146 E3
Sandford Rd IP14. . . . . .52 A1
Sandgalls Dr IP27. . . . .109 E6
Sandgalls Rd IP27 . . . .109 D6
Sand Hill CO10. . . . . . . .93 C3
Sandholme Cl IP33 . . .123 B4
Sandhurst Ave IP3. . . .139 F4
Sandlands Dr IP32. . . . .48 B5
Sandling Cres IP4 . . . .140 E5
Sandlings Prim Sch
IP12. . . . . .85 C3
Sandlings The
Aldeburgh IP15 . . . . . . .130 C6
Ipswich IP3 . . . . .138 E3
Sandown Cl ③ IP1. . . .135 A3
Sandown Rd IP1. . . . . .135 A3
Sandpath ⑤ IP1. . . . . . .39 E8
Sandpiper Cl CB9 . . . .133 A6
Sandpiper Rd
Bury St Edmunds
IP33. . . . . .123 C2
Ipswich IP2. . . . . .138 E2
① Stowmarket IP14 . .124 F7
Sandpit Cl IP4. . . . . . . .140 F5
Sandpit Dr ⑧ IP31. . . . .49 E4
Sandpit Hill IP20. . . . . .23 B3
Sandpit La
Thurstow IP31. . . . . .49 E4
Worlingham NR34. . . . . . . .9 F4
Sandpits La CO7 . . . . .103 E8
Sandringham Cl IP2 .138 F2
Sandringham Rd
NR32. . . . . .113 C1
Exning CB8 . . . . .120 D8
② Felixstowe IP11. . . .153 D6
Sandstone Way ⑦
IP22. . . . . .20 B2
Sandy Cl
⑤ Felixstowe IP11. . . .107 D8
㉔ Great Blakenham
IP6. . . . . .82 A5
Sandy Dro IP28. . . . . . . .30 F3
Sandy Drove
Brandon IP27. . . . . .5 D1
Lakenheath IP27. . . . . . .109 E7
Sandy Hill
Barham IP6. . . . . .82 B7
Worminghford CO6. . . . . .101 D3
Sandyhill La IP3. . . . . .139 E1
Sandy La
Barham IP6 . . . . .82 A6
Barningham IP31. . . . . . . .34 E8
Barsham NR34 . . . . .9 A4
Blundeston NR32 . . . . . .112 A6
② Bromeswell IP12. . . .85 A5
Bulmer CO10 . . . . .91 D3
Bury St Edmunds IP30 . . .49 A1
Bury St Edmunds IP32 . .123 A8
Cattawade CO11. . . . . . .104 E4
Diss IP22. . . . . .20 D2
Dunwich IP17 . . . . .43 B1
Gillingham NR34. . . . . .9 A7
Gisleham NR33. . . . . .11 A1
Holton IP19. . . . . .118 E4
Hoo IP13. . . . . .70 B4
Hulver Street NR34. . . . .10 C2
Iken IP12. . . . . .72 F2
Little Bealings IP13 . . .137 C5
Marlesford IP13. . . . . .71 C5
Needham Market IP6 . . .125 E6
Rendham IP17. . . . . .56 F3
Ringshall IP14. . . . . .80 D8
St Mary, South Elmham
otherwise Homersfield
IP20. . . . . .23 B7
Saxmundham IP17. . . . .128 B5
Sizewell IP16 . . . . .58 F1
Smallworth IP22. . . . . . . .18 D5
Somerleyton NR32. . . . . . . .2 F2
Sternfield IP17 . . . . .72 C8
Stowlangtoft IP31 . . . . . .50 A7
Sudbury CO10. . . . . .148 A4
Sutton IP12. . . . . .99 B8
Waldringfield IP12. . . . . . .98 E8
Westerfield IP6 . . . . .135 E5
Wickham Market
IP13. . . . . .127 D5
Witnesham IP6. . . . . . . .136 B8
Woodbridge IP12. . . . . .146 D2
Sandy Lane NR34 . . . . . .2 A2
Sanfoin Cl ㉕ IP28 . . . .30 C1
San Francisco Wlk ③
NR33. . . . . .114 C5
SANTON DOWNHAM . .6 C2
Santon Rd IP27. . . . . . . .6 D3
SAPISTON 33 F6
Sapiston Rd IP31. . . . . .33 F5
Sapling Pl IP4. . . . . . . .140 E5
Sapphire Cl IP5. . . . . . .138 D8
Saracens House Bsns Ctr
IP4. . . . . .155 C3
Sarah Ct CB9. . . . . .132 E3
Sarah Rand Rd IP7. . . .149 F7
Sarsen Cl IP19. . . . . . . .118 C4
Sascombe Vineyard★
IP13. . . . . .60 F2
Sassoon Cl CB8. . . . . . .121 A4
Sassoon Cres ⑥
IP14. . . . . .124 B8
Saturn Cl NR32 . . . . . .113 D4
Saturn Rd IP2 . . . . .138 D8

Saunders Field CO7. .104 A3
Saunders La IP31. . . . . .50 C5
Sawmill Cl ⑤ IP21. . . . .28 D3
Sawmill La IP10 . . . . . .145 B6
Sawmills Rd IP22 . . . . . .20 E2
Sawston Dr ⑩ IP2. . . .139 A2
Sawyers IP7. . . . . .80 F1
Sawyers Cl IP9 . . . . . . .150 E2
Saxes La IP29. . . . . .64 A2
Saxham Bsns Pk IP32 . .47 E2
Saxham Ct ⑬ CB9. . . . .74 A1
Saxham Rd IP29 . . . . . . .47 E2
SAXHAM ST
Broad Green IP14. . . . . . .67 C7
Mendlesham Green
IP14. . . . . .52 C1
SAXHAM STREET 67 C8
SAXMUNDHAM 128 D3
Saxmundham Free Sch
IP17. . . . . .128 C2
Saxmundham Mus★
IP17. . . . . .128 C2
Saxmundham Prim Sch
IP17. . . . . .128 C2
Saxmundham Rd
Aldeburgh IP15 . . . . . . .130 C5
Framlingham IP13 . . . . .126 E3
Friston IP17 . . . . .72 E7
Knodishall IP17. . . . . . . .57 F1
Saxmundham IP17. . . . . .57 F3
Theberton IP16 . . . . .58 A2
Saxmundham Sports
Club IP17. . . . . .128 C4
Saxmundham Sta
IP17. . . . . .128 C3
Saxon Cl
Debenham IP14 . . . . .53 F1
Exning CB8 . . . . .120 D8
⑪ Felixstowe IP11. . . .153 D6
Saxon Cres
Haverhill CB9 . . . . .132 E8
④ Hampton IP31 . . . . .33 D5
Saxon Dr ⑨ CB5 . . . . . .44 A5
Saxonfields IP17. . . . . . .72 D5
Saxon Gate ④ IP28 . . . .30 C8
Saxon Hall Rd ⑦ CB8. .46 A5
Saxon La IP8 . . . . .95 E4
Saxon Meadow
Hunston IP31. . . . . .50 D7
① The Marsh IP22. . . . . .36 E8
Saxon Pl
Lakenheath IP27 . . . . . .109 C6
① Thetford IP24 . . . . . .16 B5
Weeting IP27. . . . . .5 E3
Saxon Rd
Lowestoft NR33. . . . . . . .115 B3
Saxmundham IP17. . . . .128 B3
Saxon Rise IP33. . . . . . .122 E3
Saxon St Rd CB8 . . . . . .60 E6
SAXON STREET 60 D6
Saxons Way IP19 . . . . .118 B4
Saxon Way IP12 . . . . . .147 A2
Saxon Wlk IP26 . . . . .6 A8
SAXSTEAD BOTTOM . .55 C5
Saxstead Gn Postmill★
IP13. . . . . .55 B3
SAXSTEAD 55 C4
SAXSTEAD GREEN 55 B3
SAXSTEAD LITTLE
GREEN. 55 B5
Saxtead Rd
Dennington IP13. . . . . . . .55 D5
Framlingham IP13 . . . . .126 A5
Saxted Rd IP13. . . . . .55 A6
Sayer'S Lake Drove
CB7. . . . . .28 D6
Sayers Way ⑯ NR31. . . .3 B6
Scabious Gdns ⑬
CB7. . . . . .29 A1
Scalesbrook La IP19 .118 E7
Scales St NR35. . . . . . . .110 A4
Scaltback Cl CB8. . . . . .120 E6
Scaltback Dr CB8 . . . . .120 F5
Scama La IP22. . . . . .36 C6
Scampton ⑲ IP27 . . . . .13 F2
Scarlin Rd IP33. . . . . . .122 C3
Sceptre Dr IP3. . . . . . . .139 H1
Schneider Rd ③
IP11. . . . . .153 H11
Scholars Wlk IP22 . . . . .20 C3
School Cl ① IP30. . . . . .50 E2
School Cl
① Capel St Mary
IP9. . . . . .150 E3
Cheveley CB8 . . . . .60 E8
Hadleigh IP7. . . . . .149 E5
Kenninghall NR16. . . . . . . .19 A8
Lakenheath IP27 . . . . . .109 D6
⑧ Mendlesham IP14 . . .52 E4
North Cove NR34 . . . . . . .10 C4
Norton IP31. . . . . .50 B4
㉑ Stanton IP31. . . . . . .34 E4
Weston Ditch IP28 . . . . . .29 F7
School Corner IP19. . . .40 D6
School Cottages IP29 . .82 B6
School Cres CB9. . . . . . .133 E8
School Farm La CO10 . .78 C2
Schoolfield ⑰ CO10. . . .77 A3
School Green
Edwardstone CO10. . . . . .93 A5
Stoke by Clare CO10. . . . .89 E6
Schoolhall La IP33. . . . .154 B3
School Hill
Blaxhall IP12 . . . . .72 A4
Boxford CO10 . . . . .93 C3
Copdock & Washbrook
IP8. . . . . .95 F4
Kettleburgh IP13 . . . . . . .70 C7

School Hill *continued*
Nacton IP10. . . . . .145 B4
School La
Bardwell IP31. . . . . .34 C4
Bawdsey IP12. . . . . .99 E2
Benhall IP17. . . . . .72 C8
⑤ Brantham CO11. . . .104 E5
Bungay NR35. . . . . .8 D7
⑱ Burwell CB5. . . . . . .44 A5
Dedham CO7. . . . . .103 F4
East Bergholt CO7. . . . .151 B5
Easton IP13. . . . . .70 C6
Easton IP13. . . . . .70 E5
Fornham St Martin
IP31. . . . . .48 D6
⑨ Fressingfield IP21. . .39 D8
Great Barton IP31. . . . . .49 B6
Great Horkesley CO6 . .102 C1
Halesworth IP19 . . . . . .118 A4
⑰ Harleston IP20 . . . . .22 D6
Haverhill CB9 . . . . .132 B5
Hollesley IP12 . . . . .99 F7
Little Horkesley CO6. . . .102 B3
Long Melford CO10 . . . . .77 E1
Manningtree CO11. . . . .104 D1
Martlesham IP12 . . . . . .146 C1
④ Mistley CO11. . . . . .104 F2
Newton CO10. . . . . .92 D3
Rendlesham IP12. . . . . . .85 C7
Reydon IP18 . . . . .119 C5
Stratford St Mary CO7 .103 E5
① Stuston IP22. . . . . . .20 E1
Thelnetham IP22 . . . . . . .18 E1
Thorpe Abbotts IP21. . . . .21 D2
⑦ Thurstow IP31. . . . . .49 E4
Ufford IP13. . . . . .84 F7
Waldringfield IP12. . . . . . .98 D7
School Meadow
① Stowmarket
IP14. . . . . .124 D7
④ Wetherden IP14 . . . . .51 A1
School Rd
Alburgh IP20 . . . . .7 A1
Bedfield IP13. . . . . .54 E5
Bedingham NR35. . . . . .7 B7
Blaxhall IP12 . . . . .72 A3
Bressingham IP22 . . . . . . .19 E4
Bury St Edmunds IP32 122 A8
Button's Green IP30. . . . .78 F8
Clay Common NR34 . . . . .26 A3
Coddenham IP6 . . . . .68 B1
Coldfair Green IP17. . . . .129 A3
Dallinghoo IP13 . . . . .70 C2
Earsham NR35. . . . . .7 F4
Elmswell IP30. . . . . .50 E2
Framsden IP14. . . . . .69 B5
Great Ashfield IP31. . . . . .50 F6
Great Barton IP31. . . . . .49 B6
Great Wratting CB9. . . . .74 F3
Hinderclay IP22 . . . . .35 E7
Hollesley IP12 . . . . .99 F7
Kedington CB9 . . . . .133 E8
Kirby Cane NR35. . . . . . . .8 E8
Knodishall IP17. . . . . . . .73 A8
Langham CO4. . . . . .103 C2
Little Horkesley CO6. . . .102 B2
Little Yeldham CO10 . . . . .90 B2
Long Melford CO10. . . . . .91 D6
Lowestoft NR33. . . . . . . .114 F8
Monk Soham IP13. . . . . . .54 D4
Moulton CB8. . . . . .45 F4
Old Newton IP14. . . . . . . .52 A1
Pentlow CO10. . . . . .90 F7
Poystreet Green IP30. . . .65 D6
Ringsfield NR34 . . . . .9 B1
Risby IP28 . . . . .47 E5
St Andrew, Ilketshall
NR34 . . . . .9 C3
⑨ Shotley Gate IP9 . .107 A4
Stoke by Clare CO10. . . . .89 E6
Sudbourne IP12. . . . . . . .87 A8
Tattingstone IP9. . . . . . .142 D1
Thurstow IP31. . . . . .49 E4
Tunstall IP12. . . . . .71 F2
Waldringfield IP12 . . . . . .98 D7
Westhall IP19. . . . . .25 C4
Woodditton CB8. . . . . . . .60 D6
School St
Foxearth CO10 . . . . .91 B7
Needham Market IP6 . . .125 D4
Stoke-by-Nayland CO6 .102 E3
Sudbury CO10. . . . . .148 C5
School View NR34 . . . . .24 F5
School Yard IP33. . . . . .154 B4
Schreiber Rd IP4. . . . . .140 B7
Scofield Ct CO10. . . . . .148 E4
SCOLE. 21 A2
Scole Comm IP21. . . . . .20 F3
SCOLE COMMON. 20 F3
Scole Comm Rd IP21. . .21 A2
Scole Prim Sch IP21. . 21 A2
Scole Rd
Brockdish IP21. . . . . .21 F2
Thorpe Abbotts IP21. . . . .21 E1
Sconch Beck Rd IP20 . .23 A6
Scopes Rd IP5. . . . . . . .141 C8
Scossels ⑬ CO10. . . . . .77 A3
Scotland End CB7. . . . . .29 E1
Scotland St CO6 . . . . . .103 A7
SCOTLAND STREET . .102 F7
Scotred Cl CB5. . . . . . . .44 A4
Scott Ave IP28. . . . . . . .116 C5
Scott La ② IP12 . . . . . . .84 E6
Scott Rd
Ipswich IP3. . . . . .140 D1
⑬ Ixworth IP31. . . . . . .34 B1
Scotts Cl ⑭ NR33 . . . . .11 B1

Scotts Hall La IP17. . . . .58 D6
Scott's Hill IP14 . . . . . . .68 B6
Scott's La IP13. . . . . . . .84 C7
Scotts Yard IP14. . . . . .124 C2
Scrivener Dr IP8. . . . . . .138 B2
Scudamore Pl NR35 . . .110 B7
Scuffin's La IP21. . . . . . .22 A1
Sculthorpe ⑮ IP27. . . . .13 F2
Seabrook Cl CO10. . . . . .75 D4
Seabreeze Rd IP14. . . .124 D5
Seafield Ave ⑤
CO11. . . . . .105 A2
Seafield Rd ⑥ CO12. . .107 A1
Seafields Dr ③ NR31. . . .3 B6
Seago St NR32 . . . . . . .113 C1
Sea Lake Rd NR32. . . . .114 E8
Sealodes Rd CB7. . . . . . .28 C5
Seaman Ave IP17 . . . . .128 B2
Sea Rd IP11. . . . . .152 F2
Searsons Farm Bsns
Units IP11. . . . . .152 B6
Seaton Cl ⑱ CO11. . . . .104 D2
Seaton Rd IP11. . . . . . . .152 E5
Seavert Cl ③ NR33. . . .114 E3
Sea View NR33. . . . . .11 C1
Seaview Rd IP18. . . . . . .119 C7
Sea View Rise NR31. . . . .3 C6
Sea View Wlk NR33 . .115 B4
Seaward Ave ②
IP16. . . . . .129 D5
Sebert Rd IP32 . . . . . . .123 E8
Sebert Wood Cty Prim
Sch IP32. . . . . .123 E5
Seckford Almshouses
IP12. . . . . .146 F5
Seckford Cl ① IP4. . . . .140 F5
Seckford Hall Rd
Martlesham IP12 . . . . . .146 D3
Woodbridge IP13. . . . . .146 B3
Seckford St IP12. . . . . . .146 F5
Second Ave
Felixstowe IP11. . . . . . . .152 B7
② Glemsford CO10 . . . .77 B3
㉒ Harwich CO12 . . . . .107 B2
Sudbury CO10. . . . . .148 C7
Second Dro IP27. . . . . . .13 C7
Second Drove CB5 . . . . .44 B8
Secret Cl NR33. . . . . . . .114 B1
Sedan Wlk IP1. . . . . . . .155 A2
Sedge Fen Rd IP27. . . .109 C7
Sedge Way IP33 . . . . . .154 A4
Sedlescombe Rd ⑧
NR33. . . . . .114 D5
Seething Rd NR35. . . . . .7 D8
Sefton Way CB8. . . . . . .120 D5
Segger View IP5. . . . . . .141 C6
Segrave Place IP13 . . .126 B5
Sekynden CI NR32 . . . .112 D3
Selby St NR32. . . . . .113 C1
Self's La IP22. . . . . .18 F3
Selion Way ㉑ IP30. . . . .50 F2
Selkirk Rd IP4 . . . . .136 C1
Selvale Way IP1. . . . . . .152 E4
Selway Dr ⑧ IP32. . . . . .49 A3
Selwyn Cl
Ipswich IP2 . . . . .155 B1
Mildenhall IP28 . . . . . . .116 D6
Newmarket CB8 . . . . . . .121 A1
SEMER 79 F1
Semer Cl IP14 . . . . .124 F8
Semer Gn La IP21. . . . . .21 C6
Semere Green IP21. . . . .21 D7
Semere Green La
IP21. . . . . .21 C6
Semere La IP21. . . . . . . .21 D8
Semer Rd IP7. . . . . .80 B2
Sergeants Wlk IP33 . .154 B3
Serpentine Rd IP3 . . . .140 B2
Seven Acres NR33. . . . .115 A2
Seven Acres La
③ Southwold IP18. . . . .43 C5
Southwold IP18 . . . . . . .119 A1
Seven Cotts La IP5. . . .136 C1
Seven Gdns Rd IP13. . . .83 F6
Seven Hills (Barrow
Cemetery)★. 16 F4
Brettenham IP31. . . . . . . .16 F4
Little Livermere IP31. . . .33 A4
Sevenhills La IP31. . . . . .33 A4
Severalls Ct IP13 . . . . . .55 D6
Several Rd IP13. . . . . . . .55 B3
Severals La CO10 . . . . .101 D8
Severals The CB8. . . . . .121 B4
Severn Rd
Bury St Edmunds
IP32. . . . . .48 C5
Ipswich IP3. . . . . .139 F1
Sewells IP7. . . . . .79 E6
Sewell's La CO10. . . . . . .90 D5
Sewells The IP33 . . . . . .123 A2
Sewell Wontner Cl
IP5. . . . . .141 C8
Sexton Rd IP33 . . . . .7 D6
Sextons Cl IP33. . . . . . .122 E6
Sexton's Manor Com
Prim Sch IP33. . . . . .122 C6
Sextons Md IP33. . . . . .154 C1
Sextons Meadow
IP33. . . . . .123 B3
Sextons Mews IP33 . . .154 C1
Seymore Dr CB9 . . . . . .132 B5
Seymour Ave IP27 . . . . .14 D8
Seymour Cl CB8 . . . . . .121 C3
Seymour Rd IP2. . . . . . .155 B1
Shackeroo Rd ③
IP31. . . . . .49 A4
Shackleton ⑳
CO12. . . . . .106 F1

Shackleton Rd IP3. . . .140 B3
Shackleton Sq ③
IP3. . . . . .140 B3
Shaddick Rd IP18. . . . . .119 B8
Shade Prim Sch The
CB8. . . . . .28 C5
Shade The CB7. . . . . . . .28 C5
SHADINGFIELD 25 E7
Shadingfield Cl
NR32. . . . . .113 A5
Shadow Barn La NR34. .8 A1
Shadowbush Cl ②
IP29. . . . . .132 D7
SHADWELL. 17 C6
Shadwell Cl IP27. . . . . . .5 E3
Shadwell Wlk IP32 . . .122 B6
Shaftesbury Ave ④
CO12. . . . . .107 A2
Shaftesbury Ct ㉓
CB9. . . . . .132 C5
Shaftesbury Sq IP4. . .155 C2
Shafto Rd IP1. . . . . .134 E1
Shaker's La IP33. . . . . . .123 C5
Shakers' Rd IP29 . . . . . .47 B4
Shakers' Rd IP27 . . . . . .15 A6
Shakers' Rd IP27 . . . . . .31 D8
Shakers' Rd
Lakenheath IP27. . . . . . . .14 E1
Wangford IP27 . . . . .14 E4
Shakespeare Rd
Ipswich IP1. . . . . .134 E3
Stowmarket IP14. . . . . .124 B8
Shamrock Ave ㉗. 5 E3
Shannon Cl IP29. . . . . .133 B5
Shannon Heights
IP12. . . . . .99 F7
Shannon Rd ④ IP3. . . .144 A8
Shardlow Cl CB9. . . . . .132 A7
Sharman's Rd CB7 . . . . .29 A1
Sharon Rd IP33. . . . . . . .123 C5
Sharon Rd IP33 . . . . . . .123 C5
Sharper's Cnr IP27. . . .109 B8
Sharpes Cnr IP27. . . . . .109 C7
Sharpe's Hill IP29. . . . . .47 B2
Sharpe's Row IP30. . . . . .65 E8
Sharp Rd IP33. . . . . .122 F2
Sharp's Gn ⑪ IP29. . . . .63 A7
Sharps Green CB8 . . . . .60 F2
Shaw Ave NR33 . . . . . . .114 D3
Shaw Dr IP31. . . . . .49 D5
Shawlands Ave CO10 .148 F5
Shaw Rd CO10. . . . . .91 E8
Shawsgate Vineyard★
IP13. . . . . .126 F6
Shaw Valley Rd ⑦
IP12. . . . . .84 A1
Shearing St ⑲ IP32 . . . .48 B5
Shearman Rd IP7. . . . . .149 F5
Shearwater Way IP18 119 B7
Sheckford La IP11 . . . . .21 C8
Sheckie Meadow IP7 .80 C1
Sheepcote Farm La
CO10. . . . . .91 F1
Sheepcote Pl ㉙
IP14. . . . . .67 A5
Sheepden La IP27 . . . . .93 D8
Sheepdrift Rd IP12. . . . .85 B5
Sheepgate NR34. . . . . . .111 B5
Sheepgate La
Badwell Ash IP31. . . . . . .51 B7
Bush Green IP30 . . . . . . .64 D5
Clare CO10 . . . . .90 A8
Falkenham IP10. . . . . . . .98 F1
Sheep La IP31. . . . . .49 E5
Sheepshead Hill ②
CO10. . . . . .92 B3
Sheepwash La IP17. . . . .58 E6
Sheerwater ⑨ IP17. . . . .67 A5
Sheerwater Rd IP30 . . .123 F7
Shelbourne Cl ⑦
IP5. . . . . .141 D7
Sheldrake Dr IP2 . . . . . .138 D7
Sheldrick's Rd CB7. . . . .29 D5
Sheldrick Way IP28 . . .116 A4
SHELFANGER 20 C4
Shelfanger Rd IP22 . . . .20 C4
SHELLAND 66 A7
SHELLEY 94 C1
Shelley Ave CO10. . . . . .148 F4
Shelley Cl IP14 . . . . . . .124 F7
Shelley Rd
③ Bury St Edmunds
IP32. . . . . .48 C5
Layham IP7. . . . . .149 E1
Shelley St IP2. . . . . .155 B1
Shelley Way
Bacton IP14. . . . . .51 E5
Thetford IP24. . . . . .16 C7
Shelly Rd CO6 . . . . .103 A8
Shelterhouse Cnr
IP24. . . . . .32 C8
Shelton Hill IP21. . . . . . .39 B5
Shelton Rd ④ NR33 . . .114 F3
Shenley Rd IP3. . . . . . . .140 B1
Shenstone Dr IP1. . . . . .135 A3
Shepherd Cl CB8. . . . . .120 D8
Shepherd Dr IP8. . . . . . .138 C2
Shepherds Croft IP14 .54 B4
Shepherds Ct
CB9 . . . . .132 C6
Shepherds Dr ①
IP29. . . . . .63 D1
Shepherds Gr Ind Est
IP22. . . . . .35 B4

Shepherds Grove Pk
IP31. . . . . .34 F3
Shepherds La
Burgate IP22 . . . . .36 D7
Glemsford CO10. . . . . .77 A3
Onehouse IP14. . . . . .124 A8
Southwold IP18 . . . . .119 A6
Shephers Fold IP12 . . .99 F7
Sheppards Way 6
IP5. . . . . .141 D7
Sherborne Ave IP4. . .136 A2
Sherborne Rd IP33. . .122 D3
Sherbourne St CO10 . .93 B4
SHERBOURNE
STREET 93 B4
Sheridan Cl IP14. . . . .124 A8
Sheridan Wlk NR34. . .111 E4
Sheriffs Ct CB8 . . . . . . .59 F2
Sherrington Rd IP1. .139 E4
Sherwood Fields 4
IP5. . . . . .141 C7
Shetland Cl
5 Ipswich IP4. . . . . .136 A1
Ipswich IP4. . . . . . . .140 A8
Shetland Rd CB9. . . . .133 B5
Shetland Way 9 IP8. .81 C3
Shickle Pl IP22. . . . . . . .18 C2
Shilling St 14 CO10. . . .78 D4
Shillitoe Cl IP33 . . . .154 A2
SHIMPLING
Burston and
Shimpling. 21 A6
Shimpling. 77 E6
Shimpling Cl 7
IP14. . . . . .124 E3
Shimpling Rd
Alpheton IP29. . . . . . .78 A8
Lawshall Green IP29 . . .77 F8
Scole IP21. . . . . .21 B5
SHIMPLING STREET . . .77 E8
Shingle Hill IP21. . . . . .38 C4
Shingle La IP17. . . . . . .56 F1
SHINGLE ST IP12. . . .100 A6
SHINGLE STREET 100 A5
Shinham Bridge IP31 . .49 B5
Ship Corner IP12 . . . . .72 A4
Ship Gdns IP28. . . . . .116 B3
Ship La
Bradfield CO11. . . . . .105 C2
Bramford IP8. . . . . . .134 B1
Ship Launch Rd IP3. .139 E3
SHIPMEADOW 8 F4
Shipp Cl CB9. . . . . .132 F8
Shippea Hill Rd IP28 . .12 F3
Shippea Hill Sta
CB7. . . . . .12 C7
Ship Rd NR33. . . . . . . .115 A3
Shire Ct 11 CB9 . . . . . .132 C5
Shirehall Way IP33. . .154 C1
Shire Hall Yd IP4 . . . .155 C2
Shires The NR32. . . . . .113 B8
Shirley Cl 9 IP1. . . . . .135 A3
Shoals Wlk NR33. . . . .114 E6
Shocksham Terr 13
CB7. . . . . .28 D5
Shoebridge's Hill
CO7. . . . . .103 F4
Shoe Devil La NR35 . . .24 C8
SHOP CORNER 106 C5
Shop Drove IP28. . . . . .29 F6
Shop Green IP14. . . . . .51 E5
Shop Hill
Alpheton CO10. . . . . . .78 B6
Wickhambrook CB8. . . .61 E1
Shop La IP13. . . . . .71 E5
Shop Rd
Clopton IP13. . . . . .69 E1
Dallinghoo IP13. . . . . .70 D2
Shop St IP13. . . . . .54 D7
Shore La
Bradfield CO11. . . . . .105 C2
Harkstead IP9 . . . . . .106 A5
Nacton IP10. . . . . . . .145 B3
Shores Cl IP28. . . . . . . .29 E2
Short Beck 19 IP26. . . . .4 E5
Short Brackland
IP33. . . . . .154 B2
Shortgrove La
Hopton IP22. . . . . .18 C1
Market Weston IP22. . . .35 B8
Shortingate Rd 10
IP24. . . . . .16 D7
Short La
Feltwell IP26 . . . . .4 D5
Lowestoft NR33 . . . . .114 C2
Walberswick IP18 . . . .43 C5
Shortlands IP2 . . . . . .138 D1
Short Rd
Belton with Browston
NR31 . . . . .2 D8
Blundeston NR32 . . . . .3 A4
Snailwell CB8. . . . . . . .45 A5
Short St IP33. . . . . . . .115 B4
Shotcroft La IP22. . . . .20 A7
SHOTFORD HEATH. . . .22 D4
Shotford Rd IP20. . . . . .22 D5
SHOTLEY 106 F6
Shotley Cl
1 Felixstowe IP11. . . .152 D4
Ipswich IP8 . . . . .138 C2
Shotley Com Prim Sch
IP9. . . . . .106 F5
SHOTLEY GATE 107 A4
Shotley Mews 8 IP12 .85 B3

Shotley Rd
Chelmondiston IP9. . . .106 D8
Shotley IP9. . . . . .106 E6
SHOTTISHAM 99 C7
Shotts Meadow 6
IP17. . . . . .72 C8
Shrimpling Rd IP29 . . .77 C6
Shrubberies The
CB8 . . . . .121 D1
Shrubbery Cl
Felixstowe IP11. . . . . .152 F4
Hessett IP30 . . . . .64 F8
Shrubbery Rd IP13. . .146 B7
Shrub House Cl 1
IP28. . . . . .30 B8
Shrubland Ave IP1. . .134 E1
Shrubland Cl 2 IP6. . . .82 A6
Shrubland Dr IP4 . . . .140 F5
Shrubland Pk Gdns★
IP6 . . . . .82 A6
Shrubland Rd 11
CO11. . . . . .105 A2
Siamhall La CO10 . . . . .92 F3
Siam Pl 4 CO10 . . . . .148 C5
SIBTON. 57 A8
SIBTON GREEN 41 D2
Sibton Rd
Sibton IP17. . . . . .56 F8
Sibton Green IP17 . . . .41 E2
SICKLESMERE 63 F7
Sicklesmere Rd
Bury St Edmunds
IP33. . . . . .123 D2
Nowton IP30. . . . . . . .63 E8
Sidegate Ave IP4 . . . .140 A8
Sidegate La IP4. . . . . .136 A1
Sidegate La W IP4. . . .135 F1
Sidegate Prim Sch
IP4 . . . . .140 A8
Sidegate Rd NR31. . . . .3 A8
Sidge'S La IP20. . . . . . .7 B4
Siding Rd NR34. . . . . . .10 C5
Sidings The 5 IP24. . . .16 C6
Sienna Gr CO11. . . . . .104 D1
Signal Way CB9. . . . . .132 F5
Silent St IP4. . . . . .155 B2
Silhalls Cl 7 CB8 . . . . .60 F8
Silk Cl 13 IP32 . . . . . . .48 B5
Silk Factory Row 15
CO10. . . . . .77 A3
Silk Mill Cl 2 IP7 . . . .149 D5
Siloam Pl IP3. . . . . . . .139 E4
Slough La
Acton CO10. . . . . .78 C1
Horringer IP29. . . . . . .122 A2
Workhouse Green
CO10 . . . . .101 C8
Slough Rd
Botesdale IP22. . . . . . .36 C5
Brantham CO11 . . . . .104 E5
Slugs La NR32 . . . . .2 C4
Sluice Dro IP26. . . . . . . .4 E3
Slushy La IP9. . . . . . . .106 A6
Smaley La 1 CO10. . . .91 E8
Smallbridge Entry
CO8. . . . . .101 E4
Smallbridge Hall★
CO8. . . . . .101 E4
Small Fen La IP27. . . . . .5 E1
SMALLWOOD GREEN. . .64 F5
SMALLWORTH 18 D3
Smallworth Common
IP22. . . . . .18 D3
Smallworth La IP22. . .18 E3
Smart St IP4. . . . . .155 C4
Smear La IP18. . . . . . . .26 D2
Smear La E IP18. . . . . . .26 F1
Smeetham Hall La
CO10 . . . . .91 C3
Smithbrook La IP29. . .77 A8
Smith Cres 17 NR33 . .11 B1
Smithers Cl IP9. . . . . .150 E3
Smithfield IP12. . . . . .147 B6
Smiths Cl IP14. . . . . . . .54 E7
Smiths Dr IP21. . . . . . . .21 B5
SMITH'S GREEN 88 C3
Smiths Knoll NR35. . . . .7 D8
Smiths Orchard CB5 . . .44 A6
Smiths Pl 9 IP5. . . . . .141 D7
Smiths Rd
Hulver Street NR34. . . .10 C1
Wrentham West End
NR34 . . . . .26 C8
Smith's Wlk NR33. . . .114 C6
Smith Wlk IP33 . . . . . .123 D2
SMITHWOOD GREEN . . .78 C7
Smithy Cl
Bradfield Combust with
Stanningfield IP29. . . . .64 A3
1 Rushbrooke with
Rougham IP30. . . . . . .64 D8
Smithy Ct 2 IP30. . . . . .64 D8
Smithy Rd IP14. . . . . . .52 D2
Smock Hill Rd IP11 . . .152 D6
Smock Meadow 8
IP7. . . . . .79 F4
Smoke House Dr 25
IP28. . . . . .30 B8
Smyth Cl IP17. . . . . . . .56 F8
Snab Hill
Kessingland NR33 . . . .11 A1
Toad Row NR33. . . . . .10 F2
SNAILWELL. 45 A6
Snailwell Rd
Fordham CB8 . . . . .44 F7
Kennett CB7 . . . . .45 B7
Newmarket CB8. . . . .121 B7
Snailwell Short Rd
CB8. . . . . .44 F5
Snake La NR31. . . . . . . .2 B5
Snakes and Ladders★
IP3 . . . . .139 E5

Skelton Rd IP22. . . . . .20 D7
Skelton's Dro IP28. . . .13 A2
Skilman Hill IP18. . . .119 D4
Skimmer Chase 9
CB7. . . . . .28 E3
Skimmers La IP31. . . . .34 C4
Skinners Cl IP20. . . . . .23 C3
Skinners La IP21. . . . . .39 A5
Skinner's La
Metfield IP20 . . . . .23 C3
Starston IP20. . . . . . . .22 B8
Skinners Meadow IP20 .7 B4
Skinner St IP33. . . . . .154 B2
Skinners Vw NR35 . . .110 C3
Skipper Cl
3 Ipswich IP8. . . . . . .142 E8
19 Thurston IP31. . . . .49 E4
Skipper Rd 4 IP2. . . .138 D1
Skipper's La IP9. . . . . .74 A3
Skoulding Cl 1
NR33. . . . . .114 F7
Skoulding Pl IP19. . . .118 B4
Skye Gdns 2 IP26 . . . . .4 F6
Sky Hall Hill CO4. . . . .103 B4
Skylark Cl 1 IP32. . . . .49 A4
Skylark Dr 15 IP12 . . .84 A1
Skylark La 8 IP8. . . . .138 C2
Skylark Rise IP13 . . . . .70 E5
Skylark Way 13 IP14 .124 F6
Skyliner Way IP31. . . . .49 A3
Slack's Drove IP28. . . .13 E1
Slade La IP22. . . . . .19 E2
Slades Cl 7 CO10. . . . . .77 B3
Slade St IP4. . . . . .155 C2
Slade The IP6 . . . . .134 D8
Slater Ave IP31. . . . . . .49 A3
Slaters Dr CB9 . . . . . . .132 C8
Slaughden Rd IP15 . . .130 E2
Sleaford Cl IP2 . . . . . .139 A3
Sleepy Valley IP19. . . .118 F5
Slip Ponds IP10. . . . . . .98 A4
Sloeberry Rd IP3 . . . .144 C7
Sloe La
Friston IP17. . . . . .129 A2
Snape IP17. . . . . .72 D6
Slough Farm La CO10 .78 C1
SLOUGH HILL. 77 E7
Slough Hill IP29 . . . . . .77 E7

Snakes La NR34. . . . . . .9 A7
Snake's La
Lound NR32. . . . . .2 F6
Topcroft NR35. . . . . . . .7 A8
SNAPE. 72 D4
Snape Bridge IP17. . . .72 D4
Snape Dr NR32. . . . . . .113 A4
Snape Hill IP22. . . . . . .35 F6
Snape Maltings IP17 .72 D4
Snape Maltings Concert
Hall★ IP17. . . . . .72 D4
Snape Marshes Nature
Reserve★ IP17. . . . . .72 D4
Snape Prim Sch IP17 .72 D5
Snape Rd
Friston IP17. . . . . .129 A2
Sternfield IP17. . . . . . .72 D7
Sudbourne IP12. . . . . .131 A7
Tunstall IP12. . . . . . . .72 A2
Tunstall IP12. . . . . . . .72 D2
Snapes La CO10. . . . . . .79 A3
Snare Dro IP28. . . . . . . .12 E3
Snares La IP13. . . . . . . .54 C6
Snipe Farm Rd IP13. . .69 E1
Snowberry Way 6
CB7. . . . . .28 D5
Snowcroft IP9. . . . . . .150 E3
Snowden Gdns 1
IP16. . . . . .129 A6
Snowdens Yd 14
IP18. . . . . .119 D5
Snowdon Cl 7 CB9. . . .132 C4
Snowdon Hill IP13. . . .127 C7
Snowdon Rd IP2. . . . .139 B2
Snowdrop Cl IP32. . . .123 F5
Snowdrop Dr IP9. . . . .150 F3
Snowdrop Wlk CB7. . . .29 C4
Snowdrop Way 12
IP28. . . . . .30 C1
Snow Hill CO10 . . . . . . .76 A1
Snow Hill La CO6. . . . .103 B7
SNOW ST IP22 . . . . . . .20 A4
SNOW STREET. 20 A4
Soames Cl IP14. . . . . .124 C7
Soane St IP4 . . . . .155 C3
Soers Cl IP23. . . . . .53 B8
Soft Rd CO10. . . . . .90 F3
SOHAM. 28 A4
SOHAM COTES 28 B6
Soham Rd CB7. . . . . . . .28 A8
Soham Town Cnr
IP13. . . . . .54 F3
Soham Tunnel Drove
IP28. . . . . .12 A3
Soham Village Coll
CB7. . . . . .28 D3
Solace Cl NR35. . . . . .110 D3
Solomon Rd 10 NR33 .11 C1
Solomons Cl CB7. . . . .28 B5
Somerleyton Hall &
Gdns★ NR32 . . . . . . .2 E4
Somerleyton Prim Sch
NR32. . . . . .2 D4
Somerleyton Rd
NR32. . . . . .112 F4
Somerleyton Sta NR32 .2 D3
Somerset Ct
7 Cheveley CB8. . . . . .60 E7
12 Haverhill IP22. . . .132 C5
Somerset Gdns
CO11. . . . . .104 D1
Somerset Rd IP4. . . . .139 F8
SOMERSHAM. 81 C3
Somersham County Prim
Sch IP8 . . . . .81 C3
Somersham Rd
Bramford IP8. . . . . . . .81 F2
Flowton IP8. . . . . .81 C2
SOMERTON 76 F8
Somerton Ave NR32. .113 C3
Somerton Rd
Boxted IP29. . . . . .77 A6
Hartest IP29. . . . . .77 A7
Somerville Lea 2
IP15. . . . . .130 E5
Song Thrush Cl 3
IP14. . . . . .124 F6
Sorrel Cl
1 Great Blakenham
IP6. . . . . .82 A6
Ipswich IP2 . . . . .138 F3
Sorrel Ct 30 IP28. . . . . .30 C1
Sorrell Gn IP14 . . . . . . .51 D6
Sorrell Wlk IP5 . . . . . .141 F7
Sorrel Wlk CB9 . . . . . .132 B7
SOTHERTON 25 E2
SOTHERTON
CORNER. 25 E1
SOTTERLEY 26 A7
Sotterley Cl 7 NR32 .113 A6
Sotterley Common
NR34. . . . . .26 B7
Sotterley Rd
6 Lowestoft NR32. . . .112 F4
Sotterley NR34. . . . . . .10 C1
Sotterley NR34. . . . . . .26 A5
Stoven NR34. . . . . .25 F4
Willingham St Mary
NR34. . . . . .25 F7
Sound The NR33. . . . .114 E5
South Bank Drove
CB7. . . . . .29 A8
South Cl
Beccles NR34. . . . . . .111 A3
Bury St Edmunds IP33 .154 A1
Ipswich IP4. . . . . .139 E8
Leiston IP16. . . . . . . .129 D5
9 Melton IP12. . . . . . .84 E6

South Coast National
Nature Reserve★
IP17. . . . . .43 B4
SOUTH COVE. 26 F4
South Dr CB8 . . . . .120 F4
South Elham Hall★
IP20 . . . . .23 D6
South Elmham Terr
NR33. . . . . .114 E8
Southend Rd 4
IP17. . . . . .128 D2
Southend Road Ind Est
NR35. . . . . .110 B3
South Entrance
IP17. . . . . .128 D2
Southern Belle Cl
IP32. . . . . .123 F7
Southern La IP22. . . . . .19 A1
Southerton Corner
NR34. . . . . .25 E1
Southery Rd NR26 . . . . .4 B6
Southfield Dr IP16. . . .129 C5
Southfield Gdns
NR33. . . . . .114 F6
Southfields CO7. . . . . .103 F3
Southfields Cl CB8. . . .120 E4
Southgate 12 IP20. . . . .22 D5
Southgate Ave IP28. . .116 B7
Southgate Gdns
Bury St Edmunds
IP33. . . . . .123 C3
3 Long Melford CO10 . .91 E7
Southgate Rd IP8. . . . .138 B1
Southgate St
Bury St Edmunds
IP33. . . . . .154 C1
4 Long Melford CO10 . .91 E7
South Gn IP19 . . . . . . .119 D4
SOUTH GREEN
Hoxne. 38 B5
Pulham St Mary 21 F6
South Green Rd IP23. . .38 B6
South Hill IP11. . . . . . .152 F3
Southlands Row
Beccles NR34. . . . . . .111 D4
Ipswich IP4. . . . . .140 F4
South Lee Sch IP33. . .123 C2
South Leet Cl 4
NR32. . . . . .112 E4
South Lodge Dr 1
IP28. . . . . .48 C6
SOUTH LOPHAM 19 B4
South Lowestoft Ind Est
NR33. . . . . .114 E2
SOUTHOLT 54 B7
Southolt Rd
Athelington IP21. . . . . .38 F1
Bedfield IP13. . . . . . . .54 D6
Newtown IP13. . . . . . .54 C7
South Pier Leisure
Complex NR33. . . . . .115 E8
South Pk IP27 . . . . .5 E3
South Rd
Hockwold cum Wilton
IP26 . . . . .4 F2
Ipswich IP1 . . . . .155 A4
12 Manningtree CO11 .104 E2
Risby IP28 . . . . .47 D4
South Strand 1
CO11. . . . . .104 E5
Southview IP17. . . . . .128 C5
South View IP13. . . . . .70 B3
South View Cl 8
NR32. . . . . .113 B2
South View Gn IP19. . .104 F7
Southwell Rd NR33. . .115 B7
SOUTHWOLD. 119 C5
Southwold Bsns Pk
IP18 . . . . .119 D5
Southwold Lighthouse★
20 IP18. . . . . .119 D5
Southwold Maze★
IP18 . . . . .43 C7
Southwold Mus★ 21
IP18 . . . . .119 D5
Southwold Pier★
IP18 . . . . .119 E6
Southwold Prim Sch
IP18 . . . . .119 D5
Southwold Rd
Blyford IP19. . . . . .42 B8
Brampton with Stoven
NR34. . . . . .25 E5
Holton IP19. . . . . .118 F3
Wrentham NR34. . . . . .26 E5
Southwold Sailors
Reading Rm★ IP18 .119 D5
Southwood Cl IP17 . . .128 D2
Sovereign Ct CB8 . . . .121 B2
SOWLEY GREEN 75 A5
Spalding's Chair Hill
IP24. . . . . .17 B3
Spanbies Rd 3 CO7. . .103 E5
Sparhawk St IP33. . . .154 C1
Sparkes Cl 13 CB9. . . .132 B7
Sparkes Way 11 IP26 . .4 D5
Sparks La CO9 . . . . .89 D3
Sparrow Ct 11 IP14 . . .53 F2
Sparrowhawk Cl 18
NR31. . . . . .3 B6
Sparrowhawk Rd
IP19. . . . . .118 F7
Sparrow Rd CO10 . . . .148 F4
Sparrows Croft Rd 5
IP12. . . . . .85 E8

Spartan Cl 3 CB9. . . . .132 A6
Spashett Rd 2 NR32 .113 A4
Spearmint Ave 9
IP28. . . . . .30 C1
Speckled Wood Cl
IP8. . . . . .142 D8
Speed Cl CB7. . . . . .28 D4
Speedwell Cl
8 Hopton on Sea
NR31. . . . . .3 B6
7 Lowestoft NR33. . . .115 A3
Speedwell Rd IP2. . . .138 F4
Speedwell Way 13
IP20. . . . . .22 D5
Spencer Cres 3 IP22 .20 D3
Spencer Dr NR32. . . . .113 B6
Spencer Dro CB7 . . . . . .28 C4
Spencer Rd 4 IP12 . . .85 E8
Spencers Piece IP30 . . .65 E6
Spencer Way IP14. . . .124 B7
Spenser Rd IP1. . . . . . .134 E3
Sperling Dr CB9 . . . . . .132 C8
Sperrinks Cl CB8. . . . . .46 C3
SPEXHALL. 24 F3
Spexhall Way NR32 . . .113 B5
Spicers La 2 CO10. . . .91 E8
Spicer Way CO10. . . . .148 F1
Spiers Hill IP22. . . . . . .36 C8
Spiers Way 1 IP22. . . .20 B2
Spike's La IP14. . . . . . . .66 E7
Spilsby 5 IP27 . . . . . . .13 F2
Spindler Cl IP5 . . . . . .141 D7
Spindle Rd CB9 . . . . . .132 B7
Spinks' La NR35. . . . . . .7 D6
Spinnel's Hill CO11. . .105 D1
Spinner Cl IP1. . . . . . .138 D8
Spinners La 3 IP18 . . .119 D5
Spinney Cl NR34. . . . . .10 B4
Spinney Dr NR16. . . . . .18 D8
Spinney Gdns NR33 . .114 C4
Spinney Hill IP7. . . . . . .81 A1
Spinney Rd IP31. . . . . . .33 B3
Spinney The
Beccles NR34 . . . . . . .111 D4
Ipswich IP4. . . . . .140 F4
Spinning Cl IP17. . . . . .128 D5
Spinning La 22 NR32. . .48 B5
Spire Chase CO10. . . . .148 E8
Spirkett's La IP22. . . . .20 D5
Spitfire Cl IP3. . . . . . .140 B1
Splash La IP10. . . . . . . .98 C2
Spong La
Elmswell IP30. . . . . . . .50 F1
Silverley's Green IP19 . .40 B6
Spong The IP20. . . . . . .23 C3
Spooners Cl CB8. . . . . .59 F4
Spooners Drove IP28 . .12 B1
Spooners La 5 IP7 . . .149 D6
Spooner's La NR34. . . .26 E2
Spout La
Horner's Green CO10. . .93 C4
Little Cornard CO10 . .101 B8
Sprats Water La
NR33. . . . . .114 A5
SPRATT'S STREET 85 D5
Springbank Ave 16
CO11. . . . . .104 D2
Spring Cl
3 Bentwaters Airfield
IP12. . . . . .85 D8
Burwell CB5 . . . . .44 A5
13 Gislingham IP23 . . .36 D2
Haverhill CB9 . . . . . . .132 A6
18 Lavenham CO10. . . .78 D4
Springett's Hill CO8. . .101 B5
Springfield IP18. . . . . .119 A4
Springfield Ave
Bury St Edmunds
IP33. . . . . .154 A3
Felixstowe IP11. . . . . .153 A5
Springfield Dr IP27. . .109 D6
Springfield Gdns
NR33. . . . . .114 F7
Springfield Inf Sch
IP1. . . . . .138 E8
Springfield Jun Sch
IP1. . . . . .138 E8
Springfield La IP1. . . .138 E8
Springfield Rd
Aldeburgh IP15 . . . . .130 C5
Bury St Edmunds IP33 .154 A3
4 Somersham IP8. . . . .81 C3
Sudbury CO10. . . . . . .148 C7
Springhurst Cl IP4. . . .139 F6
Spring La
Bury St Edmunds
IP33. . . . . .154 A3
Crowfield IP6. . . . . . . .68 B3
Dennington IP13. . . . . .55 B5
5 Lavenham CO10. . . . .78 D4
Polstead CO6 . . . . .93 D2
Ufford IP13. . . . . .127 B7
Wickham Market
IP13. . . . . .127 D7
Springland Cl IP4. . . . .140 A6
Springlands Way
CO10 . . . . .148 C8
Spring Meadow
10 Glemsford CO10. . . .77 A3
Playford IP6. . . . . .137 B4
Spring Meadow Primary
Sch CO12 . . . . .107 A2
Spring Pk
Otley IP6. . . . . .69 C2
Willingham NR34. . . . .25 E8
Spring Rd
Bardwell IP31. . . . . . . .34 C5

Spring Rd continued
Copdock & Washbrook
IP8 . . . . **95** E5
Earl Soham IP13 . . . . . . **54** E3
Ipswich IP4 . . . . **139** F6
Spring Row IP14 . . . . **124** D7
Spring St 6 CO10 . . . . **78** D4
Springtail Rd IP18 . . . **142** E8
Springwood Dr IP17 . . **56** F8
Spring Wood Nature
Reserve★ IP9 . . . . . . **142** E7
Sprites End IP11 . . . . . **152** D7
Spriteshall La IP11 . . . **152** D7
Sprites La IP8 . . . . . . **138** C1
Sprites Prim Acad
IP2 . . . . **138** C2
SPROUGHTON **138** A7
Sproughton Bsns Pk
IP1 . . . . **138** D7
Sproughton CE Prim Sch
IP8 . . . . **138** B6
Sproughton Ct IP8 . . **138** A6
Sproughton Enterprise
Park IP1 . . . . **138** C6
Sproughton Ent Pk
IP2 . . . . **138** C7
Sproughton Rd IP1 . **138** C7
Spruce Cl 14 IP27 . . . . **13** F2
Spruce Ct NR32 . . . . . **113** C5
Spruce Dr IP27 . . . . **5** F1
Spur End IP12 . . . . . . **147** C7
Spurgeon Score 12
NR32 . . . . **113** E2
Spurling Cl 2 CB8 . . . . **60** E7
Square The IP14 . . . . **124** E4
Squires Ct 21 CB9 . . . **132** E5
Squires La 4 IP5 . . . . **98** A8
Squires Wlk NR32 . . . **113** C5
Squirrells Mill Rd 3
IP7 . . . . **129** E4
Squirrels The IP9 . . . . **150** E4
Stables Rd IP11 . . . . . **152** D6
Stackwood Rd CO6 . . . **93** F3
STACKYARD GREEN . . **93** C8
Stafford Ct NR32 . . . . **112** E4
Staithe Cl 4 NR35 . . . **110** B4
Staithe La
Aldeby NR34 . . . . **2** A2
Somerleyton, Ashby &
Herringfleet NR32 . . **2** C4
Staithe Rd
Bungay NR35 . . . . **110** B4
Burgh St Peter NR34 . . . **10** C7
Staithe The NR33 . . . . **114** E6
Staith Rd NR31 . . . . **2** B8
Stallode Bank IP27 . . . **13** B7
STAMBOURNE **89** B1
**STAMBOURNE
GREEN** **89** A1
Stambourne Rd CO9 . . **89** E2
Stamford Cl IP2 . . . . . **142** E4
Stamford Ct 3 IP33 . . **122** F3
Stamford St CB8 . . . . **121** B2
Stammers Pl IP5 . . . . **141** E8
Stanford Rd IP26 . . . . . **6** B5
Stanford St 3 NR32 . . **113** C1
Stanhope Cl IP17 . . . . . **72** D5
Stanley Ave IP3 . . . . . **140** A4
Stanley Drapkin Prim Sch
8 CB9 . . . . **88** D3
Stanley Rd
Diss IP22 . . . . **20** B2
Felixstowe IP11 . . . . . **153** A3
Lowestoft NR33 . . . . . **114** E7
Newmarket CB8 . . . . . **121** C3
Sudbury CO10 . . . . . . **148** C6
Stanley St NR32 . . . . . **113** D1
Stanley Wood Ave
CO10 . . . . **148** D7
Stannard Way CO10 . **148** E4
STANNINGFIELD **64** A4
Stanningfield Rd IP30 **63** F5
STANSFIELD **76** C7
Stansfield Cl NR33 . . **114** E6
Stansfield Rd CO10 . . **76** B4
STANSTEAD **77** C4
Stanstead Rd IP29 . . . **77** D6
STANTON **34** C4
STANTON CHARE **34** D5
Stanton Cl
Beccles NR34 . . . . . . **111** C3
Lowestoft NR32 . . . . . **113** C5
Stanton Com Prim Sch
IP31 . . . . **35** F4
Stanton Hughes Way 10
CO11 . . . . **104** D2
Stanton Pl 12 CB9 . . **132** F6
Stanton Postmill★
IP31 . . . . **34** F4
Stanton Rd IP31 . . . . . **34** C4
STANTON STREET **50** B5
Stanway Cl CO10 . . . . **77** B3
STANWAY GREEN
39 C1
Stanway Green IP21 . . . **39** B1
Staple Cl IP31 . . . . . . **35** C1
Staplehurst Cl 7
NR33 . . . . **114** C4
Staples La CB7 . . . . . . **28** D3
Star And Garter La
CB8 . . . . **60** E8
Starfield Cl IP4 . . . . . **140** B6
Starhouse La IP14 . . . **66** E5
Stark Cl 8 IP22 . . . . . **20** C2
Star La IP4 . . . . **155** C2
Starling Way IP14 . . **124** F7
Starre Rd IP33 . . . . . . **122** C5
STARSTON **22** C7

Starston La IP20 . . . . . **22** C5
Station App
Newmarket CB8 . . . . . **121** A2
Saxmundham IP17 . . . **128** D3
Station Approach
CO11 . . . . **105** B2
Station Drove CB7 . . . **12** B6
Station Field 11 CO10 **93** C3
Station Gate 1 CB5 . . **44** A4
Station Hill
1 Bures CO8 . . . . . . **101** C4
Bury St Edmunds IP33 **154** B4
Harleston IP20 . . . . . . **22** D6
Little Whelnetham IP30 **64** B6
Thurstow IP31 . . . . . . **49** D4
Station La 13 CO12 . . **107** B2
Station Rd
Alburgh IP20 . . . . **7** A1
Bacton IP14 . . . . **52** A6
Barnham IP24 . . . . **16** B2
Bentley IP9 . . . . **104** E7
Birdbrook CO9 . . . . . . **89** B4
Blaxhall IP12 . . . . **71** E3
Blythburgh IP19 . . . . . **42** F6
Bradfield CO11 . . . . . **105** B2
Brampton with Stoven
NR34 . . . . **25** C5
Burston & Shimpling
IP21 . . . . **20** F6
Campsea Ashe IP13 . . **71** C2
Clare CO10 . . . . **90** B8
Claydon IP6 . . . . **134** B8
8 Corton NR32 . . . . . **3** D4
Corton NR32 . . . . **113** C8
Diss IP22 . . . . **20** D2
Ditchingham NR35 . . **110** C6
Dullingham CB8 . . . . . **59** E5
2 Earsham NR35 . . . . . **7** F4
Ellingham NR35 . . . . . . **8** D7
Elmswell IP30 . . . . **50** F2
Felixstowe IP11 . . . . . **152** C7
Finningham IP14 . . . . **52** A7
Fordham CB7 . . . . **29** A1
Framlingham IP13 . . . **126** C2
Geldeston NR34 . . . . . . **8** F6
Haddiscoe NR31 . . . . . . **2** A5
Hadleigh IP7 . . . . **149** E5
Harleston IP20 . . . . . . **22** D6
Harwich CO12 . . . . . . **106** F3
1 Harwich CO12 . . . **106** F3
Haughley IP14 . . . . . . **51** D1
11 Haverhill CB9 . . . **132** C6
Hockwold cum Wilton
IP26 . . . . **4** F2
Hopton on Sea NR31 . . **3** B6
Isleham CB7 . . . . **29** C4
Kennett CB8 . . . . **45** F7
Lakenheath IP27 . . . . **109** C7
Lakenheath IP27 . . . . **109** C7
Laxfield IP13 . . . . **39** F4
Leiston IP16 . . . . **129** C6
Little Bealings IP13 . . **137** E3
Long Melford CO10 . . . **91** E7
Lowestoft NR32 . . . . . **113** D4
Manningtree CO11 . . . **104** E3
Mildenhall IP28 . . . . . **116** B3
Pulham Market IP21 . . **21** E8
Pulham St Mary IP21 . **22** A8
Risby IP28 . . . . **47** E4
Soham CB7 . . . . **28** C4
Somerleyton, Ashby &
Herringfleet NR32 . . **2** C3
Southwold IP18 . . . . . **119** C6
Sudbury CO10 . . . . . . **148** C5
Tattingstone IP9 . . . . **105** A7
Thetford IP24 . . . . **16** B6
Wetheringsett-cum-
Brockford IP14 . . . . **53** B4
Woodbridge IP12 . . . . **147** A4
Wrabness CO11 . . . . . **105** F2
Yoxford IP17 . . . . **57** D7
Station Rd E IP14 . . . **124** E6
Station Rd W IP14 . . . **124** E6
Station Sq 11 NR32 . . **115** D8
Station St IP2 . . . . . . **139** C3
Station Terr IP13 . . . . **126** C2
Station Vw CO9 . . . . . **89** F1
Station Yard
Ipswich IP2 . . . . **155** A1
Yoxford IP17 . . . . **57** E8
Station Yd
Hadleigh IP7 . . . . **149** E5
Mildenhall IP28 . . . . . **116** B3
Needham Market IP6 . **125** E4
Staverton Cl IP12 . . . . **85** B6
Staygate Wlk 7
NR32 . . . . **112** E4
Stead Dr IP19 . . . . . . **118** C3
Stearn Dr IP14 . . . . . . **66** C6
Stearn's La IP14 . . . . . **67** D6
Stebbings La IP12 . . . . **99** E7
Stedman Terr IP18 . . . **119** E8
Steeds Meadow 7
CO10 . . . . **91** E8
Steeles Rd IP30 . . . . . . **50** D1
**STEEPLE
BUMPSTEAD** **88** D4
Steeple Bumpstead Rd
CB9 . . . . **88** B4
Steeplechase CO10 . . . **75** C4
Steeple End IP19 . . . . **118** B3
Steggall Cl IP6 . . . . . **125** C6
Steggall Rd 7 IP14 . . . **51** C1
Steggles Dr 5 IP22 . . . **20** C3
Stella Maris IP2 . . . . **138** D5
Stennetts Cl IP11 . . . **152** B8

Stephen Cl
Haverhill CB9 . . . . . . **132** D6
Long Melford CO10 . . . **91** D7
Stephen George Way
NR32 . . . . **112** D8
Stephen Rd IP5 . . . . . **141** E8
Stephen's Ct IP4 . . . . **140** B6
Stephenson Pl IP32 . . **122** F8
Stephenson Place
IP32 . . . . **154** A4
Stephensons Wlk
NR32 . . . . **113** D4
Stephenson Way IP24 **16** A4
Stepping Hill 3
NR34 . . . . **111** B5
STERNFIELD **72** D8
Sternfield Rd
Benhall Green IP17 . . . **72** C8
Snape IP17 . . . . **72** D6
STETCHWORTH **60** A5
Stetchworth Rd
Dullingham CB8 . . . . . **59** F4
Stetchworth CB8 . . . . **60** B4
Stevenson App CO10 **148** F3
Stevenson Rd IP1 . . . **155** A3
Stevens St NR32 . . . . **113** C1
Steward Rd IP33 . . . . **123** C2
Stewards Field CB7 . . **29** A1
Stewart Field IP14 . . **52** A7
Stewart Young Gr
IP5 . . . . **141** D7
Stimpson Cl 3
NR32 . . . . **113** A6
Stirling Cl
Chedburgh IP29 . . . . . **62** D4
Lowestoft NR32 . . . . . **112** F4
7 Thistley Green IP28 **29** F6
Stirling Dr 12 IP18 . . **132** C6
Stirling Gdns CB8 . . . **120** E4
Stirling Rd 3 IP26 . . . **4** A5
Stirling View IP27 . . **109** D5
Stirrups La NR32 . . . . . **3** C5
Stirrup St IP13 . . . . . . **39** F3
St. Margaret's Prim Acad
NR32 . . . . **113** C3
Stobart Cl NR34 . . . . . **111** D3
STOCK HILL **50** E8
Stockley Cl CB9 . . . . . **133** A5
Stockmers End 8
IP9 . . . . **150** E3
Stocks La IP18 . . . . . . **119** A2
Stockton Cl IP7 . . . . . **149** F4
Stockton Rd NR34 . . . . **9** A7
Stoddart Rd IP8 . . . . . **134** A2
STOKE **155** B1
STOKE ASH **37** B1
Stoke Ash Community
Prim Sch IP23 . . . . . . **52** F8
STOKE BY CLARE **89** E6
**STOKE-BY-
NAYLAND** **102** E7
Stoke-by-Nayland CE VC
Prim Sch CO6 . . . . . **102** E7
Stoke Hall★ IP2 . . . . . **155** B1
Stoke Hall Rd IP2 . . . **155** B1
**Stoke High Sch -
Ormiston Acad** IP2 **139** C3
STOKE PARK **138** F1
Stoke Pk Dr IP2 . . . . . **139** A1
Stoke Quay IP2 . . . . . **155** C1
Stoke Rd
Clare CO10 . . . . **90** A7
HADLEIGH IP7 . . . . . . **94** A1
Layham IP7 . . . . **149** D1
Leavenheath CO6 . . . **102** B8
Nayland-with-Wissington
CO6 . . . . **102** D5
Stoke Ash IP23 . . . . . **37** D1
Stoke-by-Clare CO10 . **89** F7
Stoke St IP2 . . . . **155** B1
Stollery Cl IP5 . . . . . **141** B7
Stonalls IP30 . . . . **50** C1
Stonards Farm Rd
CO10 . . . . **89** D7
Stonebridge Ave
IP33 . . . . **122** F3
Stonebridge La IP14 . **67** A8
Stonechat Rd IP2 . . . **138** C3
STONE COMMON
IP12 . . . . **71** F4
Stonegrove Rd IP13 **152** D1
Stone Hall Rd IP23 . . . **36** A2
Stonehouse Rd IP7 . . **149** D6
Stone La
Blo' Norton IP22 . . . . . **18** F2
Bressingham IP22 . . . **19** F6
Wrabness CO11 . . . . . **105** F2
Stone Lodge Acad
IP2 . . . . **138** F2
Stone Lodge La IP2 . **139** A3
Stone Lodge La W
IP2 . . . . **138** F3
Stone Lodge Wlk
IP2 . . . . **139** B3
Stonemill Way CB9 . . **132** B5
Stone Pl 12 IP12 . . . . **147** A5
Stone St Ct IP7 . . . . . **149** B8
Stone St Rd 2 CO10 . . **93** C3
Stone St
Boxford CO6 . . . . **93** C3
Bungay NR34 . . . . **8** D1
Crowfield IP6 . . . . **68** C3
Hadleigh IP7 . . . . **149** B8
High Street NR34 . . . . **24** C8
Spexhall IP19 . . . . **118** C8
STONE STREET
Boxford **93** C2

STONE STREET continued
Spexhall **24** F5
Stonewell Hill IP6 . . . **68** D7
Stoney La
Barrow NR29 . . . . **47** B2
Thurston IP31 . . . . **49** F4
Stoney Rd IP13 . . . . . . **83** D6
STONHAM ASPAL **68** A6
Stonham Aspal CE VA
Prim Sch IP14 . . . . . **68** B6
Stonham Aspal Rd
IP14 . . . . **68** C6
Stonham Barns Leisure
Complex★ IP14 . . . . **68** C6
Stonham Cl 18 IP28 . . **30** B8
Stonham Rd
Cotton IP14 . . . . **52** A5
Cotton IP14 . . . . **52** B4
Crowfield IP6 . . . . **68** C5
Stony La
2 Aldringham cum Thorpe
IP16 . . . . **73** F6
Debenham IP14 . . . . . **53** D2
Wortwell IP20 . . . . **22** F8
Stopford Ct 8 IP1 . . **139** A7
Stores Hill CB8 . . . . . . **61** C8
Store St IP22 . . . . **20** C3
Storeys La IP21 . . . . . . **39** F6
Storeys Rd 16 CO11 . **104** E4
Stour Ave IP14 . . . . . **152** E3
Stour Cl
Glemsford CO10 . . . . . **77** B1
4 Harwich CO12 . . . **106** E1
Saxmundham IP17 . . . **128** C4
Stourdale Cl 27
CO11 . . . . **104** D2
Stour Gdns CO10 . . . . **148** E2
Stour Green CO10 . . . . **90** A7
Stourmead Cl CB9 . . . **133** E8
Stour Rd CO12 . . . . . . **107** B3
Stourside IP9 . . . . **107** A4
Stour St
Cavendish CO10 . . . . . **90** D8
17 Manningtree CO11 **104** E2
Sudbury CO10 . . . . . . **148** B5
Stour Vale CO9 . . . . . . **89** B5
Stour Valley Com Sch
CO10 . . . . **90** B8
Stour Valley Rd CB9 . **132** F5
Stourview Ave 4
CO10 . . . . **105** A2
Stourview Cl 6
CO10 . . . . **105** A2
Stour Wood Nature
Reserve★ CO12 . . . **106** B2
STOVEN **25** F4
Stoven Cl NR32 . . . . . **113** B5
Stoven Rd NR34 . . . . . **25** F3
Stow La IP31 . . . . **50** A8
STOWLANGTOFT **50** C7
STOWMARKET **124** E6
Stowmarket High Sch
IP14 . . . . **124** B7
Stowmarket Rd
Badley IP6 . . . . **125** A8
Great Blakenham IP6 . . **81** F6
Mendlesham IP14 . . . . **52** D3
Old Newton with Dagworth
IP14 . . . . **51** E1
Rattlesden IP30 . . . . . **65** E6
Ringshall IP14 . . . . . . **80** E7
Stonham Aspal IP14 . . **68** A6
Wetherden IP14 . . . . . **51** A1
Stowmarket Sta
IP14 . . . . **124** E6
Stow Rd IP31 . . . . **34** B1
STOWUPLAND **67** B6
Stowupland High Sch
IP14 . . . . **67** A7
Stowupland Rd
Gipping IP14 . . . . **52** B2
Stowmarket IP14 . . . . **124** F7
Stowupland St IP14 . **124** D6
STRADBROKE **39** A5
Stradbroke Bsns Ctr
IP21 . . . . **39** A4
**Stradbroke Business &
Enterprise Coll**
IP21 . . . . **39** A4
Stradbroke CE Prim Sch
IP21 . . . . **39** A5
Stradbroke Rd
Chickering IP21 . . . . . . **28** D8
Fressingfield IP21 . . . . **39** D7
Ipswich IP4 . . . . **140** A7
Lowestoft NR33 . . . . . **115** A4
6 Lowestoft NR33 . . **115** B4
Southwold IP18 . . . . . **119** D5
STRADISHALL **75** F7
Stradishall Rd CO10 . . **75** E5
Straight La 19 IP20 . . . **22** D6
Great Waldingfield
CO10 . . . . **92** D6
Straight Rd
Battisford IP14 . . . . . . **66** D1
Boxted CO4 . . . . **102** F1
Bradfield CO11 . . . . . **105** B1
East Bergholt CO7 . . . **104** D6
East Bergholt CO7 . . . **151** F4
Foxhall IP10 . . . . **141** C1
Polstead CO6 . . . . **93** F3
Whepstead IP29 . . . . . **63** C4
Strand The IP2 . . . . . **143** C8
Strasbourg Sq 11
CB9 . . . . **132** F6
Stratford Rd
Dedham CO7 . . . . **103** E4
Ipswich IP1 . . . . **134** F7
**STRATFORD ST
ANDREW** **71** F7

**STRATFORD ST
MARY** **103** D5
Stratford St Mary Prim
Sch CO7 . . . . **103** E5
Strattonhall Drift
IP10 . . . . **145** F2
Strawberry Ave 38
CO11 . . . . **104** D2
Strawberry Fields
CB9 . . . . **132** B5
Strawberry La
Westhall IP19 . . . . **25** D3
Willisham IP8 . . . . **81** B5
Straw La CO10 . . . . . **148** B5
Street Farm La 4
IP31 . . . . **34** B1
Street Farm Rd IP17 **128** D3
Streetfield Cl IP29 . . . **77** F7
Street The
Aldeby NR34 . . . . **9** F8
Alderton IP12 . . . . **99** E3
Aldham IP7 . . . . **94** E8
Ashen CO10 . . . . **89** E5
Ashfield cum Thorpe
IP14 . . . . **54** C1
Assington CO10 . . . . . **92** F1
Assington CO10 . . . . **101** F8
Bacton IP14 . . . . **51** E5
Badwell Ash IP31 . . . . **50** E7
Barnham IP24 . . . . **16** B2
Barrow IP29 . . . . **47** A2
Barton Mills IP28 . . . **116** E2
Bawdsey IP12 . . . . **99** E2
Beck Row, Holywell Row &
Kenny Hill IP28 . . . . **30** C8
Belchamp Otten CO10 . **90** E4
Belstead IP8 . . . . **142** C6
Benacre NR34 . . . . **27** A7
Birdbrook CO9 . . . . . . **89** A3
Blo' Norton IP22 . . . . . **18** E2
Blundeston NR32 . . . . . **3** A4
Botesdale IP22 . . . . . . **36** A6
Boxted IP29 . . . . **77** A6
Bradfield CO11 . . . . . **105** C1
Bradfield Combust with
Stanningfield IP30 . . **64** B4
Bramfield IP19 . . . . . . **41** F5
Bramford IP8 . . . . **134** A2
Brampton with Stoven
NR34 . . . . **25** E4
Brandon IP27 . . . . **5** E1
Brantham CO11 . . . . . **105** A5
Bredfield IP13 . . . . **84** C8
Bressingham IP22 . . . . **19** D6
Brettenham IP7 . . . . . . **65** C1
Bridgham NR16 . . . . . . **17** E8
Brockdish IP21 . . . . . . **21** E2
Brome & Oakley IP23 **117** D8
Bruisyard IP17 . . . . . . **56** D4
Brundish IP13 . . . . **39** D1
Burrough Green CB8 . . **59** E3
12 Bury St Edmunds
IP28 . . . . **48** C6
Butley IP12 . . . . **86** A6
Capel St Mary IP9 . . . **150** D3
Cavenham IP28 . . . . . . **47** A8
Charsfield IP13 . . . . . . **70** B3
Chattisham IP8 . . . . . . **95** C4
Chedburgh IP29 . . . . . **62** C4
Chelsworth IP7 . . . . . . **79** D3
Coney Weston IP31 . . . **17** E1
Copdock & Washbrook
IP8 . . . . **95** F5
Corton NR32 . . . . **3** D4
Cratfield IP19 . . . . **40** D5
Cretingham IP13 . . . . . **69** E7
Culford IP28 . . . . **48** B8
Dalham CB8 . . . . **61** B8
Darsham IP17 . . . . **42** B1
Dennington IP13 . . . . . **55** E6
Dickleburgh IP21 . . . . . **21** B5
Drinkstone IP30 . . . . . **65** B8
Earl Soham IP13 . . . . . **54** F2
Earsham NR35 . . . . **7** F4
East Bergholt CO7 . . . **151** B4
Easton IP13 . . . . **70** E5
Elmsett IP7 . . . . **80** F1
Eriswell IP27 . . . . **13** F1
Eye IP21 . . . . **38** B4
Eyke IP12 . . . . **85** B6
Farnham IP17 . . . . **72** A7
Flixton NR35 . . . . **7** E2
Framsden IP14 . . . . . . **69** B6
Freckenham IP28 . . . . . **29** E3
Garboldisham IP22 . . . **18** D4
Gazeley CB8 . . . . **46** B3
Geldeston NR34 . . . . . . **9** A7
Great Barton IP31 . . . . **49** B5
Great Bricett IP7 . . . . . **80** D5
Great Livermere IP31 . . **33** C2
Great Waldingfield
CO10 . . . . **92** D6
Great Wratting CB9 . . . **74** F3
Grundisburgh IP13 . . . **83** E5
Hacheston IP13 . . . . . . **71** A6
Halesworth IP19 . . . . . **118** E3
Harkstead IP9 . . . . . . **106** A5
45 Harleston IP20 . . . **22** D6
Hessett IP30 . . . . **64** F0
Hinderclay IP22 . . . . . . **35** E7
Holbrook IP9 . . . . **105** E7
Hollesley IP12 . . . . **99** F7
Horham IP21 . . . . **38** E3
Horringer IP29 . . . . . **122** B1
Huntingfield IP19 . . . . **41** A4
Icklingham IP28 . . . . . . **31** D4
Kersey IP7 . . . . **93** F7
Kettleburgh IP13 . . . . . **70** C7

Street The continued
Kirtling CB8 . . . . **60** E3
Lawshall IP29 . . . . **63** E1
Layham IP7 . . . . **149** E2
Letheringham IP13 . . . **70** D4
Lidgate CB8 . . . . **61** B4
Little Bealings IP13 . . **137** D4
Little Thurlow CB9 . . . . **74** D5
Little Waldingfield
CO10 . . . . **92** E8
Lound NR32 . . . . **2** F6
Lowestoft NR33 . . . . . **114** C2
Market Weston IP22 . . **35** A8
Martlesham IP12 . . . . **146** C1
Middleton CO10 . . . . . **148** C1
Mildenhall IP28 . . . . . . **30** B8
Monks Eleigh IP7 . . . . **79** C2
Moulton CB8 . . . . **45** F3
Nacton IP10 . . . . **145** C5
Newbourne IP12 . . . . . **98** D6
North Cove NR34 . . . . . **10** B2
North Lopham IP22 . . . **19** A6
Norton IP31 . . . . **50** B4
Occold IP23 . . . . **37** F1
Pakenham IP31 . . . . . . **49** E6
Parham IP13 . . . . **71** A7
Peasenhall IP17 . . . . . **56** F8
Pettistree IP13 . . . . . . **127** C4
Poslingford CO10 . . . . . **76** A3
Preston St Mary CO10 . **79** A5
Ramsey & Parkeston
CO12 . . . . **106** D1
Raydon IP7 . . . . **94** E1
Redenhall with Harleston
IP20 . . . . **22** F5
1 Redgrave IP22 . . . **36** A8
Riddlesworth IP22 . . . **18** A3
Rumburgh IP19 . . . . . . **24** C4
Rushmere NR33 . . . . . **10** E1
St James, South Elmham
IP19 . . . . **23** F4
Shotley IP9 . . . . **106** F6
Shottisham IP12 . . . . . **99** B7
Snailwell CB8 . . . . **45** A6
Somerleyton, Ashby &
Herringfleet NR32 . . **2** D4
South Lopham IP22 . . . **19** B4
Southolt IP23 . . . . **54** B7
Stanton IP31 . . . . **34** E4
Starston IP20 . . . . **22** C7
Sternfield IP17 . . . . . . **72** D8
Stoke Ash IP23 . . . . . . **52** F8
Stoke-by-Clare CO10 . . **89** D6
Stonham Aspal IP14 . . **68** B6
Stowlangtoft IP31 . . . . **50** B6
Stradishall CB8 . . . . . . **75** F7
Stratford St Mary CO7 **103** E4
Sturmer CB9 . . . . **133** D3
Thorndon IP23 . . . . . . **53** B8
Thornham Magna IP23 **37** A2
Troston IP31 . . . . **33** D3
Tuddenham St Martin
IP6 . . . . **136** C5
Ubbeston IP19 . . . . **40** F3
Walberswick IP18 . . . . **119** A2
Wattisfield IP22 . . . . . . **35** C4
Wenhaston IP19 . . . . . . **42** C6
Westleton IP17 . . . . . . **58** C7
Wetheringsett-cum-
Brockford IP14 . . . . **52** F6
Weybread IP21 . . . . . . **22** D2
Whatfield IP7 . . . . **80** C1
Wherstead IP9 . . . . . **143** A6
Winfarthing IP22 . . . . . **20** B8
Wissett IP19 . . . . **24** D2
Witnesham IP6 . . . . . **136** A8
Woodbridge IP12 . . . . **147** C7
Woodditton CB8 . . . . . **60** D5
Woolpit IP30 . . . . **50** D1
Worlington IP28 . . . . . **30** B4
Stretham Rd CB7 . . . . **28** A2
Stretton Ave CB8 . . . **121** B2
Stretton Gdns CB8 . . **121** B2
Strickland Cl 6 IP8 . . . **95** F4
Strickland Manor Hill
IP17 . . . . **57** C8
Strickland Pl 18
IP18 . . . . **119** D5
Stricklands Rd 1
IP14 . . . . **124** E5
Strickmere CO7 . . . . **103** E5
Strollers Way CB8 . . . **60** A5
Strowger's Way 6
NR33 . . . . **11** C1
Struggler's La IP6 . . **136** A8
Struston Mead IP10 . **98** D3
Stuart Cl
5 Felixstowe IP11 . . . **153** D7
Ipswich IP4 . . . . **139** F7
Stuart Dr NR34 . . . . . **111** C4
Stuarts Dr CO10 . . . . **148** C5
STUBBING'S GREEN . . **36** C5
Stubbing's La IP21 . . . **22** E3
Stubbins La
East Bergholt CO7 . . . **151** A7
Wetherden IP14 . . . . . **51** A2
Stubbin's La CB8 . . . . **46** B3
Stubb La NR35 . . . . . . **24** B6
Stubbs Cl
3 Haverhill CB9 . . . . **132** B7
Ipswich IP3 . . . . **140** A1
9 Manningtree
CO11 . . . . **104** D2
Stubbs Wood NR32 . . **113** B6
Studio Cl IP17 . . . . . . **58** C8

Studlands Bsns Ctr
CB8 . . . . 120 D6
Studlands Park Ind Est
CB8 . . . . 120 E6
Studlands Pk Ave
CB8 . . . . 120 D6
Studlands Ret Pk
CB8 . . . . 120 F7
Stud Rd IP31 . . . . 140 F4
Stump's Cross CO9 . . . 89 D1
Stump St IP13 . . . . 127 A3
Sturdee Ave IP3 . . . . . 140 B3
Sturgeon Way 22
IP31 . . . . 34 E4
Sturgeon Way 7 IP6 . . 82 A6
STURMER 133 C2
Sturmer End Ind Est
CB9 . . . . 133 A3
Sturmer Rd
Haverhill CB9 . . . . 88 F5
Kedington CB9 . . . . . . 133 D5
Wixoe CO10 . . . . 89 B5
Sturston Cl IP24 . . . . 16 C7
STUSTON 20 E1
Stuston La IP21 . . . . . 117 B8
Stuston Rd IP21 . . . . . 20 E1
STUTTON 105 D6
Stutton CE Prim Sch
IP9 . . . . 105 D5
Stutton Cl IP9 . . . . 105 D5
Stutton Gn IP9 . . . . 105 E5
Stutton La IP9 . . . . 105 D7
Stutton Rd CO11 . . . . . . 105 A5
Sub-station Rd IP11 152 D2
Sucklings St CB9 . . . . 88 E4
SUDBOURNE 86 F8
Sudbourne Rd
14 Felixstowe IP11 . . . 152 D5
Orford IP12 . . . . 131 B5
Tunstall IP12 . . . . 72 C1
SUDBURY 148 C4
Sudbury Arts Ctr
CO10 . . . . 148 D7
Sudbury Common Lands
**Nature Reserve*
CO10 . . . . 148 B6
Sudbury Rd
Acton CO10 . . . . 92 B7
Bulmer CO10 . . . . 91 C3
Bures St Mary CO8 . . . 101 C5
3 Felixstowe IP11 . . . 152 C4
Gestingthorpe CO9 . . . 90 F1
Great Whelnetham
IP30 . . . . 64 A6
Lavenham CO10 . . . . . . 78 D3
Long Melford CO10 . . . 91 D6
Newton CO10 . . . . 92 C4
Stoke-by-Nayland
CO6 . . . . 102 D7
Sudbury Ret Pk
CO10 . . . . 148 F6
Sudbury Sports Ctr
CO10 . . . . 148 D7
Sudbury Sta CO10 . . . 148 D5
Sudbury Upper Sch &
Arts Ctr CO10 . . . . . . 148 D7
Suffolk Ave IP31 . . . . . 33 D5
Suffolk Bsns Pk
IP30 . . . . 123 F4
Suffolk Cl 12 NR31 . . . 3 B6
Suffolk Coast National
**Nature Reserve*
IP19 . . . . 43 A5
Suffolk Ct 2 IP27 . . . . 5 F1
Suffolk Dr IP12 . . . . . . 85 D8
Suffolk New Coll
IP4 . . . . 139 E5
**Suffolk Odyssey Llamas*
IP19 . . . . 41 D5
Suffolk One Sixth Form
Coll IP8 . . . . 138 C3
**Suffolk Owl Sanctuary*
IP14 . . . . 68 C6
Suffolk Pl IP12 . . . . . . 147 B5
**Suffolk Punch Trust*
IP12 . . . . 100 A8
Suffolk Rd
2 Bury St Edmunds
IP32 . . . . 122 E8
Ipswich IP4 . . . . 155 C4
Lowestoft NR32 . . . . . 115 D8
Sudbury CO10 . . . . 148 C6
Suffolk Ret Pk IP1 . . 139 A6
**Suffolk Ski Ctr*
IP2 . . . . 143 B7
Suffolk Sq 5 CO10 . . 148 C6
Suffolk Way CB8 . . . . 120 E5
**Suffolk Wildlife Pk*
NR33 . . . . 11 B1
Suffolk Wr Pk* IP8 134 A5
Sulleys Hill IP7 . . . . . 103 D8
Sulleys Hill Rd IP7 . . 103 E8
Sullivan Pl IP12 . . . . . 98 D7
Summerfield Cl
14 Burwell CB5 . . . . 44 B8
Ipswich IP4 . . . . 140 D8
Summerfield Ct IP4 141 D8
Summerfield Gdns
NR33 . . . . 115 A6
Summerhill Sch
IP16 . . . . 129 C7
Summer La
Bromeswell IP12 . . . . 85 A6
Candle Street IP22 . . . 35 F5
Summer Rd 8 NR32 113 D1

Summers Pk Ave 30
CO11 . . . . 104 D2
Summers Rd IP32 . . . 122 E8
Summit Bsns Pk
IP11 . . . . 152 E1
Sumner Rd IP22 . . . . . . 35 B4
Sunbeam Cl NR33 . . . . 114 A3
Sunburst Green 5
CB7 . . . . 28 E3
Suncrest Rise 21 IP14 67 A5
Sunderland Rd 2
IP11 . . . . 153 H11
Sunfield Cl IP4 . . . . . . 140 B6
Sun La
Newmarket CB8 . . . . . . 121 A3
Woodbridge IP12 . . . . 147 A5
Sunley Cl NR35 . . . . . . 110 E8
Sunningdale Ave
Ipswich IP4 . . . . 140 D5
Lowestoft NR33 . . . . . 115 A4
Mildenhall IP28 . . . . 116 B4
Sunningdale Dr
IP11 . . . . 153 B6
Sunnybrook Cl IP23 . . 36 C3
Sunnyfields NR33 . . . 115 A7
Sunnyhill IP12 . . . . . . 98 D7
Sunnyside
Bedingham NR35 . . . . . . 7 C8
Diss IP22 . . . . 20 C3
Sunray Ave IP11 . . . . 153 B6
Sun Rd NR35 . . . . 110 D8
Sun St 4 CB7 . . . . 29 C5
Surbiton Rd IP1 . . . . . 138 F7
Surrey Cl 8 IP13 . . . . 126 C3
Surrey Rd
Felixstowe IP11 . . . . 152 F4
Ipswich IP1 . . . . 139 A6
Surrey St
5 Lowestoft NR32 . . . 113 D1
4 Lowestoft NR32 . . . 115 D8
Sussex Crof 9 IP12 . . . 85 B3
Sussex Rd
11 Fornham St Martin
IP32 . . . . 48 B5
Lowestoft NR32 . . . . . 113 D3
Sutherland Dr NR32 . . 113 B5
SUTTON 85 A1
Sutton Cl
Bury St Edmunds
IP32 . . . . 123 E5
Woodbridge IP12 . . . . 147 B5
Sutton Dr IP23 . . . . . . 35 A5
Sutton Hall Dr IP12 . . 99 A8
Sutton Hoo* IP12 . . . 147 D5
Sutton Hoo Maze
**Adventure Pk*
IP12 . . . . 146 D1
Sutton Rd
Sutton IP12 . . . . 85 D1
Woodbridge IP12 . . . . 147 F5
Suttons Rd 10 NR34 . . . 9 F4
SUTTON ST IP12 . . . . . . 99 A8
SUTTON STREET 99 A7
Swaffham Heath Rd
CB8 . . . . 59 A7
Swaffham Rd
Burwell CB5 . . . . 44 A3
Mundford IP26 . . . . 6 B8
Swainston Way IP13 . . 55 D5
Swale View 7 IP24 . . . 16 D7
Swallow Cl
Felixstowe IP11 . . . . 153 C7
12 Harwich CO12 . . . . 106 F1
Swallow Dr
Brandon IP27 . . . . 6 A1
3 Stowmarket IP14 . . 67 A4
Swallowfields NR33 . . 114 D3
Swallows Cl NR2 . . . . . 138 B8
Swallows Cl IP12 . . . . 99 F7
Swallowtail Cl
1 Ipswich IP8 . . . . 142 E4
Wicken CB7 . . . . 28 A2
Swamp La IP22 . . . . 20 A3
Swan Cl
Halesworth IP19 . . . . 118 B3
29 Martlesham Heath
IP5 . . . . 98 A8
Stowmarket IP14 . . . . 124 A6
Swan Ct 12 CO11 . . . . 105 A2
Swan Dr NR32 . . . . 112 E3
Swanfield CO10 . . . . . . 91 E8
Swan Gn La IP19 . . . . . . 40 C5
Swan Gr CB8 . . . . 120 B8
SWAN GREEN 40 B5
Swan Hill IP8 . . . . 138 A2
Swan La
Bury St Edmunds
IP33 . . . . 154 C1
Coney Weston IP31 . . . 34 D8
Cretingham IP13 . . . . . 69 E8
Exning CB8 . . . . 120 B8
Halesworth IP19 . . . . 118 B3
Halesworth CB9 . . . . . 132 E6
9 Long Melford CO10 . . 91 D8
North Cove NR34 . . . . 10 C4
Redenhall with Harleston
IP20 . . . . 22 D6
Westerfield IP6 . . . . . 135 C4
Swan Lane Bsns Pk
CB8 . . . . 120 B8
Swan Meadow CO7 . . . 103 E5
Swan Rd IP13 . . . . 54 E7
Swansea Ave IP24 . . . 139 B1
Swan St CO10 . . . . 93 B3
Swan Yard 10 IP30 . . . 50 D1
Swatchway Cl 3
IP3 . . . . 144 B8
Swaynes 1 CO7 . . . . . . 103 E5

Sweden Cl 1 CO12 . . . 106 F2
Sweet Briar Cl 8
CO6 . . . . 102 A7
Sweetbriar La NR34 . . . 26 D4
Sweethill La IP31 . . . . . 50 B4
SWEFFLING 56 E2
Swift Cl NR33 . . . . 114 D3
Swift Dr IP14 . . . . 67 A5
SWILLAND 83 A7
Swilltub La IP14 . . . . . . 52 A4
Swinburne Rd IP1 . . . 134 E3
Swine's Gn NR34 . . . . 111 C4
SWINGLETON
GREEN 79 C2
Swingleton Hill IP7 . . . 79 C2
Swinton Cl IP2 . . . . . . 138 D1
Swonnells Ct NR32 . . 114 D8
Swonnell's Wlk 2
NR32 . . . . 112 D1
Sybil Andrews Acad
IP31 . . . . 49 A3
Sycamore Ave NR33 . 114 D7
Sycamore Cl
Beccles NR34 . . . . 111 C3
3 Great Brickett IP7 . . 80 D6
Haverhill CB9 . . . . 132 D6
Ipswich IP8 . . . . 138 C1
Leiston IP16 . . . . 129 C5
6 Palgrave IP22 . . . . . 20 C1
Sycamore Dr
8 Beck Row, Holywell Row
& Kenny Hill IP28 . . . . 13 B1
6 Bury St Edmunds
IP32 . . . . 49 A3
5 Mildenhall IP28 . . . . 30 A8
Rendlesham IP12 . . . . . 85 D8
Sycamore Path CB8 . . . 75 C6
Sycamore Rd
Stowupland IP14 . . . . . 67 A6
Sudbury CO10 . . . . . . 148 F4
Sycamore View IP22 . . 36 E6
Sycamore Way
Brantham CO11 . . . . . 104 E5
Diss IP22 . . . . 20 D3
Sycamore Wlk 20
IP27 . . . . 13 F2
SYLEHAM 22 A1
Syleham Hall La IP21 . . 22 C1
Syleham Rd
Brockdish IP21 . . . . . . 22 A2
Shotford Heath IP21 . . 22 D4
Syleham IP21 . . . . 38 D8
Sylvester Rd IP16 . . . 129 D5
Symonds Rd
Bury St Edmunds
IP33 . . . . 123 C4
Risby IP28 . . . . 47 C4
Symphony Ct 4 CB7 . . 28 E3
Syres Farm IP7 . . . . . . 79 E6

T

Tacket St IP4 . . . . 155 C2
Tacon Cl IP23 . . . . 117 C2
Tacon Rd IP11 . . . . 152 E1
Tailors Green IP14 . . . . 51 F6
Takeleys CO8 . . . . 101 C2
Takers La IP14 . . . . . . 124 E4
Talante La NR35 . . . . . . 8 E5
Talbot Meadow 2
IP22 . . . . 20 E1
Talbot Rd CO10 . . . . . . 148 D7
Talbot St 11 CO12 . . . 107 B3
Talbot Wlk IP13 . . . . . . 71 C2
Tallboys Cl IP5 . . . . . . 141 C8
Tallyho Cnr 8 CO7 . . . 103 E5
Talmash Gdns IP2 . . . 139 A4
Tamage Rd CO10 . . . . . 92 B7
Tangham IP12 . . . . 85 F3
Tan House La CB5 . . . . . 44 A4
Tankard Farm Cl 13
IP7 . . . . 79 F4
Tannersfield Way
CB8 . . . . 120 F4
Tanners La CB7 . . . . . . 28 D3
Tanners Vw 1 IP14 . . 138 F7
Tannery Bsns Ctr The
IP14 . . . . 66 E2
Tannery Dr IP33 . . . . . 123 B3
Tannery Rd IP14 . . . . . 124 C1
TANNINGTON 55 A6
Tannington Long Rd
IP13 . . . . 39 D1
Tannington Rd
Bedfield IP13 . . . . 54 E6
Saxtead Little Green
IP13 . . . . 55 A5
Tanns La IP22 . . . . 19 F4
TAN OFFICE 52 F2
TAN OFFICE GREEN . . . 62 C6
Tan Office La
Chevington IP29 . . . . . 62 C5
Mendlesham IP14 . . . . 52 E1
Tansy Cl 5 NR33 . . . . 114 F3
Tansy Meadow 3
IP21 . . . . 39 D8
Tanyard St IP13 . . . . . 126 C4
Target Hill IP20 . . . . . . 23 B6
Tarn Hows Cl 1
IP11 . . . . 153 D6
Tasmania Rd IP4 . . . . 140 D6
Tasman Rd CB9 . . . . . . 133 A5
Tassel Rd IP32 . . . . . . 123 F6
TATTINGSTONE 105 B8
Tattingstone CE VC Prim
Sch IP9 . . . . 105 B8
Tattingstone Rd IP9 105 D7

TATTINGSTONE WHITE
HORSE 142 D1
Taunton Cl IP11 . . . . . 135 B4
Taunton Rd IP11 . . . . 152 F5
Tavern La
Bury St Edmunds
IP33 . . . . 154 B2
7 Diss IP22 . . . . 20 D2
Tavern St
Ipswich IP1 . . . . 155 B3
Stowmarket IP14 . . . . 124 D6
Tavistock Pl CO11 . . . 104 D1
Tawneys Ride 2
CO8 . . . . 101 D4
Tayberry Cl 38 IP28 . . 30 C1
Tayberry Pl IP13 . . . . 144 C7
Tayfen Rd IP33 . . . . . . 154 B3
Tayfen Terr IP33 . . . . 154 B4
Tayler Cl 4 IP7 . . . . . . 149 D5
Tayler Rd IP7 . . . . 149 E5
Taylor Dr 8 CO11 . . . 104 E2
Taylor Drift NR16 . . . . 18 D8
Taylor Rd 8 IP22 . . . . . 20 B2
Taylors Farm IP14 . . . 66 C1
Taylors Farm Rd CB9 . . 75 A2
Taylors Field CB8 . . . . 59 F4
Taylors La IP7 . . . . 80 C4
Taylors Rd NR34 . . . . . 10 B7
Tea Kettle La CB8 . . . . 59 F5
Teal Ave CB7 . . . . 28 C5
Teal Cl
Ipswich IP2 . . . . 138 D3
Southwold IP18 . . . . 119 B7
Teal Dr 28 IP14 . . . . . . 67 A5
Teal Wlk IP27 . . . . 6 A1
Tea Pot Corner IP7 . . . 94 C1
Teasel Cl
Haverhill CB9 . . . . 132 B7
3 Kennett IP28 . . . . . . 45 F8
Tedder Cl 3 IP24 . . . . 16 C2
Tedder Rd NR34 . . . . 113 B4
Teesdale NR33 . . . . . . 114 E3
Telesia Ct IP13 . . . . . . 113 B4
Temperance Pl 8
NR34 . . . . 111 B5
Templars Ct 20 CB9 132 C5
Temple Bar Mws 6
IP14 . . . . 124 D6
Temple Cl IP28 . . . . . . 31 C4
TEMPLE END
Foxearth 91 A6
Little Thurlow 74 C5
Temple End CB9 . . . . . 74 C5
Temple Pattle 11
CO11 . . . . 104 E4
Temple Rd
Ipswich IP3 . . . . 140 C4
Isleham CB7 . . . . 29 B4
Stowmarket IP14 . . . . 124 D5
Ten Bell La 10 CB7 . . . 28 D4
Tenby Rd IP2 . . . . 139 B1
Tennis Drove IP26 . . . . 4 E8
Tennyson Cl IP12 . . . 146 E6
Tennyson Rd
13 Bury St Edmunds
IP32 . . . . 48 C5
20 Diss IP22 . . . . 20 D2
Lowestoft NR32 . . . . . 113 D2
Saxmundham IP17 . . . 128 B4
Tennyson Way IP24 . . 16 C7
Tenter Cl IP7 . . . . 149 E6
Tenter Cl IP7 . . . . 149 E6
Tenterden Cl 6
NR33 . . . . 114 D5
Tenter Field
Bures CO8 . . . . 101 C4
4 Stratford St Mary
CO7 . . . . 103 E5
Tenter Piece 16
CO10 . . . . 78 D4
Tenth Rd IP10 . . . . 98 A3
Tentree Rd CO10 . . . . . 92 C7
Terence Airey Ct 25
IP20 . . . . 22 D6
Terence Pl 12 CB7 . . . 29 A1
Tern Cl CB9 . . . . 133 A5
Tern Pl CB8 . . . . 120 A8
Tern Rd IP2 . . . . 138 E2
Terrace The
Aldeburgh IP15 . . . . 130 E4
Snape IP17 . . . . 72 D5
Terra Cotta Place
CO10 . . . . 77 C4
Tethys Pl NR32 . . . . . . 113 D3
Tetley Cl IP13 . . . . 126 B4
Tett Terr IP13 . . . . 126 D2
Tewkesbury Pl 7
IP31 . . . . 49 A5
Thackeray Gr IP1 . . . 124 B7
Thackeray Rd IP1 . . . 134 E3
Thacker Cl IP8 . . . . . . 134 A2
Thanet Rd IP4 . . . . . . 140 B6
Tharp Way CB7 . . . . . . 29 C1
Thatchers Wlk 4
IP14 . . . . 124 D3
**Theatre Royal*
IP33 . . . . 154 C1
Theatre St IP12 . . . . 146 F5
The Ave
Lawford CO11 . . . . . . 104 D8
Martlesham Heath IP5 . . 98 B8
The Avenue NR32 . . . . 2 D6
The Barracks IP31 . . . 33 A2
The Battlies IP30 . . . . 49 B3
The Beeches
Bury St Edmunds
IP33 . . . . 122 E5
Norton IP31 . . . . 50 B4

The Beeches Com Prim
Sch IP1 . . . . 134 E3
The Benthills 10 IP16 . . 73 F6
THEBERTON 58 B4
Theberton Rd
Ipswich IP3 . . . . 140 B1
Saxmundham IP17 . . . 57 F3
The Birches
Aldeburgh IP15 . . . . 130 D5
6 Beyton Green IP30 . . 49 F2
The Blundells IP10 . . . 98 A4
The Boundaries NR34 . . 9 B7
The Briars CB5 . . . . 44 A6
The Broadway IP33 154 C2
The Brooks 8 IP12 . . 147 B6
The Carrops IP28 . . . . 45 F8
The Causeway
Lawford CO11 . . . . . . 104 D3
Sibton IP17 . . . . 57 F8
The Cedars
Somersham IP8 . . . . . 81 B4
Wrentham NR34 . . . . . . 26 E5
The Central Maltings 34
CO11 . . . . 104 E2
The Chestnuts 12
IP29 . . . . 63 A8
The Churchill Special
Free Sch CB9 . . . . . . 132 F7
The Circle 20 IP6 . . . . 82 A5
The Cl IP21 . . . . 38 C7
The Cliff IP18 . . . . 119 E7
The Close IP22 . . . . 20 A3
The Common
All Saints South Elmham
IP19 . . . . 24 B5
Mellis IP23 . . . . 36 F5
Metfield IP19 . . . . 23 C2
Sizewell IP16 . . . . 58 E2
Somerleyton NR32 . . . . 2 D4
Southwold IP18 . . . . 119 C5
Stubbing's Green IP22 . 36 B5
Tunstall IP12 . . . . 72 B1
The Copse 11 IP12 . . . 84 A1
The Cres
5 Great Blakenham
IP6 . . . . 82 A6
Westhorpe IP14 . . . . . 51 E8
The Croft IP16 . . . . . . 129 D4
The Crossroads
IP23 . . . . 117 A7
The Cygnets IP15 . . . 130 C5
The Dales 27 CO12 . . 106 F1
The Danger IP19 . . . . . 25 C3
The Daubentons
IP33 . . . . 123 C6
The Dell
Elveden IP24 . . . . 15 D2
Sudbury CO10 . . . . . . 148 E4
The Drift
Aldeburgh IP15 . . . . 130 D5
Capel St Mary IP8 . . . 150 D3
Dedham CO7 . . . . 103 F4
Kirton IP10 . . . . 98 B3
Newmarket CB8 . . . . 121 B4
Thurston IP31 . . . . 49 E3
The Driftway IP28 . . . . 29 E3
The Drive NR32 . . . . 2 E7
The Duddery CB8 . . . . 61 F1
The Dullingham Rd
CB8 . . . . 59 C1
Thedwastre Cl 8
IP30 . . . . 50 F2
Thedwastre Rd IP31 . . 49 E3
The Fen IP19 . . . . 42 F4
The Fens IP16 . . . . 129 C1
The Ficketts IP8 . . . . 134 A3
The Fields IP12 . . . . . . 71 F2
The Firs IP33 . . . . 123 D3
The Gables IP16 . . . . 129 B5
The Gates IP1 . . . . 139 A6
The Gdns
Halesworth IP19 . . . . 118 F5
Haverhill CB9 . . . . 132 C5
Norton IP31 . . . . 50 B5
Raydon IP7 . . . . 94 F1
The Glade Community
Prim Sch IP27 . . . . . . 5 F1
The Glebe CO10 . . . . . 79 A3
The Granary 11 IP30 . . 50 E2
The Grange IP27 . . . 109 D5
The Gravel IP28 . . . . . 29 F6
The Great Churchyard
IP33 . . . . 154 C2
The Green
Ashbocking IP6 . . . . . . 69 A1
Barrow IP29 . . . . 47 A2
Beyton Green IP30 . . . 49 F2
Borley CO10 . . . . 91 C5
Burrough Green CB8 . . 59 F2
Capel Green IP12 . . . . 86 A3
Cavendish CO10 . . . . . 76 E1
Depden Green IP29 . . . 62 B4
Flowton IP8 . . . . 81 C1
Gazeley CB8 . . . . 46 B3
Great Brickett IP7 . . . . 80 D5
1 Hartest IP29 . . . . . . 77 B7
Hawkedon IP29 . . . . . . 76 D8
High Street NR35 . . . . 24 E7
Hoggard's Green IP29 44 A3
Little Thurlow CB9 . . . . 74 E6
Long Melford CO10 . . . 77 C1
Monk Soham IP13 . . . . 54 D4
Moulton CB8 . . . . 45 F3
Naughton IP7 . . . . 80 C3
Newton CO10 . . . . 92 D3
Norton Little Green
IP31 . . . . 50 E5

The Green continued
Otley IP6 . . . . 69 D3
Pettaugh IP14 . . . . 68 E6
Rede IP29 . . . . 62 E2
5 Redgrave IP22 . . . . . 36 A8
Rendham IP17 . . . . 56 E3
Risby IP28 . . . . 47 D5
Rougham Green IP30 . . 64 C8
St Margaret, South Elmham
IP20 . . . . 23 F6
Saxmundham IP17 . . . . 57 E2
Saxstead Green IP13 . . 55 B3
Stowmarket IP14 . . . . 67 A6
Tannington IP13 . . . . . 55 A7
Thorpe Green IP30 . . . 64 F1
Timworth IP31 . . . . 48 D8
Tostock IP30 . . . . 50 B2
Tuddenham IP28 . . . . . . 30 F2
Walberswick IP18 . . . 119 B2
Westhorpe IP14 . . . . . 51 F7
West Stow IP28 . . . . 32 B1
Whatfield IP7 . . . . 80 B2
Wickham Skeith IP23 . . 52 D8
Woolpit Green IP30 . . . 65 D8
Worlington IP28 . . . . . . 30 A4
The Grove 7 IP26 . . . . 6 B8
The Grundle IP31 . . . . 34 E4
The Gurdons CO10 . . 101 F8
The Haven IP12 . . . . . . 99 E4
The Havens CB8 . . . . . 60 D6
The Headlands 13
IP16 . . . . 73 F6
The Heath
Bucklesham IP10 . . . . 98 B4
Honington IP31 . . . . . . 33 D4
Tunstall IP12 . . . . 72 C3
The Hill
Poslingford CO10 . . . . 76 B3
Snape IP17 . . . . 72 D5
Stanstead CO10 . . . . . . 77 C3
The Hills NR34 . . . . 25 E7
The Hindle IP22 . . . . . . 35 B6
The Hollies
Ipswich IP10 . . . . 141 C1
Ipswich IP5 . . . . 141 F8
Lawford CO11 . . . . . . 104 D1
The Horseshoes IP11 . 50 C4
Theinetham Fen Nature
Reserve* IP22 . . . . . . 18 E1
The Kennels IP12 . . . . 85 C8
The Knoll
Alderton IP12 . . . . 99 E4
Redlingfield IP23 . . . . 38 C1
The Lammas 4 IP26 . . 6 A8
The Leas IP13 . . . . 70 A7
The Leys IP30 . . . . 50 B2
The Limes
Botesdale IP22 . . . . . . 36 B7
Harleston IP14 . . . . . . 66 C6
Saxmundham IP17 . . . 128 D4
The Limes Prim Acad
NR32 . . . . 112 D3
Thellusson Rd 8
IP12 . . . . 85 E8
THELNETHAM 18 D1
Thelnetham Rd IP22 . . 18 E1
**Thelnetham Windmill*
IP22 . . . . 18 E1
The Low IP21 . . . . 39 E8
THELVETON 21 A4
The Maltings IP10 . . . 98 D2
The Manor House Estate
IP12 . . . . 99 E3
The Maples IP13 . . . . . 69 E7
The Marsh 6 IP22 . . . . 36 E8
The Mead IP33 . . . . . . 122 E4
The Meadows
Friston IP17 . . . . 72 F6
Hollesley IP12 . . . . 99 F7
9 Wickhambrook CB8 . . 61 E2
The Millers 1 CB8 . . . . 60 F8
The Oaks
Newmarket CB8 . . . . 121 D1
Wickham Market IP13 . 127 B6
Theobald Cl 5 IP6 . . . 125 D5
Theobalds Cl CO10 . . 91 D7
The Old Coaching Pl 10
IP22 . . . . 20 D2
The Old Maltings 5
IP14 . . . . 124 E5
The Old Orchard 15
CO10 . . . . 77 A2
The Old Stackyard
IP9 . . . . 106 C8
The Open Coll of Equine
Studies IP29 . . . . 62 D6
The Orchard
Ringshall Stocks IP14 . 80 F6
Wetherden IP14 . . . . . 51 A2
The Orchards CB8 . . . . 75 E7
The Paddocks
5 Cheveley CB8 . . . . . . 60 E7
Lakenheath IP28 . . . . 13 D1
Shadwell NR16 . . . . 17 D7
Stradbroke IP21 . . . . . 39 E5
The Pastures IP12 . . . . 99 E5
The Pines Prim Sch
IP28 . . . . 30 C2
The Pippins IP3 . . . . . 140 B5
The Pit IP13 . . . . 71 D3
The Planche IP31 . . . . 49 E3
The Poplars 8 IP6 . . . 68 B1
The Post Mill IP31 . . . 50 B4
The Pound IP29 . . . . . . 62 E2
The Presidents IP28 . . 3 D8
The Quay IP12 . . . . 98 E7
The Queach IP31 . . . . . 49 D8
The Ravine NR32 . . . . 113 E3

Therberton Hall Dr
　IP16 . . . . .58 B5
Therberton Hall Farm
　Dr IP16 . . . . .58 C5
The Roadways NR34 . . .10 B7
The Rose Gdns IP31 . . .49 E3
The Row
　Hartest IP29 . . . . .77 B7
　Kersey IP7 . . . . .94 A7
　4 Weeting IP27 . . . . .5 E3
The Royalls IP5 . . . . 141 D8
The Ryes CO10 . . . . . . .91 D1
The Sandlings 14
　IP12 . . . . .84 A1
The Seabrooks 16
　CO10 . . . . .77 A2
The Shrublands 2
　IP20 . . . . .116 C4
The Sidings 7 IP14 . .52 E4
The Spinney
　14 Long Melford
　　CO10 . . . . .91 E8
　Lowestoft NR32 . . . . .112 F1
　Saxmundham IP17 . .128 D4
The Sq
　Bell's Cross IP6 . . . . . .82 E7
　Hadleigh IP7 . . . . . . .149 E7
The Squires CB8 . . . . .46 B5
The St
　Ashfield IP14 . . . . .54 D2
　Bedingfield IP23 . . . . . .53 F6
　Bedingfield IP23 . . . . . .54 A6
　Boyton IP12 . . . . .86 B1
　Brandeston IP13 . . . . . .70 A7
　Burstall IP8 . . . . .95 E8
　Chillesford IP12 . . . . . . .86 C7
　Coney Weston IP31 . . . .17 F1
　Cransford IP13 . . . . . . .56 B3
　Freston IP9 . . . . .143 E3
　Herringswell IP28 . . . . .46 B8
　Kettlebaston IP7 . . . . . .79 C5
　Little Welnetham
　　IP30 . . . . .64 B7
　Stoven NR34 . . . . .25 F4
　Sweffling IP17 . . . . .56 E2
　Tannington IP13 . . . . . .55 A6
　Timworth IP31 . . . . .48 E8
　Walpole IP19 . . . . .41 C5
　Westhorpe IP14 . . . . . . .51 E8
　Wickham Skeith IP23 . .52 D8
The Stone IP6 . . . . . . .81 D5
The Street
　Ampton IP31 . . . . .33 A2
　Blythburgh IP19 . . . . . .42 F6
　Brent Eleigh CO10 . . . . .79 A3
　Charsfield IP13 . . . . . . .70 A5
　Chelsworth IP7 . . . . . . .79 E2
　Elmswell IP30 . . . . .50 E2
　Fornham All Saints
　　IP28 . . . . .48 C6
　Haverhill CB9 . . . . . . .133 E2
　Hepworth IP22 . . . . . . .35 A5
　Lindsey Tye IP7 . . . . . . .93 D8
　Metfield IP19 . . . . .23 C3
　Red Lodge IP28 . . . . . .30 E2
　Rushall IP21 . . . . .21 E5
　Shimpling Green IP29 . .77 F7
　Toad Row NR33 . . . . . .10 E2
　6 Wetherden IP14 . . . . .51 A1
　Wyverstone Street
　　IP14 . . . . .51 D6
　Yaxley IP23 . . . . .37 C4
THETFORD 16 D5
Thetford Gram Sch
　IP24 . . . . .16 B6
Thetford Heath National
　Nature Reserve★
　IP24 . . . . .16 A2
Thetford Rd
　Brandon IP27 . . . . .5 F1
　Coney Weston IP31 . . . .34 D8
　Elveden IP27 . . . . .15 D8
　Euston IP24 . . . . .16 E2
　Fakenham Magna IP24 . .33 E8
　Fornham St Martin
　　IP31 . . . . .48 D5
　Garboldisham IP22 . . . .18 C4
　2 Ipswich IP1 . . . . . .139 A7
　Ixworth IP31 . . . . .34 A2
　Ixworth Thorpe IP31 . . . .33 F3
　Mildenhall IP28 . . . . . .116 E4
　Santon Downham IP27 . . .6 B1
　Shadwell IP24 . . . . .17 C6
　South Lopham IP22 . . . .19 A4
Thetford Sta IP24 . . . .16 B6
The Thetford Acad
　IP24 . . . . .16 C7
The Timbers IP31 . . . .33 F5
The Triangle IP28 . . . .32 D2
The Tye
　Alpheton CO10 . . . . . . .78 A5
　Barking IP6 . . . . .81 A7
　Lindsey Tye IP7 . . . . . . .93 D8
The Vale NR34 . . . . . .26 D4
The Valley IP22 . . . . . .19 E4
The Village IP30 . . . . .64 A8
The Vines 6 IP28 . . . .45 F8
The Waldegraves 10
　CO0 . . . . .101 C4
The Walk IP20 . . . . . . .7 A4
The Walks
　Sutton Common IP12 . . .85 A3
　Thurston IP31 . . . . . . .147 F5
The Walnuts 13 IP13 . .84 F7
The Warren IP17 . . . . .72 E5
The Wash
　Eastbridge IP17 . . . . . . .58 B5
　Soham CB7 . . . . .28 E3

The Whinlands 9
　IP16 . . . . .73 F6
The Willows
　Ipswich IP5 . . . . .136 E1
　Mildenhall IP28 . . . . . .116 B3
The Wonder IP9 . . . . .105 B7
The Woodlands IP14 . .52 A8
The Woodyard
　Framlingham IP13 . . . .126 B3
　8 Fressingfield IP21 . . .39 D8
Thieves La IP31 . . . . . .49 F8
Thingoe Hill IP32 . . . .154 B4
Third Ave
　Glemsford CO10 . . . . . .77 B3
　19 Harwich CO12 . . . .107 B2
Third Drove CB5 . . . . .44 B8
Thirlmere CI IP14 . . . .52 E4
Thirlmere Dr IP14 . . .124 D6
Thirlmere Wlk NR32 . .113 A4
Thirlwall Dr CB7 . . . . .29 C1
Thistle CI IP2 . . . . . . .138 F4
Thistledown NR33 . . .114 D4
Thistledown Dr IP31 . .34 B2
Thistleton Hall Rd
　IP13 . . . . .83 F7
Thistle Way 14 IP28 . .30 C1
THISTLEY GREEN 29 E7
Thixendale NR33 . . . .114 E2
Thomas Arne CI 1
　IP14 . . . . .124 C8
Thomas Ave IP14 . . . . .54 D2
Thomas Bardwell Dr 4
　NR35 . . . . .110 C2
Thomas Bole CI IP22 . .18 D4
Thomas Churchyard CI
　IP12 . . . . .84 E6
Thomas CI 20 IP31 . . .34 B1
Thomas Cres IP5 . . . .141 D6
Thomas Gainsborough
　Sch CO10 . . . . .148 F2
Thomas La IP33 . . . . .154 B1
Thomas Manning Rd 12
　IP22 . . . . .20 D2
Thomas Mews CB7 . . . .28 C4
Thomas Mills High Sch
　IP13 . . . . .126 A5
Thomas Walls CI 3
　IP13 . . . . .83 E5
Thomas West Ct
　CO10 . . . . .148 A4
Thomas Wolsey Ormiston
　Academy IP1 . . . . . . .135 A4
Thomas Young CI 3
　IP14 . . . . .124 D3
Thompson CI
　19 Grundisburgh
　　IP13 . . . . .83 E5
　Haughley IP14 . . . . .51 D1
　Haverhill CB9 . . . . . . .132 F4
Thompson Rd IP1 . . .138 F8
Thompsons Meadow
　IP6 . . . . .68 C4
Thompson Wlk IP32 . .122 D7
Thomsons La IP14 . . . .69 A2
Thong Hall Rd IP13 . .127 A5
THORINGTON 42 C4
Thorington Hall La
　IP9 . . . . .142 E6
Thorington Rd IP19 . . .42 A5
THORINGTON
　STREET 103 A6
Thornapple View 46
　IP28 . . . . .30 C1
Thornbush La IP8 . . . .138 A8
Thorn CI CB7 . . . . .28 C5
THORNDON 53 B8
Thorndon Bridge
　IP23 . . . . .37 D1
THORNEY GREEN 67 A7
Thorney Gn Rd IP14 . . .67 A6
Thorney Hall CI IP14 .124 E6
Thorney Rd IP9 . . . . .150 E4
Thorney View 6
　IP14 . . . . .124 D3
Thorney Way 51 IP14 . .67 A5
Thornham CI 3
　NR33 . . . . .114 F4
THORNHAM MAGNA . . .37 A2
THORNHAM PARVA 37 B3
Thornham Rd
　Gislingham IP23 . . . . . .36 D2
　Mellis IP23 . . . . .37 A2
Thornham Walled Gdn★
　IP23 . . . . .37 A2
Thornhayes CI IP2 . . .139 A3
Thornhill Rd IP6 . . . . .82 B5
Thornley Dr IP4 . . . . .140 C8
Thornley Rd IP11 . . . .153 C4
Thorns CI 6 CB8 . . . . .61 E2
Thorns Corner 12 CB8 .61 E2
Thorns Meadow CB8 . . .61 E2
Thornton CE VC Prim Sch
　IP23 . . . . .53 B8
Thornton Rd IP33 . . . .122 E2
Thorn Way IP11 . . . . .152 E4
Thorn Wlk IP21 . . . . . .85 C2
Thornycroft Gdns
　NR33 . . . . .114 A3
Thoroughfare IP19 . . .110 D3
Thoroughfare The
　Brundish IP13 . . . . .55 C8
　Harleston IP20 . . . . . . .22 D6
　Wilby IP21 . . . . .39 D1
　10 Woodbridge IP12 . .147 A5
Thorpe Abbots Rd
　IP21 . . . . .21 D4
THORPE ABBOTS 21 E2
THORPE COMMON 107 C8

THORPE GREEN 64 F1
Thorpe Hall Rd IP21 . . .38 F4
Thorpe La
　Ashfield cum Thorpe
　　IP14 . . . . .69 C8
　Debenham IP14 . . . . . . .53 F1
　Trimley St Martin
　　IP11 . . . . .107 C8
THORPE MORIEUX 79 A8
THORPENESS 73 E6
Thorpeness Windmill★
　IP16 . . . . .73 E6
Thorpe Rd
　Aldeburgh IP16 . . . . . .130 F6
　Aldringham IP16 . . . . .129 D2
　Preston St Mary CO10 . .79 A6
　Thorpeness IP16 . . . . . .73 F6
Thorpe's Hill IP8 . . . . .95 C6
THORPE STREET 35 D8
THRANDESTON 37 B7
Thrandeston Rd
　Brome IP23 . . . . .117 F7
　Mellis IP23 . . . . .37 A6
Threadneedle St
　Dedham CO7 . . . . .103 F4
　1 Hadleigh IP7 . . . . . .149 D6
Three Chimneys La
　CO9 . . . . .89 C3
Three Counties Way 5
　CB9 . . . . .74 A1
Three Marsh La
　IP18 . . . . .119 B6
Three Stiles La IP12 . . .84 B1
Threshers Yard 5
　IP28 . . . . .116 B4
Thrift Drove CB7 . . . . .28 E5
Throckmorton Rd
　NR35 . . . . .110 D3
Through Duncans
　IP12 . . . . .146 E3
Through Jollys IP5 . . .141 D8
Thunderbird Way
　IP27 . . . . .109 F1
Thurleston La IP1 . . . .134 F5
Thurlow CE VC Prim Sch
　CB9 . . . . .74 D6
Thurlow CI IP17 . . . . .128 B3
Thurlow Ct 2 IP14 . . .124 D6
Thurlow PI 13 CB9 . . .132 F6
Thurlow Rd
　Great Bradley CB9 . . . . .74 D7
　Withersfield CB9 . . . . . .74 B2
Thurmans La IP11 . . . .152 B8
Thurne Rd NR33 . . . . .114 F5
THURSTON 49 E3
Thurston CE Prim Acad
　27 Thurston IP31 . . . . .49 E4
　Thurston IP31 . . . . .49 E4
Thurston Com Coll
　IP31 . . . . .49 D4
Thurston Ct 6 IP11 . . .152 C4
THURSTON END 76 D6
Thurston La CO10 . . . .76 C7
Thurston Rd
　1 Beyton IP30 . . . . .49 F2
　Grimstone End IP31 . . . .49 E7
　Hawkedon IP29 . . . . . . .76 D7
　Lowestoft NR32 . . . . . .113 D2
　Thurston IP30 . . . . .49 D3
　Thurston IP31 . . . . .49 E3
Thurston Sta IP31 . . . .49 D3
Thurtells CI IP17 . . . . .57 E8
THWAITE 52 F7
Thwaite Rd
　Bungay NR35 . . . . .8 A7
　Ditchingham NR35 . . . .110 C7
　Thorndon IP23 . . . . . . .53 B8
　Wickham Skeith IP23 . . .52 D7
Tibbenham's Score 6
　NR32 . . . . .3 D4
Tiberius CI CB9 . . . . .133 B5
Tide Mill★ IP12 . . . . .147 B4
Tide Mill Way IP12 . . .147 A4
Tideway NR32 . . . . . .114 E8
Tidy Rd IP12 . . . . .85 D8
Tidys Ct IP33 . . . . . . .154 B3
Tiger Hill Nature
　Reserve★ CO8 . . . . . .101 E6
Tiggins La IP17 . . . . . .128 D8
Tilbrook CI IP21 . . . . . .39 A5
TILBURY GREEN 89 E4
Tilbury Hill CO9 . . . . . .90 A2
TILBURY JUXTA
　CLARE 90 A3
Tilbury Rd
　Great Yeldham CO9 . . . .90 A2
　Ovington CO10 . . . . . . .90 A3
　Ridgewell CO9 . . . . . . .89 E4
Tile Barn La CO11 . . . .104 B1
Tilia CI NR34 . . . . .10 A3
Tillbrooks Hill CB8 . . . .61 B1
Timber Yard IP17 . . . . .71 E8
Timperley CI IP7 . . . . .149 D7
Timperley Rd IP7 . . . .149 E7
Timperleys IP8 . . . . . .95 C6
TIMWORTH 48 D8
TIMWORTH GREEN 48 D7
Tinabrook CI IP2 . . . .138 E1
Tinhouse Rd IP17 . . . .56 D7
Tinker Brook IP13 . . . .71 F5
Tinkers La NR34 . . . . .10 D1
Tinker's La
　Hadleigh IP7 . . . . .149 B2
　Tivetshall St Mary
　　NR15 . . . . .21 C8
Tinker St CO12 . . . . . .106 C1
Tintern CI 5 IP2 . . . . .139 A2
Tippet Ave IP14 . . . . .124 C8

Titan Ct 2 IP1 . . . . . .138 D8
Titchwell Dr 2 IP3 . . .144 D8
Tithe Ave IP28 . . . . . . .30 B8
Tithe CI CB8 . . . . .46 C3
Tithe Courtyard CO6 .102 C3
Title Rd IP17 . . . . .58 A6
Titlow Rd 28 IP20 . . . .22 D6
Tittle Hall La IP29 . . . .77 A5
TOAD ROW 10 F1
Toad Row NR34 . . . . . .10 F1
Todd Way 11 IP32 . . . .49 A3
Todhunter Ave NR34 . . .9 B6
Tog La CO6 . . . . .102 D2
Tokio Rd IP4 . . . . .140 A6
Tollemache Bsns Pk
　IP7 . . . . .80 E4
Tollemache Hall Rd
　IP7 . . . . .80 E5
Toller CI IP12 . . . . . . .131 C3
Toller Rd IP3 . . . . .139 E3
Tollesbury Way CB8 . . .46 B3
Tolley Cobbold St 3
　IP28 . . . . .30 A8
Tollgate County Prim Sch
　IP32 . . . . .122 F8
Tollgate Ct 17 IP6 . . . .82 B5
Tollgate La 2 IP32 . . .123 A8
Toll Gate Rd 6 IP9 . . .150 E3
Tolworth Rd IP4 . . . . .140 A6
Tom Jennings CI
　CB8 . . . . .120 F5
Tomline Ct IP10 . . . . .145 C5
Tomline Rd
　Felixstowe IP11 . . . . . .153 A3
　Ipswich IP3 . . . . .140 A5
Tomline Wlk IP3 . . . . .140 A5
Tommy Flowers Dr
　IP5 . . . . .141 E7
Tomo Bsns Pk IP14 . . .124 E4
Tomo Ind Est IP14 . . .124 E6
Tomo Rd IP14 . . . . . .124 F6
Tomtit's La IP14 . . . . . .51 B2
Tongs La IP19 . . . . . . .40 B6
Tonning St NR32 . . . .113 C1
Tooks Comm La NR34 . .8 F1
Tooks Rd 1 IP1 . . . . .134 E3
Topcroft Rd NR35 . . . . .7 A5
Top Drag Way IP22 . . . .18 F4
Toper La IP33 . . . . . . .154 C1
Top Green CB8 . . . . . . .76 A7
Toppesfield CI 3
　IP7 . . . . .149 D5
Toppesfield Gdns
　IP7 . . . . .149 D5
Top Rd
　Hasketon IP13 . . . . . . .146 B8
　Rattlesden IP30 . . . . . . .65 D5
　St Andrew, Ilketshall
　　NR34 . . . . .8 E1
　Wingfield IP21 . . . . . . .39 A7
Topsfield CO10 . . . . . .148 E2
Top St IP12 . . . . .146 C2
Tortoiseshell CI 5
　IP9 . . . . .142 E8
TOSTOCK 50 B2
Tostock Rd IP30 . . . . . .49 F2
Tot Hill IP14 . . . . .66 C8
Tots Green CO10 . . . . .92 B8
Tottington La IP22 . . . .20 B2
Touchey's La CO7 . . . .104 D5
Tovells 4 IP13 . . . . . . .84 F7
Tovell's Rd IP4 . . . . . .139 F6
Tower Ct 18 CB9 . . . . .74 A1
Tower Field Rd IP12 . . .85 D7
TOWER HILL 107 C3
Tower Hill NR34 . . . . .111 C3
Tower Hill Rd IP12 . . . .99 F7
Tower La IP15 . . . . . . .130 E4
Tower Mill La IP7 . . . .149 E6
Tower Mill Rd
　Bungay NR35 . . . . .110 B3
　Ipswich IP1 . . . . .138 F7
Tower Ramparts IP1 . .155 B3
Tower Ramparts Sh Ctr
　IP1 . . . . .155 B3
Tower Rd
　Felixstowe IP11 . . . . . .152 F4
　Lowestoft NR33 . . . . . .115 A2
　Tower St IP1 . . . . .155 B3
Town End CI 5 CB9 . . .132 D7
Town Farm CI IP20 . . . .23 C3
Town Farm Est IP12 . . .85 D8
Town Farm La IP17 . . . .57 D5
Town Hall Galleries★
　IP1 . . . . .155 C3
Town House Cnr IP14 . .68 F7
Town House La IP22 . . .35 D6
Townhouse Rd IP31 . . .35 C1
Town La
　Grundisburgh IP13 . . . . .83 E6
　Wetheringsett-cum-
　　Brockford IP14 . . . . . .52 E4
Townlands Dr NR34 . .111 B3
Townlane Rd IP33 . . . .123 B1
Townsend CB7 . . . . . . .28 C5
Townsend Way
　NR32 . . . . .113 A6
Town Stps IP15 . . . . . .130 C4
Toyse CI 1 CB5 . . . . . .44 B6
Toyse La CB5 . . . . .44 A6
Trafalgar CI IP4 . . . . .139 F6
Trafalgar Rd CO10 . . .148 E7
Trafalgar St
　4 Lowestoft NR32 . . . .113 C1
　Lowestoft NR32 . . . . . .115 C4
Trafalgar Way 3
　IP22 . . . . .20 D2

Trafford CI 2 IP14 . . . .51 E1
Tranmere Gr IP1 . . . . .134 F2
Traveller's Hill (Tumuli)★
　IP28 . . . . .32 E5
Travellers Rd IP13 . . . .69 E5
Traverse The IP33 . . . .154 B2
Treetops IP11 . . . . . . .152 E7
Treeview IP14 . . . . . . .124 B6
Trefoil CI IP2 . . . . . . .138 F4
Tremlett La IP5 . . . . . .141 F7
Trenchard Sq 8 IP26 . . .4 D5
Trent Rd
　1 Bury St Edmunds
　　IP32 . . . . .48 C5
　Ipswich IP3 . . . . .139 F2
Trevethan CI IP32 . . . .122 E7
Triangle Yd 9 NR32 . .113 C2
Trigg Way 7 IP32 . . . .48 B5
TRIMLEY LOWER
　STREET 107 C7
Trimley Marshes Nature
　Reserve★ IP11 . . . . .107 B6
Trimley Rd IP10 . . . . . .98 D2
TRIMLEY ST
　MARTIN 107 D8
Trimley St Martin Prim
　Sch IP11 . . . . .98 D1
TRIMLEY ST MARY . . .152 C8
Trimley St Mary Prim Sch
　IP11 . . . . .152 C8
Trimley Sta IP11 . . . . .152 C7
Trinity Ave
　Felixstowe IP11 . . . . . .152 B3
　Mildenhall IP28 . . . . . .116 C5
Trinity CE VA Prim Sch
　IP14 . . . . .124 F3
Trinity CI
　Fordham CB7 . . . . .29 B1
　Ipswich IP5 . . . . .140 F7
　28 Manningtree CO11 .104 E2
　16 Southwold IP18 . . .119 D5
　Woodbridge IP12 . . . .146 D3
Trinity Distribution Pk
　IP11 . . . . .152 B4
Trinity Dr 8 IP2 . . . . .121 B2
Trinity Gdns 3
　NR35 . . . . .110 B4
Trinity Gild 7 CO10 . . .78 D4
Trinity Link CB9 . . . . .132 E7
Trinity Mews NR33 . . .154 A3
Trinity Rd
　Lowestoft NR32 . . . . . .113 E1
　Manningtree CO11 . . . .104 E2
Trinity St
　Bungay NR35 . . . . .110 B4
　Rose Hill IP3 . . . . .139 E4
　15 Southwold IP18 . . .119 D5
Trinity Wlk IP14 . . . . . .67 A7
Triple Plea La NR35 . . . .7 B8
Triple Plea Rd NR35 . . .7 B8
Troon CI 5 IP14 . . . . .136 B1
Troon Gdns 3 IP4 . . .136 B1
Trossachs The 1
　NR32 . . . . .112 D2
TROSTON 33 D5
Troston Mount
　(Tumulus)★
　IP31 . . . . .33 D5
Troston Rd
　Great Livermere IP31 . . .33 D2
　Honington IP31 . . . . . . .33 E5
Trotting Horse La
　CB8 . . . . .75 A8
Trott's La CO10 . . . . . .92 F3
Trunch Hill
　Alburgh IP20 . . . . .7 B1
　Denton IP20 . . . . .7 A3
Trunch Rd IP20 . . . . . . .7 B2
Trundley CI CB9 . . . . .132 D7
Truro Cres IP5 . . . . . .141 A6
Truswell Terr 14
　CO11 . . . . .104 E4
Tubby Walk NR32 . . . .112 F5
TUDDENHAM 30 F2
Tuddenham Ave IP4 . .139 E7
Tuddenham Cnr IP28 . .46 E6
Tuddenham La IP5 . . .136 B2
Tuddenham Rd
　Barton Mills IP28 . . . . .116 F2
　Broom's Barn IP28 . . . .46 E6
　Ipswich IP4 . . . . .155 C4
　Tuddenham IP28 . . . . . .30 E2
　Westerfield IP4 . . . . . .136 A3
TUDDENHAM ST
　MARTIN 136 C5
Tudor Ave 1 IP22 . . . .20 B3
Tudor CE Prim Sch
　CO10 . . . . .148 C2
Tudor CI
　Chedburgh IP29 . . . . . .62 D5
　9 Framlingham IP13 . .126 C3
　Haverhill CB9 . . . . . . .132 F4
　3 Shotley Gate IP9 . . .107 A5
　Sudbury CO10 . . . . . . .148 C2
Tudor Ct
　1 Occold IP23 . . . . . . .37 F1
　Westhorpe IP14 . . . . . . .51 E7
Tudor Gn CO10 . . . . . .140 C8
Tudor PI IP4 . . . . .155 C3
Tudor Rd
　5 Honington IP31 . . . . .33 D5
　11 Lowestoft NR33 . . .114 E4
Tuffen La IP22 . . . . . . .35 D8

The-Ugg 187

Tuffields Rd IP29 . . . . .63 B3
Tuffs Rd IP23 . . . . . . .117 D4
Tulip Way 12 IP28 . . . .46 A8
Tumbril La IP21 . . . . . .22 A3
Tunbeck CI IP20 . . . . . .23 A7
Tunbeck Rd IP20 . . . . .23 A8
Tunbridge CI 4 CB5 . . .44 A5
Tunneys La NR35 . . . .110 C3
Tuns La IP33 . . . . .154 C1
TUNSTALL 71 F2
Tunstall Dr NR32 . . . .112 F4
Tunstall Gn IP12 . . . . .71 F2
Tunstall Rd
　Campsea Ashe IP13 . . .71 D2
　Tunstall IP12 . . . . .72 A3
　Tunstall IP12 . . . . .72 E2
Turing Ct IP5 . . . . . . .141 E7
Turino Ave IP12 . . . . . .98 B8
Turin St IP2 . . . . .155 B1
Turin Way 2 NR31 . . . .3 C6
Turkentine CI 14
　CO10 . . . . .92 B3
Turkeyhall La IP14 . . . .51 F6
Turnberry CI 3
　NR33 . . . . .114 F4
Turnberry Dr 11 IP28 . .46 C6
Turnbull CI IP5 . . . . . .141 E7
Turner Ave 1 CO11 . . .104 D2
Turner CI
　15 Cattawade CO11 . . .104 E4
　Ditchingham NR35 . . . .110 C7
　Haverhill CB9 . . . . . . .132 B7
　4 Lowestoft NR32 . . . .113 C1
　Sudbury CO10 . . . . . . .148 E8
Turner Gdns IP21 . . . .146 D3
Turner Gr IP5 . . . . . . .141 D8
Turner La 4 IP14 . . . . .51 C1
Turner Rd
　Ipswich IP3 . . . . .144 A8
　Stowmarket IP14 . . . . .124 B7
Turn La IP13 . . . . .147 A4
Turnpike Ct 3 IP14 . . .124 F7
Turnpike Hill CB9 . . . . .74 B2
Turnpike La 5 IP28 . . .45 F8
Turnpike Rd
　Chippenham CB8 . . . . . .45 F8
　Red Lodge IP28 . . . . . .30 B1
　Woodbridge IP12 . . . .147 B6
Turnstile La 7 NR35 . .110 B4
Turnstone CI 2
　IP28 . . . . .116 D4
Turnstone Dr 5 IP32 . .49 A3
Turret La IP4 . . . . .155 B2
Tutelina Rd IP30 . . . . . .64 A6
Tut Hill
　Bury St Edmunds
　　IP32 . . . . .122 B8
　Fornham All Saints
　　IP28 . . . . .48 B5
Tutt Hill (Tumulus)★
　IP24 . . . . .16 D4
Tuyar Wlk CB8 . . . . . .120 E8
Tweed CI CB8 . . . . . . .45 F3
Twelve Acre App
　IP5 . . . . .141 B7
Twinnings The IP14 . .124 C3
Twin Oak Dr IP13 . . . .56 B7
Twiss CI 5 IP22 . . . . . .20 A3
Twites Corner IP29 . . . .47 D2
Two Acres IP9 . . . . . .150 F4
Two House CI IP13 . . .127 C4
Two Pole Dro CB7 . . . .28 A7
Two Village CE Prim Sch
　CO12 . . . . .106 D1
Tydeman CI 3 IP4 . . . .139 E7
Tydemans Ct 1
　IP14 . . . . .124 D6
Tyefield PI IP7 . . . . . .149 C6
Tye Gn CO10 . . . . .77 A3
Tye Green
　Alpheton CO10 . . . . . . .78 A5
　Haverhill CB9 . . . . .81 A7
Tye Green Paddock 18
　CO10 . . . . .77 A3
Tye La IP8 . . . . .81 D2
Tye Rd
　Bell's Corner CO6 . . . .102 D8
　Brent Eleigh CO10 . . . .79 B3
　Ipswich IP3 . . . . .139 E4
Tyes Corner IP13 . . . . .54 D6
Tye Went CO10 . . . . . .93 A6
Tylers Gn IP11 . . . . . .152 C7
Tyler St
　3 Harwich CO12 . . . . .106 F3
　Ipswich IP2 . . . . .155 B1
Tylers Way 1 IP14 . . .124 C8
Tymmes PI IP13 . . . . .146 C8
Tynan Cres IP14 . . . . .124 B8
Tyndale Gdns IP11 . . .153 C5
Tyrone CI IP1 . . . . . . .134 D2

U

UBBESTON 40 E4
UDDESTON GREEN 40 D3
Ubbeston Way NR33 . .114 F4
UFFORD 84 F7
Ufford PI
　Haverhill CB9 . . . . . . .132 F4
　8 Ufford IP13 . . . . . . .84 F7
Ufford Rd
　Bredfield IP13 . . . . .84 D7
　Eyke IP12 . . . . .85 B6
UGGESHALL 25 F3

Uggeshall Cl NR32 . . . 113 A5
Uggeshall Rd NR34. . . .26 C4
Ullswater NR33 . . . . . . 114 D2
Ullswater Ave 4
　IP11. . . . . 153 D7
Ullswater Rd IP12. . . . .71 C2
Ulster Ave IP1 . . . . . . 134 D1
Una Rd CO12. . . . . 106 F2
Uncle's La IP19 . . . . . . .24 B6
Undercliff Rd E IP11 153 C4
Undercliff Rd W
　IP11. . . . . 153 A3
Underhill IP14. . . . . . 124 C5
Underwood Cl NR32. 113 A6
Underwood Rd CB8. . .59 D4
UNDLEY 13 C4
Undley IP27 . . . . 109 B5
Undley Rd IP27 . . . . . 109 B4
Unicorn Pl
　Bury St Edmunds
　IP33 . . . . 123 C6
　7 Stowmarket IP14. 124 E5
Union Hill IP7 . . . . . . .94 A8
Union La
　Lowestoft NR32 . . . . 112 E5
　Lowestoft NR32 . . . . 112 F5
　Wortham IP22 . . . . . . .20 A1
Union Pl N R33. . . . . . 115 C7
Union Rd
　Lowestoft NR32 . . . . 113 C1
　Onehouse IP14. . . . . . .66 C6
　Stowmarket IP14. . . . 124 A7
Union St E IP14 . . . . . 124 D6
Union St W IP14 . . . . 124 D6
Union St IP4. . . . . 155 C3
**Unitarian Meeting
　House**★
　Bury St Edmunds
　IP33 . . . . 154 B2
　Ipswich IP1 . . . . 155 B2
Unity Rd IP14. . . . . . . 124 D5
Unity St IP3 . . . . 139 E4
University Ave 1
　IP3. . . . . 139 E5
**Univ of Suffolk (Campus
　North)** IP3 . . . . 139 E5
**Univ of Suffolk
　(Waterfront Bldg)**
　IP3 . . . . 139 E5
Unwin Cl CO9. . . . . . . .90 B2
Upcher Cl IP26 . . . . 4 E5
UPEND 60 F5
Upend Rd CB8. . . . . . . .60 F4
UPGATE ST NR35. . . . . .7 B6
UPGATE STREET 7 B6
Upland Hall Farm Rd
　NR34. . . . . 8 A2
Upland Rd IP4. . . . . . 140 A6
Uplands Cl NR33. . . . 114 D4
Uplands Cres CO10. . 148 C7
Uplands Rd
　3 Aldringham cum Thorpe
　IP16. . . . . .73 F6
　Sudbury CO10. . . . . . 148 C7
Uplands Rd N NR33 . 114 D5
Uplands Rd S NR33 . 114 C3
Uplands The
　Aldringham cum Thorpe
　IP16. . . . . .73 F6
　Beccles NR34. . . . . . 111 D4
Uplands Way
　Diss IP22 . . . . .20 C3
　Halesworth IP19 . . . . 118 B5
Upland Terr IP20 . . . . . .7 A4
Upper Ave IP19 . . . . . 118 B5
Upper Barclay St
　IP4. . . . . 155 C2
Upper Brook La IP20. .22 B4
Upper Brook St IP4 . 155 B3
Upper Burnthouse La
　IP20. . . . . .22 A5
Upper Cavendish St
　IP3. . . . . 140 A3
Upper E St CO10 . . . . 148 C6
Upper Farm Rd CO10. .89 E4
Upperfield Dr IP11. . 153 C6
Upper Grange Rd
　NR34 . . . . 111 A4
UPPER GREEN 46 E3
Upper Green
　Mount Bures CO6 . . . . 101 B2
　Stoke by Clare CO10. . .89 D6
　Upper Green IP28. . . . .46 E3
Upper Hall Rd CO9 . . .90 C1
Upper Harmans La
　IP20. . . . . .22 B5
Upper High St IP1 . . 155 B4
UPPER HOLTON 118 E7
Upper Holton IP19. . 118 E6
UPPER LAYHAM 149 F2
Upper Meadow 12
　IP31. . . . . .35 C2
Upper Melton Terr 10
　IP12. . . . . .84 E6
Upper Moorfield Rd
　IP12. . . . . 146 F6
Upper North St CO10. .75 D4
Upper Oakley IP23. . 117 F8
Upper Olland St
　NR35. . . . . 110 B3
Upper Orwell Courts
　IP4. . . . . 155 C2
Upper Orwell St IP4. 155 C3
Upper Rd CO10 . . . . . 101 C8
Upper Rose La IP22 . .20 C1

Upper St La IP22. . . . . .35 C5
UPPER ST IP6. . . . . .81 E6
Upper St
　Brome Street IP23 . . . 117 F8
　Gissing IP22. . . . . .20 F8
　Higham CO7 . . . . 103 D6
　Layham IP7. . . . . 149 F1
　Stansfield CO10 . . . . . .76 C6
　Stanstead CO10 . . . . . .77 C4
　Stratford St Mary CO7 . 103 C4
　Witnesham IP6. . . . . . .83 A6
UPPER STREET
　Baylham 81 E6
　Dickleburgh and
　Rushall. 21 C7
　Stansfield 76 C6
　Stutton 105 B5
UPPER TOWN
　49 E7
　Pakenham IP31. . . . . . .49 E6
Upper Tumbril La
　IP20. . . . . .22 A4
Upper Tye CO10 . . . . . .92 C4
UPPER WEYBREAD . . .22 B2
UPSHER GREEN 92 D6
Upsons Way IP5 . . . . 141 E8
Up St IP31. . . . . .34 C4
UPTHORPE 34 F3
Upthorpe Rd IP31. . . .34 F4
Upton Cl IP4. . . . . 139 E6
Upton Pl IP16. . . . . . . 129 C5
Upwood 35 IP27 . . . . . .13 F2
Urban Rd IP19 . . . . . . 129 D6
Uvedale Gdns IP6. . . 125 E4
Uxbridge Cres IP3 . . 140 C1

V

Vale Ct IP27 . . . . .5 E4
Vale La
　Bury St Edmunds
　IP33 . . . . 123 C3
　Kersey IP7 . . . . .94 A6
　Stutton IP9. . . . . 105 A6
Valentine Way IP30. . .64 F7
Valerian Gdns 2 CB7 .28 E3
Valerian Rise 4 IP24. .16 D6
Vale View Rd IP8 . . . . 138 B3
Valiant St 6 IP28 . . . . .13 B1
Valley Cl
　4 Brantham CO11. . . 104 E5
　Halesworth IP19 . . . . 118 E4
　Ipswich IP1 . . . . 135 C1
**Valley Farm Camargue
　Horses**★ IP13 . . . . . 127 A8
Valley Farm La IP7. . . .94 E5
Valley Farm Rd
　Melton IP12 . . . . 147 B8
　Orford IP12 . . . . .87 B8
Valley Farm Vineyards★
　IP19. . . . . .24 C2
Valley Gdns IP16. . . . 129 D6
Valley Green CO8 . . . . 101 B3
Valley La
　Battisford IP14. . . . . . .80 F8
　Buxhall IP14. . . . . .65 F3
　Shimpling IP21. . . . . . .21 A6
　Wherstead IP9. . . . . . 143 A3
Valley Rd
　Battisford IP14. . . . . . .66 E1
　Chilton CO10. . . . . . . .92 C5
　Great Brickett IP7 . . . . .80 D6
　Harwich CO12 . . . . . . 102 E1
　Ipswich IP1 . . . . 135 B1
　Leiston IP16. . . . . 129 E6
　Little Blakenham IP8 . . .81 E4
　Wickham Market IP13 127 A8
Valley View CO10 . . . . .77 C4
Valleyview Dr IP4. . . 140 F4
Valley View Dr 16 IP6 .82 A5
Valley View Rd IP13. . .40 C3
Valley Wash CO10. . . . .75 D4
Valley Way CB8 . . . . . 120 E3
Valley Wlk IP11. . . . . 152 F5
Vallibus Cl 5 NR32 . . 112 E4
Vance Cl IP19 . . . . 118 C6
Van Dyck Cl 9 NR32 . 113 B6
Vandyck Rd 7 IP3 . . . 144 A8
Vanners Rd CB9 . . . . . 132 E5
Vansittart St 9
　CO12. . . . . 107 B3
Vaughan St IP2. . . . . 155 B1
Vaunces La IP21 . . . . . .21 E4
Vaunce's La IP21 . . . . .21 E4
Vaux Ave 15 CO12. . . 106 F1
Velda Cl NR33 . . . . . . 114 F4
Ventris Cl IP2 . . . . . . 138 D5
Venture Rd
　Badwell Ash IP31. . . . . .50 F7
　Woolpit IP30. . . . . .50 E1
Verdons La IP21 . . . . . .39 E4
Verdure Cl 27 NR32 . 112 F5
Vere Gdns IP1 . . . . . . 135 C2
Vermeer Cl 5 NR32. . 113 B6
Vermont Cres IP4. . . 155 C4
Vermont Rd IP4 . . . . 155 C4
Verna St 4 IP32 . . . . . .48 B5
Verneuil Ave IP14 . . 124 D3
Vernon St IP2 . . . . . . 155 B1
Verow Rd IP13. . . . . . 126 D2
Vetch Wlk CB9. . . . . . 132 B7
Veyses End 6 CO7 . . . 103 E5
Viburnum Gn NR32. . 113 C2
Vicarage Cl CB8 . . . . . .59 E6
Vicarage Field CO10 148 F3
Vicarage Gdns
　16 Debenham IP14. . . .53 F2

Vicarage Gdns continued
　4 Mildenhall IP28. . . 116 B4
Vicarage Hill 7
　IP12. . . . . 147 A5
Vicarage La
　Acton CO10. . . . . .92 A6
　Acton CO10. . . . . .92 B7
　Assington CO10 . . . . . .92 F1
　Bramford IP8 . . . . 134 B1
　Bungay NR35 . . . . 110 E3
　Wherstead IP9 . . . . . . 143 B5
　Woodditton CB8. . . . . .60 B6
Vicarage Rd
　Belchamp St Paul
　CO10 . . . . .90 D5
　Felixstowe IP11 . . . . . 152 D4
　Laxfield IP13. . . . . .40 B3
　Newmarket CB8 . . . . . 121 B3
　Thetford IP24. . . . . . . .16 C6
　Wingfield IP21. . . . . . . .39 A8
　Winston IP14. . . . . .69 A8
Vicars Orchard CO10. .91 C3
Vicary Estate CO10. . .92 F1
Victor Charles Cl IP27. . .5 E3
Victoria Cl
　11 Diss IP22 . . . . .20 D2
　5 Thurstow IP31. . . . . .49 E4
　Weston Ditch IP28. . . . .29 F7
Victoria Cres 2
　CO11. . . . . 104 E2
Victoria Gdns
　Needham Market
　IP6. . . . . 125 D5
　Wattisfield IP22 . . . . . .35 D5
Victoria Hill IP23 . . . 117 C4
Victoria Mews CB7. . .29 B1
Victoria Mill Rd
　IP13. . . . . 126 B2
Victoria Rd
　Aldeburgh IP15 . . . . . 130 E4
　Diss IP22 . . . . .20 D2
　Felixstowe IP11. . . . . 152 F3
　Haverhill CB9 . . . . . . 132 B5
　1 Lowestoft NR33. . . 114 E7
　Stowmarket IP14. . . . 124 E7
　Woodbridge IP12. . . . 147 A5
Victoria Row IP27. . . . .13 F1
Victoria St
　Bury St Edmunds
　IP33 . . . . 154 A2
　Felixstowe IP11 . . . . . 153 A4
　7 Harwich CO12 . . . . 107 B2
　Ipswich IP1 . . . . 139 A6
　13 Southwold IP18. . . 119 D5
Victoria Terr
　3 Fressingfield IP21. . .39 E8
　Lowestoft NR33 . . . . . 115 D7
Victoria Way CB8 . . . 120 E7
Victory Cl IP33. . . . . . 123 C2
Victory Ct IP11 . . . . . 124 D4
Victory Rd
　Ipswich IP4 . . . . 140 A7
　Leiston IP16 . . . . 129 C5
Victory Way 6 IP14 . .70 D7
View Point Rd IP11 153 H10
Viking Cl
　Little Green IP23 . . . . . .36 C2
　Martlesham IP12 . . . . . .84 B1
Viking Hts IP12. . . . . . .84 B1
Viking Rd IP14. . . . . . 124 C5
Vikings Cl IP29 . . . . . . .64 A3
Village Way
　Lowestoft NR32 . . . . . 113 B5
　Waldringfield IP12. . . .98 D7
Villa Hill IP12. . . . . .99 B7
Villiers Way 10 IP27. . . . .5 E4
Vincent Cl
　Exning CB8 . . . . 120 E7
　7 Feltwell IP26. . . . . . . .4 E5
　Ipswich IP1 . . . . 138 E4
Vincent Drift IP5. . . . 141 F7
Vince's Rd IP22. . . . . . .20 D2
Vine Cl IP31. . . . . .17 E1
Vinefields The IP33 . 154 C2
Vine Rd IP6 . . . . .69 C2
Vinery Cl IP13 . . . . . . 127 C6
Vinery Rd IP33. . . . . . 122 F3
Vinesse Rd CO10. . . . 102 B2
Vines The IP17 . . . . . . 128 D7
Vineway The 2
　CO12. . . . . 107 A2
Vine Wlk IP9 . . . . 150 E3
Violet Cl
　Bury St Edmunds
　IP32. . . . . 123 F5
　Ipswich IP2 . . . . 138 F4
Violet Hill IP14 . . . . . . .53 B6
Violet Hill Rd IP14 . . . .53 B6
Virginia Rd 11 IP28. . . .30 A8
Virginia St IP21 . . . . . 139 D3
Viscount Cl 1 IP22 . . .20 E2
Vyces Rd IP13 . . . . . . 126 B3

W

Wacker Field Rd 8
　IP12. . . . . .85 E8
Waddesdon Rd 5
　CO12. . . . . 107 B2
Wadd La IP17. . . . . .72 C6
Waddlegoose La IP14 54 D2
Waddling La NR32 . . 112 A7
Wade Cres CO10 . . . . . .92 C4
Wadehall La NR34. . . .10 B5
Wadehall New Dam
　NR34 . . . . .10 C5

Wadehall Old Dam
　NR34. . . . . .10 C5
Wades Gr IP5. . . . . . . 141 E7
Wade's La IP10 . . . . . 145 C2
Wade's La
　Raydon IP7. . . . . .94 E1
　Shotley IP9. . . . . 106 E7
Wades Wood 1 IP30. .50 E1
Wadgate Rd IP11 . . . 152 E4
Wadhurst Rd IP3 . . . . 140 D3
Waggoners Ct IP12 . . 146 F5
Wagstaff Cl IP9. . . . . . 105 F8
Wagtail Dr
　2 Bury St Edmunds
　IP32. . . . . .49 A3
　Bury St Edmunds IP32. 123 F7
Wagtail Rd IP17 . . . . 124 F7
Wagtail Way IP24 . . . .16 C4
WAINFORD 110 D5
Wainford Cl 5 NR34 . . .9 F4
Wainford Rd NR35 . . 110 E5
Wainwright Cl 4
　NR32. . . . . 113 A6
Wainwright Gdns 3
　IP6. . . . . .81 F5
Wainwright Way
　IP5. . . . . 141 D8
Wake Ave IP28 . . . . . 116 C5
Wakelin Cl 21 CO10 . .92 B3
Wakes Colne Rd
　CO6. . . . . 101 A1
Wakeshall La CO10. . . .90 B4
WALBERSWICK 119 A2
Walberswick Rd IP19 .42 F5
Walberswick Way 8
　NR32. . . . . 113 A3
WALCOT GREEN 20 D4
Walcot Grn IP22 . . . . . .20 D3
Walcot Rd IP22 . . . . . . .20 D3
Walcot Rise IP22. . . . . .20 D3
Walcott Wlk IP28. . . . 115 B5
Waldegrave Ave
　CO11. . . . . 104 D2
Waldegrave Cl 29
　CO11. . . . . 104 D2
Waldingfield Rd
　10 Acton CO10. . . . . . .92 B7
　Acton CO10. . . . . .92 C7
　Chilton CO10. . . . . . . 148 F8
　Lindsey IP7 . . . . .93 C7
　1 Sudbury CO10 . . . . 148 F8
　Upsher Green CO10 . . . .92 E6
WALDRINGFIELD
　HEATH. 98 C7
Waldringfield Prim Sch
　IP12 . . . . .98 D7
Waldringfield Rd
　Ipswich IP10 . . . . .98 B7
　Martlesham IP12 . . . . . .84 C1
WALES END 76 D4
Wales End Rd CO10 . . .76 D3
Walkbarn Farm Rd
　IP17. . . . . .58 C7
Walkbarn La IP11. . . . .98 C1
Walk Barn Rd IP10 . . 145 D7
Walker Chase IP5. . . . 141 C6
Walker Cl IP4. . . . . . . 140 C5
Walker Gdns NR34. . . .26 E5
Walks The NR34 . . . . . .10 A8
Walk The
　Bacton IP14 . . . . .51 D5
　Beccles NR34. . . . . . . 111 B6
　Ipswich IP1 . . . . 155 B3
　Walton IP11. . . . . 152 E6
Wallace Rd IP1 . . . . . 138 E8
Walled Gdn The★
　IP17. . . . . .72 B8
Waller's Gr IP2 . . . . . 138 F4
Wall La CO11 . . . . 105 E2
Wallow La IP7 . . . . .80 D4
Wall St IP5 . . . . 141 F7
Walls The CO11 . . . . . 104 E2
Walmer Cl NR33. . . . . 115 A5
Walmer Rd NR33. . . . . 115 A5
Walne Cl IP13 . . . . . . 126 C2
Walnut Cl
　Acton CO10. . . . . .92 B8
　Felixstowe IP11 . . . . . 153 D7
　Hopton IP22. . . . . .18 C1
　13 Lakenheath IP27. . .13 F2
Walnut Gr IP28 . . . . . . .30 A4
Walnutree Cl IP31. . . . .50 B4
Walnuts La IP13 . . . . 127 B5
Walnuts The
　Beccles NR34. . . . . . . 111 E4
　8 Ufford IP13 . . . . .84 F7
Walnut Tree Cl
　4 Bramford IP8. . . . . 134 A2
　18 Stowmarket IP14. . .67 A6
Walnut Tree Cottages
　CB8 . . . . .59 F2
Walnut Tree La
　Burstall IP8 . . . . .95 D7
　2 Harkstead IP9. . . . 106 A5
　Sudbury CO10. . . . . . 148 B5
Walnut Tree Meadow
　IP14. . . . . .68 B6
Walnut Tree Wlk
　IP14. . . . . 124 C6
WALPOLE 41 C5
Walpole Bridge Rd
　IP19. . . . . .41 D6
Walpole Cl NR35. . . . . 110 D7
Walpole La IP19 . . . . . .41 D5
Walpole Rd
　Bramfield IP19 . . . . . . .41 E4

Walpole Rd continued
　Cookley IP19 . . . . .41 B5
　Halesworth IP19 . . . . 118 A1
**WALSHAM LE
　WILLOWS** 35 C2
**Walsham Le Willows CE
　VC Prim Sch** IP31 . 35 C2
Walsham Rd
　Finningham IP14 . . . . . .36 A1
　6 Ixworth IP31. . . . . . .34 B1
　Wattisfield IP22 . . . . . .35 C3
　Westhorpe IP14 . . . . . .51 D7
Walsh Rise CO6. . . . . . 102 C5
Walsingham Cl 11
　CO10 . . . . .92 B3
Walsingham Rd
　IP33. . . . . 122 D3
Walters Cl 9 NR31. . . . .3 B7
Waltham Cl IP2. . . . . . 139 A2
WALTON. 152 F6
Walton Ave IP11 . . . . 152 C3
Walton Cl
　5 Fordham CB7. . . . . .29 A1
　1 Stowmarket IP14. . .124 B8
Walton Hall Dr IP11. 152 D6
Walton Rd NR32. . . . . 113 D1
Waltons CO9 . . . . 133 E1
Wamil Rd IP28. . . . . . . .30 B5
Wamil Way IP28 . . . . 116 B4
Wamil Wlk IP28 . . . . 116 B3
WANGFORD 26 B2
Wangford Rd
　Cox Common IP19 . . . . .25 A6
　Lakenheath IP27 . . . . . .13 F7
　Reydon IP18 . . . . .26 D1
　Southwold IP18 . . . . . 119 B8
　Uggeshall NR34 . . . . . .26 A3
　Westhall IP19. . . . . . . .25 B4
Wannock Cl NR33. . . . 114 D4
Wantisden Cnr IP12. . .86 A6
Wantisden Rd IP12 . . .85 F7
Warbler Way 10 IP14 124 F6
Ward Cl IP7 . . . . 149 D8
WARD GREEN 51 E3
Wardlaw Cl 10 IP14 . 153 F2
Wardle Cl 18 CO11 . . 104 E4
Wardley Cl IP2 . . . . . 138 D1
Wardley Hill Rd NR35. .8 B8
Ward Rd IP6. . . . . 138 B2
Ward's View IP5. . . . . 141 E8
Wareham Ave IP3 . . . 140 D3
Warene Cl 3 IP13 . . . 126 C3
Ware Rd IP7. . . . . .80 B6
Warham Rd CO12 . . . 106 F1
Warner Rise CO10 . . . . .92 F1
Warner Way CO10. . . 148 E6
Warnes Meadow IP13 54 E5
Warren Ave IP17. . . . 128 D3
Warren Chase IP5 . . . 141 E7
Warren Cl
　Badwell Ash IP31. . . . . .50 F7
　Elmswell IP30. . . . . . . .50 E2
　Lakenheath IP27 . . . . 109 D5
Warren Ct 14 CO12 . . 132 C5
Warreners Reach
　IP27. . . . . 109 D4
WARREN HEATH 140 F1
Warren Heath Ave
　IP3. . . . . 140 D2
Warren Heath Rd
　IP3. . . . . 140 D2
Warren Hill La IP15 . 130 D7
Warren Hill Rd IP12. . 146 E4
Warren Hills IP21. . . . .37 E8
Warren La
　Arwarton IP9 . . . . . . 106 D6
　Elmswell IP30. . . . . . . .50 E2
　27 Martlesham Heath
　IP5. . . . . .98 A8
　Woolpit IP30. . . . . .50 F1
Warren Loke NR31. . . . .2 B7
Warren Rd
　Feltwell IP26 . . . . .5 A7
　Great Yarmouth NR31. . .3 B8
　Herringswell CB8. . . . . .46 A8
　Hopton on Sea NR31. . . .3 C7
　Lowestoft NR32 . . . . . 113 D4
　Red Lodge IP28 . . . . . . .30 C1
Warren Sch NR33. . . . 114 C6
Warrens La 3 IP22 . . . .36 A6
Warren's La NR34. . . . .10 A2
Warren The IP18. . . . . 119 E8
Warrington Rd IP1. . . 155 A4
Warrington St CB8. . . 121 A2
Warwick Ave
　Halesworth IP19 . . . . 118 C5
　Woodbridge IP12 . . . . 146 F6
Warwick Cl 10 CB9. . 132 C6
Warwick Rd IP4 . . . . . 139 E6
WASHBROOK 95 F5
Washbrook Rd
　Chattisham IP8. . . . . . .95 D4
　Washbrook Street IP8 . .95 E5
**WASHBROOK
　STREET** 95 F6
Washington Cl IP2. . . 139 D3
Washington St 4
　IP28. . . . . .30 A8
Wash La
　Beccles NR34. . . . . . . 111 B2
　Boxford CO6. . . . . .93 D2
　Burgh St Peter NR34. . . .10 C8
　Frostenden NR34. . . . . .26 C3
　Great Finborough
　IP14 . . . . 124 A5
　Hinderclay IP22 . . . . . .35 E8
　Kessingland NR33. . . . .11 C1
　Mendlesham IP14 . . . . .52 E3

Wash La continued
　Redgrave IP22 . . . . . . .19 D1
　Reydon IP18 . . . . .26 D2
　St Peter, South Elmham
　NR35 . . . . .23 F7
　Shelfanger IP22 . . . . . .20 B6
　Sibton IP17. . . . . .56 F8
　Spexhall IP19 . . . . 118 A7
　Stanton IP31. . . . . .34 F3
　Thorpe Morieux IP30 . . .79 A7
　Topcroft NR35. . . . . . . .7 A8
　Wenhaston with Mells
　Hamlet IP19. . . . . . . 118 E1
　Westleton IP17. . . . . . .58 B8
　Wickhambrook CB8. . . .61 E1
　Witnesham IP6. . . . . . .83 A6
　Wrentham NR34. . . . . .26 E2
WASHMERE GREEN . . .78 D2
Wassicks La IP14 . . . . .51 E3
Watch House Hill
　NR35. . . . . 110 E4
Waterbeach Rd IP12. .85 D3
Watercourse The
　CB8 . . . . 121 A4
Water Farm Dr IP7. . . .94 C1
Waterford Rd IP1. . . . 134 D2
Waterhall Rd
　Haverhill CO9 . . . . . . 133 F1
　Wixoe CO10 . . . . .89 B5
Waterhead La IP12 . . 147 D8
Watering Cl 1 IP8. . . .81 C3
Watering La IP17 . . . . .72 C7
Watering Rd IP21. . . . .38 D5
Water La
　Athelington IP21. . . . . .38 F1
　Barnardiston IP29 . . . . .75 B4
　Barnham IP24 . . . . .16 C2
　Botesdale IP22. . . . . . . .35 F5
　3 Bures CO8 . . . . 101 C5
　Cavendish CO10 . . . . . .76 E1
　Debenham IP14 . . . . . . .53 F2
　Denston CB8. . . . . .75 F7
　Garboldisham IP22. . . . .18 D4
　Great Bradley CB8. . . . .74 C8
　Great Horkesley CO6 . 102 C5
　Great Whelnetham
　IP30. . . . . .64 A6
　Hadleigh IP7. . . . . 149 A8
　Helions Bumpstead CB9 88 B4
　Hornecreet CO4 . . . . . 103 C4
　Kersey IP7. . . . . .94 A6
　Kettlebaston IP7 . . . . . .79 C4
　Kirtling Green CB8 . . . . .60 D2
　Layham IP7 . . . . 149 E1
　Long Melford CO10. . . . .91 E7
　Lowestoft NR32 . . . . . 113 C2
　Monks Eleigh IP7 . . . . . .79 C3
　Polstead CO6 . . . . 102 F8
　Steeple Bumpstead
　CB9. . . . . .88 D3
　Sturmer CB9. . . . . 133 D3
　Thelnetham IP22 . . . . . .18 E1
　Thorndon IP23 . . . . . . .53 A8
　Thornham Magna IP23. .37 A1
　Weybread IP21. . . . . . . .22 D4
　Worlingworth IP13. . . . .54 D3
WATERLOO
　Aldeby 9 E8
　Beccles NR34. . . . . .9 E8
　Dickleburgh and Rushall 20 F2
Waterloo Ave
　Leiston IP16 . . . . 129 B6
　4 Roydon IP22 . . . . . .20 A3
Waterloo Cl CB8 . . . . 120 D8
Waterloo Mws IP16 . 129 C6
Waterloo Rd
　4 Ipswich IP1. . . . . . 139 E4
　Lowestoft NR33 . . . . . 115 D7
　Sotterley NR34. . . . . . .26 A7
Watermill Cl IP7. . . . 149 E2
Watermill Farm La
　IP19. . . . . .42 B7
Watermill La IP21. . . . .22 C4
Water Mill La IP21 . . . .38 C8
Watermill Rd IP13 . . . .98 C5
Water Run The IP7. . . .79 F7
Waters Ave NR33 . . . 114 C3
Waters Edge 6 CB9. . 132 D7
Waterside
　Burwell CB5 . . . . .44 A7
　Isleham CB7. . . . . .29 C5
Waterside Dr NR35. . 110 C6
Water Steet CO10. . . . .78 D4
Water Tower La IP22. .19 F6
Water Vole IP14 . . . . 124 E4
Waterworks Rd 12
　IP28. . . . . .30 A8
Waterworks St IP4. . . 155 C2
Watery La IP13 . . . . . 146 A8
Watson Cl IP33 . . . . . 123 B2
Watson Pl 8 CB9 . . . . .74 A1
Watsons Cl 3 NR31. . . .3 C7
Watson's Hill IP7 . . . . .79 F1
Watsons Way 19 IP29 .47 A2
Watson Way IP12. . . . . .99 E4
Watt Cl IP12 . . . . .99 E4
WATTISFIELD 35 D5
Wattisfield Rd
　Thorpe Street IP22. . . . .35 D7
　Walsham le Willows
　IP31. . . . . .35 C2
WATTISHAM 80 B6
Wattisham Airfield
　IP7. . . . . .80 C6
Wattisham Airfield Mus★
　IP7 . . . . .80 C6
Wattisham Rd
　Bildeston IP7 . . . . .79 F4

Wattisham Rd continued
Charles Tye IP14 . . . . . . .80 D7
WATTISHAM STONE . . .80 A6
Watts Cl 18 IP32 . . . . . .48 B5
Watts Ct IP4 . . . . 155 C2
Waveney Cl 3 IP17 . 128 C4
Waveney Cres NR33 . .115 B7
Waveney Dr NR33 . . . 115 A4
Waveney Hill
  Carlton Colville
    NR32 . . . . .114 B8
  Lowestoft NR32 . . . . .112 B1
Waveney Hts IP21 . . . .21 F2
Waveney Rd
  Beccles NR34 . . . . . . .111 B4
  Bungay NR35 . . . . 110 D3
  10 Bury St Edmunds
    IP32 . . . . .48 C5
  9 Diss IP22 . . . . .20 D2
  Ditchingham NR35 . . . 110 C8
  Felixstowe IP11 . . . . . .152 E3
  Ipswich IP1 . . . . .138 E8
  10 Lowestoft NR32 . . . 115 D8
Waveney Sports &
  Leisure Ctr NR32 . . 113 C3
Waveney Terr 4
  CB9 . . . . .132 E5
Waveney Valley
  Swimming Pool
    NR35 . . . . 110 D2
Waverley Pl 5 IP29 . .63 D1
Way Bank La
  Kedington CO10 . . . . .115 E7
  Stoke-by-Clare CO9 . . . .89 C7
Wayne Cl NR32 . . . . . .113 B5
Wayside Cl IP14 . . . . .124 D3
Weald The NR32 . . . . .112 E2
Weatheralls Cl 9
  CB7 . . . . .28 D4
Weatheralls Prim Sch
  The CB7 . . . . 28 D4
Weathercock Farm Rd
  CB9 . . . . .75 A4
Weaver Cl IP1 . . . . . . 138 D8
Weavers Cl
  2 Hadleigh IP7 . . . . .149 D6
  4 Lavenham CO10 . . . .78 D4
  Stowmarket IP14 . . . . .124 C3
Weavers Croft 8
  IP20 . . . . .22 D6
Weavers Ct
  13 Diss IP22 . . . . .20 C3
  12 Sudbury CO10 . . . . 148 C5
Weavers Dr 6 CO10 . .77 A2
Weavers La
  18 Fornham St Martin
    IP32 . . . . .48 B5
  Sudbury CO10 . . . . . . .148 C5
Weavers Marsh La
  IP17 . . . . .41 E2
Weavers Way 2 IP6 . .82 A5
Webb Cl CB9 . . . . .132 F8
Webb Ct IP33 . . . . . . .123 D3
Webb Rd IP14 . . . . . . .124 D3
Webb's Cl IP14 . . . . . .124 C1
Webbs Ct IP5 . . . . . . .141 C7
Webb St 1 IP12 . . . . . 139 C3
Webbs Way 6 IP26 . . .5 A3
Webster St NR35 . . . . 110 A4
Weddell Rd CB9 . . . . .133 A4
WEETING 5 E3
Weeting Castle ★ IP27 .5 E4
Weeting Heath Nature
  Reserve ★ NR35 . . . .5 C3
Weeting Heath Visitor
  Ctr ★ IP27 . . . . .6 C1
Weeting VC Prim Sch
  IP27 . . . . .5 E3
Weir Pl IP10 . . . . .98 D2
Weirs Dro CB5 . . . . . . .44 A6
Welbeck Cl
  Felixstowe IP11 . . . . . .152 C7
  North Grove NR34 . . . . .10 C4
Welbourne Way NR34 . 10 C4
Welch Cl NR34 . . . . . . .10 D3
Welham Cl 6 IP14 . . .51 C1
Welham La IP28 . . . . . .47 D5
Well Cl Sq IP13 . . . . . .126 C3
Wellesley Rd IP3 . . . . .139 F5
Wellington Cl
  Chedburgh IP29 . . . . . .62 D4
  Hadleigh IP7 . . . . .149 D7
  Thistley Green IP28 . . . .30 A6
Wellington Espl
  NR33 . . . . 115 C6
Wellington Rd
  Eye IP23 . . . . .117 D3
  4 Feltwell IP26 . . . . . .4 E5
  6 Harwich CO12 . . . . .107 C3
  2 Lowestoft NR33 . . . 115 A3
  8 Mildenhall IP28 . . . .30 A8
Wellington St
  7 Ipswich IP1 . . . . . . 139 A7
  1 Newmarket CB8 . . . .121 A3
Wellington Terr 5
  CB9 . . . . .132 C5
Well La
  9 Clare CO10 . . . . . . .90 A8
  Hulver Street NR34 . . . .10 B2
Wells Cl IP4 . . . . .139 E6
Wells Cnr IP13 . . . . . . .39 F2
Wells Ct IP28 . . . . . . .116 B5
Wells Hall Com Prim Sch
  CO10 . . . . .148 F3
Wells Hall Rd CO10 . . .148 F3
Wells' La IP20 . . . . .22 D5
Wells Rd IP20 . . . . .22 C5

Well St IP33 . . . . .154 B2
Wells Way IP14 . . . . . . .53 F1
Wellum Cl 13 CB9 . . . .132 C5
Wembley Ave NR34 . . .111 B4
Wemsey'S La CO8 . . . .101 F7
Wendy Cl 7 IP9 . . . . . 106 C8
Wenfran Meadow IP7 79 E6
Wenham La
  East Bergholt CO7 . . . .151 D8
  Wenham Magna CO7 . . .150 A2
Wenham Rd
  Copdock & Washbrook
    IP8 . . . . .150 E8
  Great Wenham CO7 . . .150 C3
  Little Wenham IP9 . . . .150 C5
WENHASTON 42 C6
Wenhaston La IP19 . . .42 D5
Wenhaston Prim Sch
  IP19 . . . . .42 C6
Wenhaston Rd IP19 . . .42 B5
Wenhaston Way 2
  NR32 . . . . .112 F3
Wensleydale 6
  NR33 . . . . .114 E3
Wensum Gdns NR32. 113 C3
Wentford Ct 7 CB9 . 132 A6
Wentford View 1
  CO10 . . . . .76 A1
Wentworth Cl
  14 Fornham All Saints
    IP28 . . . . .48 C6
  Hadleigh IP7 . . . . . . .149 F5
  Nettlestead IP8 . . . . . .81 D4
  Weeting IP27 . . . . .5 E4
Wentworth Dr
  Felixstowe IP11 . . . . . .153 C6
  7 Ipswich IP8 . . . . . .138 C2
  10 Mildenhall IP28 . . .116 B5
Wentworth Rd
  Aldeburgh IP15 . . . . .130 F4
  Ipswich IP3 . . . . .144 F8
Wentworth Terr 5
  CB9 . . . . .132 C6
Wentworth Way 2
  NR33 . . . . .114 F4
Wesel Ave IP11 . . . . . .152 D3
Wesley Cl NR34 . . . . .111 B2
Wesley End Rd CO9 . . .89 B2
Wesley Rd 37 CO11 . .144 E2
Wesley Way 3 IP1 . . .138 F8
West Bank La IP21 . . . .21 E1
West Bar 16 IP16 . . . .73 F6
WESTBOURNE 138 F7
Westbourne Acad
  IP1 . . . . .134 E1
Westbourne Ct 6
  CB9 . . . . .132 E6
Westbourne Rd IP1 . .134 F1
Westbrook Dr 5
  IP16 . . . . .129 A6
WESTBROOK GREEN . .20 C4
Westbury Cl IP33 . . . .122 D5
Westbury Rd IP4 . . . . .140 B8
West Dock Rd CO12 . .106 F3
West Dr
  Mildenhall IP28 . . . . . .116 B4
  Soham CB7 . . . . .28 C4
West Dr Cres CB7 . . . . .28 C4
West Dr Gdns CB7 . . . .28 C4
WEST END
  26 B6
  Bungay NR35 . . . . .8 F7
West End Cl CB8 . . . . . .60 B5
West End Corner
  NR34 . . . . .2 C6
Westend La CB9 . . . . .133 F8
West End La
  Great Thurlow CB9 . . . .74 B4
  16 Harwich CO12 . . . .107 A1
West End Rd IP1 . . . . .155 A3
WESTERFIELD 135 E4
Westerfield Bsns Ctr
  IP6 . . . . .135 E3
Westerfield La IP6 . . .136 A5
Westerfield Rd
  Ipswich IP1 . . . . .155 C4
  Westerfield IP6 . . . . . .135 E4
Westerfield Sta IP6 . .135 E3
Westerings The 1
  CO6 . . . . .102 C5
Western Ave
  Felixstowe IP11 . . . . . .153 D6
  Haverhill CB9 . . . . . . .132 C7
Western Cl
  4 Feltwell IP26 . . . . . .4 D5
  Ipswich IP4 . . . . .140 F4
Western's End 6
  CO11 . . . . .104 E4
Western Way IP33 . . .122 D6
West Fen Drove CB7 . .29 A6
Westfield 2 CO10 . . . .90 A7
Westfield Prim Acad
  CB9 . . . . .133 A6
Westgarth Gdns
  IP33 . . . . .154 A1
Westgate 5 IP16 . . . .73 F6
Westgate Com Prim Sch
  IP16 . . . . .73 F6
Westgate St Service Rd
  IP1 . . . . .155 B3
Westgate St
  Bury St Edmunds
    IP33 . . . . .154 C1
  Ipswich IP1 . . . . .155 B3
  Long Melford CO10 . . . .77 F1
  West Gr NR33 . . . . . . .115 A3
WESTHALL 25 C4
Westhall IP21 . . . . .39 B5

West Hall Dr IP26 . . . . .6 A8
Westhall Rd NR32 . . . .113 B5
West Hall Rd
  1 Mundford IP26 . . . . .6 B8
  Walsham le Willows
    IP22 . . . . .35 F3
WEST HARLING 18 A8
West Harling Rd
  Harling NR16 . . . . .18 B8
  Shadwell IP24 . . . . . . .17 E6
West Herne La IP22 . . .19 A1
West Hill IP16 . . . . . . .129 C2
Westholme Cl IP12 . . .146 F4
Westholme Rd IP1 . . .135 A1
WESTHORPE 51 D8
Westhorpe 3 CB5 . . . .44 A6
Westhorpe Ave IP32 .122 E8
Westhorpe Rd
  Finningham IP14 . . . . . .52 A8
  Wyverstone IP14 . . . . .51 E6
West La IP15 . . . . .130 E3
Westland 28 IP5 . . . . .98 A8
Westland Rd NR33 . . .114 E6
West Lawn IP4 . . . . . .140 C8
WESTLETON 58 B7
Westleton Heath National
  Nature Reserve ★
    IP17 . . . . .58 E8
Westleton Rd
  Darsham IP17 . . . . . . .57 E8
  Dunwich IP17 . . . . . . .43 A2
Westleton Way 17
  IP11 . . . . .152 D5
WESTLEY 122 A6
Westley Bottom Rd
  CB8 . . . . .59 A4
Westley La IP29 . . . . .122 B3
Westley Mid Sch
  IP33 . . . . .122 C5
Westley Rd
  Fornham All Saints
    IP33 . . . . .122 D5
  Fornham St Martin
    IP32 . . . . .48 B5
WESTLEY
  WATERLESS 59 E3
Westley Way IP31 . . . . .50 E7
West Meadows IP1 . . .134 C4
West Mill Gn IP9 . . . .104 F7
Westminster Dr 4 . .140 B5
Westminster Dr
  IP33 . . . . .122 D3
Westmorland Cl 8
  CO11 . . . . .105 A2
Westmorland Rd
  IP11 . . . . .153 D7
WESTON 9 D1
Weston Colville Rd
  CB8 . . . . .59 E1
WESTON DITCH 29 F7
Weston Dr 9 IP32 . . . .48 B5
Weston La IP22 . . . . . .35 B7
Weston Rd
  Lowestoft NR32 . . . . . .113 B5
  Market Weston IP22 . . . .35 D8
Weston Way CB8 . . . .120 F6
West Rd
  Bury St Edmunds
    IP33 . . . . .122 E4
  Ipswich IP3 . . . . .140 E1
Westropps 6 CO10 . . .91 E7
WEST ROW 29 F6
West Row Com Prim Sch
  IP28 . . . . .29 E7
West Row Row Rd IP28 . 116 A5
West Side Cl NR32 . . .113 C5
West St
  Harwich CO12 . . . . . . .107 B3
  Icklingham IP28 . . . . . .31 C4
  Isleham IP28 . . . . .29 B5
  Rickinghall Inferior
    IP22 . . . . .35 E3
  West Street IP31 . . . . . .35 A2
WEST STOW 32 B1
West Stow Anglo-Saxon
  Village ★ IP28 . . . . .31 F2
West Stow Cntry Pk ★
  IP28 . . . . .31 F2
Weststow Rd
  Lackford IP28 . . . . .31 F2
  Wordwell IP28 . . . . . . .32 A5
West Stow Rd
  Flempton IP28 . . . . . . .32 B1
  Hengrave IP28 . . . . . . .48 A8
WEST STREET
  Rickinghall Inferior 35 A1
  Walsham-le-Willows . . .35 E5
West Suffolk Coll
  IP33 . . . . .122 E6
West Suffolk Coll
  (Sudbury) CO10 . . . 148 D5
West Suffolk Hospl
  IP33 . . . . .123 A2
WEST TOFTS 6 E7
West Tofts Rd IP26 . . . .6 D7
West View
  Bacton IP14 . . . . .51 F6
  Burstall IP8 . . . . .95 F7
  Carlton IP17 . . . . .120 D6
  Shimpling Green IP29 . . .77 E7
  Stowmarket IP14 . . . . .124 B6
West View Gdns 4
  IP23 . . . . .36 D2
Westward Deals CB9 .133 F8
Westward Ho IP16 . . .129 C6
West Wood 9 IP31 . . .49 A5
Westwood Ave
  Ipswich IP1 . . . . .139 A8

Westwood Ave continued
  Lowestoft NR33 . . . . . .114 E6
Wetherby Cl IP1 . . . . .135 B3
WETHERDEN 51 B1
Wetherden Rd
  Elmswell IP30 . . . . . . .50 F2
  Great Ashfield IP31 . . . .51 B6
  Haughley Green IP14 . . .51 C2
WETHERDEN UPPER
  TOWN 51 B4
WETHERINGSETT 53 A5
Wetheringsett CE Prim
  Sch IP14 . . . . 53 A5
Wetheringsett Rd
  IP14 . . . . .53 C5
WETHERUP STREET . . .53 C3
Wet La CO4 . . . . .102 F3
Wexford Rd IP1 . . . . . .134 D2
Wexford Way 28 IP32 .48 C5
WEYBREAD 22 D3
Weybread Rd IP21 . . . .22 A1
Weyland Rd IP6 . . . . . .83 A6
Weylands Cl IP14 . . . . .67 D7
Whalebone Cnr CO4 . .103 C4
Whapload Rd NR32 . . .113 C1
Wharfedale NR33 . . . .114 F3
Wharfedale Rd IP1 . . .135 A1
Wharf La 3 CO8 . . . . .101 C4
Wharton St NR35 . . . .110 B4
WHATFIELD 80 C1
Whatfield CE Prim Sch
  IP7 . . . . .80 C1
Whatfield Hall Rd IP7 .80 B2
Whatfield Rd
  Aldham IP7 . . . . .94 C7
  Elmsett IP7 . . . . .80 E1
Whatfield Way IP14 . .124 E3
Whatley Cl 22 IP30 . . .50 F2
WHEATACRE 2 B1
Wheatacre Dr 3 NR32 .3 A4
Wheat Cl 4 IP1 . . . . . .134 E3
Wheatfield Rd NR33 . 114 D4
Wheatfields
  3 Botesdale IP22 . . . .36 A6
  4 Thurston IP31 . . . . .49 E4
  Whatfield IP7 . . . . .80 C1
Wheatsheaf Cl CO11 .105 E2
Wheatsheaf La CO11 .105 E2
Wheelbarrow La
  IP20 . . . . .23 F5
Wheel Chase CB9 . . . .133 E2
Wheeler's La IP31 . . . .51 A5
Wheelwright Cl
  Blackthorpe IP30 . . . . . .49 C2
  Stowmarket IP14 . . . . .124 C3
  Yaxley IP23 . . . . .37 C4
Wheelwrights Cl
  IP9 . . . . .105 D5
Wheelwrights The
  IP11 . . . . .152 C8
WHELP ST CO10 . . . . . .79 B4
WHELP STREET 79 B4
WHEPSTEAD 63 B5
Whepstead Rd
  Hawstead IP29 . . . . . . .63 B7
  Horringer IP29 . . . . . . .122 D1
  Rede IP29 . . . . .62 E1
Wherry La 4 IP11 . . . .155 C2
Wherry Quay IP4 . . . .155 C2
Wherry Rd
  3 Bungay NR35 . . . . .110 A3
  Bungay NR35 . . . . . . .110 E3
WHERSTEAD 143 B6
Wherstead Rd IP2 . . .155 B1
Whights Cnr IP8 . . . . .138 A1
Whinchat Cl IP2 . . . . .138 D3
Whincroft IP13 . . . . . .127 C5
Whinfield 13 IP5 . . . . .98 A8
Whinfield Ave 23
  CO12 . . . . .106 F1
Whinfield Ct 16 IP5 . . .98 A8
Whin La NR34 . . . . .25 D1
Whin Marsh
  6 Aldeburgh IP15 . . . .130 E5
  8 Aldeburgh IP15 . . . .130 E5
Whinneys The IP5 . . . .141 D8
Whinyard Way 3
  IP11 . . . . .153 D7
Whiskin Cl 7 NR32 . .112 D2
Whisper Wood CO10 . .92 D3
Whistle Dro IP28 . . . . .12 D5
Whitby Rd
  Bury St Edmunds
    IP33 . . . . .122 D3
  Ipswich IP4 . . . . .139 F8
Whiteacres 4 IP24 . . .16 C6
White Brick Cl IP30 . . .50 E1
White Caville CB9 . . . .132 A6
White Clover Way 13
  NR31 . . . . .3 B6
Whitecroft Dr CB8 . . . .60 E6
Whitedike Dro CB4 . . . .4 B4
White Elm Rd IP30 . . . .50 C1
White Elm St IP3 . . . .139 E4
Whitefen Drove IP27 . .13 F7
White Foot La IP13 . . .83 E6
White Gates CO10 . . . .78 D3
White Hall Cl CO10 . . .92 C5
Whitehall Rd IP14 . . . .51 F1
Whitehart Ct 5
  IP28 . . . . .116 C4
White Hart La 20 CB7 .28 D4
White Horse Cl 4
  IP11 . . . . .153 C6
White Horse Hill
  IP9 . . . . .142 D1
White Horse La IP30 . .64 D7

White Horse Rd
  Capel St Mary IP9 . . . .150 E7
  East Bergholt CO7 . . . .151 D3
  Kedington CB9 . . . . . .133 E8
White Horse St 4
  NR32 . . . . .113 E2
Whitehouse Cl CO4 . .103 B2
Whitehouse Com Prim
  Sch IP1 . . . . 134 E1
White House Farm La
  IP21 . . . . .22 B6
Whitehouse Farm Link
  CO9 . . . . .88 F2
White House Farm Rd
  Dallinghoo IP13 . . . . . .70 D2
  Hasketon IP13 . . . . . . .84 A6
White House Gdns
  NR34 . . . . 111 A4
Whitehouse Ind Est
  IP1 . . . . .134 C3
Whitehouse La
  Belchamp Otten CO10 . .90 D5
  Earsham NR35 . . . . .7 C5
  Stowupland IP14 . . . . . .67 D8
White House La IP21 . .22 A1
White House Rd
  Ipswich IP1 . . . . .134 D2
  Saxmundham IP17 . . . .57 F2
White Lion Ct IP7 . . . .149 D5
White Lion Rd NR34 . . .10 B8
White Lodge Gdns
  IP5 . . . . .141 C8
White Meadow 8
  IP14 . . . . .51 A1
White Mullein Dr 4
  IP28 . . . . .45 F8
Whiteplot La IP26 . . . . .4 D7
Whitepost Cnr IP14 . . .54 C1
Whitepost La IP21 . . . .21 F4
Whites Cl IP21 . . . . . . .39 B4
Whites Field CO7 . . . .151 B5
White's La
  Kessingland NR33 . . . .11 B1
  Westleton IP17 . . . . . . .58 C8
WHITESTREET
  GREEN 93 D2
Whitethorn Ley IP30 . .79 A8
Whitethorn Rd 2
  IP3 . . . . .140 F1
Whiteup'S La IP14 . . . .52 D3
White Womans La
  IP12 . . . . .85 B7
Whitewood Wlk 8
  IP27 . . . . .13 F2
Whithersfield Rd
  CB9 . . . . .132 C8
Whiting Ct CB9 . . . . . .132 F4
Whiting Rd NR32 . . . .112 C2
Whiting St IP33 . . . . . .154 B1
Whitland Cl IP7 . . . . . .143 A8
Whitlands 6 CO10 . . . .77 A3
Whitlock Dr CO9 . . . . . .89 F1
Whitney Cl IP3 . . . . . .144 D8
Whittle Rd IP2 . . . . . .138 F6
WHITTON 134 F3
Whitton Church La
  IP1 . . . . .134 F4
Whitton Cl NR33 . . . . .114 E6
Whitton Cl NR33 . . . . .115 A3
Whitton Green Cty Prim
  Sch NR33 . . . . 114 F5
Whitton La IP1 . . . . . .134 D4
Whitton Leyer IP8 . . . .134 C2
Whitton Sports Ctr
  IP1 . . . . .134 E4
Whitworth Cl IP7 . . . .138 D2
Whorton Ave 17 IP31 . .49 A3
Whyte Horse Mdw
  IP19 . . . . .23 F4
Whyteway IP19 . . . . . .24 B4
WICKEN 28 B1
Wicken Rd CB7 . . . . . .28 D1
WICKER STREET
  GREEN 93 E5
WICKHAMBROOK 61 E2
Wickhambrook
  Community Prim Sch
    CB8 . . . . .61 E2
Wickhambrook Ct 2
  IP11 . . . . .152 C4
Wickhambrook Rd
  IP29 . . . . .62 A5
WICKHAM GREEN 52 C8
Wickham La IP14 . . . . .52 A6
WICKHAM MARKET . .127 B6
Wickham Market
  Community Prim Sch
    IP13 . . . . .127 B6
Wickham Market Rd
  Charsfield IP13 . . . . . . .70 C3
  Dallinghoo IP13 . . . . . .70 D1
  Wickham Market IP13 . .70 F4
Wickham Mkt Sta
  IP12 . . . . .71 C2
Wickham Rd
  Finningham IP14 . . . . . .52 B8
  Thornham Magna IP23 . .37 A1
  Thwaite IP23 . . . . .52 D7
Wickham St Rd CB8 . . .76 A8
WICKHAM SKEITH 52 E8
WICKHAM STREET
  Wickhambrook 61 F1
  Wickham Skeith 52 C8
Wick La CO12 . . . . . . .107 A4
Wicklow Rd IP1 . . . . . .134 D2
Wick Rd
  Langham CO4 . . . . . . .103 C2
  Stoke-by-Nayland CO6 103 A6

White Horse Rd
Wicks La IP14 . . . . . . .67 D7
Widgeon Cl IP2 . . . . . .138 F3
WIDGHAM GREEN 60 B2
WIGGENS GREEN 88 C5
Wiggin Cl IP28 . . . . . . 116 D2
Wiggs Acre NR34 . . . . .10 C4
Wigg's Way 3 NR32 . . .3 D4
Wigmore Cl
  Ipswich IP2 . . . . .138 F1
  Stoke Park IP2 . . . . . .139 A1
Wignall St CO11 . . . . .104 C2
Wigston Rd IP33 . . . . .122 C3
Wigwam Hill IP22 . . . . .19 F1
Wilbur Cl 14 IP31 . . . .49 A3
WILBY 39 C2
Wilby CE Prim Sch
  IP21 . . . . .39 B2
Wilbye Cl IP32 . . . . . .123 E4
Wilby La IP13 . . . . .39 E2
Wilby Rd IP21 . . . . . . .39 A4
Wild Acres 13 CB5 . . .44 A5
Wilderness Cl 3
  IP20 . . . . .22 D5
Wilderness Hill IP8 . . .95 B6
Wilderness La
  Harleston IP20 . . . . . . .22 D6
  Woodbridge IP12 . . . . .147 A6
Wilde St Est IP28 . . . . .13 D1
Wilde St NR32 . . . . . . .113 E2
WILDE STREET 13 D2
Wildflower Way
  NR35 . . . . .110 B7
Wilding Dr IP5 . . . . . . .141 D7
Wilding Rd
  Badwell Ash IP31 . . . . .50 F7
  Pinewood IP8 . . . . . . .138 C1
Wildings La CB9 . . . . . .88 C2
Wildmere La IP28 . . . . .13 D1
Wild Tracks Offroad
  Activity Pk ★ CB7 . . .45 E7
Wilford Bridge Rd
  IP12 . . . . .147 D7
Wilford Bridge Spur
  IP12 . . . . .147 C7
Wilfred Hurry Cl IP8 . .134 A1
Wilfred Sherman Cl
  CB8 . . . . .121 A4
Wilkes Ct IP5 . . . . . . .141 E7
Wilkes Way IP14 . . . . .124 C6
Wilkinson Dr IP5 . . . .141 C6
Wilkinson Way IP12 . .147 A6
Wilks Rd IP33 . . . . . . .123 B2
Willbye Ave IP22 . . . . .20 D3
Willcox Ave IP33 . . . . .122 C6
Willets Pond CO7 . . . .151 D3
William Armstrong Cl 6
  IP30 . . . . .50 F2
William Blake Ct
  CB9 . . . . .132 C7
William Booth Way 11
  IP11 . . . . .152 D5
William Brown Way 2
  IP22 . . . . .20 B3
William Flack Pl IP29 .63 B5
William Groom Ave 2
  CO12 . . . . .107 A1
Williamsburg Ave 19
  CO12 . . . . .107 A1
WILLIAM'S GREEN 93 E5
Williamson Cl 16
  IP22 . . . . .20 C3
Williamsport Way
  IP6 . . . . .125 F3
William St IP1 . . . . . . .155 F3
William's Way 4 IP28 29 F6
Willie Snaith Rd CB8 .120 F6
WILLINGHAM 25 E7
Willis Cres 7 IP41 . . . .136 A1
WILLISHAM 81 A6
Willisham Hall Rd
  IP8 . . . . .81 B5
Willisham Rd IP6 . . . . .81 A4
WILLISHAM TYE 81 A6
Willis St 16 IP11 . . . . .71 A7
Willoughby Cl IP13 . . .71 A7
Willoughby Rd IP2 . . .155 A1
Willowbank IP12 . . . . .147 C6
Willowbrook Cl
  NR33 . . . . 114 A3
Willow Cl
  Badwell Ash IP31 . . . . .50 F8
  6 Claydon IP6 . . . . . .134 C8
  Haverhill CB9 . . . . . . .132 B7
  6 Holywell Row IP28 . .30 C8
  Stradbroke IP21 . . . . . .39 B5
  1 Sudbury CO10 . . . . 148 C4
  7 Walsham Le Willows
    IP31 . . . . .35 C2
  Worlingham NR34 . . . .111 F3
  Wortwell IP20 . . . . . . .23 A4
Willow Corner
  Edwardstone CO10 . . . .93 A5
  5 The Marsh IP22 . . . .36 B8
Willow Cres CB8 . . . . .121 B2
Willowcroft Rd IP1 . . .135 A2
Willow Dr IP31 . . . . . . .51 B7
Willow Farm Meadow
  IP13 . . . . .54 E7
Willowfield Cl 26
  IP28 . . . . .46 A8
Willow Gdns IP14 . . . .66 C5
Willow Gn IP13 . . . . . .54 E7
Willow Gr 3 CO6 . . . .102 C5

Willow La
Bedingham NR35 . . . . .7 B7
Broome NR35 . . . . .8 C7
Cotton IP14 . . . . .52 B6
Winfarthing IP22 . . . . .20 D8
Willow Marsh La
Darsham IP17 . . . . .42 A1
Yoxford IP17. . . . . .41 F2
Willow Rd NR33. . . . . 115 A2
Willow Rise IP11. . . . 152 D2
Willows Prim Sch The
IP2 . . . . 138 F2
Willow Tree Cl IP13..127 B6
Willowvale NR32. . . . 112 F6
Willow Way
Bury St Edmunds
IP33 . . . . 154 A3
9 Great Brickett IP7. . .80 D6
3 Harwich CO12 . . . . . 106 F1
8 Rendlesham IP12 . . . .85 D8
Saxmundham IP17 . . 128 E3
Willow Wlk
5 Harleston IP20 . . . . .22 D5
Needdham Market
IP6 . . . . 125 D6
Willrede Cl NR34. . . . 111 B3
Wilmslow Ave IP12 . .146 E5
Wilmslow Dr IP8. . . . 138 C2
WILNEY GREEN 19 D4
Wilsey Rd CB9 . . . . . .133 B7
Wilson Rd
Hadleigh IP7. . . . . 149 E5
Ipswich IP8 . . . . 138 B1
Lowestoft NR33 . . . . . 115 C5
Wilton Rd IP26 . . . . .4 E5
Wimbledon Ave IP27. .14 E8
Wimborne Ave IP3. . . 140 D4
Wimpole Cl IP5. . . . . .140 F6
Wincanton Cl IP4. . . . 136 A1
Winchester Cl IP14. . .124 B6
Winchester Gdns 4
IP6. . . . . .82 B5
Winchester Rd IP33. . 122 D4
Winchester Way IP2 .142 F8
Windell Dr 10 IP32. . . .48 B5
Windermere Pk
NR32 . . . . 113 A4
Windermere Rd
6 Felixstowe IP11. . . . 153 D7
Stowmarket IP14 . . . .124 C6
Sudbury CO10. . . . . . .148 E6
Windgap La IP14. . . . . .51 D1
Windham Rd CO10 . . .148 E6
Winding Piece 5
IP9. . . . . 150 E3
Windings Rd 4 IP7. . .80 F1
Windmill Ave IP30 . . . .50 C1
Windmill Cl
Boxted CO4. . . . . .102 F2
Lakenheath IP27 . . . . 109 D5
Ramsey & Parkeston
CO12 . . . . 106 C1
Soham CB7 . . . . .28 E2
3 Somersham IP8. . . .81 C3
Sudbury CO10. . . . . . .148 F1
Windmill Gn
Ditchingham NR35 . . . 110 C7
19 Stanton IP31. . . . . .34 E4
Windmill Hill
Capel St Mary IP9. . . . 150 C3
Exning CB8 . . . . 120 C8
Long Melford CO10. . . . .77 D1
Windmill La IP21 . . . . . .38 F8
Windmill Place CO10. .77 C4
Windmill Rise
Mistley Heath CO11 . .105 B1
Wortwell IP20 . . . . . . .23 A7
Windmill Rise
Bury St Edmunds
IP33 . . . . 154 A1
Hundon CO10 . . . . .75 D4
1 Wetherden IP14 . . . .51 A1
Windmill Row 5
CO10 . . . . .77 B3
Windmill View 5
CO12 . . . . 106 D1
Windrush Rd IP5 . . . . 141 C8
Windsor Circ
Lakenheath IP27 . . . . . .14 A3
Lakenheath IP27 . . . . 109 F1
Windsor Cl
7 Barnham IP24 . . . . . .16 C2
Lawshall IP29. . . . . . . .63 D2
Windsor Ct
1 Diss IP22. . . . . .20 D3
Needham Market IP6. .125 D5
WINDSOR GREEN 64 B2
Windsor Pl CO10. . . . .148 E5
Windsor Rd
Felixstowe IP11. . . . . .152 E3
Ipswich IP1 . . . . 138 F7
Lowestoft NR33 . . . . . 115 C7

Windsor Rd *continued*
Newmarket CB8 . . . . . .120 E4
Southwold IP18 . . . . . .119 B8
Windsor Terr
Haverhill CB9 . . . . 132 B6
12 Haverhill CB9. . . . 132 C6
Windward Way
IP33. . . . . .114 E5
Windyridge Rd IP30. . .65 D5
WINFARTHING 20 B8
Winfarthing Rd
IP22. . . . . .20 B6
Winfrith Rd IP3. . . . . 140 D4
WINGFIELD 39 B8
Wingfield Ave IP27 . . 109 D7
WINGFIELD GREEN . . .38 F8
Wingfield Green IP21 . . .38 F7
Wingfield Meadows
IP14. . . . . .68 B6
Wingfield Old Coll &
Gdns★ IP21. . . . . 39 A7
Wingfield St
Bungay NR35 . . . . 110 B3
Ipswich IP4 . . . . 155 C2
Wings Rd IP27 . . . . . . 109 D6
Wings Rd Cl IP27 . . . 109 D6
Winnipeg Rd NR32 . . 113 D2
Winsford Rd IP32 . . . .123 E6
WINSTON 68 F8
Winston Ave
Ipswich IP4 . . . . 140 C8
Lowestoft NR33 . . . . . 114 E7
Winston Cl
5 Felixstowe IP11. . .152 D5
11 Kessingland NR33. .11 C1
Winston Rd IP18. . . . . 119 C7
Wintergreen Rd 7
IP28. . . . . .30 C1
Winthrop Rd IP33. . . .122 D4
Winthrops The
CO10 . . . . .93 B4
WISSETT 24 D2
Wissett Cl IP19 . . . . . .118 B4
Wissett Rd
Chediston IP19. . . . . . . .41 B8
Halesworth IP19 . . . . 118 A5
Wissett IP19. . . . . .24 D1
Wissett Way NR32. . . 113 B4
Wissey View 2 IP26 . . .6 B8
Wissington Uplands
CO6. . . . . 102 A5
Wiston Hall La CO6. . 102 B4
Wiston Rd CO6. . . . . . 102 B4
Witch Elm 31 CO12. . .106 F1
WITHERMARSH
GREEN 103 A8
Withersdale Rd
Mendham IP20. . . . . . . .23 A5
Weybread IP21. . . . . . . .22 D4
WITHERSDALE
STREET 22 F4
WITHERSFIELD 74 B2
Withersfield Rd
Haverhill CB9 . . . . 132 B5
Withersfield CB9 . . . . . .74 C4
Withers Pl 2 CB7. . . . . .29 A1
Withindale La CO10 . . .91 D7
Withingdale Gall The★
CO10. . . . . .91 D7
Withipoll St IP4. . . . . 155 C3
WITNESHAM 83 A6
Witnesham Church La
IP6. . . . . .82 F5
Witnesham La IP6 . . . . .38 C7
Witnesham Prim Sch
IP6 . . . . .83 A7
Witney Gn NR33 . . . . 115 A3
Witney Rd 3 NR33 . . 115 A3
Wittons La IP21. . . . . . .38 C7
WIXOE 89 B6
Wix Rd CO12. . . . . 106 C1
Wlk Farm Rd IP12. . . . .72 B2
Wollaston Cl IP32. . . . 122 D4
Wollaston Rd NR32. . 113 D1
Wolsey Art Gall★
IP1 . . . . 155 C4
Wolsey Gdns IP11. . . 153 A3
Wolsey Rd 4 IP14 . . . 124 C7
Wolsey St IP1 . . . . . . .155 B2
Wolton Rd IP5. . . . . . . 141 C7
Wolves Farm La IP7. . .94 E6
Wolves Wood Nature
Reserve★ IP7 . . . . . . .94 F6
Wood Barn La
Foxash Estate CO11 . . .104 B1
Lowestoft NR33 . . . . . . .10 E5
WOODBRIDGE 146 F6
Woodbridge 3 IP27 . . .13 F2
Woodbridge Gall★
IP12 . . . . 146 F5
Woodbridge Mus The★
IP12 . . . . 147 A5

Woodbridge Prim Sch
IP12 . . . . 147 A6
Woodbridge Rd
Alderton IP12. . . . . .99 D5
Bredfield IP13 . . . . .84 C7
Butley IP12. . . . . .86 A5
Debach IP13. . . . . .70 A1
Framlingham IP13 . . . . .78 C6
Grundisburgh IP13. . . . .83 E6
Ipswich IP4 . . . . 155 C3
Sutton IP12. . . . . .85 A1
Tunstall IP12. . . . . .71 E1
Waldringfield IP12 . . . . .98 D6
Wantisden IP12 . . . . . . .85 E5
Woodbridge Walk IP12. . .99 F8
Woodbridge Rd E
IP4. . . . . 140 C7
Woodbridge Sch
IP12 . . . . 146 F5
Woodbridge Sch Prep
IP12 . . . . 147 A4
Woodbridge Sta 147 B4
WOODBRIDGE WALK . .99 F8
Woodbridge Walk
IP12. . . . . 100 A8
Woodburn Dr 17 IP32 .48 B5
Woodchurch Ave 6
NR33 . . . . 114 C4
Wood Cl
Kenninghall NR16. . . . . .19 A8
Rendlesham IP12 . . . . . .85 D8
Tostock IP30. . . . . .50 B3
Woodcock Cl IP30 . . . . .50 B3
Woodcock Rd IP2. . . . 138 E2
Woodcock Rise IP26 . . .6 A1
Woodcote IP14 . . . . . .124 B6
Woodcrofts Cl 2
IP29. . . . . .63 A1
Woodcutters Way
IP27. . . . . 109 D7
WOODDITTON 60 C5
Woodditton Rd
Kirtling CB8. . . . . .60 D3
Newmarket CB8 . . . . . . 121 A1
Woodditton CB8 . . . . . . .60 B6
Wood Farm Bsns Ctr
IP6. . . . . .68 C5
Wood Farm La
Brampton NR34 . . . . . . .25 D6
Reydon IP18. . . . . .26 C2
Wood Farm Rd IP13...83 C5
Woodfield Cl NR34. . . . .25 E7
Woodfield Dr IP14 . . . 124 E5
Woodfield La
Stowmarket IP14 . . . . 124 D4
Stutton IP9 . . . . 105 C5
Woodfields IP27 . . . . . .39 A4
Woodford Gdns
IP32. . . . . 123 A8
Woodgates Rd CO7 . . 151 D7
Woodhall Bsns Pk
CO10. . . . . 148 D8
Woodhall Cl CO10. . . 148 C7
Woodhall Com Prim Sch
3 CO10. . . . . 148 D8
Wood Hall Dr IP12 . . . .99 B7
Wood Hall La IP23 . . . .37 B1
Woodhall Rd CO10 . . 148 C7
Woodhouse La IP10. . 141 C2
Woodhouse Sq IP4 . . 155 C2
Wood La
Bedingham NR35 . . . . . . .7 C6
Bressingham IP22 . . . . .19 E6
Coney Weston IP31 . . . .17 C1
Dallinghoo IP13 . . . . . . .70 B1
Dickleburgh & Rushall
IP21 . . . . .21 C2
Fressingfield IP21 . . . . .40 A8
Henstead with Hulver Street
NR34 . . . . .26 E7
Hepworth IP22. . . . . . . .35 A6
Oulton NR32 . . . . .112 C3
Reydon IP18. . . . . .26 C1
Scole IP21 . . . . .21 C4
Thelnetham IP22 . . . . . .35 C6
Woodland Ave NR34 .111 F4
Woodland Cl
Onehouse IP14. . . . . . . .66 C6
Risby IP28 . . . . .47 D5
Thurston IP31. . . . . .49 E3
Woodland Dr
Bungay NR35 . . . . 110 B1
Ellingham NR35 . . . . .8 E7
WOODLAND GREEN . .133 C5
Woodland Pl 7 IP31 . .49 A6
Woodlands
1 Chelmondiston
IP9 . . . . 106 C4
Hadleigh IP7. . . . . 149 B7
35 Harleston IP20 . . .22 D6
Lakenheath IP27 . . . . 109 D8
Leiston IP16 . . . . .129 C4
Westleton IP17. . . . . . . .58 C8
Woodlands Ave
Felixstowe IP11. . . . . . 152 B8
4 Lowestoft NR33. . .114 C3

Woodlands Bsns Pk
IP30. . . . . .49 B3
Woodlands Dr IP24 . . .16 C7
Woodlands Rd
Chapel St Mary IP7. . . . .95 B4
Holbrook IP9 . . . . .105 B8
Raydon IP7 . . . . .94 C7
Rushbrooke with Rougham
IP30. . . . . .49 B3
Woodlands Rise IP14 .14 D8
WOODLANDS THE 95 A3
Woodlands The
NR32 . . . . 113 B8
Woodlands Way
Bramford IP8 . . . . 134 C4
Mildenhall IP28 . . . . . .116 F5
Woodlands Way IP31 . .35 A4
Woodland Valley IP7. .80 C5
Woodlane Rd IP23 . . . .38 C1
Woodlark Cl
Ipswich IP2 . . . . 138 E1
Thetford IP24. . . . . .16 C5
Woodlark Dr 4 IP14 . 124 F7
Wood Ley Com Prim Sch
IP14 . . . . 124 B7
Woodleys Yd IP18 . . . 119 D5
Woodpecker Ave 2
NR33 . . . . 114 D5
Woodpecker Cl 16
IP14. . . . . .67 A5
Woodpecker Rd IP27 . 138 D3
Woodpeckers CO10 . . 148 C4
Wood Rd
Badingham IP13 . . . . . . .56 B6
Woolpit IP30. . . . . .65 F8
Woodrush Rd IP3. . . . 140 E2
Woods Cl
Ditchingham NR35 . . . .110 B7
Sturmer CB9 . . . . .133 C3
Woodside
Beccles NR34 . . . . . . .111 D3
Brampton with Stoven
NR34 . . . . .25 E5
Martlesham Heath IP5 . .98 B8
Wood Side IP14 . . . . . 124 B5
Woodside Bsns Pk
IP31. . . . . .32 F2
Woodside Cl
IP33. . . . . 123 B1
Lowestoft NR33 . . . . . 114 C3
Woodside View IP31 . .33 D4
Woods La IP12. . . . . . . 147 B7
Woods Loke E NR32 .113 A3
Woods Loke Prim Sch
NR32. . . . . 112 F3
Woods Loke W NR32 .112 F3
Woodspring Cl 12
IP2. . . . . 139 A2
Woodstone Ave IP1. . 135 C1
Woods Walk IP5. . . . . 141 E7
Woodthorpe Cl IP7 . . 149 F5
Woodthorpe Rd IP7. . 149 E5
WOODTON 7 C8
Wood View
Dagworth IP14. . . . . . . .66 D8
4 Sibton IP17. . . . . . .56 F8
Woodville Rd IP4 . . . . 139 F5
Woodward Ave IP14 . . .51 F6
Woodward Cl IP2. . . . 138 D5
Woolhall St 2 IP33 . . .154 B2
Woollards Cl IP1. . . . . 139 A6
Woollards Gdns 3
CO10 . . . . .91 E8
Woolmers Cl IP14. . . . 124 D4
Woolner Cl
7 Claydon IP6. . . . . . .82 A5
5 Hadleigh IP7. . . . . 149 E6
Woolnough Cl 6 CB9 .88 D3
Woolnough Rd IP12. . 146 F6
Woolnoughs The 2
IP5. . . . . 141 D7
Woolpit Bsns Pk
IP30. . . . . .50 D1
Woolpit Community Prim
Sch IP30 . . . . .50 D1
Woolpit & District Mus★
IP30 . . . . .50 D1
WOOLPIT GREEN 65 D8
WOOLPIT HEATH 65 E8
Woolpit Rd
Ixworth IP31 . . . . .34 C2
Rattlesden IP30 . . . . . . .65 D6
Tostock IP30. . . . . .50 A2
Tostock IP31. . . . . .50 C3
Wool Rd IP32. . . . . .48 B5
WOOLVERSTONE 144 B1
Woolverstone Cl
IP2. . . . . 138 D1
Wooten Green IP21 . . .39 B3
WOOTTEN GREEN 39 B3
Wootton Dr IP1. . . . . . 139 C8
Worcester Cl 5
IP32. . . . . 123 E6
Worcester Rd IP3. . . . 144 A8

Wordsell Cl IP2. . . . . . 139 C3
Wordsworth Cl IP17 .128 B4
Wordsworth Cres
IP1. . . . . 134 C3
Wordsworth Dr 22
IP22. . . . . .20 D2
Wordsworth Rd
4 Bury St Edmunds
IP32 . . . . .48 C5
2 Stowmarket IP14 . .124 B8
WORDWELL 32 D3
Worell Dr NR34. . . . . . 111 C3
WORKHOUSE
GREEN 101 C8
WORKHOUSE HILL . . . 102 F2
Workhouse Hill
Boxted CO4. . . . . .102 F3
Hartest IP29. . . . . .77 B8
Workhouse La
Great Glemham IP17 . . .71 D8
Poystreet Green IP30. . .65 E5
Saxmundham IP17 . . . . .57 E2
Workhouse Rd
Little Horkesley CO6. . .102 B2
Thornham Magna IP23. . .37 A1
Workshop La IP10 . . . 145 C5
WORLD'S END 65 F2
World's End La IP14 . .65 F7
World's End Rd IP13 . .55 B4
WORLINGHAM 111 F3
Worlingham CE VC Prim
Sch NR34 . . . . 111 F3
Worlingham Way
NR32 . . . . 113 A4
WORLINGTON 30 A4
Worlington Rd
Barton Mills IP28 . . . . . .30 E3
Worlington IP28. . . . . . .116 A3
WORLINGWORTH 54 F8
Worlingworth CE VC
Prim Sch IP13 . . . . .54 D7
Worlingworth Rd
Horham IP21 . . . . .38 F3
Tannington IP13. . . . . . .55 A7
WORMINGFORD 101 F2
Wormingford Grove
CO6. . . . . 102 A1
Wormingford Rd
CO10 . . . . 101 F7
Worsley Cl IP2. . . . . . 138 D2
WORTHAM 36 D8
Wortham Ling Nature
Reserve★ IP22 . . . . . .19 F2
Wortham Pl 1 CB9 . . 132 E6
Wortham Prim Sch
IP22 . . . . .36 E7
Worthing Rd NR32 . . . 113 D3
WORTWELL 23 B8
WRABNESS 105 A2
Wrabness Local Nature
Reserve★ IP9 . . . . . 105 C2
Wrabness Rd 1
CO12 . . . . 106 D1
Wrabness Sta CO11 . 106 A2
Wragg Dr CB8 . . . . . . 121 A6
Wratting Rd
Great Thurlow CB9 . . . . .74 D5
Haverhill CB9 . . . . 132 E7
Wreford Ct 12 CO10 . .91 E8
Wren Ave IP2. . . . . . . 138 D3
Wren Cl
2 Bury St Edmunds
IP32 . . . . .49 A4
Mildenhall IP28 . . . . . .116 D4
1 Stowmarket IP14 . .67 A5
13 Thurstow IP31. . . . .49 D4
Wrens Pk 2 IP11 . . . . 153 D7
Wrens The IP24. . . . . . .16 C5
WRENTHAM 26 E5
Wrentham Rd NR34 . . .26 D7
WRENTHAM WEST
END 26 C7
Wriggle St IP13. . . . . . .70 A7
Wright Cl IP14. . . . . . . 124 D3
Wright La IP5 . . . . 141 D8
Wright Rd IP3. . . . . . . 140 C2
Wrights Way
Leavenheath CO6 . . . . 102 A7
Woolpit IP30. . . . . .50 C1
Wroxham Rd IP3. . . . . 139 F3
Wyards La IP31. . . . . . . .50 A4
Wyatt Cl IP30. . . . . .50 F3
Wyatts La CO10 . . . . . 101 B8
Wyatt Way IP24. . . . . . .16 B7
Wye Rd IP3. . . . . 140 A2
Wyken Rd IP31. . . . . . . .34 D3
Wyken Vineyard &
Gdns★ IP31. . . . . . . .34 E2
Wykes Bishop St 5
IP3. . . . . 139 E4
Wymering Rd 10
IP18. . . . . 119 D5
Wyncoll's La IP7. . . . . .94 B2
Wyndham Way CB8 . . 121 A6
Wynterton Cl IP3 . . . .140 B1
Wynton Rise IP14. . . . 124 E4

Wytchwoods The
IP14. . . . . .68 E6
Wyvern Rd IP3. . . . . . 140 C1
WYVERSTONE 51 E6
WYVERSTONE
GREEN 51 E6
Wyverstone Rd
Badwell Ash IP31. . . . . .51 B7
Wyverstone Green
IP14. . . . . .51 E6
WYVERSTONE
STREET 51 D6

Y

Yale Bsns Pk IP3 . . . . 144 F8
Yarmouth Pl 3
CB9 . . . . .132 E6
Yarmouth Rd
Bungay NR35 . . . . .8 D7
Corton NR32. . . . . 113 A8
Ditchingham NR35 . . . 110 D7
Geldeston NR34 . . . . . . .9 A7
Ipswich IP1 . . . . 139 A6
Kirby Cane NR35. . . . . . .8 E7
Lound NR32 . . . . .2 F7
Lowestoft NR32 . . . . . 113 B5
Melton IP12 . . . . .84 E6
Woodbridge IP12 . . . . .147 C8
Yarn Wlk 23 IP32 . . . . .48 B5
Yarrow Cl 21 IP30. . . .50 F2
Yarrow Dr NR33 . . . . . 114 C4
Yarrow Way IP6 . . . . . 135 C5
YAXLEY 37 B5
Yaxley Hall La IP23. . . .37 C4
Yaxley Rd
Eye IP23 . . . . .37 C3
Mellis IP23 . . . . .37 A5
Yeldham Pl CB9 . . . . . 132 E6
Yeldham Rd CO10. . . . .90 E2
Yellowhammer Cl 10
IP14. . . . . .67 A6
Yeoman Cres IP7. . . . 149 E5
Yeoman Rd IP11. . . . . 152 D3
Yeomanry Gdns
CO12 . . . . 106 E1
Yeomanry Yd IP33 . . . 154 A2
Yeoman's Cl NR35. . . 110 C3
Yeoman Way IP7 . . . . 149 E5
Yeovil Rd NR32 . . . . . 113 C2
Yerril Gdn CB9. . . . . . 132 C5
Yew Cl
1 Lakenheath IP27 . .14 B3
Saxmundham IP17 . . . 128 E3
Yewcroft IP11 . . . . 152 E2
Yew Ct IP2 . . . . 139 A3
Yewdale NR33 . . . . . . 114 D2
Yewlands Gr IP30. . . . .65 A4
Yew Tree Cl IP28 . . . . 116 D6
Yew Tree Ct 1
IP33. . . . . 122 F3
Yew Tree Gdns 9
IP28. . . . . .29 F6
Yewtree Gr IP5 . . . . . .140 F7
Yewtree Rise IP8 . . . . 138 C1
Yew Tree Rise IP13 . . 127 C7
York Cl
Bury St Edmunds
IP33 . . . . 122 E5
1 Mildenhall IP28 . . . .30 A8
Sudbury CO10. . . . . . .148 C7
York Cres
12 Claydon IP6. . . . . .82 B5
Claydon IP6 . . . . 134 C8
York Rd
Bury St Edmunds
IP33 . . . . 154 A2
Felixstowe IP11 . . . . . 153 A4
Foxhall IP5 . . . . .98 A7
Haverhill CB9 . . . . 132 C5
Ipswich IP3 . . . . 140 A4
Lowestoft NR32 . . . . . 113 C1
Southwold IP18 . . . . . .119 B5
Sudbury CO10. . . . . . .148 C6
York Terr IP33. . . . . . . 154 A2
Yorktown Cl 20
CO12 . . . . 107 A2
YOXFORD 57 C8
Yoxford Gdns★ IP17. .57 C8
Yoxford Mews 7
IP12. . . . . .85 B3
Yoxford & Peasenhall
Prim Sch IP17. . . . . .57 D8
Yoxford Rd
Bramfield IP19 . . . . .41 E4
Middleton IP17. . . . . . . .57 F6
Sibton IP17. . . . . .57 A8
Yoxwood View IP17. . .57 C8

Z

Zanetta Ct NR32 . . . . 113 C1
Zemke Way IP19. . . . . 118 C6
Zurich Cl 3 NR31. . . . . .3 C6